Ethical Issues in
Social Science
Research

Ethical Issues in Social Science Research

EDITED BY

Tom L. Beauchamp
Ruth R. Faden
R. Jay Wallace, Jr.
LeRoy Walters

THE JOHNS HOPKINS UNIVERSITY PRESS

Baltimore and London

This book was brought to publication with the generous
assistance of the National Science Foundation.

The Johns Hopkins University Press, Baltimore, Maryland 21218
The Johns Hopkins Press Ltd., London

Library of Congress Cataloging in Publication Data
Main entry under title:

Ethical issues in social science research.

  Bibliography
  Includes index.

    1.   Social sciences—Research—Moral and religious aspects—Addresses, essays,
lectures. I. Beauchamp, Tom L.
H62.E76   174'.9301   81–12419
ISBN 0-8018-2655-1   AACR2
ISBN 0-8018-2656-X (pbk.)

Contents

Preface

Methods used in social science research have led in recent years to moral uncertainty about the rights and obligations of both research subjects and investigators. For the last decade or so, members of several professions—including most of the social sciences, philosophy, law, government, public health, and organizations such as the American Association for the Advancement of Science—have become involved in discussion of the ethical issues that arise in social science research. This book provides a systematic overview of these discussions and at the same time attempts to push the issues forward and reveal their complexity. The majority of the authors are social scientists, and the book therefore exhibits a firsthand familiarity with the situations and problems researchers encounter in their work. The book is by no means exclusively the product of social scientists, however. Philosophers, legal scholars, and those involved in the administration and regulation of research in the social sciences represent a bare minority of authorship. Moreover, even the papers by social scientists reflect careful and prolonged discussion with representatives of other fields. It is the hope of the editors and contributors alike that this combination of disciplinary perspectives will render the debate about moral controversies in the social sciences better informed and more genuinely engaged.

We have been able neither to address all the important questions nor to represent all the points of view on the issues under discussion. We have tried, however, to make this volume the most comprehensive, detailed, and interdisciplinary treatment of the subject presently available. We have also insisted that the essentials of ethical theory be present at all appropriate points throughout the volume; and we have taken care to distinguish various research questions in the social sciences from questions of ethics that confront the relevant methods and uses of social science research.

Many persons have contributed to the production of this book. The authors, for example, have often generously helped each other—a form of assistance that we greatly appreciated as editors. Herbert Kelman did much to facilitate the editors' work in making Part I an integrated unit by his willingness to adopt a common terminology, by his frequent submission of drafts for further comment, and by his general willingness to extend his perceptive analyses into virtually every area of the ethical issues explored in this volume. Our special appreciation for valuable counsel, suggestions, and useful services beyond the preparation of the manuscripts is also owed to Carl Wellman, Bradford Gray, Loren Graham, Robert Boruch, Norman Bradburn, Arthur Norberg, William Blanpied, Thomas Dalglish, Leon Gordis, Patricia King, Wallace Waterfall,

Sally Finnerty, Richard McCormick, William Pitt, Mary Baker, Mary Ellen Timbol, Emilie Dolge, and Susan Dreux. This entire project was supported by the National Science Foundation (EVIST grant number OSS78-17720). Without this assistance the several hundred hours spent on editing, correspondence, compilation, and research would have been impossible. We also wish to express our gratitude to the Kennedy Foundation, whose continuing support of the Kennedy Institute of Ethics made the venture possible.

T.L.B.
R.R.F.
R.J.W.
L.W.

PART ONE

Foundations

1

Introduction

The essays in this volume have been organized topically and divided into five sections. The present section is entitled "Foundations," because chapter one introduces the reader to certain basic and recurring concepts and distinctions, and chapter two develops a typology of the ethical problems that social science researchers confront. As indicated by the section headings, the subsequent chapters treat topics of "Harm and Benefit," "Informed Consent and Deception," "Privacy and Confidentiality," and "Government Regulation." Both of the chapters in this foundation section use this scheme of classification as a basic organizational framework.

Our specific concerns in this chapter are threefold. First, we sketch the background of moral controversy in the social sciences. We consider where moral controversy in scientific research has generally arisen, the historical background of ethical argument specific to the social sciences, and some nonmoral issues that have often been mistaken for ethical ones in social research. In the second part of the chapter, an account of the structure of moral controversy and moral justification is provided. Using examples from social science research, we describe the patterns that moral controversies commonly exhibit and the principles and methods of justification appropriately invoked in moral disputes about the social sciences. In the final part of the chapter we outline some outstanding topics of moral controversy in the social sciences, setting the stage for the detailed typology of issues confronting different research methods that Herbert C. Kelman presents in chapter two.

The Background of Moral Controversy in the Social Sciences

The Sources of Moral Controversy over Scientific Research

Research in the social sciences might at first seem unremarkable in its ethical implications—a scholarly activity dealing only with empirical facts. Yet social science research is not always a morally neutral activity. On the contrary, such research raises ethical issues that distinguish the social sciences

3

from nearly all the other academic disciplines. Most of these distinctive issues stem from the involvement of persons in research conducted by social scientists. Of course, scholars in many disciplines perform research that is in some way concerned with human nature and behavior. Philosophers and historians, for instance, frequently address these and related topics. Their research, however, rarely depends on the direct scientific study of living persons which characterizes research in the social sciences. The distinctive ethical problems in the latter disciplines generally turn on how persons may properly be involved in this scientific research.

The fact that social science research usually involves the scientific study of living persons makes these disciplines distinctive, but it does not render them entirely unique. Biomedical scientists also employ human subjects in scientific research, and it is their activities rather than those of social scientists that have drawn predominant attention to the ethical problems concerning human research subjects. The reasons for the comparative prominence of biomedical research are not difficult to understand. Research practices have tended to generate controversy in proportion as the harms they pose to subjects are dramatic and dangerous. Perhaps as a matter of historical accident, it was experimentation in the biomedical sciences that first put subjects dramatically at risk of significant and irremediable harm. Not surprisingly, then, normative analyses of the ethical issues in research have long been marked by a preoccupation with cases drawn from biomedical experimentation involving human subjects.

The watershed event for the historical development of these ethical analyses was undoubtedly the series of biomedical experiments performed by Nazi researchers during the Second World War. Although they were not the earliest examples of harmful research on unwilling human subjects, the Nazi experiments were unprecedented in the extremity of the dangers to which they knowingly exposed their victims. Using subjects drawn from the populations of concentration camps, Nazi scientists explored such topics as the length of time humans can survive after ingesting poisons or being immersed in ice water. The Nuremberg Military Tribunals unambiguously condemned these activities as part of their review of Nazi "crimes against humanity" in 1945. The judges asserted that there are certain basic principles which researchers are obligated to respect in conducting experiments that involve human subjects, and they proposed a list of ten such principles that has come to be known as the "Nuremberg Code."

The Nuremberg Code proved even more influential in the years following 1945 than might reasonably have been predicted. With the profusion of biomedical research during the postwar period, researchers and their govern-ments alike began to realize the importance of fostering an appreciation of relevant ethical principles in the research community. The Nuremberg Code served as a model for many of the professional and governmental codes formulated through the mid-1960s. But it was not until the late 1960s and

1970s that normative ethical analyses of human subjects research took on a truly systematic character. As influential as the Nuremberg Code was for this later development, another precedent has been of at least equal significance: the accumulation of legal opinion in cases involving informed consent in therapeutic medicine. Malpractice suits alleging failure to obtain informed consent are not uncommon, and the law's response to them provides a refined vocabulary that has often been applied in independent ethical assessments of research practices.

The fact that ethical analyses of research practices have frequently relied on the legal vocabulary of informed consent law is symptomatic of the preoccupation with issues surrounding the biomedical sciences. As illuminating as the legal distinctions have been in normative ethical analysis, they are not necessarily equally pertinent to all types of research. There may well be many unique characteristics of social science research, and if so, the concepts and principles developed in therapeutic medical contexts need modification before being applied to the social sciences. An independent and detailed examination of allegedly unique issues in social science research therefore has an appropriate place in any comprehensive ethical analysis of scientific research. Yet to date there has been no sustained attempt to situate a detailed study of the social sciences within the framework of a comprehensive ethical analysis flexible enough to take account of the issues peculiar to the social sciences.

This generalization is most clearly illustrated by the history of U.S. government research regulation during the past fifteen years. From the start of that period, federal regulatory agencies have expressed their interest in formulating a general policy applicable to all human subjects research. When, for example, the Public Health Service established a requirement in 1966 that local institutions review research in order to protect human subjects, it specified that the requirement was applicable to social and behavioral as well as to biomedical research. But the commitment to comprehensiveness which this stipulation suggests has never been well understood, let alone consistently practiced. The trend is strikingly illustrated by one of the more recent governmental attempts to address issues of human subjects research: the President's Commission for the Study of Ethical Problems in Medicine and Biomedical and Behavioral Research. First convened in January of 1980, the commission was established to continue the work of the earlier National Commission for the Protection of Human Subjects of Biomedical and Behavioral Research. By all accounts, its own included, the national commission paid insufficient attention to the distinctive problems that arise in social science research. One would therefore expect that topic to figure prominently on the agenda of a body established to attend to issues left unresolved by the national commission. Yet the simple addition of the term "Medicine" in the title of the President's commission, as well as its mandate— which specifies a set of issues almost exclusively in the medical and biomedical domains—indicates otherwise. Moreover, its membership in-

cludes but a single social scientist. It would seem, then, that the moral problems
which may arise in social science research have still not been accorded their
proper place in the comprehensive study of research practices. The sources of
moral controversy over scientific research have predominantly been developments in the biomedical sciences.

Historical Background in the Social Sciences

The generalizations offered in the preceding section should not be taken as
suggesting that no attention whatever has been paid to the ethical issues in
social research. On the contrary, considerable work has been done on this
subject in recent years, nearly all of it by social scientists themselves. There is
no better manifestation of this trend than the extensive publications social
scientists have prepared on the ethical issues that arise in their work. Among
the first and most prominent of the social scientists contributing to this
development is Herbert C. Kelman, whose early papers were published in
1968 as *A Time to Speak*.[1] Kelman has been especially influential in focusing
the attention of many colleagues in the social sciences on the distinctive kinds
of ethical problems that they typically must confront. The breadth of interest
that characterizes Kelman's work has since been echoed in a number of book-
length studies by social scientists, including works by Robert T. Bower and
Priscilla de Gasparis,[2] Edward Diener and Rick Crandall,[3] and Paul Davidson
Reynolds.[4] In addition, the past two decades have witnessed a proliferation of
books on closely related but more narrowly focused topics, of which perhaps
the best known are those written or edited by Gideon Sjoberg,[5] Henry W.
Riecken and Robert F. Boruch,[6] Alice M. Rivlin and P. Michael Timpane,[7]
Paul Nejelski,[8] Michael A. Rynkiewich and James P. Spradley,[9] Gordon
Bermant, Herbert C. Kelman, and Donald P. Warwick,[10] Stephanie B. Stolz,[11]
Murray L. Wax and Joan Cassell,[12] Robert F. Boruch and Joe S. Cecil,[13] and
Carl B. Klockars and Finbarr W. O'Connor.[14]

Social scientists have also heavily invested in work of a more specialized
variety. Most conspicuous are the several published debates which have
emerged from controversial cases in social science research (cases that
frequently engage commentators outside the social sciences as well). The
social sciences have nothing in their history closely analogous to biomedical
experimentation under the Third Reich, but they are not suffering for want of
particular projects that have inspired heated controversy. Names such as the
Wichita Study, "Milgram's Research," "Laud Humphreys's Research," and
Project Camelot are invoked again and again, and the reader who is not already
familiar with them can expect to become so by the end of the present volume.
Each of these cases has spawned whole schools of critics and defenders, many
of whose writings perspicuously illustrate ethical principles that apply to
research and suggest alternative resolutions of moral dilemmas.

In addition to such focused debates, a steadily increasing number of scholarly articles in the journals of the social sciences and related fields have addressed moral problems in social research. The articles in the August 1978 issue of *American Sociologist* and the February 1980 issue of *Social Problems* are representative of this genre of activity. In recent years, especially as federal regulations for the protection of human research subjects have been reformulated so as to apply more specifically to the social sciences, the discussion of ethical issues by social scientists has occasionally carried over into organs of the popular press as well. Considered together, the variety of book-length studies and individual articles by social scientists represents a prodigious output. The bibliography assembled by Bower and de Gasparis for their 1978 study of *Ethics in Social Research* includes over 300 citations. And a somewhat less selective survey of the literature on ethical issues in social science research conducted in connection with the present volume turned up over 3,500 citations.

The sheer volume of work which this amount of publication represents surely bespeaks a more than perfunctory interest on the part of social scientists in the ethical dimensions of their work. That interest is further reflected in their efforts to forge a consensus on the standards of ethical behavior appropriate to research in the social sciences. The results of these efforts have been the codes of ethics formulated and reformulated by the professional associations during the past two decades. Partly in response to a political climate of acute social concern, both the American Anthropological Association and the American Sociological Association adopted new codes of ethics in 1971. At the same time, the latter organization established a standing committee to enforce the stipulations of the code and to review the ethical dimensions of continuing research in sociology, and the former group has substantially revised its ethical guidelines in the subsequent years. The American Psychological Association, too, undertook an examination of ethical issues specific to the discipline, sponsoring extensive research and discussion that culminated in a thorough revision of its fifteen-year-old code of ethics in 1977. These codes of ethics have successfully fostered an appreciation of the fact that research in the various social sciences presents important ethical problems that all professional social scientists ought to acknowledge.

Still more evidence of social scientists' concern about professional ethics may be found in the area of educational activities in the social sciences. Examining this area in his 1980 study, *The Teaching of Ethics in the Social Sciences,*[15] Donald P. Warwick has identified a heightened pedagogical interest in ethical issues in the years since 1965. Widespread indecision certainly persists concerning the appropriate place of ethical issues in the social science curricula, but a number of steps have been taken at American universities to make ethical analysis a routine part of a social scientific education. Although Warwick estimates that there are no more than fifteen courses in the United States devoted exclusively to ethical problems in any of the social sciences, he notes a significant movement (involving "several dozen" instructors at the least) to incorporate sections on ethical issues in both introductory and advanced courses. This development is of course reflected in the discussions of ethical issues that now commonly appear in many textbooks in the social sciences. In addition, recent years have seen an increase in activities that contribute to a heightened awareness of ethical problems among academicians, ranging from informal discussion between colleagues to interdisciplinary conferences.[16]

Taken together, the publications, ethical codes, and educational activities in the social sciences constitute a flourishing area of applied ethics. Yet there is still much more room for growth. In other areas of professional ethics, such as business ethics and medical ethics, the most comprehensive explorations have been thoroughly interdisciplinary. By contrast, social scientists have to this point carried forward the discussion of ethical problems in their field almost single-handedly, though this trend now shows signs of change—the present volume being but one reflection of the interest located in other quarters.

Moral and Nonmoral Issues

Our discussion in the previous section presupposed that there is a distinctive activity described as normative ethical analysis or moral argument. It may not be obvious, however, what distinguishes this activity from other analysis or debate. Indeed, at least three types of questions routinely raised in the social sciences have sometimes been confused with the issues addressed in normative ethical analysis. These include questions concerning the *empirical* results of research projects, questions about the *methodological* design of such projects, and *theoretical* issues involving the nature and limits of the knowledge attained in the social sciences. Before we consider the distinguishing characteristics of moral arguments themselves, it will be useful to determine why these three types of questions lie outside the proper domain of normative ethical analysis.

The empirical results obtained in social science research raise issues which are perhaps most easily distinguishable from the questions debated in normative moral philosophy. A certain confusion may nevertheless be induced by the topics of social scientific inquiry. Social scientists have long applied the methodologies of their disciplines in studying moral phenomena. They examine, for instance, standards of morally acceptable behavior in different cultural settings and the factors contributing to individual moral development within such settings. Important as these studies are in their own right, they provide an understanding of morality that is different in kind from the results of normative ethical analysis in philosophy. Whereas normative moral philosophy aims at determining what *ought* to be done in a given set of circumstances, social scientists intend solely to describe and explain what *is* in fact done. To invoke a familiar dichotomy, normative ethical analysis is evaluative and prescriptive, while analysis in the social sciences is empirical and descriptive. The latter analysis often generates controversies among social scientists about research data, methods, and conclusions; but these controversies tend not to involve a normative moral evaluation of the social phenomena described and explained. Instead, they are likely to center on questions of the accuracy and generalizability of the results and the explanatory power of the theories offered in analyzing those results.

Sometimes the empirical results of social scientific studies contribute substantially to normative arguments in moral philosophy, and the proponents of normative positions often welcome empirical data that they believe support their case. It is important to notice, however, that such scientific conclusions can only make a contribution when presented in conjunction with normative premises. For instance, a researcher might set out to determine the moral justifiability of a research practice by polling a sample of people in some respect representative of those who will be affected by the practice. The results of such a study, however, could not settle a moral issue in isolation from normative premises. In order to draw normative conclusions, the researcher would have to situate his or her nonnormative conclusions within a context of ethical principles and argument which determine how the views of the representative sample *could* count toward the resolution of the issue. To continue this same example, suppose the research practice in question is a procedure for obtaining the informed consent of research subjects in a psychological experiment. Moral principles would determine that consent is required and that a disclosure must be clear and comprehensible. This normative framework might raise the empirical issue of *whether* a consent form contains an adequate disclosure about the research. The purpose of the empirical survey would then be to answer this last question, determining the clarity and comprehensibility of the disclosure by testing it with a representative population. But in the absence of specified moral principles, the results of such empirical research would be quite neutral in their ethical implications.

In a similar if more subtle way, questions of methodological design should also be distinguished from topics of normative ethical analysis. These questions pertain to the methodological adequacy and importance of possible research procedures, such as the experimental deception of subjects or the collection of data in an individually identifiable form. Such questions might be confusing because they involve *evaluation* of the plans or behavior of the researcher, and this evaluative activity may initially appear to resemble moral reasoning and judgment. The resemblance, however, is superficial. The criteria invoked in a methodological evaluation of a research practice are distinct from the criteria appealed to in a moral evaluation of the practice. The methodological criteria specify how a particular procedure should function in a research design, enabling one to assess whether the procedure would screen out effects specific to the research situation that could render the results ungeneralizable, or at least unreliable. A procedure may satisfy such criteria of methodological adequacy and yet be morally unjustifiable; or the procedure may be morally justified but methodologically inadequate.

Of course, methodological questions are not always irrelevant to ethical analysis. A design adequate to achieve the objectives of the research may itself be considered a necessary condition for the *moral* justifiability of a research practice. But in arguing for such a conclusion one's reasons and justifications would include considerations other than the strict appropriateness of the research procedures to the research objectives, such as whether the research is worthwhile based on its promise. One might argue, for instance, that it is irresponsible to use resources of time and money to conduct research that is poorly designed, or that it is morally wrong to employ experimental techniques running any risk of harm whatever if a design is defective. Either justification would presume criteria for assessing the methodological adequacy of research procedures, but in both cases the reasons for making methodological soundness a condition of moral justifiability are independent of these criteria themselves.

Finally, the questions addressed in normative moral philosophy should be kept distinct from certain theoretical problems concerning knowledge in the social sciences. The theoretical questions to which we here refer have historically been grouped under the rubric of "the value controversy" in the social sciences. This grouping, however, is not altogether coherent, for the value controversy has designated a variety of specific issues. In recent years, the expression has come to describe sophisticated questions involving the characteristics of scientific knowledge. Some authors wonder, for instance, whether it is *possible* for social scientific knowledge to attain the value-free status to which it often aspires. They frequently conclude that certain value assumptions which inevitably form the basis of social scientific understanding are necessarily reflected in the results of research in those disciplines, and that the social sciences therefore cannot be perfectly objective (i.e., value free).

These last issues may appear closely related to the issues discussed in normative moral philosophy, for they center on the role of certain values and normative beliefs in social scientific knowledge. But social scientists who consider these topics do not necessarily expect to determine how research in their disciplines *ought* to be conducted (though they might have this objective in mind). The main focus of controversy is again descriptive rather than prescriptive. In this case, it is the process of obtaining social scientific understanding itself that is described, so that social scientists' own activities are the subject under investigation. Such investigations are *theoretical,* because their goal is the provision of comprehensive theories or explanations to account for the processes whereby social scientists acquire knowledge.

The methods employed in these theoretical investigations are sometimes those of the social science being studied, as is the case with R. W. Friedrichs's *A Sociology of Sociology.*[17] But theoretical analyses of social scientific knowledge also borrow freely from the analytic tools and methods of certain branches of philosophy. Philosophers interested in epistemology and philosophy of science in particular have developed refined explanations of what it is possible to know and how it can be known. These explanations are directly applicable to the processes of scientific understanding exhibited in the social sciences. But from the mere fact that some philosophical methods may be applied in such theoretical investigations, it does not follow that those investigations are pertinent to normative moral philosophy. Normative ethics represents but a small part of contemporary work in philosophy; indeed, even within the field of ethics many philosophers are interested more with the description of moral phenomena than with determining what ought to be done in particular situations. It would thus seem that prominent theoretical issues concerning social science research must also be distinguished from normative ethical analysis of the problems that arise therein.

Moral Controversy and Moral Justification

The Nature of Moral Controversy

In distinguishing empirical results, methodological questions, and theoretical issues from the topics of normative ethical analysis, we have left deliberately vague the precise characteristics of the last kind of analysis. One good way to acquire a sense for what normative ethical analysis involves is to consider particular situations which have generated moral controversies. These controversies often exhibit patterns or structures of moral argument and justification, and by examining those patterns it is possible to come to a clearer understanding of the distinctive problems addressed in normative ethical analysis. In this section, we shall attempt to identify such patterns or structures of moral argument by considering one of the aforementioned controversial cases from the history of the social sciences.

Among the best known of these cases is Laud Humphreys's pioneering study of impersonal homosexual activity, carried out as dissertation research from 1965 to 1968 and published in 1970 under the title *Tearoom Trade*.[18] Humphreys's topic was the sexual behavior and social position of men who frequent public restrooms in search of quick and anonymous sexual encounters. He developed a detailed role analysis of the behavior patterns exhibited during such encounters, and he provided a characterization of the types of people who tend to participate in them. His results suggested that, far from being the deviant and potentially dangerous social types commonly imagined, his subjects led conventional and routine public lives. Most turned out to be married (if not always happily) with children, and only 14 percent were exclusively homosexual.

Some ethical issues raised by projects such as Humphreys's derive from the consequences of the research. Humphreys himself presented an extensive defense of his study which pointed to such beneficial consequences of the research as the destruction of dangerous stereotypes held about homosexual men. He regarded these consequences as powerful factors in any moral justification of the research. It is clear from this defense and from his book that Humphreys sympathized with the plight of his subject population. He considered them a disregarded and maligned group in American society, and he believed that widespread misperceptions played a significant role in perpetuating the social injustice affecting the group. Humphreys was also careful to stress that his findings revealed no social harms that could be attributed to his subjects or even to the male homosexual community in general; on the contrary, the only dangers seemed to stem from social repression of homosexual activity. To the extent that these findings challenged prevailing misunderstandings, Humphreys argued that they would help improve the social condition of homosexual men. This appeal to beneficial consequences as conditions justifying a research project is characteristic of a structural pattern that ethical arguments commonly assume.

In defending his project, Humphreys emphasized consequences likely to stem from his research *results.* In order to obtain those results, Humphreys of course employed a particular set of research *methods,* and these methods have proved far more controversial than the results, which have scarcely aroused any controversy at all. The several extensive deceptions that the methods involved are at the heart of the controversy. Since homosexual activity in public facilities tends not to take place in the presence of external observers, Humphreys found it necessary to conceal his identity as a social researcher. He did so by playing the part of a "watchqueen," an established role which requires that one look out for intruders while men are engaged in acts of fellatio. But to study the social position and public behavior of his homosexual subjects outside the restrooms, Humphreys moved beyond deception to covert investigative activity. He recorded the license numbers of his subjects' automobiles and on that basis obtained residential information about them from police registers and phone company records. A year later, after changing his hair style and attire, Humphreys interviewed his subjects in their homes as part of an ostensibly anonymous public health survey.

Most critics of Humphreys's research built their case on the consequences of these research methods. They maintained that even if the research results entail significant social benefits, the countervailing negative consequences of the methods employed outweigh those benefits, and so render the study morally unjustifiable. Two distinct kinds of negative consequences tend to be singled out in the course of such criticisms. First, there are consequences that affect a whole society by somehow altering its values and institutions. Writers such as Donald Warwick have argued that Humphreys's deceptive methods would exacerbate a widespread erosion of trust in American society and would contribute to an increasingly cavalier attitude toward invasions of citizen privacy. But perhaps more important for Warwick and other critics are the risks of harmful consequences that must be borne by the participants in the research. Humphreys's research program required that he identify his subjects, linking particular men not only with license numbers and automobiles but with their names and residential addresses. Though Humphreys took great pains to protect his information, he himself pointed out that American society has not always been noted for its enlightened treatment of identified sexual "deviants." Focusing on this historical fact, many commentators have claimed that Humphreys's identification of his subjects, careful as it was, still exposed them to serious risks of economic harm and damage to reputation, as well as legal jeopardy.

This example illustrates some of the complexity of ethical disputes. Competing commentators make compelling claims for both the beneficial and the harmful consequences of Humphreys's research, and their appeals to such consequences constitute a distinctive pattern of moral argument. Difficult as these purely consequentialist issues are, however, they do not exhaust the range of ethical problems that arise in social science research. Even if, as Humphreys maintained, his research actually posed only a negligible risk of harmful consequences, the methods employed would still be morally controversial. Considered apart from their consequences, deceptive practices such as those Humphreys used appear to many to disrespect the people who are deceived. Most people would consider any inherently disrespectful character of deceptive actions to be morally wrong, and controversies about the moral wrong involved introduce a further complication in the structural pattern of ethical argument. These controversies raise basic questions concerning the proper justification of moral conclusions, for they call into question the justificatory relevance of consequentialist considerations. Some believe, for instance, that the moral wrong entailed by deception is of a sort that cannot be justified by appeals to beneficial consequences of any magnitude. Others agree that deception involves a moral wrong, but conclude that the wrong is simply one factor to be considered along with the harmful and beneficial consequences of the deceptive action. The structural patterns of ethical argument may thus include far more than competing calculations of an action's harmful and beneficial consequences. They often extend to the prior question of *whether* an action's consequences can have justificatory relevance at all, as Humphreys and his critics jointly assume.

Disputes over such issues are frequently couched in terms of *rights*. When it is said that deceptive actions are disrespectful of the person deceived, it is often meant that the actions fail to recognize the person's moral rights. Those rights might include a right to self-determination, encompassing in the Humphreys case the right to decide for oneself whether the risks are sufficiently compensated by other consequences of participating in the research. A related right was attributed to research subjects by the journalist Nicholas von Hoffman. In a column sharply critical of Humphreys's research, von Hoffman suggested that people have a fundamental right to privacy. He argued that Humphreys's acquisition of identifiable information about people's sexual and social lives was an unjustifiable denial of this moral right to privacy. Often enough, however, rights language becomes a two-edged sword in ethical conflicts. Irving Louis Horowitz and Lee Rainwater came to Humphreys's defense in an article that focused on the researcher's right to pursue and to communicate knowledge. To the extent that restrictions on deceptive methods would make studies such as Humphreys's impossible to perform, Rainwater and Horowitz held that those restrictions would infringe the scientist's right to illuminate still mysterious regions of human understanding.

Thus, ethical disputes about social science research can exhibit a complex and interrelated variety of forms. Controversies frequently turn on the consequences of social science research, with disputants examining the methods and results of the research and calculating the harmful and beneficial consequences of each. Additionally, controversies may focus on moral wrongs that are independent of specifiable consequences. Here, the question arises of whether certain moral wrongs render possible consequences invalid as justificatory considerations. Finally, these issues are often couched in terms of moral rights, and the rights of research subjects may then be pitted against conflicting or competing rights of researchers. As the Humphreys case illustrates, arguments assuming a highly complex structural pattern may be generated by a single controversial case. This complexity alone helps to account for the frustrating intractability that often characterizes prominent moral dilemmas.

Similarities among Moral Controversies

Research in the social sciences rarely generates controversies as intense as those that have surrounded Humphreys's project. From this fact, however, it should not be inferred that Humphreys's research is not representative of the ethical issues that can arise in routine work in the social sciences. A great deal of research involving human participants, innocuous though it frequently seems, raises similar ethical questions, and similar moral principles and rights will be mentioned in attempts to resolve these issues. Even the determination that a project is innocuous involves at least an implicit appeal to the same rights and ethical principles invoked in the more controversial cases. Ethical analysis is therefore not something to be reserved simply for the most extreme research cases.

Some social scientific studies which have aroused only muted moral controversies will serve to illustrate this point. Consider first an anthropological study of an urban bar conducted by Brenda J. Mann.[19] Mann's project grew out of a waitressing job she took at a local bar to supplement her income while in graduate school; the research possibilities presented by her position as a waitress were recognized only after she had begun working there. As Mann describes it, this situation created a tension between the various roles she assumed in her dealings with people at the bar. It required that she treat as anthropological subjects people with whom she was already involved professionally and in some cases even personally. Perhaps because of this proximity with her informants, Mann came to appreciate the importance of following the injunction in the American Anthropological Association's code of ethics to communicate the aims of her investigation to the subjects. She sought informal means to convey this information whenever possible, relying on such available mechanisms as the "grapevine" of waitresses at the bar.

Mann's efforts in this connection suggest a recognition that her informants, no less than Humphreys's, had important moral rights which would have been violated by deception about her objectives. Some might object that she revealed her identity as an anthropologist only after the study had begun, depriving her informants of an opportunity to withdraw completely from participation in the project. Mann would perhaps counter by pointing out that even after learning about her study, the people at the bar seemed generally uninterested in what she was doing. Moreover, she might add, her concern for her informants' rights and welfare took the additional form of measures to protect their anonymity and to secure the confidentiality of the information in her possession. She changed the names of all informants and locations, altered insignificant details in her descriptions while eliminating others, and waited two full years before publishing her results.

Of course, Humphreys too went to considerable lengths to protect the anonymity of his subjects and the confidentiality of his data. Furthermore, he was manifestly concerned about the rights and welfare of his subjects. In his view and in that of his advocates, the difference between the projects lay only in the relative sensitivity of the information he collected and in the methodological impossibility of obtaining that information without some misrepresentation of his purposes. The comparison of his study with Mann's reveals most clearly that beneath these differences in the controversiality of the projects, there are substantial similarities in the ethical issues that arise and in the patterns and language of moral justification that are invoked.

The impression that such similarities exist among research projects so markedly different may be reinforced by considering a recent public health survey conducted by K. Ann Coleman Stolurow and Dale W. Moeller.[20] Though this study might be regarded as "biomedical" research, the methods it employed and the results achieved are actually held in common with the social sciences. (For further exploration of the ethical problems presented by some research methods common to biomedicine and social science, see the chapter in this volume by R. Jay Wallace, Jr.) Stolurow and Moeller were interested in the frequency with which x-rays are routinely used as a part of dental check-ups. To obtain this information, they conducted a simple telephone survey of dental offices in the Boston area. They found that in 95 percent of the offices surveyed x-ray procedures are customarily ordered in connection with the initial investigation of new patients, and that in nearly half of those offices, the procedures employed involve full mouth x-rays.

The Stolurow-Moeller survey might initially appear extremely noncontroversial in its ethical dimensions. A closer examination of their survey methods, however, reveals ethical issues and patterns of justification not unlike those that have already been identified. To obtain accurate results from their survey, the public health researchers presented themselves over the telephone as new residents in the Boston area inquiring about available dental services, and they asked a series of specific questions that followed a prepared written survey instrument. There is evidence to indicate that this misrepresentation did indeed contribute to the accuracy of the results, for the data obtained showed a frequency of dental x-ray use far greater than that reported by an earlier study in which the researchers did not conceal their purposes. Despite the possible gain in accuracy of results, the use of deception raises the ethical issues of whether the researchers violated the moral rights of the participants in their study, and of whether their action was therefore morally unjustified.

Many people would likely not consider the Stolurow-Moeller study morally unjustifiable. Following an argument used by the researchers themselves, they might point to the benefits of obtaining accurate information about dental x-rays as morally justifying considerations. (The information, for instance, might form the basis on which the American Dental Association would refocus its efforts to reduce unnecessary x-ray exposure from lessening dosage levels to cutting down on the frequency of exposure.) Additionally or alternatively, they might draw an analogy with consumer surveys, noting that it is a contractual service which the Stolurow-Moeller survey sought to evaluate. It could then be argued that the terms of the contract confer a right on potential customers to possess accurate information about the service, and that this customer right overrides conflicting rights of dental office employees.

Once again, then, it seems that a relatively noncontroversial project may be shown to involve ethical issues and patterns of justification similar to those more dramatically apparent in the famous Humphreys study. A parallel demonstration could be provided for any number of historically noncontroversial research projects in psychology or social psychology. For example, in social psychology, the classic study of restaurant owners' behavior with regard to the exclusion of ethnic minorities by R.T. LaPiere[21] could be shown to present issues of misrepresentation and its justification that closely resemble those we have already identified.

Conformity to these identified patterns of argument and justification, however, is not alone sufficient to qualify a dispute as distinctively moral. In many cases, legal and political controversies exhibit similar patterns and present similar issues, and these similarities frequently complicate the task of discerning and sorting out the ethical dimensions of a particular project. An illuminating example of this source of added complexity is provided by one of the earliest social science projects to generate heated public controversy. In 1954 professors in the social sciences and the Law School at the University of Chicago performed a study of jury deliberations that has since come to be known as the Wichita Jury Study.[22] The researchers secretly recorded the discussions of six separate juries in order to obtain empirical data by which to test frequent criticisms of the jury system and the assumptions about that system implicit in American law.

The Chicago academicians stressed the beneficial consequences of possessing such data. We should not be left in the dark, they maintained, about the actual operations of an institution so fundamental to our legal system. Yet the importance of maintaining confidentiality in that institution also led many to question the justifiability of the methods used to collect the information. The Seventh Amendment to the Constitution guarantees the right of U.S. citizens to a trial by jury in criminal cases. Senator James O. Eastland echoed the opinion of a large number of commentators when he noted that secret deliberation is essential to the jury process as the framers of the Seventh Amendment conceived it. The potentially harmful consequences of recording jury discussions would on this view include the denial or erosion of a specific constitutional provision. The extent to which Senator Eastland's interpretation was shared at least by other politicians is indicated by the passage of legislation in 1956 explicitly prohibiting the recording of federal grand or petit jury deliberations.

Eastland's appeal to legislative intentions and constitutional guarantees rests on a recognizably legal argument. Yet the Wichita Study raises ethical issues that can be distinguished from the historically more prominent legal and political aspects of the case. To the extent that the jurors under investigation believed that their discussions were taking place in private, the recording of those discussions presents a now familiar moral problem. Even if that recording did not inflict any specifiable harms on the participating jurors, it may involve a moral wrong, one whose status would have to be assessed before an ethical analysis of the project could be complete.

In addition to addressing such questions of moral wrongs, a normative ethical analysis would likely take into account the reasonably anticipatable harms and benefits of the study. At this stage, the patterns of moral and legal justification may well be difficult to distinguish. For instance, a moral philosopher and a lawyer might both cite among the study's benefits the importance of information about the jury system, and among its harms the danger of eroding any aspect of such a constitutionally guaranteed institution. In so doing, they would provide an illustration of the common ground that ethical and legal positions frequently occupy. Developed ethical arguments, however, generally do differ from legal and political positions, because the respective bases of the arguments are distinct. While the latter rest on codified legislation, common law, or constitutional stipulations, ethical arguments invoke distinct rules, referred to in ethical theory as principles. It is this appeal to independent rules that distinguishes ethical from legal and political analyses of social science research.

Moral Justification

Everyone is familiar with at least some moral principles, for we are called upon almost daily to justify our behavior, to criticize new legislation that has captured our attention, or to deliberate about alternative courses of action. Moral principles are the most general moral rules used for these purposes. In recent years philosophers and others interested in ethical analysis have attempted to apply these general principles to concrete social dilemmas and to moral problems that emerge in various professional activities. Regardless of whether the field under examination is politics, business, medicine, or law, the moral principles used to discuss ethical issues remain the same, or at least there is considerable continuity across fields. Thus from a philosopher's point of view much the same principles apply in biomedical ethics, political ethics, journalistic ethics, jurisprudence, and business ethics, as well as social research ethics. For instance, moral principles of truthfulness have significance for debates about secrecy and deception in business ethics, balanced reporting, the use of placebos in medicine, and deception in psychological research. Presumably greater clarity about the conditions in general under which truth must be told and when it may be withheld would enhance understanding of what is required in each of these areas. Let us now look in a more formal way at moral principles that are especially applicable to the ethical issues in social science research, and at how the justification of moral positions may appeal to such principles.

Perhaps most common of the specific moral principles invoked in analyses of human subjects research is the principle of autonomy, often referred to in literature on ethics in the the social sciences as the principle of self-determination, or respect for persons. Though this principle has historically been formulated in a variety of ways, the central demand constant in the diverse formulations is that we respect the values and decisions of other people. Of course, the liberty implied by the principle of autonomy is not unlimited, for actions that physically harm unwilling parties are rightfully restrained. Nor does the principle prevent us from recognizing that certain people, such as children and the mentally infirm, are not in a position to act in a fully autonomous manner. But to the extent that a competent person's unconstrained actions are self-regarding (i.e., affecting only the actor), the principle of autonomy requires that the reasons for the actions be respected and the actions themselves not interfered with. To obtain this attitude of respect and noninterference is, in the expression of Immanuel Kant, to treat other people as ends in themselves and not solely as means to the ends of others. The most obvious and immediate application of this principle to problems of social research comes in the requirement that the informed consent of research subjects be obtained, and thus that appropriate disclosures be made prior to their involvement in research and prior to the use of any deceptive practices. We will have occasion later in this Introduction to return to the principle of autonomy and its application to theories of informed consent.

A second ethical principle pertinent to social science research is the principle of nonmaleficence. This principle stipulates that it is wrong intentionally to inflict harm on another person. Like the principle of autonomy, nonmaleficence at this general level of formulation is vague in its specific implications; its applicability will turn, for instance, on the way "harm" is defined and the consequent scope it is given. The principle of nonmaleficence is usually presented in conjunction with a related ethical principle, that of beneficence. Beneficence specifies a positive obligation to remove existing harms and to confer benefits on others. The principle of beneficence thus suggests a more active and far-reaching category of moral obligations than does nonmaleficence, but the two obviously fit together, especially when we must weigh the possibility of doing harm by an intervention against the possibility of a benefit from the same intervention. This problem raises questions about the appropriateness of risk-benefit analysis for ethical issues in social research, a topic to be taken up later in this Introduction together with further discussion of these two principles.

In addition to autonomy, nonmaleficence, and beneficence, a fourth ethical principle is sometimes applicable to research situations in the social sciences. That is the principle of justice. In its purely formal statement, this principle stipulates that people who are equal in relevant respects should be treated equally, while those who differ in such respects should be treated differently. As should be evident, this formal statement leaves great latitude for differences in the interpretation of how justice applies to particular situations, especially on the question of the respects considered relevant for purposes of comparing individuals. Philosophers have accordingly developed remarkably diverse theories of justice even when they share the same starting point. One theme common to many theories, however, is that programs or services designed to assist people of a certain class should be made available to all members of that class. To provide some with access to such programs, while denying access to others who are equally qualified, simply seems unfair, and the notion of fairness is on most construals closely allied with the principle of justice. The principle of justice thus understood is particularly applicable to problems of program experimentation, where the methods of the social sciences are used to evaluate innovations in public policy and in the administration of justice (e.g., by empirically testing the effects of alternative parole policies with certain classes of criminals). It may also be pertinent to social research on deviant behavior or primitive societies, in which the research subjects are exposed to various types of harm without, in some cases, standing to benefit from the conduct of the research or the publication of the research results.

The reader may wonder at this point about the foundation giving authority to such ethical principles as autonomy, nonmaleficence, beneficence, and justice. It would be easy to assert in response that, at least in Western societies, these principles have a long historical heritage, and that in some respects they constitute the moral basis of our cultural tradition. Such a response describes an acceptable starting point, but moral philosophers are generally not content to rely upon historical givens. Their professional tendency is to develop broad moral theories intended to justify particular moral principles and sets of principles. These moral theories generally follow one of two distinct patterns. *Utilitarian* theories hold that actions are justified by reference to only one of their characteristics. That characteristic is the action's consequences. According to such theories, the primary moral rule from which all others are derived is that one should always act to produce the greatest possible balance of value over disvalue for all affected persons. The papers in this volume by Alan C. Elms and by Jay Wallace provide especially clear examples of utilitarian justification applied to research practices in the social sciences. By contrast, *deontological* theories maintain that features of an action other than its consequences are relevant to the moral assessment of the action. On Kant's deontological theory, for example, moral principles should be adopted if they meet the formal conditions of universalizability stipulated by his "categorical imperative." On other deontological accounts, ethical principles are said to be grounded in natural law or derived from a hypothetical social contract. These arguments too will become familiar to the reader in working through papers in this volume by Ruth Macklin, Terry Pinkard, Alasdair MacIntyre, and others.

In thus broadly characterizing moral theories, we may seem to suggest that substantive ethical principles such as autonomy and beneficence figure prominently in all utilitarian and deontological philosophies. That is not in fact the case. One common version of utilitarianism maintains that it is not moral rules but particular acts that are to be evaluated strictly on the basis of their consequences. For proponents of this "act utilitarianism," the formal requirement of maximization of value over disvalue in particular settings itself becomes the only controlling ethical principle. Even moral theories that do develop and rely on substantive ethical rules must allow for considerable distance between general principles and particular circumstances of action. As one might expect from principles as broad as autonomy, nonmaleficence, beneficence, and justice, the specific meaning and precise scope of an ethical principle will not always be easy to discern in its (necessarily) broad formulation. Most ethical theories permit and encourage subsidiary moral rules, social institutions, or procedures that could in some degree bridge this apparent gap. A single ethical principle might then eventuate in a number of less general moral rules, the application of each of which would be stipulatively restricted to a particular range of circumstances. We may call these subsidiary rules moral requirements.

The aforementioned procedures of informed consent and risk-benefit analysis are the requirements most commonly derived from general ethical principles, at least for application to research involving human participants. The professional codes of ethics mentioned in the second section of this Introduction are more systematic attempts to define the moral requirements applicable to particular disciplines. The code of the American Anthropological Association, for instance, stipulates that "There should be no exploitation of individual informants for personal gain. Fair return should be given them for all services." This rule can be seen as an application of the principle of justice to situations likely to arise in anthropological research. Still, there is no unanimous consensus as to the moral requirements that apply to research in the social sciences, and many of the controversial questions in social science research turn on this question of which requirements are appropriate in the various disciplines.

To summarize, then, the ethical principles most pertinent to moral justifications in social science research are the principles of autonomy, nonmaleficence, beneficence, and justice. Various philosophers have defended a similar set of principles by both utilitarian and deontological arguments, and such arguments have in turn been used to legitimate moral rules of greater specificity that we shall call "moral requirements." Let us now turn to some prominent topics of moral controversy in the social sciences and see how these principles and methods of justification may apply in their analysis.

Topics of Moral Controversy in the Social Sciences

Professional Obligations and Their Limits

For the professional in any field of activity, there are likely to be certain requirements or rules so basic and broadly presupposed that they rarely need be made explicit. It is taken for granted, for instance, that the business executive incurs an obligation to promote the interests of the company for which he or she works. Similarly, the social science researcher, and indeed the researcher in any academic discipline, is expected as a matter of course to advance the systematic understanding of a field of inquiry. Such fundamental professional obligations may be considered instances of the broader class of duties imposed by what sociologists refer to as role norms. According to this conception, people exhibit distinctive patterns of behavior in conformity with the implicit rules of the social institutions or organizations to which they belong, their professional obligations being but one conspicuous set of duties and responsibilities incurred through institutional associations.

Such terms as *obligation, duty,* and *responsibility* are often employed to explicate the notion of role norms. This terminology suggests a common normative vocabulary for expressing role requirements and moral requirements. The connection may be more than merely linguistic, for professional obligations are usually of sufficient importance that the fulfillment of those obligations is viewed as a matter of *moral* urgency. This perception of the relationship is often reflected in codes of ethics, where it is common to find basic role obligations and duties to a profession mentioned prominently among the rules of the code. Each of the codes of ethics that we mentioned in the second section, for instance, makes some reference to the researcher's obligation to contribute objectively to the acquisition of scientific knowledge.

Within such codes of ethics, the requirement that the researcher contribute to the acquisition of knowledge is generally advanced in conjunction with a commitment to academic freedom of inquiry, for only under conditions of free inquiry can scholarly pursuits optimally flourish. Researchers should be free to pursue their studies in accordance with their perception of scholarly importance, unhindered in such determinations by political considerations or social pressures at either the institutional or political level. Of course, this description of academic freedom depicts an ideal seldom realized in practice. Academicians in any field encounter more or less subtle boundaries restricting their activities. The obligation to advance knowledge is only one among a large number of social obligations that affect the researcher, and these other obligations can easily impose alternative and conflicting imperatives.

Such conflicts emerge frequently in the social sciences. This phenomenon may be explained in large part by the topics naturally of interest to social scientists. Those topics often touch on issues that attract widespread attention in the larger society, such as homosexuality, professional thievery, prison conditions, voter preferences, obedience to authority figures, routine cheating on taxes, and decision making in the jury system. The controversial nature of such topics make social scientists particularly susceptible to the pressures of political and private interests in the society, especially when results are disapproved or regarded as trivial wastes of public monies. While many social scientific studies of prominent social issues have been and continue to be performed, some have maintained that certain studies are or will prove too controversial for society to permit, no matter how important the knowledge gained might be.

Dorothy Nelkin takes this position in her essay, "Forbidden Research: Limits to Inquiry in the Social Sciences." She argues that the social scientist's pursuit of knowledge can extend only as far as prevailing social values and power relationships permit. According to Nelkin, these restrictions of academic freedom generally assume two distinct forms: limitations imposed because of the ends (the knowledge) pursued by researchers, and those imposed because of the means employed to attain such ends. Falling under the former category, for instance, are studies social scientists refrain from undertaking in deference to the interests of powerful groups in the society such as corporate leaders, university administrators, or politicians. The latter category of prohibited research would include, for example, projects modeled after the Wichita Jury Study, where it is not the findings but the means employed to obtain those findings that are thought to threaten the jury system. In Nelkin's view, then, the social scientist's professional obligation to pursue knowledge is restricted by the nexus of social values and external forces in which the research must be conducted.

Nelkin's observation that certain kinds of social scientific studies tend not to be undertaken is noncontroversial. More controversial is her thesis that this phenomenon is a consequence of the restriction of academic freedom through social pressures and powerful interests. Alasdair MacIntyre's commentary contrasts sharply with Nelkin's interpretation on precisely this point. That the debate over this issue should still be focused on the question of how best to explain an agreed-upon social phenomenon perhaps reflects the relatively youthful character of this area of applied ethics. Only when these interpretative issues have been settled will such normative questions as the following likely be addressed: Under what (if any) conditions should social science research be prohibited? How should the social scientist respond when academic freedom of inquiry is wrongly circumscribed by powerful social pressures?

One approach to these normative issues begins by considering the specific moral principles described in the previous section of this Introduction. If certain restrictions on scientific inquiry could be shown to reflect a reasonable public apprehension that the restricted research was morally impermissible, then the restrictions might seem defensible rather than arbitrary. But how could it be shown that research practices are morally impermissible? Minimally, a demonstration that the research violates some fundamental ethical principle would be required. Consider first the principle of nonmaleficence. As we saw, this principle imposes a moral duty not to harm other people, and it thus suggests a rough and basic criterion that a research practice would have to meet in order to be considered morally impermissible. To the extent that research runs the risk of inflicting significant harms on people, (prima facie) grounds exist for supposing it to be morally impermissible (though, as we shall see in the next section, other principles suggest a need to weigh harms against countervailing benefits).

The question *whether* social science research does harm people, however, is not as straightforward as it may at first appear. On one side of the controversy that has erupted over this question are those who maintain that the possibilities of harmful consequences from social science research are manifold, significant, and common. The paper in this volume by Donald Warwick on "Types of Harm in Social Research" is representative of this point of view. Warwick presents an elaborate typology of possible harmful effects in the social sciences, identifying consequences that range in severity from death to minor and ephemeral psychological reactions such as irritation, annoyance, and frustration. Many other social scientists would dispute at least the implications of Warwick's position. Focusing on differences between biomedical and social scientific research, these commentators argue that the latter activity is relatively harmless. Whereas biomedical experimentation often presents a risk of irreversible physical damage or disfigurement, the social sciences are seen as involving risks of harm no greater than those entailed by quotidian social interactions. Some representatives of this position, such as E. L. Pattullo, in his essay, "Modesty is the Best Policy: The Federal Role in Social Research," concede that Warwick has identified conceivable consequences of social research, but argue that those consequences are so unlikely in the vast majority of projects that they need not be taken into account. It is of course possible to hold a middle position on this issue, as evidenced in Herbert Kelman's essay in this volume. Kelman argues that the likelihood of concrete harms to interests varies markedly by the type of research method employed.

Normative issues raised by the principle of nonmaleficence are thus clouded by disagreements over the largely empirical question of whether social science research is a harmful activity. To some extent, these disagreements turn on the conceptual question of criteria for harm in making moral evaluations. (Should the term be restricted to physical consequences that are damaging and irreversible, or should it also embrace impermanent and less dramatic psychological effects? Legal effects? Economic effects?) Even if agreement could be reached on all empirical and conceptual issues, however, the normative implications of the principle of nonmaleficence could remain unresolved. As we shall see in the next section of this Introduction, the presence of harmful consequences does not alone provide sufficient grounds for judging social research projects morally impermissible.

Harm and Benefit

Our consideration of the principle of nonmaleficence has left open the following normative question: Is research that involves risk of harms to people ever morally justified? Most people would answer this question in the affirmative. Defenders of Laud Humphreys's project, for instance, admit that it posed some risk of harming the men under investigation; yet, they still maintain that the research was morally justifiable. As we have seen, advocates of this position frequently build their case around the beneficial consequences of Humphreys's research. These benefits include most prominently the improvements in the social condition of homosexual men that presumably would result from a clearer understanding of their activities and values.

In focusing on the beneficial consequences of the research, Humphreys's defenders at least implicitly make an appeal to the principle of beneficence, as described earlier in this Introduction. Their appeal suggests that the professional obligation to advance human understanding may not be the only positive duty applicable to the social science researcher. In addition to that professional obligation, the principle of beneficence specifies a moral duty to provide social benefits. It is important to observe, however, that the duty to produce benefits is commonly held in moral philosophy to be supererogatory rather than strictly obligatory. That is, while the production of social benefits is always in itself laudable, people are not *morally* deficient if they fail on some occasion to produce certain possible benefits. This characterization of beneficence is consistent with our present endeavor, which is not to determine those actions that the researcher *must* perform, but to ascertain the classes of actions that it is morally *permissible* for the researcher to perform. In other words, we are principally concerned with moral prohibitions.

An action is not determined to be morally permissible simply by demonstrating that it is in conformity with the requirements of beneficence. Indeed, the principle of nonmaleficence is more directly pertinent to the question of what risky actions are morally permissible. The interesting problem is that actions that provide social benefits frequently transgress the limits suggested by nonmaleficence, presenting risks of harm that must be taken in order to secure the benefits. Such conflicts between beneficence and nonmaleficence arise frequently in social science research, the Humphreys case being particularly celebrated in this connection only by virtue of the public controversy it aroused.

Given these conflicts, it would seem a formidable task to forge a consensus about when social science projects are to be considered morally permissible. Yet on one common approach to the treatment of such conflicts, their resolution appears to be a straightforward matter of common sense. As we noted earlier, the moral *principles* of beneficence and nonmaleficence are generally taken to justify a moral *requirement* of risk-benefit analysis. According to this requirement, apparent conflicts between the obligations of beneficence and nonmaleficence are to be negotiated by weighing projected possible harms and possible benefits of a proposed procedure that is under consideration. If the risks of the procedure are "reasonable" in relation to the benefits hoped for, the action may be considered morally permissible (at least with respect to the principles of beneficence and nonmaleficence).

The ostensibly straightforward character of this moral requirement, however, is belied by the difficulties that can attend its application to research situations in general (and perhaps to research in the social sciences in particular). Three such difficulties warrant brief consideration: First, moral problems could arise if the requirement of risk-benefit analysis were not supplemented by an assessment of the justice of the distribution of the harms and benefits in question. As Alasdair MacIntyre points out in his commentary, considerations of justice have seemed to many to establish independent limits on the moral permissibility of the patterns by which risks and benefits are distributed. Thus, a project whose benefits clearly outweighed its risks might nevertheless be morally impermissible if the risks were unjustly borne by economically disadvantaged members of the society. There is some evidence to suggest that the need to supplement risk-benefit analysis by attention to distributive justice has been appreciated at least by academic social researchers in recent years, for very few instances can be cited of academic social research in which the distribution of risks and benefits violates notions of justice. Bradford H. Gray, in his paper on "The Regulatory Context of Social and Behavioral Research," describes a prestigious survey which found that "risks and benefits [of research] are not distributed in the aggregate in a way that raises serious ethical concern."

The case is somewhat different, however, with social research in applied or nonacademic contexts. There, the distribution of risks and benefits has on occasion come into conflict with the dictates of the principle of justice. As we noted above, the application of that principle is perhaps least controversial in cases involving service delivery programs and innovations in the administration of justice. It stipulates that the benefits of such programs should be available equally to all people who meet the specified qualifications. Yet social experimentation—the use of social science methods to test proposed programs and innovations—frequently proceeds by systematically excluding certain qualified individuals from a program whose effects are under investigation. This is done, of course, in order to create a control group, the data from which can be compared with the data obtained about the experimental program itself. Even though the practice may thus be justifiable on scientific grounds, the question remains whether the principle of justice renders disparate treatment of like individuals *morally* impermissible. That question is likely to generate particular controversy when the benefits conferred by the experimental program are considered substantial, as was the case with the New Jersey-Pennsylvania Income Maintenance Experiment discussed by several of the authors in this volume.

A second problem with the risk-benefit approach has proved equally controversial in the social sciences. That problem concerns the question of whether it is appropriate to justify social research in terms of the social benefits it promises to produce. In considering this question (the debate over which in many respects parallels the debate about whether social research is a harmful or risky activity) a comparison with biomedical research involving human subjects is instructive. Risk-benefit analyses have long been undertaken in reviewing research projects in the biomedical sciences, and proponents of these projects regularly cite anticipated improvements in health or cost reduction as important social benefits. Many have wondered whether it is possible to invoke comparable social benefits in performing risk-benefit assessments in the social sciences. After all, considerable social research aims primarily at the acquisition of knowledge, and only secondarily, if at all, at the beneficial applications which may result from that knowledge. Risk-benefit analysis may therefore be critically deficient or even inapplicable as a tool for determining the moral permissibility of many research projects in the social sciences. Focusing on the case of social science research conducted with public funds, Gordon Bermant explores this question in his essay "Justifying Social Science Research in Terms of Social Benefit." Bermant concludes that publicly supported social research both can and should be justified by reference to anticipated benefits. But he is careful to observe that one's answer to this question will hinge on how one settles the related conceptual issue of what a social benefit is.

A third set of difficulties historically associated with the risk-benefit re-quirement also involves issues of the practicality of using the technique. Perhaps the most frequently voiced objection to risk-benefit analysis is that it is extremely difficult, if not altogether impossible, to discover a common standard in terms of which to compare harmful and beneficial consequences. A dramatic example in this connection would be one taken from cross-cultural research in anthropology, where some would maintain that differences in cultural values make it impossible to assess the projected risks and benefits in a way that would permit an informative comparison between the two. Compounding these problems of comparative assessment are the difficulties involved in predicting harms and benefits even in their own terms. Risk-benefit analyses are of course useful guides to anticipated conduct only if they are performed in advance of the actions whose harmful and beneficial consequences are being analyzed. According to some commentators, such as Joan Cassell in her paper "Does Risk-Benefit Analysis Apply to Moral Evaluation of Social Research?" this characteristic makes risk-benefit analysis doubtfully applicable to much social research. In Cassell's view, advance assessment of research harms and benefits requires predictions that cannot reliably be made in the labile context of fieldwork in anthropology, sociology, and social psychology.

Many would no doubt admit that risk-benefit analysis presents practical problems of comparison and prediction without concluding that the requirement is an inapplicable, useless tool for assessing social research. For them, the requirement provides a practical method for answering the question of when research projects involving ineliminable risk are morally permissible according to the imperatives of beneficence and nonmaleficence. Yet even if risk-benefit analysis is applicable to the social sciences and supplemented by considerations of justice, its use may still not decisively determine whether a research project is morally permissible. In the following section of this Introduction, we shall consider whether the principle of autonomy sets further limits on the moral justifiability of social science research.

Informed Consent and Deception

In the light of the preceding discussion, consider for a moment a hypothetical research project from the social sciences: The project is expected to bring substantial social benefits that (uncontroversially) outweigh the various identifiable costs. On the grounds of beneficence and nonmaleficence, the project would seem justifiable. But suppose that the researcher finds it impossible to inform the participants in the project that they are the subjects of social science research without compromising the scientific validity of the results. Even if the research were likely to have benign effects for those involved, many would consider the project nonetheless morally unjustifiable. The reason would be that the researcher failed to afford the participants an opportunity to decide whether or not to contribute to the research in question. And this failure, they would maintain, violates the requirements of the principle of autonomy.

As suggested above, autonomy is perhaps the principle most frequently mentioned in discussions of the ethical issues in social research. Its scope and implications, however, are disputed. The principle is often associated with the deontological moral theory of Kant and is formulated in Kantian terms as requiring that people be treated as ends in themselves and never solely as a means to the ends of others. Indeed, Kant's account of the importance of autonomy has achieved such prominence that the principle is sometimes taken to be the leading weapon with which to attack a utilitarian approach to moral problems. Such interpretations are, however, simplistic. Philosophically, any rule utilitarian could consistently hold that the greatest proportion of value over disvalue would be achieved if the principle of autonomy were included among the set of basic moral rules. And historically, the prominent utilitarian philosopher John Stuart Mill provided in his work *On Liberty* a defense of the principle nearly as influential as Kant's.

It is not, however, the general formulation of the principle of autonomy that has proved most controversial in the social sciences. Disputes have instead centered on the moral requirement of informed consent, which is commonly derived from that principle and applied to research involving human partici-pants. The requirement of informed consent has been developed as a means of ensuring that potential participants in a research project are given an opportunity to assess the methods, risks, and purposes of the project and to decide on that basis whether to participate. To satisfy this goal, informed consent has generally been taken to require disclosure of accurate, comprehen-sible, and sufficiently comprehensive information about the research project in question. It is further understood to involve the removal of potentially con-straining circumstances and inducements that could unduly influence the potential participant's decision. When these broad requirements of informed consent are satisfied, participation in a research project should become a matter of the exercise rather than the violation of a person's autonomy; the consenting participant is not being treated merely as a means to the researcher's ends, because the participant has to some extent chosen to adopt those ends as his or her own.

This argument provides the general moral rationale for the informed consent requirement, a rationale few would find objectionable in itself. As we mentioned above, the requirement has nonetheless generated controversy in the social science research community. The grounds for the controversy are various, ranging from practical considerations of convenience and efficiency to questions of the incompatibility of the requirement with the methodological demands of research. Some maintain that a rigid insistence on the requirement would render much research prohibitively and unreasonably costly in time and money, while bringing only minimal advantages. They cite, e.g., research involving review of public records and observation research conducted in public settings, such as surveys of seat belt usage conducted *in situ*. Others contend that regardless of its expense, the requirement would inject an element of participant self-consciousness which is incompatible with the social scientist's quest for an objective understanding of human behavior, and which would effectively preclude valuable research such as that of Laud Humphreys. Still others contend that imposing an informed consent require-

ment on certain kinds of social science research that involves direct questioning of participants is in violation of First Amendment rights to free speech.
Ruth Macklin, in her essay, "The Problem of Adequate Disclosure in Social
Science Research," describes and assesses these various claims that informed
consent is sometimes an inappropriate requirement for the social sciences. She
concludes that none of the claims adequately appreciates the force of the moral
principle of autonomy (or respect for persons) that underlies the informed
consent requirement. Macklin's own interpretation of the strong imperatives of
autonomy suggests a deontological approach to the moral problems in social
science research and illustrates the possible implications of a deontological as
opposed to a utilitarian construal of this widely accepted moral principle. It
also provides a comprehensive introduction to the lines of controversy that
have emerged on the question of informed consent requirements.

Macklin's approach and conclusions contrast instructively with those
presented by Alan C. Elms in his essay, "Keeping Deception Honest:
Justifying Conditions for Social Scientific Research Stratagems." Elms
focuses on the case of active deception, where social scientists not only do not
inform research participants about the nature and purposes of their projects,
but systematically misinform them in order to control aspects of the research
situation. Stanley Milgram's studies of *Obedience to Authority* provide a
much discussed illustration of this research procedure. Elms presents an
avowedly utilitarian defense of deception in Milgram's research and in other
analogous contexts. He maintains, more specifically, that the social benefits of
research in the social sciences can be so significant as to justify deceptive
methods, but only when those methods are necessary to carry out the research
and when certain procedural safeguards are present. Viewed from this
utilitarian perspective, a departure from the requirements of informed consent
becomes one of the consequences—albeit an extremely significant one—to be
entered into the risk-benefit analysis of a proposed research project. Commentators such as Macklin and MacIntyre would presumably take the very
different position that a departure from informed consent requirements is
morally impermissible regardless of the calculated ratio of risks to benefits.
For them, in other words, the principle of autonomy sets limits on the moral
permissibility of research practices—limits that are both independent of and
prior to those set by the principles of nonmaleficence and beneficence alone.
Elms in effect challenges this position by focusing on its implications for the
viability and scientific integrity of research in the social sciences.

A second alternative to Macklin's position is suggested by Alexander
Capron's discussion in his essay "Is Consent Always Necessary in Social
Science Research?" Capron attempts to find a middle ground between the
insistence that informed consent requirements strictly and literally be
observed, and the contention that departures from them are justifiable when
the consequences are sufficiently beneficial. To this end, he develops a
functional analysis of informed consent requirements, arguing that once the

functions of informed consent have been identified, alternative procedures more compatible with the methodological imperatives of research can be assessed. Capron evaluates several possible alternatives (e.g., proxy consent, debriefing), and concludes that while many of these alternatives hold out some promise, none of them is likely to more than approximately serve the traditional functions of informed consent. Still another way of approaching these issues is presented by Gerald Dworkin's commentary, "Must Subjects be Objects?" Dworkin maintains that it is not necessary to obtain informed consent in all research situations, but bases this conclusion on decidedly nonutilitarian grounds. Dworkin argues that it is the context in which research is conducted, rather than the consequences of performing the research, that needs to be assessed in order to determine whether informed consent must be obtained. The contexts in which the formal requirement can be waived are in his view precisely those which involve "implied consent" to the sort of activity which the researcher wishes to perform.

The essays by Macklin, Elms, Capron, and Dworkin thus clearly illustrate the variety of positions that can be taken on the controversial question of informed consent requirements in social science research. While a commitment to the principle of autonomy is consistent with a rule-utilitarian no less than with a deontological moral theory, it is evident from these essays that one's general theoretical approach is likely to determine the strength of one's insistence that the applicable moral requirement be strictly enforced. Those unwilling to allow departures from the informed consent requirement under any circumstances must consider the implications of their position for the scientific integrity and viability of social science research, especially in situations where the research itself is unlikely to be stressful or otherwise damaging to the interests of research participants. Conversely, those who would allow departures from the requirement must convincingly demonstrate that the moral considerations they invoke do not legitimate similar departures in cases where they clearly would not wish to condone them. Given the difficulty of either project, it is not altogether surprising that this area of social research ethics is still beset with a polarization of opinion.

Privacy and Confidentiality

While the specific factual background of discussion varies markedly between the two areas, many of the questions so far canvassed about the appropriateness and scope of basic moral requirements have proven equally controversial in biomedicine and in the social sciences. The same cannot be said, however, about all the controversial moral issues that arise in connection with social research. A set of issues discussed under the labels "privacy" and "confidentiality," for instance, is generally considered of greater importance in the social sciences than in biomedicine. Questions of privacy and confidentiality certainly do arise in biomedical research, but they do not there occupy the same central position that they assume in the social sciences.

The reason for the comparative prominence of these issues in debates about the social sciences most probably concerns the methods and purposes of research in those disciplines. Because social scientists are interested principally in human behavior, they are attracted to the study of activities that many persons consider private. Indeed, theirs would be a rather limited and uninformative pursuit if it were on all occasions restricted to behavior and activities that are uncontroversially public. There would then be no social scientific examination of such matters as marital relations, the effects of mental disability, doctor-patient relationships, etc. In addition, the methods employed in social research frequently raise privacy and confidentiality problems of their own that are to some extent independent of the activity or behavior under examination. The various methods of data collection and analysis, for example, sometimes require access to information contained in confidential records, and questions arise about the conditions, if any, under which such access to private records is morally justifiable.

Before such questions can be treated, it is necessary to come to some understanding of the moral foundations and implications of privacy and confidentiality. One approach is to formulate these issues in the language of moral *rights,* and to ask what ethical principles and practical concerns underlie an imputed right to privacy. This approach might then lead us, for example, to treat the right to privacy as grounded in the broad principle of autonomy. This principle confers a right to self-determination that, as we have seen, may be protected by informed consent requirements, and the right to privacy might easily appear to be derivative from this more general right to self-determination. That is, the right to privacy might seem to consist in the right to self-determination in contexts involving personal information, giving moral authority to the individual's interest in determining what will be known about him or her. If the right to privacy were thus viewed as derivative from the principle of autonomy, controversies about privacy and confidentiality in the social sciences could borrow from the terminology developed in discussions about autonomy and informed consent.

This straightforward approach initially appears promising, but there is reason to doubt that it provides an adequate basis for analysis of privacy and confidentiality issues. One objection to the approach is presented by Arthur L. Caplan in his essay, "On Privacy and Confidentiality in Social Science Research." Caplan argues that to see privacy as derivative from any more basic or comprehensive moral principle is to mistake its own fundamental nature and importance. Citing empirical evidence from the social sciences, Caplan contends that privacy is a universal human need. All cultures allow their members at least some spheres in which the privacy of their activity is protected, and in Caplan's opinion this fact suggests that privacy is essential to the human sense of identity and well-being. The universality of privacy is in turn said to give it a special importance in moral deliberations; since privacy itself is a basic human need, the moral right to privacy achieves a primacy superior to that of other rights grounded in relatively controversial ethical principles (such as the principle of autonomy). From Caplan's perspective, then, data gathered from social scientific research ironically provide reasons for protecting individual privacy against the possible intrusions of social researchers.

Even for people more sympathetic to the approach of grounding the right to privacy in an ethical principle such as autonomy, serious obstacles remain. Discussions of moral rights have had a notorious history of elusiveness and indeterminacy in philosophy and politics, and the right to privacy in particular has been invoked in contexts too diverse to be subsumed exclusively under a single ethical principle such as autonomy. As Terry Pinkard suggests in his essay, "Invasions of Privacy in Social Science Research," it may simply be the case that the notion of privacy has no single fixed and identifiable meaning (or even a fixed core of meanings), but is rather inherently or essentially susceptible of being disputed or contested. Pinkard himself, however, eventually retreats somewhat from so thoroughly despairing a conclusion. He argues that the right to privacy can be given a coherent formulation adequate at least for purposes of application to social science research. According to this formulation, the right to determine what other people will know about oneself is immune to compromise merely in the interests of greater social utility. Indeed, the right to privacy *requires* that people be given a chance to decide when and under what circumstances information about them will be revealed. This requirement need not, however, be seen as the equivalent of a formal rule of informed consent to the disclosure of personal information. Taking controversial situations from the social sciences as his examples, Pinkard (recalling Dworkin in this regard) shows how the *context* in which research is conducted—including the normal expectations associated with that context— can indicate a person's implicit or informal consent to the disclosure of personal information.

If Pinkard's analysis is correct, then the terminology of autonomy and informed consent should after all be applicable to right-to-privacy cases, even though such a right may not be fully explicable by reference to autonomy rights. It follows that only the observation of behavior and the use of data without implied or explicit consent would constitute a violation of the right to privacy in social research. To some extent, of course, this approach still leaves the notion of an invasion of privacy or a violation of the right to privacy indeterminate. If, for instance, implied consent is accepted as a criterion of a research procedure *noninvasive* of privacy, questions will persist as to which circumstances actually signal a research participant's implicit consent. Did Laud Humphreys's subjects consent to being observed when they agreed to have him stand guard as their "watchqueen"? What about the participants in Brenda Mann's study of barroom activity? The difficulty presented by such questions suggests that hard and fast distinctions between public and private behavior will remain elusive even where agreement has been reached as to the proper general analysis of the moral right to privacy.

Nonetheless, some activities are uncontroversially private, and some kinds of information clearly confidential, irrespective of which theoretical approach is taken to these issues. A familiar question then arises: Are there any circumstances under which the observation of such private behavior and the use of such confidential information is morally permissible? Pinkard argues that actions which uncontroversially violate privacy rights are justified only in cases where there is a competing right strong enough to override the privacy right at issue, and concludes that such situations rarely occur in social research. But arguments can be offered that without access to private or confidential sources of data, research in the social sciences is likely to be seriously compromised and to produce far less useful information. While arguments stressing these consequences do not alone provide good *moral* grounds for proceeding with the study of private behavior and the use of confidential information, a broad moral defense of those practices (many of which are now institutionalized) could be constructed on the basis of predictions about the likely consequences of curtailing research into private behavior or of prohibiting the research use of confidential information. Jay Wallace, in his essay, "Privacy and the Use of Data in Epidemiology," presents such a moral defense of research methods that allegedly violate people's right to privacy. Like Elms, he stresses the beneficial consequences made possible only by research methods that in some respects "invade" privacy, thus explicitly building his case on utilitarian moral grounds. While he defends methods of data collection that have their broadest applicability in the social sciences, he does so by focusing on their use in epidemiology, a context commonly categorized as biomedical rather than social scientific. Wallace's essay thus suggests a way in which common investigative methods can present similar moral problems for biomedical investigators and social scientific investigators. (Whether the *methods* involved are those of the biomedical or the social sciences—or both together—is a separate issue about scientific methodology.)

Wallace's utilitarian arguments take for granted, of course, that research methods will in some cases violate participant rights to a certain extent. Both for those sympathetic to his utilitarian approach and for those opposed to it, a far preferable solution to actual rights violations would be to find *alternative* research procedures that do not involve such violations. Wallace contends that, at least in the context of epidemiology, such alternative procedures are not available and affordable at the present time. It is possible, however, that this conclusion is unduly pessimistic. As Robert Boruch illustrates in his essay, "Methods for Resolving Privacy Problems in Social Research," many research procedures have been developed which permit the use of *identifiable personal information* without giving researchers easy access to the identities of the people to whom the information pertains. The widespread adoption of such procedures would go a considerable way toward satisfying the twin imperatives of scientific integrity and moral justifiability (although, as Caplan observes, questions can be raised regarding just how widely Boruch's procedures *can* be adopted in social research).

It might be thought that the approach Boruch outlines provides a way of simply eliminating moral controversy from the social sciences. If statistical and methodological techniques—the techniques of the social sciences themselves—can so neatly resolve seemingly intractable moral dilemmas, what need is there for a distinctively moral analysis of the problems that arise in social research? To see Boruch's approach in this way would, however, be to mistake the nature of his proposals. His statistical and methodological solutions constitute not an elimination of privacy and confidentiality issues from the social sciences, but an imaginative *response* to those very issues. That is, his proposals presuppose a sophisticated understanding of the moral problems that can and do commonly arise in social research. If further progress is to be made in addressing the privacy and confidentiality issues in the social sciences, it will require conceptual and moral analyses of the sort Pinkard and Wallace attempt no less than the methodological approach taken by Boruch.

Government Regulation [23]

The issues canvassed in this Introduction have so far been heavily philosophical in character. We have been interested in the ethical justifiability of various research practices, and appeal has therefore been made to ethical principles and their derivative requirements. This focus on distinctively ethical analysis should not, however, be taken as suggesting that the topics treated in the present volume are without implications in contexts that are not strictly philosophical. As earlier noted in connection with the Wichita Jury Study, legal and political issues and patterns of argumentation often bear a close resemblance to ethical issues and arguments. This fact alone suggests that it may not always be possible to attain an exclusive focus on the ethical dimensions of problems in social research. But there is a still more direct connection between ethics on the one hand and law and politics on the other. Many fundamental legal injunctions that governments enforce are directly supported and at least partially justified by ethical principles and arguments. One need look no further for an example than the universal moral injunction against murder and its correspondingly universal legal codification.

To recognize that enforced legal rules can thus be buttressed by ethical considerations is not, however, to deny that this direct relation between the two areas is sometimes controversial. Governments—both dictatorial and democratic—are prone to invoke spurious ethical justifications in defense of laws and policies whose actual justification is drawn on the narrowest grounds of self-interest. Even when a democratic government makes a genuine appeal to ethical principles and requirements, the resulting legal codification can be highly controversial. Laws prohibiting or discouraging such "victimless crimes" as pornography and homosexuality are prominent contemporary cases in which the legitimacy and propriety of legal appeals to ethical considerations are far from clear and straightforward.

Another area where the relation between ethical principles and the law has proved increasingly controversial is government regulation of social research. Indeed, this topic has attracted more prominent public attention than any of the others treated in the present volume. Debate about U.S. government regulation in the social sciences is rapidly spreading from the pages of scholarly journals into the popular press. At issue are a set of federally stipulated requirements concerning the justifiability of research practices (including qualified formulations of the moral requirements of risk-benefit analysis and informed consent), and a network of locally controlled Institutional Review Boards (IRBs) charged with ensuring that the stipulated requirements are satisfied.

In the main, this regulatory framework is meant for application primarily to social research projects that are funded directly by the federal government. John Robertson, in his paper "The Social Scientist's Right to Research and the IRB System," presents a defense of this aspect of the government's involvement in the control of social research. As Robertson sees it, the central question here concerns the scope of the government's freedom to attach restrictions or conditions on the use of government-supplied money. At least some limitations on this freedom are suggested by ethical considerations. If the government included among its funding conditions a requirement inconsistent with an accepted moral point of view, a strong ethical argument could be mounted against the requirement. Important limitations on the government's freedom in this connection are of course also set by stipulations of the U.S. Constitution. Addressing both possible limitations, Roberston argues that the existing federal regulatory structure conflicts with no pertinent ethical or constitutional principles; he concludes that the issues in this area should therefore be couched in terms of prudent public policy rather than in terms of moral or jurisprudential legitimacy.

Defenses of government research regulation such as Robertson's, however, have not commanded universal assent. Particularly controversial is the extension of the regulations to cover all social science research conducted at institutions receiving federal research funds, not just those projects that are directly funded by the government. Many contend that this extension represents a meddlesome and simplistic attempt to legislate about questions of the greatest ethical complexity and importance—an attempt that may well amount to an unconstitutional intrusion into the protected spheres of personal deliberation and choice. Robertson argues, however, that existing constitutional precedent provides no warrant for such a view. He suggests that funding conditions applicable even to nonfunded research are likely to be ruled constitutional as long as they can be shown to promote goals—such as protecting the moral rights of research participants—reasonably desired of funded research. That the attachment of regulatory conditions to nonfunded research does indeed promote such goals is a factual point that many of Robertson's opponents would doubtless not concede.

Arguments against government regulation are often drawn on less narrow grounds. Many commentators have recently held that government research regulations are unconstitutional and perhaps immoral, even in the case of social research directly supported by government funds. E. L. Pattullo defends such a view in his chapter "Modesty is the Best Policy: The Federal Role in Social Research." Drawing attention to similarities between everyday human interactions (e.g., the relations of journalists to the people they interview), and typical situations in social research, Pattullo contends that the risks presented by most research projects in the social sciences are no greater than the risks posed by everyday social relations. Indeed, Pattullo argues, the risks in both cases are precisely those which *must* be accepted as the cost of life in a liberal society. In his opinion, the social scientist has a moral and constitutional right to carry out research that is derivative from widely recognized rights to freedom of thought and expression, and the dangers of governmental interference with that right far surpass the risks to participants posed by unregulated social research. Of course, many other writers (including, for instance, Donald Warwick in this volume) would dispute Pattullo's assessment of the risks presented by research in the social sciences. For them, the need to protect the rights of research participants is probably at least as strong as the conflicting need to protect the rights of social researchers. It is perhaps to the credit of Pattullo's approach that it puts the case against social research regulation in such a way that the discussion can proceed in terms of *competing* moral and legal rights held by different parties.

While some critics have maintained that the U.S. government has remained passively oblivious to problematic issues raised by its regulatory activities, this claim is dubious. Since the inception of government-mandated ethical review of research proposals, the regulatory structure has undergone repeated modification and refinement in the light of both internal and external scrutiny. As noted in the first section of this Introduction, however, this process has not always reflected a recognition of the special problems posed by the applicability of government regulations to research in the social as well as the biomedical sciences. The precise and changing implications of the developing regulations for social research are therefore difficult to distinguish, and the reader interested in assessing these implications might do well to start with Bradford Gray's paper, "The Regulatory Context of Social and Behavioral Research." Gray provides an illuminating sketch of regulatory history which is attentive to the peculiar problems and demands of social science research.

The development and refinement of government research regulations is of course an ongoing process. Gray's paper accordingly moves beyond its purely descriptive task to present an evaluative commentary on the most recent regulatory developments. Richard Tropp's chapter, "A Regulatory Perspective on Social Science Research," also provides an analysis of the federal regulatory approach in the 1970s and includes constructive suggestions for future government regulation. Identifying a series of "conceptual problems" embodied in the formulation of the regulations, Tropp advocates the distinctive position that the solution to these problems will at once require more extensive regulation in some areas of the social sciences and less regulatory coverage in others. He recommends, for example, that provision be made for IRB review of certain types of social research after projects are well under way, while advising that other classes of social science research be exempted from IRB review altogether.

The suggestions made by Gray and Tropp are not exhaustive of the positions that can be taken on the future course of government regulation in the social sciences. Those sympathetic with Pattullo's position would presumably advocate still more extensive exemptions from IRB review than do either Gray or Tropp. In evaluating these alternative recommendations, the reader should keep in mind the ethical issues raised and discussed in the first three sections of the volume. The positions taken on those issues do not automatically entail corresponding positions on the questions of government regulation. It could for instance consistently be held that informed consent is an applicable and important ethical requirement for social research, but that the government should not be in the business of enforcing such ethical rules. Nevertheless, the resolution of the ethical issues of harm and benefit, informed consent, and privacy does have some bearing on the debate about government regulation. People who consider social science research a significantly risky but sometimes justifiable activity are unlikely to object in principle to the government's attachment of ethical requirements to government-funded research. Even where the legitimacy of regulation itself is not in question, the earlier ethical disputes can have an important bearing on determinations of the precise nature and scope of the regulations. If, as Elms and Wallace argue, deception and invasions of privacy are ethically justifiable under certain specified conditions, then the regulations should not prohibit such practices in research that satisfies those conditions. Here as elsewhere in the present volume, the difficult problems can be solved only by careful reflection on both the ethical and public policy aspects of social science research.

Notes

1. Herbert C. Kelman, *A Time to Speak* (San Francisco: Jossey-Bass, 1968).
2. Robert T. Bower and Priscilla de Gasparis, *Ethics in Social Science Research* (New York: Praeger Publishers, 1978).
3. Edward Diener and Rick Crandall, *Ethics in Social and Behavioral Research* (Chicago: University of Chicago Press, 1978).

4. Paul Davidson Reynolds, *Ethical Dilemmas and Social Science Research* (San Francisco: Jossey-Bass, 1979).

5. Gideon Sjoberg, ed., *Ethics, Politics, and Social Research* (Cambridge, Mass.: Schenkman Publishing Co., 1967).

6. Henry W. Riecken and Robert F. Boruch, eds., *Social Experimentation* (New York: Academic Press, 1974).

7. Alice M. Rivlin and P. Michael Timpane, eds., *Ethical and Legal Issues of Social Experimentation* (Washington, D.C.: Brookings Institution, 1975).

8. Paul Nejelski, ed., *Social Research in Conflict with Law and Ethics* (Cambridge, Mass.: Ballinger Publishing Co., 1976).

9. Michael A. Rynkiewich and James P. Spradley, eds., *Ethics and Anthropology* (New York: John Wiley & Sons, 1976).

10. Gordon Bermant, Herbert C. Kelman, and Donald P. Warwick, eds., *The Ethics of Social Intervention* (Washington, D.C.: Hemisphere Publishing, 1978).

11. Stephanie B. Stolz and associates, *Ethical Issues in Behavior Modification* (San Francisco: Jossey-Bass, 1978).

12. Murray L. Wax and Joan Cassell, eds., *Federal Regulations: Ethical Issues and Social Research* (Boulder, Colo.: Westview Press, 1979).

13. Robert F. Boruch and Joe S. Cecil, *Assuring the Confidentiality of Social Research Data* (Philadelphia: University of Pennsylvania Press, 1979).

14. Carl B. Klockars and Finbarr W. O'Connor, eds., *Deviance and Decency: The Ethics of Research with Human Subjects* (Beverly Hills, Calif.: Sage Publications, 1979).

15. Donald P. Warwick, *The Teaching of Ethics in the Social Sciences* (Hastings-on-Hudson, N.Y.: Hastings Center, 1980).

16. Recent conferences in this area have included sessions conducted by Murray Wax and Joan Cassell at the American Association for the Advancement of Science meeting in 1977 and at the American Anthropological Association meetings in 1977 and 1978; the Conference on Solutions to Ethical and Legal Dilemmas in Social Research organized by Robert Boruch, Joseph Cecil, and Jerry Ross; a Hastings Center conference in fall of 1978 on ethical problems in survey research; and the conference held at the Kennedy Institute of Ethics in September of 1979 that was the starting point for the present volume. See ibid., pp. 10-12.

17. R. W. Friedrichs, *A Sociology of Sociology* (New York: Free Press, 1970).

18. Laud Humphreys, *Tearoom Trade: Impersonal Sex in Public Places* (Chicago: Aldine Publishing Co., 1978). All articles referred to in the subsequent discussion are reprinted in this enlarged edition.

19. A firsthand account of the ethical dimensions of this study is provided in Brenda J. Mann, "The Ethics of Fieldwork in an Urban Bar," in Rynkiewich and Spradley, *Ethics and Anthropology,* chapter 7.

20. K. Ann Coleman Stolurow and Dale W. Moeller, "Dental X-Ray Use in Boston," *American Journal of Public Health* 69 (July 1979): 709–10.

21. R. T. LaPiere, "Attitude vs. Actions," *Journal of Social Forces* 13 (1934): 230–37.

22. For a good introduction to this case, see Jay Katz, *Experimentation with Human Beings* (New York: Russell Sage Foundation, 1972), pp. 67–109.

23. Government regulation in this area has been in a state of regular flux and modification. The discussion of research regulation in the present volume has as far as possible attempted to address the fundamental issues underlying the regulation of social science research, in any form the regulation might assume. Nevertheless, reference to the latest stage in regulatory development has at many points proven unavoidable. As the papers in this volume were substantially completed by January of 1981, such references to the latest regulations generally reflect only those developments that had taken place by that time.

However, on January 26 and 27, 1981, the Department of Health and Human Services and the Food and Drug Administration issued important amendments to their regulatory requirements for research involving human participants (see *Federal Register* 46, no. 16 (January 26, 1981): 7933–8015). These revised regulations do not alter the basic system whereby research projects are reviewed by locally controlled institutional review boards, but they do specify broad categories of research that are exempted from the requirement for IRB review (including all research not funded or conducted by HHS). Other broad categories are specified that need only go through an expedited review process.

These categories of expedited and exempted research include much social science research that presents little or no risk to participants. Their specification in the revised regulations reflects an appreciation of many social scientists' arguments—made, for example, by Joan Cassell and E. L. Pattullo in the present volume—that relatively risk-free social research is not an appropriate target for full IRB review. While this latest turn of events may not be reflected at every point in the present volume, the fundamental moral issues that are discussed should remain of interest to anyone concerned to understand the justification and appropriate limits of any government involvement in this area.

2

Ethical Issues in Different
Social Science Methods

HERBERT C. KELMAN

The ethical issues arising in social science research tend to vary as a function of the particular research methods employed. For example, certain genres of social-psychological experiments have created ethical concerns because they involve misrepresentation of the purpose of the research to the participants or because they subject participants to stressful experiences. Some organizational or large-scale social experiments have been troubling because participation may be seen as damaging to the long-term interests of certain groups. Survey research has on occasion been criticized for probing into sensitive areas, such as sex, religion, or family relations. Participant observation research may constitute invasion of privacy, particularly when investigators gain access by misrepresenting themselves or make covert observations. Cross-cultural studies have been charged with exploitation of Third World populations and disrespect for their cultural values.[1]

The purpose of the present chapter is to provide an overview of the types of ethical issues that confront the different methods used in social research. The overview is intended to be more than a checklist, ticking off the problems that arise with each research method, but less than a comprehensive, overarching scheme for categorizing and organizing all of the problems. Instead, it takes the form of a rudimentary framework, designed to highlight some of the problems that will be discussed more fully in subsequent chapters and to suggest possible relationships between them.

The framework is itself rooted in a social science analysis, relevant to our concern with problems of social institutions (including the professions and the institution of scientific research), of social relations, and of social control. This kind of analysis may provide a systematic basis for answering some of the questions that have been central to the debate about the ethics of social research. One is the question of the appropriateness of a risk-benefit analysis to the ethical issues that arise in social and behavioral research. Such an analysis may or may not be useful for biomedical research, but perhaps a modified version of risk-benefit analysis or an entirely different approach—such as an analysis in terms of rights (including, of course, the right to protection against injury)—would be more appropriate to social research.[2] Another issue to which the present framework might contribute concerns the appropriateness of government regulations for the control of social research. Should social research be subject to government regulation at all? Should at least certain types of research be specifically exempt from regulation? If government regulations are indicated, should they take a form different from those designed for biomedical research or should they be applied in different ways? The framework may help us address such questions in a systematic way.

In the discussion that follows, I shall (1) present the framework and identify the ethical issues that it brings to the fore; (2) examine which of these issues arise for each of the different methods of social research that can be distinguished; and (3) draw out some of the general implications suggested by this analysis. Before turning to this discussion, however, I shall summarize the general approach to the problem of moral justification that underlies my analysis.[3]

Approach to Moral Justification

My ultimate criterion for moral evaluation of an action, policy, or institution—as well as of a general rule of conduct—is its effect on the fulfillment of human potentialities. Fulfillment of people's potentialities depends on their well-being in the broadest sense of the term: Satisfaction of their basic needs— including needs for food, shelter, security, love, self-esteem, and self-actualization—is both a condition for and a manifestation of such fulfillment. Furthermore, fulfillment of human potentialities depends on the availability of capacities and opportunities for self-expression, self-utilization, and self-development. We therefore have a moral obligation to avoid actions and policies that reduce others' well-being (broadly defined) or that inhibit their freedom to express and develop themselves. This is essentially a consequentialist view, in that it judges the moral rightness of behavior on the basis of its consequences. It differs from some standard utilitarian theories in the *particular* consequences that form the center of its concern—namely, consequences for the fulfillment of human potentialities. This definition of "the good" in turn implies a broader conception of human well-being that includes the satisfaction of such needs as self-actualization.

Most commonly accepted moral principles can be derived directly from analysis of the consequences of their acceptance or violation for the fulfillment of human potentialities. Clearly, violations of the principles of autonomy, nonmaleficence, and beneficence, described in the preceding chapter, have direct negative consequences for the fulfillment of potentialities. The importance of truth telling or keeping promises is not so obvious. Breaking a promise or telling a lie *may* inhibit fulfillment of the other's potential, depending on the precise nature of the benefit or the information of which that person is thereby deprived. But, to justify a general rule of truth telling or promise keeping, one would have to introduce the additional notion that lying and breaking promises undermine interpersonal trust within the society, thus depriving everyone of one of the conditions necessary for fulfilling human potential. In this sense, then, lying and breaking promises are always (prima facie) wrong, regardless of the *specific* consequences for the individual so treated. In calculating the effects of lying, it is therefore not enough to weigh the harm caused to the individual subjected to the lie against the benefits (perhaps to many others—e.g., through the increase in knowledge produced by deceptive experiments) that the lie might bring in its wake. One must also take into account the larger effect of the lie in undermining interpersonal trust in the society.

More generally, I subscribe to the rule-utilitarian view that adherence to moral rules is important in order to maintain the integrity of the rules themselves. Thus, the mere violation of the rules against lying or breaking promises entails a social cost in that it weakens these rules and hence reduces the predictability and trust necessary for the fulfillment of human potentialities within a society. The same reasoning can be used to rule out certain classes of action entirely, regardless of any calculation of specific harms and benefits, on the grounds that these actions violate rules that are of paramount social significance. The presumption is that the larger social harm caused by the mere violation of these rules always outweighs any potential benefits that the actions might produce. On this presumption, I would argue, for example, that the act of killing or enslaving another can never be justified on the grounds that it would produce a greater good, although it might be justified on the grounds that it would prevent an even greater evil.

The last example underscores a difficulty in using the fulfillment of human potentialities as the criterion for moral evaluation. A rule that I regard of paramount social significance—namely, that we must never kill or enslave another on the grounds that such an act would produce some greater good—rests on the mere *presumption* that the larger social harm caused by the violation of this rule always outweighs whatever benefits the action might produce. Although a moral principle may be conceptually linked to the fulfillment of human potentialities, it is often very difficult to demonstrate empirically that violation of this principle—in a specific case or in general—has negative consequences for human fulfillment. The difficulty arises in large part from the fact that the predicted consequences are often due to the cumulative effect of violations of the principle. For example, a single lie may not have any demonstrable negative consequences, but the accumulation of lies may damage the self-esteem of the individual to whom these lies are directed, may lower the level of trust in the society, and may undermine the integrity of a rule essential to harmonious and effective social interaction. Such cumulative effects cannot be readily proven, and it is even more difficult to disprove them. We could avoid unnecessary ambiguity, therefore, by using a criterion for moral evaluation based on description of the action rather than on prediction of its consequences.

For this reason, I prefer to use consistency with human dignity as my working criterion for moral evaluation of an action, policy, or institution. The principle of human dignity is very closely linked to the fulfillment of human potentialities. On the one hand, the fulfillment of one's potentialities is one of the determinants of personal dignity.[4] On the other hand, respect for human dignity—as reflected in the treatment people receive from others and in social policies and institutions—is a necessary condition for the maximal fulfillment of human potentialities. But, while the principle of human dignity is conceptually linked to—and indeed derivable from—principles demanding fulfillment of human potentialities, it can be treated as though it were an end in itself in moral decision making. The principle holds whether or not its acceptance or violation has demonstrable consequences for self-fulfillment.

I define human dignity as "the status of individuals as ends in themselves, rather than as means toward some extraneous ends."[5] Two components of human dignity can be distinguished, which serve as both operationalizations and conditions of dignity: identity and community.[6] Identity refers to our capacity to take autonomous action, to distinguish ourselves from others, to live our lives on the basis of our own goals and values; community refers to our inclusion in an interconnected network of individuals who care for each other and protect each other's interests.[7] According identity to others means respecting and fostering their autonomy and freedom of choice; according community to them means treating them as fellow humans and caring actively for their well-being.[8] At the level of social policies and institutions, one can roughly equate the provision of identity with the prevalence of individual freedom and the provision of community with the prevalence of distributive justice, although I would stress that freedom and justice (and, indeed, identity and community themselves) are inseparable and interdependent conditions for realizing human dignity. The extent to which people are accorded identity and community (in interpersonal relations, in social policies, and in institutional arrangements) determines their (objective) level of dignity, as well as their (subjective) sense of dignity. To deny them identity or community is to treat them as means rather than ends and thus to deprive them of dignity, from both an objective and a subjective point of view. Moreover, implicit in the principle of human dignity is the requirement to accord others identity and community on a basis of equality: If individuals are ends in themselves, then each one—by virtue of being human—has equal worth.

My conception of human dignity places it clearly within a consequentialist framework: Respect for others' dignity is important precisely because it has consequences for their capacity and opportunity to fulfill their potentialities. However, to subscribe to consequentialism as a framework for justification does not mean to adopt act-utilitarian consequentialism as a method for moral decision making. I go on the *assumption* that violations of people's dignity reduce their capacity and opportunity to fulfill their potentialities. To some extent, this assumption can be evaluated empirically. For example, we can show in a particular situation that lying deprives people of information needed to protect their interests and meet their needs or contributes to an atmosphere of distrust within a community—thereby lowering the capacity for self-fulfillment. Even in the absence of such demonstrable consequences, however, I assume that lying degrades and diminishes the person so treated and undermines the principle of truth telling—and thus generally weakens, at the individual and societal level, the conditions for fulfillment of human potentialities. According to my view of human nature and of the social order, these are necessary and immediate consequences of the action itself, consequences usually manifested only in their cumulative effects. Whether or not such consequences can be demonstrated in a given instance, I regard them as sufficient justification for evaluating the action as morally wrong.

The principle of human dignity, along with its two components, serves as a "master rule" from which other rules of moral conduct can be derived. Some of these rules—such as the rules against killing, injuring, or enslaving others—govern actions that are not only obviously inconsistent with respect for human dignity, but also have direct negative consequences for the fulfillment of human potentialities. This category includes actions that deprive others of their basic human needs (broadly defined), that reduce their freedom of self-expression and self-development (including their capacity and opportunity to pursue their own goals and protect their own interests), or that deny them equal access to such benefits and freedoms. Other rules—such as the rules against lying or breaking promises—govern actions that are also inconsistent with respect for human dignity but that may or may not have directly demonstrable consequences for the fulfillment of human potentialities. These rules ultimately derive their moral force from the *presumption* that the actions they proscribe have adverse consequences for the individual capacities and social conditions essential to personal fulfillment.

In any particular situation, moral conflicts may arise because two different moral rules require conflicting actions. To resolve such conflicts, we must make a judgment about the relative importance of the two rules—in general and in the particular situation—to the preservation of human dignity. Such judgments are not easy, particularly when they must take account of the long-term and systematic effects of violation of a rule, including effects on the continuing integrity of the rule itself. Equally difficult dilemmas, however, are faced by the act utilitarian, trying to assess (quantitatively) which action maximizes utility, or by the deontologist, trying to decide which is the overriding duty. Conflicts may also arise because an action that presumably contributes to creating the conditions for enhanced human dignity in the society at large (e.g., the advancement of social research) may deprive particular individuals of dignity (e.g., by lying to them). In many cases of this sort (such as the decision whether or not to carry out an important experiment that involves some deception of the participants), I would accept the need for weighing the relative costs and benefits of taking or not taking the action and choosing the one that is most consistent with the preservation and enhancement of human dignity. In calculating costs, however, I would consider not only the cost to the individual who is deceived, but also the long-term cost to the larger society. In other cases (such as the decision about an important experiment that entails some risk of death or serious injury to the participants), the action represents so fundamental a violation of the principle of human dignity that it can virtually never be envisioned, no matter how valuable its social contribution may be.

Harm-benefit considerations clearly play a central role in my approach to moral justification, if harms are defined as experiences that detract from well-being and benefits as experiences that enhance well-being, and where well-being in turn refers to meeting one's needs, attaining one's goals, and having the capacity and opportunity to express and develop one's self. Human dignity, which is closely linked to the fulfillment of human potentialities, can be seen as a manifestation and condition of well-being. Thus, actions, policies, and rules deemed consistent with human dignity represent either ways of enhancing well-being, or ways of maintaining people's ability to assure their own well-being (i.e., protect their own interests, pursue their own goals, express and develop themselves). But, to say that harm and benefit considerations are central to moral justification does not mean—as it does for the act utilitarian—that the procedures for arriving at ethical decisions involve a calculation of immediate risks and benefits without reference to rules and other moral considerations. Risk-benefit analysis is a useful tool in ethical decision making, but it is not relevant, and certainly not conclusive, under all circumstances. For many purposes, I would consider a rights-based analysis as the most appropriate procedure for arriving at ethical decisions.

Rights, in my approach, are derivative from consequential considerations, and thus are not the ultimate source of justification for moral action. The use of fulfillment of human potentialities and of respect for human dignity as criteria for moral evaluation implies a right to self-fulfillment and dignity. And from this "right," one can derive various other rights, corresponding to the various "duties" implied by the moral rules based on respect for dignity. Thus, for example, one can speak of a right not to be lied to, corresponding to the rule against lying. But I do not postulate a set of rights as *independent* bases for moral action. I see rights as socially accepted and enforced protective devices, which assure people access to certain benefits, defense against certain harms, and continued ability to safeguard their interests, pursue their goals, and express and develop themselves. The value of rights is that they reduce the dependence of an individual's (or group's) well-being on others' calculations in particular circumstances of what is best for that individual (or group) and for society at large. They represent, in principle, noncontingent entitlements to certain resources or opportunities. In practice, of course, rights are not absolute. Judgments have to be made about competing rights, both in the sense that it may not be possible to grant a given right (e.g., the right to food or police protection) fully to everyone, because of limited resources; and in the sense that the right of one person (e.g., to speak freely) may conflict with a competing right of another (e.g., to be protected against intimidation). In weighing competing rights, one of the considerations is the relative cost of violating one as compared to the other, including the relative social cost entailed by the reduced integrity of whichever right is being violated.

Rights, then—although their origin is ultimately in harm-benefit considerations—become functionally autonomous in that they retain their moral force whether or not, in any given case, it can be demonstrated that their violation will cause harm. Furthermore, maintaining the integrity of the rights is itself an important consideration in ethical decision making, because of the long-term, systemic consequences of their violation. In short, operationally, we take or avoid certain classes of action (defined by general moral principles) in order to conform to a right and to maintain the integrity of that right, not (or not *only*) in order to avoid the harm against which the right is designed to protect people. It is enough to say that the right is being violated; there is no need to prove that its violation causes measurable harm. Calculation of harms becomes especially important when the right conflicts with another right and some way of assigning priorities must be found.

A Framework for Identifying Ethical Issues in Social Research

The primary task of this chapter is to identify and classify ethical issues in social research in a way that would enable us to evaluate and compare the role different research methods play in creating or perpetuating these issues. In order to make the resulting scheme maximally useful for the present volume, I selected, as one of the bases for classifying ethical issues, the four issue areas around which the volume is organized: harm and benefit, informed consent and deception, privacy and confidentiality, and social control. These four issue areas constitute the rows of table 2.1, which summarizes the classificatory scheme. Of these four issue areas, the first three represent broad categories of

TABLE 2.1
A CLASSIFICATION OF ETHICAL ISSUES IN SOCIAL SCIENCE RESEARCH

Issue Areas	Types of Impact of the Research		
	Concrete Interests of Participants	Quality of Inter-personal Relationships	Wider Social Values
Harm and benefit	Injury (physical, psychological, material)	Stress and indignity (discomfort, embarrassment, feelings of inadequacy)	Diffuse harm (perversion of political process, inequity, manipulation, arbitrariness)
Privacy and confidentiality	Public exposure	Reduced control over self-presentation	Reduction of private space
Informed consent and deception	Impaired capacity for decision making	Deprivation of respect (lack of candor, choice, reciprocity)	Erosion of trust (cynicism, anomie)
Social control	Government regulation	Professional standards	Social policy

ethical problems that social research confronts, while the fourth refers to socially patterned ways of dealing with such problems. For the fourth area, it should be noted, I am using a more inclusive description than the one used in the organization of this volume (social control instead of government regulation), since I want to cover a wider range of control mechanisms, of which government regulation is only one form.

The three categories of problems overlap to a considerable degree. Specifically, issues of privacy and deception could both be analyzed within a harm-benefit framework.[9] There is heuristic value, however, in separating them out, particularly since they encompass some of the special problems that are inherent in certain methods of social research.

Harms and benefits here refer to certain effects of a piece of research on the well-being of individuals and society. Well-being, in turn, can be gauged by the attainment of goals or valued states. Any effect that reduces people's well-being, by blocking achievement of a goal or interfering with a valued state (such as health, security, or social cohesion), constitutes a harm.[10] Any effect that enhances well-being, by promoting the attainment of goals or valued states, constitutes a benefit. The clearest examples of harms that might result from scientific research are lasting injuries or damages suffered by the research participants themselves. The term *harms,* as used here, however, also encompasses temporary experiences of stress or discomfort, even if they cause no measurable long-term damage. Furthermore, harms may accrue not only to the research participants themselves, but also to other individuals and groups affected by the process or products of research.[11] More generally, one may speak of harms to the society at large insofar as the process or products of research tend to reduce the integrity and effectiveness of social institutions in achieving societal goals and values.

Benefits may accrue to individual research participants in the form of improvements in health, help with personal (psychological or social) problems, specific services (such as child care, educational enrichment, and income supplementation), financial remuneration, new insights, enjoyable experiences, advantages to their groups or communities, or the satisfaction of contributing to the research enterprise. Benefits may also accrue to individuals and groups who do not personally participate in the research, and to society at large, "in the form of contributions to scientific knowledge and the general social welfare or public enlightenment generated by this knowledge."[12] Since ethical concerns are frequently generated by the potential of harmful effects in social research, I shall be emphasizing harms much more than benefits in this chapter. Benefits, of course, affect the amount of concern engendered by a piece of research, on the assumption that the greater its potential benefits to participants or to the larger society, the greater the justification for risking certain harms. As was noted in the previous chapter, however, ethical judgments are not based solely on the ratio between harms and benefits. There are certain kinds and degrees of harm that most of us would consider unacceptable no matter how large the potential benefits might be (unless perhaps the risk of harm had been consented to by those affected). Moreover, calculations of the risk-benefit ratio are complicated by the fact that those who are most likely to benefit from a research study are often not the ones who bear the attendant risks.

Turning to the second row of table 2.1, the issue of privacy and confidentiality relates to a harm-benefit framework in two ways: Invasion of privacy and violation of confidentiality can be viewed, in their own right, as harms of a special type; or they can be viewed as conditions that subject people to the possibility of harm. Oscar M. Ruebhausen and Orville G. Brim, Jr., define privacy as "the freedom of the individual to pick and choose for himself the time and circumstances under which, and most importantly, the extent to which, his attitudes, beliefs, behavior and opinions are to be shared with or withheld from others."[13] Since social research, by its very nature, focuses on precisely such personal information, it inevitably runs the risk of invading the participants' privacy. "Invasions of privacy occur to the extent that participants are unable to determine what information about themselves they will disclose and how that information will be disseminated."[14] Violations of confidentiality occur when information about a participant is disseminated to audiences for whom it was not intended. They constitute a subclass of invasion of privacy, exacerbated by the breaking of a promise that was made—explicitly or implicitly—at the time the data were obtained.

Invasion of privacy cannot be described as a harm in the obvious sense of a lasting injury or measurable damage to the research participants. It can, however, be subsumed under the category of harms that Alasdair MacIntyre designated "moral wrongs,"[15] i.e., acts that subject people to the experience of being morally wronged, whether or not their interests are damaged in specifiable ways. Similarly, in terms of the approach to moral analysis that I presented above, invasion of privacy, by violating people's autonomy, is inconsistent with respect for their dignity and hence a presumptive cause of harm. In evaluating consequences of this variety, we move away from a standard risk-benefit analysis toward an analysis related to the concept of individual rights. Thus, when we speak of the invasion of privacy as a moral wrong, we are postulating a correlative right—the right to privacy—that is being violated. Invasion of privacy. when known by subjects, also tends to create a certain degree of stress and discomfort. In this sense, too, it can be viewed as a harm in its own right. More importantly, however, the discomfort engendered by invasion of privacy may be a function of its *indirect* relationship to harm: Within a harm-benefit framework, invasion of privacy is troubling primarily because it subjects the individual to the *possibility* of harm. Privacy provides people with some protection against harmful or unpleasant experiences—against punishment and exploitation by others, against embarrassment or lowered self-esteem, against threats to the integrity and autonomy of the self. Invasions of privacy increase the likelihood of harm because they deprive the individual of that protection.

Turning to the third row of table 2.1, we can link informed consent and deception to a harm-benefit framework in three ways: deception and curtailments of informed consent can be viewed as harms in their own right, as multipliers of harms due to other causes, and as conditions that subject research participants to the possibility of harm. Deception refers to any deliberate misrepresentation of the purposes of the research, of the identity or qualifications of the investigator, of the auspices under which the research is conducted, of the experiences to which participants will be subjected, or of the likely uses and consequences of the research. Deception curtails the participants' opportunities to give informed consent insofar as it deprives them of information that might be material to their decision to participate. Withholding of potentially relevant information—even in the absence of active deception (in the sense of misrepresentation)—would also constitute a violation of the requirement of informed consent. Furthermore, informed consent is compromised insofar as the individual's freedom to agree to or refuse participation is limited—whether it be through outright coercion or undue pressure, through threats of punishment or the offering of irresistible inducements.

When viewed as harms in their own right, deception and violation of informed consent—like invasion of privacy—belong in the category of "moral wrongs" or deprivations of dignity. Whether or not individuals suffer specifiable damage as a result of these procedures, they are wronged in the sense that their basic rights to the truth and to freedom of choice are violated. Deception and coercion can also be viewed as multipliers of harms due to other causes. In the calculation of the risk-benefit ratio for a stressful psychological experiment, for example, the injury or discomfort resulting from participation would be multiplied if participants were misled about the nature of the experiment or unduly pressured to take part in it and therefore prevented from making an informed, voluntary decision about whether or not to subject themselves to a potentially stressful experience. Finally, deception and coercion—again, like invasion of privacy—are linked to a harm-benefit framework in that they are conditions that subject the individual to the *possibility* of harm. The norms of truthfulness and informed consent afford us some protection against harmful or unpleasant experiences by enhancing our ability to make decisions in line with our interests, preferences, and values. They do so by providing the opportunities and the tools for making such decisions, and by maintaining an atmosphere of predictability, trust, and mutual respect, in which such decisions can be made. Deception and violations of informed consent increase the likelihood of harm because they reduce research participants' ability to protect themselves against it.

In sum, the issues of privacy and informed consent can both be addressed within a harm-benefit framework. Not only can invasions of privacy and violations of informed consent be viewed as harms in their own right, but—most important for a risk-benefit analysis—they constitute conditions that subject research participants to the possibility of various other harms. Nevertheless, there are some advantages in treating these two issue areas as separate categories. First, they highlight concerns that are of critical importance to the protection of research participants in general—concerns reflected in the regulation of confidentiality and informed consent. Concerns in these two issue areas are particularly likely to be aroused by certain methods of social research, which—in the interest of enhancing the validity of the data—are especially intrusive in nature or rely on deceiving participants about the purpose (or even the occurrence) of the research. Second, separating out these two issues suggests an additional procedure, complementary to risk-benefit analysis, for arriving at ethical decisions: a procedure based on the specification of rights, including the right to privacy and the right to all material information and to freedom of choice. Thus, separate consideration of the issues of privacy and deception is useful, despite the inevitable overlaps, precisely because these issues bridge two approaches to ethical decision making, one based on calculation of risks and benefits and the other based on protection of rights.

Cutting across the four issue areas is a distinction between three types of impact that social research may have, each of which is a potential source of ethical concern (see the columns of table 2.1): the impact on the concrete interests of research participants, on the quality of the interpersonal relationships between investigators and participants, and on wider social values. The distinction is conceptually linked to distinctions that I have made in my earlier work among three processes of social influence (compliance, identification, and internalization) and three types of orientation to social systems (rule, role, and value orientation).[16]

The first column of table 2.1 refers to the possible impact of social research on the concrete interests of research participants. The concern here is that participation in the research may work to the disadvantage of the individuals involved, leaving them worse off at the end of the experience than they were at the beginning. In other words, the research may entail risks of injuries— physical, psychological, or material—that are of a relatively enduring nature. Involved here is more than momentary stress or discomfort, but a lasting damage to the individual's interests. The risk of such injuries may stem from the research procedures themselves (e.g., ingestion of potentially harmful drugs or confrontation with potentially disturbing revelations about one's self) or it may stem from the research findings (e.g., data showing inefficiencies in work organization that may lead to layoffs of some workers, or data on family organization that may lead to cuts in welfare payments). In some cases, risks are created or magnified by public exposure of information obtained from research participants; that is, the interests of participants are jeopardized if the information is widely disseminated or revealed to certain specific individuals or agencies. Risks of injury—and ethical concerns about such risks—are generally increased when the norm of informed consent is in any way violated or sidestepped, since research participants are then deprived of the full opportunity to protect their own interests.

Questions about the impact of social research on the interests of participants become more complex when we consider the interests, not only of the individual participants, but also of the groups from which they are drawn. This immediately calls attention to the impact of the products of social research, in addition to the impact of the processes of research themselves. Much of the thinking about research ethics—particularly the logic behind the regulatory approach to research with human subjects—is predicated on the assumption that one is dealing with specific effects on identifiable individuals. The model is taken from the type of biomedical research in which injection of certain substances or performance of certain procedures exposes research participants to the risk of disease or other injury. This model is insufficient even for biomedical research, which may well have an impact on the interests of specific groups within the population, such as research on genetic diseases that disproportionately affect certain ethnic groups, or research on environmental hazards that affect certain regions and occupations. It is clearly insufficient for social research, which often focuses on group differences and has implications for social policy.

The very conduct of social research, and particularly its findings, may adversely affect the interests of some groups within the population—typically those who are already most vulnerable. Research suggesting that the performance of individuals from minority groups or lower social classes compares unfavorably with that of the majority or middle-class participants (perhaps—though not necessarily—because of biases in measurement or interpretation) may serve as a basis for practices or policies that place these groups at a distinct disadvantage. Thus, in considering the impact of a piece of research on the concrete interests of the participants, it is necessary to take group interests into account—to project the possible harms that may accrue to the group, to assure adequate protection of the group in the dissemination and use of the findings, and to assess effects on the group as part of the process of informed consent. The issues here are far more complex than those relating to the impact of the research on the specific individual who provides the data: Effects on the group are more remote and harder to predict; confidentiality of group data cannot readily be preserved; and there is no obvious way of determining who speaks for the group in giving informed consent. These issues go beyond the impact of the research on the specific individuals involved and are, to some extent, within the domain of the third column of table 2.1—the impact of the research on wider social values—to be discussed below.

The second column of table 2.1 refers to the possible impact of research procedures on the quality of the interpersonal relationship between investigators and participants. There is general consensus—to a large extent universally shared—about the way in which people ought to deal with each other in a variety of interaction contexts. In a professional relationship, which can serve as a model for interaction between investigators and research participants, it is expected that each party will show concern for the other's welfare and that they will treat each other with dignity and respect. Each tries to be helpful to the other and to avoid actions that might cause the other stress or discomfort. They are careful not to insult, degrade, coerce, exploit, frighten, or shock each other.

They make every effort to protect each other from humiliation and embarrassment, from feelings of pressure or hurt. To this end, we generally accept the way in which others present themselves and we try not to be overly inquisitive or intrusive, leaving others adequate room for maneuver. One of the guiding principles of a respectful relationship is honesty and candor about our own purposes and intentions. Another is reciprocity in both obligations and benefits. Social research engenders concerns insofar as it violates these standards for good interpersonal relations. Such concerns are aroused by procedures that subject research participants to discomfort, embarrassment, or other forms of stress; that deliberately deprive them of control over their self-presentation; or that involve deception or undue pressure.

The second column differs from the first in that it does not refer to long-term damages to the participant's interests. Rather, it encompasses experiences that are largley confined to the research situation itself—experiences of temporary stress or of wrongful treatment, without any measurable effect on the participant's well-being beyond this situation. Of course, there is always the possibility that such experiences may leave a residue that influences the person's future relationships. The experience of being humiliated, deceived, or coerced may lead to a lowering of the person's self-esteem or a wariness about interpersonal relationships that carries over into subsequent situations. In such cases, we could properly speak of damage to the person's concrete interests in the form of a psychological injury. But even when the psychological impact is only temporary, a sacrifice in the quality of interpersonal relationships is not devoid of ethical significance. First, respect for human dignity ought to be treated as though it were an end in itself, quite apart from any particular consequences. I base this requirement on the view that depriving others of dignity leads to a presumptive decline in their well-being, even in the absence of calculable damage to their interests. Second, social research cannot be isolated from the rest of social life, particularly as it becomes more widespread and thus enters into the lives of a large number of people on a large number of occasions. Thus, any lowering in the quality of interpersonal relationships in research situations has a wider effect on the quality of life throughout the society.

Finally, the behavior of social scientists within their research situations has implications for the role of social science in the society. When social scientists violate the norms of good interpersonal relationships, they contribute to forces of exploitation, deception, coercion, and intrusion that are already at work. Moreover, the conditions under which the data are collected may affect the nature of the findings; thus, research procedures that rely heavily on manipulation of the participants may reinforce a manipulative conception of human relations and organizational functioning.[17] The impact of social research procedures on the quality of interpersonal relationships, therefore, raises questions about the larger social impact of social science. This concern, as well as the concern about the spread of effects from the research situation (as one type of interaction situation in our society) to the general quality of life in our society, brings us directly to the kinds of issues that are the focus for the third column of table 2.1.

The third column refers to the potential impact of social research on wider social values. The procedures and the products of social research—and indeed the prevalence or even the very existence of certain lines of research—may affect social values in a variety of ways. Social research may help to create, reinforce, and legitimize certain values within the society—and, conversely, to undermine and delegitimize other values. It may have an effect on the social atmosphere in which we live, contributing to the development of general moods and expectations. It may influence patterns of interpersonal relations, the functioning of various social institutions, the shape of political and economic processes. It may affect the relationships between different groups within the society and the satisfaction of their separate and competing needs. It may contribute to the relative emphasis given within the society to diverse and often conflicting social goals. Concern is aroused here by the possibility that social research may thus have a deleterious impact on important values of the society. Judgments of this impact are likely to differ among different analysts, not only because they may make different predictions about the probable consequences of various procedures or findings, but also because they may differ in their value preferences or in the priorities they assign to them. Thus, it is entirely possible that a type of research considered socially harmful by some will be deemed beneficial by others.

The third column differs from the other two in that it does not focus on the direct impact of the research on the individuals who participate in it or even on the groups from which they are selected, but on its impact on the society at large. The concern here is, essentially, with diffuse harm to the entire body politic.[18] However, the way individuals—or groups—are treated in the process of collecting the data and disseminating the findings is an important source of the diffuse harm that research may cause to wider social values. For example, research procedures that systematically deceive participants, subject them to undue pressure, or intrude on their privacy may result in the weakening of such social values as trust and personal autonomy. Research that exploits relatively powerless and vulnerable groups, whose members find it difficult to refuse participation, and that disseminates findings in a way that may place such groups at a disadvantage, may have a deleterious effect on the values of equity and social justice. Other potential sources of diffuse harm are the products of social research—i.e., some of its specific findings. For example, research that suggests genetic differences in intelligence between different racial groups may undermine societal efforts to promote equal opportunities in education and employment.[19]

Finally, the prevalence or even the very existence of certain lines of research may itself constitute a source of diffuse harms to important social values. For example, opinion polls that focus on the intentions of the voters over the course of an election campaign may distort the political process, for the poll results themselves may become major determinants of the behavior of both citizens and candidates.[20] To take a different example, the prevalence of field experiments on helping behavior may have the effect of reducing such behavior by providing an additional justification for bystanders' failure to intervene in a crisis situation on the grounds that it is probably just another experiment. Proponents, of course, can cite countervailing social benefits that might accrue from both of these lines of research, but the examples illustrate the possibilities of diffuse harm that must be taken into account.

In sum, the columns of table 2.1 distinguish three types of impact of social research that bring three distinct (though interrelated) sets of ethical concerns to the fore. These ethical concerns, in turn, reflect general social concerns about the functioning of any profession that is recognized and supported within a society: How are the competing interests of the professionals and their publics to be balanced and reconciled? How are standards of professional conduct, consistent with the social norms that govern interpersonal relations, to be established and maintained? And, how are basic social values to be enhanced and protected by the role the profession occupies and the ways it functions within the society? With these general concerns in mind, I shall proceed to examine the implications of the three types of impact distinguished by the columns of table 2.1 for each of the four issue areas defined by the four rows. For the first three rows, these implications follow directly from the descriptions of these three rows, as well as of the three columns, that have already been given. From my summary and elaboration of the three-way distinction as it applies to each of these three rows, I shall then draw further implications for the fourth row, proposing the form of social control that seems most appropriate in response to each of the three types of ethical concern.

Harms and Benefits

From a harm-benefit perspective, the three columns simply represent a classification of three types of harm that might result from social research (or, indeed, any research with human participants). For each of these types of harm, one can also cite a corresponding type of benefit. There is no assumption, however, that the justification for a particular study depends on the separate harm-benefit ratios for each column. For example, there could be a justification for risking harms of the first or second type if the potential benefits of the third type were sufficiently great. On the other hand, a favorable risk-benefit ratio—within a column or across columns—would not automatically justify a study because, as has already been noted, certain kinds and degrees of harm cannot legitimately be risked, no matter how great the potential benefits might be.

The three types of harm have already been defined above, in the discussion of the columns of table 2.1, and they will only be summarized here with some further elaboration.

Injury

Research may cause damage to the concrete interests of the participants or of the groups from which they are drawn in the form of relatively enduring physical, psychological, or material injuries.[21] Physical injuries in social research could conceivably occur if the research procedures generated violent reactions among participants themselves, if the research findings caused others to direct violence against the participants or their groups, or if participation in the research subjected people to penalties from authorities or revenge from adversaries. Physical injuries could also occur in studies involving the use of drugs or alcohol, various forms of deprivation, or exposure to the elements.[22] Psychological injuries could take the form of psychotic reactions in vulnerable individuals, as a result of stress, anxiety, painful self-discovery, or rejection experienced in the course of the research. They may also take the form of experimentally induced losses in self-esteem or self-confidence, which persist beyond the research situation.[23] Material injuries may take the form of losses in certain resources or opportunities as a result of participation in the research—for example, by those who receive the "less desirable" treatment in educational, criminal-justice, or large-scale social experiments. The findings of social research may also have a deleterious effect on the material well-being of research participants, since they could lead to changes in policy with negative consequences for their incomes, fringe benefits, working conditions, or living conditions. It is the findings of research that represent the most obvious risks of damage to group interests. Thus, research findings on group differences in intelligence could cause injury to disadvantaged groups—both materially, through their effects on social policy, and psychologically, through their effects on the groups' reputation and self-esteem.

Corresponding to these different kinds of potential injuries, there are various ways in which social research may produce concrete benefits to the interests of participants and their groups. Such benefits may take the form of financial remuneration, special services, improvements in health and psychological well-being, and access to material resources and opportunities. Similarly, the findings of social research may advance the concrete interests of the participants as well as their groups, through their effects on organizational practices, social policy, and public understanding.

Stress and Indignity

Research may cause stress and indignity to the participants within the research situation. While such experiences may not constitute long-term harms to their interests, they do represent violations of the standards of good interpersonal relations. Stress may take the form of specific fears or general anxiety, physical or interpersonal discomfort, feelings of inadequacy or uncertainty, embarrassment, frustration, or internal conflict. Research participants may, for example, experience discomfort, embarrassment, and a sense of inadequacy because they do not know how to handle the situation in which they find themselves or because they believe—sometimes because they have been deliberately led to believe—that they are not performing well. These typically are temporary, situational reactions, although the line between short-term and long-term effects cannot always be sharply drawn. As has already been noted, the self-doubts and lowered self-esteem induced in such situations may at times—depending on the characteristics of the individuals involved and the nature of the precipitating experience—carry over into future situations; short-term stress and discomfort would, in these cases, shade into psychological injury. Even when the stress is only temporary, it does constitute a harm: Clearly the accumulation of stressful experiences represents a lowering in the quality of a person's life, even though the harm contributed by any single stressful experience—because of its short-term nature—cannot be easily calculated for purposes of risk-benefit analysis.[24]

Research participation may also produce situational effects that are less palpable and more elusive than stress or discomfort and hence even more difficult to enter into risk-benefit calculations. These can best be described as indignity—i.e., being subjected to an experience that is degrading and that deprives the person of the respect with which we generally treat fellow humans. Such experiences may arise, for example, when research procedures cause people to lose control over their reactions, to violate their own values, or to appear foolish, or—more generally—when they employ deception and psychological manipulation. Perhaps the limiting case of short-term harm, involving at least a mild form of indignity, is the imposition that results from taking up people's time in an activity that they find useless and lacking in interest. Though the relationship between investigator and participant in this case may be free of stress and degradation, it lacks reciprocity in that it serves the interests of the investigator but provides no benefits to the participants commensurate with the time they are asked to invest. Again, it should be noted that indignities constitute harms—in the form of insults, rather than injuries. While it may not be possible to demonstrate the damaging effect of any single instance of indignity, the accumulation of such indignities (whether or not they are experienced as stressful) is likely to lower the person's self-esteem, self-confidence, and capacity for autonomous action.

Corresponding to the different kinds of short-term harms that have been described, there are potential benefits to participants resulting from their involvement in an experience that may be enjoyable, interesting, or instructive, and may enhance their self-esteem. The latter effect is likely to the extent participants are treated with respect, assured that they are participating in an important enterprise, and made to feel that their personal contribution to the enterprise is valuable and appreciated.

Diffuse Harm

Research may cause diffuse harm which does not directly affect the individual participants or even the groups from which they are drawn, but which is damaging to the society at large. Such damage may take the form of reducing the integrity and effectiveness of social institutions in achieving societal goals and values, or of creating an atmosphere—a set of beliefs and expectations—antagonistic to important and widely shared social values. A prime example, already mentioned, is the perversion of the political process that might result from the excessive use of opinion polling in election campaigns. Under the guise of assessing the views of voters, polls may actually shape the preferences of voters; consequently, the activities of candidates may in turn be geared to raising their standing in the polls rather than to addressing the issues. Disproportionate and sometimes exploitative use of minority group members as research participants and dissemination of data about group differences in ability and achievement may increase the level of inequity in the society and undermine efforts to enhance equality of opportunity. The value of equity may also be compromised by social experiments—e.g., in housing, income maintenance, or the administration of criminal justice—in which certain advantages are differentially allocated to different segments of the population. The prevalence of field experiments on helping behavior, mentioned above, in which experimental confederates feign injury or other kinds of disability in order to observe bystander reactions under varying circumstances,[25] may add to the level of arbitrariness and irrationality within society and compound the ambiguity of real-life situations that call for bystander intervention. These and other types of social research that are intrusive or deceptive may also cause diffuse harm by reducing the private space and the level of trust in the society—effects to which I shall return momentarily.

Corresponding to the different kinds of diffuse harms that have been described, there are potential benefits that social research may bring to the larger society. Research advances the development of scientific knowledge, which is a social value in its own right, and which, in turn, may contribute to social welfare and public enlightenment. Increased understanding of human behavior and social institutions may both directly enhance the quality of life and contribute to the solution of social problems, to the effectiveness of institutional functioning, and to the development of sound and just social policies.

Privacy and Confidentiality

For the issue of privacy and confidentiality, the three columns of table 2.1 correspond to three types of concerns about invasion of privacy that social research brings into play.[26] In each case, invasion of privacy can be viewed both as a harm in its own right, particularly in the sense of a moral wrong, and as a condition that subjects people to the possibility of harm by depriving them of the protection that privacy offers. However, as we move from the first to the third column, the emphasis shifts somewhat from invasion of privacy as exposure to the risk of specific harms to invasion of privacy as violation of a basic right.

Public Exposure

An obvious source of concern about the potential invasiveness of social research is the fear that information revealed by participants in the course of the research may be disseminated beyond the research setting itself. Such wider public exposure of the participants' views or actions may subject them to the possibility of damaging consequences. Research participants may be concerned, for example, that the information might become accessible to authorities who are in a position to penalize or harass them. Individuals engaged in illegal activities, welfare recipients whose private lives are always subject to scrutiny, or political dissidents in a repressive environment are among those who are particularly likely to feel such anxieties. Participants may also be concerned that the information might become accessible to specific others in their daily environments, particularly their superiors in a status hierarchy (such as their bosses, teachers, parents, officers, or keepers), who might retaliate against them if they disapproved of their opinions or actions. Potentially damaging consequences of public exposure include not only the risk of penalty or reprisal, but also the possibility of embarrassment and disapproval, affecting people's reputations and relations with their associates.

Concern about public exposure may also extend to group data. For example, information about the performance or attitudes of a particular unit within an organization or community may subject its members to possibly damaging or embarrassing consequences, even if the responses of individual participants are not identified. Similarly, information about the practices of an organization, institution, or community may have deleterious effects on its reputation and the resources it can command. Sometimes, of course, research is specifically designed to increase public knowledge about the practices of an organization (or type of organization) and to evaluate its performance. In such cases, public exposure does not present an ethical problem, unless respondents were misled about the way in which the data were to be used, or unless observations were made covertly, as in David L. Rosenhan's pseudopatient studies in which the investigators gained admission to psychiatric hospitals by pretending to have heard voices.[27] Public exposure of group data may also be an issue in studies of ethnic minority communities or foreign societies, carried out by outsiders with insufficient understanding of the cultural context. Members of these groups may view the dissemination of information obtained in such studies as invasive of their group's privacy, with the consequence of reinforcing negative stereotypes about them and justifying policies that are irrelevant or detrimental to their interests.

At the level of the individual, the risks of public exposure can be virtually eliminated by spelling out precise procedures for maintaining confidentiality of the data and scrupulously adhering to them (as Robert F. Boruch discusses in this volume). In most cases, it is even possible to protect confidential data against involuntary exposure (resulting, for example, from forced entry or court orders) by removing identifying information as soon as possible. Maintaining the confidentiality of group data is far more complex. Even when research reports attempt to disguise the identity of an organization or community or of its subgroups, it is often impossible to prevent recognition by many readers. In studies focusing on large groupings (such as ethnic minorities) or on entire societies, disguising the identity of the population is generally both impossible and inconsistent with the purposes of the research. In the case of group data, then, the main issue shifts from maintaining confidentiality to introducing safeguards—in the choice of research topics, the design and procedures of the research, the solicitation of the participants, and the reporting of the findings—to assure that the group's interests will be maximally protected against potentially harmful consequences of public exposure.[28]

Reduced Control over Self-Presentation

A second source of concern about the potential invasiveness of social research is that it may reduce participants' control over their self-presentation in the research situation proper. Self-presentation and impression management are central preoccupations in most of our interpersonal relationships.[29] Efforts to control our self-presentation are partly designed to protect ourselves against humiliation, embarrassment, disapproval, and rejection. According to the norms that govern social interaction, people generally accept and support the identity that others seek to project and respect the others' desire to maintain control over their self-presentations. To maintain this control, they must be free to pick and choose what information about themselves to disclose and what information to withhold. There are a number of ways in which the structure of the research situation and the procedures of social research may have the effect of restricting this freedom, thereby reducing participants' privacy. Research participants lose a measure of control over their self-presentation to the extent they are unaware of the conditions under which they are being observed—because they do not know that they are being observed at all, or who it is that is observing them, or what aspects of their behavior are the focus of observation. Control over self-presentation is also reduced to the extent that participants feel under pressure to reveal personal information that they would prefer to withhold. Finally, control over self-presentation is reduced to the extent participants are caught unawares, being confronted by an unexpected or disturbing event or a violation of social norms.

Confrontation with such circumstances, which reduce people's control over their self-presentation, is not unique to social research situations, but is a common feature of everyday life. It is one of the risks we take whenever we venture out into the public arena and engage in social interaction. Even though the resulting reduction in control over our self-presentation is experienced as a loss in privacy, the events that cause it—whether in real life or in the research situation—do not in themselves constitute ethically objectionable invasions of privacy. Serious ethical concerns arise only insofar as the reduced control over participants' self-presentation is brought about by deliberately deceptive, coercive, or intrusive means.[30] The problem is that social research, in at least some of its manifestations, is prone to employ precisely such questionable means in its quest for valid, spontaneous reactions from respondents. There is often an inherent tension between the participants' desire to maintain control over their self-presentations and the investigator's goal to obtain accurate information about their motives, attitudes, behavior patterns, or personal histories, which may require circumventing their efforts at control and penetrating their facades. For example, unobtrusive measurement and experimental deception are specifically designed to counteract respondents' tendencies to manipulate their self-presentations by keeping them unaware of the behavior being observed. Thus, the issues raised by the second source of concern over privacy are more difficult than those relating to public exposure. We are dealing not merely with the introduction of safeguards to minimize threats to privacy (by protecting confidentiality of data), but with the question of the inherent invasiveness, and hence the ethical propriety, of certain research procedures that social scientists consider essential to the methodological soundness of their work.

Reduction of Private Space

The third source of concern about the potential invasiveness of social research is that it may reduce the overall amount of private space available to individuals. Private space protects the integrity and autonomy of the self. Preservation of the sense of an autonomous self depends on maintaining a recognized boundary between self and environment, which assures the individual a private space, both physical and psychological. Violations of this space—what Erving Goffman has called "contaminative exposure"[31]— threaten our capacity to develop an autonomous self and to maintain its integrity. The definitions of the boundaries of private space differ across individuals and across cultures, but it generally includes our own bodies and personal possessions, our intimate relationships, biographical facts, and personal thoughts. Societies develop and maintain social norms designed to minimize personal and institutional actions that overstep these boundaries. The inviolability of private space as a social value, however, often comes into conflict with the functioning of various social institutions in the pursuit of other social values—such as the functioning of a free press, of the criminal justice system, of consumer credit systems, or of airport security systems.

Social research is one societal enterprise that, by its nature, comes into conflict with the value of preserving an optimal amount of private space within the society. Some of the controversies about intrusive research have centered on studies that involve direct observations of behavior that is quintessentially private (even though it may occur in semipublic places)—such as Laud Humphreys's study of male homosexual activities in public restrooms[32] or the

R. Dennis Middlemist et al. study of micturition.[33] Critics of these studies have focused on the surreptitious nature of the observations and the fact that they were obtained without informed consent—procedures that are generally troublesome, but become more so when used to gain access into people's private space.[34] The problems of balancing the social values represented by social research with the value of preserving private space are more fundamental, however, than these more dramatic examples would suggest. Significant research on human behavior and social institutions inevitably must inquire into matters that at least some individuals, some groups, or some societies place within the boundaries of private space—such as love, personal health, death, religion, ethnicity, politics, money, or family relations. To declare such topics categorically off limits to social science would trivialize the enterprise and greatly reduce its potential benefits to human welfare. While no topic ought to be considered taboo for social investigation, social controls are essential to assure care and sensitivity in the choice of occasions and procedures for investigating areas that might constitute part of private space for the individual, group, or society involved.

Informed Consent and Deception

When applied to the issue of deception and informed consent, the three-way distinction reflected in the columns of table 2.1 corresponds to three types of concerns generated by the use of deception and by violations of informed consent in social research. I shall use the term *pressure* as a shorthand designation of the various ways in which an individual's freedom of choice in the situation may be curtailed. At the extreme, this refers to the use of coercion or direct threats of punishment to induce participation in the research. Less extreme forms of pressure include efforts to induce participation by indicating that powerful authorities expect it, by offering irresistible rewards, by implying that failure to participate would result in penalties or place the individual in a bad light, by putting the individual on the defensive, or by identifying refusal with a lack of courage, courtesy, or patriotism. Both deception and pressure may occur at the point at which participation in the research is solicited, where they have a direct impact on the individual's capacity to give voluntary, informed consent. They may also occur at different points throughout the research process itself. For example, participants may be misled about various features of the situation or given false information about their performance; and they may be pressured to reveal information that they would prefer to withhold, or to engage in activities they would prefer to avoid, or to continue in the research when they would prefer to quit.

Impaired Capacity for Decision Making

One reason for concern about pressure and deception is that they impair participants' capacity to make voluntary, informed decisions in line with their own interests. Decisions about participating in the research at all, about continuing participation, about cooperating with certain of the activities or procedures involved in the research, and about revealing certain kinds of information may all have a bearing on the concrete interests of the participants. Insofar as they are subjected to pressure or coercion, they are denied the opportunity to weigh these considerations and decide accordingly. Insofar as they are subjected to deception or misrepresentation, they are denied information that may be material to the decisions they have to make. As a consequence, their ability to protect themselves against possible injury is restricted.

The problems in this category are not completely resolved by full disclosure and mechanical adherence to the principle of informed consent. Full disclosure of the purposes and conditions of the research may provide information that is not material to participants' interests and the decisions they have to make, while adversely affecting the validity of the findings. Voluntary, informed consent is illusory if the participants lack the capacity to evaluate the information given (e.g., because of age, intelligence, or mental and physical state) or if they are in a highly coercive environment (such as prison). The primary concern is that participants have all the opportunity and information that they need and that they can utilize for making decisions and protecting their own interests.

An added element of complexity is introduced when we consider the effects of deception and pressure on participants' capacity to protect the interests of the groups to which they belong. The problem takes on special urgency when we remember that the groups whose interests are most likely to be affected by social research—groups characterized by disadvantage, dependence, deviance, or captive status—are also the groups that are most subject to pressures and least able to resist demands to participate in research.[35] When group interests are at stake, therefore, it is particularly important to avoid procedures that would further impair research participants' capacity to make voluntary, informed decisions. Given the difficulty in predicting the probable consequences of a piece of research (including its products) for the interests of the group, it may often be useful to bring representatives of the group's leadership into the decision-making process. This would lessen the individual participants' burden of deciding what is or is not in the best interest of their groups, although it might also subject them to an additional set of pressures coming from their own (perhaps self-appointed) group leaders.

Deprivation of Respect

A second reason for concern about deception and pressure is that they deprive participants of the respect to which fellow humans are entitled as a basic assumption of decent interpersonal relations. By deliberately misrepresenting their own purposes and intentions and by restricting participants' choices through manipulative and coercive means, investigators are violating some of the guiding principles on which a respectful relationship rests. The resulting relationship is marked by a lack of reciprocity in obligations and outcomes, which is tantamount to the use of others as means rather than as ends in themselves.

This concern is independent of the possibility that deception and pressure may expose research participants to specifiable harmful consequences. Even if they suffer no injury or even temporary discomfort (except for the discomfort that generally accompanies the experience of being pressured), they have been subjected to a moral wrong. Their right to respectful treatment, including associated rights to candor, to freedom of choice, and to reciprocity, have been violated. Violation of these rights subjects people to the possibility of harm in the long run. The principle of mutual respect and the rights associated with it provide a set of social norms and an interpersonal atmosphere that help to protect individuals from injurious and stressful interactions. Systematic violations of these norms undermine the principle of respect and create an atmosphere in which disregard for the well-being of participants is legitimized and their vulnerability to harm is heightened.

Erosion of Trust

A third reason for concern about the use of deception and pressure in social research is the cumulative effect that such procedures have on the integrity of certain social values. Specifically, by the systematic use of deception and pressure, social research may contribute to the erosion of trust in social institutions and interpersonal relations. Extensive reliance on deception and manipulation by various institutions in our society—including government, business, the professions, and the media—has already created widespread distrust in social institutions. Concomitants of this distrust are a cynical attitude and a sense of anomie. The message seems to be that deception and manipulation are expectable and hence acceptable as long as you manage to avoid being caught; in any event, you would be wise to assume that people, particularly those in authority positions, cannot be trusted or believed. It is especially troublesome when social scientists contribute to this message, since they implicitly lend their own professional authority to the view that such behavior is an inevitable feature of human nature and social relations.

Trust is an important social value in its own right, basic to our conception of desirable relationships among people generally, as well as between citizens and authorities. It is also of great instrumental significance, in that trust is a condition for the legitimacy and effectiveness of social institutions and for the smoothness and reliability of social interaction. Trust provides the sense of security and predictability that allows us to plan and arrange our activities so as to maximize our values and protect our interests. Thus, the erosion of trust within the society or any of its component institutions subjects us to the possibility of harm by undermining our ability to protect ourselves against it.

Social Control

The term *social control* is used loosely here to refer to the entire range of processes and mechanisms employed by a society through its various agencies to prescribe, guide, monitor, and restrain the behavior of its members—for present purposes, the ethical conduct of social scientists. The concerns aroused by each of the three types of impact mapped in table 2.1 call for some kind of social control. What I am proposing, however, is that the most appropriate form of social control varies from column to column, depending on the particular nature of the problem we are confronting. Specifically, I maintain that government regulation becomes less appropriate as one moves from concerns about the concrete interests of research participants to concerns about the quality of interpersonal relationships and wider social values (which affect more ephemeral and remote interests).

Government Regulation

When our concern focuses on the impact of research on the concrete interests of the research participants, government regulation is probably the most appropriate form of social control, although it should not be seen as a substitute for the development of professional standards and broader social policies to protect the interests of participants. A good example of government involvement in social control is the system of Institutional Review Boards, with its associated regulations and procedures, established by the U.S. Department of Health, Education, and Welfare (now Health and Human Services) in recent years. The primary purpose of government regulation is to protect research participants from palpable injuries, such as physical harm, psychological breakdown, or financial loss. To this end, regulatory mechanisms are designed to ensure that research studies do not expose participants to undue risks of injury; that the confidentiality of data is protected, so that injuries resulting from public exposure can be avoided; and that informed consent procedures are adhered to, so that participants are in a position to protect themselves against injury.

The role of government in protecting citizens against palpable injuries (through such diverse agencies as the police, the courts, and the regulatory commissions) is well established. Introducing government regulation, backed by the government's coercive power, into the research process can thus be justified when one is dealing with the risk of harms that are enduring, direct, and measurable—that is, injuries comparable to those for which one might claim damages in court. Historically, government intervention in research with human subjects began in the United States with the revelation of abuses in certain biomedical studies, which placed patients at serious risk to their health and perhaps even their survival, without adequate procedures for obtaining their informed consent. The involvement of government agencies can be attributed in part to the failure of professional associations and institutions to do a satisfactory job of self-policing. But even if they had done so, total reliance on self-regulation by the profession does not seem appropriate in a situation that clearly involves conflicting interests between investigators and research participants. While the two parties do have some common interests, the research participants have a special interest in avoiding injury to themselves, and the investigators have a special interest in advancing their scientific work and their personal careers. Complete reliance on self-regulation, under these circumstances, would be tantamount to leaving the task of adjudicating competing interests to one of the interested parties. Thus, involvement of a third party—in the form of a public agency—is not only appropriate but clearly necessary where such conflicting interests are at issue.

Government regulation becomes more problematic when the concern focuses on group interests rather than the interests of individual participants; and when the concern is generated by the products of the research rather than by its processes. In these situations, it is considerably more difficult to predict the impact of the research (as it interacts with other social forces), to specify the nature of the injury that might result, and to identify the populations that are at risk. If government regulation is appropriate at all under these circumstances, it should apply only to special cases, in which important interests of particularly vulnerable groups are at stake, and it should set only very general guidelines (e.g., mandating that some type of consultation or "socioenvironmental impact study" be undertaken). In general, however, it would seem more appropriate to rely on the social policy process, rather than the regulatory process, for the protection of group interests in social research.

Professional Standards

When our concern focuses on the impact of social research on the quality of interpersonal relationships, without risk of significant injury, government regulation does not appear to be the appropriate form of social control. While it is possible to set out general criteria for the respectful, solicitous treatment of research participants, it is very difficult to translate them into specific requirements that can be enforced by an IRB (beyond such requirements as ensuring confidentiality and informed consent, which are designed to protect the participants' concrete interests, but of course also have a bearing on the quality of the relationship). Furthermore, violations of the norms that govern social interaction do not constitute palpable, demonstrable, enduring injuries of the kind that justify intervention by the government's regulatory apparatus with its coercive backing. Finally, maintaining the quality of interpersonal relationships with clients requires professional judgment, which is an essential ingredient of the professional role and an important criterion for professional certification. While government intervention may be necessary to protect clients from the consequences of gross violations of the norms of professional conduct (essentially, from malpractice), it would totally undermine the professional role if it were aimed at regulating the details of the professional-client relationship.

To say that the quality of the relationship between investigator and research participant is not an appropriate subject for government regulation is not to imply that it should be entirely exempt from social control. Rather, in keeping with my view that the quality of the relationship with clients is a central feature of the professional role, I propose that this is precisely a domain in which professional standards must exercise the major control function. At the most formal level, professional standards for the treatment of research participants may be communicated in the form of ethical guidelines or codes adopted by professional associations, to serve an advisory or a binding function for their memberships. An excellent example of such an effort is the rather detailed document on ethics of research with human participants developed by the American Psychological Association.[36] Documents of this type contribute to social control by sensitizing the profession to the standards to which members are expected to adhere and introducing these standards into the training of new professionals. Often, professional associations may also develop mechanisms for enforcing their codified standards. For example, the ten general principles formulated by the American Psychological Association's Committee on Ethical Standards[37] were formally adopted by the association and incorporated in its code of ethics. Violations of the code can be the subject of formal charges brought against a member and can lead to various penalties, of which the most extreme is expulsion from the association.

The primary function of professional standards, however—whether or not they are formally codified—is not to serve as the basis for enforcement procedures, but to express the profession's consensus about the proper ways to enact the professional role. Professional standards governing the relationship of investigator and research participants are conveyed in professional training, in research supervision, in discussions at professional meetings, in debates in the literature, in special conferences and publications. Standards can be raised by introducing various practices that legitimize and institutionalize concern with ethical issues as part of the professional role—e.g., by including units on research ethics in the curriculum, by requiring a section on ethical considerations as a standard feature of research reports,[38] or by establishing committees and task forces devoted to these issues.[39] Professional standards (whether for the quality of scientific work or the quality of investigator-participant relationships) exercise social control by virtue of the effect that adherence to such standards has on the professional careers, reputations, and self-images of investigators.

Social Policy

When our concern focuses on the impact of social research on wider social values, government regulation again does not appear to be the appropriate form of social control. We are dealing with the risk of diffuse harms to the body politic, rather than concrete injuries to identifiable individuals, whose interests government regulations are designed to protect. The consequences of research for social values are remote and hard to predict, and the links of existing social trends to earlier research activities (as distinct from other social forces) cannot readily be established. Not surprisingly, observers disagree in their speculations about the probable wider impact of certain lines of social research. Moreover, there is often disagreement about the desirability of certain anticipated consequences: Effects seen as harmful by some may be seen as beneficial by others. Under these circumstances, given the absence of a clear and present danger, the possible effect of government regulation on the integrity of social science itself becomes a particularly important consideration. Much of social research involves observation of ongoing events, interviewing, and the study of public records, and is thus more comparable to journalistic than to biomedical investigation.[40] Regulation of social research, therefore, can be seen as imposing constraints not only on the freedom of scientific inquiry, but also on freedom of speech and freedom of the press. Such constraints are hard to justify in a democratic society when their only purpose is to reduce the risk of diffuse harm.

To an important degree, reducing the risks of diffuse harm is the responsibility of the profession. Social scientists must consider the impact of their research on wider social values in the collection and dissemination of their data, as well as in their teaching and other professional activities. One of the functions of professional associations is to monitor the uses to which social science is put and to anticipate the long-term consequences of social research. Professional standards need to include norms regarding research sponsorship, the presentation of research findings, and follow-ups on completed research, all designed to minimize the possibilities of misinterpretation and misuse of the findings. But social controls in this domain cannot be left entirely to the profession itself. To a large extent, we are dealing here with the place of social science in the larger society, and this is of necessity a concern that engages the public interest.

Social control, under these circumstances, is most appropriately exercised through the processes by which social policy is formulated. These processes, in a democratic society, involve extensive public debate at different levels, in which social scientists—individually and through their organizations—must take an active part. By way of this debate, policies affecting the status of social science in the society are hammered out. This policy process yields decisions, for example, about the amount of public financial support that is to be given to social science and about its allocation to particular lines of research; about the extent to which social research (e.g., in the form of social experiments or evaluation studies) is to be commissioned or mandated in conjunction with the development of social programs; about the use of social science data in the implementation of social policies (such as school desegregation or court reform); about the establishment of new research or training institutions in the social sciences (such as a National Peace Academy); or about the special rights, privileges, and protections that are to be extended to social scientists (such as the right to maintain the confidentiality of their sources). In the course of this policy process, which clearly represents an effective source of social control over social science, assessments of the impact of social research on wider social values legitimately play a central part. The debate, of course, must carefully balance the risks of diffuse harm created by certain types of social research against the potential benefits to the society, not only of the scientific knowledge to be produced, but also of maintaining a free, vigorous, independent social research enterprise.

Ethical Issues Confronting Different Research Methods

Within the framework presented in table 2.1, we can now look more specifically at the different methods used by social scientists. We can ask what impact each method is likely to have on the concrete interests of research participants, on the quality of the interpersonal relationships between investigators and participants, and on wider social values. Each of these types of impact will be examined in terms of the amount and kind of harm that is risked by a given method, the degree to which it threatens violations of privacy and confidentiality, and the degree to which it involves deception or other curtailments of informed consent. This examination will also suggest the major issues to which social controls need to be directed for each method.

For present purposes, I have divided the methods of social research into three broad categories that represent different ways in which the data are obtained: experimental manipulation, questioning of respondents, and direct observation. Each of these three categories, in turn, has (for the sake of symmetry) been further divided into three subcategories. The resulting nine types of research methods are listed in the left-hand column of table 2.2.

Within the category of experimental manipulation, the first subcategory that can be distinguished is the laboratory experiment. In controlled laboratory experiments, which are particularly popular among psychologists, the experimenter creates different psychological or social conditions by varying the definition of the situation, the experimental instructions, or the participants' activities or experiences in the situation, and observes the effects of these variations on the participants' behavior. I also include in this subcategory laboratory simulations in which participants are asked to play such real-life roles as those of national decision makers, business executives, or prison guards and inmates. Though such simulations are generally not controlled experiments, they do involve the deliberate staging of a set of events or experiences in order to study their effects on participants' behavior. A second use of experimental manipulation occurs in field experiments in which the experimenter—unbeknownst to the research participants—introduces ex-

TABLE 2.2
MAJOR ETHICAL ISSUES CONFRONTING DIFFERENT TYPES
OF SOCIAL RESEARCH

Types of Research	Types of Impact of the Research		
	Concrete Interests of Participants	Quality of Interpersonal Relationships	Wider Social Values
Experimental manipulation			
Laboratory experiments and simulations	Impaired capacity for decision making	Stress and indignity	Erosion of trust
Field experiments	Impaired capacity for decision making	Reduced control over self-presentation	Erosion of trust
Organizational and social experiments	Risk of material injury	Deprivation of respect	Inequity
Questioning of respondents			
Questionnaires and tests	Public exposure	Deprivation of respect	Inequity
Surveys and interview studies	Public exposure	Reduced control over self-presentation	Perversion of political process; manipulation
Records and secondary analysis	Public exposure	Deprivation of respect	Reduction of private space
Direct Observation			
Structured observation	Impaired capacity for decision making	Stress and indignity	Reduction of private space
Unobtrusive (public) observation	Impaired capacity for decision making	Reduced control over self-presentation	Reduction of private space
Participant observation	Public exposure	Deprivation of respect	Erosion of trust

perimental manipulations in a natural setting, as in the studies of helping behavior cited earlier. A very different type of field experiment, which I am including in the third category (with the designation "organizational experiment"), deliberately introduces alternative experimental treatments in an ongoing organization or group of organizations and compares their effects on various behavioral, attitudinal, or organizational dimensions. An extension of this type of research, also included in the third subcategory, is the large-scale social experiment, such as the New Jersey—Pennsylvania Income Maintenance Experiment, designed to evaluate new social policies by studying their effects on sample communities, each of which is selected to participate in one or another version of the program being tested or to serve as a control group.[41]

The second category involves the questioning of respondents about their personal characteristics, life histories, experiences, interpersonal relations, attitudes, beliefs, values, fantasies, past behaviors, or behavioral intentions. This type of research may rely on written questionnaires and tests (of aptitude, achievement, or personality), which have been used on a variety of populations for a variety of purposes—ranging from studies of child-rearing practices, as reported by school children, to studies of creativity in artists and scientists. The second subcategory of this type includes the sample survey, which is used in opinion polling, market research, and a wide variety of theoretical and applied studies, to assess the attitudes, expectations, or practices of a population through interviews with a representative sample of that population. I also include in this subcategory the use of personal interviews with special populations, as in studies of job satisfaction among workers in a particular factory, of inner conflicts among psychiatric patients, or of political attitudes among legislators. The third subcategory of "questioning" research includes the use of records—such as those kept in hospitals, schools or municipalities— as a source of data, and the secondary analysis of data collected in earlier surveys or questionnaire studies. The distinguishing feature of this subcategory is that the data consist of information obtained from (or about) respondents on an earlier occasion and for a different purpose.

Direct observation of ongoing behavior can be subdivided into structured, unobtrusive, and participant observation. In structured observation, the investigator assigns special tasks to research participants or arranges special interaction situations—such as group discussions or mother-child interactions—in a laboratory setting and then observes and records the participants' performance, usually in terms of a systematic set of behavioral categories. I would also include in this subcategory systematic observations carried out in relatively structured nonlaboratory situations—such as classrooms, encounter or therapy groups, and conferences—in which the investigator is a nonparticipating observer. Unobtrusive observation refers to naturalistic study of ongoing behavior in public places, such as the play behavior of children, the interactions of strangers on trains or lovers in the park, and the reactions of crowds at football games or political demonstrations. In participant observation, used extensively by anthropologists and sociologists, the investigator studies a community, organization, institution, or social movement, by participating in its regular activities. Participant observers may in fact be members of the groups they are studying, or they may deliberately become members for the purposes of the research, or they may join the group temporarily as acknowledged outsiders.

My listing of the ethical issues that may arise in each of these types of research is not based on a systematic survey of studies in the genre and is certainly not intended to provide a statistical picture of prevailing practice. I will cite a problem for a given type of research whenever the logic of the methods it employs, or the context in which it is generally carried out, or the nature of the data it collects, creates the potential for that problem to arise. I will give special emphasis to a problem when there is evidence that it has manifested itself with relative frequency in the actual experience with this type of research. Thus, deception is presented as a major issue for laboratory and field experiments, since it flows from the logic of the method (i.e., the requirement of keeping participants unaware of the purpose of the experimental manipulation) and is rather widespread. For participant observation research, deception is presented as a less central issue because it is not as pervasive as in experimental research, even though disguise and misrepresentation have been used fairly often for methodological purposes (to gain entry into situations that might otherwise be inaccessible to the observer). By contrast, deception hardly arises as an issue at all with respect to survey research, because investigators working in that tradition have not had any systematic reason for its use, nor are there any indications that it has often appeared in practice. This does not mean that deception could never be used in survey research, or even that it could not, under different circumstances, become a standard procedure. Conversely, there is no implication that deception is a necessary component of laboratory or field experiments, or even that it is ubiquitous in current practice. It is important to remember that many lines of experimental research—and certainly of participant observation research—do not rely on deception at all. In short, citing a problem for a particular type of research does not suggest that certain abuses are inherent in its methods; omitting the problem for another type of research does not suggest that its methods are immune to these abuses.

Table 2.2 summarizes the major ethical issues posed by each of the nine types of research with respect to participant interests, interpersonal relationships, and wider social values. For each cell of the table, I make a judgment about the most important problem, choosing in each case between magnitude of potential harm, threat to privacy and confidentiality, and potential violation of informed consent. These choices are somewhat arbitrary, particularly since the three issue areas often overlap and interact. They are forced choices, whose main purpose is to make a tabular overview of major issues more manageable. A fuller statement of the problems associated with each type of research can be found in the text that follows.

Laboratory Experiments and Simulations

At the level of participant interests, the risk of physical injury becomes an issue only in those laboratory studies that involve pharmacological or physiological interventions. In studies involving strictly psychological or social interventions, there is the hypothetical possibility that experimentally induced aggression, for example, might expose participants to the risk of physical attack, but there is virtually no evidence that this problem has in fact arisen. A possible exception is the prison simulation study by Philip G. Zimbardo and associates, in which student participants became so involved in their roles that the "guards" actually began to subject the "inmates" to physical (in addition to psychological) abuse.[42] Shortly thereafter, however, the study was prematurely terminated. The risk of psychological injury is more serious, although there is no evidence that participants in laboratory experiments have actually experienced psychotic reactions or long-term psychological damage. Yet, one cannot rule out the possibility that the self-doubts and lowered self-esteem that participants often experience, as a direct or indirect result of experimental manipulations, may endure beyond the laboratory situation. This issue is raised, for example, by several experiments in which college-age participants were given false information that created doubts about their sexual identities (although they were subsequently debriefed),[43] and by studies in which participants are induced to act in ways that violate their values and self-concepts, such as Stanley Milgram's well-known obedience experiments[44] or the Zimbardo et al. prison simulation.

Public exposure due to violations of confidentiality has not been an issue in laboratory experiments, largely because the information they obtain from individuals is quite esoteric and usually of no interest to anyone other than the experimenter. Impairment of the capacity for decision making, on the other hand, is a major issue—in fact, I am suggesting, *the* major issue when our concern focuses on the concrete interests of research participants—because of the heavy reliance on deception in this research tradition. While the risk of injury—even psychological injury—may be relatively small, participants have a right to decide for themselves whether or not they are prepared to take that risk, and deception may deprive them of the opportunity to do so. I would argue that, in the case of laboratory experiments, deception and other possible constraints on informed consent are the primary issues to which government regulations (and IRBs) need to address themselves. The use of deception immediately raises the question whether the participants' capacity for decision making is impaired—a question that takes on special importance in experiments that are stressful and experiments in which there is even a remote possibility of enduring psychological injury. Regulations are *necessary* to ensure that participants have all the information and freedom they need to protect themselves against undue stress and possible injury. For laboratory experiments involving only psychological and social intervention, regulations ensuring informed consent are probably also *sufficient* to provide the needed protection.

At the level of interpersonal relationships, the possibility of stress and indignity is a major issue for laboratory experiments. In many laboratory studies, the experimental manipulations are specifically designed to induce such stressful states as fear, anxiety, internal conflict, frustration, feelings of failure or inadequacy, embarrassment, confusion, or unpleasant interactions, in order to explore their behavioral consequences under different conditions. In other cases, participants may be subjected, over the course of the experiment, to experiences that are stressful or demeaning—for example, when they are induced to engage in actions that they and others consider unworthy.[45] Invasion of privacy is not a serious issue in laboratory studies, since participants know that they are under observation and can exercise some control over their self-presentations. Control over self-presentation is reduced, however, to the extent that participants are deceived about the purposes of the experiment (which is precisely why experimenters often resort to deception) and to the extent that they are exposed to disturbing experiences or to instructions that violate common expectations. Deception and manipulation threaten the quality of the experimenter-participant relationship—even in the absence of acute stress—because they deprive participants of the respect to which they are entitled. I have listed stress and indignity as the major issues confronted by laboratory studies in the second column of table 2.2, since in effect they encompass the problems of deception and manipulation. Controls at this level call for continuing refinement of professional standards, in the search for alternative approaches that would meet the research objectives without sacrificing participants' dignity, for ways of mitigating deception and stress if they are to be used, and for debriefing procedures designed to alleviate stress and restore trust.

At the level of wider social values, the major concern generated by laboratory experiments is that, in their extensive reliance on deception and manipulation, they may be contributing to the erosion of trust in authorities and social institutions. As a further consequence, they may reinforce an attitude of cynicism and help to legitimize the practices of misinformation and manipulation within the society. These potential implications of research that uses deception are appropriate subjects for policy debate, to be considered in the context of other societal activities—such as politics, advertising, and news reporting—that may similarly contribute to the erosion of trust.

Field Experiments

The profile for field experiments is similar to that for laboratory experiments, with some differences in emphasis. At the level of participant interests, the risk of injury is negligible in those experiments that involve the introduction of only minor variations in an ongoing public activity (e.g., variations in the race, sex, appearance, or attire of individuals collecting signatures for a petition). When the manipulation involves the staging of an unusual, disturbing event, there is the hypothetical, but far-fetched, possibility of physical injury (e.g., if somehow a melee were precipitated). More realistic is the possibility of psychological injury; for example, unwitting research participants confronted with a feigned accident might be deeply shocked, or might experience losses in self-esteem because they found themselves incompetent or unwilling to help. Even in such disturbing situations, however, the likelihood of enduring psychological harm is rather low. The experience is more likely to produce temporary effects, though it may cause considerable inconvenience, annoyance, and conflict.[46] The possibility of material injury may arise in field experiments in which the manipulation has differential effects on the participants in a real-life setting. For example, in the Robert

Rosenthal-Lenore Jacobson study of self-fulfilling prophecies,[47] teachers were led to expect that certain children (in fact, randomly selected for the experimental group) would show unusual intellectual gains; the teachers apparently interacted with these children in ways that actually facilitated their intellectual development. It can be argued that the control-group children were not only deprived of benefits extended to the experimental group, but were denied opportunities they might have had in the absence of the experiment.

As in laboratory experiments, public exposure due to violations of confidentiality is not an issue here, since participants are not even identified. Public exposure becomes an issue only in the sense that some of the participants' shortcomings may be revealed in a public situation; but this is more a matter of embarrassment and shame (relevant to the quality of relationships) than a threat to concrete interests. The major threat to concrete interests comes from impairment of participants' capacity for decision making, which is inherent in this line of research. A central feature of the variety of field experiments that I have included in this category is that participants are not even aware that an experiment is in progress, so that informed consent in the usual sense of the term is virtually impossible. The intrusion and deception represented by this procedure are not particularly problematic when the experimental manipulation "falls within the range of the respondent's ordinary experience, merely being an experimental rearrangement of normal-level communications."[48] The curtailment of informed consent becomes problematic, and a suitable subject for government regulation, when the manipulation involves the staging of a dramatic event that borders on the creation of a public nuisance.

Such potentially disturbing field experiments also raise the issue of stress and indignity, at the level of interpersonal relationships. At the least, they may constitute an imposition on unsuspecting passers-by and cause them inconvenience. Beyond that, they may generate anxiety, internal conflict, guilt, embarrassment, feelings of inadequacy, and unpleasant interactions. The deception and manipulation involved deprive participants of their right to respectful treatment. Perhaps the most important issue is that such procedures, without giving people the opportunity to give or withhold their consent, intrude on their privacy, in the sense of reducing their control over their self-presentations. By misrepresenting themselves and the situation and by catching people unawares, experimenters restrict participants' ability to pick and choose the aspects of themselves they wish to reveal. While people may be confronted with similar experiences in the usual course of events, professional standards must specify the extent to which investigators are entitled to stage them deliberately for experimental purposes.

At the level of wider social values, the major concern generated by field experiments—and hence the major issue for social policy consideration—is again the erosion of trust. Whereas the prevalence of deceptive laboratory experiments would contribute primarily to distrust and cynicism regarding authorities and social institutions, the prevalence of intrusive field experiments would also affect the level of trust in ordinary relationships. Since field experiments, unlike laboratory experiments, are injected without warning into everyday life, their prevalence may reinforce people's sense of the arbitrariness and irrationality of daily existence and compound the ambiguity of real-life situations that call for bystander intervention.

Organizational and Social Experiments

Research in this category is generally designed to evaluate organizational processes or social policies, which have a bearing on the material well-being of the research participants themselves and of others similarly situated in the organization or the society. Therefore, the major ethical issue that arises at the level of participant interests—and hence the primary focus for government control—is the risk of material injury to the participants and their groups. In large-scale experiments, control-group members may not only be denied the benefits extended to the experimental group, but may actually be worse off as a consequence of the experiment. For example, an experiment that provides housing allowances to some members of a community may contribute to competition and to inflated costs in the housing market for the entire community, thus leaving members of the control group (or, in a community saturation experiment, those who do not meet the criteria for participation)[49] worse off than they were before. Even members of the experimental group, who do receive the intended benefits, may find themselves worse off. Peter G. Brown has demonstrated how participants in a health insurance experiment may actually experience a decline in the quality of their health care.[50]

Moreover, participants risk material (and to some extent psychological) injury at termination of the experiment. For example, individuals who decide to change their employment patterns as a result of their participation in an income maintenance experiment may find, at termination of the experiment, that they can no longer return to the jobs they had given up (or no longer find them as satisfying as in the past).[51] In organizational experiments, some of the participants may be subjected to experimental treatments—such as new ways of organizing the work process or new incentive systems—that they find disadvantageous. Not only the procedures, but also the findings of such studies may cause material injury to participants (and to other present or future members of the organization). For example, as mentioned earlier, the findings may suggest changes in policy with negative consequences for their incomes, fringe benefits, working conditions, or living conditions.

The material interests of participants in social and organizational experiments are further jeopardized by the possibility of public exposure of some of the data they provide. In the New Jersey—Pennsylvania Income Maintenance Experiment,[52] for example, the investigators experienced considerable difficulty in maintaining the confidentiality of the data in the face of pressures from official agencies.[53] In organizational experiments, even if the confidentiality of individual data is preserved, I have already noted the complexities in disguising the identities of subunits and protecting their members against damaging consequences. Participants' capacity to protect their interests may also be impaired by informed consent procedures. There have been no reports of deliberate deception, but it is often difficult in a complex social experiment to give participants enough information to understand the implications of the rules to which they are committing themselves or to predict the long-run consequences of their participation.[54] Moreover, in experiments sponsored by the government or by their employers, people often are not free— or at least do not feel free—to refuse participation. Obtaining informed consent from control groups and from nonparticipants affected by the experiment may prove particularly troublesome.[55]

Consent, in a broader sense, is the major ethical issue at the level of interpersonal relationships. As Donald P. Warwick points out: "Few social experimenters would disagree with the broad ethical principle that those to be affected by the policies tested by social experiments should take part in their design. Yet none of the experiments conducted to date has been based on anything resembling real participation by target groups."[56] The same holds true for most organizational experiments. In research that has such a direct bearing on the fate of the participants and their groups (usually the disadvantaged segments of the society or the rank and file of an organization), it is important that their "consent" be sought, not only to their personal participation, but also to the definition of the problem and the selection of the options to be subjected to experimental test. At the very least this requires consultation with representatives of the target groups in the design of the experiment (as well as in the subsequent interpretation of the findings). To assume that participants lack the capacity or the authority to contribute to this process is to deprive them of the respect that we owe to autonomous, responsible adults. The issue raised here has ramifications for other types of research as well, underscoring the need for encouraging, within the profession, the development of "participatory research" models.[57]

At the level of wider social values, the major ethical issue raised by social and organizational experimentation is that of inequity. The issue arises particularly in large-scale experiments, in which the government, in effect, provides certain benefits to some citizens (the experimental group) and withholds them from others (the control group), or subjects different groups to more and less desirable treatments. Insofar as participation in the experiment is mandatory—as it is, for example, in experiments within the criminal justice system—such differential treatment raises not only ethical issues, but also the constitutional issue of equal protection of the laws.[58] Potential inequities may arise, not only in the assignment of individuals to different conditions, but also in the selection of the target populations for the experiment. Participation in social experiments may be risky and burdensome, even when it offers certain short-term benefits to some of the participants. Since the disadvantaged and the poor are more likely to be targeted for research, social experiments may "impose greater burdens on the poor, for the sake of gaining information about human behavior in various markets (such as labor, housing, or health care) that may be useful in formulating policy that will be beneficial to poor and nonpoor alike."[59] Inequities may also arise from the fact that different segments of the population differ in their degree of influence on the definition of the research problem and the design of the experiment; those groups whose points of view dominate the formulation of the alternatives selected for study may also be more likely to benefit from the resultant findings. Debates on social policy need to address the impact of social experiments on the value of equity and need to develop ways of reducing and counteracting their possible contributions to the level of inequity in the society.

Questionnaires and Tests

At the level of participant interests, it is difficult to conceive of injuries that might result from the process of completing a questionnaire or test, other than the loss of time. Perhaps some respondents might be shocked by a highly personal question, or disturbed by an association to a projective test item, or distraught by their poor performance on an intelligence test, but the likelihood that such reactions would cause enduring psychological harm is so remote that it does not call for protective regulation. There is a real possibility that the *findings* of research using test or questionnaire data for group comparisons may be deleterious to the interests of certain groups, particularly minority and disadvantaged populations, but this issue is more appropriately considered under the rubric of wider social values. For individual participants, the threat of injury arises if some of their responses are publicly exposed—through inadvertence or under legal compulsion—subjecting them to the possibility of punishment, harassment, social disapproval, or denial of certain benefits and opportunities. Even if individual responses are not identified, the disclosure of subgroup data (e.g., data for a given work unit or for welfare recipients in a particular neighborhood) may expose the members of that subgroup to damaging consequences.

For these reasons, the primary purpose of government regulation of studies relying on questionnaires or tests is to ensure that investigators maintain the confidentiality of the data and adequately inform participants of any constraints on their ability to maintain confidentiality. Failure to inform participants of such constraints, of course, reduces their capacity to protect their own interests when deciding on participation. Participants' capacity for decision making is also impaired if they are given the explicit or implicit message that they are required to complete the research instruments—an issue that is particularly likely to arise if the research is sponsored by an official agency or conducted in institutional settings with captive populations. The issue of consent is further complicated when there is controversy about participants' competence to give informed consent. For example, some critics have argued that the distribution of questionnaires in schools—particularly if they deal with such controversial topics as sex, religion, or parent-child relations—requires the consent of the parents, even if the students themselves are clearly informed that they are free to refuse participation.

At the level of interpersonal relationships, there is some possibility that questionnaire or test respondents may experience a degree of stress or discomfort, even though there is no deliberate attempt to induce such reactions. For example, they may feel confused by the instructions, disturbed by some of the questions, annoyed by the choices offered, inadequate because of their inability to answer, or simply bored and imposed upon. Since respondents often do not know precisely what dimensions the instruments are designed to tap, their control over their self-presentation is reduced and they may unwittingly reveal information about themselves that they would prefer to withhold. This is particularly likely to happen when attitude scales or personality tests deliberately disguise the dimensions of concern—through the use of indirect questions or projective tasks—in order to circumvent re-spondents' tendency to give responses they consider socially approved and mentally healthy. While such procedures withhold information that respon-dents could use in controlling their self-presentations, I would not regard them as unduly deceptive and invasive, as long as respondents are not given false information and freely enter into the research contract on the basis of the minimal or vague information that they have received about the precise dimensions under scrutiny. More serious ethical problems, amounting to deprivation of respect, would arise if the purpose of the research were deliberately misrepresented or if respondents were subjected to direct or subtle pressures to participate. I list this as the major issue in the second column of table 2.2, not because it is inherent in the use of questionnaires and tests or represents a prevalent practice, but because these instruments are often used in settings in which people are habitually asked to do things without explanation and find it difficult to say no. There may be a temptation, therefore, to take shortcuts in informed consent, which has to be curbed by professional sensitivity to the issue.

At the level of wider social values, the major issue that has confronted this type of research is its potential for reinforcing inequities within the society. This issue, as I have already indicated more than once, has emerged from the interpretation that is often placed on group differences found in studies using questionnaires or psychological tests—such as racial and social-class dif-ferences in intelligence, national differences in attitudes toward work, or differ-ences between "deviants" and "normals" on various personality char-acteristics. There has been a tendency to attribute such differences to enduring characteristics of the groups (i.e., to "blame the victim"), which encourages social policies likely to perpetuate the systemic inequities that may largely account for the differences. There is nothing inherent in questionnaires or tests—even when they are used to compare demographic groups—that produces such interpretations and policies. However, they readily lend themselves to dispositional attributions because they focus on characteristics of individuals and because they produce quantitative data on objective instruments that are presumed to have the same meaning for the different groups compared. Since the products of this particular line of research play a significant role in the policy process, the research itself becomes a relevant focus for policy debate. A more general impact on wider social values of the proliferation of questionnaires and tests, probing into a variety of personal matters, is that it reduces the amount of private space available in the society. The policy implications of this issue need to be explored in the context of debates about the entire range of social processes and institutions (including, for example, the mass media) that contribute to the reduction of private space in modern society.

Surveys and Interview Studies

Many of the issues raised by survey research and the use of personal interviews are identical to those raised by questionnaires and tests, but some special considerations are introduced by the collection of data through face-to-face interactions, and by some of the social uses to which surveys are put. At the level of participant interests, the risk of injury resulting from the interview process is as low as it is in questionnaire studies, and the possibility that the findings of the research may be injurious to group interests is as real as it is in questionnaire studies. Again, the major concern is public exposure of an individual's responses, and the primary focus for government regulation is therefore to ensure confidentiality of the data and communication to participants of any constraints on the investigator's ability to maintain confidentiality. The capacity of respondents to protect their own interests when deciding on participation is impaired if the interviewer misrepresents the organization that is conducting the survey or the overall purpose of the survey. Such misrepresentations, however, are completely contrary to the norms of survey methodology and are frowned upon by reputable survey organizations. Respondents may be subject to some pressures deriving from the dynamics of a face-to-face request; to turn down such requests is considered discourteous and places the individual in a bad light. Yet, there is evidence that many people do feel free to refuse an interview. This feeling is reinforced by one of the important features of survey research: Interviews are typically carried out in the setting of the respondent's home—or, increasingly now, over the telephone.

At the level of interpersonal relationships, the interview situation may create some stress and discomfort, although a skilled interviewer can keep these to a minimum. Still, respondents may feel inadequate because they lack information on the topic on which they are being questioned or because they have no opinions on matters on which they feel they are expected to have opinions; they may feel embarrassed and uncomfortable about the opinions they do have, expecting the interviewer to disapprove of them; they may feel constrained by the form of the interview and frustrated because they are not given the opportunity to discuss the topic on their own terms; or they may feel anxious because of uncertainties about the organization that is asking all these questions and its purposes. Respondents' control over their self-presentation is reduced by the fact that the interviewer may not always give them complete information about the study and may ask questions that are indirect or not obviously related to the topic of the interview. Such procedures, however, are generally within the terms of the contract formed when the respondent agrees to be interviewed, assuming there was no misrepresentation. Respondents' control over their self-presentation is further reduced by the interpersonal aspects of the interview situation. Respondents may prefer not to answer certain questions because they are embarrassed about their opinions or their lack of opinions, but they may feel under pressure to respond. Failure to do so would itself be embarrassing because it would both violate the implicit contract they agreed to and reveal something about their areas of sensitivity or ignorance. Such subtle pressures, which are normal features of social interaction, do not represent serious ethical problems as long as the interviewer does not use coercive or manipulative tactics. Nevertheless, I list reduced control over self-presentation as the major issue here, to which professional standards need to be addressed, because it bears directly on the sensitivity with which the interrogation itself—the central tool of the survey method—is carried out. Blatant deprivations of respect for the respondent, in the form of deception and coercion, are rare in survey research, in part because the typical setting in which interviews are carried out is the respondents' home territory.

At the level of wider social values, the proliferation of surveys—along with questionnaire studies—contributes to the reduction of private space. What I see as the major issue at this level, however, to which public debate needs to address itself, relates to some of the special uses to which survey methods are being put in our society. It must be stressed that these uses are not inherent in survey methodology and characterize only a small proportion of the research based on sample surveys or other interview procedures. I have in mind surveys whose primary purpose (or at least practical purpose) is to find out how best to sell to the public a product, a political candidate, a program, or a policy. I do not refer to the use of surveys in the development of a program or policy (or even a commercial product), where there is a genuine interest in exploring public needs and concerns to ensure that these are being seriously considered and adequately met. Rather, I refer to surveys designed to help in the packaging of the product (commercial or political) and in projecting the desired image. Such surveys often try to discover people's vulnerabilities, prejudices, and secret dreams, so that these can be exploited in selling the product. Ethical concerns are likely to differ, as a function of the nature of the product that is being sold and the interests that are being served. For example, we may not be too concerned about public-health research seeking the best ways to "sell" the public on the importance of regular blood pressure tests or the dangers of smoking. But, at least in the political arena and in market research, there is concern that survey methods may be used to manipulate the public in the interest of political power and corporate profit. In the political sphere, as I mentioned above, such uses of surveys and electoral polls may contribute to the perversion of the political process, shifting the focus from debating the issues to selling the candidate. Not only may surveys provide information on how best to accomplish that, but the results of polls taken in the course of a political campaign may themselves shape the preferences of voters and the activities of candidates. I do not wish to suggest that the use of surveys in politics and marketing is always destructive of wider social values, but it does raise the issue of possible perversion of the political and economic process and, more generally, of contributing to the level of manipulation in the society.

Records and Secondary Analysis

At the level of participant interests, the major issue that arises in the analysis of records and documents, or in the secondary analysis of data from earlier surveys or questionnaire studies, is the risk of public exposure. The primary purpose of government regulation, therefore, is to ensure that the confidentiality of the data is maintained, preferably by removing all identifying information. Another issue that needs to be considered is whether respondents' consent is required to the new use of the data they originally supplied. Assuming they did not know that their data would be used in subsequent studies, their capacity to protect their interests was clearly impaired when they originally consented to providing the information. The question is whether their tacit consent to the subsequent analyses can be taken for granted. It can be argued that individuals are generally aware (or should be aware) of the possibility that personal information they provide to hospitals, schools, or agencies may be used for subsequent statistical analyses, since such analyses are routinely performed and often reported in the press. An even stronger case for tacit consent can be made with respect to secondary analysis, on the presumption that people agreeing to participate in a study have no particular expectations about who will perform what analyses to test which hypotheses. Serious ethical problems arise only when respondents agree to provide information for one specific purpose and the data are then used for a clearly different purpose.

The failure to obtain consent for a clearly different use of the data than the one originally agreed upon would also represent an ethical problem at the level of interpersonal relationships. Investigators working with data collected by others do not have a direct relationship with the respondents, but in accepting their data they incur an obligation to honor the original contract. Failure to do so deprives the respondents of the respect to which they are entitled.[60]

At the level of wider social values, the major issue raised by research based on records and secondary analysis is the reduction of private space. The practice of opening people's records to research and widening the circle of those to whom personal information about them is made available may weaken the boundaries that the society sustains between private and public domains. It may help to create the feeling that personal data revealed in a restricted context will sooner or later become public property. On the other hand, it can be argued that the sharing and recycling of data help to preserve privacy by reducing the number of intrusions by researchers into people's lives. Although this type of research probably does not represent a serious invasion of privacy (as long as the confidentiality of the personal data is scrupulously protected), it ought to be considered in the context of policy debates on the entire range of threats to privacy within the society.

Structured Observation

At the level of participant interests, the risk that people taking part in a structured-observation study might be injured in any way is quite low. It is conceivable that in certain of the interaction situations that are especially arranged for the purpose of systematic observation, psychologically vulnerable people might experience a high level of anxiety. This could happen, for example, if participants in a self-analytic group are induced to go too far in self-revelation or find themselves scapegoated by fellow participants; or if participants in a stress interview are subjected to relentless pressure or hostile attack. Although it is unlikely that such experiences will result in enduring psychological injuries, it is important for investigators to monitor participant reactions carefully when the interaction situations they observe have the potential for producing anxiety. The risk of public exposure is not much of an issue in this type of research, since the observations typically focus on behavior in the situation, producing data about the participants that are of little interest to outside parties.

Impaired capacity for decision making, on the other hand, may well arise as an issue, particularly when the observations focus on interactions in structured real-life settings such as classrooms, therapy or encounter groups, and conferences. In such situations, the investigator—though making no secret of the fact that observations (or recordings) are being made—may be casual about obtaining participants' consent or may subtly discourage participants from raising objections. The problem becomes more serious if the investigator (in laboratory or nonlaboratory studies) deliberately keeps the participants uninformed of the presence of observers; or if the observers or listeners are hidden, perhaps using mechanical devices (such as one-way mirrors or hidden recorders) to extend their vision or hearing without the participants' knowledge; or if other deceptions are introduced, such as the use of a preinstructed "stooge." Although such deliberate deceptions appear to be quite rare in structured-observation studies, they represent the main potential threat to the interests of the participants and hence the primary focus for government regulation.

At the level of interpersonal relationships, I have already raised the possibility that some of the interaction situations arranged for laboratory observation may be stressful. In nonlaboratory situations, particularly situations in which people express intense personal feelings and reveal their conflicts and vulnerabilities—as in therapy or encounter groups—participants may experience the mere presence of uninvolved observers as stressful and degrading and may consider it an invasion of their privacy. Their control over their self-presentation is reduced by the sometimes contradictory requirements of impressing the observers and impressing fellow participants. Hidden observation and other deceptions, of course, reduce their control over self-presentation in different ways and also raise the issue of deprivation of respect.

At the level of wider social values, the major issue arising in this type of research is that the proliferation of observation studies in a variety of real-life settings may contribute to the reduction of private space within the society.

Unobtrusive Observation

The issues raised by unobtrusive observation depend very much on the particular context in which the observations are made. Serious ethical problems arise when people are secretly observed in a situation that they had a right to consider private, particularly if hidden mechanical devices are employed.[61] Another set of problems arises in the typical field experiment, in which the investigator makes unobtrusive observations after introducing certain experimental manipulations into the natural setting. For the present purposes, however, I refer only to unobtrusive observation focusing on ongoing behavior in a *public* situation, not manipulated for experimental purposes. In this context, unobtrusive observation does not present any risks of injury to the unwitting participant. There is also no risk of public exposure of individuals, since the participants are not identified, although there is the possibility of public exposure that might prove embarrassing to the group being observed. The only serious issue, at the level of participant interests, is the impairment of participants' capacity for decision making. By definition, there is no informed consent in this type of research, since participants are not aware that they are systematically being observed. On the other hand, as long as the investigators do not hide, or misrepresent themselves, or intervene in the situation, their observations consist essentially of public behavior, accessible to anyone who happens to be present. It can be assumed, in such a situation, that people know their behavior is potentially observable by others (even if they do not know that these others include social scientists) and that they already do what is necessary to protect their interests in view of this possibility.

At the level of interpersonal relationships, the fact that participants are not aware that they are systematically being observed raises the issue of invasion of privacy, in the sense of reduced control over self-presentation. If they knew they were being observed, they might wish to act differently. It can be argued, however, that whenever people act in a public situation, they are in effect waiving their right to privacy, since they must (and do) accept the possibility that they will be observed by others. The right to privacy is never completely relinquished: Social norms (such as those against eavesdropping and staring) set limits to the kinds of observations that are permissible even in public situations. However, when social scientists make systematic observations of public behavior that would be accessible, within the limits set by social norms, to anyone else who took the trouble to look, they are not being unduly invasive of people's privacy.

At the level of wider social values, the major issue again is that the proliferation of studies in this genre may contribute to the reduction of private space. Even though we are dealing with public behavior, there is a difference between knowing that random passers-by may be able to observe what we are doing and feeling that, at any time, a professional social scientist may be out there, systematically focusing on particular categories of our behavior, counting their frequency and rating their intensity. Such observations of naturally occurring behavior by social scientists are not unlike those made by journalists, novelists, travel writers, and moralists. They are equally legitimate, but also at least equally likely to impinge on the sense of privacy in a society.

Participant Observation

At the level of participant interests, the risk of injury of any kind resulting from the interaction between participant observers and the people they observe (as distinct from injury resulting from publication of the data) is minimal, and indeed there is no evidence that such studies have caused long-term damage.[62] The major risks of injury stem from the possibility of public exposure. The participant observer is often privy to personal information about individuals and to sensitive information about groups, organizations, and communities, disclosure of which might cause them embarrassment and damage their material interests in a variety of ways—e.g., by subjecting them to legal action or to withdrawal of financial support. Thus, the primary concern for government regulation of this type of research is to ensure that investigators maintain confidentiality or provide clear information about any external limits on their ability to protect the confidentiality of the data and about their own plans for publication.

The problem of public exposure in field studies is illustrated by the controversial Springdale study,[63] in which community members and other critics felt that the investigators broke their promise of anonymity. Although the publication used pseudonyms, the town and many of its inhabitants were readily identified, which caused them considerable embarrassment and hurt. Publication of reports of anthropological field studies, of community studies (particularly if they involve minority communities), and of studies of deviant groups and their organizations may damage the group interests of the populations observed, by creating or reinforcing stereotypes and adversely affecting public opinion and public policy.[64] Of course, such reports may also benefit the groups involved, by correcting commonly held stereotypes, by providing a sounder understanding of their realities and their problems, and by thus creating a more favorable climate for public opinion and public policy.

The risks of public exposure are intensified when the observation is disguised, the investigator having gained access to the people observed through misrepresentation. The research in this genre that has aroused the greatest amount of debate and controversy is the study by Humphreys, who was able to observe male homosexual activities in public restrooms by posing as a "watchqueen," or lookout.[65] He also recorded the automobile license numbers of a sample of the men he observed, traced the men through police license registers by posing as a market researcher, and interviewed them in their homes a year later by adding them to the sample of a health survey. Other examples of disguised observation come from the various studies in which investigators join an organization under false pretenses in order to gain access to activities from which nonmembers would normally be excluded.[66] These misrepresentations clearly impair people's capacity to decide what to reveal or not to reveal to an outsider and hence to protect themselves against the possible consequences of wider exposure. The ethical problems here parallel those raised by deception in experiments, but they are even more serious because the risk of injury (in the event of public exposure) is generally greater.[67] In many of these studies, for example, the disguised observer gains access to information that the group members deliberately want to keep secret—because their behavior is illegal, socially disapproved of, or part of an organizational strategy. Disguised observation can be justified more readily if the behavior observed is in principle subject to public scrutiny. For example, in defense of Rosenhan's[68] and other pseudopatient studies, it can be argued that the hospital staff's treatment of their patients is not protected by the right to privacy: Staff members have in effect waived that right in adopting their professional and institutional roles. Alternatively, insofar as such studies are undertaken to increase the accountability of public institutions, it can be argued that the staff's right to privacy is outweighed by the clients' rights to protection against abuse or neglect. Still, the observers' covert entry into the situation remains ethically troublesome.

Disguised observation also raises the issue, at the level of interpersonal relationships, of reduced control over self-presentation. Even when they are not particularly concerned about potential damages to their concrete interests, people tend to relate differently to fellow members of their own groups than they do to outsiders. By pretending to be group members, the observers induce them to say or do things in their presence that they may wish to reserve for fellow members. Control over self-presentation is also reduced if the observers are themselves genuine group members, but do not acknowledge the fact that they are making systematic observations. The ethical problem in this case is much less severe, as long as the observations focus only on activities in which the observers participate as part of their normal membership roles. Group members must always reckon with the possibility that someone in their midst might write about their experiences—in a novel or a memoir, if not in a social science monograph. The way in which member-observers subsequently use their observations has more critical implications for privacy than the fact that they make unacknowledged observations. Even when participant observers acknowledge their research interest and are accepted on that basis, some reduction in group members' control over their self-presentation may ensue because of the ambiguities inherent in the participant observer role. Group members may come to accept the observers as part of the scenery and act unself-consciously in their presence, revealing information they might prefer to keep private. However, such an eventuality raises ethical problems only if observers deliberately take advantage of the ambiguity of the role—e.g., by implying a greater level of commitment to the group than they actually feel— and thereby seduce group members to confide in them more than they otherwise would.[69]

Disguised observation clearly constitutes a deprivation of respect, which I see as the major ethical issue raised by participant observation research at the level of interpersonal relationships. In some ways, deception in participant observation is more profoundly disrespectful of others than it is in laboratory experiments, since it is not confined to a special experimental situation, which can be isolated from the rest of life, but enters into real-life and sometimes continuing relationships. It should be noted, however, that disguised observation is only one of several models of participant observation (or fieldwork), and the one that raises uniquely knotty ethical problems.[70] The other models, of course, are not entirely free of their own ethical complexities. In one of the models distinguished by Joan Cassell, the *verandah* model, disrespect for the people studied manifests itself in the coercive, exploitative, patronizing, and nonreciprocal relationship that the investigator tends to establish with them.[71] On the whole, however, participant observation research—particularly as it has evolved in anthropological fieldwork—has been more respectful of the people from whom it obtains its data than many other research traditions. It has been characterized by a greater degree of reciprocity between investigator and participant, equality of power, and two-way interaction, thus approximating a model of participatory research.[72]

At the level of wider social values, participant observation research may contribute to prevailing inequities within the national and the global society, insofar as it reinforces stereotypes about minority and deviant communities or

Third World societies and encourages policies focusing on group "deficiencies" rather than on inequalities rooted in social structure. The proliferation of participant observers in a variety of groups and organizations may contribute to the reduction of private space in the society. However, the most important threat of diffuse harm to social values comes, again, from disguised observation. The knowledge that hidden observers may insinuate themselves into various private relationships and group activities, often on a continuing basis, is bound to contribute to the erosion of trust. Although their purpose is social research, the cumulative effect of such practices must be examined in the context of the widespread use of spies and undercover agents (and perhaps the even more widespread suspicion of their use) for many other legitimate and illegitimate purposes.

Implications

The analysis presented in this chapter has relied heavily upon a harm-benefit framework. I consider the harm-benefit approach, if broadly conceived, as a useful and probably necessary tool for making ethical decisions in social research. Our primary concern is with protecting and enhancing the well-being of research participants and of others who are, or may in the future be, affected by the research. We therefore have an obligation to minimize the risk of harm caused by the research and to forgo research that carries unacceptable risks. Not even minimal risks can be justified unless the probable benefits outweigh them. (The converse does not hold true: Certain risks cannot be justified no matter how large the probable benefits.)[73] Harm-benefit considerations are also central to our notions about the rights of research participants. Such rights as the right to informed consent or the right to privacy are not mere abstractions, but conditions for maintaining people's well-being. That is, these rights are ultimately linked to our concern with meeting our basic needs and interests and protecting ourselves against harm.

Even though I regard harm and benefit considerations as basic to the analysis of ethical issues in research with human participants, the particular model of risk-benefit calculation as it has evolved in biomedical research is of only limited usefulness in social research. In biomedical research itself, the model applies most clearly to the decision whether a given experimental treatment procedure should be used on a particular patient. One can reasonably base such a decision on the ratio between the risks entailed by the procedure and its probable benefits, relative to the risk-benefit ratio for the standard treatment procedures that are available. These estimates may be difficult to make, but the logic of the approach is straightforward. As one moves from this situation to biomedical research in which the experimental procedure is not related to the subject's own treatment, the calculations become considerably more complicated, since they involve balancing risks to the subject against potential benefits to future patients and/or to science. Still, at least with respect to the risks, one is dealing with measurable physical injuries that can be entered into the calculation. Even within the biomedical sciences, however, there seem to be other lines of research in which risk-benefit calculations are not particularly relevant to the ethical issues raised.[74] Whether or not this is so, I would argue that, at least as far as social research is concerned, risk-benefit analyses are often not particularly relevant to the ethical decision about whether or not to proceed with a given piece of research. There are several reasons for this conclusion, which I hope have emerged from previous sections of this chapter.

1. By and large, the probability that participants in most social research will incur concrete injuries in the course of the research process is low, as is the magnitude of the injuries that might occur. I have pointed to the possibility that certain laboratory experiments and observations, as well as certain field experiments, might cause psychological injury, although there is no evidence that enduring damage has actually resulted from participation in such studies. Only in one type of research—social and organizational experiments—are participants, in principle, exposed to serious risks of injury, in the form of material losses, since the experimental manipulations may affect such significant life resources and opportunities as income, housing, health care, working conditions, educational programs, or conditions of parole. At the same time, the magnitude of potential concrete benefits accruing to participants is generally low—again, with the possible exception of participants in large-scale social experiments. The benefits to be derived from social research largely take the form of contributions to science and society; these contributions are not readily predictable or demonstrable—and, in any case, they do not directly advance the well-being of the participants themselves. Under these circumstances, the calculation of risk-benefit ratios in social science studies—with some notable exceptions—may largely be a hypothetical exercise that hampers research without really addressing the critical ethical issues.

2. The major threats to the concrete interests of participants in social research do not come from the research procedures themselves, but from the possibility of public exposure of information about identifiable individuals or groups. Public exposure may seriously affect people's reputations and may subject them to the possibility of harassment and punishment—even to the point of imprisonment or death, if, for example, the research is done in an area of intense domestic or international conflict. The real concern in this context, to which regulation must address itself, is to ensure that investigators maintain the confidentiality of the data or clearly inform participants of any limits to their ability to do so. The urgency of maintaining confidentiality varies, of course, as a function of the magnitude of the danger to which participants would be exposed if their responses were publicly identified. But, except in extreme cases, it is very difficult to predict what might happen as a consequence of exposure. The principles of confidentiality and privacy are

designed to protect participants against the possibility of harm caused by unforeseeable as well as foreseeable future circumstances. If they were made conditional on calculation of the magnitude of harm anticipated, they would lose much of their protective value. Thus, although the right to confidentiality and privacy is ultimately rooted in concerns about the possible harms to participants, it must be treated as functionally autonomous. That is, the right has moral force regardless of whether, in any given case, it can be *demonstrated* that its violation would cause harm. It is *presumed* that any violation of this right is damaging—if not in the short run, then in the long run; if not to the particular individual involved, then to the larger society (by weakening an important protective mechanism). In the ethical evaluation of procedures used to protect participants against unacceptable public exposure, therefore, the primary issue is the risk of violations of confidentiality (and the concomitant requirement that participants be fully informed of such risks) rather than the risk of harm *if* confidentiality were violated.

3. The requirement of informed consent, like that of confidentiality, is ultimately rooted in concerns about possible harms to participants' concrete interests. The requirement is designed to ensure that participants have the opportunity and the capacity to decide for themselves what is in their best interest and what risks they are prepared to take. The urgency of ensuring informed consent varies, of course, as a function of the magnitude of the potential harm entailed by a given piece of research. But, in the final analysis, the decision of how large an injury is too large and how much of a risk is too much must be left to the individual. If the availability of the informed consent procedures were made conditional on calculation of the magnitude of harm by others (IRBs, for example), it would lose much of its value as a protective device for participants themselves. The right to informed consent, therefore, must also be treated as functionally autonomous. Thus, in the ethical evaluation of informed consent procedures, impairment of participants' capacity for decision making is an issue that must be considered independently of the magnitude of demonstrable harm to which participation might expose them.

Appropriate procedures for informed consent are relatively straightforward when it is possible to spell out in advance the risks entailed by participation. In social research, it is often impossible to predict the consequences of the research (particularly the consequences of publication of the findings) or even to describe in advance what will happen in the course of the research. Furthermore, there are some types of social research that would not be feasible if standard procedures for obtaining informed consent were to be used. Examples are those studies in which participants are not even informed that they are being observed, or in which some information about the research is withheld or deceptions are introduced in the interest of obtaining valid data. The mere fact that such studies may entail only negligible risks of injury is not in itself sufficient reason to sidestep informed consent. On the other hand, there may be justifications for modifying or even omitting informed consent procedures in certain instances, particularly as one moves away from research that involves manipulations of the person or the environment. In any event, risk-benefit analysis is of only limited utility in devising procedures that would uphold participants' capacity to protect their own interests in social research.

4. In much of social research (and in a fair amount of biomedical research, as well), the findings may have harmful consequences for the groups that are studied. Since potential damage to group interests affects the individual participant only indirectly, it cannot readily be incorporated in the standard risk-benefit calculation, which focuses on the individual. Similarly, procedures for obtaining informed consent from individual participants will not in most cases provide proper protection against possible harms to group interests; concerns in this domain have to be addressed through other means, such as consultation with group representatives. On the whole, group interests are probably not as well protected as individual interests by the regulatory process, as embodied in IRBs, because their definition is often a matter of controversy both within and between different groups in the society. The protection of group interests, therefore, requires particular attention at the professional and public policy levels.

5. The harm that participants may experience in the course of their involvement in social research may often take the form of stress and indignity. These are temporary situational effects, which debase the quality of the relationship between investigator and participant, but do not cause long-term measurable damage to the participant's interests. Exposing people to stress and indignity is certainly a harm, since respectful treatment by others is a condition for personal well-being. Furthermore, the difference between temporary effects and enduring injuries is often merely a quantitative one. For example, a single instance in which a person is made to feel inadequate or degraded may be a source of temporary discomfort; but the cumulative effect of repeated experiences of this kind may well be a chronic lowering of the person's self-esteem, constituting psychological injury.[75] Nevertheless, it is difficult to enter temporary discomforts into risk-benefit calculations in the absence of measurable injuries that can directly be attributed to these experiences. By the same token, these are not the types of harm for which government regulation, with its coercive backing, is an appropriate form of social control. Instead, I have argued, they should be controlled through the development and refinement of professional standards. At that level, we are less bound to the negative emphasis of the risk-benefit model, which links regulation to evidence that certain procedures are potentially harmful; we can instead focus on the positive task of defining the contours of a good investigator-participant relationship as a matter of continuing professional attention.[76]

6. Another type of harm that may be caused by social research—and by many lines of biomedical research, as well—takes the form of diffuse harms to

the body politic. Such harms may result not only from the procedures of the research, but also from its findings. They can generally not be traced to a particular study, but represent the cumulative impact of a continuing line of research. They do not involve direct effects on the individual participants in the research, but effects on the larger society and on wider social values. They are typically subject to disagreements within the society, both about the occurrence or nonoccurrence of a particular impact and about its harmful or beneficial implications. For all of these reasons, diffuse harms cannot readily be entered into the standard risk-benefit calculations that are undertaken as part of the regulation of individual research projects. The issues raised by the possible impact of social research on wider social values clearly require a balancing of potential harms against potential benefits, but within the context of public policy debate rather than within a regulatory framework.

In pointing out the limitations of the standard risk-benefit requirement, I am not suggesting that government regulation of social research is unnecessary. I have already stressed the appropriateness and clear necessity of such regulation when the protection of the participants' concrete interests is at stake. I am suggesting, however, that the scope, the focus, and the specific form of government regulation have to be adapted in view of the special characteristics of different types of social research and the nature of the ethical issues raised by each. Furthermore, I am suggesting that government regulation is only one form of social control, which cannot substitute for the development and refinement of professional standards and broader social policies designed to enhance the well-being of research participants and the integrity of social values.

My review of ethical issues confronting different research methods indicates that the risk of injury resulting directly from research participation is not a major concern for the vast bulk of social science studies. Only in social and organizational experiments are the material injuries to which participants are potentially subject of sufficient magnitude to become a central consideration in regulation and prior review. Though of lesser magnitude, the risks of psychological injury resulting from laboratory experiments and simulations and from structured observations in laboratory settings, and the risk of psychological or material injury resulting from field experiments, also must be considered; generally the risks involved in these studies are of such a nature that informed consent would be sufficient to provide the needed protection.

The two major issues in social research that have direct implications for participant interests and to which regulation must address itself are public exposure and impaired capacity for decision making. The risks entailed by public exposure and hence the need to regulate the confidentiality of the data are a central concern in research based on questionnaires and tests, in surveys and interview studies, in studies based on records and secondary analysis, and in participant observation studies, as well as in social and organizational experiments. Impairment of participants' capacity for decision making is a central issue in laboratory experiments employing deception, in intrusive field experiments, in structured observation using hidden observers, and in disguised participant observation. The problem may also arise in social or organizational experiments and in questionnaire and test studies, if people are led to believe (by virtue of the setting or the auspices) that their participation is required; and in studies based on records and secondary analysis, if the data are used for purposes that clearly diverge from those for which consent was originally granted. Studies using unobtrusive observation of public events, by their very nature, do not offer participants the opportunity for informed consent, but I take the view that in such public situations people give tacit consent to observation of their behavior.[77]

The review of ethical issues confronting different research methods also highlights practices that bear on the quality of the investigator-participant relationship, even though they may not cause demonstrable long-term injuries. Participants may be subjected to stressful or degrading experiences in laboratory experiments and simulations, particularly where deception is also involved; in intrusive field experiments; and, less frequently, in structured-observation studies. They may also experience a certain degree of discomfort—arising from the nature of the questions or from their own sense of inadequacy—when responding to questionnaires, tests, or personal interviews. Invasion of privacy, in the sense of reduced control over self-presentation, is potentially a central issue in field experiments; in structured observation studies, particularly when they use hidden observers; in participant observation studies, particularly when the observer is disguised; and in studies based on unobtrusive observation, particularly when they violate social norms against eavesdropping and staring. Respondents' control over their self-presentation is also reduced by the use of indirect or projective items in questionnaires or tests and by the dynamics of the interaction process in many interview situations.

Similarly, there are a variety of ways in which participants' choices may be restricted, depriving them of respect for their personal autonomy. This may happen in laboratory and field experiments, whenever participants are deceived and manipulated; in organizational and social experiments, whenever participants or their representatives are excluded from the process of selecting the options to be investigated; in questionnaire or test studies, whenever investigators take advantage of the setting to induce participation without giving people much choice or explanation; in studies based on records or secondary analysis, whenever investigators violate the contract under which the data were originally collected; and in participant observation studies, whenever investigators misrepresent themselves or treat informants in a patronizing, exploitative way.

This review brings to the fore a number of issues to which the social science professions must address themselves, as we continue to develop and refine professional standards governing the investigator-participant relationship.

What are the limits of stress and deception that an investigator can impose on research participants? What are the limits of permissible intrusion and interference in real-life settings? How do investigators avoid taking advantage of positions of power within the society, within a particular institutional setting, and within the research interaction itself, to manipulate research participants? What special obligation do investigators have to protect the rights and interests of disadvantaged and powerless populations on whom they carry out research? What obligations do investigators have in debriefing research participants, in feeding back to them the findings of the research, in reciprocating the help that they have received? What obligations do they have to people whose data they use when these data were collected by others? To what extent are they responsible for the ways in which others interpret and use their own findings? What alternative approaches can be developed to replace procedures that are deceptive, coercive, or intrusive, or violate in other ways the standards for good interpersonal relationships? How can social science further develop research models and practices that are based on the principles of participation and reciprocity and that enhance the autonomy of the research participant? Concern with these issues at the level of professional practice makes it possible, as I suggested above, to move from an emphasis on avoiding harm through professional misconduct to an emphasis on the positive task of developing a reciprocally enriching relationship between the investigator and the participant.

Finally, the review of different types of research helps us focus on the impact of social science on wider social values. There are various ways in which social research may cause diffuse harm by contributing to the weakening of certain values on which the integrity of social institutions and social relations is based. The level of privacy in the society may be reduced by the proliferation of questionnaires, tests, and interviews, particularly when these probe into areas that most people consider parts of their private space; by the use of personal records for research purposes; and by observation studies in real-life settings, especially when they interfere with ongoing activities or intrude on relationships from which outsiders are generally excluded. The erosion of trust may be furthered in a number of ways: trust in authorities and institutions by the proliferation of deceptive laboratory experiments; trust in ordinary day-to-day relationships by intrusive field experiments; and trust in one's associates in various groups and organizations by research using disguised participant observers. The value of equity may be compromised by social experiments that provide unequal treatment to different groups; by questionnaire and test studies focusing on group differences; and by participant observation studies featuring the characteristics of minority or Third World communities. Some of the uses of survey methodology—particularly in electoral polling and market research—may contribute to the perversion of political and economic processes and, more broadly, to manipulation of the public. In fact, the potential that their methods and findings may be used for manipulative purposes runs through many areas of social research that contribute directly or indirectly to creating knowledge about the control of human behavior.[78]

Social control with respect to these potentially harmful effects of social research on wider social values must be exercised, I have argued, through the public policy process, in which such effects have to be balanced against the potential social benefits of social research and of particular investigations. In the debate of these issues, the potential diffuse harms of social research have to be seen in the context of other societal processes that contribute to the erosion of trust, the invasion of privacy, the spread of manipulation, and the perpetuation of inequity. As a committed social scientist, I hope—and continue to believe—that social research will contribute more to the solution of these problems than to their aggravation.

Notes

This chapter was completed while I was a Fellow at the Woodrow Wilson International Center for Scholars and I gratefully acknowledge the Center's support. I also wish to express my appreciation to Tom Beauchamp, Ruth Faden, and Jay Wallace for their exceptionally careful and creative editing of the chapter and their thoughtful and stimulating questions and suggestions. Their comments and my discussions with them both forced and helped me to clarify my thinking on a number of central issues.

1. For a review of these issues, see Herbert C. Kelman, "Research, Behavioral," in Warren T. Reich, ed., *Encyclopedia of Bioethics* (New York: Macmillan and Free Press, 1978), vol. 3.

2. The intention here is not to contrast a utilitarian framework with a deontological one as bases for justifying moral decisions. I refer to risk-benefit analysis and to a rights-based analysis not as different ways of *grounding* moral decisions, but as different *procedures* for arriving at such decisions. Either one of these procedures may be used, in my view, whether one subscribes to a utilitarian or to a deontological theory. Moreover, these two procedures are not mutually exclusive and may well be used in complementary fashion.

3. The argument in the following section is not essential to an understanding of the rest of the chapter. Readers who are not particularly interested in the nature of moral justification as such may, therefore, prefer to skip this section.

4. I speak here of "having" dignity in a descriptive, behavioral sense. I also believe that humans have dignity in the ontological sense, but—though this may be the ultimate justification for the moral principles I favor—my present concern is with the conditions for dignity as behaviorally manifested.

5. Herbert C. Kelman, "The Conditions, Criteria, and Dialectics of Human Dignity: A Transnational Perspective," *International Studies Quarterly* 21 (1977): 531.

6. Ibid., pp. 531-33.

7. A person's sense of identity and sense of community are closely related to, but not synonymous with, objective identity and community. They can be viewed as both determinants and consequences of the objective states.

8. In terms of the three principles described in the preceding chapter, identity corresponds to the principle of autonomy and community corresponds to the principles of beneficence and nonmaleficence, and the just distribution of harms and benefits.

9. Kelman, "Research, Behavioral," pp. 1472-74, 1476-78.

10. An exhaustive categorization of potential harms resulting from social research can be found in Donald P. Warwick's chapter in the present volume.

11. See Kelman, "Research, Behavioral," as well as Herbert C. Kelman, "The Rights of the Subject in Social Research: An Analysis in Terms of Relative Power and Legitimacy," *American Psychologist* 27 (1972): 989-1016, for an elaboration of the distinction between ethical problems relating to the processes of social research and those relating to the products of social research.

12. Kelman, "Research, Behavioral," p. 1474.

13. Oscar M. Ruebhausen and Orville G. Brim, Jr., "Privacy and Behavioral Research," *Columbia Law Review* 65 (1965): 1189.

14. Herbert C. Kelman, "Privacy and Research with Human Beings," *Journal of Social Issues* 33, no. 3 (1977): 169.

15. Alasdair MacIntyre, "Risk, Harm, and Benefit Assessments as Instruments of Moral Evaluation," in the present volume. See also Donald Warwick's chapter in this volume.

16. Herbert C. Kelman, "Compliance, Identification, and Internalization: Three Processes of Attitude Change," *Journal of Conflict Resolution* 2 (1958): 51-60; idem, "Processes of Opinion Change," *Public Opinion Quarterly* 25 (1961): 57-78; idem, "Patterns of Personal Involvement in the National System: A Social-Psychological Analysis of Political Legitimacy," in James N. Rosenau, ed., *International Politics and Foreign Policy,* 2nd ed. (New York: Free Press, 1969), pp. 276-88; and Herbert C. Kelman, "Social Influence and Linkages between the Individual and the Social System," in James Tedeschi, ed., *Perspectives on Social Power* (Chicago: Aldine, 1974), pp. 125-71.

17. Chris Argyris, "Dangers in Applying Results from Experimental Social Psychology," *American Psychologist* 30 (1975): 469-85.

18. See the discussion of harms to society in Donald Warwick's chapter in this volume.

19. The entire tradition of research rooted in the ideology of "blaming the victim" is subject to this criticism. See William Ryan, *Blaming the Victim* (New York: Pantheon, 1971).

20. For a discussion of some of the issues see Charles W. Roll, Jr., and Albert H. Cantril, *Polls: Their Use and Misuse in Politics* (New York: Basic Books, 1972).

21. I use the term *injury* to refer to a subcategory of harms, namely, harms that are of a relatively enduring nature (as distinguished from momentary stress or discomfort), that affect the individual in a direct and personal way (as distinguished from diffuse harm), and that constitute measurable, demonstrable losses to the individual. The enduring, personal, and measurable character of injuries is what qualifies them as damages to the *concrete* interests of research participants, as specified in the first column of table 2.1. The term *concrete* is meant to distinguish such interests from those that are more ephemeral (e.g., a person's interest in making a good impression) or more remote (e.g., a citizen's interest in a sound foreign policy). The cumulative effects of experiences and policies bearing on these less concrete interests may be quite damaging to the individual, but they do not constitute demonstrable losses that can be attributed to a specific action.

22. These examples are mainly designed to illustrate what is meant by physical injury in social research. There is no implication that these kinds of injury—or some of the other harms discussed in this section—are frequent outcomes of social research or even that they have occurred at all.

23. Several specific examples of research with the potential of lasting psychological harm are described in chapter 8, "The Human Use of Human Subjects," of Herbert C. Kelman, *A Time to Speak: On Human Values and Social Research* (San Francisco: Jossey-Bass, 1968), pp. 212-15.

24. Hence I distinguish such harms from injuries, which refer to more enduring and demonstrable losses. See note 21.

25. See Irving M. Piliavin, Judith Rodin, and Jane A. Piliavin, "Good Samaritanism: An Underground Phenomenon?" *Journal of Personality and Social Psychology* 13 (1969): 289-99, for an example of research of this genre.

26. See Kelman, "Privacy and Research with Human Beings," for a fuller treatment of these three types of concerns.

27. David L. Rosenhan, "On Being Sane in Insane Places," *Science* 179 (1973): 250-58.

28. See June L. Tapp, Herbert C. Kelman, Harry C. Triandis, Lawrence S. Wrightsman, and George V. Coelho, "Continuing Concerns in Cross-Cultural Ethics: A Report," *International Journal of Psychology* 9 (1974): 231-49, for a proposal of safeguards, as they might apply to cross-cultural research.

29. Erving Goffman, starting with his first book, *The Presentation of Self in Everyday Life* (New York: Doubleday-Anchor, 1959), has given particular emphasis to this feature of social relations.

30. I am here subscribing to the view that the right to privacy—at least in the sense of control over one's self-presentation—is derivative: Actions that limit people's control over their self-presentation violate their right to privacy only when they violate some other right in the process. For an exposition of this view of privacy, see Judith J. Thomson, "The Right to Privacy," *Philosophy and Public Affairs* 4 (1975): 295-314.

31. Erving Goffman, "On the Characteristics of Total Institutions," in *Asylums: Essays on the Social Situation of Mental Patients and Other Inmates* (Chicago: Aldine, 1962).

32. Laud Humphreys, *Tearoom Trade: Impersonal Sex in Public Places,* enl. ed. (Chicago: Aldine, 1975).

33. R. Dennis Middlemist, Eric S. Knowles, and Charles F. Matter, "Personal Space Invasions in the Lavatory: Suggestive Evidence of Arousal," *Journal of Personality and Social Psychology* 33 (1976): 541-46.

34. Donald P. Warwick, "Tearoom Trade: Means and Ends in Social Research," *Hastings Center Studies* 1, no. 1 (1973): 24-38 (reprinted in Humphreys, *Tearoom Trade*); Gerald P. Koocher, "Bathroom Behavior and Human Dignity," *Journal of Personality and Social Psychology* 35 (1977): 120-21.

35. See Kelman, "Rights of the Subject in Social Research," for a discussion of the disproportionate use of disadvantaged populations in social research and its implications for informed consent.

36. Ad Hoc Committee on Ethical Standards in Psychological Research, *Ethical Principles in the Conduct of Research with Human Participants* (Washington, D.C.: American Psychological Association, 1973).

37. Ibid., pp.1-2.

38. This is one of E. L. Pattullo's proposals at the end of his chapter in the present volume.

39. Interestingly, the government's increasing involvement in research ethics and the development of government regulation have helped not only to draw professional attention to these issues, but also to legitimize such attention.

40. E. L. Pattullo, "Who Risks What in Social Research," *IRB: A Review of Human Subjects Research* 2 (March 1980): 1-3, 12. Pattullo's chapter in this volume considerably expands the arguments of this earlier paper.

41. See Peter H. Rossi, Margaret Boeckmann, and Richard A. Berk, "Some Ethical Implications of the New Jersey-Pennsylvania Income Maintenance Experiment," in Gordon Bermant, Herbert C. Kelman, and Donald P. Warwick, eds., *The Ethics of Social Intervention* (Washington, D.C.: Hemisphere Publishing Corp., 1978), pp. 245-66. For a general review of issues in social experimentation, see Alice M. Rivlin and P. Michael Timpane, eds., *Ethical and Legal Issues of Social Experimentation* (Washington, D.C.: Brookings Institution, 1975).

42. Philip G. Zimbardo, Craig Haney, W. Curtis Banks, and David Jaffe, "The Psychology of Imprisonment: Privation, Power, and Pathology," in Zick Rubin, ed., *Doing unto Others* (Englewood Cliffs, N.J.: Prentice-Hall, 1974), pp. 61–73. It is worth noting, incidentally, that this study did not involve deliberate deception.

43. Dana Bramel, "A Dissonance Theory Approach to Defensive Projection," *Journal of Abnormal and Social Psychology* 64 (1962): 121-29; idem, "Selection of a Target for Defensive Projection," *Journal of Abnormal and Social Psychology* 66 (1963): 318-24; Allen E. Bergin, "The Effect of Dissonant Persuasive Communications upon Changes in a Self-Referring Attitude," *Journal of Personality* 30 (1962): 423-38.

44. Stanley Milgram, *Obedience to Authority* (New York: Harper & Row, 1974).

45. The obedience experiments by Milgram, ibid., and the prison simulation study by Zimbardo et al., "Psychology of Imprisonment," can serve as illustrations here.

46. It has been suggested, however, that, from a legal point of view, the inconvenience and annoyance caused by such staged events may serve as the basis for legal action against the investigator. See Irwin Silverman, "Nonreactive Methods and the Law," *American Psychologist* 30 (1975): 764-69.

47. Robert Rosenthal and Lenore Jacobson, *Pygmalion in the Classroom: Teacher Expectation and Pupils' Intellectual Development* (New York: Holt, 1968).

48. See Donald T. Campbell, "Prospective: Artifact and Control," in Robert Rosenthal and Ralph L. Rosnow, eds., *Artifact in Behavioral Research* (New York: Academic Press, 1969), p. 371.

49. See Peter G. Brown, "Informed Consent in Social Experimentation: Some Cautionary Notes," in Rivlin and Timpane, *Ethical and Legal Issues,* pp. 94-95.

50. Ibid., pp. 87-89.

51. For additional examples of risks of termination, see ibid., pp. 89-90; and David N. Kershaw, "Comments," in Rivlin and Timpane, *Ethical and Legal Issues,* pp. 61-62.

52. Rossi, Boeckmann, and Berk, "Some Ethical Implications."

53. Donald P. Warwick, "Ethical Guidelines for Social Experiments," in Bermant, Kelman, and Warwick, *Ethics of Social Intervention,* pp. 285-86.

54. Brown, "Informed Consent," pp. 86-90.

55. Alice M. Rivlin and P. Michael Timpane, "Introduction and Summary," in Rivlin and Timpane, *Ethical and Legal Issues,* pp. 12-13.

56. "Ethical Guidelines for Social Experiments," p. 271.

57. Kelman, "Rights of the Subject in Social Research," pp. 1003-5.

58. Alexander Morgan Capron, "Social Experimentation and the Law," in Rivlin and Timpane, *Ethical and Legal Issues,* pp. 155-63.

59. Ibid, pp. 159-60.

60. The issue of consent has also been raised in connection with pyschohistorical or psychobiographical studies—another variety of research that is largely based on personal records and documents but that I see as closer to history and biography than to social science. A task force of the American Psychiatric Association has recommended that informed consent be obtained from the subjects of such studies if they are living, or from their next of kin, if they are recently deceased. "Psychoprofiles" completed by intelligence agencies (particularly the CIA) are apparently exempt "in the service of the national interest." See Philip Nobile, "Psychohistory: A Controversial Discipline," *New York Times,* October 10, 1976. Respectful treatment of the subjects of such research is clearly a matter of professional concern, as is the propriety of clinical analysis in the absence of clinical data. I am not persuaded, however, that the principle of informed consent (with the implication that the biographees or their next of kin have veto power over the work) is applicable when one is writing about public figures on the basis of publicly available records and documents. (The situation is different, of course, if the investigator is given interviews or access to confidential materials.) On the other hand, although I understand why the task force did not expect CIA psychiatrists to obtain consent from the subjects of their psychoprofiles, I would be less inclined to endow their work ("in the national interest") with professional legitimacy.

61. An example here is the use of a periscopic prism for observation in a lavatory in the experiment by Middlemist, Knowles, and Matter, "Personal Space Invasions."

62. Joan Cassell, "Risk and Benefit to Subjects of Fieldwork," *American Sociologist* 13 (1978): 134-43. See also Cassell's chapter in this volume.

63. Arthur J. Vidich and Joseph Bensman, *Small Town in Mass Society* (Garden City, N.Y.: Doubleday, 1960). For a review of some of the issues raised by this study, see Myron Glazer, *The Research Adventure: Promise and Problems of Field Work* (New York: Random House, 1972), pp. 130-34; and Edward Diener and Rick Crandall, *Ethics in Social and Behavioral Research* (Chicago: University of Chicago Press, 1978), pp. 61-62.

64. These issues are discussed and illustrated by Glazer, *Research Adventure,* chap. 4.

65. Humphreys, *Tearoom Trade.*

66. An early example of research in this genre is Leon Festinger, Henry W. Riecken, and Stanley Schachter, *When Prophecy Fails* (Minneapolis: University of Minnesota Press, 1956).

67. For a discussion of these issues see Kai T. Erikson, "A Comment on Disguised Observation in Sociology," *Social Problems* 14 (1967): 366-73; and Cassell's chapter in this volume.

68. Rosenhan, "On Being Sane." Rosenhan's reports did not identify the hospitals in which the research was carried out, but it was probably difficult to protect their anonymity, at least in professional circles.

69. See Kelman, "Rights of the Subject in Social Research," p. 998.

70. See Cassell's chapter in this volume for a very helpful distinction between five models of fieldwork and a discussion of the ways in which what she calls "the undercover agent" model differs from the others.

71. Ibid.

72. Ibid. See also Margaret Mead, "Research with Human Beings: A Model Derived from Anthropological Field Practice," *Daedalus* 98 (1969): 361-86.

73. My assumption here is that the social harm caused by the mere violation of certain rules—the most obvious being the rule against seriously injuring or killing others—always outweighs the potential benefits.

74. Biomedical research in epidemiology may be a good case in point. As Jay Wallace argues elsewhere in this volume, epidemiological research is closely related to social research.

75. Similarly, at the societal level, the cumulative effect of disrespectful treatment of research participants may be a reduction in the level of trust within the society, constituting a diffuse harm.

76. For an illustration of such an exercise, see Cassell's chapter in this volume, or my own discussion of participatory research models in Kelman, "Rights of the Subject in Social Research," pp.1003-5.

77. This analysis suggests that it should be possible to allow exemption from prior review for all research based on the questioning of respondents, *provided* confidentiality of the data is ensured (preferably by the removal of identifying information); and for all research based on direct observation, *provided* there is no deception, misrepresentation, or hidden access. However, I am inclined to agree with Judith Swazey that it would be preferable to make exemptions a category of an expedited review process, since this would make it possible for an IRB to spot the rare case in which the consent procedure is inadequate in a "questioning" study or in which there are serious risks of psychological or material injury in an observation study. See Judith P. Swazey, "Professional Protectionism Rides Again: A Commentary on Exempted Research and Responses to DHEW's Proposed Regulations," *IRB: A Review of Human Subjects Research* 2 (March 1980): 4-6. Prior review is clearly required, in my opinion, for laboratory experiments that involve deception, particularly if they subject participants to a potentially stressful experience; for field experiments, particularly if they involve a highly intrusive and potentially disturbing intervention in a natural situation; and for social and organizational experiments, particularly if access to significant resources and opportunities is at stake (although it may be that the IRB is not the appropriate agency to carry out the review process for large-scale social experiments). An *expedited* review process may be quite appropriate for laboratory experiments and simulations that do not employ deception, and for field experiments that introduce only minor variations in an ongoing activity.

78. Herbert C. Kelman, "Manipulation of Human Behavior: An Ethical Dilemma," in *A Time to Speak*, pp. 13-31.

PART TWO

Harm and Benefit

3

Types of Harm
in Social Research

DONALD P. WARWICK

Does research in the social sciences produce any serious harm, or are its effects largely innocuous? One school holds that concern about harm in social research is ill founded, for there is really very little harm done. There may be occasional bruised egos, temporary discomfort, pique, and minor irritations, but no serious damage to the individual or to the society.[1] Others see a broader range of potential harms, including physical injury, emotional stress, damage to the image of minority groups, and heightened cynicism in the society at large. This paper presents a taxonomy of potential harms arising from social science research and illustrates each variety with real or hypothetical examples. Its aim is not to resolve the debate about the frequency or severity of harms, but to provide a framework for a more careful analysis of the issues at stake.

Prefatory Comments

The discussion of harms should be prefaced by four observations about the present subject matter. The first concerns the elusive boundaries of "social science research." Most social scientists would have little difficulty in defining a laboratory experiment on group behavior as research. But what do we do with action projects or other interventions that become research at the point where they are subjected to systematic evaluation? The New Jersey–Pennsylvania Income Maintenance Experiment, for example, was introduced to test the effects of a negative income tax on, *inter alia,* the recipients' willingness to work. The difference between this and many social programs was that it was designed as a controlled experiment from the outset. Hence from the standpoint of harms and benefits it was difficult to separate the effects of *program content* from those of *social research,* for the two came together in practice.[2] For present purposes I will define social science research as any deliberate attempt to gather data on individuals or groups through such systematic means as experimentation, observation, testing, or interviewing. Income maintenance programs would thus be considered a form of social research only if they included systematic attempts at evaluating program processes and consequences. Encounter groups conducted with no explicit research component would not be regarded as social research, while those including systematic data gathering on consequences would meet the present definition. Although the focus of this paper is on harms generated by social research in itself, it should be recognized that it is often hard to disentangle the research component and the contents of the intervention being studied. This problem is particularly acute in evaluation research.

Second, research on the harms and benefits produced by social scientific research is inadequate and often biased. Some argue that, since few harms have been documented in the literature, social research must be largely benign. In a notable non sequitur, one author proclaims: "Given the large number of subjects who have participated in personally stressful experiments, if such participation did have egregious effects, there is little doubt that cases of harmed subjects would have been brought to our professional attention by now."[3] While the writer does not define "egregious effects," he implies that the absence of data about harm to subjects is a sure token of the absence of harm.

There are several reasons for questioning such attributions of benignity. Given their weak position in the university and their reluctance to offend faculty members whose good opinion they desire, student subjects may lack the motivation and the opportunity to protest. Most researchers are also not anxious to collect data showing that they may have injured their research subjects. And even where data are collected on the impact of research, they are often biased against the revelation of harm. Typically participants are asked on a self-report form whether they were glad or sorry that they participated in the experiment, whether they would do it again, and whether they experienced any ill effects.

The use of self-report data is particularly ironic in studies using deception, since the usual justification for deception is that the reports of subjects are not to be trusted in sensitive areas of behavior. In his famous studies of obedience, Stanley Milgram surely would not have used an item such as the following as the basis for his conclusions: "If you were put in a situation where you were told by an experimenter to give electric shock to other people, how much shock would you be willing to give?" (very strong, fairly strong, fairly weak, none at all). Yet in testing for subject reactions to his experiments—including areas of behavior notably susceptible of bias—Milgram used precisely that approach.[4] To follow the logic of the original experiment, deception would have to be used to test for the effects of deception because people are not likely to tell the truth when it is injurious to self-esteem. To complicate matters, theories of cognitive dissonance predict that under certain conditions individuals experience psychological pressure to justify their behaviors to themselves and that a common mode of justification is underestimation of the costs and harms involved. Regrettably, the quality of most follow-up surveys is quite low; if they were to be evaluated as independent studies rather than as codas to other projects, they would not pass muster within the professions. The only fair conclusion is that very little is known about the specific effects of social scientific research, in good part because that topic has not been carefully studied.

Third, the notion of harm implies an evaluative framework for assessing damages to individuals and social groups. This framework entails fundamental assumptions about the nature of persons and society, about the individual and collective conditions constituting well-being or its absence, about what is most and least valued by persons, groups, professions, and governments, and about the specific impact of social research on these constituencies. Much of the disagreement about the harms of social research stems not from inconclusive data but from quite disparate assumptions about the fragility or durability of a typical person, the goods that are sought and the harms that are feared by members of society, and the conditions promoting or retarding collective welfare.

To cite but one example, most experimental social psychologists practicing deception seem to assume that the ordinary research subject is a hardy species who is not easily harmed by the machinations of a laboratory experiment, and whose trust can easily be restored through a short postexperimental briefing. Given their optimism about the lack of harms produced and their focus on the individual subject, these social scientists typically do not consider the cumulative harms of their research on the larger society (though they will often cite the cumulative beneficial effects of increased knowledge). Those who take a different view of human nature, of the persistence of ruptured trust, and of the links between social research and the society will come to other conclusions.[5]

Fourth, as Alasdair MacIntyre has pointed out, the concept of "harm" is a very blunt instrument for appraising the effects of social science research.[6] It brings together in one category a heterogeneous assortment of actions and consequences without drawing appropriate distinctions about their moral salience. Within the broad notion of harm, for instance, we may distinguish four kinds of damage.[7] One is *physical or mental injury,* such as burns suffered from electric shock or prolonged depression resulting from abuse in a social-psychological experiment. A second is *harm to interests,* seen, for example, when the results of social scientific research harm the image of a corporation or of an ethnic group. A third kind of harm is *being wronged* through being subjected by others to the violations of moral principles. Research subjects suffer wrongs when they are deceived about the purposes of a study or when promises of confidentiality about their responses are broken. Finally, individuals or groups may suffer harm to their *moral integrity,* as when they are encouraged by the research process to lie to others or when they are trained to be more insensitive to human suffering. The point to be underscored is that these different forms of harm vary in their ethical implications. Thus research subjects who accidentally suffer physical injury in an experiment are not necessarily wronged, while those who are deceived may be wronged but suffer no physical injury, harm to their interests, or moral harm. I shall return to these distinctions at the conclusion of the paper, where they will be relevant to judgments made about the justifiability of harms in social research. For simplicity of presentation, the more global notion of harm will be used in the typology that follows.

A taxonomy of harms can be organized in different ways, such as according to the constituency suffering the damage or the agent through which the harm is inflicted (the experimenter, the research procedures, the research findings, etc.). The scheme presented here follows the first principle, that of audiences affected. I will argue that the effects of social science research—harms as well as benefits—reach three main audiences: the research participants, the research enterprise, and the society.

Harms To Research Participants

Research participants include subjects in laboratory experiments, respondents in surveys, informants in anthropological studies, and, in general, those who provide the primary data for social scientific investigations. Harms to these individuals may range from death or severe physical injury to minor irritation and discomfort. The evidence to date suggests seven kinds of potential harm to participants

1. Death. Social scientists rarely think of their research as a matter of life and death, but it can become so, especially when all of the consequences of the research are considered. In the reprinted version of *People of Alor,* the anthropologist Cora DuBois reports that when some of her informants told Japanese invaders that they were under the protection of an American, they were publicly executed.[8] Similarly, although there are no such cases on record, certain kinds of social research conducted during the Allende regime in Chile, such as applied research on community mobilization, could easily have formed grounds for the execution, torture, or imprisonment of research participants after the coup of 1973. It is well known that social scientists working on development programs under Allende were forced to leave the country, often in fear of their lives. Individuals who collaborated with them in certain kinds of social experiments may have been less fortunate, but not sufficiently visible to be recorded as fatalities of such research. Though documented cases of death to research participants are few, this category of harm is hardly far-fetched in the contemporary world.

2. Physical Abuse or Injury. There are also few recorded cases in which research participants have suffered physical abuse, injury, or significant damage to their health, but some such instances have occurred. The clearest example of physical abuse is found in P. G. Zimbardo's simulation of a prison environment.[9] His attempts to have subjects role-play guards and prisoners was so successful that the study had to be prematurely ended after six days. Zimbardo decided that it would be unethical to continue the study after volunteer prisoners suffered hour after hour of physical and psychological abuse at the hands of the "guards." Studies of stress have also put participants in circumstances where cardiac arrest or other medical breakdowns were a distinct possibility. In one case army recruits were placed in an apparently disabled aircraft, told that they were about to crash-land, and then asked to fill out questionnaires relating to their insurance policies. Others were sent into simulated "war games" giving the realistic impression that artillery shells were falling closer and closer to them, or that they were being bombarded with radioactive fallout.[10] The youthful age of the recruits probably spared them serious physical injury; or will we yet discover some casualty buried deep in the files of the Defense Department?

3. *Psychological Abuse or Injury.* More common in the literature than physical damage are participant reactions of acute anxiety, stress or guilt; damage to self-respect and self-confidence; and less severe forms of psychological harm. A now classical case of observed stress among research subjects is Stanley Milgram's laboratory study of obedience to authority. Subjects who obeyed the experimenter's instructions to administer what seemed to be electric shock to another person showed clear signs of strain. Milgram himself reports: "Subjects were observed to sweat, tremble, stutter, bite their lips, groan, and dig their fingernails into their flesh. These were characteristic rather than exceptional responses to the experiment."[11] A review article on the effects of encounter groups also cites evidence of serious negative reactions. Participants suffered increased anxiety or depression lasting several weeks, were more psychologically distressed and/or employed more maladaptive defenses as a direct result of the experience, and suffered an unspecified "emotional disturbance."[12] Encounter groups can be considered a form of social research when they are organized in part for that purpose, although usually they are carried out for their own sake.

Laud Humphreys's study of male homosexuality in public restrooms may have touched off a more focused anxiety among participants who knew they had been observed—an apprehension about being apprehended.[13] Through careful observation of about one hundred men and a later follow-up survey (based on a deceptive explanation), Humphreys amassed a wealth of data on each individual. When information about the research reached a local newspaper, several cooperating respondents phoned him to ask if they were in danger. Humphreys assured them that they were not, for all the data containing personal identifiers had been burned. In 1970, Humphreys gave this optimistic assessment: "Subsequent contacts with these men, as well as with several others who later came to realize their role as subjects in my research, have left me confident that they remained unscathed by the negative publicity my work received."[14] Though Humphreys himself felt confident about the effectiveness of his safeguards, some of the men involved may have suffered continuing anxiety about potential exposure or prosecution. Indeed, when Humphreys published a "Research Retrospect" in 1975, he seemed far less sanguine about the efficacy of his measures to protect clients against prosecution.[15] While neither he nor anyone else tried to assess the degree of anxiety among clients— a step that would undoubtedly have increased that anxiety—it is plausible that some of the men continued to be distressed.

Certain kinds of social scientific research may further leave participants with strong feelings of guilt about their own actions during a study. Examples would include subjects who, so they thought, administered large doses of electric shock to a fellow participant, beat "prisoners" while role-playing as guards, failed to help those in obvious need, stole money from a charity box, or participated in illegal acts brought on by experimental entrapment.[16] In a remarkably honest account of subject reactions to a study in helping behavior, Thomas Murray reports clear evidence of anxiety mixed with guilt. In this study subjects were met by a phony "experimenter," given a deceptive explanation of the research, and then asked to watch a TV monitor in a tiny booth. They soon saw the "experimenter" receive an apparently severe electric shock and drop to the floor. The subjects were then timed to determine how long it would take them to come to the "experimenter's" aid. If they did nothing for six minutes Murray retrieved them from the booths. He reports:

> I knew that when six minutes had passed I would have to face someone who might be trembling, who might have trouble talking, and who would have probably fabricated some fantastic explanation of what had happened to the "victim." Among the 99 subjects I put through the procedure, I saw individuals whose faces were drained of color, who were reduced to stuttering, or who could barely force words through their clenched teeth. These subjects had many versions of what had happened: the "victim" had sneezed, or tripped, or just maybe there was something wrong. Virtually every subject who had not responded showed some anxiety.[17]

Writers such as Stanley Milgram vehemently deny that subjects suffer any lasting harm from such experiences, but the strength of their convictions is much greater than the rigor of the corroborating data.[18] Given the normal human tendency to deny inhumanity to others it may be virtually impossible to obtain valid data on participant reactions to their behavior during an experiment. Still, observations such as those reported by Murray suggest ample cause for concern.

Social science research may also cause harm to a participant's self-esteem or self-respect. One study deliberately manipulated feelings of self-worth among female participants and then related these changes to romantic liking.[19] College students were given a "personality test" and then told, on the basis of rigged results, that their personalities were either healthy or constricted, unimaginative, and uncreative. While they were sitting in a waiting room after receiving the test results, a handsome male graduate student posing as another subject struck up a conversation with each woman. He acted interested in her, told her something of his own background, and then asked her out to dinner in San Francisco. But the conversation was itself a key part of the research design. Through this ruse the experimenters hoped to test the effects of increases or decreases in self-esteem on the women's attraction to the graduate student. At the end the subjects were told that it was all a hoax and that there would be no date. Although the women were debriefed about the entire experiment, we do not know if the information given removed the experimentally induced harm to self-esteem. If the manipulation had its intended effects, they may well have lasted beyond the debriefing.

A final set of psychological harms to the individual participant includes temporary and minor feelings of irritation, annoyance, frustration, or discomfort. Their common characteristic is that the amount and duration of psychic damage is small. Examples would include a respondent's feeling that a survey interviewer has been pushy, or that the survey itself asks too many personal questions and takes too long. Also within this range of harm would be minor physical discomforts during a laboratory experiment, and a general sense among subjects that they have been treated in a demeaning or mildly insulting manner. Although they may do no great damage to individual participants, such harms are not by that fact morally justified or to be counted as trivial. Individuals have been known to be highly resentful of minor slights, and feelings of being tricked or used may make participants more wary in their dealings with others. Moreover, such reactions of displeasure or aggravation can have a significant and cumulative impact on public attitudes toward social science research, a point to be explored later.

4. Damage to Interpersonal Relations. Beyond harms manifesting themselves mainly as personal reactions, research participants may suffer damage to their relationships with others. For example, experimental "team building" efforts among members of the same work organization may lead to ruffled or ruptured relationships on the job when the research is concluded. Persons who tell their superiors, subordinates, or peers exactly how they feel about them in the "here and now" of the research intervention may encounter a chilly atmosphere in the "then and there" of everyday work relations.[20] Similarly, individuals who volunteer to be subjects in certain kinds of sex research may, if that fact is disclosed, find their morality called into question by key individuals in their lives. In anthropological studies persons who volunteer to serve as informants on community life may be ostracized or subjected to other sanctions if the research suddenly becomes controversial. The difference between an informant and a spy is often a matter of political definition.

5. Legal Jeopardy. Social research often gathers data on behavior that is illegal, immoral, or acutely embarrassing. Given that this research enjoys no legal protection or privilege, and that leaks may occur with even the most careful safeguards, the presence of such information in research files constitutes a real danger to some participants. Subpoenas from local prosecutors, the General Accounting Office, or even the Congress may pose the threat of legal jeopardy. Access to the data by blackmailers can put the participant at risk in other ways.

The threat of criminal investigation and prosecution was long cited as only a hypothetical problem for social research. But the last decade has shown it to be a clear and present danger in studies collecting sensitive information. In the New Jersey–Pennsylvania Income Maintenance Experiment, a prosecuting attorney bent on exposing welfare cheaters requested data about individual participants in the study. Since the experiment prohibited, but did not audit for, the acceptance of welfare payments, the participants were handy targets for investigation. The matter was finally settled out of court when the project directors agreed to supply the names of income recipients and the actual amounts received from the project.[21] To my knowledge no participant was ever prosecuted on the basis of this information, but prosecution was a distinct possibility. Later the General Accounting Office tried to audit and verify the interviews from this experiment, a step that further endangered confidentiality. These examples underscore the legal risks for participants in social research, especially when the study is highly visible and the data collected hold significant potential for prosecutors, journalists, private investigators, "plumbers," or blackmailers.

A striking instance of legal jeopardy to participants arose in Laud Humphreys's research on male homosexuals in public restrooms.[22] By recording the license numbers on the cars of men entering the restrooms, Humphreys was able to identify them by name. Each name was then linked to detailed observations on homosexual practices as well as other data collected through a follow-up survey. With the research conducted in a single city and on a subject of some interest to law enforcement officials, Humphreys created a gold mine for an enterprising district attorney. In a critique of this research published in 1973, I wrote: "This is one of the few social scientific studies which would have lent itself directly to a grand jury investigation."[23] In a 1975 "Research Retrospect" Humphreys cited this sentence and commented on the situation in question:

> In the wake of front-page publicity, fostered by members of the administration and faculty at Washington University soon after the completion of the research, I am surprised that no such investigation followed. Even with the care I took to safeguard my data, I spent some weeks early in the summer of 1968 burning tapes, deleting passages from transcripts, and feeding material into a shredder. . . .
>
> As I pondered during sleepless nights what I would do to protect my respondents if I was called to court, my resolve was to plead the Fifth Amendment and risk contempt citations rather than reveal the identity of a single tearoom participant. . . . My lawyer, my advisers, and I spent some time discussing these matters, and I now realize that they were not as placid as I was about the prospects. Since those days of uncertainity, however, I have spent three months of a Federal sentence in a county jail and am no longer so certain that I could have withstood the pressures of the criminal justice system.[24]

This statement hardly inspires confidence in the ability of social scientists to shield participants against the hazards of research data. Similar questions arise in sex research, where information on pedophilia and other illegal sexual activities could serve as the basis for criminal prosecution or civil suits.[25]

6. *Career Damage or Economic Harm.* Research participants may likewise suffer career liabilities or other kinds of socioeconomic harm. Organizational surveys, for instance, commonly include questions tapping the attitudes of workers toward their supervisor, the supervisor's management abilities, and other aspects of the supervisor's performance. If the data are tabulated by work groups that are identified by name, the top leadership should have little difficulty evaluating certain aspects of management performance at lower levels. Although researchers often counsel against such punitive use of study findings, an unpopular supervisor in a low-performing work group could easily be dismissed or sidetracked as a direct result of organizational surveys.

Participants can suffer economic harm from social research when, as a direct or indirect result of the study, they earn less money or must pay more for certain goods or services. One criticism of income maintenance experiments is that, by providing participants with a boon of short-term income, they may encourage people to drop out of their existing places in the labor force. When the windfall has passed, these individuals may find themselves without jobs and yet ineligible for welfare. Families in communities participating in a housing experiment may also find that the experiment itself has so inflated housing costs that purchases are beyond their reach. While such effects remain largely speculative, they do point up the possibilities of economic damage to participants and others affected by the research.[26]

7. *Invasions of Privacy.* One of the most frequently discussed consequences of social research is the invasion of participants' privacy. While privacy has many meanings, the definition offered by Ruebhausen and Brim will serve present purposes: Privacy is "the freedom of the individual to pick and choose for himself the time and circumstances under which, and most importantly, the extent to which, his attitudes, beliefs, behavior, and opinions are to be shared with or withheld from others."[27]

As Herbert C. Kelman has suggested, social research may violate privacy in three ways.[28] First, it may expose to legal authorities or others damaging information obtained through the research. The examples of legal jeopardy cited earlier could also be considered violations of privacy. Similarly, disclosing the name of a community involved in ethnographic research may reduce the privacy of individuals and groups discussed in the resulting report. A case in point is the community identified as "Springdale" in the book *Small Town in Mass Society.*[29] Although the project director had pledged anonymity to those studied, the small size of the town and its proximity to the university conducting the research made it difficult to conceal the name of the community and the identities of key figures. With passages reminiscent of *Peyton Place,* this work undoubtedly reduced the privacy of individuals so identified.

Second, research methods may diminish the participant's control over self-presentation in the research setting. "Loss of control is tantamount to a deprivation of privacy in the sense that our freedom to pick and choose what information about ourselves we disclose and what information we withhold is restricted."[30] Clear examples of reduced ability to control self-presentation are seen in studies relying on covert observation techniques. In his study of male homosexuality in restrooms Humphreys used a series of misrepresentations to penetrate the defenses of participants against discovery by outsiders.[31] To gain access to the homosexual behavior itself he posed as a "watchqueen," or lookout, in the restrooms. By claiming to be a market researcher he was able to trace the license numbers of the participants and thereby obtain their addresses. After waiting a year from his initial observations, he entered the participants' homes by identifying himself as an interviewer for a health survey. In the end he managed to record his observations of these men not only at the scene of their deviant behavior, but in a major setting of their "straight" lives. Other social scientists have studied private behavior by pretending to join groups or organizations.[32] "As a result, members are induced to say or do things in their presence that they may wish to reserve for fellow members, particularly if they are intent on keeping all or part of their activities secret."[33]

A third violation of privacy arises when social research intrudes into a participant's private space, including the individual's bodily functions, sexual activity, secret thoughts or actions, or intimate family relations. A classic case of such intrusion is an observational study of bathroom behavior.[34] By placing a periscope in a stack of books on the floor of a toilet stall, R. D. Middlemist et al. gathered detailed data on "micturition" *in situ*. Even if the participants were never to become aware that these observations had been made, their private space would have been violated. Should they become aware, damage to privacy could be compounded by outrage, injured self-respect, or the psychological harms previously noted.

Harms to Society

Discussions of harms and benefits in social research show a curious inconsistency in the choice of reference points. In specifying the benefits of a given study, social scientists typically cite its potential advantages for the society, such as the advancement of knowledge in a key area or the provision of solid data for use in setting policy. But when noting risks or harms the same commentators usually confine their attention to individuals. Thus much of the literature on adverse effects, including the handful of empirical studies on this question, has focused on harms to research participants, particularly in laboratory settings. Yet the processes, contents, and results of social research can bring harms as well as benefits to the society and its subgroups, and the harms done can be substantial. The following discussion considers harms to three overlapping collectivities: the total society, subgroups of the society, and government.

The Total Society

Social research may have various kinds of reactive effects on the total society in which it is carried out. Some of these effects, such as the advancement of knowledge, are often cited as the foremost benefits of research, and used to justify the risk of harm to individual participants. But others may be far less benign and at times positively pernicious. The following are the most significant negative consequences for the society as a whole.

1. Cynicism, Mistrust, and Wariness. One of the strongest arguments against deception in social research is that it undermines the trust necessary for a decent social order. Political philosophers have long maintained that without trust there can be no democracy, no neighborliness, no friendship, nor much of what makes human existence worthwhile. Deception undercuts trust by weakening the normal expectation that what another person says will be true. Deception always presumes and then violates trust. If I try to deceive you the only way in which the deception will work is if you believe that I am speaking the truth. If you do not, the deception will be foiled, for you will either disregard the message or seek to corroborate it through other channels.

The harm wrought by research deceptions is not only that they violate the trust of persons to whom lies are told, but that they weaken the societal expectation that communication is normally truthful. The greater the number of research deceptions, the greater the harm done to this expectation. And the more frequent the lies in one sphere, such as research, the easier it is for others, such as credit checkers, to follow suit on the grounds that "everybody's doing it." J. S. Mill was one of many philosophers to see this spillover effect of the single lie:

> Thus it would often be expedient . . . to tell a lie. But inasmuch as the cultivation in ourselves of a sensitive feeling on the subject of veracity is one of the most useful, and the enfeeblement of that feeling one of the most hurtful, things to which our conduct can be instrumental; and inasmuch as any, even unintentional, deviation from truth, does that much toward weakening the trustworthiness of human assertion, . . . we feel that the violation, for present advantage, of a rule of such transcendent expedience, is not expedient.[35]

In her recent book on lying, Sissela Bok has also argued cogently about harms done to trust by deception.[36] Of course here, as with discussions on the putative benefits of social research for the total society, we have no "hard data" about consequences. But the testimony of human experience is sufficient to make damage to trust from research deceptions a plausible hypothesis. If one were to reject this hypothesis on the grounds of no data, one would have to do the same for allegations of benefit premised on evidence of roughly the same quality.

2. Reduced Helping Behavior. Closely linked to trust is the willingness of one human being to help another in times of need or distress. If I find that you have collapsed in an intersection and are about to be run down by a truck, I will be willing to offer help if (a) I am so disposed by personal conviction; and (b) I am convinced that you are genuinely in need of help. If I suspect that the scene is a ruse for social psychological research or is otherwise inauthentic, I will hesitate to step in.

Deceptive studies investigating the willingness of human beings to help each other have been conducted inside research laboratories as well as in public places. One study had a stooge fall in a moving subway train in Philadelphia. As he fell he released a trickle of "blood" from an eyedropper in his mouth.[37] This melodrama was replayed about fifty times on the same subway line to test passengers' reactions to medical emergencies. In Florida other psychologists tested responses to a different kind of emergency as they cried "Shark" on a well-populated beach.[38] Stanley Milgram has turned "lost" children out on the streets to determine whether passers-by will help them call home. Milgram also plays on public willingness to help others in his "lost letter technique," a procedure in which researchers drop several hundred stamped letters bearing such names as Friends of the Nazi Party.[39]

Such violations of public trust may weaken the very tendency to help that they try to study. For example, at the University of Washington in 1973 a male student approached another male student on campus and shot him. Others making their way across the campus saw the incident but did not stop to help. When asked later why they did nothing, some students reported that they thought it was just another psychology experiment.[40] Repeated many times and over a long period of time, such incidents could greatly reduce the willingness of people to be of help to others.

3. Undermined Social Institutions. Certain kinds of research can raise doubts about the legitimacy of key institutions within the society. A critical objection to the recording of jury deliberations for research purposes was precisely that knowledge that the proceedings *might* be recorded could change the nature of the jury's behavior. In federal hearings held on the Wichita Jury Recordings, Senator James A. Eastland stated to one of the researchers: "Now, do you not realize that to snoop on a jury, and record what they say, does violence to every reason for which we have secret deliberations of a jury?"[41] Eastland asserted that members of the jury might hesitate to state their frank opinions if they thought that recordings were being made and might be released later. As a result of these hearings legislation was passed expressly prohibiting the recording of federal petit or grand juries for any purpose whatever.

Similar concerns have been expressed about the harmful consequences of rigged or slanted public opinion polls on the legitimacy of American elections. Such polls, which are based on social science methodology and are thought by many to influence election outcomes, are designed to produce results supporting the image or position of the candidate by whom they were commissioned while maintaining the veneer of scientific respectability. The net effect may be to create public doubt about the honesty of the elections and about the trustworthiness of the candidates running for office.[42]

4. Living for the Record.   Coupled with the proliferating data banks and other records maintained on individuals, social science research may reinforce the tendency of people to live "for the record." The legal scholar Arthur Miller writes:

> As the populace becomes increasingly aware that a substantial number of facts are being preserved "on the record," people may start to doubt whether they have any meaning apart from the profile in the computer's files. As a result, they may begin to base their personal decisions, at least in part, on whether it will enhance their record image in the eyes of third parties who have control over important parts of their lives.[43]

The specific social harm here is the collective sense that someone may be snooping, prying, covertly watching or listening, or otherwise invading one's private space. This is not just a matter of single invasions of privacy, as discussed earlier, but of the very atmosphere in which members of the society must live. It is proper to speak of social harm when, in a society that values individualism, individuals must constantly look over their shoulders or under their beds to be sure that they are not being observed. This harm is accentuated when citizens must learn to be wary not only of observers who are readily identified as such, but of social scientists and others who gather data under false pretenses. Such fears grow in direct proportion to the decline of public trust in the society.

Subgroups in the Society

Social scientific research may also bring harm to subgroups in a society, including racial or ethnic minorities, religious groups, members of political parties, and individuals defined as deviants. Indeed, one of the most powerful effects of social research—for weal or woe—may be to single out certain groups for attention. By identifying one set of individuals as "deviant" and another as "disadvantaged," social research communicates a message about what is problematic to the rest of society. Such research may inflict five types of harm on social groups.

1. Death or Serious Injury.   Just as individuals can be killed or severely injured as a consequence of social scientific research, so may entire groups within a society. Systematic research on politically insurgent ethnic groups, for instance, could be turned over to military authorities and used as a guide for bombing out entire communities. This possibility was raised in connection with the tribal data center proposed for the Lanna Thai Research Center in Thailand.[44] The purpose of this facility was to collect, process, and store very detailed data on the tribal peoples of Northern Thailand and contiguous areas. The Village Data Card proposed for the project requested information on the exact village location, the names of the headman and other key influentials, the names, racial affiliations, and occupations of the residents, and the weapons on hand. While there is no evidence that social scientific data of this kind were used in bombing operations, the experience of the Vietnam War leaves little doubt about the possibility of such use.

2. *Victimization or Scapegoating.* Social research may intentionally or unintentionally create or reinforce the conditions for the victimization of certain groups within the society. Sociologists during the Hitler regime were undoubtedly under strong pressure to provide evidence of the deleterious effects of Jews on German society. Psychiatrists in the Soviet Union have also been used to define political dissidents as mentally disturbed. Research portraying the "feebleminded" as criminally dangerous, sexually uncontrolled, and a hazard to the gene pool could also set the stage for repressive actions against that group. The enthusiasm shown by some for the compulsory sterilization of retarded persons may have been abetted by earlier journalistic and scientific portrayals of their alleged excesses. Current definitions of social deviance may also shape attitudes toward the treatment of individuals within institutions. Stephanie B. Stolz argues that specialists in behavior modification in effect wreak vengeance when they apply their most painful techniques to those considered by society to be the greatest offenders, such as child molesters.[45] Research on deviance almost always carries a freight of moral judgment which can affect subsequent attitudes toward the groups under investigation.

3. *Blaming the Victim.* Social science research has also been accused of presenting interpretations that blame the victims of social injustice for their present position in the society. By arguing that the current situation of black Americans or Indians is the result of laziness, poor achievement motivation, or other individual deficiencies, the analyst implies that their deprivation results from their own inadequacies rather than defects in economic and social structures. This point was raised with considerable vehemence in the debate surrounding the "Moynihan Report" on "The Negro Family: The Case for National Action."[46] Using a variety of government and social scientific studies, Moynihan concluded that the Negro family (as it was then called) suffers from instability, a propensity to produce illegitimate children, and a matriarchal structure. Experience in this family setting, the report argues, has harmful effects on all children, but especially on boys, who come to feel that men are good-for-nothings. The psychologist William Ryan took sharp issue with this report, claiming that "it draws dangerously inexact conclusions from weak and insufficient data, encourages (no doubt unintentionally) a new form of subtle racism that might be termed 'Savage Discovery,' and seduces the reader into believing that it is not racism and discrimination but the weaknesses and defects of the Negro himself that account for the present status of inequality between Negro and white."[47]

Population research has likewise been charged with suggesting that the poor are poor because of excessive fertility rather than because of unjust social and economic conditions in the society at large. In these as in many other spheres of research, implicit assumptions about human nature, the social order, and what constitutes a "problem" in the society can greatly affect the way in which groups are depicted in social scientific studies.[48] These portrayals, in turn, redound upon the unspoken and often unexamined assumptions about who is responsible for the society's ills, and why.

4. *Stereotyping and Adverse Images.*   Even where social science research does not serve to victimize or blame social groups, it may stereotype them or otherwise create unfavorable images of their members. Consider the following statement from a well-known empirical study on the sociology of religion:

> Our overall impression is that Catholics and Protestants alike have assimilated the materialistic values of contemporary society to the point where they equally value a good job with high income, and are equally likely to aspire to such a position. However, Catholics seem to be at a disadvantage in the competition because of a series of values to which they apparently become committed as a result of their involvement in the Catholic Church and subcommunity. For example, they seem to become more strongly attached to the kin group than Protestants, and therefore less able to make the break with home and family that is required in many of the more demanding, and hence better-paid, positions in contemporary American society. Also, involvement in the Catholic group apparently fosters a de-emphasis of intellectual independence which is ill-adapted to the more creative and responsible positions in our rapidly changing social order. In addition, involvement in the Catholic group leads to higher-than-average fertility, which certainly creates difficulties in securing higher education, and which may also have some effect on I.Q., or problem-solving ability, hence further handicapping Catholic youth.[49]

This passage could easily be read as saying that as a result of their religious involvement, Catholics do not work as hard as Protestants, suffer from conformity to their authoritarian Church, and have too many children who are not bright enough for today's world. One need not go very far in the social science literature to find the Catholic Church portrayed as monolithic and authoritarian, and its members as suffering from exposure to its values, precepts, and controls.

Similarly, until quite recently studies on the attitudes of white ethnic groups, many of which are predominantly Catholic, regularly portrayed them as bigoted, insular, and politically reactionary. Sometimes the groups so portrayed have fought back, as when Italian Americans vigorously protested the image of Italians conveyed in Edward Banfield's book *The Moral Basis of a Backward Society.*[50] Typically, however, weaker groups do not have the resources to counteract unflattering images, and in some cases, as with certain very remote and illiterate groups, may not even be aware of them. Yet adverse images can shape attitudes toward the groups in question, and in many cases affect public policies.

5. *Manipulation and Control.*   A charge often leveled against social science research is that it provides economically and politically powerful groups in the society with information and other means to control the weak. In

a now famous address to the 1968 convention of the American Sociological Association, Martin Nicolaus proclaimed:

> Sociologists stand guard in the garrison and report to its masters on the movements of the occupied populace. The more adventurous sociologists don the disguise of the people and go out to mix with the peasants in the "field," returning with books and articles that break the protective secrecy in which a subjected population wraps itself, and make it more accessible to manipulation and control.[51]

Opponents of organizational research have argued that morale surveys and similar exercises can provide management with crucial tools for identifying pockets of opposition, channeling discontent, and otherwise fortifying the position of management vis-à-vis workers and their unions. Armed with surveys showing morale problems in certain divisions, management can engage the services of organization development specialists to "cool out" opposition before it stirs up confrontations with the union. Union leaders, who usually do not have access to comparable information, may find that they are outflanked in their efforts to provide viable issues and grievances for use in the next round of collective bargaining talks. Similar harms may arise in income maintenance experiments when the options chosen for testing include only those of interest to government policymakers rather than possibilities of interest to other constituencies, such as welfare rights organizations.[52] These examples illustrate the ways in which social research can be used to strengthen the power position of some groups and undermine that of others.

Government

Another party that may suffer harm from social science research is the government, whether of the researcher's home country or of another nation. At least three kinds of harm are at issue.

1. Reduced National Sovereignty. One of the strongest criticisms of Project Camelot by commentators in the developing countries was that it would have severely undermined the political sovereignty of the nations investigated. By gathering data on domestic insurgency and discontent, the critics charged, the project would have supplied the U.S. government with intelligence data damaging to the interests of the countries studied.[53] Some feared that such information would be used to mount paramilitary operations not approved by the government, perhaps in collaboration with the Central Intelligence Agency. And even if nothing quite so drastic occurred, the mere fact that the American government possessed vital information not available to the country itself could weaken the latter's bargaining position in negotiations with the United States. Even with allowances made for a certain amount of political paranoia in these reactions to Project Camelot, they do bring out various ways in which social research might infringe national sovereignty.

2. Domestic Conflict. Project Camelot also shows that social research can be a source of conflict and dissension within the country studied.

Disclosure of this study's existence and of preliminary negotiations with local social scientists touched off heated debate in the Chilean legislature. In India similar debates arose around the Himalayan Borders Country Project, an undertaking also financed by the U.S. Department of Defense. Given the strategic importance of the Himalayan area for India's conflicts with China, it is not surprising that the opposition used this incident as proof of governmental ineptitude.[54]

Even research óstensibly unconnected with politics may set the stage for domestic confrontations. In 1974, the University of Texas proposed to conduct a straightforward archaeological study in one region of Mexico. Not long afterward, the Mexican Association of Professional Anthropologists published a long newspaper ad attacking the project. After noting that the research sites were dangerously close to Mexican oil fields, the ad proclaimed (in Spanish):

> We historians and anthropologists reject this project as being potentially dangerous in view of its ambiguity, and because it is in the hands of persons and institutions which the majority of us repudiate for their depreciatory, discriminatory, and divisive attitudes toward Mexican anthropology, and because of the importation of foreign researchers who have displaced nationals in the anthropological institutions of the government of Mexico.[55]

Behind this debate was apparently a tangled set of personal and political jealousies going well beyond the project in question. The continuing exchanges suggest that any research project can become explosive if it ventures into the right minefield.

3. Misleading or Inadequate Policy Guidance. Governments frequently hire social scientists, or research organizations using social scientists, to gather data for use in formulating, implementing, and evaluating public policies. Harm can be done to those governments when the studies so commissioned are of low quality, do not address themselves to the policy issues at hand, or draw improper conclusions from the data collected. Evaluation studies, for example, often err in a direction favorable to the programs under review, typically because the evaluators do not wish to displease their sponsors with unflattering data. While the sponsors are often complicit in biased evaluations, the costs to the government can include continued investment in programs that either do not produce their intended effects or that produce side-effects canceling out such benefits as do occur. Governments often set the stage for low-quality research by pressuring the investigators to restrict the scope of their studies to "acceptable" alternatives or to come up with results presenting the program evaluated in the most favorable or least unfavorable light.

Harms to Researchers and the Research Professions

Most discussions of the effects of social science research have ignored two groups intimately linked to the conduct of such research: the researchers and the research professions. In the case of researchers a common, if unstated, assumption is that they emerge largely unharmed and emotionally unaffected by their work. Research reports often portray experimental social psychologists as but another set of stimuli in the laboratory setting. They read instructions, adopt prearranged roles, and record data, but more in the fashion of an experimental robot than an interacting human being. Hence the notion that experimenters themselves can be harmed by the manipulations and interactions in the research setting falls outside the conventional paradigms of social science. The same reasoning seems to be applied by extension to the research professions. According to the prevailing view, both they and their members are best seen as stagehands rather than actors in the drama of science. What happens to them is therefore considered of little moral consequence. I will argue here that both researchers and the research professions can be harmed by social research, and that these harms are of ethical import.

The Researcher

Researchers may suffer harm ranging from torture or death to mild doubts or regret about their professional activities. The most grave form of harm was noted in connection with individual participants: they may be executed or tortured for conducting studies considered by national authorities to be a threat to security. Three other harms may also result.

1. Legal Jeopardy. In at least one case a social scientist was imprisoned for his failure to divulge confidential information collected from research informants. Samuel Popkin, then a political scientist at Harvard University, was found guilty of contempt and jailed when he refused to disclose his sources during a federal grand jury investigation of the Pentagon Papers case. The same fate could have befallen the director of the New Jersey-Pennsylvania Income Maintenance Experiment when a local prosecutor subpoenaed project data, or Laud Humphreys, had a district attorney demanded his files on male homosexuals.

2. Callous and Manipulative Attitudes toward Others. What impact does the practice of deceptive and manipulative research have on the researcher involved? Until recently few, if any, social scientists asked that question about themselves. In 1980 Thomas Murray, a social psychologist, published the first article giving a personal account of the effects of deception and manipulation on the experimenter. After recounting his own experiences in a deceptive study on helping behavior, he came to the following conclusion:

> The deception researcher's personal dilemma is this: either one successfully dissociates the carefully crafted manipulativeness that characterizes the relationship with research subjects from relationships with people outside the laboratory, or one does not. In the first case, we should worry about the impact of the inauthentic relationship on the subject, and about the researcher's learning to systematically shut off ethically central aspects of his or her personality, as for example, learning to

lie with a completely straight face *and* a clear conscience. . . . In the second case, it follows analytically that one's relationships outside the laboratory are colored by the way one treats subjects. Neither option looks morally attractive.[56]

The basic question is whether learning theory applies to social scientists themselves, or only to others.

3. Guilt, Regrets, and Self-Doubt. Social researchers may also experience regrets, doubts, or guilt about their treatment of others. In the article cited, Thomas Murray gives clear evidence of his own misgivings about deception research:

> You try to convince yourself that, yes, all harmful effects have been removed. But I did not believe it then, and I do not today. . . . To the extent that my simulated emergency was realistic, my nonresponding subjects could make the inference that they were *not* the sort of person who acts courageously to help others in a crisis. And I doubt that my attempts to reassure them, including my willingness to encourage their rationalizations, could really undo all the damage to their self-esteem. . . .

> That I might be making some individuals, volunteers in innocence and ignorance, judge themselves cowardly or callous, troubled me deeply.[57]

One other published report indicates that social scientists who engaged in deceptive research later had second thoughts about their actions.[58] This involved the previously mentioned study of self-worth and romantic attraction among female college students. The experimenter subsequently admitted regret over cancelling the dates made with research subjects, while the graduate student proposing the dates said he was sorry he had ever participated in the study.[59]

The Research Professions

A final party affected by social science research is the researcher's profession and allied professions. But why should we be concerned about these professions? What claims do they have to be protected against harm? One answer derives from the frequent attributions of benefit to social research. To the extent that social scientific studies bring benefits to the society, to research participants, and to others, and to the extent that the research professions are responsible for those studies, these professions deserve to be shielded against harms arising from the research itself. Harms to the professions take three major forms.

1. Legal or Administrative Restrictions on Research. An extreme form of harm to professions results when entire areas of social research are flatly banned by law or administrative edict. One example is the curb on jury research mentioned earlier. Legislation has also prohibited or curtailed survey research in many parts of the United States.[60] The restrictions range from outright prohibitions to requirements that interviewers register with local law enforcement officials. The reasons for these laws vary, but often they grow out of public outrage over such deceptions as salesmen posing as survey interviewers. Administrative regulations, such as federal requirements for the protection of human subjects, can also be traced to public protests over perceived abuses to participants.

   2. Public Hostility toward Research. Even where there are no laws or administrative regulations governing social science research, public suspicions of social scientists can hamper their work. In recent years directors of survey research centers in the United States have reported great difficulties in obtaining satisfactory response rates in urban areas. The main difficulty appears to be a generalized fear of harm from strangers, but suspicion of deceptive surveys may also play a part. Hostility toward anthropological research in some North American Indian communities has likewise created barriers to field research by that profession. Indians have complained about invasions of privacy by anthropologists, the failure of their research to bring any tangible benefits to the communities studied, and sometimes even the failure to make the research findings available to those communities.[61] Similar reactions have been reported among the Aborigines of Australia.[62] The practical effect in many cases, one that many social scientists would consider salutary, is tough negotiation between researchers and the communities over what is to be studied, how, and by whom.

   3. Lowered Quality of Research. Practices such as deception and misrepresentation may reduce the quality of social research and the theories which it generates. Participants who suspect that they are being tricked or deceived, for example, may take their own defensive actions, including trickery and deception.

> Many subjects have become sophisticated about research deception from college courses, friends, previous research experience, and even the public media. Subjects' sophistication about a study ranges from vague knowledge that research deception occurs to specific foreknowledge of the particular experiment. When participants suspect that they are being hoodwinked, they may sabotage the study.[63]

Studies conducted on rates of suspicion report a steady rise over the past two decades, with between 50 and 90 percent of participants voicing doubts in some experiments.[64]

   There is also the distinct possibility that subjects who deceived their deceivers will do the same to those evaluating their deceptions. A few years hence we may discover that lies and counterlies have been so rampant in some types of research that entire areas of inquiry have to be written off as worthless. But, then, how can we ever know? Wiring subjects to portable polygraphs might be one option, but it poses problems for generalizing findings to an outside world lacking such encumbrances. And subjects might learn to manipulate the lie detectors to play yet more pernicious tricks on the experimenters. Once the cycle has begun it is very difficult to stop deception. And once the scientific value of deception is eroded, its justification even on utilitarian grounds will be defunct.

Conclusions

This paper has presented an anatomy of harms brought on by social scientific research. The presentation has been deliberately one-sided, focusing on harms rather than trying to cover corresponding benefits. The question of benefits deserves equal attention, and for a consideration of this question the reader should turn to Gordon Bermant's paper in this volume. Let me conclude with three observations on the uses and limitations of the framework I have provided.

First, establishing the presence of one or more harms in social research implies no necessary conclusion about whether or not that research is morally justifiable, or at least morally permissible. Judgments about the ethics of research require, as a minimum, information about the severity of the harm; how and by whom it was produced (e.g., deliberately or accidentally); the presence or absence of informed consent among those affected; the legal authority of those responsible, as in an income maintenance experiment; and other considerations. Information about benefits would also be essential in evaluating many kinds of harm, especially for those using a utilitarian framework of ethics. Thus, a sociological analysis of a multinational corporation could tarnish its image by disclosing examples of bribery in other countries, but such harm would not necessarily be morally unjustifiable. Determination of harm is an essential component but not the only element necessary to a moral evaluation of social research.

Second, this framework of harms should not necessarily be viewed as a set of "costs" to be traded off against a comparable set of benefits from social research. I do not accept the simple version of utilitarianism lying behind the cost-benefit analyses typically carried out for social research. Rather, I side with those who reject the notion that the deception of research subjects should be "traded off" against the presumed benefits to society of a social-psychological experiment. Alasdair MacIntyre, for instance, argues in this volume that deception, which is a moral wrong, cannot be compensated by a benefit to society's interest, for the two are incommensurate.[65] At the same time, harm to one's economic interests, such as a reduction in earnings brought on by a social experiment, can theoretically be compensated by providing a commensurate amount of money. It is thus essential to draw appropriate moral distinctions among the types of harm at stake in social research.

Third, in evaluating the ethics of social research it is helpful to distinguish between harms that are *intrinsic* to the research process and those that are *extrinsic* to that process. An intrinsic harm is one that flows immediately and directly from the research arrangements, and thus is under the control of the researcher. The clearest example is the use of deception in a social psychological experiment. Extrinsic harms are those originating outside the research context but using the findings or other elements of the study. A classic case is the use of intelligence test data by racists to establish the inferiority or superiority of certain racial groups. Many of the harms to subgroups noted earlier arise when parties not connected with the research itself use the findings to the detriment of a subgroup.

While it is certainly not watertight, this distinction between intrinsic and extrinsic harms can be useful in evaluating the overall ethical acceptability of research methods. Those methods involving intrinsic harm, such as laboratory deceptions without informed consent, may be morally unjustifiable whatever their corresponding benefits to participants, researchers, or society. If we accept MacIntyre's stipulation that wrongs, such as deception, can never be counterbalanced by benefits to interest, deceptive research would always be intrinsically unjustifiable. With extrinsic harms, the ethical picture is more complicated. In some cases, as with research on racial differences in intelligence, the social scientist can reasonably expect that almost any findings will be used by one or another disputant in the public domain. Some would argue that, under these circumstances, the social scientist should be extremely careful to prevent likely misinterpretations and other misuses of the data. But in other cases it is almost impossible to know how research findings will be used or misused, so that moral responsibility for harms is largely out of the researcher's hands. The point is that while harms may indeed arise in many forms, the causal conditions of those harms and moral responsibility for their occurrence is often a complex matter.

Notes

1. Cf. E. L. Pattullo, "Who Risks What in Social Research," *Hastings Center Report* 10 (April 1980): 15-18; and his "Modesty Is the Best Policy: The Federal Role in Social Research" in the present volume.

2. This point is discussed further in Henry W. Riecken and Robert F. Boruch, eds., *Social Experimentation: A Method for Planning and Evaluating Social Intervention* (New York: Academic Press, 1974), esp. p. 246.

3. D. S. Holmes, "Debriefing after Psychological Experiments. II. Effectiveness of Postexperimental Desensitizing," *American Psychologist* 31 (1976): 874.

4. Stanley Milgram, "Subject Reaction: The Neglected Factor in the Ethics of Experimentation," *Hastings Center Report* 7 (October 1977): 19-23.

5. Cf. S. G. West and S. P. Gunn, "Some Issues of Ethics and Social Psychology," *American Psychologist* 33 (1978): 30-38.

6. Alasdair MacIntyre, "Risk, Harm, and Benefit Assessments as Instruments of Moral Evaluation," in this volume.

7. The following distinctions build on notions introduced by Alasdair MacIntyre, ibid.

8. Cited in George N. Appell, "Basic Issues in the Dilemmas and Ethical Conflicts in Anthropological Inquiry," *Module* 19 (1974): 1-28.

9. P. G. Zimbardo, C. Haney, W. C. Banks, and D. Jaffe, "The Mind Is a Formidable Jailer: A Pirandellian Prison," *New York Times Magazine* 122 (April 8, 1973), sec. 6, pp. 38-60.

10. M. Berkun, H. M. Bialek, P. R. Kern, and K. Yagi, "Experimental Studies of Psychological Stress in Man," *Psychological Monographs: General and Applied* 76 (1962): 1-39.

11. Stanley Milgram, "Behavioral Study of Obedience," *Journal of Abnormal and Social Psychology* 67 (1963): 375.

12. D. Hartley, H. B. Roback, and S. I. Abramowitz, "Deterioration Effects in Encounter Groups," *American Psychologist* 31 (1976): 247-55. The most thorough research done to date on the effects of encounter groups is found in M. A. Lieberman, I. D. Yalom, and M. B. Miles, *Encounter Groups: First Facts* (New York: Basic Books, 1973).

13. Laud Humphreys, *Tearoom Trade: Impersonal Sex in Public Places,* enl. ed. (Chicago: Aldine Publishing Co., 1975).

14. Laud Humphreys, quoted in M. Glazer, "Impersonal Sex," in Humphreys, *Tearoom Trade,* p. 215.

15. Laud Humphreys, "Retrospect: Ethical Issues in Social Research," in Humphreys, ibid., pp. 223-32.

16. See S. Cook, "Ethical Issues in the Conduct of Research in Social Relations," in C. Selltiz, L. S. Wrightsman, and S. W. Cook, eds., *Research Methods in Social Relations* (New York: Holt, Rinehart & Winston, 1976).

17. Thomas Murray, "Learning to Deceive," *Hastings Center Report* 10 (April 1980): 12.

18. Milgram, "Subject Reaction."

19. E. Walster, "The Effect of Self-Esteem on Romantic Liking," *Journal of Experimental Social Psychology* 1 (1965): 184-97.

20. Cf. R. E. Walton, "Ethical Issues in the Practice of Organization Development," in Gordon Bermant, Herbert C. Kelman, and Donald P. Warwick, *The Ethics of Social Intervention* (Washington, D.C.: Hemisphere Publishing Corp., 1978), pp. 121-45.

21. D. N. Kershaw and J. C. Small, "Data Confidentiality and Privacy: Lessons from the New Jersey Negative Income Tax Experiment," *Public Policy* 20 (1972): 257-80.

22. Humphreys, *Tearoom Trade.*

23. Donald P. Warwick, *"Tearoom Trade,* Means and Ends in Social Research," in Humphreys, *Tearoom Trade,* p. 205.

24. Humphreys, ibid., pp. 229-30.

25. Cf. William H. Masters, Virginia E. Johnson, and Robert C. Kolodny, *Ethical Issues in Sex Therapy and Research* (Boston: Little, Brown & Co., 1977), esp. pp. 52–69.

26. For a more thorough discussion of these issues see Alice M. Rivlin and P. Michael Timpane, eds., *Ethical and Legal Issues in Social Experimentation* (Washington, D.C.: Brookings Institution, 1975).

27. Oscar M. Ruebhausen and Orville G. Brim, Jr., "Privacy and Behavioral Research," *American Psychologist* 21 (1966): 426.

28. Herbert C. Kelman, "Privacy and Research with Human Beings," *Journal of Social Issues* 33 (1977): 169-95.

29. Arthur J. Vidich and Joseph Bensman, *Small Town in Mass Society* (Garden City, N.Y.: Doubleday, 1960).

30. Kelman, "Privacy and Research," p. 177.

31. Humphreys, *Tearoom Trade.*

32. Studies in which social scientists have posed as group members to gather data include Leon Festinger, Henry W. Riecken, and Stanley Schachter, *When Prophecy Fails* (Minneapolis: University of Minnesota Press, 1956), and J. F. Lofland and R. A. Lejeune, "Initial Interaction of Newcomers in Alcoholics Anonymous: A Field Experiment in Class Symbols and Socialization," *Social Problems* 8 (1960): 102-11.

33. Kelman, "Privacy and Research," p. 179.

34. R. Dennis Middlemist, Eric S. Knowles, and Charles F. Matter, "Personal Space Invasions in the Lavatory: Suggestive Evidence of Arousal," *Journal of Personality and Social Psychology* 33 (1976): 541–46. This study has been criticized in Gerald P. Koocher, "Bathroom Behavior and Human Dignity," *Journal of Personality and Social Psychology* 35 (1977): 120-21.

35. J. S. Mill, "Utilitarianism," in *Great Books of the Western World* (Chicago: Encyclopedia Britannica, 1952), vol. 43, p. 455.

36. Sissela Bok, *Lying: Moral Choice in Public and Private Life* (New York: Pantheon Books, 1978).

37. Jane A. Piliavin and Irving M. Piliavin, "Effects of Blood on Reactions to a Victim," *Journal of Personality and Social Psychology* 23 (1972): 353-61.

38. Example cited in Edward Diener and Rick Crandall, *Ethics in Social and Behavioral Research* (Chicago: University of Chicago Press, 1978), p. 72.

39. S. Milgram, L. Mann, and S. Harter, "The Lost Letter Technique: A Tool of Social

Research," *Public Opinion Quarterly* 29 (1965): 437-38. See also S. Milgram and L. Shotland, *Television and Antisocial Behavior* (New York: Academic Press, 1973).

40.   C. Gay, "A Man Collapsed outside a UW Building. Others Ignore Him. What Would You Do?," *University of Washington Daily,* November 30, 1973, cited in Diener and Crandall, *Ethics in Social and Behavioral Research,* p. 87.

41.   T. R. Vaughan, "Governmental Intervention in Social Research: Political and Ethical Dimensions in the Wichita Jury Recordings," in Gideon Sjoberg, ed., *Ethics, Politics, and Social Research* (Cambridge, Mass.: Schenkman Publishing Co., 1967), p. 61.

42.   Cf. L. Nedzi, "Public Opinion Polls: Will Legislation Help?," *Public Opinion Quarterly* 35 (1971): 336–41. See also L. Bogart, *Silent Politics: Polls and the Awareness of Public Opinion* (New York: Wiley-Interscience, 1972).

43.   A. R. Miller, "Personal Privacy in the Computer Age: The Challenge of a New Technology in an Information-Oriented Society," *Michigan Law Review* 67 (April 1969): 1150.

44.   E. Wolf and J. Jorgensen, "Anthropology on the Warpath," *New York Review of Books* 15 (November 19, 1970): 26-35.

45.   Stephanie B. Stolz, "Ethical Issues in Behavior Modification," in Bermant, Kelman, and Warwick, *Ethics of Social Intervention,* pp. 37–60.

46.   Daniel P. Moynihan, *The Negro Family: The Case for National Action* (Washington, D.C.: Office of Planning and Research, United States Department of Labor, 1965).

47.   W. Ryan, "Savage Discovery: The Moynihan Report," in Lee Rainwater and W. L. Yancey, *The Moynihan Report and the Politics of Controversy* (Cambridge, Mass.: MIT Press, 1967), p. 463.

48.   For a discussion of what constitutes a "problem" and the politics of problem definition see Gordon Bermant and Donald P. Warwick, "The Ethics of Social Intervention: Power, Freedom, and Accountability," in Bermant, Kelman, and Warwick, *Ethics of Social Intervention,* pp. 377–418, esp. pp. 382–84.

49.   G. Lenski, *The Religious Factor: A Sociologist's Inquiry* (Garden City, N.Y.: Doubleday & Co., Anchor Books, 1963), p. 344.

50.   Cf. Edward Banfield, *The Moral Basis of a Backward Society* (New York: Free Press, 1958). Among the numerous critiques of this work is J. Lopreato, *Peasants No More* (San Francisco: Chandler Publishing Co., 1967).

51.   Martin Nicolaus, "Remarks at ASA Convention," *American Sociologist* 4 (1969): 155.

52.   Donald P. Warwick, "Ethical Guidelines for Social Experiments," in Bermant, Kelman, and Warwick, *Ethics of Social Intervention,* pp. 267-88.

53.   For a discussion of the political implications of Project Camelot for national governments see Irving Louis Horowitz, ed., *The Rise and Fall of Project Camelot: Studies in the Relationship between Social Science and Practical Politics* (Cambridge, Mass.: MIT Press, 1967), esp. pp. 3-44 and 281-312.

54.   G. Berreman, "Not So Innocent Abroad," *Nation,* November 10, 1969, pp. 505-08.

55.   *Excelsior,* December 15, 1974, p. 29A, translated by the author.

56.   Murray, "Learning to Deceive," p. 14.

57.   Ibid., p. 12.

58.   Walster, "Effect of Self-Esteem."

59.   Z. Rubin, "Jokers Wild in the Lab," *Psychology Today* 4 (1970): 18-24.

60.   R. G. Arnold, "The Interview in Jeopardy: A Problem in Public Relations," *Public Opinion Quarterly* 28 (1964): 119-23.

61.   E. Maynard, "The Growing Negative Image of the Anthropologist Among American Indians," *Human Organization* 33 (1974): 402-4.

62.   Statement issued to the Australian Institute of Aboriginal Studies under the code name of Eaglehawk and Crow. I am indebted to Dr. Maria Brandl of Australia for bringing this and related documentation to my attention.

63.   L. J. Stricker, S. Messick, and D. N. Jackson, "Suspicion of Deception: Implications for Conformity Research," *Journal of Personality and Social Psychology* 5 (1967): 379-89; and "Evaluating Deception in Psychological Research," *Psychological Bulletin* 71 (1969): 343-51.

64.   Ibid. and P. S. Gallo, S. Smith, and S. Mumford, "Effects of Deceiving Subjects upon Experimental Results," *Journal of Social Psychology* 89 (1973): 99-107.

65.   MacIntyre, "Risk, Harm, and Benefit Assessments."

4

Justifying Social Science Research in Terms of Social Benefit

GORDON BERMANT

This chapter is about social science research and, in particular, why public financial support for it is inevitably and appropriately problematic. To my considerable surprise, I have found it most useful to begin with a brief account of an expedition by American astronomers during the Revolutionary War. Following that, I discuss other topics that may initially strike readers as quite irrelevant to the major themes. There is a chance that the veil of obscurity will not dissipate before the reader's patience does. Therefore I provide in the next paragraph a synopsis of the main points along the way to my conclusions.

There is a tradition that science transcends politics, even war between nations. But historical developments in industrial technology, science, and government have diminished the independence of science from politics. The scientific elite and their expert knowledge have become less trustworthy in the eyes of numerous critics. A valid conception of *social benefit* must allow for the current pluralism of strong views about the value of science and technology in society; a definition of social benefit is proposed in this essay to meet that criterion. The distinction between pure and applied research, which is important in assessing the social benefit of research, is also defined. The benefits of the sciences are described in relation to religion and ethics, commerce, and exploration. Given a pluralism of strong views about the social benefits of science, government funding of research is, inevitably, determined through political processes that are overdetermined and not completely rational. This characteristic does not necessarily discredit the processes as a way of deciding about the support of social science research. For, whatever its flaws, the legislative process does express the prevailing public conception of social benefit. The legislator's dilemma is to act on principle without alienating the constituency. The bureaucrat's dilemma is to honor the legislative mandate without restricting freedom of inquiry. The scientist's dilemma is to find support for research without misrepresenting it. For some social science, perhaps the most important, the scientist's obligation is not to justify public support, but to reject it.

State Support of Astronomy during the Revolutionary War

In 1780, John Hancock, acting in his capacity as speaker of the House of Representatives in Massachusetts, wrote a remarkable letter to the commander of the British forces at Penobscot Bay.[1] Hancock's letter requested safe passage across the bay for the Reverend Samuel Williams and his party, of Harvard University, who wished to sail to an island for the purpose of observing a total eclipse of the sun predicted for October 27 of that year. The terms and justification of the request were brief and forthright:

> If he [Williams] shd. judge your Post or any other place within your Command most suitable for making his observations, it is not doubted that as a Friend of Science, you will not only give him yr. permission for that purpose, but every assistance in your power to render the observations as perfect as possible. Though we are politically enemies, yet with regard to Science it is presumable we shall not dissent from the practise of civilized people in promoting it either in conjunction or separately as occasions for it shall happen to offer.

Though Britian and America were fully at war, the British honored the request, and Williams's expedition proceeded into enemy territory without interference.

Hancock's letter was the consequence of an affirmative vote by the legislature to provide the Williams expedition with the supplies it requested, including transportation on a publicly owned ship. The observations of the eclipse were thus made possible by a direct government grant. Further, the grant was made on the basis of a petition to the legislature which outlined the goals and listed the benefits expected from the research. The first benefit was an improved reckoning of the dates of "ancient transactions." Observations of eclipses "have been applied with great advantage by Divines in determining ye important point of the Christian era." The second benefit was improvement in calculations of longitude and predictions of the positions and phases of the moon. "With these last two objects navigation, and of consequence, commerce, must always be very nearly connected." And as a final benefit, the petition noted that a total solar eclipse had not yet been seen in that part of America and that another opportunity would not occur for many years; the current opportunity should not be lost.

Society and the Definition of Social Benefit

Hancock's appeal to the British is based on a "practise of all civilized people" to support science. Obviously, he placed both the British and the Americans within that class. It hardly needs stating that the Americans were still British in many ways, so that the sense of community to which Hancock appealed was very strong. The research and its results could be appreciated by both sides as a continuation of their shared heritage which advanced common interests. Presumably, Hancock might have made the same appeal to the French, had they been the enemy and in control of Penobscot Bay, for the French heritage contained a similar scientific tradition. It is likely that a French officer would also have granted the request. On the other hand, it is not likely that Hancock would have directed an appeal on these grounds to the commander of an Algonquin war party, had such a group controlled access to Penobscot Bay. The New England colonists considered the local Indians to be "potential Christians"; they would not have included them among the already civilized people to whom appeals could be made for the primacy of science over warfare.[2]

These hypotheticals clarify a sense of the word *social* as I want to use it in the phrase "social benefit." In this sense, a *social* benefit is an activity or product that is cherished, respected, or otherwise approved within a particular historical tradition. What makes the activity or product a *benefit* is the repeated affirmation of its value by established groups within a society—often, but not always, associated with other leadership roles, be they poets, politicians, priests, or professors. Other members of society may or may not participate in the activity or consume the product, but they will have been exposed, at least, to the idea that the activity or product is to be respected and supported.

The society in which something counts as a social benefit may be, but need not be, closely tied to other boundaries or divisions between groups of persons, such as language differences or national borders. There is a sense of "society," for example, that implies material, cultural, and educational advantage, whose members are influential in the preservation and transmission of traditions close to home and are also likely to be acquainted with, and influenced by, similar persons living in other places and speaking other languages. In European history, for example, the ubiquity of Latin usage among the intellectual elite facilitated a community of traditions across national and ethnic boundaries.

Having defined social benefit by reference to historical traditions, I must note immediately that there is more than one tradition of ideas with claims about the benefits of science and scholarship. On the grand historical scale, there is a tradition that exalts the free pursuit of scholarship and another that subordinates intellectual pursuit in favor of the quest for equality and justice. Lewis Feuer identifies the two traditions as Hellenic and Hebraic, claiming that

> The Bible, the book of the masses, is the supreme anti-intellectual book. It has stirred the people with . . . its demand for justice . . . [but it] begins with curses against Adam for seeking knowledge, and it ends with populist prophets denouncing the culture of the cities. . . . Plato and Aristotle exalted the sciences and pure knowledge, but though they wrote of justice they were moved by no sympathy for the slaves and the downtrodden. . . . The values of free science were born in Hellenism, the values of equality and justice in Hebraism. This has been history's dualism.[3]

The dualism is maintained today, though I am not prepared to trace unbroken lines from Socrates and the Bible. Don K. Price, for example, argues that the close link between physical science and technology has been overemphasized as a rationale for government support of pure science. He wonders, rhetorically, if "it would have been more ethical (and indeed more effective) for scientists to present their case for special support on a frankly elitist basis, affirming the value of basic knowledge in its own right, even though this value would never be shared by the average voter?"[4]

As if in deliberate response to Professor Price's question, the Belgian physicist Georges Thill argues that claims for special treatment are based on an illusion of scientific autonomy. Scientists have become, "like it or not, accomplices of the industrial ideology." Claims for elite status serve only to foster the industrial ideology against other theories of social and political organization, and are unjust:

> The scientists, or rather a large majority of them, honor the confidence the industrial ideology has in them by professing their insularity. . . . When they believe that they carry out research which is autonomous and irreducible by nature, they are victims of the ideology which conceals the relation between sciences and politics, which hinders them from seeing that the sciences are also action (critique and/or manipulation).[5]

A variation on Thill's theme could be heard a dozen years earlier when Theodore Roszak described the position held by countercultural Americans in 1968:

> If we are foolishly willing to agree that experts are those whose role is legitimized by the fact that the technocratic system needs them in order to avoid falling apart at the seams, then of course the technocratic status quo generates its own internal justification: the technocracy is legitimized because it enjoys the approval of experts; the experts are legitimized because there could be no technocracy without them.[6]

The intensity of countercultural expression has diminished. Yet strong opposition remains against definitions of progress made solely in terms of high technology. The resulting tensions are expressed, for example, in arguments over how Americans should meet, and change, our requirements for energy.

To summarize, I have defined a social benefit as an activity or product that is cherished, respected, or otherwise valued within an historical tradition. We are the inheritors of traditions that differ markedly in their valuations of expert knowledge, science, and technology. The prevailing tradition confers a special status on science that is validated, in large part, by scientific contributions to technology and social progress. Other traditions, with religious or political rationales, do not similarly respect expert scientific knowledge and its products.

My definition of social benefit differs greatly from the meaning of the term in economics, where, as I understand, it refers to external economies of a transaction, as distinguished from the external diseconomies or social costs of the transaction.[7] As economists use it, social benefit is one term in a calculus that is constrained by substantial normative and empirical assumptions, which are themselves disputed between different traditions in economics and politics. To use the economist's sense of the term here would cripple our effort. Economics is currently the most powerful of the social sciences. We should like to know whether its theories, predictions, and applications are worth pursuing and supporting. We cannot do that by relying on definitions of key concepts that are *internal* to economics, but need instead an independent approach to describing its worth to society.

Pure Science, Applied Science, and the Justification of Public Support

I have already noted that the Reverend Mr. Williams's grant request listed three social benefits to be expected from his research. Each of these benefits remains in some modified form plausible as a potential characteristic of scientific research, including that in the social sciences. Williams's list will therefore serve as a useful framework for discussing contemporary justifications of social science research.

Science in Relation to Religion and Ethics

The first benefit on the list was an improved ability to fix the dates of historical events, the life of Jesus in particular. Placing science in the service of religious history was, apparently, a significant, socially approved argument in favor of the research. It was not, however, a novel argument. The service offered to Christianity by the Reverend Mr. Williams was relatively minor and technical, when compared with the role astronomy had played in philosophy and theology during the preceding centuries. It had been 250 years since Copernicus published his heliocentric theory, only 150 years since Galileo had been called to account by the Inquisition for supporting Copernican theory in a book for nonspecialists, and just slightly longer since Kepler published his three laws and, in the account of Arthur O. Lovejoy, analogized the Sun to the Father, the sphere of the fixed stars to the Son, and the intermediate planetary volume to the Holy Ghost.[8] Still more recently, Newton had spent the majority of his publishing career laboring over theological matters and relating them to the physical sciences.

New answers to the old question about the location of our planet in the universe opened the door for intensified speculation about human significance in relation to God, heaven, hell, and other sentient creatures in the universe. It may be true, as Professor Lovejoy argues, that the major innovations in philosophy and theology of those times were not dependent upon the Copernican theory.[9] But this is a historian's argument that takes full advantage of hindsight. During the period itself, I think, neither the purveyors, the consumers, nor the censors of revolutionary ideas would have made such scholarly distinctions.

Thus, there have been times when the connection between science and theology was closer than it now appears to be.[10] New observations and theories in astronomy could facilitate or force challenges to traditional conceptions of our relationship to God. This influence was an ultimate application of science, challenging society's most fundamental beliefs. It is a prime example of what I will mean, in general, by applied science, which is the influence of science on the lives or work of nonspecialists, given the efforts of engineers and explicators. The difference between basic (pure) and applied science, at any time, is the extent of the influence of the science on nonspecialists.

Two additional interrelated attributes of scientific work also contribute to the distinction between basic and applied science. One is the time horizon of applicability: how long will it be before the research will be influential? The other is the intention of the scientists: to what extent are they pursuing an inquiry totally internal to their discipline, instead of conducting the work with applications in mind? Of course an individual scientist or a research team may be working with combinations of intentions. Moreover, there is no necessary connection between scientists' intentions and the usefulness of their scientific products. But when contributing to applications is part of the scientists' plan, the scientists serve as the explicators of their own work and hasten the appreciation of it by others.

These measures of applied science could be brought to bear on other great scientific achievements, for example the theory of evolution by natural selection. No one doubts that social and political consequences followed from the publication of *The Origin of Species* in 1859 and *The Descent of Man* in 1871. I suppose one might argue in this case, as Professor Lovejoy did in the earlier one, that there are only loose analogical links between evolutionary theory and new programs for guiding human behavior. But one would at least be obliged to have the argument with Edward O. Wilson, who suggests, after overwhelming his reader with 561 pages of evolutionary biology, that "scientists and humanists should consider together the possibility that the time has come for ethics to be removed temporarily from the hands of the philosophers and biologicized."[11] Indeed, philosophers and nonphilosophers alike have taken up the challenge of sociobiology, thereby demonstrating its potency as applied science even as they argue to deny it. For, as Lovejoy says at the conclusion of *The Great Chain of Being,* "the utility of a belief and its validity are independent variables; and erroneous hypotheses are often avenues to truth."[12]

Behavioral scientists have also made explicit claims on the turf of the moral philosopher. A sustained and highly publicized example of this intellectual imperialism was B. F. Skinner's argument in *Walden Two* (1948) and *Beyond Freedom and Dignity* (1971).[13] The first book, a novel of ideas, describes life and decision making in a community that is run according to principles that

Professor Skinner extrapolated from studies of animals behaving under highly controlled laboratory conditions. The cultural implications of behaviorist principles are discussed further in the second book, which also contains a critique of the traditional language of values. The book was widely, and heatedly, reviewed when it appeared. Its lasting impact on moral, social, or political thought, i.e., its value as applied science, remains to be discerned.

Now, at last, I can ask two questions about social science, though the answers must be deferred still longer. The questions are these: Given the conceptions of pure and applied science developed here, what is the social benefit of pure social science? Indeed, what would pure social science be?

Science and Commerce

The second social benefit the Reverend Mr. Williams offered the legislature was an enhancement of commerce through improved navigation. This was an appealing justification in the context of eighteenth-century values, and similar projects are still welcomed today, particularly if they offer commercial competitors equal advantage. Federal and state governments spend a great deal of money on the engineering and construction of wider highways, new and deeper waterways, improved air safety control systems, and so on. Research in support of any of these programs—for example, on local geology or new guidance systems—would bear the same relation to commerce that Reverend Williams's expedition did. Another example will also be familiar: publicly supported research on the causes and predictability of earthquakes is justifiable as a response to proposals for the siting of nuclear power stations.

The triangular connection between commerce, government, and science suggested by these examples becomes a matter of dispute when there is no consensus on the social benefits promoted or degraded by the relationship. Illustrations include public research policy on the development of alternative sources of energy, government-supported agricultural research that allegedly favors concentrated agribusiness, and genetic research leading to patentable life forms. A case study of any of these would reveal strongly conflicting theories of social benefit, each supporting a different proposal for aligning the interests of government, business, and research. There is another element to disputes involving commerce that adds further complexity to their resolution. Obviously enough, at least some of the parties to the dispute have considerable sums at stake in it, and they naturally tend to act to protect their investments. Disagreements expressed in terms of social benefit may be camouflage to cover competition over narrower financial interests. It is not uncommon in such circumstances for one disputant to present an argument to which the other disputants would concede, were investments not at stake. Nor will the "investments" at issue always be those of corporate capital and expenditure. For example, a farm worker, as a consumer, benefits from reduced food prices. The worker also understands that applied genetic research on tough-skinned tomatoes and engineering research on automated tomato pickers will, other things being equal, reduce the price of tomatoes at the market. But this benefit to the worker as consumer is hardly worth the cost of losing his or her job picking tomatoes by hand. In such a situation, the worker is unlikely to consider the research straightforwardly justifiable, especially if it is undertaken at a state tax-supported university that is also heavily financed by federal grants and contracts. Government research in this situation is disputable not because the applied science is poor or wasteful, but precisely because it is effective and "economical."

Where does social science fit in the connections between science, commerce, and government? Even a preliminary answer requires analysis of social science into its disciplines—what one says about economics is not what one would say about comparative ethnology. And even the briefest treatment of a discipline should acknowledge that it comprises several theories and areas of emphasis: in economics, for instance, there are neoclassical and Marxian theories, marcro and micro levels of analysis, monetary and fiscal issues, and so on. But constraints of space, and the even more serious limitations of my competence, require rapid progress to two assertions that are, I think, indisputable: first, government acts in important ways to stimulate and regulate commerce. Second, among social scientists, professional economists in particular are involved, increasingly, in guiding these actions of government.

The Federal Reserve System interest rate is one prominent example of the sort of intervention I have in mind; the structure of tax systems is another. Every consumer, worker, investor, and entrepreneur has a stake in the skill with which government makes decisions in these areas. If economic theory gives valid guidance to decision making, then public support of research in economics is a sound public investment.

Some economists claim that their theories are universally applicable; other economists dispute this contention.[14] There are many factions among the economists who advise on government policy. Their disagreements raise appropriate doubts about the independence of economics from strong political, psychological, and moral suppositions. Economics is touted by some of its practitioners as the queen of the social sciences, and perhaps it is. But nonspecialists are bound to wonder, as they labor to reconcile conflicting prescriptions from economists for the cure of stagflation, whether the queen is wearing the emperor's new clothes.

The important issue here, I believe, is what a lack of consensus among economists on policy issues implies about the social benefit of economic research and the justifiability of public funding for it. Part of that issue can be resolved simply. Not all applications of economics in government are controversial. Input-output analysis, for example, presumably clarifies relationships between resources and products for private and public planning. Improvement in the analytic method through research is like sharpening a useful tool, and can properly be paid for on that basis. But what about economic research that is either clearly influenced by partisan political theory, or, alternatively, is not related to any matter in the world that a nonspecialist can appreciate? This question, like the two at the end of the preceding section, will be addressed at the chapter's conclusion.

Rare Events, Unusual Places: Science and Exploration

The third and last benefit on the Reverend Mr. Williams's list appealed as much to historians' as to scientists' values. Williams desired to make the first report of total solar occlusion observed in that region, and thirty years would pass before another opportunity would arise.

There is an appeal to the observation and description of rare events that goes beyond the pleasures and applications of systematic science. Rare events naturally arouse scientific curiosity, because they seem to challenge the normal order of things. Once subjected to scientific investigation, rare events have different sorts of fates. Some become comprehensible and predictable within a theory, like eclipses. Others, like earthquakes, volcanic eruptions, and meteorites striking the earth, are not strictly predictable, but their capriciousness does not weaken our trust in the correctness of the scientific frameworks through which we study them. A third class of rare event, perhaps peculiar to science, is the new or anomalous observation that was previously unseen or unattended to because prevailing theory could not encompass it. Anomalous events of this sort have been crucial in the development of sciences as diverse as physics and experimental psychology.[15] Once seen and rationalized, the rare or anomalous can become the common or expected. Still another class of rare event is the vanishing opportunity, for example, to observe the behavior of many species of large African mammals before their numbers and habitats are irrevocably destroyed by the growth and exploitation of the human population. A fifth class of rare event, very useful to science, are the extremes of natural populations: geniuses and idiots, dwarfs and giants, neonates and centenarians. Sixth and finally, there are events, reported as miracles, that are offered by some people and rejected by others, as defying or transcending scientific explanation altogether.

The rarity of a class of objects or events is a characteristic of its frequency or duration relative to the time frame of human observation. The spatial analogue of the rare event is the unusual place. We are heir to a long tradition of valuing travel to unusual places: The more distant they are, the more interesting they become. Explorers have been admired for their courage and audacity; they have been rewarded for the commerce they stimulated and the riches they plundered; and they have been esteemed for their accounts of their travels. Years of the *National Geographic,* carefully arranged at home on bookshelves containing as well only a Bible and *Readers' Digest Condensed Books,* provide quiet testimony to the social benefit Americans ascribe to the explorations and accounts of distant places. There is an abiding sense that these things matter; they enrich the lives of oneself and one's children.

What have rare events and unusual places to do with social science, and vice versa? The answer comes, in part, from an appreciation of the close connection between the description of particulars—including those which are most rare and exotic among the data of our experience—and the discovery of generalities. Whatever aspirations we may have for the systematic rigor and generality of the social sciences, we should remain attentive to the benefits provided by careful descriptions of rare events and unusual places. The continuation of exotic field work in anthropology is a case in point. As described elsewhere in this book, great sensitivity is required to pursue ethnography with the appropriate balance of scholarly detachment and adherence to the norm of reciprocity in social relations. The message here is that the work has a strong claim, as a social benefit, that establishes the basis for its public support.

Government's Decisions about Scientific Research

To this point in the chapter I have treated "government" as if it were an undifferentiated entity. Of course this is false, and in more ways than one. The ideas in the remainder of the chapter are based on quite a different, more accurate portrayal of government and its role in scientific research, social science in particular.

First, consider the bulk and variety of research conducted or supported by the federal government. During fiscal year 1979, for example, the federal government expended 3.833 billion dollars for university research, ranging from traditional grants to broad institutional support programs.[16] These funds were channeled through more than a dozen agencies both inside cabinet departments (e.g., NIH, within what is now the Department of Health and Human Services, and AID, within the State Department) and independent of them (e.g., NSF, EPA, NASA). In addition to academic research, there are federally supported research programs conducted in profit and nonprofit research organizations. Finally, the government conducts its own research programs in a number of natural and social scientific fields. Though regularization of funding procedures is effected through the operation of the Office of Management and Budget, great variety in research direction and emphasis remains.

Second, consider how the language of legislation, including appropriations, is translated by government employees (bureaucrats) into regulations, standards, guidelines, and other decision-making apparatus and criteria. There is some bureaucratic discretion at every stage of the translation process; out of this comes a variety of approaches to the conduct of the government's business, in research as in everything else.

The British physicist John Ziman has described differences between patterns of organization of scientific research establishments in France, Britain, and the United States:

> In France the scheme is rational and centralized, like the whole French government machine; in Britain it is empirical, opportunist and greatly dependent on the personal linkages between the top people in various spheres of influence; in the United States it is pluralistic and competitive, reflecting the division of power between semi-autonomous agencies and corporations.[17]

The idea of American pluralism, with its competition between conflicting conceptions of social value and benefit, emerged earlier in the chapter; here it reappears in the structure of the American research establishment.

Government's Obligations to Science

In his illuminating constitutional analysis of the scientist's right to conduct research, John A. Robertson states that the first duty of government is "the negative duty not to interfere" with the scientist's choices of research ends and means.[18] The negative duty corresponds to the scientist's right to determine the topics and methods of investigation. Neither the duty nor the right is absolute. The government's scope of legitimate interference is greater in regard to research methods, particularly the treatment of human subjects, than to research topics. Government's lawful authority to forestall publication of research results is limited to very narrow grounds.

The ultimate expression of the government's negative duty to science would be, I suppose, for the the government to eliminate its support of science altogether. This extreme position has been advocated by economists Milton and Rose Friedman, who call for elimination of the National Science Foundation, the National Institutes of Health, and the National Endowment for the Humanities, as well as discontinuation of all federal support of arts and higher education.[19] The Friedmans' position does not reflect disaffection with science, but rather disdain for the ability of government to support good science economically. The Friedmans believe that private enterprise would pick up the bill for the basic work now supported by the government. In addition to being more efficient, they argue, private funding would be fairer, particularly to the low-income taxpayer. The Friedmans' proposals have been criticized by former astronaut and now Senator Harrison Schmitt (R.—N.M.). While granting that excessive public support can inhibit private research enterprise and stifle academic freedom, Senator Schmitt argues that the proposed reforms will lead us into deeper trouble: "To advocate the abolishment of the National Science Foundation (NSF), the National Institutes of Health (NIH), and federal support of higher education is like treating brain tumors with a guillotine."[20]

It is difficult for me to imagine strong physical and biological science in this country without support from NSF and NIH. I do not share the Friedmans' optimism that other sources of funding would be forthcoming, and I reject the tautology that work that cannot find private support is not worth doing. Much of behavioral and social science also depends currently on public support. It is even more difficult for me to imagine private sources providing support for much of this work, dissertation research in cultural anthropology for example. It appears, given the budgetary aspirations of the administration of President Reagan, that we will have an opportunity to observe the consequences of reduced support for the social sciences.

Social science presents additional dimensions of concern in respect to public funding; these are the focus of the chapter's conclusion.

Government's Authority over Science

The government's authority to specify the content, method, and published form of research increases markedly when the research is supported by public money. Robertson puts the matter succinctly:

> The constitutional right to research will seldom protect against the power of the purse. That power allows the government to choose the science it wishes to sponsor and the knowledge it wishes to produce. . . . Here the first amendment right to research is no help to the scientist who wants both government funds and total discretion on how to use them.[21]

Though this passage accurately describes the legal consequences of public funding of research, it may seem to imply, inaccurately, that there is a monolithic, remote, or authoritarian government in control of science. One example that helps to correct a perception of government as Leviathan is the heavy reliance placed on reviews and recommendations by academic and industrial scientists for grants made by the NSF and NIH. In the case of NSF, the regular ad hoc and peer panel review procedures are supplemented by the appointment of "rotating" program and division directors. These individuals assume substantial administrative and policy responsibilities within the Foundation during their tenure of, say, two years, then return to their parent institutions. The direct influence on Foundation policy of the communities served by it is thus continuously sustained and periodically refreshed.

Legislation and the Legislator's Dilemma

Article I, Section 9, paragraph 7, of the Constitution defines the law and codifies the morality required in the stewardship of public funds: "No Money shall be drawn from the Treasury, but in Consequence of Appropriations made by Law; and a regular Statement and Account of the Receipts and Expenditures of all public Money shall be published from time to time." The morality of this position will be accepted as axiomatic, I hope: People entrusted with other people's money ought not to distribute it except in accordance with the procedures, and for purposes, agreed on in advance. The apparatus of representative democracy, especially the authorization and appropriations processes, are the tools we use to determine how public money is to be spent.

A wise and thoughtful judge, who has also served in Congress and the executive branch, characterizes the life and temper of the legislator as follows:

> Variety, breadth, respect, and influence on the one hand; lack of time, depth, privacy, security, and serenity on the other. Only Faust could appreciate the trade. . . . One does not ask of a legislator: Is he or she brilliant? Is he an expert? Is he systematic and well-organized? Is he objective? But, rather: Where does he stand? Does he work for the people? How effectively does he foresee, understand, and discuss issues? Can he ferret out common interests and mobilize diverse groups to support socially valuable goals?[22]

What is striking about this description is just how different, even opposed, are the requirements and rewards of the legislator and the scientist. If Judge Coffin's description is correct, the expression *antilegislator* would accurately characterize the contrasting norms of scientists: scientists are expected to be brilliant experts with systematic habits and objective standards of judgment. Is it any wonder, then, that scientists and legislators misunderstand each other more often than either would wish? But there is more to the relation of legislation and science than differences between model personalities, and what remains is of greater ethical and practical significance.

In a particular and important sense for science and research, the legislative process is not rational. By this I do not mean that it is irrational, nor that it cannot be rationalized, i.e., explicated and understood. I mean, rather, that bills become law, or do not, for all kinds of reasons, only some of which have to do with the merits of what the bills propose. To take a crass but clear example, a bill authorizing the construction in some district of a marina, or a courthouse, or a postoffice, may pass *because* the legislator representing that district is retiring, and his colleagues wish to pay tribute to him. The Congress is remarkably frank in avowing this sort of reason for spending public money, in part no doubt because of confidence that it could provide a more "rational" justification for the expenditure if pressed to do so: the district needed its marina or courthouse. Another example is the trading of votes, where a legislator votes against his or her inclination on one bill, to gain a similar concession from a colleague on another bill. More serious examples are easily cited.[23] In general, a number of factors will contribute to the nonrationality of the process, including venality, special interest, and the need to compromise: what is reasonable is not necessarily rational, and vice versa. Legislation is almost always overdetermined; that is, it is the product of numerous causes or intentions, of which one or several may be used as justifications at the convenience of a legislator who is called upon to provide them.

Congressional oversight of governmental activities is also an overdetermined activity, and one that has recently been of particular concern to behavioral and social scientists. The Supreme Court's decision in *Hutchinson v. Proxmire* appears to have clarified, and perhaps diminished, the scope of legitimate congressional criticism of publicly funded research.[24] But, in any event, the publicity and influence wielded by the Golden Fleece awards are blunt instruments compared with the razor-like precision with which particular projects may be sliced out of a budget. Consider, for example, what happened to the proposal of Professor Harris B. Rubin of Southern Illinois University to study effects of marijuana on male sexual response to erotically explicit films. The sensitivity of the public to the topic was well understood by Rubin and the NIMH, so they took every precaution in following the proper procedures for peer review, legal authorizations, and so on. Funding was granted in June 1975. Subsequent editorial comment on the project was mixed; two St. Louis newspapers took opposing positions. The controversy came to the attention of Rep. Robert Michel (R.—Ill.), who eventually introduced a provision into the DHEW Appropriations Bill of April 13, 1976, that prohibited further funding for the research and demanded return of the funds already awarded. The House did not debate the provision, but the Senate Appropriations Committee did, on May 12, 1976. Senator Hathaway of Maine offered an amendment to remove the provision, arguing that Congress ought not to intervene in the established scientific review process. Though his view received vocal support from other senators, his amendment failed.[25]

This is a useful example in two respects. First, it illustrates the conflict I mentioned above between the conceptions of social benefit purveyed by competing traditions in our pluralistic culture. Providing a justification for paying men, with tax dollars, to strap on a penile plethysmograph and watch erotic films while inhaling a controlled substance is, to say the least, not the easiest task on a scientist's agenda. Not easy, but not impossible either. There is a justification, and Rubin made it successfully to the NIMH. It was, however, a justification containing normative and empirical assumptions that are not shared by the general public, even though they are acceptable and even routine in scientific and medical communities. The response in the Congress was argued for in terms of social benefits that are much closer to mainstream American traditions than to those of the scientific research community. Even Senator Hathaway's argument was procedural rather than substantive. Few legislators could afford to support Rubin's work during public debate without fear of alienating their constituencies. This is often the legislator's dilemma.

The example is also useful as an illustration of the way intragovernmental disagreement can reflect conflicts between competing traditions of value and benefit. Here, the broader conflict is played out by the legislative and executive branches (the latter represented by NIMH in this case). Such disagreement is especially significant for science and the ethics of research, and it leads to a dilemma for the responsible bureaucrat.

The Bureaucrat's Dilemma

As the final part of the present volume clearly indicates, the language of legislation always requires interpretation in regulations, standards, guidelines, and the other procedural paraphernalia of the executive branch; and all these, in turn, must be interpreted by those who must conform to their stipulations. The aims of Congress may be gleaned from legislative histories as well as from the language of the law itself, but it remains an elementary fact of government that congressional intent is open to interpretation by executive agencies and the courts. The scope of interpretation, or discretion, depends on the specificity of the legislative language, which in turn will depend on congressional confidence in its own substantive expertise. For example, the terms of Title I of the Speedy Trial Act of 1974 are much more explicit and operational than the language of the law that established the National Science Foundation.[26] There are many more lawyers than scientists in the Congress and on congressional staffs; it is not surprising to find greater specificity in legislation pertaining to legal issues.

The bureaucrat in a science-funding agency is likely to be trained in science and sensitive to the theories of value and social benefit accepted pervasively among scientists. The bureaucrat is also bound, morally and legally, to carry out the legislative mandate as interpreted by the agency. The task of the bureaucrat, which sometimes presents a dilemma, is simultaneously to honor both the legislative or executive mandate *and* the norms of the scientific community. When the Congress and the scientists invoke the same standards (for example, ones that justify the construction and operation of a new telescope or particle accelerator), the bureaucrat's job is not morally problematic. When, however, congressional intent and scientific norms clash, the bureaucrat faces a difficult task, which is to weigh the worth of the research according to the conflicting conceptions of social benefit, act on the result, and accept the consequences (including those that threaten the agency's budget).

The Scientist's Dilemma

The scientist, like the bureaucrat, may face dilemmas posed by competing traditions of social benefit. Consider, for example, a scientist who wishes to pursue a line of basic research in biochemistry. The research is expensive, and funds are unavailable from private sources or public agencies that fund basic research directly. Money is available, however, from a federal agency that requires justification of the research in terms of its potential contribution to medicine. The scientist may be able to fashion a medical justification for the research, but he or she knows that the justification iş speculative and shallow. It is, at least partially, a cover story to justify work that cannot find support on its merits as basic research. The scientist's dilemma in this example is to choose between doing the work under speculative and perhaps partially false pretenses, and not doing it at all. Unlike the legislator who, for later advantage, votes for a bill he or she in fact opposes, the scientist has no procedural norm to justify this deceit.

The morally responsible social scientist has a special problem relating to government and public money. Everything written so far in this chapter has been structured to set a context for appreciating what the problem is. Clearly stating the problem is the aim of the conclusion of the chapter.

Conclusion: Justifying Public Funding of Social Science Research in Terms of Social Benefit

I have defined social benefits as activities or products that are cherished, respected, or otherwise approved within an historical tradition. I have distinguished applied science from basic (pure) science by the degree of influence the science has on the lives or work of nonspecialists, after the efforts of engineers and explicators. I have avoided an explicit definition of social science and any listing of the social sciences. Now I will define social science as *any systematic description or explanation of individuals, aggregates of individuals (however abstractly characterized), or activities of individuals or aggregates, in relation to each other.* This definition will, I trust, exclude nothing of interest. Certainly it includes everything normally considered to fall within the purview of traditional social science disciplines.

With these definitions in hand, I can return to the questions raised earlier in the chapter. The first two questions were these: What is the social benefit of pure social science, and, indeed, what would pure social science be? Taking the second question first, pure social science is, by definition, systematic description or explanation that, after efforts by explicators, remains without influence on the lives or work of everyone except the people who promulgated it. As to the first question, because pure social science is mute to nonspecialists, it speaks to no important traditions; i.e., it neither contains nor is relevant to any social benefit. Public funding of this research is, on this account, not justified. However, I must emphasize the following point about basic research: as I have defined it, quite a lot of applied social science research would be called pure or basic under previous usage. The clearest example is comparative ethnography, but I could supply others. I emphasize this because I am concerned that my position will otherwise be misunderstood as a denigration of all social research heretofore considered "pure." My position is far from that.

The third question raised earlier in the chapter was, what could be the justification for public funding of economic research that is based on disputed or partisan political theory or, alternatively, is based in no context at all to which the nonspecialist can relate? Again taking the second case first, if the work, after all attempts at explication, remains obscure to all but the specialists who produced it, then it neither contains a social benefit nor is contained within an important tradition. There is no basis for public support.

The question of partisan research, not only in economics but in any social science, is more interesting and important, and its answer less transparent. Important social science research will speak to important social issues. "Issues" here means matters of concern or contention. Matters become issues when people disagree about the way things are or should be. The appropriate standards or methods for resolving such issues are themselves sometimes subjects of dispute. Systematic efforts to describe or explain the first level issues may be accomplished without raising issues at the second or deeper level. In that case, social science may be applied without being partisan. Social science that investigates the criteria for resolving deeper issues is partisan. The most important social science may be the most partisan. Its importance—its influence on the lives of nonspecialists—stems precisely from its creation of the most serious challenges to existing traditions of value and belief.

At stake in the relation between social science and government are the issues of rights and responsibilities to influence social and political life through sytematic collection and dissemination of information. Conor Cruise O'Brien has noted that there are two great risks in research and scholarship: *revolutionary subordination,* in which research is performed completely in the service of a revolutionary cause; and *counterrevolutionary subordination,* in which research is performed completely in the service of the established order.[27] At the time of his writing, 1967, O'Brien believed that "the real danger" came from counterrevolutionary subordination. Regardless of how perspectives may have changed in the years since O'Brien expressed this view, his concern for the dark side of government funding for social science research should not be put aside in order to press the argument that social science receives inadequate public support.

The social scientist who explores the most important issues will, by definition, address conflicting theories of social benefit. If the research is partisan, i.e., based on controversial criteria for the resolution of first-order issues, it will approximate one or the other of the extreme conditions described by O'Brien. In either case, the position of the social scientist relative to the government's support of research is morally problematic. If the research intentionally represents "professionalized disrespect for the established order," a position some scholars advocate as the proper role of sociology,[28] its integrity will be less suspect if the researchers shun support from the order they disrespect. Similarly, if research supports increased government control over aspects of our lives now free from regulation, its authenticity, and the credibility of the scientists who conduct it, will be greater if it is in no way part of the government's research enterprise.

In the end, then, the question for social scientists aspiring to do the most important work, is not whether they *can* justify public support for their research, but whether they should try. In my view, they should not.

Epilogue.   I approached my main idea slowly and tried to surround it so that it would not elude me and, like the Cheshire cat, disappear, leaving behind only a derisory grin. The reader will decide whether I succeeded. I hope I have done a little better than the Reverend Mr. Williams, whose calculations about the point from which to observe the total eclipse were erroneous. He was never totally forthright in owning up to that. In 1788 he forged a receipt of repayment, and was subsequently forced to resign his Harvard professorship.

Notes

This chapter has been thoroughly rewritten twice since I presented the first draft at the conference in 1979. I am indebted to several colleagues, Michael Leavitt in particular, for their constructive criticism along the way. My primary debts are to the editors of this volume, especially Ruth Faden, for encouraging me to try again, and again, to get things right. The opinions I express are my own, not those of the Federal Judicial Center.

1. This account, and the quotations, are taken from Robert F. Rothschild, "What Happened in 1780?," *Harvard Magazine* 83 (January-February, 1981): 20-27.

2. Samuel E. Morison, Henry S. Commager, and William E. Leuchtenberg, *A Concise History of the American Republic* (New York: Oxford University Press, 1977), pp. 5-7.

3. Lewis S. Feuer, "Introduction," in *Basic Writings on Politics and Philosophy: Karl Marx and Friedrich Engels* (Garden City, N.Y.: Anchor Books, 1959), pp. xv-xvi.

4. Don K. Price, "The Ethical Principles of Scientific Institutions," manuscript prepared for Nobel Symposium No. 44, *Ethics for Social Policy* (Stockholm, August 21-25, 1978).

5. Georges Thill, "Democratic Control of the Sciences," *International Philosophical Quarterly* 20 (1980): 90–91.

6. Theodore Roszak, *The Making of a Counter Culture* (Garden City, N.Y.: Doubleday & Co., 1969), p. 207.

7. See, for example, "Externalities," in *The Harper Dictionary of Modern Thought* (New York: Harper & Row, 1977); C. E. Ferguson, *Microeconomic Theory* (Homewood, Ill.: Irwin, 1966), pp. 391-94; Lester C. Thurow, "Government Expenditures: Cash or In-Kind Aid?" in Gerald Dworkin, Gordon Bermant, and Peter Brown, *Markets and Morals* (Washington, D.C.: Hemisphere Publishing Corp., 1977), pp. 86-106; Richard A. Posner, *Economic Analysis of Law,* 2nd ed. (Boston: Little, Bown & Co., 1972), p. 18.

8. Arthur O. Lovejoy, *The Great Chain of Being* (New York: Harper Torchbooks, 1960), p. 106.

9. Ibid., p. 110.

10. There is still contention, however. See, for example, Dorothy Nelkin, *Scientific Textbook Controversies and the Politics of Equal Time* (Cambridge, Mass.: MIT Press, 1977).

11. Edward O. Wilson, *Sociobiology* (Cambridge, Mass.: Harvard University Press, Belknap Press, 1975), p. 562.

12. Lovejoy, *Great Chain of Being,* p. 333.

13. B. F. Skinner, *Walden Two* (New York: Macmillan, 1948); *Beyond Freedom and Dignity* (New York: Alfred A. Knopf, 1971).

14. E. K. Hunt, "The Normative Foundations of Social Theory: An Essay on the Criteria Defining Social Economics," *Review of Social Economy* 36 (1978): 285-309.

15. Thomas S. Kuhn, *The Structure of Scientific Revolutions,* 2nd ed., enl. (Chicago: University of Chicago Press, 1970), chapter 6; William A. Mason and Dale F. Lott, "Ethology and Comparative Psychology," *Annual Review of Psychology* 27 (1976): 129-54.

16. National Commission on Research, *Funding Mechanisms: Balancing Objectives and Resources in University Research* (Washington, D.C.: National Commission on Research, May 1980), p. 6

17. John Ziman, *The Force of Knowledge* (Cambridge: Cambridge University Press, 1976), p. 339.

18. John A. Robertson, "The Scientist's Right to Research: A Constitutional Analysis," *University of Southern California Law Review* 51 (1977): 1203-79. Robertson's conclusions are expanded to include other considerations in the final section of the present volume.

19. Milton Friedman and Rose Friedman, *Free to Choose: A Personal Statement* (New York: Harcourt Brace Jovanovich, 1980); Nicholas Wade, "Why Government Should Not Fund Science," *Science* 210 (1980): 33.

20. Harrison Schmitt, "The Federal Government's Role in Basic Research," *Science* 211 (1980): 226.

21. Robertson, "Scientist's Right to Research," p. 1279.

22. Frank M. Coffin, *The Ways of a Judge* (Boston: Houghton Mifflin Co., 1980), pp. 5-6.

23. See, for example, David B. Truman, *The Governmental Process* (New York: Alfred A. Knopf, 1958), chapter 12; Robert Sherrill, *Why They Call It Politics* (New York: Harcourt Brace Jovanovich, 1972), chapter 4.

24.   441 U.S. 111 (June 26, 1979).

25.   *Congressional Record, S7054-7057* (May 12, 1976). I thank Professor Harris Rubin for sending me other background documents.

26.   For the NSF, see Title 42 of the *United States Code,* sections 1861-1863, section 1862 in particular. The Speedy Trial Act and its various amendments are in Title 18 of the code, sections 3161-3174. See also Anthony Partridge, *Legislative History of the Speedy Trial Act of 1974* (Washington, D.C.: Federal Judicial Center, 1980).

27.   Conor Cruise O'Brien, "Politics and the Morality of Scholarship," in Max Black, ed., *The Morality of Scholarship* (Ithaca, N.Y.: Cornell University Press, 1967), pp. 59-74.

28.   James H. Laue, "Advocacy and Sociology," in G. H. Weber and G. J. McCall, eds., *Social Scientists as Advocates: Views from the Applied Disciplines* (Beverly Hills: Sage Press, 1978), p. 177; Laue is making reference to the position of Alvin Gouldner.

5

Does Risk-Benefit Analysis Apply to Moral Evaluation of Social Research?

JOAN CASSELL

At first glance, risk-benefit analysis seems appropriate to the moral evaluation of social research. Social research has been known to harm those studied and to benefit them, and, theoretically at least, potential harms could be analyzed and weighed against benefits. More interesting are the issues of whether such analysis is equally applicable to every variety of social research and, if so, how and when it should be applied.

These questions have not been asked by those who framed the HHS Regulations for the Protection of Human Subjects which at one time applied to almost every variety of biomedical, behavioral, and social research. These regulations require that "risk" to human subjects be weighed against "benefit" before research is carried out.

What Is a Subject?

Let us explore some implicit assumptions found in the HHS regulations and their interpretation by the National Commission for the Protection of Human Subjects of Biomedical and Behavioral Research. One way to examine these assumptions is to use the familiar sociological concept of *role* to analyze the term *subject*. Roles can be defined as "series of behavioral attributes, each with its peculiar content of aims, tasks, expectations, entitlements, obligations; relationships, in turn, referred to the constancies of behavior, still conceived

In partial consequence of the critical analyses presented at the 1979 Kennedy Institute conference on ethical issues in social science research, the Department of Health and Human Services issued a revised version of the human subject regulations in January 1981. As a result, some of the critical passages of the present essay have lost their relevance to contemporary issues in the politics of science and have become of historical interest. The nature of such essays makes it impossible to suspend them in time for purposes of book publication; nevertheless, I believe that the arguments and analyses developed herein have validity beyond the initial occasion for their writing.

with this kind of content, between people defined in role terms."[1] Some roles come in pairs; they are "relational" or "reciprocal": "thus, there can be no role called 'patron' unless it is opposed by the correlative role of 'client'."[2] One reason that a "human subject" is very different from a "human being" is that "subject" is a *role*. Conventionally, it is part of a reciprocal pair of roles: the role of "subject" being contraposed to the correlative role of "experimenter," with the appropriate set of reciprocal rights, obligations, entitlements, and behaviors. Linguistic confusion appears when "subject" is characterized outside of this reciprocity, for even when the term is scrupulously defined so that it applies to someone studied by a wide range of research methods (National Commission for the Protection of Human Subjects, 1978: pp. xx-xxi), those who use the *term* tend to gravitate toward a discussion of the *role* and the reciprocal relationship involved in that particular pair of roles.[3]

Research Roles and Relationships

Other reciprocal role relationships in social research are those between interviewer and respondent, ethnographer and informant, observer and observed. All involve particular relationships which differ significantly from one another.

Differences in research relationships become apparent when they are compared along four dimensions: (1) the relative power of the investigator as perceived by those studied;[4] (2) the relative magnitude of control over the research setting; (3) the relative magnitude of control over the context of research; and (4) the relative magnitude of control over research interaction (guiding the flow of interaction in one direction or two). The first two dimensions refer to the asymmetry (or parity) of the relationship; the second two, to the investigator's conceptual control, or narrowness of focus. Control over the context of research measures how many contextual features—physical, situational, cultural, and structural—are defined in advance as relevant, and how many are excluded. Narrowly focused research excludes, ignores, or controls for contextual features, while broadly focused research includes the context as well as the behavior.[5] Control over research interaction measures how many features of the interaction between investigator and investigated are defined in advance as relevant or irrelevant. Although interaction between researcher and researched inevitably flows in two directions, it is the investigator's conceptual control that determines how much of that interaction is included within the research paradigm. Narrowly focused research defines all but a limited number of responses by subjects as "irrelevant." Thus, the reactions of a subject to the personality, ethnic background, or loving attention of an experimenter—when these variables are not being studied—are considered "noise" to be controlled for. In narrowly focused research, significant interaction flows primarily in one direction, from the investigator, who applies stimuli, to the investigated, who produce responses. All other interaction is at worst "interference," and at best—as Gatsby said of Daisy's love for her husband—"merely personal."

I am now going to review several ideal typical forms of research, comparing the relationships in biomedical experimentation, psychological experimentation, survey research, fieldwork (ethnographic research), nonreactive observation, and secondary analysis of data. Table 5.1 summarizes my argument.

The relationship between *biomedical experimenters and subjects* provides the paradigm for recent HHS human subject regulations—and evidence indicates that these regulations were originally intended to apply solely to such research.[6] When research relationships are located upon a spectrum, using these four dimensions, biomedical experimentation occupies one extreme of the spectrum.[7] Experimenters are perceived as having great power by subjects, who frequently rely upon these physicians for medical care. The experimenters control the hospital or laboratory setting where research takes place. The investigators have high conceptual control; the research design controls for as much contextual interference and interpersonal variation as possible. As a result, the research interaction flows in one direction: experimenters act; subjects, or their diseases or physiologies, react.

The relationship between *psychological experimenters and subjects* subdivides into laboratory and field experiments. In laboratory experimentation, the investigator is perceived as having high-to-medium power. The experimenter controls the research setting and exerts high conceptual control, with a narrow focus on a limited number of relevant variables. In field experimentation, the perceived power of the investigator is medium to low; here, the researcher has no control over the research setting. The experimenter has less contextual control than in the laboratory; it is difficult to exclude or control completely for contextual features in the field. Control of interaction is comparatively high, however; the experimenter focuses narrowly on a limited number of relevant behaviors, although there is, perhaps, more possibility of "noise" than in a laboratory.

The relationship between *interviewer and respondent* must be examined separately for face-to-face and mail surveys. The perceived power of the face-to-face interviewer is comparatively low; the investigator has little ability to exact compliance or punish for noncompliance. The interviewer rarely controls the research setting. When structured and close-ended questionnaires are used, conceptual control is relatively high, since this technique preselects those contextual and interactive features considered important and minimizes or suppresses those considered irrelevant. Research interaction is, in effect, one-way: the interviewer applies verbal stimuli and those interviewed supply responses. Control over context and interaction is reduced when an open-ended questionnaire or an unstructured interview is used. The researcher who uses mail surveys has less perceived power than in a face-to-face situation, where charm or cajolery may elicit responses. Respondents control the

TABLE 5.1

Relationships between Investigators and Those Studied

	Biomedical Experimentation	Psychological Experimentation		Survey Research			Nonreactive Observation	Secondary Analysis of Data
		Lab	Field	Face-to-Face (structured close-ended)	Mail (structured close-ended)	Fieldwork (Participant Observation)		
Investigators' power as perceived by those studied	H	H-M	H-M	L	O	=	O	O
Investigators' control over research setting	H	H	O	O	negative (control by those studied)	negative (control by those studied)	O	O
Investigators' control over context of research	H	H	M	H-M	H-M	O	M-L	M-L
Investigators' control over research interaction (direction of interaction)	H I → S one-way	H I → S one-way	H-M I → S one-way	H-M I → S One-way	? I — S no interaction	= I ⇄ S two-way	? I — S no interaction	? I — S no interaction

I - Investigator
S - Those Studied
H - High
M - Medium
L - Low
= - Equal
O - None

research setting, and the investigator must rely upon the goodwill of the investigated to obtain data. With structured questionnaires, the investigator has fairly high control over the context of research. There is no interaction between investigator and investigated, but the research instrument exerts a relatively high control over interaction, with only a limited number of preselected responses defined in advance as relevant.

When we examine the relationship between *fieldworker and informant,* we find that the ethnographer has little power over those studied: informants are usually free to leave the situation or to decline interaction. Fieldwork is traditionally carried out over an extended period of time, in a setting controlled by those studied. As a result, the hosts may exert some power over the ethnographer, who may depend upon them for shelter, food, and protection.[8] The investigator's conceptual control is low. Contextual features cannot be controlled for or excluded; fieldwork is carried out amidst the "blooming buzzing confusion" of everyday life, with that confusion being part of the ethnographic data. Unlike other research relationships, few aspects of interaction are placed outside the fieldwork paradigm; instead, *the paradigm is based upon human interaction in all its richness, variety, and contradiction.* In consequence, it is frequently difficult to separate the human relationship from the research relationship; the role and the persona of the fieldworker are linked. Research interaction thus flows freely in two directions, with investigator and investigated participating on a comparatively equal basis. On some occasions it is the researcher, on others the researched, who initiates interaction, with the extent of participation determined by individual situations and personal predilections. Fieldworkers have their research agenda; areas of particular interest have been noted in advance, and they enter the field with a trained ability to initiate interaction and elicit information. This might be considered a type of conceptual control, but informants also have their own agenda, and frequently exhibit remarkable skills in elicitation.[9] The informant may well be playing a role in the fieldworker's script, but the researcher is often cast by informants in scenarios of their own. Contradictory definitions of the research enterprise and its relationship, by fieldworker and hosts, may lead to conflict or misinterpretation—but these contradictions can also lead to deeper understanding by the ethnographer of how informants organize and define reality. Compared with the asymmetrical, hierarchical, and limited role relationships between investigators and investigated in most varieties of research, the classic fieldwork relationship consists of meaningful encounters between humans in a real-life setting.[10] Fieldworkers are their own measuring instruments; interaction is their method.

In fieldwork, then, power is shared between ethnographers and their hosts, with those studied having somewhat more power to frustrate research than do researchers to compel them to participate. The hosts control the research setting, and investigators exert little control over the context of research or interaction.

The last two categories of research relationships occupy the end of our spectrum opposite the highly controlled biomedical experiment. For both the *nonreactive observer of public behavior* and the *investigator involved in secondary analysis of anonymous data,* there is limited control and no functioning relationship between researcher and researched. Because this absence of real interaction makes for few distinctive moral problems, I shall confine my subsequent discussion to the more substantive categories of role relationships in social science research.

Weighing Harms against Benefits

I have examined differences in the reciprocal roles of experimenter and subject, interviewer and respondent, fieldworker and informant, nonreactive observer and observed, and analyst and anonymous provider of secondary data. Similar differences are found when the risks associated with various types of research—or more accurately, the harms[11]—are weighed against benefits.

Thus, subjects of biomedical experimentation are exposed to a high probability of harm as well as a probability of serious harm. Potential benefits are also high: symptoms may be ameliorated, diseases cured, lives saved. Subjects of psychological experimentation are not exposed to the same degree of easily calculable harm as biomedical subjects, but then rarely do they stand to benefit to the same degree, although a larger class of individuals might possibily benefit and the findings may contribute to human knowledge.[12] Survey research would seem to have less potential for serious harm than biomedical or behavioral experimentation, with the greatest injury being violation of anonymity or confidentiality. The benefits to respondents are often less substantial than those of experimentation, with the greatest benefit accruing to science or human knowledge.

In the conduct of fieldwork, there is a comparatively minimal level of harm—again, primarily violation of anonymity or confidentiality. The most serious harms occur when findings are disseminated or published.[13] In this discussion, however, I am following the recommendations of the National Commission for the Protection of Human Subjects, and examining primarily the conduct, and not the consequences, of fieldwork. It may also be difficult to calculate the tangible benefits of fieldwork; these are primarily in correcting misperceptions about various groups and in advancing human knowledge.

The high perceived power of biomedical exprimenters and their control of the research setting facilitates coercion: subjects may find it difficult to refuse to take part in research or to request to leave an ongoing project. The high conceptual control of experimenters, leading to a narrow focus on relevant variables and a one-way flow of relevant interaction, facilitates prediction: biomedical researchers can predict with some reliability physical and psychological responses and side-effects. (The testing of products and procedures upon animal subjects increases predictability.) We have, then, a situation where there is a high potential for harm and benefit to subjects, a high possibility of coercion, and a fairly good chance of predicting what may occur. When investigators have the ability to cause serious harms, confer sizable benefits, strongly coerce and predict with some reliability, it makes good sense to require that harms be weighed against benefits before research takes place, and that subjects be informed of the harms and benefits to which they may be exposed, being allowed to decide for themselves whether they wish to participate.

As we move across the spectrum of research relationships, the power of the investigators and their control of the research setting diminish, minimizing their ability to coerce those studied to participate. The investigators' conceptual control—their control over the context of research and over research interaction—also diminishes, making it more difficult to predict what will occur during interaction. Because investigators at the far end of the spectrum have little ability to predict what is going to occur during the course of research interaction, it becomes close to impossible for them to secure "informed" consent before research is initiated.

As we move across the spectrum, then, calculable harms become less serious and benefits less immediate. In addition, those who stand to benefit from research frequently bear little relationship to those who run the risk of injury. In this situation, cataloging potential harms and weighing them against benefits before research is carried out becomes primarily an exercise in creativity, with little applicability to the real ethical difficulties that may emerge during the conduct of research. In research where the relationship between investigator and investigated is comparatively symmetrical, where the investigator has little ability to predict what will occur during interaction, and where harms and benefits are comparatively minimal, consequentialist risk-benefit calculations are neither effective nor appropriate for the moral evaluation of research.

A more useful framework for evaluating fieldwork might be founded on respect for autonomy based upon the fundamental principle that persons always be treated as ends in themselves, never merely as means—Kant's categorical imperative.[14] (In considering autonomy, Gerald M. Dworkin's formulation, that autonomy consists of authenticity plus independence, is helpful.[15] In this view, anything which threatens authenticity or diminishes independence violates the principle of autonomy.)

Before I compare this imperative with risk-benefit analysis, it would be helpful to examine ethnographic research in more detail. I have discussed fieldwork as though it were composed of a comparatively homogeneous set of interactions. Fieldwork can, however, be separated into a number of different relationships between ethnographer and informant, and these can be measured against the same dimensions used to examine the broader modes of research.

Varieties of Fieldwork

The relationship between ethnographer and hosts unfolds over time, growing and changing as do the participants. The relationship is social as well as professional, expressive as well as instrumental—or more accurately, we might say that the relationship is professionally social, instrumentally expressive. This gives field relationships a certain tension and ambiguity, leading some fieldworkers (and critics) to speak of ethnographers as hypocrites, or as "using people."[16] But it is rarely a matter of the fieldworker simply using people as a means to a predetermined research end. The interaction is mutual: each side uses and is used; each side gives as well as getting.[17]

Relationships between fieldworkers and informants differ in various types of ethnographic research. These too can be located on a spectrum, when measured against our four dimensions. Table 5.2 summarizes my argument.

At one extreme—and by now, historically obsolete in many parts of the

TABLE 5.2
Relationship between Fieldworkers and Informants

	Verandah Model	Noblesse Oblige	Going Native	Undercover Agent	Advocate
Fieldworkers' power as perceived by informants	H	H-M	L-O	O	H-M
Fieldworkers' control over research setting	H	M	L-O	L-O	L
Fieldworkers' control over context of research	H-M	L	L-O	L	M
Fieldworkers' control over research interaction (direction of interaction)	M-L F ⇄ I limited two-way	= F ⇄ I two-way	= F ⇄ I two-way	M F ⌢ I distorted	L-negative variable

Note: The varieties of fieldwork are rated relative to each other, and the categorizations are not comparable to those of Table 5.1.

F - Fieldworker
I - Informant
H - High
M - Medium
L - Low
= - Equal
O - None

world—is what Murray L. Wax and I have called the *verandah* model of fieldwork.[18] Think of the researcher, seated on the verandah of the government station, sending for a "native" who will be subjected to intense questioning about his—usually "his," not "her"—exotic language and customs. The modern version is carried out in prisons, mental hospitals, drug treatment centers, and other institutional settings, where inmates can be summoned to the office of the researcher for interrogation. This relationship is characterized by the relatively high perceived power of the researcher, comparatively high control of the research setting, medium-high contextual control—since interviews are employed rather than observation in a natural setting—and some control over interaction, since the situation is constrained (resulting in somewhat one-sided interaction).

Next is the *noblesse oblige* model, exemplified by the fieldworker who moves into a substantial residence, with a body of retainers, coming to play in local society the role of wealthy and influential *patron.* Although the classic version of the role is associated with the imperialist era of the European presence, it still can be played—and is on occasion expected by hosts—in many areas of the world. It works most easily when the fieldworker is able to establish a peer relationship with the local elite, and indeed in many situations it is difficult for a relatively wealthy, higher-status researcher not to be cast in such a role. The fieldworker, here, has high-to-medium perceived power, some control of the research setting, no contextual control, and little or no control over interaction, which flows freely in both directions.

In the next model, *going native,* the researcher tries in every conceivable fashion to adopt the way of life of the common people being studied, to live as they do, speak their language, and share their hardships. Such conduct is frequently hazardous, because the researcher is attempting to learn the role of a responsible adult—itself a time-consuming task—while at the same time conducting research and maintaining field notes. This role is most easily handled when the researcher is, or can be cast by those studied as, a "native," as I was when I studied the contemporary American women's movement.[19] The fieldworker here has little or no perceived power, little or no control of the setting, which is controlled by those studied, no control over the context of research or over interaction, which flows in two directions.

In the next model, the *undercover agent,* the ethnographer seeks to expose the activities of persons who are, for one reason or another, concealing important parts of their lives. This infiltration is described as "penetrating fronts" and "exposing the backstage." Undercover agents invent fraudulent identities for themselves and conceal the fact that they are doing fieldwork.[20] Undercover agents have little perceived power, but they have more power, because of their deceit, than is realized by those studied. They do not control the research setting and have little control over the context of research. They exert some control over interaction, however, since informants may not behave as they would if they knew they were being studied. Because of their masks, it is possible that undercover agents send distorted signals and receive distorted responses, thus blocking the free flow of interaction.[21] It is also possible that their masks distort their perception of social reality.

At the far end of the spectrum is the *advocate* model of fieldwork, where the ethnographer works to help those studied improve or transform their destinies. Advocacy can range from the liberal—or relatively conservative—approach known as "applied anthropology" to varieties of insurgency, and advocates can range from those scarcely familiar with the hosts to those both familiar and deeply committed. Frequently, advocates attempt to transfer power or knowledge—their own or that of the group or milieu from which they come—to their hosts.[22] Although advocates rarely control the research setting, they may influence the context of research by their definition of the situation as one where their task is to aid or empower those studied. Interaction flows in two directions, and certain varieties of advocacy research are so set up that those who are studied exert control over interaction—by determining the goals of research and helping to decide the methods that will then be used.[23]

The Moral Evaluation of Fieldwork

Because most of the ethical dilemmas faced by ethnographers cannot be predicted in advance or analyzed within a utilitarian framework, I have suggested that respect for autonomy—based on the principle that people be treated as ends in themselves, rather than solely as means—might be more effective for the moral evaluation of fieldwork.

Let us examine the various models of fieldwork and see when during the research process they might be evaluated, and what principles are most appropriate for such evaluation. Is it ever effective to judge fieldwork protocols before research is conducted, for example, as HHS regulations once required? Are risk-benefit calculations useful for such prior review, or is the categorical imperative more effective?

Prior to the actual conduct of research, risk-benefit analysis can be applied only with great difficulty to the *verandah* model of fieldwork. In fact, harms and benefits are most effectively weighed only some years after publication, when one can judge whether those studied were harmed or helped by the conduct of research and by its products. Unfortunately, by the time we know whether a particular investigation has benefited human knowledge, the direct consequences of research become difficult to document. I believe that most verandah fieldwork results in few harms, some minimal benefits to those studied, and (from some studies) substantial benefits to knowledge. Nevertheless, despite the absence of calculable harms, the relationship between the fieldworker and those studied feels intuitively *wrong*. One feels, today, that those who were studied were treated as less than human, and that such treatment is not ethical, even when people are otherwise unharmed. Thus, despite the fact that benefits often outweigh harms, certain varieties of the verandah model might be judged questionable beforehand when evaluated by the categorical imperative. Because of the "imperial" context, the asymmetry between ethnographer and informant facilitates coercion: Those studied have little ability to refuse to participate. It is thus too easy for the fieldworker to treat informants primarily as means, and thereby to violate their autonomy.

The *noblesse oblige* and *going native* models of fieldwork cannot be evaluated in advance, by risk-benefit calculations or the categorical imperative. Incidents and relationships must be weighed on an individual basis after research is completed. Even then, it is difficult to calculate harms to those studied and weigh them against the various benefits. It would be easier, and more effective, to judge whether people were *wronged,* and their autonomy violated. Here, the quality of interaction is evaluated, not the results of research.

Undercover agent research can be judged in advance; it is questionable by both utilitarian and Kantian criteria. The purpose of the deception is to lead people to reveal secrets which they would not reveal if they knew they were being studied; consequently, the information has a high potential for harm. The investigator, too, may be harmed by a gradual coarsening of moral sensibilities, and the research may be damaged if those studied pick up unconscious cues from the investigator that they are being deceived, and reorient their behavior accordingly.[24] Science itself may also be harmed when social scientists are thought of as liars and snoopers. The controversy over Humphreys's work illustrates one shortcoming of utilitarian calculations.[25] Humphreys did not deny that his covert research on impersonal homosexual activities in public restrooms had potential for harm; instead, he argued that those studied were, in fact, not harmed, and that the understanding gained from this work benefited homosexuals specifically and knowledge generally. If his arguments were true, then such research might be justified on utilitarian grounds. In this respect, I find the categorical imperative more satisfactory: Using people as means rather than ends cannot be justified by lack of harm, or by benefits—it is categorically *wrong.* Undercover agent research uses people primarily as means. In addition, the covert fieldworker presents an inauthentic self, and consequently the research interaction is not authentic. Thus it violates the autonomy of those studied.[26]

The effective application of risk-benefit calculations to *advocacy* research is an almost impossible task. Advocates are confident that the potential benefits of their work outweigh the harms; that is precisely why they are practicing. But such benefits cannot be calculated beforehand, and often cannot be measured after the fact. When examining advocacy research, we usually find that some groups were benefited at the expense of others, a state of affairs that raises questions of justice with which utilitarian calculations may not be able to cope. When advocacy research is measured by the categorical imperative, we see that there are many different varieties of advocacy, and that some use those studied as a means to the researcher's ends. Thus, an advocate whose fieldwork is really a species of revolutionary agitation is violating the autonomy of others, using the hosts as a means to attain the researcher's own revolutionary goals. A similar critique can be applied to the researcher who insists upon keeping the hosts "untainted" by the larger world, even when they are eager to obtain modern techniques, ideas, and goods. Because this posture regards only the desires and values of the investigator, not those of the host population, it treats people solely as means to alien ends and so violates their autonomy. We might agree with an advocate's contention that a specific project, if successful, would benefit a particular group, but if that "benefit" is not desired by that group, then the fieldworker's effort is ethically questionable. The categorical imperative cannot be applied to a research protocol, however, until one knows the relationship between the researcher's wishes and hopes and those of the hosts.

In contrast with research where people are treated as means to the fieldworker's ends are advocacy programs where the investigator works closely with the study population, helping them determine the relevant problems, methods, and goals, and then helping them achieve these goals.[27] Such research might be viewed as a paradigm of the ideal relationship between investigator and investigated. Before examining this relationship further, let us briefly explore some reasons why fieldwork is evaluated and regulated.

Evaluation, Regulation, and Improvement

I have argued that because the relationship between fieldworker and informants is more symmetrical and broadly focused than that found in other modes of research, the investigator's ability to coerce and predict is diminished. As a result, consequentialist analysis does little to improve the ethical adequacy of most varieties of fieldwork. In fact, because most harms come from dissemination or publication of findings—or from extremely long-range consequences of events occurring in the field—a risk-benefit analysis carried out at the completion of fieldwork is still likely to be ineffectual.[28] If we wish to *regulate* fieldwork effectively so that people are neither harmed nor wronged, most projects (with the exception of covert research) must be judged only after publication.

If, however, we are more concerned with improving the ethical quality of fieldwork than with regulating it, then we must realize that the most important person who evaluates research is the investigator. The more guidance we give fieldworkers, the less likely they will be to harm or wrong those studied. Calculating potential harms versus benefits offers little guidance to actors under the intense pressures of the field. Few fieldworkers wish to harm those studied; most are eager to help them. Predicting the consequences of one's actions, however, is even chancier in the field than at home. Surrounded by foreign beliefs and behaviors, faced by an opaque chain of causality, fieldworkers stand at the interface of two "worlds of morals and meaning."[29]

Some of their most perplexing ethical dilemmas come from the question of whether to intervene. Should a woman dying in childbirth be taken to the hospital if her people believe death would be supernatural retribution for her transgressions? Should an exploitative local official be unmasked when informants ask the ethnographer for help? If, after modern medical care, the woman lives, those studied have been benefited. If, after the researcher leaves the field, the dishonest official's brother gains political power, those studied have been harmed.[30] Blanket injunctions such as "never intervene" offer no practical aid. In the reciprocal relationship that arises between fieldworker and hosts, it seems immoral—and perhaps is—to stand back and let those who have helped you be menaced by danger, exploitation, and death.

Although it is not a panacea, the principle of respect for autonomy does offer some guidelines for the hard-pressed fieldworker, who wishes to behave ethically but is not sure what constitutes ethical behavior in a particular situation. Concentrating on intent rather than consequences, in a situation where consequences are unknown and probably unknowable, helps the fieldworker weigh decisions and most fully respect the humanity of those studied.

The principle of respect for autonomy also helps the fieldworker come to terms with the uniquely *communal* concerns of ethnographic research. Unable perhaps to treat whole communities under investigation as ends in themselves,[31] the ethnographer can nevertheless respect and even enhance the autonomy—the authenticity and the independence—of these groups. In this formulation, then, the fieldworker must treat informants as ends, not solely as means, and must thus respect their individual autonomy, as well as that of the group or community to which they belong.

An Ethics of Aspiration: Knowledge as Power

Federal regulations, such as those of HHS for the Protection of Human Subjects, are designed to prevent abuses. As a result, they tend to lead to a minimalist ethics, consisting primarily of prohibitions—thou shalt not harm, thou shalt not treat people primarily as means. But ethics consists of more than prohibitions, it includes an active search for moral excellence.[32] Although it cannot be enforced, the goal of a professional should be to help or benefit those studied. The principle of respect for autonomy can direct us beyond minimalist ethics. We might then say that not only should fieldworkers respect autonomy, their goal should be to help those studied enlarge their sphere of autonomy.

Biomedical research affects the "biological person"; harms and benefits are tangible, physical and, most frequently, measurable. The harms and benefits of social research, on the other hand, are psychological or social and rarely measurable. *In social research, harms and benefits come from knowledge.*[33] "Psychological harm" comes from self-knowledge: those studied learn something about themselves they prefer not to know. "Social harm" comes from knowledge by others: outsiders learn of matters those studied prefer to keep private. Knowledge confers benefits, too. Self-knowledge may bring insight and understanding, enhancing the autonomy of an individual or group, while others' knowledge about oneself may be a source of pride. Knowledge by others may also give them greater understanding of, and sympathy for, previously stigmatized persons and groups. Science and society also benefit from knowledge.

Knowledge also benefits the social researcher. Not only in the vulgar sense of career advancement, but also because it gives the investigator power to help those studied by sharing what has been learned, or to help some at the expense of others.

One can debate the issue of whether knowledge is value-neutral, but I think most people would agree that its use is value-laden: knowledge can be consciously (and unconsciously) used to help or harm those studied.

Programs of advocacy research—where the function of the investigator is to help the hosts determine the goals and methods of research, and then work with them to achieve these goals—are illuminating. Although such research has its own set of ethical problems, involving power, factionalism, and the allocation of scarce resources within the host community, it does illustrate the *use* of knowledge to enlarge the sphere of autonomy of those studied.

I wish, then, to propose that fieldwork findings deliberately be used to help those studied by being returned to them in a way that can enhance their autonomy.[34] (If we view autonomy as composed of authencity plus independence, then ethnographic data is particularly appropriate for enlarging its sphere. Authenticity is enhanced when people learn more about themselves, their group or community; independence is increased when people learn new alternatives for, and possible consequences of, specific actions.) Feedback of research results is much discussed by ethnographers, and some do it as a matter of course. The goal here must be *autonomy*, not simply feedback of research. Information in the wrong form at the wrong time can injure, and the rigid or unthinking researcher, who forces findings upon people clearly unready and unwilling to receive them, is both harming those studied and using them as means to the fieldworker's own "moral" and emotional ends.[35] The ethnographer, then, must return research results at a time and in a form where they are most likely to augment the autonomy of those studied.

Feedback to enhance autonomy is a kind of reciprocity that can be analyzed in terms of the exchange relationship between the fieldworker and those studied.[36] In a classic analysis, Marcel Mauss points out that the gift relationship involves not only a short-term obligation to reciprocate, but also a long-term relationship involving solidarity between participants, and obligations that extend into the future.[37] The fieldworker, placed in a gift relationship with those studied, feels a deep sense of obligation. Charles W. Lidz believes this sense of obligation leads to a dilemma: The fieldworker is faithful either to informants, or to the norms of the discipline. If faithful to

informants, the fieldworker must relinquish "professional norms of dispas-
sionate analysis" when analyzing data; if faithful to the norms, the researcher
feels guilty about carrying out objective analysis and consequently "betray-
ing" those studied.[38] The objective, and therefore guilty, fieldworker then
tends to justify this course of action by overemphasizing negative findings
and feeling so alienated from those studied that the researcher has difficulty
empathizing with them.

In this view, what has been called "over rapport" is seen as interfering with
scientific objectivity.[39] The solution is prefigured by the term "over rapport,"
which implies too much of a good thing. The fieldworker is cautioned to be
wary of identifying him or herself symbolically and emotionally with those
studied, and advised to minimize close involvement whenever possible.[40]
Unfortunately, symbolic and emotional identification with those studied is one
way to gain ethnographic insight and understanding, and the fieldworker who
stays at a distance may learn less.[41] Lidz states that this dilemma stems from
the absence of "a single clear cut reciprocal payment" for the favors done for
the fieldworker by the observed.[42]

I suggest that the knowledge gained by the ethnographer, returned *in a form
designed to enhance the autonomy of those studied,* might provide such a
payment. In this case, feedback to enhance autonomy becomes a moral
obligation. Students must be taught that they will receive gifts from those they
study, and that they must be prepared to reciprocate at a later date, returning
the knowledge they get from their hosts in a way that will benefit those studied.
Feedback must also be built into research proposals, with sufficient time and
funds allocated so that it becomes a recognized and feasible part of the
ethnographic research process.

At this stage in the development of the disciplines of anthropology and
sociology, feedback of research results is an individual option for the
fieldworker. Although regarded with favor, there is no "theory" or "ethics" of
feedback. I would suggest that developing such a theory of feedback may be a
task to which the methods and focus of ethnography are peculiarly well suited.
In the experimental social sciences, as we have seen, most dimensions of the
relation between researcher and subject are considered irrelevant for purposes
of experimental results. Yet it is precisely the irrelevant human dimensions—
the specific needs, desires, and situation of the subject—that are important in
determining when and how feedback of results is appropriate. By contrast, the
fieldworker must regard all dimensions of the relation to those studied as both
relevant and significant. Thus, the information and conceptual tools crucial in
the feedback process are already the presumed possession of the accomplished
ethnographer. On this basis, it should be possible responsibly to refine and to
generalize the methods according to which gifts given the fieldworker by the
host people—knowledge and aid—can be returned in the form of further
knowledge and aid. The feedback process would then become a consistent
extension of the fieldwork methodology itself.

In certain ways, the notion of feedback to increase autonomy blurs the distinction between pure and applied research. The fieldworker is enjoined to work not only to benefit knowledge but also to benefit those studied. I am beginning to think\ that the distinction—in fieldwork, at least—between "pure" and "applied" research is unproductive, and that "knowledge" and "aid" should not be conceptualized as unrelated categories. In the 1960s many radical critics pointed out the potential for harm in knowledge, and some went so far as to advocate suppressing results and becoming revolutionaries rather than researchers. If the fieldworker conceives of knowledge as something that he or she is morally *obliged* to return, in ways that will enhance the autonomy of those studied, perhaps some of its harmful potential may be neutralized.[43] Feedback, then, rather than being part of a personal transaction between researcher and researched, would become part of recognized research practice. By solving problems of over rapport, and guilt because the gift relationship has not been reciprocated, the return of the gift can improve not only the ethics of fieldwork but also its methods.

Notes

1. S. F. Nadel, *The Theory of Social Structure* (London: Cohen & West, 1957), p. 102.
2. Ibid., p. 82.
3. Thus, when Engelhardt examines basic ethical principles to guide biomedical and behavioral research involving human *beings*, he limits his discussion almost entirely to experimentation, as though "research involving human *subjects*" and *experimentation* were identical. H. Tristram Engelhardt, Jr., "Basic Ethical Principles in the Conduct of Biomedical and Behavioral Research Involving Human Subjects," in National Commission for the Protection of Human Subjects of Biomedical and Behavioral Research, *The Belmont Report: Ethical Principles and Guidelines for the Protection of Human Subjects of Research,* DHEW Publication no. (OS)78-0014 (Washington, D.C.: Government Printing Office, 1978). In point of fact, of 26 articles by philosophers and scientists, addressing ethical principles and guidelines for the protection of human subjects of research, in *The Belmont Report* appendixes, only 7 specifically discuss nonexperimental research. The same experimental bias was shown when the National Commission for the Protection of Human Subjects of Biomedical and Behavioral Research was formed; despite the fact that biomedical research was broadly interpreted as including social research, no (nonexperimental) social scientists were appointed.
4. I stress the perception of those studied because investigators may have less power than perceived. It is the perception of this power by those studied, however, which affects their behavior and consequently alters the relationship.
5. Narrowly focused research methods are characterized as "context stripping," by E. G. Mishler, "Meaning in Context: Is There Any Other Kind?," *Harvard Educational Review* 49 (1979): 1-9.
6. Richard A. Tropp, "What Problems Are Raised When the Current DHEW Regulation on the Protection of Human Subjects Is Applied to Social Science Research?," in National Commission for the Protection of Human Subjects of Biomedical and Behavioral Research, *Belmont Report,* appendix, vol. 2; Lauren H. Seiler and James M. Murtha, "Federal Regulation of Social Research Using 'Human Subjects': A critical assessment," *American Sociologist* 15 (1980): 146-57.

7. The varieties of research discussed here are ideal types, and actual research projects may differ from them in many ways. The point is that the greater the perceived power and control of the investigator, the easier it is to coerce those studied to participate, while the narrower the research focus, the more reliable are the investigator's predictions of what will occur during the research interaction.

8. Murray L. Wax, "On Fieldworkers and Those Exposed to Fieldwork: Federal Regulations and Moral Issues," *Human Organization* 36 (1977): 323.

9. See Rosalie H. Wax, *Doing Fieldwork: Warnings and Advice* (Chicago: University of Chicago Press, 1971), pp. 181-220.

10. Thus, when Jean Briggs (1970) lived for seventeen months with an Eskimo family, her temperamental inability to conform to the role requirements of adopted "daughter" was not merely a "personal" difficulty, outside the research paradigm; instead, the resulting friction was an integral part of her data, illustrating the emotional and social dynamics of Eskimo life. One could conceive of a narrowly focused research project requiring an investigator to live in a similar situation. Here, the same difficulties would be relevant only insofar as they interfered with the collection of "real" data.

11. William F. May notes that the terms *risk* and *benefit* are asymmetrical, "The Right to Know and the Right to Create," *Science, Technology and Human Values Newsletter* (Boston, 1978). " 'Risk' implies the mere possibility or probability of harm, while 'benefit' seems to describe virtually certain payoffs." What is really being discussed is *risk* of *harm* versus *hope* of *benefit*, and the choice of terms loads the dice.

12. For a discussion of these issues, see Herbert C. Kelman, *A Time to Speak: On Human Values and Social Research* (San Francisco: Jossey-Bass, 1968), and "The Rights of the Subject in Social Research: An Analysis in Terms of Relative Power and Legitimacy," *American Psychologist* 27 (1972): 989-1016.

13. For a discussion of these harms, see Joan Cassell, "Risk and Benefit to Subjects of Fieldwork," *American Sociologist* 13 (1978): 134-43.

14. Immanuel Kant, *Foundations of the Metaphysics of Morals* (Indianapolis: Bobbs-Merrill, 1959 [1785]).

15. Gerald Dworkin, "Autonomy and Behavioral Control," *Hastings Center Report* 6 (1976): 23-28.

16. See Myron Glazer, *The Research Adventure: Promise and Problems of Field Work* (New York: Random House, 1972), pp. 88-96.

17. For a discussion of these issues, see Wolf Bleek, "Envy and Inequality in Fieldwork: An Example from Ghana," and a rejoinder by Wim van Binsbergen, "Anthropological Fieldwork: 'There and Back Again,' " *Human Organization* 38 (1979): 200-209.

18. Murray L. Wax and Joan Cassell, "Fieldwork, Ethics and Politics: The Wider Context," in Murray L. Wax and Joan Cassell, eds., *Federal Regulations: Ethical Issues and Social Research* (Boulder, Colo.: Westview Press, 1979).

19. Joan Cassell, *A Group Called Women: Sisterhood and Symbolism in the Feminist Movement* (New York: David McKay Co. [Longmans], 1977).

20. For an extreme example, see Mortimer A. Sullivan, Stuart A. Queen, and Ralph C. Patrick, "Participant Observation as Employed in the Study of a Military Training Program," *American Sociological Review* 23 (1958): 660-67.

21. See Joan Cassell, *A Fieldwork Manual for Studying Desegregated Schools* (Washington, D.C.: National Institute of Education, 1979), p. 72.

22. See Alan Holmberg, "The Role of Power in Changing Values and Institutions of Vicos," in H.F. Dobyns, ed., *Peasants, Power and Applied Social Change* (Beverly Hills, Calif.: Sage Publications, 1971), p. 47.

23. Sue-Ellen Jacobs, "Action and Advocacy Anthropology," *Human Organization* 33 (1974): 209-15; Stephen L. Schensul and Jean J. Schensul, "Advocacy and Applied Anthropology," *Social Scientists as Advocates* (Beverly Hills, Calif.: Sage Publications, 1978); Richard M. Hessler and Peter Kong-Ming New, "Toward a Research Commune?," *Human Organization* 31 (1972): 449-51.

24. For a discussion of these issues, see Margaret Mead, "Research with Human Beings: A Model Derived from Anthropological Field Practice," *Daedalus* 98 (1969): 361-86.

25. Laud Humphreys, *Tearoom Trade: Impersonal Sex in Public Places* (Chicago: Aldine Publishing Co., 1970); Nicholas von Hoffman, Irving Louis Horowitz, and Lee Rainwater, "Sociological Snoopers and Journalistic Moralizers: An Exchange," *Transaction* 7 (May 1970):

4-8; Donald P. Warwick, "Tearoom Trade: Means and Ends in Social Research," *Hastings Center Studies* 1 (1973): 27-38.

26. Covert research is not the only kind of deception found in fieldwork. Deception ranges from the "white lies" necessary to keep interaction flowing fairly smoothly in fieldwork as well as friendship; through behaviors such as agreeing with informants, or at least looking as though one agrees with them, just to keep them talking (this can include adapting specific clothing or mannerisms in order to "fit in"); to not reminding people that one is studying them at critical moments when something interesting, and possibily confidential, is occurring; to making friends with people from whom one needs information. The question of implicit and explicit deception in fieldwork is serious, and merits separate examination.

27. See note 23. Also Stephen Schensul, "Anthropological Fieldwork and Sociopolitical Change," *Social Problems* 27, no. 3, (1980): 309-19; Laura Thompson, "The Challenge of Applied Anthropology," *Human Organization* 38 (1979): 114-19.

28. Let me point out that the notorious cases, discussed in the literature, seem to have exhibited potential for harm but little documented injury, save for breach of anonymity and hurt feelings. See Humphreys, *Tearoom Trade;* Gideon Sjoberg, "Project Camelot: Selected Reactions and Personal Reflections," in Gideon Sjoberg, ed., *Ethics, Politics and Social Research* (Cambridge, Mass.: Schenkman Publishing Co., 1967); Seymour J. Deitchman, *The Best-Laid Schemes: A Tale of Social Responsibility and Bureaucracy* (Cambridge, Mass.: MIT Press, 1976); Edward Diener and Rick Crandall, *Ethics in Social and Behavioral Research* (Chicago: University of Chicago Press, 1978). If there have been instances where it has been demonstrated that fieldwork caused more serious injury, they have not been cited in the literature—leading one to conclude that they have successfully been kept from the public eye.

29. Murray L. Wax and Rosalie H. Wax, "Fieldwork for Educational Researchers" (Paper presented at the meetings of the American Educational Research Association, San Francisco, April 1979).

30. These examples come from G. N. Appell, *Ethical Dilemmas in Anthropological Inquiry: A Case Book* (Waltham, Mass.: Crossroads Press, 1978).

31. William May notes that ethnographers must respect the integrity of communities as well as individuals, and argues that the individualistic bias of the categorical imperative creates problems when applying it to fieldwork. "The Bearing of Ethical Theories on Fieldwork," *Social Problems* 27, no. 3 (Special issue on Ethical Problems of Fieldwork, edited by Joan Cassell and Murray L. Wax) (1980): 358-70.

32. The phrase "an ethics of aspiration" is borrowed from May, as is the discussion of a two-tiered ethics, composed of moral precepts and "counsels of perfection." William May, remarks as a discussant in a session on Ethical Problems of Fieldwork, American Anthropological Association meetings, Los Angeles, November 1978.

33. The relationship between harm, benefit, and knowledge in social research was pointed out to me by Nancy McKenzie.

34. My argument about feedback to enhance autonomy was influenced by Schensul, "Anthropological Fieldwork."

35. I interviewed a fieldworker who, before starting research, had promised to show her results to the administrators of the institution studied. After the project was completed, the administrators made it clear that they did not want to see the findings, and the fieldworker said she knew her report would upset them. Nevertheless, she felt that her violation of a promise, and of the principle of reciprocity, was more important than the desires of those studied. She said: "I don't feel professionally clean—for my own professional ethics." One way to avoid such a mechanical formulation of "ethics" is to emphasize the enhancement of autonomy rather than feedback in and of itself.

36. Charles W. Lidz, "Rethinking Rapport: Problems of Reciprocal Obligations in Participant Observation Research" (Paper presented at Eastern Sociological Association meeting, New York, 1977, pp. 2-3); Charles L. Bosk, *Forgive and Remember: Managing Medical Failure* (Chicago: University of Chicago Press, 1979), pp. 203-6.

37. Marcel Mauss, *The Gift* (New York: Norton, 1954).

38. Lidz, "Rethinking Rapport."

39. S. M. Miller, "The Participant Observer and Over Rapport," *American Sociological Review* 17 (1952): 97-99.

40. Ibid.; Lidz, "Rethinking Rapport."

41. For some striking examples of ethnographic insight based upon symbolic and emotional

identification, see Renee Fox, *Experiment Perilous: Physicians and Patients Facing the Unknown* (New York: Free Press, 1959), p. 231; Barbara Myerhoff, *Number Our Days* (New York: Dutton, 1979), p. 189.

42.   Lidz, "Rethinking Rapport."

43.   James Laue and Gerald Cormick discuss "empowerment" as a value of social intervention. I prefer the concept of autonomy to empowerment, first, because I am not discussing conflict situations as are they, but, more importantly, because "empowerment" involves a zero-sum game. Power is a limited good, which means that when one group is empowered, it is at the expense of another. Laue and Cormick, for example, exhibit no moral qualms about empowering blacks and Puerto Ricans at the expense of "antidemocratic" blue-collar workers. "The Ethics of Intervention in Community Disputes," in Gordon Bermant, Herbert C. Kelman, and Donald P. Warwick, eds., *The Ethics of Social Intervention* (New York: Halsted Press, John Wiley & Sons, 1978), p. 227. Autonomy, on the other hand, does not appear to be a limited good; I do not believe that enhancing the autonomy of one group will reduce that of another.

6

Forbidden Research: Limits to Inquiry in the Social Sciences

DOROTHY NELKIN

Science is increasingly under public scrutiny. The moral implications of scientific research—its procedures, and its immediate and long-range consequences—are subject to vigorous debates. Difficult questions are posed in such debates: Are there moral limits to scientific inquiry? What social or political constraints should be placed on research? Is some research so risky or so reprehensible that it should not be done at all?[1]

While these questions touch diverse areas of science, they are increasingly directed to the social sciences, where research findings have immediate human interest and often carry long-term social policy implications. Moreover, social science procedures pose troublesome ethical dilemmas whenever investigators invade the privacy of individuals and institutions or manipulate the subjects of research.[2] Thus, many areas of social science research are, if not forbidden, at least severely constrained.

A network of control mechanisms is presently in place to protect the rights of human subjects involved in social as well as biomedical research. Federal guidelines for the protection of human subjects and procedures of the local institutional review boards that implement these guidelines have placed effective controls, if not absolute limits, on inquiry. These controls are under debate, as researchers complain of the "medicalization" of social science and decry constraints that they feel are unnecessary, irrelevant, and obstructive. Those who view science as a value-free intellectual activity, "progressing by means of its own norms of consensual validity,"[3] argue that freedom of inquiry is essential for healthy research and is perhaps even a constitutional right. For them, the idea of "forbidden knowledge," or even of external constraints on research, raises the specter of McCarthyism, Lysenkoism, and the Inquisition. They see at stake the freedom of the scientific endeavor from external political control.

While the concept of freedom in scientific inquiry has a venerable history as a basis for the health and integrity of science, there are many cases where the

This paper has gained enormously from criticism by Rose Goldsen, Rebecca Logan, Michael Pollak, and David Sills.

goals of inquiry conflict with prevailing social norms. The premise that scientific freedom overrides other social values would place scientists beyond the judgments of the larger social system.

I will argue that freedom of scientific inquiry is a relative concept that is interpreted and implemented in terms of the prevailing social values and power relationships in a society at a given time. While scientists continually negotiate for autonomy, their work is embedded in a cultural and political context that in fact constrains their choice of research topics and the boundaries of acceptable practice. Some research is questioned because the knowledge pursued is judged to be of dubious social or political merit. In other cases, the ends may be interesting and valued, but the methods of acquiring knowledge—the research procedures—invade privacy, require deception, or pose other problems that are judged to be socially unacceptable. In the following analysis of controversial areas of research, the extent to which such judgments in fact fetter research practices will be seen to vary under different social and political conditions.

Political Acceptability of Research

In 1953 a scholar working under a U.S. Air Force contract published a book on the conditions under which "strategic surrender" is appropriate.[4] Drawing cases from World War II, he concluded that it is a fallacy to expect unconditional surrender in the modern international political context. His study became so controversial that Congress legislated against the use of public moneys for any research dealing with a U.S. surrender. This example is clearly a case where political values have explicitly limited research.

More often, political values impose indirect but nevertheless real limits to inquiry. In 1962 Walter Laqueur observed that in the seventeen years following World War II, scholars in the Soviet Union had not produced a single study of the Nazi regime or of the rise of German fascism, despite a presumably widespread Soviet interest in this topic, and despite its relevance to Soviet political ideology. Laqueur argued that the rise of fascism in a society with a large industrial proletariat contradicted the premises of Soviet political philosophy at the time, and that Soviet scholars therefore avoided the topic.[5]

The political acceptability of social science research is often questioned because of the source of research funding. In the late 1960s the Office of the Secretary of Defense funded a project at Harvard and at MIT to develop a new computer methodology which could handle large quantities of social science data. Project Cambridge became the focus of a heated controversy, with faculty and students seeking to prevent Harvard from doing research which might give the government immediate access to a vast body of social information. In the political climate of the 1960s people were especially wary of social technologies which might be used to collect dossiers on individuals and to suppress dissent. The source of funding for Project Cambridge, the

Department of Defense, only reinforced these suspicions. Nevertheless, the funds were accepted and the project launched, although participation in the research was made the responsibility of individual scholars rather than of the university as an institution.[6] Despite intense controversy over the acceptability of research at a time when military policies were widely suspect, no constraints were imposed.

Similar questions about the political acceptability of military sponsored research provoked the famous controversy over Project Camelot. The Department of Defense supported this project to study patterns of revolution and insurgency in developing countries and to find ways to predict and cope with these problems. Described as "insurgency prophylaxis," the project employed many social scientists, not all of whom were aware of its military auspices. Camelot enraged many Latin American scholars who warned that people under its scrutiny would suspect all future research. The ensuing debate hinged on the acceptability of doing academic research to further military goals. Should social scientists under military sponsorship accept the mission of penetrating a culture and investigating the details of its institutions? Critics argued for limiting such research when done by academic scholars. Supporters countered that the research, which would be carried out in any case, would be done better by a "disinterested" community of scientists than by those directly employed by the military.[7] It is important to emphasize here that similar research in collaboration with the military during World War II did not provoke criticism because of the prevailing political consensus against fascism. For the political limits on research are defined in the context of political goals.

The Potential Misuse of Knowledge

In 1972, UCLA proposed to open an interdisciplinary research center to study criminal violence. The Center for the Study and Reduction of Violence was intended to advance understanding of the sources of pathologically violent behavior, to identify "violent predispositions" in individuals, and to develop techniques of preventing violence and of treating criminal offenders. Among the proposed research projects were studies of the families of disturbed adolescents, investigation of the relationship between chromosomal abnormalities and violent behavior, and evaluation of proposals to improve behavior control therapies. The center's objective was to provide alternatives to incarceration and to reduce violence in society. The researchers regarded their work as a benefit to potential criminals, to victims of violence, and to society as a whole. Critics, however, perceived this project in a different light, attacking the researchers as "racist," "Nazi butchers . . . sprinkling the perfume of scientific legitimacy over the stench of experimentation on prisoners."[8] And they vilified the project as "fascism," "eugenics," and "genocide."

Behavior control can be seen as a way to bring recalcitrant individuals into a more "normal" or productive life, or as a means to maintain order at enormous cost to those who do not conform to establishment expectations. Research on the genetic basis of criminal behavior can be seen as a way to prevent crimes or as a means to facilitate social control. One's judgments on such matters depend on the definition of violent or antisocial behavior that is employed and on normative assumptions about the causes of violence. Depending on one's conceptions and assumptions, research on genetic bases of behavior or on behavior control appears as a public service, or as so pernicious in its potential for abuse that it should not be done at all. In the social climate of the early 1970s, one suffused by a heightened awareness of social injustice and a growing mistrust of authority, the opposition prevailed and the UCLA project was dropped.

The possibilities of pernicious abuse have also supported arguments for restricting studies of the relationship between genetics and intelligence. In response to Jensen's claims that differences in IQ reflect genetic differences more than environmental factors, critics have argued that "the wise scientist will not devote himself to research on the relationship between race and ability; the wise university will not honor those who do, or disseminate their work."[9] Quite apart from the many methodological criticisms of this research, it has been attacked on the grounds that its findings, appealing to racist bias, could result in labeling that would reduce our respect for individuals and promote egregious social policies.

Social scientists often look to hereditary factors to explain human behavior, tracing genetic influences on the development of personality, on criminality, and even on vocational interests.[10] Those who would limit such research maintain that, although causal explanations can never be definitive, emphasis on genetic and therefore intractable bases of human behavior will discourage public policy makers from alleviating existing inequities.[11] Such arguments have had little effect on the direction of research; while few would deny that the results of research can be manipulated and abused, this possibility is generally rejected as a reason for forbidding research.

The extent to which arguments based on the potential social impact of research actually affect the boundaries of acceptable research practice depends on the structure of power relationships in a society. These relationships often impose only subtle constraints—less a question of forbidden research than a discreet avoidance of sensitive topics. Sociologists working in state universities that rely on legislatures dominated by agricultural interests will often study rural and agricultural issues, but avoid the politically sensitive problem of migrant farm labor. Relatively little social science research has focused on the tenure system at universities, or on the decision-making procedures in research foundations.

Analyzing such research biases, Laura Nader has observed that anthropologists always focus on underdogs or the poor.[12] Yet their research methods and their insight could also enrich our understanding of the way power and responsibility are exercised in established elite institutions. Why not study *up* instead of *down*? Nader contends that key institutions—law firms, corporate boardrooms, major agencies, industries—are often "off limits" because they do not want to be examined; they therefore determine practical restrictions on the scope of scientific inquiry. On the other hand, as minority groups have become aware of their rights, they too have imposed limits on research which they feel might have implications for social policy. And, like the elites, minorities have insisted that they must also derive tangible benefits from such research.

These demands and constraints reflect a view of science as a commodity, indeed as a political resource that may be used to enhance the power and control of specific social groups. As various groups either restrict access to knowledge, or conversely seek to employ science to justify their political claims, their vision of science invariably affects the boundaries of research— the issues addressed, the questions raised, and the interpretations of scientific findings.

Science as a Threat to Values

In 1974, protest spread throughout the country against an elementary school course called "Man: A Course of Study" (MACOS).[13] This course was based on contemporary research into animal behavior and on ethnographic studies of human behavior. It explored fundamental questions about the nature of animal and human life, discussing social relations, child-rearing practices, reproductive aggression, and religion. It drew parallels between animals and human beings, and it conveyed a highly controversial message—that neither behavior nor beliefs can be understood and valued independently of their social or environmental context.

MACOS aroused intense opposition from certain groups, who objected to the course on religious and moral grounds. The dispute revealed a social polarization between those who share the outlook of science and those who appeal exclusively to religious and moral considerations that stand opposed to a scientific mode of analysis. Critics of MACOS sought to remove the course from public schools because it promoted "an evolutionary and relativistic humanism." Social science, they argued, is "inseparable from people's beliefs, from their theology, from their morality." They contended that MACOS undermined traditional interpretations of reality, violated sacred assumptions (for example, about the uniqueness of man), and fostered pernicious arguments about cultural relativity. They questioned the validity of such knowledge, claiming that it was based on a dubious belief in "secular humanism," and they sought to forbid its distribution among the "vulnerable" populations of public schools. Social scientists defended MACOS as a well-tested and significant educational advance. The issue, they argued, centered on academic freedom. Can educators' access to the fruits of scholarship be so easily limited? Despite these concerns about educational freedom, federal support for MACOS was eventually withdrawn. The MACOS controversy illustrates how much power "textbook watchers" can wield in the determination of American educational policy.

This dispute and others (over the teaching of evolution theory in public schools or over the books to be used in West Virginia classrooms) focus less on limitations on scientific research than on science education, less on forbidding the acquisition of knowledge than on limiting its distribution to protect the public against "dangerous" or threatening ideas. But similar arguments based on concern about the religious or moral values threatened by science have limited research as well. Some areas of research are officially off limits in any society at a given historical time; others are simply not perceived as worthy of investigation. Moral norms have always clearly identified certain topics as forbidden. For years sexual behavior, rape, and sexual perversion were not legitimate subjects for research, but even as these areas have emerged as researchable topics, other taboos persist. Incest and childhood sexuality are just now becoming acceptable areas for research. Societies often find it convenient to avoid recognizing certain facts of life, and freedom to conduct research into such facts is accordingly curtailed.

By What Means?

Not long ago, a team of social scientists wanted to evaluate a questionnaire that purported to test people's comprehension of moral principles. They proposed to administer such a test to teen-agers at a male juvenile delinquency rehabilitation center, and then to tempt them to lie or to steal. The test, if valid, would predict the boys' behavior. The methods employed in this research posed a number of problems. The investigators could not elicit the informed consent of the research subjects because the design of the study *required* deception. Moreover, the procedures themselves could cause harm. By tempting boys in a rehabilitation center to lie or to steal, the researchers reinforced the socially undesirable activities that had brought their subjects to the center in the first place. Even in an experimental setting, to tempt youths to steal violates basic values and borders on entrapment. What might be the impact of this test on the rehabilitation of these boys? On their self-image? What, in any case, could be the possible application of the research findings? If a test to judge one's moral understanding were in fact found to correlate with criminal behavior, would this test be administered widely to teen-agers in order to predict who might eventually become a criminal?

This project illustrates several problematic aspects of social science research, but it provides a particularly clear example of the risks to research subjects that may be caused by certain methods of research. These methodological risks may even include legal sanctions. Sociologists study problems such as drug addiction, illegal immigration, criminal behavior, and homo-sexuality, gathering information that could be used against research subjects. There have yet been no definitive constitutional tests of the legal protection afforded subjects involved in such research.

Some of these problems achieved notoriety in the case of a study of transient homosexual contacts in public restrooms. A sociologist loitered near public urinals, and established himself as a "lookout" willing to watch for police. This gave him a chance to observe people engaged in acts of fellatio. He noted license plate numbers, using them to trace names and addresses of the men involved. Later, he appeared at their homes and secured permission to interview them, ostensibly conducting research for a social health survey. By way of this subterfuge, he accumulated data on their personal characteristics, such as social and economic background, employment status, health con-ditions, and marital relations. The investigator defended the research as a means to destigmatize homosexual behavior as a social problem. He took great care to protect the identity of the unsuspecting research subjects. Still, the project required considerable deception and invasion of personal privacy, and any lapse in the discretion of the investigator could have brought harm to many of the research subjects. When ethical questions were later raised about the research procedures, the "right of scientists to conduct their work" was vigorously defended by eminent sociologists.[14]

The risks to human subjects in social science research are often vague and difficult to define; they may involve less physical harm than psychological distress, invasion of privacy, or social embarrassment. The research design of many studies requires systematic deception; informing the subject of what is to occur would necessarily invalidate the research results. Research on con-formity to group pressure, on individual reactions in emergency situations, on illegal or socially questionable behavior is routinely based on deception. In cases where open research would not be feasible, social scientists often employ techniques of participant observation, which similarly preclude consent. Festinger, Riecken, and Schachter's famous study of "cognitive dissonance" within millenial cults required that psychologists join the cult as believers. Had they identified themselves as social scientists they would not have been admitted to the group.[15]

According to current estimates, between 19 percent and 44 percent of social psychology and personality research involves direct lying to subjects, and one study of psychology experiments suggests that complete information was given in only 3 percent of the cases reviewed.[16] Much of this research would not have been possible without deception. The extension of re-quirements for informed consent to social research is therefore vigorously opposed within the field. Even when an investigator does seek consent, the vague and intangible nature of psychic risk may preclude informed under-standing of the potential consequences of research. Yet much social science research can have a far-reaching impact on the personal lives of research subjects. One of the more dramatic examples is Stanley Milgram's experiment on obedience to authority. Experimenters ordered reséarch subjects to give a series of progressively higher electric shocks to a "subject" (who in fact was a professional colleague) in order to test their obedience to scientific authority. Most subjects obeyed the commands of the researcher and continued to administer apparently dangerous shocks even when the supposed victim appeared to be in pain and losing consciousness. The research created an ethical furor, and a major point of criticism was the personal anxiety and humiliation that subjects could experience following such a graphic demonstration of their willingness to do violence.[17]

In another experiment, Professor P. G. Zimbardo created a prison environment in a building at Stanford University in which students role-played prisoners and guards. Their intense involvement in these roles ("prisoners" became docile and subservient; some "guards" became cruel and abusive) was sufficiently traumatic that the experiment was prematurely terminated because of possible psychological damage to the subjects.[18] For the research subjects, the traumatic nature of both the above experiments resembles that of a psychotherapeutic experience. But in a setting supervised by scientists, not clinicians, this resemblance called into question the moral legitimacy of the experiment.

Research procedures may pose risks to social institutions as well as to individual subjects. In 1952 a team of researchers at the University of Chicago Law School undertook a project to study the way the American jury system actually works. As a part of this broad empirical study, the research team obtained permission to observe a jury by recording jurors' deliberations without their knowledge or consent. The researchers sought to understand how the interaction among jurors influenced both the outcome and the play of deliberation in the legal system. Extending our knowledge about these legal processes is an important research objective, and the Chicago investigation included careful precautions to protect all parties involved. But while the goals of research were important and the quality of results high (two famous books resulted from the study), the means were inherently suspect. The jury is by law inviolate—out of bounds to external intrusion by the public, the press or the research community. The violation of privacy entailed by "bugging" as a research procedure, employed to scrutinize a widely venerated and legally protected American institution, turned this research into a social science scandal. The project became the focus of a Congressional investigation, and legislation was passed prohibiting further studies of its kind. "In effect the jury study sought to lay bare a structure that the society has viewed as indispensable, even sacred . . . and the threat to fundamental values led to a reassessment of the police power of the state."[19]

Such taboos express a society's desire to maintain the sacred quality of certain social arrangements and conventions. Researchers are legally forbidden from placing hidden recorders or cameras in jury rooms or in confessionals, however useful the information obtained might be. Those who violate these fundamental taboos are open to sanction from the scientific community as well as from the law. In effect, our culture considers techniques of scientific investigation inapplicable to certain subjects of unchallenged social importance, regardless of the potential benefit of studying them.

Most constraints, however, affect research done in academic contexts, funded by the government and subject to federal guidelines as well as institutional controls. Considerable research with a similar potential for risk takes place in industrial contexts where proprietary interests preclude public scrutiny.

Recent research, for example, has differentiated the way the brain's two hemispheres process information. As part of this research, psychologists, working for marketing or advertising firms, seek to understand the mechanisms through which the brain remembers images without deliberate effort. Testing is done on television viewers wired to electrodes as they watch proposed commercials. The tester observes brain waves to find out whether the images are registering, and the results are used to help advertisers create images that can be remembered without conscious thought.

Social science research provides significant guidance to the media and its industrial sponsors.

> Psychologists, sociologists, motivation researchers . . . devise ever more sophisticated ways of attracting attention, arousing excitement, and discovering which symbols evoke the kinds of emotions to be packaged with the product image.[20]

Social science research can be employed to develop subliminal techniques of "coercive persuasion,"[21] to influence beliefs, and to break down personal defenses so as to heighten responsiveness to the messages conveyed. The sociological and psychological techniques developed to facilitate media advertising raise ethical questions at least as serious as those projects generating the conflicts and constraints described above. The research violates notions of privacy. It employs procedures that in an academic setting would be promptly subject to criticism and review. Experiments in the psychological manipulation of a television audience are sometimes done without obtaining voluntary informed consent. Moreover, claims of benefit are colored by the fact that support for research in this area often comes from organizations with clearly self-serving purposes—to change consumer behavior, to dull critical sensibilities, or simply to create markets. However, such unquestioned research usually takes place under private auspices and in industrial settings removed from the control and professional sanctions that constrain federally funded research. Thus the ethical questions that would immediately be raised in an academic setting can easily be avoided. As a result, the participation of social scientists in research endeavors involving direct or indirect collaboration with industry remains largely unchallenged and unconstrained.

Conclusion

Political conventions, laws, the availability of funding, and social taboos have long placed many limits on both the ends and the means of research in the social sciences. The choice of research areas and the acceptability of certain procedures are sometimes strongly, but more often subtly, constrained in ways that serve to protect prevailing social values and existing political relationships. But public concerns about the limits of inquiry are increasing. This trend is in part an extension of the preoccupation with the risks of biomedical research; but it also reflects significant changes in the techniques available for social science research and the possibilities inherent in the utilization of research findings.

First, the scope of social research has broadened. Many areas of human behavior formerly out of bounds have become subjects of social science investigation. Second, the technology of data collection has become more sophisticated, increasing the risk to research subjects. Recording devices and one-way screens facilitate violations of privacy; new data-processing techniques permit analysis case by case rather than by aggregation and so enhance the possible abuses of research findings; and the use of computer data banks confers extraordinary power on the organizations controlling them. Third, in the prevailing social climate many activities previously considered acceptable have been challenged. In the early post-Sputnik years it would have been difficult to imagine a serious discussion of limits to scientific inquiry. But by the mid-1970s the "ideology of progress" had given way to an "ideology of limits." Questions of ethics and of individual freedom of choice enter the public evaluation of scientific research just as they enter the assessment of any other social activity, and the unquestioned acceptance of science as an unmitigated benefit has given way to a far more critical view.

Finally, the preoccupation with the limits of social science research reflect the increased use of social science as a basis for social policy. Governments increasingly rely on specialized expertise to meet the complex demands of social planning or to resolve social problems. Social scientists are closely involved in decision making through advisory boards, special commissions, and consultant groups, as well as through increased employment within government bureaucracies. Between 1960 and 1970, federal government employment of social scientists grew by 52 percent (total federal government employment grew by only 30 percent during this period). In this context, social science research itself becomes a source of political power and social control, and its boundaries thus assume increasing social importance.

Despite existing constraints that are seldom questioned by scientists, the very notion of limiting research provokes a defensive response. Scientists continually negotiate for autonomy, arguing that "ethical decisions are best made by educated scientists who understand the value implications of their decisions, carefully consider the moral alternatives when making choices, and then accept responsibility for their actions."[22] But this plea for self-governance is based on an image of science that does not take into account the potential impact of research and its increased use as a political resource. As the role of science changes so does the justification for scientific autonomy. And in this changing context, control over knowledge, its production, and its codification, becomes a focus of political negotiation and public dispute.

Notes

1. See the issue of *Daedalus* on the "Limits of Scientific Inquiry" (Spring 1978).
2. Edward Diener and Rick Crandall, *Ethics in Social and Behavioral Research* (Chicago: University of Chicago Press, 1978).
3. Morris Janowitz, *The Last Half Century* (Chicago: University of Chicago Press, 1978), p. 324.
4. Paul Kecskemeti, *Strategic Surrender* (Palo Alto, Calif.: Stanford University Press, 1958).
5. Walter Laqueur, "Russia and Germany," *Survey,* nos. 44-45 (October 1962).
6. Harvey Brooks, "The Federal Government and the Autonomy of Science," in Charles Frankel, *Controversies and Decisions* (New York: Russell Sage Foundation, 1976), pp. 235-58.
7. Irving Louis Horowitz, ed., *The Rise and Fall of Project Camelot* (Cambridge, Mass.: MIT Press, 1967); Irving Louis Horowitz and James E. Katz, *Social Science and Public Policy in the United States* (New York: Praeger, 1975), chap. 6; and K. H. Silvert, "American Academic Ethics and Social Research Abroad: The Lesson of Project Camelot," *American Universities Field Staff Reports,* West Coast South American Series, 12 (July 1965).
8. See the review of this controversy by Dorothy Nelkin and Judith P. Swazey, "Science and Social Control," in Ruth Macklin, ed., *Research on Violence* (New York: Plenum Press, 1981).
9. In a letter to the *New York Times* (September 21, 1969), p. 4; cited in Lee Cronbach, "Public Controversy over Mental Testing," in Frankel, *Controversies and Decisions,* p. 133.
10. See, for example, Robert Dworkin et al., "Genetic Influences on the Organization and Development of Personality," *Developmental Psychology* 13 (1977): 164.
11. Ann Arbor Science for the People Collective, *Biology as a Social Weapon* (Minneapolis: Burgess, 1977).
12. Laura Nader, "Up the Anthropologist: Perspectives Gained from Studying Up," in Dell Hymes, ed., *Reinventing Anthropology* (New York: Pantheon, 1969), pp. 284–311.
13. Dorothy Nelkin, *Science Textbook Controversies and the Politics of Equal Time* (Cambridge, Mass.: MIT Press, 1978).
14. Laud Humphreys, *Tearoom Trade: Impersonal Sex in Public Places,* enl. ed., (Chicago: Aldine Publishing Co., 1975). See also *Transaction* 7 (January 1970): 10-25; Nicholas von Hoffman, Irving Louis Horowitz, and Lee Rainwater, "Sociological Snoopers and Journalistic Moralizers: An Exchange," *Transaction* 7 (May 1970): 4-9; Letters to the Editor, *Transaction* 7 (May 1970): 12-13 and (July 1970): 7-8.
15. Leon Festinger, Henry W. Riecken, and Stanley Schachter, *When Prophecy Fails* (Minneapolis: University of Minnesota Press, 1956). A review by M. Brewster Smith, "Of Prophecy and Privacy," *Contemporary Psychology* 2 (1957): 89-92, first raised the ethical issues involved in the infiltration of an organization.
16. Diener and Crandall, *Ethics in Social and Behavioral Research.*
17. Stanley Milgram, "Behavioral Study of Obedience, " *Journal of Abnormal and Social Psychology* 67 (1963): 371-78; and "Issues in the Study of Obedience," *American Psychologist* 19 (1964): 848-52.
18. P. G. Zimbardo, "On the Ethics of Intervention in Human Psychological Research," *Cognition* 2 (1973): 243-56.

19.   Gideon Sjoberg, *A Methodology for Social Research* (New York: Harper and Row, 1968), p. 115. For a review of the case, see Ted Vaughan, "Government Intervention in Social Research: Political and Ethical Dimensions in the Wichita Jury Recordings," in Gideon Sjoberg, ed., *Ethics, Politics and Social Research* (Cambridge, Mass.: Schenkman Publishing Co., 1967), pp. 50–76.

20.   See Rose Goldsen, "Why TV Advertising Is Deceptive and Unfair," *Et Cetera* (Winter 1977): 355-61.

21.   Janowitz, *Last Half Century,* p. 324.

22.   Diener and Crandall, *Ethics in Social and Behavioral Research,* p. 5.

7

Risk, Harm, and Benefit Assessments as Instruments of Moral Evaluation

ALASDAIR MACINTYRE

On Warwick's "Types of Harm in Social Research"

The social sciences are moral sciences. That is, not only do social scientists explore a human universe centrally constituted by a variety of obediences to and breaches of, conformities to and rebellions against, a host of rules, taboos, ideals, and beliefs about goods, virtues, and vices, some explicit and some tacit, but their own explorations of that universe are no different in this respect from any other systematic form of human activity. Hence, to invite the social scientist to consider the moral dimensions of social research is in no way to ask him or her to recognize some external, intrusive, limiting factor, threatening his or her freedom of inquiry from without. It is primarily to ask him or her to bring the social scientist's own activities into the same moral focus that the best social scientific work provides for whatever it studies.

It is no criticism of Professor Donald P. Warwick's paper to remark that it reveals how little has as yet been achieved in this area. As social scientists so often do in the early stages of an inquiry, he offers us a taxonomy, but one whose point and purpose are not entirely clear. The unclarity emerges in the way in which his assigning of a particular piece of research—or of some particular aspect of a particular piece of research—to a particular class of harm, injury, or wrong does not as yet tell us clearly how to respond to it. The force of his taxonomic verdicts thus remains unclear. My quarrel is not, therefore, generally with the verdicts themselves, and least of all with the taxonomic approach. The making of taxonomies is the social scientist's permanent temptation, and I shall myself follow Oscar Wilde's advice that the only way to get rid of a temptation is to give in to it, by suggesting one way of amplifying, rather than emending, Warwick's taxonomy.

I shall not, within the limits of the space assigned to me, be able to offer anything but the simplest and most compressed arguments for adopting the schemes of moral classification which I will outline; but part of my purpose is to suggest that those who disagree with my classificatory scheme will presuppose, by the very fact of their disagreement, adherence to some rival scheme of moral classification. Moreover, although disagreement on those matters is endemic in a pluralist moral culture such as our own, it is perhaps worth emphasizing at the outset that the extent of the moral agreement on which we can rely is very far from insignificant.

For I take it that we almost all agree—Professor Warwick certainly agrees—that some types of experiment with human subjects are *absolutely prohibited*. Nazi scientists, for example, tested the capacity of human beings to endure the loss of body heat by immersing prisoners for longer and longer periods in freezing water in order to discover at what point they died.[1] The information derived from such experiments was and remains useful, and members of an indefinitely large number of future generations may benefit from it. But no matter how great the number of beneficiaries throughout the years and no matter how predictable it might have been at the time of the experiments that the number of beneficiaries would be whatever it will be, such experiments clearly fell, and fall, under an absolute prohibition. If anyone does not agree with this, then he or she and I would have to argue at a more fundamental level than is possible in this commentary; although I am strongly inclined to believe that anyone who did not so agree would turn out, like the Nazi scientists, to be too morally corrupt for fruitful argument.

If we presuppose agreement that certain types of experiment with human subjects are absolutely prohibited, the problem of classification is in part that of showing in what place to draw the relevant line. We may notice at once that all objections even to the Nazi experiment would have been removed if adult and sane experimental subjects had given fully informed and free consent to their participation in the experiments, or if, for example, the Nazi scientists had experimented on themselves, as J.B.S. Haldane courageously did in order to discover if changes in the alkalinity of the blood caused certain types of difficulty in breathing. It does not, of course, follow that full and free consent by adult, sane experimental subjects will make *any* well-designed experiment morally acceptable; but the importance of consent is a clue to where the line of absolute prohibition ought to be drawn.

When I invite the consent of a sane adult to some course of action for the sake of the good to be achieved by pursuing that course, I treat him or her as a rational agent. I invite him or her to consider how the relevant criteria ought to be applied. I presuppose some substantial shared understanding of what a good reason is in the relevant area. But when I coerce other rational adults, or lie to them, or take their property by force, fraud, or stealth, or kill them, I violate this relationship between rational agents. I treat myself as to some degree an arbitrary sovereign ruling over their lives. It is actions that involve this kind of violation and usurpation that I wish to class as wrongs. Is the class of wrongs coextensive with the class of actions that are absolutely prohibited? Some moral philosophers have adduced strong grounds for asserting that the answer is "Not quite." I may, in spite of Kant's argument to the contrary, avert an immediate grave wrong, such as an imminent murder, by committing a lesser wrong such as a lying to the person who, if he learns the truth, will be able to implement his murderous intention. But it is rarely if ever going to be the case that the performance of a social scientific experiment which involves wronging the experimental subjects by, for example, lying to them, will prevent some imminent grave wrong. Therefore in practice, so far as social scientific experiments are concerned, to classify an experiment as involving the doing of a wrong to someone is to say that this experiment ought not to be done.

The notion of a *wrong*, thus defined, contrasts sharply with that of a *harm to someone's interests. Harms to interests*, actual or potential, may always be weighed against *benefits to interests*, so that doing that which brings about such a harm can generally—although, as I shall suggest in my comments on Dr. Joan Cassell's paper, not always—be justified if the benefit clearly outweighs the harm. Wrongs cannot be weighed or justified in this way. Harms of course, like wrongs, can be more or less grave, just as benefits can be more or less substantial. But even if I harm someone's interest gravely—by, for example, setting up a candy store next door to his or her candy store—I do not thereby do him or her any wrong. Certain types of action—stealing your watch, for example—may be both wrongs and harms to your interests. But in wronging you—by lying to you, for example, when the lie has no consequences or even beneficial ones—I do not necessarily do you any harm at all.

Warwick uses a terminology that is very close to my own; but I do not know how close. For in distinguishing wrongs and harms he does not make it clear what kind of prohibition or possible justification attaches to each, and the concluding remarks in his paper are too brief to be clear. Whereas if I allocate particular proposed experiments to either of these categories, defined as I have defined them, I partially specify the burden of justification placed upon the would-be experimenter. Consider two of Warwick's examples: that of the physician who encounters a case of venereal disease while participating in research into sexual behavior and reports it, and that of the exposure of the person cheating on welfare in the course of an income maintenance experiment. Neither the person whose venereal disease is reported nor the welfare cheat has been wronged, although their interests may have been substantially harmed. Of course, if either the infected person or the welfare cheat had been promised by the researchers that they would be protected from any damaging disclosure, they would have been wronged. But the wrong would have arisen from the breach of the promise and not from the harm to their interests.

Since harms and benefits are commensurable, harms can be compensated for. And this is clearly important for the justification of certain types of social scientific research. For if a program experiment involves harm to the participants, the experiment can nonetheless be justified not only by citing the benefits which will arise from the experiment in the form of new knowledge and its practical applications, but also by providing the participants with compensating benefits. Clearly *no* experiment which does not have a reasonable prospect of producing significant new knowledge can be justified anyway; but some experiments in which the benefits of such knowledge might not by themselves be thought adequate to justify the necessary harm to the interests of the participants could be justified—and are—by providing compensation to the experimental subjects.

The categories of *wrongs* and *harms to interests* do not, however, of themselves provide an adequate moral taxonomy. We need a third category, that of *moral harm*. Moral harm is inflicted on someone when some course of action produces in that person a greater propensity to commit wrongs. If a course of action will predictably inflict moral harm, will predictably make some person or persons morally worse, then even if the action which produces the moral harm is not itself the infliction of a wrong, it is prohibited for reasons that arise clearly from the wrongs that will be produced. Inducing others to look for the quick and undeserved reward and teaching others to behave in ways that will produce cynicism are clearly examples of the infliction of moral harm. Thus *moral harm* is incommensurable with benefit in just the way that *wrong* is. Once again I am unclear whether Warwick intends his use of the expression "moral harm" to carry this implication or not. And once again the remarks in the concluding section of his paper fail to make clear where he stands.

It is not, of course, only a particular moral stance that I have been defending in these remarks. It is also a particular type of philosophical understanding of moral judgments. And consequently there are moral philosophies which are incompatible with the position I have urged. Most, and perhaps all, forms of utilitarianism are incompatible with the distinction between wrongs and harms, drawn as I have drawn it. Since many social scientists are, explicitly or implicitly, utilitarians, their natural response to what I have defended will be one of rejection. To note this, however, is to reemphasize what I said at the outset: Their rejection will be based on an alternative moral view already embodied in their approach to their research, and it could not be otherwise. For every systematic approach to social inquiry already presupposes some particular moral stance and some particular moral philosophy. And this is why it would be quite wrong to understand what I have been suggesting as an attempt to impose moral constraints on social scientific research from some external point of view. The morality is always there already in the work of social science. The only question is: *which* morality is it to be?

On Bermant's "Justifying Social Science Research in Terms of Social Benefit"

Dr. Gordon Bermant argues that public funding of social scientific research acknowledges that there are conflicting conceptions of social benefit, which he defines in general as "an activity or product that is cherished, respected, or otherwise approved within an historical tradition." However, it also deserves notice that rival and different conceptions of social benefit would entail very different views not only of what social science research ought to be publicly funded but also of what dangers need to be guarded against in such funding. At one end of the scale, it is difficult to see that very much, if any, public funding of social scientific research would be justified on a libertarian view; at the other, a classical view of government would warrant inquiry into areas that many liberals would hold ought to be protected against governmental intrusion. The choice of one particular conception of social benefit thus will have strong implications for Bermant's theses, and his loose definition of social benefit and subsequent analysis somewhat obscure this fact.

My own conclusion is that the concept of social benefit is, in the context of our particular intellectual and political culture, essentially debatable and contestable. This view is not inconsistent with Bermant's own culture-bound analyses, but it is at the very least a refinement of his proposals. I derive this conclusion not only, of course, from the fact that there are so many different and incompatible conceptions available, but from the way in which each of them is powerfully represented both within the larger community and within the social scientific professions. We simply do not share a single agreed view of what counts as social benefit, and we possess no way of settling our disputes. Fundamental disagreement is at the heart of our political and social order.

That this is so is often concealed from us by the way in which political transactions, including those political transactions that concern the public funding of research, are carried on through coalitions organized for the most part without regard to the issues attention to which would lay bare our fundamental conflicts. Our modes of political association to a remarkable degree bypass areas of large disagreement. One way they do this is by substituting some accepted form of rhetoric for argumentative substance. Indeed, the whole process of funding research may be even less susceptible to an infusion of rationality than Bermant suggests in saying that "the legislative process is not rational." I do not mean by this to suggest that the vast majority of individuals involved in the funding process, whether the social scientists or bureaucrats he discusses, do not behave rationally almost all the time. But the social sciences have made us aware of how often a multiplicity of individual rational decisions may produce a process itself not susceptible to rationality as a whole. My suspicion that the public funding process is a process of this kind is strengthened by noticing some peculiarities of governmental bureaucratic funding. In private corporations rationality in funding research is generally held to require a good deal of retrospective accounting. How much did we invest in this research project? What return did we receive from our investment? How do different research projects compare in respect of such return? How do research projects compare with other projects in respect of such return? These questions are, so far as I know, rarely asked about past episodes in the public funding of research, and there are therefore no answers to them which may rationally guide future funding.

The failure to ask such questions could have at least two different sources. It may arise simply from the lack of any agency in government which systematically holds bureaucracies accountable for failing to ask and answer such questions. Bureaucracies respond to what they have to respond to and neither the Congress nor the GAO nor anyone else holds them responsible in this way. But it may also be the case that such questions go unasked because they are systematically unanswerable and that they are systematically unanswerable because we lack any rationally usable and defensible *conception* of social benefit, or the public interest, so that we have no way of evaluating, even in crude terms, the return on our investment in research. Thus my initial doubts about that concept turn out to be far more than doubts about Bermant's appeal to it.

On Cassell's "Does Risk-Benefit Analysis Apply to Moral Evaluation of Social Research?"

What I have to say about Dr. Cassell's paper falls into two parts. She has suggested that methods of research in the social sciences vary systematically in the kind of benefits and the kind of costs that each characteristically produces; I shall argue what is an obvious corollary, namely, that the applicability of cost-benefit analysis to uses of research methods varies in the same systematic way across the same spectrum. I therefore shall first focus attention on some— although only some—of the limitations inherent in cost-benefit analysis in order to identify a little more precisely the reasons why in the spectrum of research methods it is a fruitful type of evaluation at one end of the spectrum, but a sterile one at the other. So far I shall be in substantial agreement with Cassell. But I shall then proceed to argue that precisely as and to the extent that cost-benefit evaluation ceases to be applicable, the role-playing of the researcher becomes open to question in a new way and that it is precisely some of those features of fieldwork that make the application of cost-benefit evaluation to it a relatively fruitless enterprise that raise moral questions about ambiguities in the researcher's role. So that although, in the second part of my comments, I shall follow Cassell in her emphasis upon role-playing, my conclusions will be a little different.

The paradigm case for an effective use of cost-benefit analysis in social science research is the well-designed controlled experiment, conducted with a view to an immediate decision between alternative policies. If the experiment is well-designed, then the population affected by the experiment, whether in the experimental group or the control group, will be clearly identifiable. If any harm is done to them, we shall surely be able to say with a useful degree of clarity *who* paid certain costs and *what* costs they paid. If the experiment provides a reasonably adequate test for deciding between alternative policies, then we shall surely be able to say with a useful degree of clarity *who* will receive certain benefits and *what* benefits they will receive. Relevant examples would be a parole board's experiments with shortening—or lengthening—the time spent in prison by a particular class of prisoner, with a view to framing a general policy for all future prisoners of the relevant kind, or a school system's experimenting with different methods of teaching pupils to read, with a view to adopting one method rather than another for subsequent generations of pupils.

Notice that even in that type of case, where it is most clearly applicable, cost-benefit analysis *never* by itself provides us with sufficient reasons for deciding what we ought to do; and that this is because we need in our decision-making process to set limits to the application of cost-benefit analysis in at least two ways. The first limit will be set by our response to the answer to the questions of *who* will pay the costs and *who* will receive the benefits in this particular case and of whether the distribution of costs and benefits violates the principles of a just distribution. What is clear is that some forms of distribution are morally intolerable, in the light of the requirements of justice.

Second, justice also imposes a constraint on what kinds of cost are held to be morally tolerable. I am not referring here only to the exclusion of what in my comment on Professor Warwick's paper I called wrongs; there are also types of harm to people's interest which place so great a burden on them that almost no benefit will justify it. If nobody offers a particular unemployed individual a job and he simply cannot find a job, nobody may have done him any wrong; but the harm to interests which is involved in long-term unemployment is so great for those who suffer it that it is difficult to see that any degree of compensation to the individuals involved (let alone of justification in terms of benefits to others) could be adequate.

Cost-benefit analysis, then, always needs both to be supplemented and limited by an application of the principles of justice; it is always by itself an incomplete instrument. A second relevant limitation—I am not trying to give an exhaustive list of such limitations— is that it is only an effectively usable instrument where we are dealing with the more rather than the less predictable, with the more rather than the less quantifiable, with the more clearly rather than the less clearly definable. It is for this reason that various types of experimental and quasi-experimental research, various types of survey research, and various types of fieldwork can be placed on a spectrum such that cost-benefit analysis becomes, as we move across that spectrum, a progressively less useful method of evaluation. Note that this is *not* because there are not both costs and benefits at the fieldwork end of the spectrum, but because if they are to be mobilized effectively in an overall evaluative argument, it will have to be in some way other than within the framework of cost-benefit analysis.

Cassell illuminatingly relates the applicability or inapplicability of cost-benefit analysis in different methods of research to the differences in the role of the researcher in each method. Let me concentrate on the differences between—using Professor Cassell's elegant terminology—the *verandah* model and the *patron* or *noblesse oblige* model, on the one hand, and the *going native* model on the other. What the difference between these modes of role-playing raises is the question of the morality involved in passing between cultures, in presenting myself, a self whose identity is defined for me by my own culture, in some guise provided by the culture which I am visiting. I take it that one role with which it is illuminating to compare the role assumed by the fieldworker who "goes native" in another culture is that of the *spy*. And that therefore it is relevant to the moral evaluation of such fieldwork to ask: what is wrong, if anything, with *being a spy?* What we need to answer this question, and what unfortunately we lack, is any adequate philosophical account of pretending and of the moral differences between various species of pretending. When we do finally possess such an account, it will have been able to draw on many sources already available to us: the sociological insights of Erving Goffman and more especially of Elizabeth Burns, and the philosophical analyses of J. L. Austin and G.E.M. Anscombe, for example. But we do not as yet, even with these resources, understand pretending well enough. What, however, we can already understand is the socially disruptive character of that kind of pretending which undermines all our most taken-for-granted assumptions about the interpretation of the behavior of others, such as the pretenses and disguises involved in spying. Moreover, this disruption may not be any the less in the case where we know or suspect that someone pretending to innocence is in fact a spy. Goronwy Rees has movingly described what friendship with Guy Burgess did to aspects of his life.[2] For behind the overt surfaces and disclosures of the spy's behavior lie a whole set of undisclosed motives and intentions; moreover, while the spy tries to withhold himself or herself systematically in his or her encounters with others, he or she at the same time characteristically tries to discover more about those others than they would willingly or ordinarily disclose. In so doing the spy corrupts the very basis of those human relationships which afford to social life the possibilities of trust, security, and intimacy.

In a similar way the fieldworker who in Cassell's terms "goes native" in an alien culture both has an undisclosed set of motives and intentions hidden behind the overt surfaces of behavior and seeks to make others reveal themselves in such a way that he or she will, if possible, understand them and their practices better than they do themselves. Thus the fieldworker in this research mode resembles the spy in operating under false pretenses, false pretenses that may be not at all diminished by the announcement "I am a visiting anthropological fieldworker," since in many cultures this announcement cannot be interpreted as the fieldworker interprets it. Spies too have been known to announce "I am a spy" and have been taken not to be confessing but to be joking. Guy Burgess once again provided examples. I do not want to exaggerate the parallel between the fieldworker and the spy; Margaret Mead was in some ways palpably unlike Mata Hari. But the spylike aspects of the fieldworker in an alien culture are strengthened in their disruptive effect by an additional feature of the encounter.

Our culture has one idiosyncratic feature that distinguishes it from most and perhaps all other cultures. It is a culture in which there is a general desire to make social life translucent, to remove opacity, to reveal the hidden, to unmask. Examples abound. It never seems to have occurred to Victorian explorers that forbidden cities such as Lhasa or Mecca perhaps should *not* be entered. When Freud published his work, it was read as a summons to do away with what his readers took him to be stigmatizing as irrational taboos—and this from the man who thought that his fiancée should not learn to skate because she would have to lean on the arm of her skating instructor. "Behind the manifest, look for the latent" was the public reading. So Lytton Strachey unmasked the Victorians, D. H. Lawrence unmasked Bloomsbury, and collections of private letters became fodder for writers of dissertations. A secret in our culture has become something to be told. And social science research cannot hope to avoid being in part an expression of this same tendency.

Thus the fieldworker who tries to understand the alien culture in a systematic and unlimited way will, by the very act of trying to understand, be apt to commit an act of aggression wherever that culture is one which itself sets boundaries to, and imposes taboos upon, acts of cultural understanding. Some Victorian anthropologists understood this very well: their self-appointed task was explicitly to expose primitive superstition from the vantage point of civilization. Modern anthropologists blush at their crudity; what they do not always ask is whether a far less crude, but thereby in some ways more seductive, version of the same attitude is not implicit in the whole enterprise of fieldwork, with its assumption that understanding an alien culture is a good even when that culture does not think that such kinds of understanding are good.

The experimenter's role is relatively morally unambiguous then; the costs and benefits of his work, if it is well-designed, can be assessed with reasonably adequate precision; but the fieldworker's role—if the fieldworker "goes native" in an alien culture—is far less easy to evaluate. Moreover there is one further reason why cost-benefit analysis cannot be applied in the case of the fieldworker, which highlights the problem.

I remarked earlier that even when cost-benefit analysis is applicable, it needs to be supplemented. But this is of course not the only limitation of such analysis. It is a commonplace that before we—whoever we are—can apply cost-benefit analysis, we must first decide what is to count as a cost and what as a benefit; and in order to decide that, we must first decide who is to have a voice in deciding what is to count as a cost or a benefit. When the fieldworker approaches an alien culture, the fieldworker will often be confronted by alien conceptions of cost and benefit, thus encountering the question of whether such harm as the fieldworker may bring with him or her is to be assessed on the scale of the fieldworker's own culture or on that of the culture being studied. In other words, the fieldworker's allegiance to the culture of anthropological inquiry may be put in question by the alien culture; the spy, as so often, faces the possibility of being transformed into a double agent.

What, however, is more likely to happen is that the fieldworker will look for some culturally neutral criteria of value by which the issue between the two cultures may be judged. And the danger here is that what is taken to be culturally neutral by the anthropologist may be merely what his or her own culture takes to be culturally neutral. Cassell herself has perhaps not escaped this danger entirely. For she urges us to use the findings of fieldwork "to enlarge the sphere of autonomy of those studied." She defines autonomy as "authenticity plus independence." But the value of authenticity belongs distinctively to the culture of the modern West, while the notion of independence is far from clear.[3] Certainly the promise of autonomy is a distinctive feature of modern Western culture. So that Cassell may, in the guise of protecting those whom the fieldworkers study from the effects of intrusion, be assisting in undermining their cultural integrity in the most subtle way, something that she clearly does not intend.

The implications of the general point, however, are not exhausted by its relevance to fieldwork. For if the applicability of cost-benefit analysis depends on some prior agreement—not only on the conception of costs and benefits to be applied, but also on *whose* conception of costs and benefits is to prevail—then it becomes relevant that our own society is a milieu in which a number of cultures, some of them very alien to each other, coexist *and* that any agreement on a conception of costs and benefits may well signal the victory of one of those cultures over the other. Social scientists are necessarily part of an academic intelligentsia whose subculture is more powerful in Cambridge, Berkeley, and Manhattan than in South Boston or Roxbury, South Carolina or the Dakotas. Cost-benefit analysis itself is therefore always at least liable to be an instrument whereby the social hegemony of Cambridge over South Boston and Roxbury is expressed. And if cost-benefit analysis is not culturally neutral, can it be a morally neutral instrument of appraisal either?

On Nelkin's "Forbidden Research: Limits to Inquiry in the Social Sciences"

"I will argue that freedom of scientific inquiry is a relative concept that is interpreted and implemented in terms of the prevailing social values and power relationships in a society at a given time. While scientists continually negotiate for autonomy, their work is embedded in a cultural and political context that in fact constrains their choice of research topics and the boundaries of acceptable practice." If this is Dr. Dorothy Nelkin's conclusion from her examples, then I remain unclear both as to what she means by it and as to how she thinks that the examples which she cites support it. Notice first the unrestricted generality of her conclusion. She is not pointing to a contrast between those times and places where science has developed in a relatively unrestricted way and those in which social and political restriction has hedged it around. The crucial differences between Nazi Germany and Wilhelmine Germany or between the United States in 1930 and the United States in 1943 are rendered invisible by this extreme generality.

Notice secondly that the cultural and political context in Nelkin's view "constrains" the scientist. But in societies where science flourishes, scientists themselves, their habits of work and modes of thought, their forms of association and their pressures upon government *are* a substantial part of the cultural context and at times a not insignificant part of the political context. Nelkin's deterministic idiom reifies the notions of "prevailing social values," of "power relationships," and of "cultural and political context," so that these appear as external forces impinging upon and constraining individual scientists. It is not surprising that she speaks of guidelines and committees as "control mechanisms." The suspicion is inevitably sown that her conclusions arise from her initial choice of terminology and not at all from the evidence that she cites.

The generality of Nelkin's conclusion is matched by her failure to classify her examples adequately. They are in fact examples of very different types of social phenomena, and they certainly do not all point us in the same direction. Indeed, we need to distinguish at least five different types of case. There are first of all her examples of hostile perceptions of particular pieces of scientific work and of attacks upon them, where it is not science itself, but the use of the results of science by government or some other agency, that is in question. Project Camelot is a notorious case in point. In such cases scientists are sometimes paying the price for their own earlier and continued involvement with government or with private corporations. By accepting support for their work they have implicitly or explicitly agreed to make the results of that work easily available to those who support it. When this is so, what is being attacked or criticized, and perhaps in the end limited, is not the autonomy of scientists, but their own failure to safeguard that autonomy. Thus what appear at first sight as attacks on the freedom of particular scientists to pursue a particular course of action may in fact be a defense of the freedom and autonomy of science. This is a possibility that Nelkin never recognizes.

Second, there are what she treats as examples of avoidance behavior by scientists, or failure to inquire about certain subject matters. Missing here is any adequate recognition by Nelkin herself or by those whom she cites of how difficult it is to provide sufficient evidence for the truth of any judgment of the forms "X is deliberately not doing such-and-such" or "X is refraining from doing such-and-such from certain specific motives." People do indeed sometimes do what they do partly or very largely to avoid doing something else. But we need positive evidence of such avoidance, evidence strong enough to rule out alternative and incompatible explanations of why people are doing what they are doing. The contention that "relatively little social science research has focused on the tenure system at universities" (p. 166) because social scientists find this too sensitive an area has, for example, to meet the objection that you need very little social science research to understand the tenure system and its consequences completely.

Third, Nelkin cites at least one case—the legislative prohibition of certain types of research into the activities of juries—where the argument is not primarily about science or scientists at all, but about the social and legal importance of a particular kind of institution. It has in the past been important

both to jurors themselves and to others that they could speak to each other fully
and frankly in the security of the knowledge that their proceedings were
completely private. Here the value of freedom of scientific inquiry is being
weighed against the value of the traditional jury system. To take this kind of
problem seriously does not necessarily involve any hostility to or criticism of
science or scientists at all. Consider a parallel type of example. There is a whole
range of problems about the carrying out of social scientific experiments in the
justice system which arise from the fact that it is of the essence of a well-
designed, controlled experiment using randomization that groups who are
alike in certain relevant respects should be treated differently, while it is a basic
constitutional and legal principle of our justice system that like cases shall be
treated alike. An experiment in which some prisoners guilty of a certain type of
crime were given probation and others guilty of the same type of crime were
sent to prison for three years (individual prisoners being randomly assigned the
one sentence or the other) might be scientifically—and socially—valuable in
informing us of the deterrent effect of a certain kind of sentence for a certain
kind of crime, but it would violate elementary principles of justice.

Social scientists have for the most part understood very well that there is
this kind of problem in this kind of area; the conflict is thus usually not between
social scientists on the one hand and adherents of the justice system on the
other. For most social scientists *are* adherents of the justice system in the
required sense; indeed, social scientists who work in the area of the justice
system largely do so because they care, sometimes passionately, that social
science should serve the cause of justice. For such social scientists the
argument therefore is not between them and the representative of some
external power; it is an argument with themselves, an argument internal to their
social scientific activity.

Fourth, there are cases—Nelkin cites Laqueur's speculations about Soviet
social science in the forties and fifties—where research and teaching is limited
in the interest of preserving some set of beliefs, by shielding the beliefs from
possible counterexamples. Such cases must be carefully distinguished from a
fifth type where it is not science and ideology that are in conflict, but rather two
ideologies, one of them masquerading as science. Nelkin believes, for
example, that the controversy over MACOS was between "those who share
the outlook of science" and "those who appeal exclusively to religious and
moral considerations that stand opposed to a scientific mode of analysis" (p.
167). I am not here concerned with whether her characterization of the
MACOS controversy is historically correct, but rather with her claim that to
be on the side of science is to affirm "that neither behavior nor beliefs can be
understood and valued independently of their social or environmental
context." For if this were so, science would be committed, as Nelkin is, to what
is plainly false. How, for example, does my belief that from p and if p, then q, I
may validly infer q, but that from p and if q, then p, I may not validly infer q—
one of my most firmly held beliefs—depend for its comprehension or its

evaluation in any way on any social and environmental context? What Nelkin is identifying with the cause of science is a particular ideology which claims—falsely—to speak in the name of science.

The generality of Nelkin's conclusions and her failure to classify her examples adequately combine to prevent her from raising such interesting questions as "When is it reasonable and when unreasonable to limit scientific inquiry?" and "Under what conditions is a reasonable stance on these matters likely to be effective?" Underlying these questions is an even more fundamental set of questions about the ways in which knowledge is or is not a good. Because Nelkin does not even pose these questions, she deprives herself of any normative framework that would enable her to classify her historical examples in an instructive way. The barrenness of her paper is a tribute to the sterility of the sociology of knowledge when it is not pursued as a normative inquiry.

Let me finally therefore state—necessarily briefly and dogmatically—one possible answer to these questions. If this answer is false, it must be because some other normative position on these matters is true. But until we find good reasons for adopting *some* normative position, we shall be unable to make any use of historical materials in an illuminating way. The premises from which I am going to derive my conclusions are of two different kinds. The first concerns the conditions under which knowledge is a good; the second concerns the reasons which underlie and explain the existence of social taboos or prohibitions. Their conjunction will, so I shall suggest, show that certain areas of human life are per se morally protected from research inquiry.

Knowledge *as such* is not a good; there is of course a tradition which appears to assert that it is, but the words used in that tradition, words such as *episteme* or *scientia,* identify knowledge that has the status of *science,* knowledge that is the fruit of, and itself contributes to, systematic intellectual inquiry. But there is much knowledge that has not this status, the learning of which can do nobody any good. Such are for example the facts used by subeditors to fill up newspapers on insufficiently disaster- and atrocity-ridden days. There are indeed, so I want to argue, four and only four types of knowledge the possession of which is a good. To learn that such-and-such is the case is a good first if in learning it I test a hypothesis or learn a truth of theoretical or metaphysical importance; second, if in learning it I upset some substantial preconception or prejudice of my own or of some group to which I belong; third, if in learning it I discover the truth or falsity, or move nearer to discovering the truth or falsity, of some assertion about causal connection in the natural or social world, so that I or others do or may become more effective either in changing the world or in preventing it from being changed; and fourth or finally, if in learning it I learn something that is important to my having more adequate beliefs, attitudes, and feelings about other human or animal individuals or groups than I do now. Knowledge that falls outside these four categories may interest, titillate, or merely fill a vacancy of the mind. But it is not thereby a good. It follows that a certain type of journalism is simply unjustified, and I take it that entering upon the career of a journalist is a morally dubious action in much the same way that entering the career of an actress was held to be in the reign of King Charles II.

The mention of the journalist is not of course fortuitous; some inferior social science is not at all unlike journalism. And indeed the degree and kind of resemblance are such that if we ask why some types of journalism are morally offensive we shall be likely to find out why certain areas are or ought to be morally prohibited to social scientific inquiry. Consider three such areas: it is wrong for anyone, and therefore for both journalists and social scientists, to intrude upon the grief of a recently bereaved person or family; and it is wrong for me or any other stranger to read without permission other people's diaries or letters; and it is wrong to violate the integrity of the jury process. Why? The study of taboos by anthropologists and of privacy by sociologists show how important it is for a culture that certain areas of personal and social life should be specially protected. We need sanctuaries, we need to be able to protect ourselves from illegitimate pressure, we need places of confession, and we need to disclose ourselves in different degrees to people to whom we stand in different degrees of relationship. Intimacy cannot exist where everything is disclosed, sanctuary cannot be sought where no place is inviolate, integrity cannot be seen to be maintained—and therefore cannot in certain cases be maintained—without protection from illegitimate pressures.

Now let me bring together my two points. My classification of the kinds of knowledge the acquisition of which is indeed a good and my characterization of the areas of human life into which we ought not to enter, when conjoined show that invasion of those areas would in fact yield substantial goods in terms of knowledge. Grief, for example, the stress of bereavement, the effect of death upon the most private recesses of human life, are areas the investigation of which might very well yield knowledge which would contribute to the overall structure of the human sciences and almost certainly *would* challenge some of our preconceptions and prejudices and almost certainly *would* strengthen our knowledge of important causal connections. Hence it is substantial goods of knowledge that we are to be denied by this kind of prohibition. But in the light of my argument on Professor Warwick's paper this conclusion should not be surprising. For using the terminology of my commentary on his paper, what I have argued both here and there is that certain types of social scientific research of an important and substantial kind cannot be carried through without wronging someone; and no good, no benefit, not even the benefit of one of those three kinds of knowledge, can make it right to do a wrong to anybody. What some of Dr. Nelkin's examples—especially the jury example—seem to show, perhaps unintentionally, is that this conviction is more widely shared in our society than we might at first suppose.

Notes

1. For a useful summary of the areas in which Nazi scientists experimented unjustifiably—for the most part without making any significant contribution to knowledge—see William L. Shirer, *The Rise and Fall of the Third Reich* (New York: Simon & Schuster, 1959), p. 979.

2. Goronwy Rees, *A Chapter of Accidents* (London: Chatto & Windus, 1972).

3. See on this Lionel Trilling, *Sincerity and Authenticity* (Cambridge, Mass.: Harvard University Press, 1972), esp. chaps. 1 and 5.

PART THREE

Informed Consent
and Deception

8

The Problem of Adequate Disclosure in Social Science Research

RUTH MACKLIN

The Problem

Biomedical scientists are not the only researchers today who complain of overregulation. Social scientists and others who use human subjects in research have bridled at the proliferation of committees, federal regulations, guidelines, review boards, and other constraints on the exercise of free inquiry. Some social scientists have responded by trying to separate their disciplines from the biomedical domain. One writer, referring to the Human Subjects Protective System (National Research Act, P.L. 93-348; DHEW regulations, Federal Register 1975), claims that:

> Since fieldwork involves such a different methodology, with unique and often unpredictable benefits and risks (for both researcher and researched), this regulatory system is inappropriate in many ways, particularly on the issue of consent, to the ethical dilemmas of fieldwork.[1]

Another anthropologist argues:

> The comparative irrelevance of protective regulations based on a biomedical model to the most serious ethical problems facing fieldworkers may have been obscured by advocates of "scientific" sociology or anthropology. The terminology of these behavioral scientists reflects their desire that the research situation resemble that of natural science.[2]

To cite one more example of a similar contention, in a book devoted to the topic of ethics in social and behavioral research, the authors write:

> Despite the desirability of gaining informed consent in most research, there are problems with its *automatic* use in all social science studies. . . . The concept of informed consent was originally developed for biomedical research, and laws requiring consent were formulated mainly with this in mind. . . . Informed consent should not be made an absolute requirement for all behavioral research just because it is accepted practice in medical research.[3]

It is worth noting that these contentions are all by social scientists who think ethics is an important and appropriate concern in conducting research in their respective disciplines. They object not to all use of ethical constraints in social science research, but, rather, to the inappropriate use of a biomedical model to devise standards for research participation. Since social scientific research differs in a number of fundamental respects from biomedical research, they argue, the informed consent requirement should differ as well.

How ought this claim be assessed? To begin with, it is obvious that various forms of social science research differ to a greater or lesser degree from the usual forms of biomedical research. The type of social science research closest to the biomedical model is probably clinical research in psychology, social work, and other counseling fields. But when it comes to cross-cultural fieldwork in anthropology, for example, the departure from standard biomedical research is strikingly evident. Yet even if it is true that social science research differs in a number of ways from biomedical research, it need not follow that standards for disclosure should differ. Indeed, what follows from the differences between social science research and biomedical research, if anything, is uncertain. For one thing, the issue is complicated by the existence of varying types of social science research: clinical research in therapeutic or counseling settings; laboratory experiments in social psychology; fieldwork or ethnography, including participant-observer research; and social experimentation. Even within these categories, some studies involve experimental manipulations, others employ some alteration of the natural environment, still others examine aggregate group behavior rather than individual responses.

As a result, the differences between the various social science methodologies appear at least as great as the general difference between research in the social sciences and in biomedicine. Those who argue that the requirements for disclosure in social science research should differ from those accepted in biomedical research might well reflect on whether such requirements should vary accordingly *within* the domain of social science research. If the regulations themselves differ from one area of scientific research to another, does this mean they embody different *moral* standards regarding the need for disclosure to research subjects? The term "standard," here and throughout this paper, refers to a moral basis from which specific regulations may be derived. Standards are developed themselves from ethical principles (i.e., very general moral rules) such as those central to major ethical theories. Two leading examples of such principles are the utilitarian principle and a version of Kant's categorical imperative—examples I shall rely on in the argument of this paper. The most general version of utilitarianism can be put as follows: Right actions (or practices) are those that maximize overall happiness, benefit, or welfare. Because Kant himself formulated the categorical imperative in different ways, with neo-Kantians offering still other versions, I propose the following amalgam: right actions (or practices) are those that demonstrate respect for persons; in particular, they never treat people as means solely, they do not violate autonomy, and they prohibit exploitation.

These general principles are obviously in need of further elucidation, as are their basic terms: *benefit, welfare, autonomy,* and *exploitation.* To attempt such elucidation would consume the remainder of this paper, so I will reluctantly leave basic moral principles and terms unanalyzed, relying on examples to make them clear. This procedure is not intended to diminish their importance. The utilitarian principle and the respect-for-persons principle provide the moral basis for two different yet plausible standards that might govern the conduct of scientific research. I shall confine the discussion below to these two standards, both because they arise from two significant moral traditions in Western philosophy and because they compete directly in the areas of greatest debate concerning the ethics of research using human subjects.

The overall standards embodied in HHS regulations are blends of the utilitarian and the respect-for-persons principles. The requirement that IRBs assess the risk-benefit ratio of proposed research, for example, expresses the utilitarian standard. An absolute prohibition of gruesome research methods, or of enlisting research subjects by coercive methods, embodies the "respect-for-persons" standard. Since the topic of this paper is the problem of adequate disclosure in social science research, the conclusions I draw concerning standards are meant to apply only to the issues surrounding informed consent. On balance, I believe a blend of utilitarian and Kantian principles should prevail in the overall conduct of research using human subjects. Yet different blends are possible, depending on what standards one adopts for various aspects of research practice. On the specific topic of informed consent, I embrace the respect-for-persons standard, as the remainder of the paper makes clear. Adherence to this standard is compatible with the use of a variety of particular procedures for obtaining consent, such as getting "group consent" for a sociological study where that is the only feasible alternative.

Several conclusions might plausibly be drawn from the fact that various types of social science research depart significantly from biomedical experiments: (1) standards for adequate disclosure should vary accordingly; (2) standards should be identical, so some forms of social science research would have to be abandoned; (3) standards should be the same, but procedures for gaining informed consent may vary; for example, certain pieces of pertinent information may be withheld until the research is completed. In this paper, I shall defend the third conclusion, recognizing that one possible implication is the need to accept the second as well.

What argument might be offered in support of the contention that the standard of disclosure in social science research should be different from that in biomedical research? The following is a list of the chief claims that, taken singly or together, have been used to show that the differences between research in these two areas are so profound that at least some requirements placed on biomedical researchers should be abandoned for investigators in the social sciences.

1. Harm to subjects is not as likely in social science research as it is in biomedical research, so protection of subjects by means of consent requirements is not nearly as important in the social sciences.[4]

2. A good deal of significant social scientific research simply could not be done if the standard for gaining informed consent were the same as that in biomedicine.[5]

3. The power and authority of the investigator vis-à-vis the subjects are much less in social science research (e.g., fieldwork) than in biomedical research, and perhaps are wholly reversed in some cases.[6]

4. Much social science research is conducted on groups, rather than on individuals, so the requirement for obtaining individual consent, drawn from biomedical research, is inapplicable.[7]

The bulk of this paper is devoted to assessing these claims, to see whether they succeed in showing that standards of disclosure should vary. Where relevant, the analysis will refer to the six basic elements necessary for informed consent included in HHS regulations governing research on human subjects. Since it is impossible to discuss in full detail each of the above claims for each type of social science research, it is necessary to be selective. Accordingly, I shall draw on examples from some but not all types of social science research. One type is excluded at the outset: clinical research in psychology, social work, and counseling. The ethical issues that arise in this type of research so closely resemble the problems connected with clinical research in medicine that no special treatment of them is required. Instead, the chief focus will be on various forms of fieldwork (participant-observer and observer research), since it is in this area that the strongest case can be made for a difference between biomedical research and social science research. Furthermore, it is the field from which most of the antiregulatory claims decrying inappropriate imposition of the biomedical model have emanated. I shall also refer to examples from psychology experiments in a laboratory setting and instances of social experimentation. Since other papers in this volume focus directly on the topic of deception, remarks on that subject are kept to a minimum. But no discussion of adequate disclosure would be complete without some reference to those experiments in social psychology that notoriously involve forms of deception.

The following four sections, then, will explore the list of claims offered to support the contention that the standard or standards of disclosure should be different for social science research than for biomedical research.

Harm to Subjects and Informed Consent

A number of writers have claimed that harm to subjects is not as likely in social science research as it is in biomedical research, and thus protection of subjects through the mechanism of informed consent is not nearly as important. Edward Diener and Rick Crandall observe that

> the risks involved in social science research, in contrast to medicine, are usually trivial. In the overwhelming majority of behavioral studies subjects are not exposed to any greater dangers than they undergo in the course of everyday life . . . "unusual levels of temporary discomfort," such as high anxiety or fear, are rare in social

science investigations, and "risk of permanent damage" is virtually nonexistent. Indeed, there has never been a documented case of permanent harm as a direct result of behavioral science research. Because most social science research is nonharmful, it makes little sense to automatically impose strict guidelines of informed consent on every behavioral study regardless of its potential risk.[8]

It is clear from these remarks that the authors construe harm somewhat narrowly, confining the concept to physical harm or to the psychological harm that may result from experiencing strong emotions such as high anxiety or fear. Yet even on a broader construal of harm, the question remains whether the probability or degree of harm is a feature of social science research relevant to the formulation of a standard for adequate disclosure. Before exploring that question, however, let us look briefly at some classic cases that serve as counterexamples to the view that social science research is nonharmful and that subjects therefore do not need protection through strict requirements of informed consent.

In the well-known studies of obedience conducted by Stanley Milgram, subjects exhibited a great deal of stress in the experimental situation. In Milgram's abstract of his own experiment, he reported:

> The procedure created extreme levels of nervous tension in some Ss. Profuse sweating, trembling, and stuttering were typical expressions of this emotional disturbance. One unexpected sign of tension—yet to be explained—was the regular occurrence of nervous laughter, which in some Ss developed into uncontrollable seizures.[9]

These signs of emotional distress fall within the category of physical and/or psychological harm—surely not the only species of harm with which Milgram's experiments have been charged. Numerous writers have cited the dangers stemming from lowered self-esteem—a concern to which we shall return shortly.

Another experiment that exposed subjects to conditions of extreme stress was one in which researchers induced in their subjects a temporary interruption of respiration through the use of a drug. The experiment, designed to study conditioned responses in a situation that is traumatic but not painful, yielded reports in which subjects stated that it was a "horrific" experience for them. "All the subjects in the standard series said that they thought they were dying." These subjects were not warned in advance about the use of the drug, since that information would have reduced the traumatic impact of the experience.[10]

A series of studies on the effects of psychological stress exposed subjects to experimental situations in which they were convinced that their lives were in danger.

> In one situation, the subjects, a group of Army recruits, were actually "passengers aboard an apparently stricken plane which was being forced to 'ditch' or crash-land." In another experiment, an isolated subject in a desolate area learned that a sudden emergency had arisen (accidental nuclear radiation in the area, or a sudden

forest fire, or misdirected artillery shells—depending on the experimental condition) and that he could be rescued only if he reported his position over the radio transmitter "which has quite suddenly failed." In yet another situation, the subject was led to believe that he was responsible for an explosion that seriously injured another soldier.[11]

In these, as in the examples cited earlier, the subjects were not exposed to direct physical harm, yet without their knowledge or consent they were nonetheless subjected to conditions of extreme emotional stress.

On a somewhat broader construal of harm than Diener and Crandall appear to be using, even more examples are forthcoming. In the experiments referred to as "emergency bystander studies," events are staged and the behavior of bystanders is observed. These are often conducted in crowded public places, as were the studies in which the researchers faked collapses on subways and let blood trickle from their mouths. Assessments of the kind and degree of probable harm are likely to vary considerably from one person making the judgments to another. Here is one speculation, referring to the subway experiments:

> Such events are not common in the lives of most subjects and may expose them to stress and risk of harm. For example, it is conceivable that upon seeing a person who is apparently bleeding internally, an onlooker could have a heart attack. And it is possible that a mentally unstable person could be unnerved by these faked scenes. Even the healthiest of subjects could be injured in a rush to help. If no one helps, the self-esteem of the individuals may be lowered when they reflect on what they should have done.[12]

These examples are sufficient to show that the risk of significant harm to subjects in social scientific experiments is greater than some would have us believe. Yet it is probably correct to judge the general level of harm—construed in the narrow sense—to be less than in biomedical research. Much more likely than physical or emotional harm, however, are species of harm falling under a broader conception—those variously termed psychological or sociological. Lowered self-esteem, mentioned in connection with the Milgram obedience study and the emergency bystander studies, falls into this category.

What now is the relevance of these observations to the problem of adequate disclosure? Recall again the point of introducing the degree and likelihood of harm in social science research: this factor is often cited as a reason why the standard of disclosure derived from the biomedical model is inappropriate for use in social science research. Whether in biomedical or social scientific contexts, the requirement for obtaining informed consent is often held to be based on the need to protect research subjects from harm. The very notion of protecting human subjects suggests that there is risk of harm of some sort that may befall the individual. But it would be a mistake to think that the informed consent doctrine as it is understood and adhered to in the biomedical domain rests *solely* on the ethical principle demanding that people be protected from undue harm. A strong Kantian strain pervades the doctrine of informed consent—a strain expressed in language such as "the dignity of human beings," "the need to respect personal autonomy," and an individual's "right to decide" what shall be done to his or her person. This last element—the individual's right to decide—often has little to do with the probability or degree of harm that may befall that person as a result of participating in an experiment. In the biomedical arena, it is sufficient that a person decide not to participate when asked, regardless of the probable harmful consequences of the research. The "respect-for-persons" standard thus prevails in the requirements for obtaining informed consent in biomedicine.

If the relevant difference between biomedical experiments and social scientific research is held to be the higher risk of harm posed by the former, this surely cannot be solely sufficient grounds for claiming that standards of disclosure to subjects should be different, unless the value of contributing to human knowledge outweighs other salient values. Concern for the autonomy of persons suggests that if individuals are to decide rationally whether or not to participate in research, they must be presented with all relevant evidence. Rational choice requires full presentation of alternatives. To lessen the opportunity for rational choice is to fail to respect the autonomy of persons when they serve as research subjects.

There is a further problem of consistency that arises here. In biomedical research, as well as in social science, different types of research and even different instances of the same type of research pose varying risks to subjects. Biomedical studies posing few or no risks of harm need not obtain subjects' informed consent at all, by the reasoning used to justify a different standard of disclosure in social science research from that governing biomedicine. Now if this seems problematic, it is not because practice is more or less standardized within the biomedical arena. It is because risk of harm is not the only factor that underlies the need to gain informed consent. The same considerations that mandate "full and frank disclosure" in the biomedical area, even when the risk of harm is slight, obtain in the field of social science research. If participants are not to be used as mere means to researchers' chosen ends, they should be afforded a full explanation of procedures to be followed in the experiment (element 1 in the HHS list of six basic elements of information), of any attendant discomforts and risks reasonably to be expected (element 2), and of benefits reasonably to be expected (element 3).

While it thus seems clear that the lower probability of harm to subjects is not *the* relevant feature of social scientific research that renders inappropriate the use of the biomedical standard for disclosure, there is room for disagreement about whether it should be considered relevant at all. Since no single feature is likely to be conclusive, let us turn now to the second claim in support of the contention that standards of disclosure should differ.

Strict Standards and the Foreclosure of Social Research

Much hangs on the term *significant* in the claim that a good deal of significant social scientific research simply could not be done if the standard for gaining informed consent were the same as that in biomedicine. Many detractors find little that is significant anywhere in social scientific research. In contrast, some practitioners within the field adopt a wholly uncritical stance, finding any piece of research important, however small the alleged advance in knowledge. I am eager to circumvent this entire debate, recognizing that disagreement exists among social scientists themselves on questions of significance and triviality of much research. Yet a few things should be said here about the difficulty of resolving abiding disagreements concerning the value of social science research.

Claims that a particular piece of research is or is not of great significance can rarely be defended objectively. Even so, it is far easier to gain agreement on the value of completed research than of proposed research, in the natural sciences as well as in the social sciences. It is not at all surprising to find social scientists arguing in support of their research, however trivial, arcane, or valueless it may appear to scholars and critics outside their disciplines. Two chief factors contribute to the gap in assessments of the significance of social science research. The first is so obvious it hardly deserves mention. It is a characteristic that researchers in the social sciences share with those in the biomedical and physical sciences: scientists are naturally biased in favor of efforts to advance knowledge in their own field. This bias is probably a combined result of researchers' self-interest (continued funding and prospects for success of their own work) and their acquired beliefs concerning the importance of inquiry in the discipline into which they have become socialized. Lack of objectivity in assessing the value of one's own field is, of course, not unique to social scientists and natural scientists. Similar charges can correctly be leveled at philosophers, historians, and devoted scholars in a variety of disciplines.

The second factor contributing to disagreements about the value of proposed research in the social sciences stems from a feature much more characteristic of those fields than of the natural sciences, namely, the lack of systematic theory into which new research findings can be integrated. While it is true that a good deal of research in psychology, sociology, and anthropology rests on a growing body of established work, there is nothing like a general theory linking these fields, or even a widely held and accepted theory forming the foundation of any of these disciplines. This lack of a general theory, or even a few highly confirmed subtheories, makes the task of objectively evaluating the importance of proposed research projects extraordinarily difficult. The more "basic" the research, the harder the task, since not only is there no theory against which to judge isolated research efforts, but there is also no clearly apparent application of the research results.

This digression into the factors that contribute to persistent disagreements about the value of much social science research should serve to explain why there can be no objective resolution of the debate—at least not in the foreseeable future. The question of the benefits to be derived from such research appears to be a "burden of proof " question. On whom should that burden fall? On the social scientists, who have expertise in the relevant disciplines, but who lack the objectivity to judge probable benefits? On the skeptic about the significance of social science research, similarly lacking in objectivity? Or should such judgments be made by seemingly "neutral" parties, whether outside or within the field of social science? The difficulty of resolving this cluster of issues bears directly on the problem of adequate disclosure, since the greater the probable benefits of the research, the more justifiable are risky procedures and underdisclosures that in other contexts would be morally questionable or even clearly immoral.

Adherents of both the utilitarian viewpoint and the "respect for persons" standard need to make some assessment of the value of social science research. For utilitarians, the clearer the likely benefits to be derived from such research, the more justifiable are acts of deception—whether in the form of outright lying to subjects, disguised participant observation, or manipulation of the natural environment. For Kantians (excepting "absolutists," who reject certain types of action *whatever the consequences*), it is necessary to judge the benefits of research in order to determine the *possibility* that particular benefits could justify transgressions of accepted moral norms, such as rules prohibiting lying. Having already revealed my preference for the respect-for-persons standard on the matter of adequate disclosure, I must confess an abiding uncertainty about the significance of much social science research. (A major exception is social experimentation—the introduction of novel social or institutional programs on a trial basis—where the potential applications are apparent before the research is begun.) This uncertainty is compounded by the absurdity of trying to make a global assessment of *research in general* in the social sciences. It is hard enough, for reasons already noted, to evaluate the importance of particular research efforts in the various disciplines. But it is a nearly impossible demand to require an overall assessment of social science research as compared with, say, biomedical research. If a measure of skepticism is warranted, it is because the burden of proof lies with social scientists themselves. They must either show what theoretical advances are likely to follow the pursuit of a particular line of inquiry; or else they should indicate some probable, fruitful applications of their research findings. An inability to provide some solid support for judgments concerning the significance of social science research will only confirm the skeptic's contrary biases.

As a case in point, consider Alan C. Elms's defense in this volume of the significance of Milgram's obedience studies. Elms writes:

> it is reasonable to assume that laboratory research on destructive obedience could make a useful contribution to the understanding of destructive obedience on a large scale. . . . Further, it is reasonable to assume that better and wider public understanding of the conditions most likely to promote destructive obedience on a small scale could have a prophylactic effect with regard to destructive obedience on a large scale. . . . Thus, I think Milgram made a good case concerning potential benefit.[13]

It is surely true that Milgram's results were surprising. But doubts have been raised about the extent to which the results of his study could be generalized beyond the laboratory, doubts that call into question any sweeping claims concerning the significance of the research. Elms also refers to "the genesis of Holocaust-like phenomena," yet it is not at all clear how Milgram's information helps to *explain* the behavior of obedient Nazis or how it might be used to predict or control human behavior in other contexts. It is an easy matter to make claims about the significance of particular pieces of research, but far more difficult to demonstrate systematically their possible applications or links to a broader theoretical framework.

A final remark on this point. It should be clear that my own skepticism about the *benefits* of social science research is not an expression of doubt about the worthiness of this field as a scholarly endeavor. I believe that contributions to knowledge are valuable for their own sake. Were that not so, I should have to cast serious doubt on scholarly work in the humanities, where it is most difficult to demonstrate "applications" or even long-term social benefits. But the humanities rarely use human subjects in the service of contributions to knowledge, so we need not worry about the lack of clear social benefit resulting from such research. The use of morally dubious research methods, however, is the concern that prompts my expression of skepticism about the benefits to be derived from social science research. The only way deception and manipulation of people can be justified—on either the utilitarian or the respect-for-persons standard, in the context of research or elsewhere—is by pointing to readily apparent, likely benefits to human beings.

Central to the problem of adequate disclosure is that a great many investigations in the social sciences rely on deception in a way essential to their experimental design. This is especially the case in social psychology research and in the activity known as disguised participant observation, employed by sociologists and anthropologists. In a paper prepared for the National Commission for the Protection of Human Subjects, Diana Baumrind notes that "the use of deception continues to be the rule rather than the exception in social psychological research today."[14] Baumrind presents statistics documenting the widespread use of intentional deception in social psychology research. Many of these studies could not be done at all without withholding information from subjects or actively deceiving them, whether about the purpose of the study, the procedures to be followed, or the risks that might be encountered.

The degree to which withholding information from subjects is considered necessary varies with the type of social science research and also with just what information is withheld. A careful examination of disclosure practices in the various kinds of observation research will illustrate the ethical implications of methodologically necessary deception. It would aid us in our quest for appropriate ethical standards for disclosure to distinguish among three types of observation research: *(a)* scrutiny of public records; *(b)* observation of public behavior; and *(c)* participant observation research. These types fall along a continuum ranging from extremely low-level invasiveness to high-level invasiveness. Scrutinizing public records intrudes not at all into the ongoing activities of those whose records are under study. Observing people's behavior in public places without further intrusion is somewhat more invasive since, among other things, it allows for the possibility that subjects will discover and be negatively affected by some response to the researcher's activity while the study is taking place. Participant observation research is, in general, the most invasive of these three types since it establishes a relationship of some sort between researcher and subjects—a relationship that may set up legitimate expectations, create a bond of friendship or trust, or give rise to deep personal feelings. In placing these three types of social science research along a continuum, I do not mean that the "least intrusive" method may not reveal data about subjects as intimate or potentially damaging (if not more so) than that gained through direct observation of behavior. Information in records may be far more damaging to subjects, if their anonymity is not preserved, than a variety of trivial facts learned about people in the course of participant observation research. This possibility underscores the importance of maintaining the anonymity of those whose records are scrutinized. If the records are public, however, there is no need to obtain informed consent from subjects for use of such data, because using published information about people is not at all the same thing as using people themselves. Examining public records without the consent of those whose records they are is not an instance of treating people as a means solely. It is not human beings who are used as a means to a researcher's ends, but rather, written information about those individuals. Observation of public records, then, does not violate the Kantian ethical standard. If two conditions are met in this type of research—first, that the records under study are truly public, and second, that the anonymity of subjects is strictly preserved—then it is not unethical to scrutinize public records without gaining informed consent.

In studies employing observation of public behavior—the next step along the continuum—matters are somewhat more complicated. On the one hand, observation of behavior in public places for the purpose of doing research is no more an invasion of privacy than watching people in those same settings out of mere curiosity. It may be rude—especially if the onlooker stares—but it does not violate privacy, nor does it harm in any way those who are observed. On the other hand, one who is observed and whose behavior is recorded without having been asked, may well *feel* intruded upon. If in the course of going about one's normal activities, one learns that every movement is being watched, every word recorded, he may justifiably feel resentful. Such resentment can be expressed in the words, "What I do is none of your business—even if I do it in public!" That such resentment is often justifiable can be traced to the notion of people's legitimate expectations. It is reasonable to expect that whatever one does in public, curious onlookers will be present. It is, however, not a legitimate expectation that social scientists are likely to be lurking about at any moment observing one's actions and taking notes. If one of the aims of such observational research is to watch and record people's spontaneous behavior in natural settings, with subjects unaffected by the knowledge that they are being observed, it is no doubt true that research results would be altered if informed consent were first obtained. Here, the methodological requirements for doing good science appear to clash with at least one prominent ethical precept embodied in the Kantian moral standard: people should be treated as ends, never solely as means. Diener and Crandall suggest, however, that not only would it be methodologically undesirable to seek informed consent in observation research; it would also be "ethically undesirable."

> When field studies do not significantly affect subjects' lives, informed consent becomes irksome and time-consuming for all parties. . . . The investigator could scarcely justify waylaying people in public places to describe a study that had little or no effect on their lives and of which they were totally unaware. Gaining informed consent would require a substantial amount of the experimenters' and subjects' time, probably more time than the observation took. . . . Where public behavior is observed and subjects are exposed to no dangers or substantial costs, it is normally sufficient to clear the study with reviewers.[15]

While it remains true that to observe people in public places without their knowledge or consent is to treat them as means to the researchers' ends (and not as ends in themselves), it is not at all clear that such observation is unethical. Perhaps this uncertainty suggests that the Kantian ethical standard is sometimes too stringent. It does seem inappropriate to require of researchers that they refrain from making observations open to ordinary citizens in the course of everyday life. The rude onlooker who stares, or who watches others for unusually long periods of time, is violating a precept of etiquette, not a moral norm. Why should it be different for social scientists? Here again, preserving anonymity is the key to ethical behavior. Like the scrutiny of public records, the observation of public behavior need not require that informed consent be obtained, so long as the subjects' anonymity is strictly maintained and so long as the setting is truly public. (Guests at a party in someone's home may behave openly and unself-consciously, but the locus of that behavior is a private setting, and so would be ruled out by this condition.) Obviously, any research employing audio or video recording or filming would be ruled out by these conditions, since it is impossible to preserve the anonymity of those filmed or recorded.

Diener and Crandall acknowledge that ethical problems do become serious in disguised participant observation research. Apart from the lack of spontaneity that would affect results in this research, subjects might not reveal information or speak as freely with a social scientist present as they would if they were surrounded only by their peers. Disguised participant observation is not possible in some forms of research, such as cross-cultural field studies, since the anthropologist is clearly from another culture, speaks a different language, and so could not pass as a "native." The most common form of research in these settings is either undisguised participant-observer research or simply observational study. Urban anthropologists studying their own cultures, however, can easily use the technique of disguised participant observation. They attempt to justify their use of this technique by appealing to the absence of risk to subjects in the study itself, principally achieved through scrupulous care in preserving anonymity in published results.

Absence of risk and maintenance of anonymity are not always sufficient, however, for convincing subjects (after the fact) that research has not violated any ethical precepts. Betrayal of trust is the factor most often cited by subjects who were unwittingly involved in a study using disguised participant observation. One woman, a member of a women's group that met regularly, later discovered that someone who had participated in a number of group meetings was really an urban anthropologist—not participating primarily for feminist objectives—studying the feminist movement and women's groups. Following the discovery, the group member said she felt "ripped off " by the experience.[16]

This example raises the question of whether such practices are unethical insofar as subjects *feel* harmed by their knowledge that trust has been violated. Thomas C. Schelling surmises that there may be at least three kinds of people:

> those whose sense of personal identity and integrity is so strong that no amount of anonymity can keep them from feeling personally violated if their intimate activities or thoughts are captured or recorded; those who don't care as long as anonymity is assured; and those who positively adore confiding intimate personal information as long as their identities will be protected.[17]

But it would be an ethics of expediency to hold that rightness or wrongness of conduct is a function only of whether or not persons *feel* harmed by a particular course of action. Not only would lying, deceiving, withholding information, and other research practices be morally neutral until it was discovered how the subjects in various instances actually felt about them. This position would preclude, more generally, the ability to make moral judgments on grounds other than the particular feelings of people affected by another's actions. Recent writers have given an account of the concept of injury that includes protection of the "psychological self." Case law now includes deceit, invasion of privacy, and violation of civil rights in the concept of liability.[18] If research activities such as disguised field experimentation and covert manipulation truly violate one or more of these values, investigators have abused a fiduciary relationship, ethically if not legally.[19] The moral judgment that this constitutes an abuse does not depend on first ascertaining whether the subjects themselves *felt* abused.

There is, however, a variation on the claim under discussion in this section. Some have argued that certain groups could never be studied without using covert or disguised methods. In particular, "bad" groups that it would be valuable to know about have been cited. One social scientist who adopts this stance writes as follows:

While all people may be worthy of the same respect as human beings, it does not necessarily follow that their activities merit the same degree of protection and respect. It is questionable whether the files of the American Nazi Party are deserving of the same respect as any other data source; must one secure the active cooperation of the Ku Klux Klan, or for that matter of the Pentagon, before conducting research in their organizations or with their personnel? The question is, how much honor is proper for the sociologist in studying the membership and organization of what he considers an essentially dishonorable, morally outrageous, and destructive enterprise? Is not the failure of sociology to uncover corrupt, illegitimate, covert practices of government or industry because of the supposed prohibitions of professional ethics tantamount to supporting such practices?[20]

This position urges the adoption of different standards of disclosure for different sorts of groups: "good" groups or institutions merit high ethical standards; "bad" groups or institutions do not. One obvious difficulty with this view is that assessments of groups or institutions vary with who is doing the judging. There would be little quarrel with the judgment that the American Nazi Party or the Ku Klux Klan are bad groups, devoted to the pursuit of evil ends. Much less agreement would exist, however, and fewer compelling arguments could be offered in the case of other groups or institutions. Consider the groups cited by another researcher who echoes the view described above:

An arguable case for covert research can be made in studying some aspects of authoritarian total institutions, such as mental asylums or the military service. With the connivance of high authority, Mortimer Sullivan and his colleagues introduced a field researcher into an Air Force basic training camp. I do not find myself morally perturbed by their account, which emphasizes the diagnostic value of comprehending the experience of enlisted men and thus redesigning the basic training program.[21]

What is not morally perturbing to this writer may seem morally outrageous to another—who not only supports the institution of the military in society, but also subscribes to the arduous techniques of basic training and other disciplinary features necessary to the proper functioning of the military.

Still another writer adopting this position dismisses the idea of rules in the professional code that would prohibit disguised participant observation.

A professional rule to this effect would not only make for great past, present and future loss to the discipline, but would be an active violation of many people's moral standards who think that there are some groups, such as professional crime and fascist groups, that should be studied whether they are asked and given permission or not. In other words, in accepting this rule, we could not study "bad" groups, which, as it happens, are also especially likely to be "groups that do not want to be studied."[22]

The basic contention of this argument—that deception opens to fruitful study certain "bad" groups that could not otherwise be studied—should be considered. There is little doubt about the truth of the factual premise in this argument: the likelihood of researchers gaining access without deception to groups such as the KKK, American Nazi party, certain police and military units, and so on, is extremely small. Does this fact, conjoined with the normative premise that these are "bad" groups, yield the conclusion that deceptive methods are justifiable in social science research? My answer is a reluctant "no," for the following reasons.

First of all, it is extremely difficult to know in advance whether a piece of research will yield significant information that would not come to light by other means. Even if the problems cited earlier concerning the difficulty of making objective judgments of significance are set aside, it is entirely possible that information about "bad" groups will be uncovered by others—investigative reporters or undercover agents, for example. There are, then, two uncertainties that bear on this issue: (1) indeterminacy about what is or is not truly significant; and (2) ignorance of the possibility that such information would come to light by other means. To justify deceptive research methods, a utilitarian calculation would have to yield a much higher probability of a "successful" outcome than (1) and (2) together permit.

Secondly, to sanction the use of deceptive research methods on "bad" groups is to open the door to likely abuse. As already mentioned, the variation in judgments about which groups are bad enough to warrant outright deception leaves matters up to the subjective evaluation of each researcher. Social science investigators whose views fall anywhere along the political spectrum may justify their use of deceptive methods by appealing to the "badness" of the groups under study. Nothing in the education or training of social scientists affords them any special expertise to make such judgments. That such circumstances have a high potential for abuse is readily apparent when we reflect on the widespread use of deception in social science research of all sorts.

Finally, we need to acknowledge that applying the respect-for-persons standard consistently will sometimes conflict with a utilitarian outcome. An ethical standard that prohibits direct lying to research subjects is easier to apply consistently than one requiring a calculation of benefits for each research effort in order to determine (1) if the results will be significant; (2) if they would not come to light by other means; and (3) if the group is sufficiently bad to warrant deception. It is no doubt true that on at least some occasions the most desirable outcome will be sacrificed: significant information about a bad group will be lost by adhering to a standard that rules out deception in social science research. This is the reason for my reluctance to draw firm conclusions about what should be permitted in investigating bad groups. I believe, however, that a consistent adherence to the Kantian standard is morally preferable—in spite of this potential loss—to a utilitarian standard that would permit selective deception of research subjects. It may also be the case that social scientists overstate their contributions from the study of "bad" groups. Even on a utilitarian standard, it could well be that little would be lost to human knowledge or to the prospects for reform if the requirements for disclosure remained the same for all individuals or groups serving as subjects of social scientific inquiry.

The Power and Authority of Investigators and Subjects

The claim that the power and authority of investigators in social science research differ from those of biomedical researchers is stated by Murray L. Wax as follows:

> In some situations of biomedical and psychological research, the investigator occupies a position of such social superiority and moral power over the research subjects that they may feel coerced into complying with the experimental procedures, even when these involve risks to their physical and mental well-being. In contrast, most fieldwork places the *investigator* in a position of social inferiority and moral dependency. In the most extreme case of ethnographic research among an exotic people, the researcher is ignorant of the language and customs, yet desirous of learning them, so that socially his position (in this respect) is like a child's. In addition, he is often dependent for basic needs like food, shelter, water, and physical safety.[23]

Even if this assessment of the situation in fieldwork is true, how does it bear on the question of adequate disclosure? Wax argues that consent in fieldwork (or, more accurately, some analogue of consent) must continually be renegotiated. Not only the differences in power and authority between biomedical and ethnographic investigators, but also the differences in the nature of the research itself suggest the need for a different model of consent. Noting that a major purpose of federal regulations is to compensate for the imbalance of power between researchers and subjects in biomedical research, Wax holds that in fieldwork, the requirement that the subject be provided with detailed information about the research is an obstacle to initiating a human relationship.[24] Wax ends by recommending as an appropriate procedure *ex post facto* consent, rather than requiring prior written consent from those about to be studied. Using this method, the investigator would prepare a detailed accounting at the close of the fieldwork period, stating whom he studied, with whom he discussed, and to whom he explained, his research, from whom and how consent was obtained. Such a report could then be read by a critical jury of one's academic or professional peers, according to Wax. While this procedure might succeed in being a "full and frank report," as Wax suggests, it is surely a misnomer to refer to it as "consent," *ex post facto* or otherwise.

Making a point similar to that of Wax, Myron Glazer writes:

> the anthropologist representing simply himself is much more often closer to the bungling fool than to the omniscient and omnipotent manipulator. While in the field, I have felt at least as often the object as the initiator of manipulative acts. Again and again, people in the field have tried to deceive, exploit, and control me for their own selfish ends. . . . Actually, if any cards are being stacked, it is not on the side of the

anthropologist. . . . It is on the side of the "natives" who know the rules of the game which the anthropologist is trying to discover.[25]

Glazer denounces the code of ethics of the American Anthropological Association as both "impractical and undesirable."[26] Noting that the Association's stand condemns the use of widespread techniques that involve any modicum of deception, Glazer claims that researchers would speak "as if " they adhered to these principles, when, in fact, they and others would know that this is simply not feasible.[27] Glazer does not make clear whether adherence to these principles is not feasible because fieldworkers will simply ignore them, regardless of their inclusion in the AAA code, or because it would be impossible to continue many forms of anthropological research if they were adopted, or both. In either case, Glazer's own conclusion is that strictures drawn from the biomedical model for adequate disclosure are too stringent to be used in fieldwork.

It is difficult for me to see why a difference in relationships of power and authority among people should dictate the use of different ethical standards for disclosure. While it is true that regulations governing research are devised to protect subjects from harm, other features of human interaction enter into an evaluation of what is ethically permissible. General moral principles are not designed solely for the protection of the weak at the hands of the strong. They govern relationships among equals as well. The Wax-Glazer argument amounts to a claim that it is all right for the weaker to deceive the stronger, but not the other way around. This is, of course, a caricature of the position discussed in this section, and one that the researchers quoted above would no doubt reject. My point is that regardless of differences in power and authority between researchers and subjects, the rules governing human interaction should not vary from one branch of research to another. Weaker or dependent researchers are no more warranted in deceiving their more powerful subjects than physicians are in manipulating patients, since respect for persons as an ethical principle is not contingent on people's relative positions of strength or power.

The Issue of Group Consent

Diener and Crandall make the general observation that one "difference between biomedical and social research is that many social science studies deal mainly with groups, not individuals, and therefore a model of individual informed consent may be difficult to implement or may be inappropriate in protecting participants' rights."[28] Consider, for example, observation research where the behavior of a large group of persons in a natural environment is being watched and recorded. Other relevant cases include experiments in which letters, stamped and addressed to fictitious organizations at the same post office box number, are dropped in various locations, as if they had been lost on the way to being mailed.

Special difficulties arise in social experimentation. Discussing the suggestion that community consent for an experiment could be decided by majority rule, Thomas C. Schelling writes:

That may be satisfactory, but only if there are no significant ethical considerations involved, and no serious disproportions in the way the experiment affects different people who, whether they like it or not, end up participating. If 10,000 school children are going to be experimented on with high-cholesterol lunches, tobacco and marijuana and placebo cigarettes, or uniformed policemen in the school corridors, the decision may have to turn on whether or not 5,000 parents, or some more commanding number, say yes. But this should probably not be referred to as "consent."[29]

Schelling concludes that there is a general problem, "to which no solution has ever been found and probably no satisfactory solution ever can be found, in interpreting the notion of consent for a group of people who disagree."[30] This conclusion leaves open the question of appropriate standards for disclosure in social experiments.

Still another difficulty with group consent is noted by Diana Baumrind in connection with anthropological research. Often conducted on tribes or other non-Western groups whose ethical systems differ radically from the ones on which federal regulations in this country are based, anthropological research contains an "intrinsic problem." Baumrind asks: "In obtaining informed consent does one abide by the code of an authoritarian tribal society which places no intrinsic value on the individual, or by a Western ethic that ostensibly does?"[31] I do not find this a particularly vexing problem, since in matters other than gaining consent, a researcher would not be expected to abandon the general ethical dictates of his or her own culture. In going about the affairs of everyday life, researchers will often find it necessary to adhere to mores and customs in the culture they are studying—mores and customs that would not even fall within the domain of morality in their own culture. But adopting the customs of the host culture need not entail abandoning the moral practices of one's own country. It is only when the moral rules or the mores of the two cultures come into direct conflict that a serious problem arises for the researcher. Thus, only if gaining consent from each individual is morally proscribed in a particular culture will the researcher have to resort to another strategy.

This reply to Baumrind's worry does not, of course, address the broader concern about what is the appropriate mechanism for gaining group consent. While the biomedical model does seem truly inapplicable here, it does not follow that standards for disclosure should be abandoned altogether. I am unable to come up with a solution to the problem of group consent but remain unwilling to conclude that because it is so difficult, it is a problem we need not worry about. This is an area that could profit from attention by social scientists, especially in devising new strategies or mechanisms for obtaining consent.

The Distinction between Standards and Procedures

To conclude, as I do, that standards for disclosure should be the same in social science research as they are in biomedical research is not to insist that procedures for gaining informed consent must be identical. To say that the standards should be the same is to insist that the same moral principles apply and should not be altered or abandoned on the grounds that certain types of research are impossible where detailed disclosure is required. A number of the social scientists whose writings I have cited in this paper agree with my conclusion that some forms of social science research simply ought to be abandoned. For example, in discussing Humphreys's participant observation study of homosexual encounters in public restrooms, Cassell acknowledges that "if investigators must deceive to obtain such information, social science will survive very well without it."[32] Diana Baumrind is another who comes out strongly against forms of research involving outright lying to subjects. In discussing attempts to decrease the costs of deceptive research by debriefing, she writes: "In my view, the investigator must forego the opportunity to engage in research that permits only two possible alternatives: *deceptive debriefing* (in which the truth is withheld from the subject because full disclosure would lower the subject's self-esteem or affect the research adversely); or *inflicted insight* (in which the subject is given insight into his flaws, although such insight is painful to him and although he has not bargained for such insight)."[33] And one can infer from Herbert C. Kelman's writings that while he would allow deception in experiments that promise a significant contribution to knowledge, he would be prepared to rule out trivial research that uses deception in its methodology.

More promising for social scientists than the abandonment of entire lines of research are efforts to develop alternative research strategies or consent strategies. Kelman and Baumrind urge this approach, as does Alexander Morgan Capron in this volume. They offer some suggestions of their own for consent procedures and research design of particular experiments.[34]

How should standards be determined for disclosure in social science research? In the above analysis of the various claims, a number of relevant considerations emerged: assessments of probable harm to subjects; Kantian principles such as respect for persons and the notion that people should be treated as ends, never as means solely; contributions to knowledge; and generally accepted research practices. Each of these is likely to yield different standards for disclosure; some are likely to be viewed as too stringent and others as too lenient. The general principle I think should govern social scientific investigations is this: contributions to knowledge, however great, do not justify treating human subjects in a manner that fails to respect them as persons. Even if no measurable physical or psychological harm is likely to befall research subjects, acts of outright deception, withholding information that might affect a subject's decision to participate, and disguised participant observation are violations of trust, privacy, or autonomy. As in the conduct of biomedical research, procedures should adhere to what has become known as "the reasonable person" standard for disclosure—what the reasonable person would want to know before granting consent. My supposition is that, minimally, the reasonable person would *not* want to be lied to.

There are, nevertheless, two considerations that justify incomplete disclosure in advance of the research. The first is the recognition that the purpose of an experiment or study need not always be revealed in advance; the second is the observation that disclosing to subjects the reasons for selecting them might itself cause some harm to the subjects.

Concerning the first of these exceptions, Diana Baumrind discusses cases in which revealing the purpose will invalidate the experiment:

> The investigator should not be required to disclose to the subject the purpose of the experiment. The requirement that in effect the investigator share his hypotheses with subjects would invalidate most social science research. Obviously subjects' behavior will be affected by explicit knowledge of the investigator's hypotheses. It is deceitful for the investigator to misinform the subject as to the purpose of the experiment, but not to explicitly withhold information.[35]

This position differs from HHS regulations in that the first element of informed consent states that the purpose, as well as the procedures, must be disclosed to subjects of research. But if prospective research subjects are informed in advance of possible risks and procedures to be followed, told that they may withdraw at any time and that the purpose of the experiment will be revealed upon completion of the study, this would meet the "respect for persons" standard: there is no violation of trust, no exploitation of persons, and no invasion of privacy. Potential subjects who hesitate to participate on the grounds that they don't know the purpose of the study are free to refuse. The purpose can be withheld, yet even with a change in the usual procedures for informing subjects, the standards for disclosure remain the same. Subjects may be informed that they cannot be told the purpose in advance; or else they may be told in a very general, nondeceptive way that does not jeopardize results.

As for the consideration that telling subjects everything may actually have negative effects on them, Diener and Crandall cite the example of informing people why they have been selected, where the criterion is social undesirability in the wide society.

> A researcher could hardly justify informing subjects that they were selected for a study because they are latent homosexuals, or neurotic, or retarded. Although such a procedure would be required by the concept of full information disclosure, it would be unethical in many cases.[36]

I am inclined to agree with this judgment, since subjects who would otherwise agree to participate in a study should not suffer lowered self-esteem by being told (or reminded) that their personal characteristics are undesirable or deviant. Rather than being considered "full and frank disclosure," imparting such information might instead be called "brutally frank disclosure."

Although social science research differs in a number of respects from biomedical research, these differences do not warrant adopting another standard for adequate disclosure. This conclusion is supported by an adherence to the respect-for-persons standard—a standard that rules out lying to subjects as well as other forms of deceptive covert research. Federal regulations governing biomedical research adhere to this standard, especially in stating the basic elements of information necessary to informed consent. Element (1) includes a fair explanation of the procedures to be followed, and their purposes; element (2) mentions a description of any attendant discomforts and risks reasonably to be expected; element (5) cites the offer to answer any inquiries concerning the procedures; and element (6) cites an instruction that the person is free to withdraw his consent and to discontinue participation in the project or activity. These provisions succeed in preserving the autonomy of research subjects and in enabling them to refuse or to withdraw from a study if they wish. Incomplete disclosure makes a significant inroad into that autonomy, and deceiving subjects prevents their being able to choose rationally whether or not to participate in research. Even taking all of the claims discussed above together, there is no compelling reason why the standard of disclosure in social science research should not be the same as that governing biomedical research.

Notes

1. Murray L. Wax, "Fieldwork and Research Subjects: Who Needs Protection?," *Hastings Center Report* 7 (August 1977): 29.

2. Joan Cassell, "Risk and Benefit to Subjects of Fieldwork," *American Sociologist* 13 (August 1978): 140-41.

3. Edward Diener and Rick Crandall, *Ethics in Social and Behavioral Research* (Chicago: University of Chicago Press, 1978), pp. 50-51.

4. See ibid., p. 51, and Cassell, "Risk and Benefit," p. 138, for statements of this claim.

5. See, e.g., Leonard Berkowitz, "Some Complexities and Uncertainties Regarding the Ethicality of Deception in Research with Human Subjects," in National Commission for the Protection of Human Subjects of Biomedical and Behavioral Research, *The Belmont Report: Ethical Principles and Guidelines for the Protection of Human Subjects of Research,* DHEW Publication no. (OS) 78-0014 (Washington, D.C.: Government Printing Office, 1978); and Diener and Crandall, *Ethics in Social and Behavioral Research,* p. 44.

6. See, e.g., Wax, "Fieldwork and Research Subjects," p. 29; Joan Cassell, "Ethical Principles for Conducting Fieldwork," *American Anthropologist* 82 (March 1980): 29–33; and Myron Glazer, *The Research Adventure* (New York: Random House, 1972), pp. 94-95.

7. See, e.g., Diener and Crandall, *Ethics in Social and Behavioral Research,* p. 51; Thomas C. Schelling, "General Comments," in Alice M. Rivlin and P. Michael Timpane, eds., *Ethical and Legal Issues of Social Experimentation* (Washington, D.C.: Brookings Institution, 1975), pp. 171–72; Diana Baumrind, "The Nature and Definition of Informed Consent in Research Involving Deception," in National Commission for the Protection of Human Subjects of Biomedical and Behavioral Research, *Belmont Report,* appendix, vol. 2, pp. 23–52.

8. Diener and Crandall, *Ethics in Social and Behavioral Research,* p. 51.

9. Cited in Baumrind, "Nature and Definition of Informed Consent," p. 29.

10. Herbert C. Kelman, *A Time to Speak* (San Francisco: Jossey-Bass, 1968), p. 214.

11. Ibid., p. 215.

12. Diener and Crandall, *Ethics in Social and Behavioral Research,* pp. 40-41.

13. Alan C. Elms, "Keeping Deception Honest: Justifying Conditions for Social Scientific Research Stratagems," this volume, pp. 239–40.

14. Baumrind, "Nature and Definition of Informed Consent," p. 3.

15. Ibid., p. 39.

16. Personal communication.

17. Schelling, "General Comments," p. 166.

18. Baumrind, "Nature and Definition of Informed Consent," p. 35.

19. Ibid.

20. John F. Galliher, "The Protection of Human Subjects: A Reexamination of the Professional Code of Ethics," *American Sociologist* 8 (August 1973): 96.

21. Wax, "Fieldwork and Research Subjects," p. 30.

22. J. Lofland, quoted in Galliher, "Protection of Human Subjects," p. 94.

23. Wax, "Fieldwork and Research Subjects," p. 29.

24. Ibid., p. 30.

25. Glazer, *Research Adventure,* pp. 94–95.

26. Ibid., p. 96.

27. Ibid., pp. 95-96.

28. Diener and Crandall, *Ethics in Social and Behavioral Research,* p. 51.

29. Schelling, "General Comments," pp. 171-72.

30. Ibid., p. 172.

31. Baumrind, "Nature and Definition of Informed Consent," pp. 23–52.

32. Cassell, "Ethical Principles for Conducting Fieldwork," p. 36.

33. Baumrind, "Nature and Definition of Informed Consent," pp. (23–38) – (23–39).

34. Ibid., pp. 44-46; Kelman, *A Time to Speak,* pp. 223-25.

35. Baumrind, "Nature and Definition of Informed Consent," pp. (23–7) – (23–8).

36. Diener and Crandall, *Ethics in Social and Behavioral Research,* p. 51.

9

Is Consent Always Necessary in Social Science Research?

ALEXANDER MORGAN CAPRON

Federal regulations, which apply to all studies conducted at institutions receiving research support from the Department of Health and Human Services (HHS, formerly DHEW), require that investigators obtain and document the "informed consent"* of each "subject at risk" in their studies. Although the regulations originated from a concern to safeguard the bodily integrity and well-being of participants in biomedical experiments, they now apply to situations far beyond these limited boundaries. Encompassed are "psychological or social injury" arising from "any research, development or related activity which departs from the application of those established and accepted methods necessary to meet [the subjects'] needs, or which increases the ordinary risks of daily life."[1]

We may thus for the moment assume that, properly read, the HHS regulations require that all persons whose interests may adversely be affected

---

*45 C.F.R. § 46.103(c) provides:

"Informed consent" means the knowing consent of an individual or his legally authorized representative, so situated as to be able to exercise free power of choice without undue inducement or any element of force, fraud, deceit, duress, or other form of constraint or coercion. The basic elements of information necessary to such consent include:

(1) A fair explanation of the procedures to be followed, and their purposes, including identification of any procedures which are experimental;

(2) A description of any attendant discomforts and risks reasonably to be expected;

(3) A description of any benefits reasonably to be expected;

(4) A disclosure of any appropriate alternative procedures that might be advantageous for the subject;

(5) An offer to answer any inquiries concerning the procedures; and

(6) An instruction that the person is free to withdraw his consent and to discontinue participation in the project or activity at any time without prejudice to the subject.

by social science research conducted under the auspices of institutions with HHS grants must have given prospective, voluntary, informed consent.[2] This conclusion elicits howls of protest from many social scientists. For them, a misplaced concern to protect people from the exaggerated risks of innocuous social science studies actually increases their probable harm and deprives everyone of the benefits that might have been derived from studies now rendered too costly.

One is tempted to dismiss such complaints as self-serving and probably grossly exaggerated. Ten years ago the medical literature resounded with denunciations of the increasing insistence on obtaining informed consent from participants in experiments. Although it was predicted then that the consent requirement would do more harm than good to subjects and would cripple research, the biomedical research enterprise has since accommodated itself (however grudgingly) to HHS rules, court decisions, and other codes of conduct. Some investigators can even be heard to remark that obtaining informed consent is not only feasible, but positively beneficial.

Nevertheless, there are good reasons not to brush off social scientists' protests. Attitudes, behavior, knowledge, and emotions are often central concerns of social science work, so the importance of having naive subjects is obvious. Further, the scope of social science research and the difficulty of defining both the "risks" it creates—and hence of identifying the "subjects" who must be consulted—are frequently much greater than in biomedical experiments.

Consequently, it seems plausible to conclude that the application of the HHS regulations, including the requirement of informed consent, imperils much social science research, particularly studies employing deception, participant observation, and secondary analysis of existing data. If one values social science research, one is then led to ask, "Is consent always necessary in social science research?" Several responses to this question are possible.

At one extreme, all of the ethical and public policy considerations—as well as the sorry history of behavior under less rigorous requirements—that led to the imposition of the federal regulations would support the reply, "Yes, consent *is always* necessary." Although that is my own intuitive answer to the question, it will not be explored further in what follows because it is already the "accepted wisdom," and the factors sketched previously suggest that a different regulatory response to social science research deserves serious consideration.

By the same token, the opposite response, "Consent ought *never* to be required," can also quickly be dismissed. It is true that social science research presents conceptual issues that may result in practical problems under the existing regulations. Such research, particularly social policy experiments (e.g., giving rent supplements in cash to some poor people to see whether they move to better housing), may, among other things, alter the lives of—or place "at risk"—many people besides those who are the direct objects of the investigators' concern. (In the rent supplement example, the group of affected people would include all of those who are competing for the same housing and who are likely to be faced with some increase in prices.) It would be extremely difficult to get consent from any of these people, even if agreement could be reached on who they are. It seems, however, better to meet this problem with a careful definition of "subjects," which would, quite reasonably in my view, exclude those only indirectly affected,* than to scuttle the whole set of requirements on the ground that a less precise reading of the term "subject at risk" would lead to such onerous requirements as to make a great segment of social science research impossible.

This essay will be concerned, then, with responses to the question "Is consent always necessary in social science research?" that fall between these poles. The intent is to see whether, in particular, there are any situations in which a negative answer to this question is acceptable *within* the rationale of the present HHS regulations. I group the responses into two categories, the utilitarian (e.g., "consent may be omitted when to do so will maximize the collective good," etc.) and the functional (e.g., "consent may be omitted when other means are available to fulfill its purposes," etc.) and conclude that some responses in the latter category seem satisfactory. †

*One means of drawing a line might derive from the legal notion of "proximate cause," which turns on the complex and somewhat circular interrelationship of such notions as "foreseeability" and "duty." For the social science investigator, the implication of this analysis might be that consent ought to be sought from anyone exposed to a harm serious enough that a reasonable person would anticipate it and would be obliged to avoid it. On the other hand, one would not regard as subjects those whose legally protected interests are not at foreseeable risk or those cases in which any exposure to possible harm is too remote (in probability or degree). Thus, in the rent cash-supplement example, since one owes no duty to avoid creating changes in a market by distributing gifts to some participants in that market, those people whose only connection with the research was that they did not get money while their neighbors did would *not* be "subjects." On the other hand, those people who are eligible for subsidies but are instead merely studied in order to provide comparison data *are* "subjects," because (a) they are directly exposed to some risks (those that inhere in information collection, etc.) and (b) they are owed the duty (at least if the research is sponsored by the state) of treating like cases alike (which is not to say that they must also, to assure strict equality, be given rent supplements—that is a separate issue—but merely that since they are a part of the group being studied, the fact of unequal treatment makes it clearer that they are "directly" affected by the experiment and ought to be considered "subjects").

† To flesh out these responses, I suggest several "strategies," about which a word of caution is in order. The purpose of this chapter is to explore principled (and, perhaps, provocative) responses to the question about the necessity of consent rather than to write new regulations. The strategies proposed would require much further refinement (such as the specification of structures and procedures) before they could be incorporated into the regulatory framework. Furthermore, in

Utilitarian Responses

Suppose that some potentially valuable information about family stability and economic resources could be gained by performing a correlative analysis of unemployment and welfare information with marital and vital statistics, all originally collected by the government. It would, on the one hand, be slow and costly to ignore the existing data and begin the research by asking for permission to use newly accrued information; on the other hand, it would be impossible to contact each individual source of the existing data to gain his or her permission at this point. Would it be acceptable to conduct the research without obtaining consent from the people whose records were being studied?

A utilitarian might be inclined to answer this question affirmatively since the development of new, useful knowledge and the efficient use of resources are important objectives and would probably be promoted if the research were permitted. One approach would be to estimate the magnitude of the potential harm to the "subjects" (e.g., embarrassment from disclosure of personal information; loss of government benefits if fraud or overpayment were discovered; etc.) and to society (e.g., increased suspicion and uncooperativeness because of public dissatisfaction with unconsented disclosure of information; etc.), as discounted by the probability that each type of harm would actually occur (e.g., procedures planned to protect confidentiality; past experiences of researchers; etc.). This estimate could then be compared with the predictable costs of other methods of gaining the same results; the research plan would be undertaken if the total benefits it would provide outweighed the harm it is expected to generate and alternative plans did not present better cost-benefit ratios. This method of searching for "optimificity" in decisions is associated with the school of philosophy known as act utilitarianism.

The question then arises whether the existing HHS regulations incorporate act-utilitarian analysis. There are some indications of a case-by-case search for the results that are "right" in the sense of maximizing total utility (although one must recognize that the HHS regulations provide no better means of quantifying "utility" than the various and often contradictory utilitarian theorists have provided). The clearest example in the HHS rules is the requirement that an institutional review board, before approving a protocol, satisfy itself that the "risks to subjects are reasonable in relation to anticipated benefits to subjects and importance of the knowledge to be gained."[3] Despite this bow to optimificity, it is apparent that the HHS regulations do *not* invite those deciding about experimentation to engage in act-utilitarian calculations. Were the contrary the case, there would be no requirement—as there is—that "informed consent will be sought from each prospective subject,"[4] for the net benefit of getting (or not getting) informed consent is just one factor an act

---

addressing solely the issue of consent, I do not intend to suggest that this exhausts the universe of morally relevant concerns that must be addressed before research may be undertaken. Just as there may be some studies that are *acceptable without* consent, so there are some that would be *impermissible even with* consent.

utilitarian would consider in deciding about each experiment individually. Since the HHS regulations fit the practice conception of rules[5] (in that the relationships of researchers to society and the relationships of citizens to government as a collector of confidential information are created, and not merely summarized, by the rules), we must look beyond act utilitarianism to discover strategies for the consent problem that are acceptable *within* the rationale of those regulations.

The alternative utility-based explanation employs rule utilitarianism: the hypothetical research project would be proper without consent if "no consent" was an optional *rule* that passed the test of utility. Since rule utilitarianism regards rules as compulsory rather than as mere rules of thumb, it better describes the framework established by the HHS regulations than does act utilitarianism. A central issue remains, however. Is the regulation of experimentation premised on utilitarian calculus? That is, were the regulations adopted because they were believed likely to maximize the net utility of the research enterprise? A negative answer appears likely on both historical and analytical grounds. The consistent theme of rules about human subjects, at least from the time of the Nuremberg judgment, has been a refusal to allow benefits to the collectivity to supplant basic rights or interests of the individual.[6] The philosophy of the present rules is incompatible with an analysis that would accept unconsented harm to a few people as the price that must be paid to help many, whether the research is in the biomedical or social sciences.

Yet even if the rules governing human experimentation embody, at least in part, notions about inherent rightness or wrongness in relations between the various participants in the research process, utilitarian thought may still be helpful if we are attempting to determine situations in which consent might not be necessary. In philosophical vocabulary, a teleological (or utilitarian) supplement to the basic deontological approach of the regulations would suggest that dispensing with consent will be most acceptable when the harm to which each subject is exposed is so small as to be virtually nonexistent and the research involved is of predictable and appreciable value.[7] It is important to remember that the concept of harm must encompass not only endangering the individual's physical, psychological, and social well-being but also the damage to the individual and society that results from a breach of the social expectation of consent (i.e., harm to feelings of dignity, personal security and, perhaps, equality, especially if the poor or powerless are disproportionately represented in the group chosen as subjects).

As an alternative to the above utilitarian approaches, one might say that certain rules about disclosure and assent have been adopted because they serve important functions having specific objectives. If it were possible to reach these same objectives by other routes, might it not then be acceptable to suspend the consent requirement? The answer to the question may depend on whether one can actually *reach* the same goals or only *approximate* them. Since I view the possibilities surveyed below as falling short of true equivalence in most cases, the alternatives (even in combination) would represent at least some sacrifice of the interests now served by informed consent. To aid in analyzing these alternatives, it may be helpful to distinguish four groups of purposes: promoting participants' autonomy, improving research, regularizing relationships, and protecting privacy. In the following four sections, various functional approaches will be assessed by attending in turn to each of these groups of purposes.

Promoting Autonomy and Self-Determination

On the surface the doctrine of informed consent may appear pragmatic, arising primarily from a concern to reduce bodily harm and the like. But the doctrine also reflects nonpragmatic ethical principles that find application in many spheres besides biomedical interventions. In the soil in which the law of consent first grew—that of medical litigation—the underlying principle was expressed as the "right to determine what shall be done with [one's] own body."[8] The elaboration of the law that began with *Salgo*[9] and *Natanson*[10] "recognized that for the right to self-determination to be meaningful. . . , it must be conjoined with a right to the information one needs to formulate an intelligent opinion."[11] The doctrine of informed consent thus gives form not only to the wish for mastery over one's fate but also to the desire, in the words of Sir Isaiah Berlin, "to be conscious of [oneself] as a thinking, willing, active being, bearing responsibility for his choices and able to explain them by reference to his own ideas and purposes."[12] The requirement of consent only partially protects autonomy, of course. Barriers of communication, of unarticulated and perhaps unrecognized hopes and preconceptions, and of uncertain knowledge stand in the way. But the goal itself is important and reflects the further function of the consent process in protecting the human status of research participants.

> To fail to acquaint a subject of observation or experiment with what is happening— as fully as is possible within the limits of the communication system—is to that extent to denigrate him as a full human being and reduce him to the category of dependency in which he is not permitted to judge for himself.[13]

To put it in other words, the doctrine of informed consent reminds all involved in research of a categorical imperative against violations of autonomy. Arguments that justify dispensing with consent on the grounds of social or scientific benefit deny subjects' status as human beings by treating them solely as means rather than as ends in themselves. Consent (in theory, at least) overcomes the means/ends problem because the subject who has truly consented has adopted the goals of the research program as his own; as a "collaborator" with the investigators, the subject is no longer merely a means to someone else's ends but a participant in a process to reach his own ends. Alternatively, if the subject does not recognize the ends of the research project to be merged with his own, at the least it can be said that the subject has consented to being used as a means.

Finally, besides these philosophical aspects, "the requirement serves practical functions as well. One consequence of truly informed consent is to remove, or at least avoid, the danger of fraud and duress."[14] There would be little value in an abstract notion of autonomy if social scientists were in practice free to mislead the subjects of their studies.

Is it possible to approximate these several aspects of "promoting autonomy" through means other than obtaining actual, advance consent from subjects of social science research? There are at least four strategies that, singly or together, might serve to approximate the various functions of consent. If the consent requirement is justified because it promotes autonomy, for example, departing from the requirement might be justified if the objective of promoting subjects' autonomy were satisfactorily served in some alternative manner.

First, in certain types of social research investigators who believe they must preserve the "naivete" of their actual subjects could use what Diana Baumrind has termed "peer consultants, selected in the same manner as public opinion poll respondents," to review the proposed experimental or observational procedures.[15] By taking the subjects' peers into their confidence, scientists would minimize the appearance of fraud. Although the actual subjects would be deceived, the deception would lose much of its bad odor were it publicly aired in advance (not just among the *investigator's* peers, in which circle the cleverness of the planned duplicity may be regarded as a sign of professional merit rather than of wrongdoing). More important, the use of peer consultants would symbolize that the investigator regards the general class from which the research participants will be drawn as rational agents worthy of consideration. By treating them as collaborators with a say in the design of research, the investigators may also approximate one function of "self-determination," which is to minimize risks unacceptable to the subjects.

The adequacy of the first strategy turns, however, on the problematic assumption that peer consultants are accurate "proxies." Some have suggested that the goal of self-determination could more adequately be approximated by a second strategy, debriefing. I am somewhat skeptical that this procedure is as valuable for subjects as its proponents claim, despite its obvious role in quieting a researcher's conscience. In any event, debriefing and "after-the-fact consent" cannot be regarded as the equivalents of informed consent. For purposes of distinction, they may instead be considered as conferring a form of "veto" power. The subject, having been told facts about a research project he did not know when participating in the research, is afforded the opportunity to forbid any retention or use of the data, although it is too late to withhold consent for the manipulation or observation itself. The debriefing-veto procedure goes far to promote the three aspects of autonomy described previously: (*a*) it gives the subject an opportunity to exercise self-determination about at least a portion of his or her relationship with the research, (*b*) it symbolizes the investigator's respect for the subject's autonomy by offering the chance to accept (or refuse) the role of collaborator and by explaining the reasons for the deception, and (c) assuming that the opportunity to veto is genuine, it avoids duress and minimizes the fraud implicit in concealed research.

The two remaining strategies, which ought to be viewed in tandem, are to conduct research without consent only in cases of negligible risk (as described during the discussion of the utilitarian approach) and to compensate subjects for all harm. Although these devices do not provide functional replacements for the philosophical aspects of autonomy (the respect owed to each individual as a human being with a right of self-determination), they may approximate the more practical function that consent serves in promoting self-determination: that an individual ought not to be subjected to harm that he or she has not chosen to risk.

Use of the "negligible harm" strategy means that if a bad result occurs that a subject has not chosen, at least it ought not to be *very* bad. Hand in hand with this, the "compensation" strategy means that reimbursement must be made for any injury, however minimal, that occurs when consent has not been obtained. Dangers certainly lurk in any too ready acceptance of these procedures as substitutes for individualized consent. Who is to say what harm is "negligible"? Is not the subjective nature of such evaluations one important reason that originally justified first-party consent requirements, lest some persons' peculiar sensitivities go unnoticed? Furthermore, the establishment of a workable compensation system will be very difficult.* Nevertheless, the use of these "strategies," particularly in combination with each other, would go a long way to approximate the function that informed consent serves in promoting the autonomy and self-determination of research subjects.

Improving Research

A second set of objectives advanced by the requirement of informed consent might be described as those associated with good research design and education. First, the requirement of candid disclosure to subjects will provoke investigators to review what they know about the research; this in turn may lead them to discover unknown risks and to understand, from the literature or

---

*Although probably a desirable adjunct to any scheme for "no consent" research (or even, at the opposite extreme, for consented research on a strict liability basis), compensation does present problems in the case of some social science research. First, the increments of harm are likely to be small, such that they will either be shrugged off by most subjects or be extremely costly to ascertain, relative to the amount of compensation actually paid. Second, the harm is likely to be of a sort (social or psychological) that is much more difficult to measure than the physical harm usually thought of as arising in biomedical research. Finally, the nature of the harm may lead many to view it with suspicion; this, in turn, is likely to cause those wishing to pursue compensation to exaggerate their claims, which will only increase the skepticism of those called upon to judge claims for recompense.

even from original inquiry and simulation, as much as possible about the research and its possible consequences. (Of course, even with a fertile imagination and a conscientious intent to make full disclosure, a social science investigator may not be able to anticipate *all* the risks or problems of a proposed study.) Moreover, the scientific validity and safety of a study may further be enhanced by what Paul Freund has termed the "reflexive effect [of the obligation to obtain consent] on the management of the experiment itself."[16]

Second, "the beneficial effects of informed consent in terms of rationality in the process of decision making . . . go beyond influencing the investigator. Rationality in resource allocation is possible only when the individuals who bear the costs and receive the benefits from the allocation determine the value of the outcome."[17] In the case of research, if choice is taken away from subjects, then it is possible that the benefit-risk calculations on which the decision to proceed were premised misevaluate the actual effects as perceived by the subjects. Of course, subjects' perceptions themselves are not immutable; indeed, one beneficial effect of a truly *informative* consent process can be to alter subjects' preconceptions that particular outcomes or procedures are unacceptable. Furthermore, in certain types of social science research (e.g., longitudinal studies of developments within families), the active collaboration of knowledgeable participants may increase the accuracy and pertinence of the data collected.

Similarly, the prospects for good social science research will be improved if the public is favorably inclined toward the research enterprise. The requirement to obtain informed consent serves this purpose by occasioning disclosure about the study in an affected population. Understanding the "purposes of the research," one of the HHS requirements that has engendered particular controversy among social scientists, is particularly valuable for this goal.

Again we may ask, are there strategies that might approximate these same functions in the absence of consent? Several of those suggested in the preceding section may be relevant here as well. For example, investigators may be prompted to scrutinize research design and explore its risks if they have to prepare what they will say in debriefing participants in a study. Indeed, the fact that the explanations come *after* the experiment, when the actions of the investigator have precluded real choice about participation, increases the need for careful attention to the "scenario" of disclosure. Even when no adverse consequences have occurred, an investigator would not welcome the prospect of being caught flat-footed during debriefing by a subject who points to a serious weakness in the research design and says, "Why didn't you think of that?"

Sensitive debriefing can also diminish adverse public reaction to research that has been conducted without prior consent. Indeed, by explaining the difficulties that the investigators faced in trying to resolve the conflict between principles of sound research design and of informed consent and the care they took in doing so, the process of debriefing may actually increase public sympathy for researchers. The use of "peer consultants" ought also to increase the community's awareness and approval of properly designed and conducted research, especially if the protocol includes provision for compensating subjects who are harmed (so that their care is not thrust upon the community).

Consultation with peers or with "a variety of community leaders, including clergymen and elected officials, such as councilmen or aldermen," or the leaders of "a single well-recognized organization that can speak for the community" under study might also improve the rationality of project design and execution.[18] It could lead social scientists to revise or abandon projects involving risks which they did not realize would be unacceptable to the group of people affected. Further, if the process of informing the community precludes complete naïveté on the part of future subjects (i.e., where, prior to an observational study, the investigators make their presence and general objectives known to the community as a whole), it may at least have the beneficial effect of *equalizing* the preconceptions that the subjects will have about their role in the project. It must be admitted, however, that any strategy making use of formal review by an official public body such as a city council runs the serious risk of resulting in disapproval, since a small number of vocal opponents can exercise disproportionate influence in such bodies.

Hence, the important ways in which informed consent improves the quality of research design and execution may to some degree be achieved through the use of alternative methods. Again, if the requirement of consent derives from its tendency to promote the relevant objectives—such as investigators' self-scrutiny, rationality in decision making, and public understanding—then it would be acceptable to waive that requirement when these objectives are met through other means that are more compatible with social science experiments.

Regularizing Relationships

Informed consent can also be viewed as a means of bringing the unusual relationship of investigator and subject within the norms of more typical social interactions. Although this function of consent is not articulated in the case law, it provides a good description of the role consent might play in social science research and suggests some intriguing theories for modifying consent requirements.

The notion I want to scrutinize here may be illuminated by several examples. First, consider a study in which randomly selected subjects from the target population are given something novel, to test its benefit. Another group from the same population is randomly selected as the control, but is merely observed to provide comparison data as a monitor for extraneous sources of apparent benefit in the subject group. To develop the notion of "regularization of relationships," I want to take issue with a conclusion of the Social Science Research Council Committee considering social experimentation as it would apply to this hypothetical experiment. The committee concluded that there was no "general obligation to inform controls that they are controls, particularly if they are being compensated in some way for their cooperation."[19] Several reasons for finding this conclusion mistaken are unrelated to the regularization point. For example, observation of the subjects is itself a form of intervention, and hence one is obliged to inform them that they are being used as controls. More to the point, greater use is being made of them than they would have reason to believe if "left with the impression that they were involved in survey research rather than in an experiment."[20] Most people do not expect to undertake one set of tasks for other people while being paid to do something else. In other words, deception (at least in circumstances where custom has not made it routine, and thereby probably accepted) is one type of conduct that falls outside social norms; if subjects are being deceived, their relationship with the investigators is "irregular." Through the use of informed consent processes (preferably consent prior to randomization) the relationship between control subjects and researchers could be returned to the norms that (at least in ideal circumstances) are supposed to prevail.

A second illustration can be found in purely observational research. Suppose a social scientist wishes to study the reactions of women between ages eighteen and thirty to personal appearances by leading presidential contenders. Suppose further that the women are all to be observed at public outdoor rallies attended by many people, including representatives of the media. Need the formal consent of these women be sought for the collection of data when the persons are not identified by name? If one answers "no," as I would, one is pointed to a strategy for answering the overall question about the necessity of consent: None may be required where it is not needed to conform the interaction of investigator and subject to already accepted norms of social relationships. In the instance given, the researchers' observations differ neither in kind nor in intensity from those we can normally expect other people to take.

Another alternative is to say that one is permitted to dispense with explicit informed consent in those instances of social science research in which the potential subjects give *implied consent.* Such an exception to the usual consent requirements has a firm place in the law of informed consent; indeed, it is the overwhelming basis for physicians' interventions in their common, everyday interactions with patients. To be acceptable, however, the implication of consent has to rest on something more than the subjects' obliviousness to the investigators' activities. In the previous example, a researcher's open and undisguised taking of notes on crowd response at the political rally would seem to provide an adequate basis for implied consent, if we may assume that anyone sensitive to being observed had ready means for avoiding the observer, such as moving elsewhere within the crowd, or leaving it entirely. (In the case of social science research it would seem advisable to limit this alternative, less formal means of obtaining consent, to situations in which the relationship of the investigator and subject already approximates that typifying normal interpersonal relations. After all, social science research subjects, unlike patients, have not actively sought the interaction to satisfy their own needs.)

I trust that these examples have served to flesh out the notion of "regularizing relationships." The function of explicit or implied consent here is to return power over the research interaction to the subjects. By conducting their research, investigators have changed the normal relationship of equality between freely associating individuals in a society into one in which they have usurped power over aspects of the subjects' lives and personalities. Surreptitious observations of illegal or immoral activities provide one illustration. The "staging" of fake incidents to measure the "Samaritan" response of individuals in different types of crowds is another.*

Again, if informed consent is not sought prior to commencing the study, are there other steps that can be taken that will approximate the function consent serves as a means of normalizing the relationship? One such alternative might be debriefing-with-veto-power. If subjects, following debriefing, are enabled to extricate themselves from the relationship and reassert their control over their own "participation" by forbidding any use of data concerning themselves, then, assuming other concerns do not pertain in that particular instance, an acceptable alternative to consent may have been found. This strategy will be especially useful when it is the possible results of the research (e.g., studies addressed to the behavior, attitudes, and so forth of identified subgroups in society) that most concern the subjects. If they are in a position to stop the research "after the fact" of observation or manipulation, but before data compilation and publication, their major concerns about not having had the opportunity to "consent" may be allayed.

Another strategy for conducting research without formal, prior consent is to establish true reciprocity in the relationship between investigators and subjects. By reciprocity, I mean that the conduct of the researchers should be similar to other conduct that the subjects, or people similarly situated, engage in toward the researchers and each other. This alternative will be particularly applicable to survey research and nonmanipulative and nonintensive participant observation.[21] The reasoning is that to make more equitable the balance of power and control in the investigator-subject relationship will return it to normality, in much the same way that holding to the requirement of informed consent would.

Other strategies that have been discussed previously may also serve to approximate the function of regularizing relationships. Insistence on a negligible level of risk and on provision for compensation would make a social science investigator's relationship to subjects being used without consent more

---

*It seems to me, incidentally, that it is the staging of the event, not the falsity of the actions, that disrupts usual social expectations. For example, to hire actual epileptics as confederates to have seizures on subway cars is, in my opinion, no different from having a nonepileptic confederate fake seizures.

like an ordinary social interaction, since most such interactions either involve a very low level of risk or at least implicit consent to a higher risk. (Often implied consent to moderate or greater risk is part of a situation of reciprocity, such as that of drivers on highways, who expose themselves and each other to comparable dangers.)[22] Moreover, even when mutual consent is implied by participation in a social interaction, there is an increasing expectation that funds will be available from insurance mechanisms or the public exchequer to cushion any heavy losses.

Finally, it should be noted that the regularizing-relationships approach is a criterion both of inclusion *and* exclusion. That is, when researchers operate without consent, the "regularizing" approach will exclude conduct that is unacceptable in ordinary social dealings, such as extensive reliance on deception. On the other hand, it may lead to the conclusion that certain questionable conduct is permissible because it would be acceptable in non-researchers. (Diana Baumrind illustrates this point with the example of not telling children the full truth about the purpose of an observer's presence in their classroom.)[23]

Protecting Privacy

One of the undeniable functions of the informed consent requirement has been to protect subjects from unwanted invasions of their privacy. The concept of "privacy" now carries a good deal of legal freight.[24] In constitutional law it has been expanded to encompass a general notion of broad—albeit not unlimited—self-determination, especially insofar as one's body is concerned.[25] (This aspect of privacy is thus included within the notion of autonomy previously described.)

In tort law the protection afforded by "privacy" may have some additional light to shed on social science research. As mentioned at the outset, the notion of consent first concerned the protection of bodily integrity; an unconsented touching is a battery, a species of intentional tort.[26] The aspect of privacy closest to this is the protection against physical invasion of a private sphere. This concept has now been expanded and would encompass research intruding on subjects, even in a nonphysical fashion, when the intrusion would be offensive or objectionable to a reasonable person (as by eavesdropping or persistent surveillance).[27]

Two other aspects of the privacy tort that may limit social science research would be appropriation and public disclosure of private facts that falls short of defamation. The offense here is a subtle one, for as Charles Fried has written: "Privacy is not simply an absence of information about us in the minds of others, rather it is the control we have over information about ourselves."[28] Although appropriation is normally thought of in commercial terms, Fried's analysis suggests the propertylike quality of personal information. Even in public settings, people may reasonably expect that others are deriving only x

amount of personal information about them as a matter of custom. Someone who through intense or coordinated observation derives $x + y$ may be taking something that most people do not intend to give. The harm is compounded if information thus obtained (or obtained on the basis of "consent" without adequate disclosure) is published and injures the reputation of subjects or the group of which they are a part.[29]

This analysis of the privacy interests that the consent requirement is designed to protect suggests that some of the strategies set forth previously may again approximate the role played by consent. It also underlines several pitfalls in those strategies. On the positive side, a compensation plan would quiet some concerns that an important right of subjects might be left permanently injured. On the other hand, the use of "peer consultants" appears less attractive when privacy interests are included in our calculations, since these interests are usually regarded as very personal and not to be exercised by one person for another (outside of one's family, for example). Moreover, any notion of slight or negligible harm must take into account the harm inherent in a privacy invasion, independent of resulting embarrassment or injury to reputation. If this view prevails at face value, then compensation would have to be made to each subject whose privacy had been intruded upon without prior consent, unless a "forgiveness" procedure is incorporated into the debriefing-and-veto strategy.

In sum, it is very hard to conceive how any strategy could substitute for the role that prior consent serves in making each person the gatekeeper for others' entry into the realm of his or her personal privacy. Nevertheless, if social scientists do not intrude into this sphere, perhaps the concerns about privacy fall away, and on that ground, at least, no substitute for an advance process of informed consent need be sought for research so limited.[30]

Conclusion

In this chapter, bases for a negative answer to the question, "Is consent always necessary in social science research?" have been sought. Whether they have been found is for the reader to say; the author remains skeptical, if not entirely unconvinced.

Were the regulations mandating subjects' consent as a precondition of research—and, indeed, the entire regulatory apparatus—constructed along utilitarian lines, it would not be difficult to find reasons for exempting at least some social science research from adherence to the consent requirement. But even a cursory evaluation of the regulations and their history leads to the conclusion that they cannot be justified in either act- or rule-utilitarian terms. If, instead, the consent requirement is based upon certain purposes that it is said to serve, then logic suggests that consent might be dispensable were these purposes capable of being met through other means. A review of some plausible functions of consent—promoting autonomy and self-determination, improving research, regularizing relationships, and protecting privacy—produces several "strategies" for approximating these functions.

Four of these strategies—identification of negligible risks to subjects, the existence of true reciprocity of power and authority between investigator and subject, a subject-investigator relationship that resembles "regular" (or "normal") social interactions, and the absence of any invasion of subject's privacy—are substantive. They depend upon someone's determination that a particular study falls into the category in which formal consent requirements are properly either waived or at least substantially modified. Several other strategies are procedural. Investigators would have to convene a group of peers of their proposed subjects as consultants (or turn to a formally organized body) or they would have to work out procedures to debrief subjects following their participation in the project and to allow the subjects to veto any use of data about themselves in the research. Finally, at least one palliative strategy emerged, which is simply to establish a compensation procedure for anyone injured in social science research without his or her consent.

As the difficulty of actually working out such a scheme suggests, much would remain if these strategies were to serve as the basis for an IRB's implementation of the newly revised regulations so as to permit social science research previously precluded because of the consent requirement. Furthermore, concern over the difficulty of measuring harm should not only alert us to the underlying notions of privacy and autonomy, which may be injured in intangible fashion, but also remind us that harm done in losing control over aspects of one's life (as represented by others having unconsented knowledge of it) may not be retrievable through after-the-fact requests for assent or offers of compensation. Given my initial skepticism, I would be comfortable employing these "strategies" in place of consent only if convinced that a very valuable research project could definitely not be conducted if ordinary consent requirements were maintained.

Notes

The federal regulations on which this chapter is based are those in force in September 1979, when it was first presented, and in 1980, when it was revised. With the exception of note 7 below, the numbering and content of the federal regulations cited in the remainder of this chapter refer to these regulations. On January 26, 1981, new regulations were issued that permit much social science research to be treated differently from biomedical research. Although an IRB's ability to waive both the informed consent requirement (new § 46.116 [c] and [d]) and the usual procedures for documenting consent (new § 46.117 [c]) is spelled out more explicitly in the new regulations, many of the same questions remain, particularly if one is looking for underlying justifications for an IRB's actions.

In many respects, the issues raised in the sections of this paper on functional alternatives to informed consent are relatively independent of any particular regulatory structure. These sections focus on the moral problems that IRBs and investigators face when they contemplate conducting social science research without informed consent. By expanding the options open to an IRB, the new regulations have increased rather than decreased the moral burden on IRBs as they develop consent policies at the institutional level.

1. Department of Health, Education, and Welfare, Protection of Human Subjects, 45 C.F.R § 46.103(b)(1979).

This chapter focuses on the necessity of consent from "subjects at risk" in social science research and not on the nature of that risk. Suffice it to note that besides the possible harmful side effects (in social or psychological, as well as physical, terms) that constitute "risk" for such subjects just as they do for subjects in biomedical research, subjects in social science research may also be exposed to such additional harm as the withdrawal effects consequent to the ending of the research (as, for example, the termination of an "income supplement" in an experiment on the effect of additional income on the desire to work) or intrusions into areas of the subjects' lives (and the lives of their friends and relations) not encompassed in the research design.

2. But see notes 1 and 7 and the discussion by Richard A. Tropp in this volume. Consent is not required when the federal government formally dispenses with it in social policy experimentation, as through legislative permission 42 U.S.C. § 1315, which allows the Secretary of HHS to permit experimental deviation for some participants in certain programs. See, e.g., *Aguayo* v. *Richardson,* 473 F.2d 1090 (2d Cir. 1973); *California Welfare Rights Organization* v. *Richardson,* 348 F.Supp. 491 (N.D. Cal. 1972); but see *Crane* v. *Matthews,* 417 F.Supp. 532 (N.D. Ga. 1976) (requiring IRB approval, and informed consent if subjects are found to be "at risk," in Medicaid copayment experiment).

3. 44 Fed. Reg. 47,895 (1979) (to be codified in 45 C.F.R. § 46.110(a) (4), replacing 45 C.F.R. § 46.102(b) (1) (1979), which varies slightly in wording).

4. 44 Fed. Reg. 47,895 (1979) (to be codified in 45 C.F.R. § 46.110(a) (5)).

5. John Rawls, "Two Concepts of Rules," *Philosophical Review* 64 (1955): 3-32.

6. See, e.g., Nuremberg Code, Section 1: "The voluntary consent of the human subject is absolutely essential."

7. Under the recent revisions in the HHS regulations (46 Fed. Reg. 8366–8391 [January 26, 1981]), no IRB approval is needed for survey and interview research and observation with subjects who are not identified or are not exposed to criminal or employment risks or are not involved in sensitive matters (e.g., alcohol use, sexual behavior, etc.) (45 C.F.R. § 46.101[b][3] and [4]). Furthermore, research coming within a list of procedures announced by the secretary of HHS as of "no more than minimal risk" may be approved by an IRB through "expedited review procedures" (45 C.F.R. § 46.110). It seems reasonable to question whether "no consent" should be permitted in those cases where expedited review is employed. In other words, the notion of "minimal risk" should not be allowed to do double duty; if it is proposed to dispense with advance consent because risks are seen as low, the institutional review board ought carefully to inquire: Is risk really negligible? Should peers of the subjects be consulted to help evaluate the risks and benefits? And so forth.

8. *Schloendorff* v. *New York Hospital,* 211 N.Y. 127, 129, 105 N.E. 92, 93 (1914).

9. *Salgo* v. *Leland Stanford Jr. Univ. Bd. of Trustees,* 154 Cal. App. 2d. 560, 317 P.2d 170 (1957).

10. *Natanson* v. *Kline,* 186 Kan. 393, 350 P.2d 1093, *clarified and rehearing denied,* 187 Kan. 186, 354 P.2d 670 (1960).

11. Jay Katz and Alexander Morgan Capron, *Catastrophic Diseases: Who Decides What?* (New York: Russell Sage Foundation, 1975), p. 80.

12. Isaiah Berlin, *Two Concepts of Liberty* (Oxford: Clarendon Press, 1958), p. 16.

13. Margaret Mead, "Research with Human Beings: A Model Derived from Anthropological Field Practice," *Daedalus* 98 (1969): 375.

14. Katz and Capron, *Catastrophic Diseases,* p. 85.

15. Diana Baumrind, "Nature and Definition of Informed Consent in Research Involving Deception," in National Commission for the Protection of Human Subjects of Biomedical and Behavioral Research, *The Belmont Report: Ethical Principles and Guidelines for the Protection of Human Subjects of Research,* DHEW Publication no. (OS) 78-0014 (Washington, D.C.: Government Printing Office, 1978), appendix, vol. 2, pp. 23-42.

16. Paul Freund, "Legal Frameworks for Human Experimentation," *Daedalus* 98 (1969): 323.

17. Katz and Capron, *Catastrophic Diseases,* pp. 88-89.

18. Henry W. Riecken and Robert F. Boruch, eds., *Social Experimentation: A Method for Planning and Evaluating Social Intervention* (New York: Academic Press, 1974), p. 248. It is important to keep in mind that, particularly as regards minority groups, whose voices may not be well heeded in official political bodies, there remains a distinct advantage in dealing with prospective subjects' *true* peers, rather than with formally elected "representatives."

19. Ibid, p. 254.

20. Ibid.

21. See also the discussion of Cassell in this volume.

22. See generally George Fletcher, "Fairness and Utility in Tort Theory," *Harvard Law Review* 85 (1972): 537–73.

23. Baumrind, "Nature and Definition of Informed Consent," pp. 23-58.

24. See generally Terry Pinkard, "Invasions of Privacy in Social Science Research," in this volume.

25. See e.g., *Roe* v. *Wade,* 410 U.S. 113 (1973).

26. See generally Alexander Morgan Capron, "Informed Consent in Catastrophic Disease Research and Treatment," *University of Pennsylvania Law Review* 123 (1974): 346-47, 404-23.

27. William L. Prosser, *Handbook of the Law of Torts* (St. Paul: West Publishing Co., 1971), p. 808. This and other senses of "privacy" are discussed by Terry Pinkard, "Invasions of Privacy."

28. Charles Fried, "Privacy," *Yale Law Journal* 77 (1968): 482.

29. See Prosser, *Handbook,* pp. 809-12.

30. See 45 C.F.R. § 46.101(b)(4) and (5) (exemption for research involving only observation of public behavior or uses of publicly available sources of information).

10

Keeping Deception Honest: Justifying Conditions for Social Scientific Research Stratagems

ALAN C. ELMS

The Problem of Deception: A Consequentialist Middle Ground

Deception is a word used to end arguments, not to begin them. To accuse researchers of deception is to remove them from the ranks of those with whom legitimate human relationships can be pursued. The term is so sweeping that it includes Satan's lures for lost souls, the traitor's treachery, the false lover's violation of a pure heart. How could any deception ever be considered ethically justifiable if it keeps such company?

The use of so broad a term as *deception* is itself deceptive when applied without qualification to certain common procedures in social scientific research. It muddies issues, biases ethical debates, lumps together a vast array of practices that differ in intent, execution, and outcome. Because of such radical differences among various practices labeled "deception," social scientists have suggested other terms for the kinds of stratagems used in their research, such as "staging" or "technical illusions."[1]

But stage plays and magic tricks are not quite on the same order as our research stratagems, either. The researcher hopes that subjects will not realize an illusion is being created. If the experiment is to work, they should perceive the stage scenery through which they are walking, the memorized speeches of the actors around them, as genuine. When the curtain falls, they are not likely to break into spontaneous applause—any more than they are likely to call the Bunco Squad or the Consumer Fraud Division. So "staging" and similar terms are as problematic as "deception." In lieu of a better word, I will continue to use "deception" for the practice of misleading research subjects, even though it obliterates important distinctions among forms of deception.

Certain ethicists refuse to differentiate social scientists' attempts to mislead subjects from any other kind of deception, conceptually as well as terminologically. For them, the argument is already over: there are no circumstances under which social scientific deception is ethically permissible. Non-absolutists are likely to find such an absolutist stance worth little attention, and I do not have the space to examine it closely here. For those who are interested, Sissela Bok has summarized the basic philosophical arguments against it.[2]

232

Certain others—I hesitate to call them ethicists, though they do hold down the other end of the ethical scale from the moral absolutists—insist that normal rules do not apply to science, that the end knowledge fully justifies the deceptive means. In extreme form, these people appear to us as Nazi eugenicists or as the mad scientists of Hollywood—much beloved by the moral absolutists, who need such opponents to justify their own extremist stance. In milder form, they include simple corner-cutters, Machiavellian careerists, and earnest believers in the primacy of scientific truth.

The position in the middle of the scale is the hard one to hold. Here are those who see life as filled with moral conflicts, rarely easy to resolve, and who see social scientific research as a necessary part of their ethical life. They see such research as the best route to certain ethical goals, and an element of deception as essential to certain kinds of research. They do not accept deception easily, and so they are the ones who might ask, and who need to know, what conditions make deceptions sometimes ethically tolerable in social scientific research. They are the ones to whom I am mainly speaking, and whom at the same time I am trying to represent.

In so doing, I am taking what is variously called a consequentialist, risk-benefit, or cost-benefit position. Shakespeare neatly dramatized the classic case for this position in *Measure for Measure,* where he presented a novice nun with a moral dilemma: should she yield her virginity to a rapacious judge in order to save her brother's life, or should she deceive the judge and thereby save both her brother and her sexual virtue? The Duke of Vienna, apparently voicing Shakespeare's own sentiments, counsels her to deceive the judge. He assures her that "the doubleness of the benefit defends the deceit from reproof."[3] The Duke and Shakespeare are making a cost-benefit analysis, and they conclude that in this instance the benefits of deception considerably outweigh the costs. Most people other than the strictest moral absolutists would agree: when the value of honesty conflicts with other values, certain circumstances may make those other values more important than honesty, and deception then becomes tolerable.

"Tolerable" does not mean "ethically neutral." Deception is, as Bok argues, never a neutral practice.[4] It always carries potential harm to the interests of the deceived, in this case to the research subjects who might have chosen to avoid research participation had they been fully and accurately informed. It always carries potential harm to the deceivers, in this case the researchers and their assistants, whose reputation for veracity may be harmed and whose own character may be affected negatively by repeated deceptive practices. It carries potential harm to the deceivers' profession, since social scientists in general may become less trusted as the deceptive practices of part of the profession become well known. And it carries potential harm to society, in that it may contribute to a general lack of trust and to the willingness of nonprofessionals to act deceptively themselves. Perhaps none of these potential harms will be realized, if social scientific deception remains on a small scale and is surrounded by various kinds of constraints and counteractive efforts. But given the potential for harm, deception in social scientific research is not something to be employed casually. It must be carefully justified and any negative effects must be offset as much as possible.

What, then, are the boundary conditions under which deception can be considered ethically justifiable in social scientific research? I will state the major conditions in a single sentence, and then expound upon each term: *deception is justifiable in social scientific research when* (1) *there is no other feasible way to obtain the desired information,* (2) *the likely benefits substantially outweigh the likely harms,* (3) *subjects are given the option to withdraw from participation at any time without penalty,* (4) *any physical or psychological harm to subjects is temporary,* and (5) *subjects are debriefed as to all substantial deceptions and the research procedures are made available for public review.* All of these conditions are by now familiar to researchers and ethicists; some have already been built into federal law. Most social scientists who use deception have accepted the conditions as reasonable and even necessary components of their own ethical decision-making processes. But not all ethicists have accepted the conditions as *sufficient* justification. I would like to argue that these five conditions are both necessary *and* sufficient justifications for the use of deception in social scientific research.

Lack of Feasible Alternatives

Henry A. Murray stated the primary justification for social scientific deception some forty years ago, in the opening pages of his classic work *Explorations in Personality.*[5] Among "the few general principles that our [research] experience invited us to adopt," he lists two that are immediately relevant:

> [A.] The experimental session should be as life-like as possible. This is important because the purpose of personological studies is to discover how a man reacts under the stress of common conditions. To know how he responds to a unique, unnatural laboratory situation is of minor interest.
>
> [B.] The subject's mind should be diverted from the true purpose of an experiment. This is usually accomplished by announcing a plausible but fictitious objective. If a subject recognizes the experimenter's aim, his responses will be modified by other motives: for instance, by the desire to conceal the very thing which the experimenter wishes to observe.

Deception is at times necessary, Murray says, in order to create a laboratory situation that will seem life-like rather than artificial, since situations that strike the subject as artificial will tell us little about human behavior and may even mislead us. We need experimental control over relevant variables because neither naturalistic observation nor the subtlest statistical manipulations of available data will in all cases allow us to sort out the crucial psychological variables; but, paradoxically, we must sometimes use deception to make an experimentally created situation *seem* real, so that subjects will give genuine, generalizable responses.

Elliot Aronson and J. Merrill Carlsmith make a useful distinction in this regard between "experimental realism" and "mundane realism."[6] An experiment is realistic in the first sense "if the situation is realistic to the subject, if it involves him, if he is forced to take it seriously, if it has impact on him." It is realistic in the second sense "to the extent to which events occurring in a laboratory setting are likely to occur in the 'real world.' . . . The mere fact that an event is similar to events that occur in the real world does not endow it with importance. Many events that occur in the real world are boring and uninvolving." Thus an experiment may be trivial because it is unrealistic in any sense; or it may be trivial because it merely presents some version of mundane reality. But it may transcend triviality by the "stress of common conditions," through the creation of an invented but emotionally involving experimental reality. The latter kind of experiment may be an important route to valuable information about human behavior (whereas the former kinds will never be); and it may be possible to pursue such a route only through the use of deception.

But what of alternative routes? Why not, for instance, simply approach people honestly and ask them to tell us about themselves? This is in some circumstances the best procedure to follow, and I certainly find it a more *comfortable* procedure than deceptive experimentation. But Murray points out its weakness as an exclusive approach, in his Principle B. Wittingly or unwittingly, a subject's knowledge that particular aspects of his or her behavior are under study will almost certainly lead to modifications of that behavior. Enough data are available on the powerful effects of "demand characteristics," the subtle and unintended cues from researchers concerning their intentions and expectations, to indicate that explicit acknowledgement of such intentions and expectations could seriously disrupt normal behavior patterns. Further, subjects may have less than admirable reasons for trying intentionally to mislead researchers about their behavior—particularly about those aspects of behavior that society might have a strong interest in understanding and perhaps in working to modify. Destructive obedience, child abuse, racial and sexual prejudice, authoritarianism—the list could easily be extended of important psychological patterns that many people would be reluctant to admit, but that we need to understand much better if we wish to build a more satisfying society for all. If individuals will not talk about such matters honestly when they are asked straightforwardly, some form of research deception may be essential in order to gain the information we need.

Moreover, people may simply not know how they would behave in certain socially important but seldom encountered situations. Concerning such matters, it may be useless to ask people what they would probably do, and impossible to observe them in relevant real-life situations where the major variables are sufficiently unconfounded to let us make sense of the psychological processes at work. Once again, some use of deception to create an experimental reality may be the only effective means to collect essential knowledge.

But what about simulation? The word here refers not to creating an experimental reality by artificial means, but to asking research subjects to *pretend* they are participating in a realistic experiment and having them report how they think they would behave if they really were in such an experiment. This kind of simulation has often been recommended by people who do not wish to abandon the strengths of experimental research but who find deception to be an unacceptable aspect of such research. Unfortunately, simulation has proven to be an inadequate alternative both methodologically and ethically. If the simulation is relatively undetailed, it is not much different from simply asking people directly to describe how they would behave in various circumstances in the real world, and it has the same flaws as that approach— people often don't know, or don't want to tell, how they would behave.[7] If the simulation closely reproduces each step of a genuine experiment, however—if for instance, as in Don Mixon's[8] or Daniel Geller's[9] simulations of the Milgram obedience studies, subjects are walked through every stage of the experiment, being given only the information available to genuine experimental subjects at each stage—it may gain in accuracy of subjects' self-reports at the expense of ethical losses. Simulation subjects may undergo stresses similar in quality if not in intensity to those experienced by genuine subjects, and at the end they may feel similarly misled as to the actual scope or intent of the experiment they have helped to simulate. Using another example, the fact that Philip Zimbardo's prison study[10] was a simulation does not divest it of the ethical dilemmas originally confronted in nonsimulation experiments. Further, even though simulation studies rendered sufficiently close in detail to the original experiment may yield similar data from their "as-if " subjects, serious doubt would always remain about the validity of a simulation study if no "real" experiment were available for comparison. The substitution of simulation studies for experiments experienced by their participants as real thus appears to be a commendable but unrealizable dream.

The Harm-Benefit Calculus

Here is where I must take an explicitly consequentialist position. Most social scientists are consequentialists, as least to some degree; otherwise they would not take the trouble to do social scientific research. The difficulty of framing and executing empirical studies, the high level of ambiguity that must be tolerated in the typical results, the ethical distress that never quite goes away—all these must be offset by the hope that some kind of social benefit will derive from the research in the long run. Otherwise, you might as well become a philosopher.

Remarkably little direct harm has ever come to subjects from academic social scientific research. I say "academic" because I am not willing to attempt any general ethical justification for the research programs of the CIA, General Mills, or the Church of Scientology, social scientific though they may be at times. They are not subject to the same kinds of regulations as academic research, and they are not open to free discussion or to the informal influence of scientific peer pressure. In terms of *academic* research, a potential subject is in far less physical danger during virtually any kind of research participation than in driving across town to an experimental session, or in spending the research hour playing tennis instead. Psychologically, as researchers have often pointed out to institutional review boards, the principal danger to the typical subject is boredom. The individual is at much greater psychological risk in deciding to get married, to have a baby, or to enroll as a college student—all activities typically entered without truly informed consent—than in participating in practically any academic research study ever carried out by a social scientist.

But what of the more notorious examples of psychologically stressful research? I worked behind the scenes of the most notorious of all, the Milgram obedience studies,[11] and I interviewed a substantial sample of the participants later,[12] as did (independently) a psychiatrist.[13] The remarkable thing about the Milgram subjects was not that they suffered great persisting harm, but that they suffered so little, given the intensity of their emotional reactions during the experiment itself. Through a combination of careful debriefing and their own standard coping mechanisms, nearly all subjects were able to process the Milgram experience as interesting but as basically irrelevant to their long-term psychological comfort. Though some commentators refuse to believe this, they must ignore not only the data on the Milgram subjects but also a great deal of evidence about human psychological resilience under much more traumatic conditions—from birth, through adolescence, to terminal illness. It may be possible to find an occasional individual who suffers some kind of lasting distress from an encounter with an inept experimenter, or from some unwanted self-insight induced by research participation.[14] But a botched debriefing cannot be held against the bulk of responsibly conducted studies, and a psychologically fragile individual's reactions to carefully managed research participation are unlikely to be any worse than to an emotionally involving movie, a fire-and-brimstone sermon, or a disappointing job interview.

And what of the indirect harms that might come from a deceptive study? I have already mentioned the possibility that deceptive research will generate a greater distrust of social scientists and of other people in general. Researchers should take such concerns into account in limiting deceptive research practices to a necessary minimum. But these concerns are often exaggerated, at times by elevating social scientists into sacred protectors of the truth who must never be caught in even momentary deception. The general public does not see social scientists that way, according to various public opinion polls. Furthermore, abuses of public trust by politicians, physicians, lawyers, ministers, business leaders, and other supposedly trustworthy individuals touch much more directly on people's lives than the encapsulated deceptions of social scientists.

Indeed, it could reasonably be argued that certain social scientific research practices, such as prompt debriefing after deception, should work to *promote* trust, in contrast to the attempts of these other societal leaders to maintain deceptions for as long as possible.

Given the generally minor harms of properly conducted social scientific research, what are the benefits? It must be acknowledged that few social scientific research studies will produce any *immediate* major benefits to participants or to society. Unless the researcher is testing a specific aspect of a carefully formulated social program, itself derived from earlier and more basic research, the findings are likely to be useful only in terms of adding to the broad body of social scientific knowledge, much of it tentative and even contradictory. That is the way of science, and it appears to be the way still more of social science, for reasons which we need not examine here. Any insistence that social science research always meet criteria of immediate utility would make it a mere adjunct of business, government, and military interests and would frustrate forever its development as a source of basic scientific discoveries useful in a broad range of applications.

Such preclusion of basic social scientific research would carry its own long-term ethical costs, usually ignored or dismissed by those intent on eliminating short-range costs. It is on this point that the ethical commitment of many social scientists is often misunderstood by professional ethicists. If your planned research clearly has some short-term ethical costs in terms of subject stress or deceptive practices, say the ethicists, why not use a less intrusive methodology or change your research topic entirely? Were researchers mainly concerned with professional respectability or academic advancement, one of those alternatives would indeed be the sensible course to take, and in fact some researchers have made such a shift—or have quit doing research altogether—in the face of difficulties with critics and IRBs. But other researchers continue to feel ethically obligated to investigate serious human issues in ways that are powerful enough scientifically to contribute to the expansion of basic knowledge, not merely in ways that will generate another journal publication as inoffensively as possible. These researchers are usually concerned with the immediate welfare of their subjects, and with the potentially negative social effects of such practices as deception; their critics have no monopoly on such concerns. But these researchers also perceive the dangers in sins of omission, of failures to do the responsible basic research that may contribute to major long-run social benefits. Such commitment to the active pursuit of usable, slowly cumulative information about human behavior may not be shared either by the more urgently involved practitioner or by the more contemplative philosopher; but its ethical foundations are genuine.

Research projects do differ, however, in their degree of potential benefits, and the differences may be important for our ethical decision making. How do we decide whether a proposed study has enough potential benefits to outweigh its potential harms—given that both are potential rather than actual? If there were easy answers to this question, we would not still be debating it. Our estimates of potential harms and benefits must be very crude at best, informed to some extent by previous experience but retaining a greater margin for error than any of us would like. Unless we decide simply to close down large areas of social scientific research, we must continue making such crude estimates and acting upon them, as individual researchers or as peer reviewers of research by others. Some kind of peer review is essential in assessing potential benefits, though it need not always be as extensive or as formal as certain government agencies now insist. If, by rough estimate, a piece of proposed research may potentially yield minor harms offset by minor benefits, it is not worth much ethical agonizing by anyone. If the rough estimate suggests minor benefits and major harms, we can easily reject the research as ethically unacceptable. If the estimate suggests minor harms and major benefits, most of us would be willing to approve the research, though we might wish to assess its actual harms and benefits later and to revise our judgmental criteria accordingly. It is only when our rough estimates suggest major potential harms *and* major potential benefits that we really begin to worry about the crudity of our estimates—and about what specific meaning to invest in such admittedly ambiguous terms as "major potential benefit."

We have already considered the question of harm with regard to the specific example of the Milgram obedience studies. Let us look at the question of benefit in the same context, since estimates of "major benefit" have been more disputed there than in perhaps any other example. Several of Stanley Milgram's critics appear to assume that his claims for the social value of his research were post-hoc justifications intended to quiet criticisms of his deceptive and stressful experimental practices. But Milgram had made a rather detailed case for substantial potential benefit in his original research proposals, and his research was funded on that basis. He had read widely concerning the events of the Holocaust and the various attempts to explain its origins. He did not propose yet another intellectual analysis, or a psychological study of some phenomenon previously much studied and perhaps vaguely related to the Holocaust, such as conformity to peer pressures. Instead, he proposed a series of studies that would examine specific contextual variables associated with greater or lesser obedience to a realistic command to administer severe physical pain to another individual. Doubtless there are many steps between such displays of individual obedience and the occurrence of a social phenomenon as broad and intense as the Holocaust. But it is reasonable to assume that laboratory research on destructive obedience could make a useful contribution to the understanding of destructive obedience on a large scale, even though it might not be the only way or even the single best way to proceed in elucidating the genesis of Holocaust-like phenomena. Further, it is reasonable to assume that better and wider public understanding of the conditions most likely to promote destructive obedience on a small scale could have a prophylactic effect with regard to destructive obedience on a large scale—although, again, there are surely many forces working in a complex society to strengthen or weaken tendencies toward genocidal Final Solutions. Thus, I think Milgram made a good case concerning potential benefit, on the basis of the issues involved and the means by which he proposed to study them. It is hard to conceive how anyone could make a better case, before the fact, for major benefits from basic social scientific research.

Furthermore, I think a case can now be made that the Milgram research has actually yielded substantial benefits in the years since its publication. Most ethical discussions of deceptive social scientific research heavily stress harm and lightly sketch benefits, as if any negative effects would reverberate through all of human society, while any positive effects would hardly resound beyond laboratory walls. That is not the way the diffusion of knowledge works in our society. I would suggest that Solomon Asch's deception-based research on social conformity helped sensitize a generation of college students to the dangers of conformism. I would suggest that Asch's student, Stanley Milgram, has helped to sensitize another generation, well beyond campus boundaries, to the possibility that they themselves could under certain circumstances be as obedient as the sternest Nazis. As much as Milgram's research offends certain moral sensibilities, it has also dramatized serious ethical choices so provocatively that virtually every introductory psychology and social psychology textbook of the past decade has prominently featured Milgram's findings.[15] Some social scientists and ethicists find it implausible that laboratory studies of individual psychological phenomena could yield any useful understanding of the dynamics of a Holocaust. I find it even more implausible to assume that research with the broad dissemination and emotional impact of Milgram's studies has not already generated enough introspection and discussion to diminish significantly the likelihood of another Holocaust-like phenomenon, at least in this country.

Few social scientific studies are likely to have the individual force of Milgram's obedience research. But judgments about their potential benefit can be made in similar fashion, on the basis of the researcher's serious consideration of factors likely to play a role in major social phenomena, the choice of apt research strategies, and the social implications of anticipated (or unanticipated but possible) research findings. At no time can these judgments be so definitive or so overwhelming as to outweigh certain kinds of research harm. But in combination with the remaining criteria, they may lead to a reasoned decision that limited potential harm deriving from deception and other aspects of the research design are outweighed by the likely long-term benefits of a particular research project as a part of the ongoing social scientific research enterprise.

The Option to Withdraw

One of the objections most often raised against research deception is that it prevents subjects from deciding whether to give their fully informed consent to research participation. "Informed consent" is a concept that grew out of medical experimentation, where the only way for patients to make an effective decision about research participation is to know well in advance what kinds of physical interventions might be imposed upon them. Many medical interventions have potentially serious and virtually irrevocable consequences, and if the patient fails to say "No" before being anesthetized, cut open, injected with cancer cells, infected with bacteria, etc., there may be no way of effectively saying "No" later. The situation is usually very different in social scientific research. As already suggested, the intervention is most often minor and the consequences are temporary or reversible (as by post-research debriefing). Perhaps even more important in an ethical sense is the possibility of an ongoing process of informed consent. Even if, for purposes of conducting a study, subjects must be asked to give their consent to participation partly on the basis of misleading or incomplete information, they can continue their assessment of the study's costs to them as it proceeds, and can be guaranteed the right to quit at any point where they decide that the costs are becoming greater than they wish to bear. This process of "ongoing informed consent" is implicit in many research situations, including interviews and questionnaires where the subject is fully in control of the information he or she supplies. In circumstances where the possible harms are greater—as when a questionnaire deals with particularly sensitive issues, or when an experiment manipulates social or other pressures to continue participation beyond normally tolerable limits of stress—the subject should clearly and emphatically be informed in advance of the right to stop participating at any time without penalty.

In some instances, a research procedure may have the potential to impose upon a subject a psychological harm well outside those encountered in normal social interactions, under circumstances where the subject is misled as to what is about to happen and is unable to withdraw his ongoing consent in time to avoid the harm. Such instances more closely resemble physical intervention without informed consent in medical research than does the usual social scientific study, and they should be placed under the same constraints as medical interventions. I am thinking here of such studies as those in which a subject fills out a personality questionnaire, then is suddenly and falsely told that the questionnaire reveals hidden homosexual tendencies or other characteristics that are highly discrepant from the subject's own self-image. Most subjects appear to accept rather easily, during debriefing, the information that an apparently realistic experimental situation has been fabricated or that a recently introduced stranger is not nearly as bad a person as the experimenter has made him out to be. But I suspect that a false imputation of homosexuality or neurosis, made by a psychologist, may continue to raise self-doubts well after the psychologist has changed stories. The characterization is not a consequence of the subject's own behavior, and its sudden attribution to the subject is made without an opportunity for ongoing informed consent.

The Milgram obedience studies have been criticized on somewhat similar grounds. But I do not see the Milgram studies as falling in the same category, since subjects in those studies were never falsely characterized. Subjects who shocked the "victim" unmercifully did so with little persuasion from the experimenter and much resistance from the "victim." They had the choice throughout the experiment of quitting at any time, and in fact a substantial portion of subjects did quit. A continuing opportunity was provided subjects to make a moral decision, and no force or unusual psychological technique was brought to bear to interfere with that choice. In such instances, where research participation brings unsought self-knowledge, I do feel that the researcher has a responsibility to help the subject cope with such self-knowledge and to give the subject some guidance in integrating it satisfactorily into his or her self-concept over the long run. Milgram's debriefing procedures were designed to do that, and the follow-up research suggests that they were effective in that regard. Self-knowledge in itself, even unsought self-knowledge, does not seem to me an ethically negative "risk." Ethically concerned individuals of many persuasions and cultural roles, including preachers, teachers, novelists, and charismatic leaders, have attempted throughout history to induce such knowledge in anyone whose attention they could momentarily catch, even by deceptive devices (such as embedding lessons about human nature within an apparently innocuous entertainment). The induction of unsought self-knowledge need not be seen as a major mission of social scientists, but neither should it be seen as an evil from which research subjects must be protected at all costs.

Temporary versus Lasting Harm

Though I am primarily a consequentialist rather than a deontologist, I am unwilling to balance the certainty of lasting harm to a misinformed subject against the possibility of general benefits as a result of a particular study. But temporary discomfort, anxiety, or even pain may fairly be weighed among the harms in a harm-benefit ratio, as long as the subject is permitted to cease participation whenever the distress becomes personally intolerable and as long as no lasting scars (physical or psychological) result. The generation of temporarily intense anxiety or pain should not be employed casually, even if these terms are met; it must be more than offset by the potential value of the research. Furthermore, as with unsought self-insight in the previous section, the researcher is obligated to take an active role in restoring the anxious or agitated subject to his or her normal emotional state. The debriefing period is usually the opportune time to do this.

Debriefing and Publicity

The debriefing period, properly used, is a time for limiting or eliminating several potential harms of deceptive research practices. First, it provides the occasion to diminish anxiety and other unpleasant emotional reactions, and to give the subject a sense of the true value of his or her participation as a research subject. Instead of leaving the subject with a sense of having been tricked, the researcher should honestly communicate the difficulty or impossibility of doing research on the topic at hand with full subject foreknowledge, and should describe the efforts necessary to give subjects a realistic—if deceptive—experience in a controlled setting. Second, the debriefing process restores a sense of honesty to the researcher, and by interrupting the role of arch-manipulator, it brings him or her back toward the human level of the subjects. Third, it provides an ethical model to researchers, subjects, and others of how a necessary deception can be limited in its consequences, how deception can be used without destroying the integrity of human social contacts or the autonomy and self-esteem of the individuals involved. Given the vast amounts of deception which occur in ordinary social life *without* any intentional debriefing, the use of deception linked with debriefing might even have a salutary effect upon the public sense of ethical standards, as already suggested, rather than producing the invidious effects predicted by certain critics of deceptive practices.

Finally, the requirement of debriefing is ethically advantageous in that it increases the level of publicity connected with the research. I am not referring to publicity in the usual sense of newspaper headlines and talk-show appearances, but to publicity as the term has been used by John Rawls and subsequently by Sissela Bok. As Bok puts it, "According to such a constraint, a moral principle must be capable of public statement and defense."[16] The general requirement of debriefing means that a researcher must at some reasonable point publicize his or her deceptive research procedures to the individuals most likely to be at risk as a result, namely, the subjects, and must therefore be able to justify the deceptions to them or risk some kind of retaliation from them. But publicity must involve more than the researcher's interactions with the subject, as the latter part of boundary condition 5 suggests.

Peer review and reviews by institutional review boards mean more publicity, more occasions when the researcher must be able to offer an acceptable ethical defense of any deceptive practices he or she feels to be required in the chosen research area. Still other professional practices common in the social sciences involve further publicity: peer reviews for academic promotions; peer reviews by granting agencies, in addition to IRB reviews; presentations of research procedures and findings at professional meetings; journal review and publication of research papers.

Conclusion: The Salutary Consequences of Publicity

Several years ago I wrote a short piece for *Psychology Today* in which I compared and contrasted experimental social psychologists with professional con artists.[17] The similarities, which were considerable, mainly concerned the practice of deception. The differences, which were also considerable, included such things as the principal motivations of psychologists vs. those of con artists and the attitudes of the two groups toward "subjects" or "marks." The *major* difference concerned the matter of publicity. Con artists avoid publicity as much as possible, and thus their deceptive practices can grow unchecked except by sheer force of law. Social psychologists, however, ordinarily seek publicity in the form of professional presentations, and have also by and large accepted its necessity in such forms as debriefing. Publicity of a perfectly ordinary professional sort was how the Milgram studies and others became the focus of a great deal of professional discussion of ethics, eventually widening to include discussion in the news media, on television drama programs, and in various circles of government. I say "publicity of a perfectly ordinary professional sort" because no scandal was involved, no hidden deceits were dramatically revealed, no damage suits came to court. Milgram talked and wrote about his research, and other people responded with their views on the ethical considerations involved, and Milgram responded in turn with his, and the dialogue continues.

The dialogue has by no means been a useless one. Deception in social science research has become much more constrained over the past fifteen years, in large part as the result of such voluntary publicity rather than through the coercion of federal regulations and financial threats. The federal government may ultimately outlaw deception in social scientific research altogether, in response to political pressures stronger than social scientists can muster—in which case I would not be surprised to see the spread of bootleg deception research on and off university campuses, conducted by researchers who feel they cannot study certain major issues effectively by any other means. That would be the ultimate ethical disaster for deception research, since in secret it would be hardly more constrained than the con artist's trade. The ultimate condition under which deception research is ethically justifiable is *out in the open,* where its practitioners are continually forced to present their justifications to others and where their critics must resort to reason rather than coercion. Ethical decision making is not a closed system in which a set of rules can be ordained once and applied to all situations forever after. I do not have all the answers about deception, its effects, and its reasonable limits; nor does anyone else. Continuing publicity about the kinds of deception social scientists see as necessary, and about the controlled conditions under which deception should be tolerated in research, will feed the ongoing dialogue about deception in such a way as to make our decisions about it increasingly more realistic, more sophisticated, and more ethical.

Notes

1. Stanley Milgram, "Subject Reaction: The Neglected Factor in the Ethics of Experimentation," *Hastings Center Report* 7, no. 5 (1977): 19.

2. Sissela Bok, *Lying: Moral Choice in Public and Private Life* (New York: Vintage Books, 1979), pp. 34-49.

3. *Measure for Measure,* act 3, scene 1. In William Shakespeare, *The Comedies* (New York: Heritage Press, 1958), p. 267.

4. Bok, *Lying,* pp. 32-33.

5. Henry A. Murray, *Explorations in Personality* (New York: Oxford University Press, 1938), pp. 26-28.

6. Elliot Aronson and J. Merrill Carlsmith, "Experimentation in Social Psychology," in G. Lindzey and E. Aronson, eds., *The Handbook of Social Psychology*, 2d ed. (Reading, Mass.: Addison-Wesley, 1968), vol. 2, pp. 22-23.

7. Jonathan L. Freedman, "Roleplaying: Psychology by Consensus," *Journal of Personality and Social Psychology* 13 (1969): 107-14.

8. Don Mixon, "Instead of Deception," *Journal for the Theory of Social Behavior* 2 (1972): 145-77.

9. Daniel M. Geller, "Involvement in Role-Playing Simulations: A Demonstration with Studies on Obedience," *Journal of Personality and Social Psychology* 36 (1978): 219–35.

10. Philip G. Zimbardo, "Pathology of Imprisonment," *Society* 9, no. 4 (1972): 4-6.

11. Stanley Milgram, *Obedience to Authority* (New York: Harper & Row, 1974).

12. Alan C. Elms, *Social Psychology and Social Relevance* (Boston: Little, Brown, 1972), pp. 153-54.

13. Stanley Milgram, "Issues in the Study of Obedience: A Reply to Baumrind," *American Psychologist* 19 (1964): 848-52.

14. Diana Baumrind, "Metaethical and Normative Considerations Covering the Treatment of Human Subjects in the Behavioral Sciences," in E. C. Kennedy, ed., *Human Rights and Psychological Research* (New York: Crowell, 1975), pp. 37-68.

15. In a recent tabulation of frequency of citations in introductory psychology textbooks, Milgram was found to be twelfth in rank among all psychologists, just below Carl Jung and higher than William James, John B. Watson, Abraham Maslow, or Leon Festinger. Daniel Perlman, "Who's Who in Psychology," *American Psychologist* 35 (1980): 104-6.

16. Bok, *Lying,* pp. 97-112.

17. Alan C. Elms, "Alias Johnny Hooker," *Psychology Today* 10, no. 9 (1977): 19.

11

Must Subjects Be Objects?

GERALD DWORKIN

The previous three papers on consent and deception all refer to the use of some kind of cost-benefit analysis, to some variety of consequentialism in ethics, and to some form of utilitarian moral theory. Each paper mentions the opposition between this predominantly utilitarian perspective on ethical issues raised by social science research and that perspective which makes use of various ideas put forward by Kant. Increasingly in the literature of ethics we find references to the Kantian idea of treating people as ends, and not simply as means, or respecting the autonomy of persons, or regarding people as ends in themselves. The extremely influential work of Rawls on justice, for example, is explicitly claimed to be a working out of such Kantian insights into the nature of morality. Although Rawls's theory is best viewed as a social contract theory of the hypothetical-consent variety, the determination of the various aspects of what he calls the original position (the nature of the parties to the contract, the requirement of universal consent, the absence of various kinds of information to the parties) is constrained by Kantian notions of autonomy and equality.

But the application of Kantian ethics to the resolution of particular moral dilemmas by natural and social scientists does not proceed by way of either Kantian or Rawlsian theory. Both in their theories and in the theories of those who attempt to apply them, it is simply assumed that we have a good idea of what the notion of "using people" or "treating them solely as means" comes to, and that the application of this idea is fairly straightforward. I wish in these comments to challenge both of these assumptions, with special application to the preceding papers.

The Use of Persons as Means

The first thing to note is that there are many things we can do to people which are bad, and are not to be identified with or subsumed under the idea of using people solely as means. We can insult, be spiteful toward, be unfair to, fail to be candid with, be cruel toward, ignore the needs of, steal from, murder, deprive of rights, humiliate, harm the interests of, be negligent toward, be indifferent to the welfare of, disappoint the legitimate expectations of, hurt the feelings of, verbally or physically abuse, or betray other people. I would argue that none of these categories of bad treatment is (necessarily) a case of using people as means. They are certainly not identical with that notion.

There is, however, a set of again quite different things we do to people, many of which are at least prima facie wrong, which do seem to be more closely related to the idea of using people as means. These include as central cases manipulation, deception, exploitation, and coercion. Again it is useful to note that none of these necessarily involves using people as a means only. For each of these things might be done to another person exclusively for that person's own good. Such paternalistic measures do involve treating a person as a means, but since they are done for the sake of the person (toward the end of his or her best interest), we are also treating the person as an end. So none of these situations is, in and of itself, a sufficient condition for using people as means.

Let us for simplicity exclude all such cases in the discussion to follow. We may suppose that what is done to the other person is not done for the sake of that person at all. Clearly none of these (manipulation, deception, exploitation, coercion) is necessary for using people to occur. Yet it does seem as if these conditions are closely connected to the idea of using people. My suggestion is that what explains the wrongness of such actions (when they are wrong) is that they *are* instances of using people as means. They constitute a particular way of treating other people wrongly. What is this way? What makes its different forms wrong?

It is important that, unlike most of the categories of wrongdoing I listed earlier (humiliation or cruelty), these ways of treating people may not involve an awareness of being so treated on the part of the victim. (This is less true of coercion than of the three other cases.) So what makes these things wrong cannot be explained in terms of perceived distress on the part of those subject to the treatment. My suggestion is that they share a common element of wrongness because they bypass the normal decision-making capacities of the agent. They interfere with the voluntary character of his or her actions.

Manipulation and deception limit voluntariness by keeping the agent in ignorance of facts that are relevant to choosing one action rather than another. Exploitation and coercion do so by providing reasons for action which force the person to act one way rather than another. Treating people in these ways involves ignorance and compulsion—the two factors Aristotle spoke of as making a person's actions involuntary.

My hypothesis is that all instances of using people as means will involve, broadly conceived, force or fraud. The converse is not true. If I come up to you and punch you in the nose, out of revenge, this may be wrong and it is force, but it is not using you as a means. It is only if I use force to get you to do something you would otherwise refuse to do or to accomplish some other end (as when the bank robber uses the teller as a shield to prevent the police from firing) that using as a means is involved.

What links interfering with the voluntary character of someone's actions to using someone as a means? Well, why does one resort to deception or force? Chiefly because the use of incentives or persuasive argument or exhortation or appeal will not work. We bypass the normal methods of influence because such methods appeal to common goals or aims or sentiments or convictions or instincts or purposes, and in these cases they are not present. We use people as means to our ends when we cannot expect them to share our ends or to share some other ends which only incidentally promote ours—as when we pay a person to perform some service for us.

It is not the case that using people as means involves simply making use of another person without reciprocation. A number of writers on topics of Kantian ethics suppose that if I ask you, a perfect stranger, to drive me to the nearest gas station (when I run out of gas on the highway) I am using you as a means. This is plainly false in the Kantian philosophy and as any reasonable person uses the word *means* in these contexts. It is false even if there is no expectation of possible reciprocity from me. It is false because I have left the decision to you, without interfering in any way with your ability to make the decision you want. If you are altruistic enough to want to promote my ends without direct reciprocation, then I have not used you as a means to my ends in the morally relevant sense.

Nevertheless, the idea of reciprocity is intimately linked with the notion of treating people as ends rather than simply means. Kant says a number of things about this, particularly in connection with his four examples about violations of the categorical imperative (lying promises, not developing one's talents, not rescuing a person from danger, suicide). He says that one treats people as ends if they are treated as "beings who must themselves be able to share in the end of the very same action."[1] A lying promise is wrong because "the man whom I seek to use for my own purposes by such a promise cannot possibly agree with my way of behaving to him, and so cannot share the end of the action."[2] Again, in the *Critique of Practical Reason,* Kant states that a person's autonomy is respected when he or she is subject to no purpose unless it is in conformity with a law that might arise from the will of the person affected.

What is wrong with manipulation, deception, exploitation, and coercion (when they are wrong), then, is that the person being treated in these ways cannot share the end of such action. But what is it to share the end of an action? This is a problem which requires further analysis. At this point the prudent philosopher usually mumbles something about lack of time, space (never ability, it should be noted), says this would require another paper, and is never heard from again. I forswear such evasions.

Sharing the Ends or Purposes of Actions

What is it to share the end of an action? I take it that for Kant this is a reference to the purpose for which the action is performed. In his example of making a lying promise to a creditor, the end or purpose is to obtain money without repaying it. In his discussion of suicide the end or purpose is to shorten life because it promises to bring more evil than pleasure. So for someone to share in the end of an action is for him to share in its purpose.

What is it to share in the purpose of an action? Again it is useful to look at what is not meant. It does not mean that one has to welcome the purpose in the sense of wanting that particular purpose to be accomplished in that particular case. For Kant, the criminal cannot justifiably complain about being punished. Yet he or she surely does not wish to be punished and, therefore, does not wish to be punished in order to secure greater compliance with the law or for retributive purposes. Yet, for Kant, the criminal could as a rational being share in the end of the action. The criminal would not be acting in any way inconsistently if he or she agreed that anyone who violated the law should be punished in order to secure compliance with the law.

Sharing the purpose of the action does not mean sharing, so to speak, all the purposes. If this more stringent condition were adopted then no commercial transactions could occur without people being used as means. If I work for you, I need not share your purpose of retiring at forty to a South Sea island. It is sufficient that I am willing to exchange my services for your wages. It is clear, then, that any useful application of this notion of sharing the purpose of an action, like the application of the categorical imperative with which it is so closely linked, depends upon a very specific formulation of the purposes of the action in question.

The notion of an inconsistency in willing (expressed in the categorical imperative as willing one's maxim of action as a universal law of nature) is just another way of putting this point. The chain goes from treating people as a means, to treating them in such a way that they cannot share the purposes of one's action, to treating them according to a principle to which they could not, as rational agents, consent, to treating them according to a principle which they could not will as universal.

The application of the idea of treating people as a means to the specific moral issues raised by social science research will rely on arguments about what rational subjects would or could or might will as universal, public standards or principles. Let us look at some of the particular issues raised by the papers.

The Observation of Public Behavior or Records

Consider those social science studies which involve the observation of public behavior or public records. I think that neither of these cases—and here I agree with Ruth Macklin—need be thought of as a violation of Kantian principles about immoral uses of persons as means.

In the case of public records there already should be an adequate reason why the records are open rather than closed. The argument will certainly depend upon the function of the institution concerned, such as the courts, and the need of the public to have access to the records. To be cogent, such an argument should already have taken into account the possibility that the records might be used for other purposes (commercial, scientific) than those of the institution itself. To demand that the subject have consented to the specific purposes for which the social scientist is using the record is too strong, for reasons mentioned earlier with respect to commercial transactions. It is sufficient that there is a justification for the public character of the records and that their public character is known.

With respect to observation of public behavior, I agree with many of Alexander Morgan Capron's suggestions in his paper, although my rationale for it not being necessary to obtain informed consent is slightly different. Since my normal expectations are that others are able to observe me when I am in public, if the purposes of the scrutiny are not intended to harm my interests, I can (though I need not always) share the purposes of the scrutiny. I would distinguish this case from that of the FBI man following me in the street in order to determine my political movements and contacts. Here I do not share the purpose of the scrutiny and cannot, therefore, be said to have consented to such observation.

What I have been appealing to here, and what Capron refers to in his paper, is what philosophers will recognize as some notion of tacit consent; what one implicitly agrees to by doing or refraining from doing various things. I think that for social scientists this is an important notion, particularly in connection with related notions of what is private and what is public. Let me give one familiar example: in Laud Humphreys's study of homosexual activity in public restrooms, he was able to observe the behavior he wished to study by taking advantage of the fact that a lookout was required because of fear of the police. Humphreys served as a "watchqueen" (the homosexual argot for this role) and observed hundreds of homosexual acts. The second part of his study consisted in tracking down some of the men via their license plates a year later and, in disguise, asking them various questions as part of a general social health survey. In reply to the objections that this study constituted an immoral invasion of privacy, Humphreys replied:

> Since one's identity within the interaction membrane of the tearoom is represented only in terms of the participant role he assumes, there was no misrepresentation of my part as an observer; I was indeed a "voyeur," though in the sociological and not the sexual sense.[3]

He went on to justify the second stage by asserting that since he was getting data for a genuine survey he was simply making multiple use of the data.

I believe Humphreys is right about the first stage of his study. By their acceptance of Humphreys's participation, the individuals tacitly consented to his knowing a certain bit of information about themselves. There was, in effect, a voluntary exchange of services. It is true that there are individuals who would have been excluded from performing this service (the police for example). But the fact that Humphreys's voyeurism was sociological in nature did not in any immoral way exceed the provisions of the implicit contract.

I think serious questions can be raised, however, over Humphreys's identification of the individuals concerned. Here too there was a tacit agreement, but one which was violated rather than adhered to. The agreement was that participants would remain anonymous. It was this implicit agreement that Humphreys violated.

Of course, like any scheme for resolving moral disputes, the idea of tacit consent can be abused. Perhaps the clearest case of abuse is the following quotation from a doctor:

> I think that when a patient goes to a modern physician for treatment, regardless of whether he consciously consents to it, he is also unconsciously presenting himself for the purpose of experimentation.[4]

We might call this the notion of unconscious consent!

Disguised Participant Observation

Let me turn now to the case of disguised participant observation. It is very difficult to decide the legitimacy of disguised participant observation in the abstract. There are diverse considerations which vary from case to case. While all such studies involve deception (implicit in the word *disguised*), it needn't be the case that they all involve the same breach of trust. The Festinger, Riecken, Schacter study of a spaceship cult is at one end of the spectrum. Here the observers infiltrated the group, reinforced the group's beliefs by relating dreams that seemed to bear out the prophecy, indicated that they shared the beliefs of the group, and so forth. Necessarily in such a setting personal relationships are formed, friendships assumed, loyalties taken for granted. It would be thoroughly implausible to hold that such a group could accept this degree of manipulation. A minimal test, necessary but not sufficient, for the legitimacy of such research should be its acceptability after the fact to the persons studied. Imagine how such a justification might sound in this case: "We were interested in studying people with weird and bizarre beliefs, and we didn't think you would let us study you if we asked, and there was no other way to learn about you; so we joined your group and pretended to agree with you while we took notes on your behavior."

In contrast, consider the David L. Rosenhan study which sent "pseudo-patients" into mental hospitals to see if the staff could make accurate diagnoses. Here there was no formation of personal relationships between patient and staff, no expectation of loyalty to the staff by the patient, no attempt to imply common goals, and so forth. Here there is deception but no betrayal. And I think one could muster some kind of ex post facto justification to the staff: "We were trying to find out how good hospital staffs are at diagnosing patients. We suspected there would be a bias towards interpreting patients' behavior as pathological. We couldn't tell you our hypothesis because that would affect the outcome. So we deceived you temporarily." It isn't obvious that such a justification is sufficient, but it certainly makes more sense than that hypothesized in the preceding paragraph. What would make even more sense, in my view, is for the hospital staff to be informed some time in advance that as part of an attempt to monitor performance such an experiment would be done and that the staff members would be informed of the results of the study. My guess is that this would have very little methodological effect on the study (though I am aware of methodological grounds for challenging this guess), and it has the moral advantage of building the public character of the research into the nature of the institution.

Experimental Deception

I think the case with experimental deception is somewhat different. Assuming that there is no harm (however broadly construed) to the subjects and that there is adequate debriefing plus post factum consent, and given the rather widespread knowledge that one is likely to be fooled when going into a psychology lab (one might want to distinguish between Stanley Milgram's work at Yale and that in the community in New Haven), the argument is basically similar to that for congressional immunity, i.e., not holding congressmen civilly or criminally liable for what they say on the floor of Congress. We normally hold people accountable for the things they say about others, but because we value the freest possible political debate, we carve out a sphere of immunity for certain people playing certain political roles. If we feel similarly about social scientists—i.e., if we agree that they play an important role in acquiring knowledge that is important for all of us to have, and if we agree that "immunity" from the normal moral course of events is required in order for them to carry out this function—then we can legitimately hold that the role of social scientist confers, so to speak, a license to deceive (provided various other requirements are met).

Notice that although there is an appeal to consequences in this argument, I am not putting forward a consequentialist argument. I am not saying that since the benefits outweigh the costs, social scientists are entitled to deceive. I am saying that we could agree about a role, publicly stated and defended, which legitimized deception in certain circumstances. It is the agreement and not the consequences that are crucial to the claim. In this respect, my position differs from that of Alan C. Elms, who bases his defense of certain deceptive research practices on an explicit appeal to the consequences of those practices. Although this consequentialist approach is of course a legitimate moral alternative, it seems inadequate to handle all cases of treating people as a means, for reasons I shall mention in the next section.

Alexander Capron has mentioned the idea of "after-the-fact" consent and pointed out that it gives the subject an opportunity to exercise self-determination if it is linked with the possibility of vetoing the use of the data gathered from the subject. I think that there is another function as well, namely ensuring that the rationale for the investigation, its importance, and the selection of means are such that the investigators are comfortable with the prospect of explaining them to the subject. I think such a requirement is plausibly regarded as a necessary condition for issuing the kind of license that I have spoken about. But it is important to remember that after-the-fact consent is only partial self-determination at best. It cannot erase the use of the subject without his prior consent, and therefore to this extent the use of the subject as a means. Only an argument along the lines I have sketched can support a claim that a subject has not been used as a means.

Three Justificatory Strategies

Let me close with some methodological remarks about my approach to this question. If one regards using others solely as means as morally dubious and in need of justification, then attempts to justify the kinds of research we have been considering can basically take three forms. First, one can concede that a particular research design does involve using people as means but argue that some other value outweighs this fact or is more important. This is the way consequentialists such as Elms would reason, and I would not deny that in some cases this is the most plausible way of thinking about a specific case. Its defect is that it provides no insight into the moral significance of the specific value that is being violated. Lying and manipulation and assault and disloyalty are all simply ways of diminishing human welfare, and on consequentialist grounds each may be justified by a showing that, in the particular case, welfare is promoted, not lessened, by its appearance. As Alasdair MacIntyre shows in this volume, consequentialism cannot distinguish between harms and wrongs.

The second strategy is to analyze the particular case in order to show that what appears to be an instance of using a person as a means is not. A nice example with respect to deception is the context of games. In poker it is understood that the purpose of speech is not simply to convey what the speaker believes. Since all the players are aware of this, and share the purpose of making the game more interesting in this way, they are not using one another. I have suggested that something analogous to this agreement to be deceived may take place in other areas as well. We may "license" people to deceive.

A third strategy is to analyze a particular situation at a deeper level in order to show that the very considerations which explain why using people is wrong may themselves generate exceptions. In the infamous Kantian example of the assassin who asks you where his or her intended victim is hiding, one can argue that the assassin knows that if you are aware of his purpose it cannot be shared. He or she has no right to the information and cannot expect a moral person to give it to him. Therefore, in the relevant sense, he cannot expect to be told the truth.

Philosophically this last approach is the most illuminating, for it deepens our understanding of the ground and nature of the moral prohibitions themselves. But from the standpoint of practical justification such a defense usually occurs when those who are treated as exceptions have themselves initiated some wrongdoing. Since this is generally not the case of subjects of social research, the last mode of reasoning will rarely be applicable.

Notes

1. Immanuel Kant, *The Moral Law; or, Kant's Groundwork of the Metaphysic of Morals,* trans. Herbert James Paton (London: Hutchinson, 1948), p. 97.

2. Ibid.

3. Laud Humphreys, *Tearoom Trade: Impersonal Sex in Public Places,* enl. ed. (Chicago: Aldine Publishing Co., 1975), p. 112.

4. Walter Modell, "Comment on 'Some Fallacies and Errors,' " *Clinical Pharmacology and Therapeutics* 4 (1962): 146.

PART FOUR

Privacy and Confidentiality

12

Invasions of Privacy in Social Science Research

TERRY PINKARD

It is not difficult to get agreement that privacy is a good thing and deserves protection. It is notoriously difficult, however, to get any agreement on what privacy is and just how much of a good it is. In many arguments about privacy, a familiar pattern emerges: agreement that privacy is good, disagreement about whether or not this or that properly belongs under the concept "privacy," and disagreement about whether some other good (e.g., effective law enforcement) outweighs the good of privacy. Several issues are tied up with the pattern. First, it is unclear what the concept means. (I take the question "What does the word *privacy* mean?" to be equivalent to the question "What is privacy?") Second, it is unclear what kind of good privacy is and how one evaluates or compares that good with others. Third, if there is a *right* to privacy, then some account must be given of its goodness in order to see what the basis of the right is. Finally, there is the problem of providing criteria for the justification or criticism of imputed invasions of privacy.

In this paper, I consider these issues in turn. Only to the extent that we can become clear on each can we begin to formulate a helpful answer to the more pertinent question, "What constitutes an invasion of privacy in social science research?" A specific focus on the social sciences therefore emerges only gradually as the paper proceeds. The general and abstract argument in the early sections receives detailed application to the social sciences in the later sections.

Legal Analyses of Privacy

Both the *concept* of privacy and the idea of a *right* to privacy are puzzling, and no less puzzling are the notions of *invading* privacy and *violating* a right to privacy. Philosophers have often disagreed on the analysis of these notions, but in this respect they are in no worse shape than lawyers, legislators, and social scientists. Indeed, it is in these latter contexts that the puzzling complexity of the concept has most starkly been exhibited, for people have there been forced to grapple with practical moral and social issues, and thus have not been allowed the luxury of unending philosophical discourse on the subject. Legal writings on the topic are in many respects the most extended and useful, and a brief look at some competing senses of "invading privacy" that have emerged in the law will both illuminate the conceptual issues and prove a helpful guide in the struggle for a more adequate analysis.

In the law "privacy" is conceptually linked to "being let alone," and an "invasion of privacy" is often treated as a tort, a harm visited upon an individual.[1] This particular tort occurs in four forms: (1) intrusion, (2) disclosure of "private" embarrassing facts, (3) publicity placing one in a false light, and (4) appropriation of another's name or likeness for one's own benefit. We may briefly consider these in order. First, the tort may take the form of an intrusion into the solitude or the private affairs of people, harming them by inflicting "mental" distress on them. A classic case is *Demay* v. *Roberts*, 46 Mich. 160, 9 n.w. 146 (1881), where a young man intruded upon a woman in childbirth, gaining her consent only through fraud. Here the person was not "let alone"; presumably, the young man did not disclose what he saw, but the act was an invasion of privacy nonetheless. In the *Demay* case, then, "being let alone" means not having one's solitude violated, in ways that would be "offensive or objectionable to a reasonable" person.[2]

This particular conception of "being let alone" and of the harm being done should be a bit unnerving to social scientists who study such easily intruded-upon areas as sexual beliefs and activities, family relationships, private clubs, and forms of secrecy. A good bit of social science research involves participant-observer methods. By pretending, e.g., to be a fully believing member of a cult, a social scientist may be given access to the private affairs or solitude of members of the cult, who may be manipulated into doing or saying things they wish to reserve for fellow members only. Since the researcher does not actually believe the tenets of the cult, he or she is intruding on privacy and gaining entrance by deception as well. The well-known studies on homosexual relations revealed by Laud Humphreys in *Tearoom Trade* are a case in point.[3] By posing as a "watchqueen" and later as a public health researcher, Humphreys was able to gain access to homosexual activities in public restrooms and to learn the identities of the various people he observed. This activity constituted intrusion through deception. Psychological studies involving covert observation of micturition behavior in bathrooms constitute another such intrusion, though there may be no overt deception in such studies. What, if anything, distinguishes these forms of social science research from the *Demay* case? The phrase "offensive or objectionable *to a reasonable person*" suggests one (not flattering) answer. The phrase marks the fact that the judgment is made to some extent relative to social practices or individual beliefs. It suggests that "reasonable" people do not find deceptions offensive when persons in "unreasonable" cults are deceived. But this judgment is merely a tip-off as to how troublesome such concepts as solitude and privacy really are.

Second, the tort of invasion of privacy may take the form of public disclosure of private facts. In *Melyvin* v. *Reid*, 297 Pac. 91 (1931), a former prostitute and defendant in a sensational murder trial, who had forgone a life of prostitution for one of eminent respectability, had her story made public and her new, respectable life thereby ruined. This constituted, so the court said, an invasion of privacy. Here being "let alone" means not having certain pieces of *information* about yourself disclosed; it too rests on what "reasonable" people find offensive. Herbert C. Kelman has shown that social scientists can invade privacy in this way by exposing information to legal authorities and by disclosing damaging facts about groups or communities.[4] This conception is different from the first conception in that it is a harm to *reputation*. The first sense involves *intruding* on one's solitude or private affairs; the second sense involves *disclosing* or *publicizing* embarrassing private facts. It can be argued that Laud Humphreys's studies fall under this second category as well, for although he did not reveal the names of his research subjects, the danger of such revelation was always present.

Social scientists can thus cause harm when, after observation and record collection, they disclose embarrassing facts either about members of a group or individuals. This harm may be avoided by some alteration of approach, such as disguising names or randomizing survey responses. Recent work in setting up retrieval systems that maintain the anonymity of the persons involved are important developments in the avoidance of disclosure harms. For example, where a person feels that since his or her *identity* is not being disclosed, a perusal of "private" records and publication of data based on them is not a disclosure of embarrassing facts. But this avoidance is easier to project than to accomplish.

Third, one can wrongly invade privacy by putting someone in a false light in the public eye. In 1816 Lord Byron sued on these grounds, attempting to stop the circulation of an inferior poem falsely attributed to him. The tort in question is not intrusion, as the first kind is, nor is it disclosure of true but "private" facts, as the second case is. It is, however, not being "let alone," for one's reputation is damaged. The interest at stake in both the second and third cases is the same (i.e., reputation) but the *kind* of harm done is different. (Privacy can also wrongly be invaded when someone's name or likeness is appropriated for another's use without their permission, e.g., using a person's picture on the cover of a box of flour. Again, someone is being interfered with and thus not being "let alone," but this fourth sense does not especially concern the social scientist as a social scientist.)

Harm to reputation through the second and third kinds of invasion of privacy is clearly a danger in much social science research. Participants in, e.g., sex research studies may suffer various kinds of social stigma if their participation in the study is disclosed without their consent. Similarly, in the book *Small Town in Mass Society,* a community fictitiously called Springdale was described and the chronicle of happenings that was presented subsequently proved embarrassing to its inhabitants. One can only guess how many individuals were wrongly identified with the anonymous individuals of the study. (This phenomenon is discussed by Kelman and by Donald P. Warwick in this volume.)

In addition to these several senses of "invasion of privacy" found in tort law, there is another sense found in constitutional law. In *Griswold* v. *Connecticut*, 381 U.S. 479 (1965), a Connecticut statute forbidding the sale of contraceptives was declared unconstitutional because it invaded the privacy of adults. In *Roe* v. *Wade*, 410 U.S. 113 (1973), antiabortion laws were struck down because they were held to invade a woman's privacy. In this conception of privacy, which also turns on "being let alone," the harm is deprivation of liberty (presumably in an illegitimate way) through a blockage of control over one's "private" affairs. Indeed, this sense of "being let alone" has led some to hold that privacy and liberty are always intimately connected.

Must one look in vain for what is common to all these cases? At first, they might seem to have nothing in common beyond their being ways in which one is not let alone. Perhaps, but one might offer as a promising generalization that two conceptions emerge from these senses and the idea of being let alone: (1) a *liberty* conception of privacy, specifying areas of personal liberty that should not be interfered with by invasions or intrusions, and (2) an *informational* conception of privacy, where "being let alone" is taken to imply noninterference with personal or group control over *what* can be known, witnessed, or disclosed about oneself (and as to who may know it). It is the latter, and not so much the former generic conception of "privacy" that is most relevant to social scientists. For example, objections to participant-observer research such as that involving pretense to join a cult generally require that information be disclosed to a researcher which would otherwise not be available. We should, moreover, expect disputes to emerge over this conception of privacy, as the phrase "what a reasonable person finds offensive" should have warned us. It also seems not implausible to conclude from these discussions that "privacy" is a "value-laden" concept. In order to say what privacy *is*, we must specify what an *invasion* of privacy is. We cannot understand the nature and value of privacy until we also appreciate the nature and value of its invasion, as we have seen the law to suggest.

The Multiple Meanings of "Privacy"

I shall now argue that the term *privacy*—in its general as well as legal uses— is embedded in social practices whose history has inevitably led to layers of meaning surrounding the concept. Privacy, on this account, has multiple meanings that are both practically and semantically connected. (Those readers who wish to see merely the upshot of these more abstruse philosophical considerations might skip this section and proceed on to the next section, or even to the final section.)

If we take the question "What is privacy?" as equivalent to the question "What does *privacy* mean?" it might seem that we are in trouble at the outset. Before we can go to the specific cases of privacy and its invasions, it would seem that we must first give an explanation of the meaning of the concept. This task might, however, seem to be either futile or worthless. It might appear worthless because all that we might be able to provide as the *meaning* of the concept is something uselessly general, such as the bare sense encountered in the previous section: "being let alone." Yet surely being told that privacy amounts to "being let alone" is not very helpful. The search for the meaning of "privacy" might appear futile, because it might be the case that there *is* no core meaning to privacy, but only (in Wittgenstein's phrase) a "family resemblance" between different uses of the word *privacy*. A set of things may be said to bear a family resemblance to one another if there are no properties that they all commonly share, but each thing shares at least one property with another member of the related set. The first thing (A) may have properties *m, n,* and *o*; the second thing (B) *n, o,* and *p*; the third thing (C) *p, q, r*. We might group A, B, and C together on the basis that B resembles A and C resembles B, although A and C do not resemble one another at all. Thus, siblings Tom, Mary, and Roger may be said to have a family resemblance because Tom has a Roman nose and a high forehead, Mary has a Roman nose and high cheekbones, and Roger has high cheekbones and a large mouth—but Roger and Tom have nothing in common. Given this possibility, we might despair of getting an argument about privacy per se; instead, we should focus on multiple meanings, as expressed in privacy$_1$, privacy$_2$, privacy$_3$, and so on.

In his illuminating work on privacy, Herbert Kelman has suggested three senses of *invasion* of privacy directly relevant to social science research. These senses include exposure of damaging information, diminishing a person's control and liberty, and intrusion into a person's private space.[5] These are similar to the legal senses previously canvassed. This limited survey of different senses of invasion of privacy might easily lead one to think that privacy itself is simply a fragmented concept of the family resemblance variety. One might think, for example, that little more is held in common by the informational and the liberty conceptions of invasion of privacy than the word *privacy* itself. Intrusion into private affairs has something in common with disclosure of embarrassing facts, for both involve being revealed in inappropriate ways to others; disclosure of embarrassing facts is similar to being put in a false light in the public eye, for both are damaging to reputation; and the latter is like being denied control over private aspects of one's life, as in *Griswold*, where state regulation of one's sexuality is in question. But between the first case and the last case (intrusion and the interference in private matters), there appears to be *nothing at all in common*.

This suspicion that all we have is a common word and no common properties is suggestive and may be difficult to dislodge. The family resemblance model, however, is not the only way to view these matters.

Indeed, in my judgment it is neither the most promising nor the most illuminating approach to the multiple meanings of "privacy." This term seems more aptly analyzed as one of those concepts described by W. B. Gallie as *essentially contested*. If a concept is essentially contested, then dispute (the "contest") about its meaning is not an accidental feature but is a necessary ("essential") feature because of the *kind* of concept that it is. In Gallie's words, they are concepts "the proper use of which inevitably involves endless disputes about their proper uses on the part of their users,"[6] not as a matter of happenstance but of necessity. They are thus concepts for which there will necessarily be competing conceptions.

A concept belongs to the class of essentially contested concepts if it satisfies the following conditions: (1) it must be appraisive in character, i.e., its use must involve the evaluation of some human achievement (e.g., in art, politics, or religion); (2) the achievement to which the concept refers must be internally complex, i.e., it cannot be understood simply by translation into a set of synonyms but must be analyzed into a complex set of properties and conditions; (3) the worth of the achievement must admit of different descriptions, or, to put it another way, how its parts contribute to its worth is variously describable; and (4) the description of the relevant achievement must be capable of (perhaps unpredictable) modification in light of changed circumstances.

These conditions are met by the concept of "art," which provides a useful example outside the normal scope of issues about privacy. When Marcel Duchamp autographed a newly acquired urinal and had it hung in a museum, there was some dispute as to whether his hanging was *really* art, just as a few years before, people wondered if Monet's paintings were *really* art. Is art *essentially* an expression of the artist's world view, a means of communication, an object for purely aesthetic appreciation, or an object which produces a certain type of response? Such questions tend to make all but the most optimistic aestheticians nervous, and for a good reason. Each one of the features is important to art; nonetheless, one often finds both artists and aestheticians firmly denying that one or the other of them is alone constitutive of "art." This controversy is a tip-off that we are dealing with an essentially contested concept. It certainly fits the criteria: (1) "art" is a term of appraisal; (2) almost any piece or type of art will be internally complex; (3) it will be variously describable (e.g., in terms of its expressive quality, as an aesthetic object on its own, etc.); and (4) the institution of art (and, correspondingly, what counts as art) changes over time.

One reason that certain concepts are essentially contestable is found in the historical situation in which language and beliefs are formed together. Over time and because of changing circumstances, an institution such as the enterprise of art itself evolves, and divergent traditions emerge. Each tradition claims to be carrying on the project of its forebears. Thus, one group says, "We are the real heirs to the artistic tradition, for we are concerned with the production of objects which can be considered for their aesthetic value alone." The other group claims, "No, we are the rightful heirs; we produce expressions of our world view," or "We are the rightful heirs; we produce works which communicate some cultural message and evoke such and such responses." Each group is in a sense right, but given the divergent traditions, their use of the term "art" will be essentially contested. Generally, a revisionist attempt at accommodation will fail, for each group can protest, "No, *why should* properties A and C and not B be so important?"

It is likely that many terms describing social life will similarly refer to essentially contested concepts. Terms such as "political party" and "democratic system" are examples.[7] Assessing *what* something is—such as privacy—will be no straightforward matter, and not necessarily because there is *only* a "family resemblance" between the various uses of the term. "Privacy," like "art," bears all the marks of an essentially contested concept. Based only on the few senses of *invasion* of privacy we have encountered in examining the law, plus Kelman's suggestions about invasions in social science research, privacy seems likely to satisfy all the criteria. It is an appraisive concept; the explication of *what* counts as an instance of privacy (what privacy *is*) necessarily involves some reference to what counts as an invasion of it (and probably a violation of the right to it)—and thus to some normative evaluation. As both the legal treatment of the concept and Kelman's analysis show, it is also an internally complex concept. The worth of privacy and the disvalue attached to its violation admit of many different descriptions, depending on the ethical model at work. Thus, invasion of privacy *might* for *some* social researchers count for little in light of possible gains in knowledge of human behavior, but for a great deal with others. Privacy will also be changeable over time, for terms like "privacy" and "art" are embedded in a broad range of social practices with a history of language and belief formation.

The image of a family resemblance between the uses of the terms is thus not as apt as that of a contest. A more useful metaphor than family resemblance would be the geological notion of land being historically "sedimented," only the land would here be "layers" of meanings acquired over time.[8] If this analysis applies as well to privacy as we have suggested in this minimal analysis, then there will be no "one thing" which is privacy; rather, there will be *many* things that involve privacy, each of which will exhibit both a historical connection with the others and a certain historical fragmentation. Let us now see how this general conceptual analysis can be applied to the idea of a right to privacy.

The Right to Privacy

The preceding discussion has centered on the concept of privacy and what it is to be an invasion of privacy. Now required is an account of the *right* to privacy, which presumes some account of the *goodness* of privacy. I have already appealed, at least intuitively, to such notions. The strategy for this section will be first to elucidate the goodness of privacy and to argue for the basis of the right to privacy. An attempt will then be made to account for the importance of the right, in order to set the stage for the final sections on criteria for assessing what constitutes morally unacceptable invasions of privacy.

Rights and goods belong together. A *right* to some good x shall be understood here as a valid claim to do or have x, where the claim satisfies the following two conditions: (1) the person who has the claim is permitted to do or have x (i.e., it would not be wrong for the person to do or have x); (2) the claim is the basis for another's obligation to the person, an obligation which can take two forms: (*a*) a positive obligation to provide the person with x or the means to do x; or (*b*) a negative obligation not to interfere with the person's doing or having x.[9] To have a right to do or have a good x thus presupposes a system of rules that imposes an obligation on someone to act or refrain from acting so that one is enabled to do or have something (if one wishes it); and a theory of rights requires a theory of obligation for its justification. This analysis accords with the widely accepted idea that the language of rights is translatable into the language of obligations—that is, that rights and obligations are logically correlative.

Moral rights are claims derivable from some set of moral principles or rules, and this distinguishes them from institutional and legal rights, which are claims derivable from some set of institutional and legal rules. Seen in this way, rights in general function to protect certain *goods*. A moral right to privacy is a claim derivable from one or more principles of morality to the effect that "being let alone" is a good with which it would be wrong to interfere. One of the basic such principles to which we might appeal in defending the validity of a claim to the protection of privacy is respect for persons—a principle Ruth Macklin discusses in some detail in her essay in this volume. This principle is notoriously difficult to ground in a general ethical theory, and may be, as Joel Feinberg has argued, " 'groundless'—a kind of ultimate attitude not itself justifiable in more ultimate terms."[10] Setting aside this grounding issue, perhaps the most important component of the concept of respect for persons is respect for their autonomy. To see people as autonomous is to see them as capable of forming conceptions of their own good and of how they should lead their lives; to *respect* this autonomy is to allow individuals, so far as possible, to act according to those conceptions. It is surely a truism that control over one's life entails control (to some degree) over what is known by others about oneself and control over some set of crucial (private) areas of one's life. From the general moral principle of respect for persons an *abstract* right to privacy thus follows. It is a somewhat elastic basis, of course, because the principle is unusually broad and because privacy is an essentially contested concept. We should therefore expect disputes about the commitments of this abstract right and its basis to surface wherever claims to *concrete* rights are at stake. There will be disputes as to its importance and goodness, as to *what* one is entitled by holding the right.

Consider, for example, the interactions that illustrate how the right to privacy may be *violated*, some of which we previously encountered. One person may violate another's right to privacy by intruding and obtaining information about the other, revealing information that is embarrassing, eavesdropping on another's conversation, peeking in open windows, spreading certain kinds of gossip (even if true), entering closed doors without knocking, and so on. Some are trivial, some weighty, and not all are legally protected, but all contribute to the overall sense of privacy, as "being let alone."

Although it is a substantial good, privacy is only one good among many. Moreover, not all aspects of privacy are equally important. Rational people can agree (and have agreed) to sacrifice some dimension of privacy for other goods. In this respect, privacy is somewhat like liberty: liberty is not unrestricted, and particular liberties are commonly surrendered in order to secure other goods. The claim that not all aspects of privacy are equally important amounts, then, to little more than the view now accepted almost everywhere that rights are not absolute; the right to privacy can legitimately be exercised and can create duties for others only when the right has an overriding status. While there is disagreement concerning the conditions sufficient to justify intruding upon privacy—as there is bound to be since privacy is an essentially contested concept—it is widely and properly recognized that some conditions are specifiable. I shall attempt such a specification for social science research in the concluding section of this paper.

The Justification of Invasions of Privacy

We have seen that a moral right to privacy must be derived from some set of moral principles or rules that require persons to leave others alone. However, we have not addressed either the problem of valid restrictions on this right or the problem of its theoretical justification. This section explores these two problems in order, with particular emphasis on whether certain privacy-invading activities of social science investigators can be justified.

The analysis of the preceding sections might be thought sufficient to support the following strong criterion for limiting invasions of privacy in social science research (where, we shall assume, there is no consent to the invasion):

C_1:   Social scientists unjustifiably invade their subjects' privacy whenever they manipulate subjects into doing something embarrassing or disclosing private embarrassing facts, and thereby place their subjects in a false public light or intrude into their private domains.

This criterion will strike many social scientists as indefensibly strong, for some methodologies *necessarily* involve deception or manipulation leading to embarrassment and intrusion into private domains. Without the use of such techniques the validity of their research would be imperiled. If Stanley Milgram had been forced to tell his subjects that his experiment was about obedience and that investigators actually were not shocking people, the experiment would have been lost. Likewise, the element of deception is crucial in most participant-observer experiments that invade privacy—such as those in which people feigned heart attacks on Philadelphia subways to study "helping behavior." Social scientists who study cults and fringe groups by posing as believing members rely on deception that can involve revelations of private information. It would seem from the investigator's point of view, then, that criterion C_1 is too stringent and would, as the cliché goes, throw the baby out with the bathwater. Surely, one can hear the social scientist insisting, it cannot be *much* of a justification for prohibiting social science research involving human subjects if the only grounds are that it violates some loosely formulated idea of a right to (the essentially contested idea of) privacy, with no history of case law behind the formulation presented. But is the social scientist justified in this complaint about strong criterion C_1?

In order to address this question, let us first consider reformulating our "strong criterion," substituting the phrase "under certain conditions when" at the very beginning of the criterion for the word "whenever," so as to make the criterion weaker. Let us call this criterion C_2.

C_2: Social scientists unjustifiably invade their subjects' privacy under certain conditions when they manipulate subjects into doing something embarrassing or disclosing private embarrassing facts, and thereby place their subjects in a false public light or intrude into their private domains.

This formulation would make the proposed criterion far more acceptable to social scientists, though specification of the actual exceptive conditions would then of course make all the difference. This strategy will naturally seem to offer a more promising criterion than C_1, for no one would claim that *all* deceit or intrusion on privacy is wrong or that deceit or manipulation are *always* wrong when they lead to invasions of privacy. One may justifiably deceive one's opponents in poker, the enemy in wartime, even sometimes deceive and invade the privacy of one's spouse—as when one plans a surprise party. Journalists are often regarded as justified in and admired for disclosing private embarrassing facts (under certain conditions, as in C_2). If deceit and invasion of privacy are not always wrong in these contexts, perhaps they are sometimes permissible in similar contexts of social science research, and for similar reasons. Still, the question remains: Can justifying conditions be added to C_2 that improve it over C_1—so as to permit enough social science research without permitting too much in the way of invasions of privacy?

One general answer has been given to these problems of justification by Justice William H. Rehnquist, who argues for a utilitarian approach to problems of privacy.[11] His argument does not uniquely apply to the social sciences, but it provides a perspective on the present issues that may be generalized to the social sciences. Rehnquist argues as follows: Government cannot escape certain conflicts between freedom and order. Both are respectable goods, and on some occasions we cannot have both. Efficient, intelligent law enforcement, which is necessary for the achievement of both goods, requires some sacrifice of privacy—e.g., in dissemination of arrest records. So, Rehnquist argues, one must *balance* the goods of privacy and efficient law enforcement when rights to privacy conflict with rights to be protected. If damage to the individual in the dissemination of criminal and arrest records to relevant authorities is slight (with strictures on the use to which the information may be put so as to avoid abuse), while the gain in social utility is great, then even those whose privacy has been invaded ought not to object.

Rehnquist supports this position with the following example.[12] If a police officer parks in front of a tavern each evening from 5:30 to 7:30 and records the license numbers of cars coming and going into the tavern's parking lot during that time, many would consider the action a violation of the right to privacy, an unwarranted invasion. But suppose that on the previous two evenings a patron of the tavern had been killed shortly after leaving it, and evidence suggested that the culprit had been present at the bar when the patron left. Suddenly the picture changes; it is no longer so clear that privacy has been invaded, or at least not so clear that it has been wrongly or unjustifiably invaded.

Justice Rehnquist takes these conclusions to be justified on utilitarian grounds. I agree with him that they are justified, and I heartily endorse his example, but I do not think the proper justification is utilitarian, and I do not think the justification supports C_2 over C_1 either. Let me, then, offer a different justification, one that leads to a defense of C_1—a justification also suitable to handle privacy invasions in social research. This justification naturally starts from the conclusion reached in the previous section on the right to privacy. The analysis of rights as valid claims that are presumptive (or prima facie valid) does not mean that rights never have an overriding status. As Ronald Dworkin has pointed out in his *Taking Rights Seriously,* some rights are so basic that ordinary justifications for state interference—such as lessening inconvenience or promoting utility—are insufficient justifications for overriding rights.[13] In Dworkin's terms, the individual rights of citizens "trump" the reasons why we generally permit state control and planning over our lives. Indeed *everything* is trumped by a right *except another right with which it conflicts.* The citizen who bears a right does not hold a privilege and is not subject to the charity or professional etiquette of another. The right can justifiably be demanded as one's due precisely up to that point at which it comes into conflict with another right. There are numerous examples in social science research to illustrate this point. Elsewhere in this section of the present volume, Robert F. Boruch presupposes that rights function to control dissemination of data collected by social scientists, government, and industry. Similarly, R. Jay Wallace, Jr., discusses conditions that limit the data collection and statistical analyses sought by epidemiologists. The conditions listed in the latter paper effectively specify the rights of citizens to control private information pertaining to their beliefs, habits, and history. However, I shall argue for stronger individual rights than does Wallace in his explicitly utilitarian analysis.

It is necessary for social justice and the institution of morality that what may be called "safe" areas of social life be carved out that are almost entirely free from intrusion. These are areas strictly protected by "rights," our most demanding moral rules. Within these areas, invasions of privacy, lying, and deception are virtually always wrong, especially where certain intimate relationships with important goods attached are at stake, because there is so seldom a warrant powerful enough to override a right. The "safe" areas are, however, only protected *areas;* they do not encompass the whole of everyday life and so cannot be protected against conflict with *other* areas that are also "safe." Rights, as we earlier remarked, can conflict with other rights. The alternative—that there are no "safe" areas protected by rights—is morally perilous, for it threatens to put morality on a shifting basis where clever legalistic reasoning with exception clauses can justify anything (e.g., on grounds of social utility).

The issues, then, turn out to be the following: no "safe" area has an ironclad safety about it, because someone's rights may always be of sufficient power to override someone else's rights in any given safe area. Social research leading to violations of rights (protected in a safe area) can *in theory* sometimes be morally justified, even when it involves deception and invasions of privacy. Thus, "in theory" C_1 may seem wrong and indefensible, and C_2 therefore preferable. However, "in theory" is not good enough. I prefer C_1 over C_2 because I do not believe social science is actually justified in its practices of deception and invasion of privacy in safe areas where rights are violated. Accordingly, I shall now argue that social science research that invades a safe area is *always* morally unjustified.

Applications to Social Science Research

There are, no doubt, goods intrinsic to the pursuit of social science, knowledge being the obvious one. The *utility* of social science—its being a significant means to some other valued end such as the efficiency of police work sought by some criminologists—is less apparent. Certainly it is difficult to justify the involvement of human subjects where risk and no obvious benefit to the subjects is involved. (These problems are discussed by Gordon Bermant and others in the "Harm and Benefit" section of this volume.) However, we can address both the invasion of privacy and the deception some social science research involves by placing them in the context of the obligation to respect persons and the right to privacy, as discussed above. First, we can quickly pass beyond the uncontroversial observation that with proper informed consent much research, including research that poses significant risks, would have nothing against it, even if it involved privacy invasions or deceptions. (Our strong criterion at the beginning of the previous section, it is to be remembered, excluded activities having the prior consent of subjects.) If an investigator discloses to subjects in advance that there is a possibility of deception or invasion of privacy, then research becomes like a poker game—a structured situation where deception or invasion of privacy not only may occur but is expected. Adequate disclosures, provided to voluntary participants and informing them of the possibility of an invasion of privacy or deception, should satisfy the moral requirements of respect for persons.

Where obtaining such informed consent is impossible, as is often the case in social science research, the problem of justification is correspondingly stickier. Research into "helping behavior" by feigning heart attacks on subway trains is again a case in point. Here reasonable expectations are interfered with by deliberate intrusions. People in subways have their "private sphere" intruded upon much as they would by eavesdroppers or con artists. It is difficult to imagine an agreement among rational agents on this point that would permit such intrusions into their private sphere. Who could agree to conferring rights on people to manipulate others or oneself, where either oneself or the others are unwittingly manipulated, merely on grounds that knowledge of "helping behavior" would be accumulated?

This situation differs from the other situations where consent legitimated deceit and invasion of privacy. In the poker analogy, a socially structured situation is present in which deceit or intrusion into a private sphere is to be *expected* and in which the anticipated manipulation contributed to the value of the enterprise for the participant. Any rational agent would easily agree to such deception or limitation of privacy. Deceit to plan a surprise party for one's spouse is similar and easily endorsed by rational agents. But the subway case is significantly different. It is not a structured, understood, and consensual situation like a game of poker. It is not even like an antagonistic international conflict such as war or a structured interpersonal relationship. In the latter contexts, there exist principles—however general—broadly delineating what is permitted and what is not. People studied in deceptive social science research are duped in a situation without familiar rules into revealing something about themselves that very likely they would rather not reveal. Their solitude—even though they are in public—is thus invaded. (The notion of "solitude in public" should not be troublesome. The earlier example of the police noting license plate numbers without any overriding justification is an example.) Such invasions are not covered by even tacit understandings, let alone by governing principles; and of course there is no prior expectation.

Participant-observer research where the researcher pretends to be a member or sympathizer of a group in order to elicit certain responses from the real participants provides another case in point, for here too no favorable analogy exists to the structured and consensual situations where deceit and invasion of privacy are legitimate. Typically, people studied feel both betrayed and invaded. As remarked earlier, structured social roles often carry with them an understanding of the amount of privacy *proper* to each. To have had someone pose as a friend only to extract private information from you is not only to have been deceived; it is to have had the bounds of what can legitimately be known about you overstepped. A gain in knowledge no more justifies this violation of one's rights than it could justify having a person pose as a lover to a member of a corporation so that the board of directors could discover his or her "real" attitude toward a task. One should add: no matter how much that knowledge furthered the aims of the corporation. Our judgments in these cases thus should be set in the context of a model of moral reasoning that focuses on principles that are *shared* between people and to which we can imagine people *contractually* agreeing. It is not the *consequences* (in the utilitarian sense) of adopting a principle that justifies it, but its being (at least hypothetically) *agreed upon*. This idea of hypothetical agreement rests on what we called earlier the principle of respect for persons, for the validity of the contract depends upon the consent of the contracting parties. Moral principles are justified when they are contracted to in order to balance conflicting interests and competing points of view.[14]

Of all people, social scientists do not need to be reminded of the complex ways in which societies are structured so that behavior which in one case is excusable may in another case be reprehensible. Lying to a close friend about a surprise party is among the excusable cases, but here one has already been granted access and privilege beyond those of the social *researcher* by virtue of a nondeceptive ongoing personal relationship. It is worth noting that no favorable analogy with governmental invasion of privacy exists here. The government has a right to collect certain types of potentially embarrassing information such as the information gathered in the census or that needed at IRS. Often there may be conflicts between rights of government and rights of individuals. But the social science researcher has no moral right to his or her investigations corresponding to the rights of government. At best, the researcher can argue that the research will have some great yield (in social utility, e.g.) and should be supported. But he or she cannot validly argue that the investigation should be supported even in face of its violating individual rights to privacy by intruding into our "safe" areas. In Ronald Dworkin's earlier mentioned phrase, rights trump utility, and certainly they trump the needs and interests of social science researchers. One can validly adjust or "balance" matters *only when rights compete*. However, there is no *right* to perform research which competes with the individual's right to privacy, and hence there is nothing to balance. Or, to state the thesis in a somewhat milder form: there may be *thin* constitutional grounds for claiming some form of first amendment right to perform research (a claim explored by John A. Robertson and E. L. Pattullo in the final section of this volume), but I know of no moral or legal grounds whatever that would support a right to perform research sufficient to override individual rights to privacy.

Of course I earlier acknowledged that IRS, the Census Bureau, and other branches of government have a right to private information—and indeed a right to information that may place citizens in situations of legal and economic risk. The research done by such agencies is often social scientific; and thus it certainly appears that *at least in these contexts* social scientists (and society) have a right that can conflict with the ordinary citizen's right to privacy, one which trumps the individual's right to privacy. This thesis will not do, however, precisely because of the consent and contractual components of the analysis that has been presented above. The government obtains its rights through the consent (tacit or otherwise) of the governed, and in this respect promulgated government rules, regulations, and actitivies are unlike unanticipated or deceptive social scientific interventions—as represented by the example of studies into helping behavior.

Milgram's experiments occupy in the minds of some a deliciously grey area here, which might explain why so many people have conflicting intuitions about these experiments. They certainly did involve manipulation and deceit, and they do prompt people to reveal things about themselves that one would assume they would rather not have revealed. Yet they also took place in a laboratory setting voluntarily consented to by participants—a facility that was outside, so to speak, the normal course of life. In this respect, Milgram's investigations differ from those into helping behavior, or even those in *Small Town in Mass Society*. But does this laboratory setting and the limited consent of subjects make a morally significant difference? I take it that some of the conflicting intuitions concerning Milgram's works are conflicts about whether or not the laboratory setting is enough like a poker game for the deception in it to be justified. To me, this seems implausible. Had a general warning been available to the participants beforehand that deception might be employed, intuitions about the rightness or wrongness of the experiments would no doubt have been considerably less divided. One would not expect this kind of change in intuition to occur if the laboratory were indeed the kind of "structured situation" in which deceit is to be suspected.[15]

To be sure, giving such a general warning would in some cases hamper or render impossible certain forms of research. But remember that putting restrictions on the admissibility of evidence hampers police work, and putting restrictions on the use of confidential information hampers banks. That restrictions hamper or prevent certain activities from reaching valuable goals efficiently should not be surprising; nor should it be surprising that morality as the regulation and guidance of life puts restrictions on even important constructive activities. We all complain and grouch with some good reason that *our* activities (whether they be law enforcement, social science, legislation, or what not) are restricted to the point of inefficiency or the diminishment of their final goal; and it should not be surprising that this complaint is pervasive. We should not, however, be blind to the cogency of ethical reasons for these restrictions when they exist. That clearly valuable work such as Milgram's might be hampered or rendered impossible by the desiderata introduced here may be unfortunate, but not on that account unjust.

In this final section, it has been shown that many examples of social science research fall into the category of unjustified invasions of privacy, that they may not be justified by appealing to a similarity with situations from everyday life where deception or invasions of privacy are justified, and that if research occurs in a laboratory situation as opposed to an everyday one it is not *obviously* excused, though its justification cannot a priori be closed to further discussion. On the basis of the preceding sections, we can also surmise that since "safe" areas of life will be in part conventionally defined, while "privacy" is an essentially contested concept, disputes about privacy (about *what* is safe) will continue.

The argument of this paper is in the end a simple one: there is a right to privacy, even if vaguely defined and subject to challenge in *some ways*. Social scientists do not have a right to invade our privacy; they have no *right* to override our rights. And, on the view presented here, there can be no alternative utilitarian or knowledge-based justification for overriding the right to privacy. Some papers that follow in this volume, particularly those by Alan C. Elms and R. Jay Wallace, provide utilitarian justifications for the rights-violating methods of social research. Their conclusions contrast sharply with the ones I have reached. Naturally I have had the views expressed in these papers in mind as I have proceeded.

Notes

1. This discussion draws on Dean Prosser's treatment of the issue. This treatment appears in the many editions of his *Torts: Cases and Materials* and in "Privacy," *California Law Review* 48 (August 1960): 383-423.
2. Prosser, "Privacy," p. 391.
3. Laud Humphreys, *Tearoom Trade* (Chicago: Aldine Publishing Co., 1975).
4. Herbert C. Kelman, "Privacy and Research with Human Beings," *Journal of Social Issues* 33 (1977): 169-95. See also his chapter in the present volume.
5. Ibid.
6. W. B. Gallie, "Essentially Contested Concepts," *Aristotelian Society Proceedings* 56 (1956): 169.
7. Cf. Alasdair MacIntyre, "The Essential Contestability of Some Social Concepts," *Ethics* 84 (October 1973): 1-9.
8. This is a term adapted from Husserl's writings on the subject. Cf. especially Edmund Husserl, *Experience and Judgment,* translated by James S. Churchill and Karl Ameriks (Evanston, Ill.: Northwestern University Press, 1973).
9. This conception of the nature of rights is taken from Joel Feinberg, "The Nature and Value of Rights," as reprinted in David Lyons, ed., *Rights* (Belmont, Calif.: Wadsworth Publishing Co., 1979), pp. 78-91.

10. Joel Feinberg, *Social Philosophy* (Englewood Cliffs, N.J.: Prentice-Hall, 1973), p. 93.

11. William H. Rehnquist, "Is an Expanded Right of Privacy Consistent with Fair and Effective Law Enforcement?" *Kansas Law Review* 23 (1974).

12. Ibid., pp. 9-11.

13. Ronald Dworkin, *Taking Rights Seriously* (Cambridge, Mass.: Harvard University Press, 1978).

14. We can place this approach to the justification of invasions of privacy in a more general theoretical framework: society is a cooperative enterprise that requires public rules and principles of cooperation. Here, the *justice* of the terms of cooperation in the society is morally paramount. The terms of cooperation will be those established by legal, moral, and cultural rules and principles that structure the society and that individuals find binding on their behavior. How does one assess the justice of these "terms of cooperation"? One way might be to evaluate them in terms of their efficiency in promoting some overall goal such as utility (measured in terms of happiness or satisfaction of preferences). The way presupposed in this paper is to assess rules and principles in terms of their *fairness*. "Do the rules allow some persons to take undue advantage of others?" and "Is respect given to individual autonomy?" are typical questions that can be asked about the fairness of particular "terms of cooperation." The point of evaluating and justifying rights to privacy is to set them into the larger context of the terms of cooperation found in a particular society. The structure of justification which I am recommending, then, is the following: justice is a matter of fairness, specifically of the fairness of the terms of cooperation in a social order; what *counts* as fair, however, depends in large part on the conventions of that social order—on, as we have called them, "structured situations." The reason for the qualification "in large part" is that one must appeal to abstract principles of justice, such as those offered by John Rawls, which are *not* dependent on social convention, even though any understanding of how in a concrete case these principles are to be applied will involve some appeal to some set of conventions. Any justification of a right will thus appeal to both abstract principles of fairness and their mediation through a concrete social ordering. It follows from this argument that one must locate moral distinctions within the context of everyday social life.

15. One might, of course, still argue that a laboratory situation is in fact like many situations in life in which deceit is built into the rules of the game. But like what situations? Like selling used cars? Like real estate? These are not flattering analogies, and one would hardly expect social scientists to accept them.

13

Privacy and the Use of Data in Epidemiology

R. JAY WALLACE, JR.

Commentators on ethical problems in social science research have spent considerable effort analyzing the differences between the biomedical sciences and the social sciences. Those differences can of course be significant. The methodologies and concerns of researchers in the two domains vary appreciably, and that fact has led many to question whether such moral requirements as informed consent and cost-benefit analysis are uniformly applicable to research involving human subjects. It is possible, however, that the differences between the social and biomedical sciences have been overestimated, for the lines demarcating the social sciences from biomedicine are not always rigid and distinct. In at least some instances, social and biomedical scientists use identical research methods, and when this is the case the ethical problems can be expected to remain similar across the two broad areas.

This paper treats a group of research methods common to the social and biomedical sciences—those of data collection and statistical analysis. In particular, the ethical problems of privacy and confidentiality that these methods present for both biomedicine and social science are explored. The procedure employed in analyzing these ethical problems is largely that of the case study of a field of inquiry. The methods and results characteristic of research in epidemiology are alone pursued. While epidemiology is generally considered a biomedical field—as evidenced by its residence in schools of medicine and public health—the ethical problems it presents are typical of the privacy and confidentiality issues that have increasingly preoccupied social scientists in recent years.

This case-study analysis proceeds through five stages. First, the nature of epidemiologic research and the methods employed in its performance are treated. Particular attention is paid to the extreme difficulty of obtaining the informed consent of epidemiologic research subjects to the use of identifiable

I am greatly indebted to Professor Leon Gordis for technical advice and suggestions useful in preparing this essay. I have relied particularly heavily on the paper Professor Gordis presented at a conference on "Ethical Issues in Social Science Research" held at the Kennedy Institute of Ethics in September 1979.

information about them. Second, a basic moral dilemma created by this difficulty of obtaining informed consent is examined. The dilemma involves a conflict between the obligation of beneficence and the right to privacy, and it is argued that considerations of beneficence generally override the duty to respect another's privacy in epidemiologic research. This contention will by no means appear intuitively obvious, especially in light of the notorious invasions of privacy by data collection agencies in contemporary society. In the third part of the essay, possible objections are met and the argument is shaped with greater precision. To this end, four conditions are defended as necessary and sufficient for the moral justifiability of epidemiologic research in which the consent of subjects is not obtained. The fourth part of the paper describes and discusses a general procedure designed to ensure that individual epidemiologic projects meet the four specified conditions. In conclusion, two alternative approaches to the conflict between obligations of beneficence and obligations to respect privacy are explored.

The Nature and Methods of Epidemiologic Research

Epidemiology may be defined as the study of the distribution and causal dynamics of diseases that affect human populations. Its main purpose is to identify social or environmental factors that cause disease. This information provides the basis for broad public health programs and policies, for once the importance of a specific factor in producing disease has been discovered, steps can be taken to reduce or eliminate exposure of the general population to that factor. Epidemiologic research also seeks to identify particular segments of the population which stand at a high risk of contracting certain diseases, thereby permitting more precisely targeted preventive and therapeutic measures. Additionally, epidemiologists frequently evaluate new or alternative preventive procedures and health care delivery systems. Thus, epidemiologic research includes studies of the etiological and risk factors of disease, the natural history and prognosis of disease, and the effectiveness of preventive and therapeutic interventions.

Epidemiologists consult a diverse array of information sources in performing research. They use medical records most of all, but their sources also include vital records, employment records, original research records, and information already culled from such sources for research purposes. The information provided by these sources is usually only useful to epidemiologists if it is obtained in an individually identifiable form, because of the research procedures employed in epidemiology. Those procedures typically include techniques of longitudinal investigation, since the isolation of the agents of disease often requires a comparative study of the health of particular populations at different points in their history. Such longitudinal study involves the linkage of information collected from discrete sources, a process that is possible only when the information has been collected in an individually identifiable form. In addition, epidemiology frequently proceeds by contacting and interviewing individuals about whom information has been obtained, and these investigative methods obviously require that the information be individually identifiable.

These methodological characteristics of epidemiology do not necessarily entail that researchers in the discipline always be able to infer the actual identities of the subjects they study. As Robert F. Boruch demonstrates elsewhere in the present volume, certain statistical and other procedures permit the provision of identifiable *information* to researchers in ways that would frustrate any attempts to determine the real identities of the *people* in question. Nonetheless, there are many situations in epidemiology, such as record review to identify eligible subjects who are later contacted and interviewed, in which these methods for preserving absolute anonymity are either inapplicable or extremely impractical. For purposes of argument, I shall therefore assume that epidemiologists' use of identifiable information generally gives them access to the actual identities of the subjects whose records they consult.

This assumption immediately suggests a source of the privacy and confidentiality problems alluded to at the start of the essay. Before those problems are considered, however, it is important to notice a second methodological feature of epidemiologic research. That feature concerns the possibility of obtaining informed consent to the use of identifiable information in epidemiology. In much of human subjects research, of course, informed consent is now regularly secured prior to the execution of research designs. Yet that procedure is simply impossible to carry out before a great many epidemiologic projects; and even when its execution is not impossible, considerations of time and expense often render informed consent a highly impractical requirement for epidemiology.

Valid informed consent can perhaps most nearly be approximated in epidemiologic research involving information originally collected for other research purposes. When such information is first obtained, it is often possible to secure the subject's "blanket consent" to further research use of the information. A blanket consent typically specifies the subject's willingness to allow later uses of the recorded information for purposes consonant with the goals of the initial research. Despite the pejorative implications of its name, the procedure goes at least part of the way toward serving the functions of informed consent. If nothing else, it warns subjects that the information they divulge may be consulted by other researchers, resulting in a condition of awareness preferable to total ignorance about the possibility of later research uses. But the deficiencies in the informational components of these warnings are great enough to render the validity of blanket consents questionable. Subjects cannot reasonably be expected to understand the objectives of research projects that have yet to be designed, and the intentions they express through blanket consents should consequently not be considered in all cases relevantly "informed" about subsequent protocols.

Furthermore, original research records occupy a restricted position on the spectrum of sources that epidemiologists must consult, and even blanket consents are unlikely to have been obtained for research use of information in medical, vital, and employment records.

As an alternative to relying on blanket consent, it might be possible to obtain the names of people on whom records are known to be kept before the records themselves are consulted. Those people could then be traced, contacted, and given an opportunity to consent to the use of their records in research whose specific objectives would have been disclosed. Attractive as this possible procedure may seem, however, its costs in time and expense make it quite impractical for widespread use in epidemiology. Furthermore, there are many situations in which the identification of individuals on whom particular records are kept would itself violate the traditional purposes of informed consent. When, for example, specialized records such as cancer registries are in question, the very fact that information about a person is contained in the record may be a strong clue to the *content* of the information. Subsequent attempts to obtain the person's consent might therefore lose much of their point. A similar difficulty arises when epidemiologists plan to interview individuals whose records have first been perused in order to determine whether they are eligible for inclusion in the study. While it is both possible and desirable to secure the subjects' prior consent to be interviewed, the previous use of identifiable information will in most cases already have proceeded without the subjects' valid informed consent.

Thus, at least given the temporal and fiscal constraints within which researchers labor, it is often not possible for epidemiologists to obtain valid informed consent to their use of identifiable information. The remainder of this paper explores the implications of this characteristic for the moral justifiability of epidemiologic research.

The Right to Privacy and Beneficent Obligations:
A Basic Moral Dilemma

The fact that epidemiologists are unable to obtain informed consent seems to present the sort of moral problem that commonly arises in human subjects research in connection with the principle of autonomy, for the application of that principle is generally at stake when the informed consent of subjects cannot be secured. I would submit, however, that the virtual impossibility of obtaining consent to epidemiologic research can more precisely be characterized as raising moral problems of privacy and confidentiality. Such problems are closely related to issues generally involving the principle of autonomy; indeed, they are best regarded as particular instances of the broader class of autonomy issues. In the language of moral rights, the principle of autonomy can be understood to confer a moral right to individual self-determination. Such a right can more precisely be construed to entail a particular moral right to determine what will be known about oneself (including to some extent the circumstances in which, and the people by whom, it will be known). That construal accurately captures at least one sense of the moral right to privacy frequently invoked in contemporary Western societies. Following Terry Pinkard's suggestion in chapter twelve of this volume, I shall call this meaning the *informational* sense of the right to privacy.

The right to privacy in this informational sense is directly pertinent to the methodological features of epidemiologic research sketched above. If people have a moral right to determine what will be known about themselves, they should be given the opportunity to approve or disapprove plans to use information that reveals something about them. Hence, the use of identifiable information without the consent of the person identified will violate that person's moral right to privacy. It is important to note that this problem is not posed by the *fact* that identifiable information must be appropriated by epidemiologists. Rather, it arises because the subjects of epidemiologic research are not given a chance to determine if and how that information will be used.

The moral problem thus presented can be further specified in terms of confidentiality, a property of information. Information is often given to doctors, employers, and researchers with an implicit understanding that it will not be divulged to other parties. If further disclosure occurs, the use of the information by other parties may amount to a violation of the person's desire that the information remain confidential. The failure to respect such desires is one form that the ethical problems in epidemiologic research could possibly take, and we may call these problems confidentiality issues. Nevertheless, since what is fundamentally in question in this possible situation is a person's determination that information be used in a certain way (i.e., that it remain confidential), confidentiality problems are best considered subsidiary instances of the more comprehensive class of moral problems that involve the violation of a person's right to privacy.

That epidemiologic research methods violate subjects' rights to privacy complicates any program for justifying such research. This violation suggests that regardless of the possible harms and benefits associated with epidemiology, research in the discipline will in some degree always involve a moral wrong. All who recognize a moral right to privacy, formulated as the right to determine what will be known about oneself, will find some degree of violation involved. It does not follow, however, that epidemiologic research is necessarily a morally unjustifiable practice. Ethical principles describe duties—in this case, a duty to respect another's moral right to privacy—but the duties they define are not always absolute. In contemporary ethical theory it is generally acknowledged that fundamental principles define a number of specific moral duties, and there is nothing to guarantee that these duties will not conflict in particular circumstances. Indeed, it is because duties conflict that moral dilemmas often assume an intractably controversial character. A viable ethical theory therefore cannot insist that action always conform with every obligation pertinent in a given situation; such a strict requirement would effectively make it impossible to act morally in the most difficult circumstances. Instead, most ethicists would characterize moral principles as imposing prima facie duties, i.e., applicable duties that are nonobligatory when they conflict with other overriding moral duties.

I hold that the duty to respect another's right to privacy is best treated as a prima facie duty. This assertion is not likely to prove controversial, for no one would seriously maintain that the moral duty in question is absolutely binding in all circumstances. (Imagine a situation in which a person's life could be saved only by divulging information about the person that he or she had conveyed to you in confidence.) What is bound to be more controversial is my contention that the duty to respect another's privacy is overridden by duties governed by the principle of beneficence. This last principle specifies an obligation minimally not to harm other people, and more positively to remove existing harms and produce social benefits. My own preference in this essay for beneficence in certain cases of conflict results, then, in the following general position: the epidemiologist is justified in using methods that invade privacy when such methods present the only promising means for achieving the significant social benefits epidemiologic research can yield.

Discerning readers will immediately detect a utilitarian cast to this preference for obligations of beneficence. It means that the moral duty to respect privacy will be overridden whenever the benefits of doing so are sufficiently great. Even within the utilitarian camp, however, my preference for duties of beneficence over duties to respect privacy will initially seem implausible. Objections based on utilitarian grounds will probably assume two distinct forms. Invoking a "slippery slope" line of argument, some might contend that my approach need only be applied to activities other than epidemiology for its flaws to become apparent. The same utilitarian calculations that justify scholarly, benign epidemiologic research might seem to justify other invasions of privacy that are less congenial. Highly objectionable CIA investigative activities, for example, could be justified by reference to the fundamental social benefit of national security. Even if lines could be drawn that would appropriately restrict my utilitarian approach and so meet the slippery slope objection, my position might seem open to a second line of utilitarian criticism. According to this second argument, the approach would be deficient because of its significant untoward consequences as a matter of social policy. To permit any invasions of privacy on cost-benefit grounds might contribute to a dangerously cavalier attitude toward invasions of citizen privacy more generally. A consequence of regarding privacy violations in epidemiology as justifiable would then be the cultivation of a climate of opinion in which people routinely condoned unjustifiable privacy violations.

Of these objections to my approach, the second is the more difficult to counter. It turns on an untested prediction about the social consequences of a specific practice, a prediction that could only be falsified by assessing the actual consequences of the approach recommended. On the strength of existing evidence in this connection, I am prepared to admit that the erosion of citizen privacy in contemporary society presents a disturbing problem; the notorious activities of commercial credit companies come all too quickly to mind. But the contribution of epidemiologic practices to this problem remains more arguable. In response to this issue, I can only venture a similarly predictive generalization: once the precise specifications of the utilitarian approach taken here are made explicit—as they will be in the following section of the paper—the distance between epidemiology and the worst CIA or credit company abuses will be evident. At the same time, such a specification will demonstrate that appropriate line drawing can foreclose the slippery slope objection, and that a utilitarian justification is therefore possible which yet stops short of formally justifying the most flagrantly objectionable invasions of privacy in our society.

The Moral Justifiability of Epidemiologic Research

As a first step toward rendering my justifying argument more precise, I should be more specific as to the nature of the utilitarian calculation proposed. The position to be defended is not simply that epidemiologic research is justified whenever, and because, its benefits minimally outweigh its costs. Rather, I maintain that for the invasion of privacy in epidemiology to be morally justifiable, the benefits of the research must promise to exceed its costs considerably, and there must be no reasonable alternatives. Only when these conditions are satisfied are the duties described by the principle of beneficence strong enough to override the important moral duty to respect another's privacy. This argument can be rendered still more precise by formally listing the necessary conditions that justified research must satisfy. The following four conditions, I shall argue, are individually necessary and jointly sufficient for the moral justifiability of epidemiologic research that invades privacy by not obtaining the informed consent of subjects:

1.   The invasion of privacy involved must be necessary to the conduct of the research.

2.   The invasion of privacy must involve only a minimal intrusion.

3.   The research must additionally present only an insignificant risk of specifiable harms to the interests of subjects.

4.   The results of the research must be likely to bring social benefits of a significant nature.

The following pages take up each of these four conditions in its relation to epidemiologic research.

1.   *The Invasion of Privacy Involved Must Be Necessary to the Conduct of the Research.*   An important initial stipulation is that any invasion of privacy in epidemiology would not be morally justifiable if alternative methods were available that did not invade privacy. Of course, the stringency of this

condition will turn on the interpretation of the adjective "available." If it is taken to specify the mere possibility of incorporating alternative noninvasive methods, without regard for considerations of cost and efficiency, then this condition would be excessively stringent. So construed, it would render unjustifiable research that manifestly ought to be conducted. Instead, this condition stipulates only that there must not be alternative noninvasive procedures that would be practical, given the financial and temporal constraints under which research is typically conducted. This is what is intended by the characterization of justifiable invasions of privacy as "necessary to the conduct of the research."

It should be clear from the first section of this essay that epidemiologic research generally meets this condition; any invasion of privacy caused is an unavoidable consequence of the methods epidemiologists must (in the circumstances) employ. This condition suggests, however, that the development of practical statistical and procedural solutions capable of ameliorating the privacy violations in question should be encouraged. Warnings about the possible research uses of recorded information could be a salutary first step toward improving the level of understanding of potential research subjects. And any cost-efficient techniques for preserving both the individual anonymity of subjects and the individual identifiability of information would eliminate the troublesome privacy violations entailed by the need for certain types of data. For reasons mentioned above, I remain skeptical that such procedures will so neatly avoid all privacy problems in epidemiologic research, at least in the near future. I am even more skeptical, however, that the most notorious invasions of privacy in contemporary society could satisfy a moral requirement comparable to this first condition.

2. *The Invasion of Privacy Must Involve Only a Minimal Intrusion.* To admit that epidemiologic research invades the privacy of subjects is not to concede that the intrusion involved must be of a more than minimal order. By considering the various ways in which the desires of subjects *can* be disregarded in research, it is possible to discriminate between minimal invasions of privacy and intrusions of a more serious nature. Only when a subject has specifically stipulated that he or she expects certain information to remain strictly confidential would the later use of that information violate a person's clearly stated intention. In such instances, the research use of the information would entail an unjustifiably severe moral wrong; it would disregard an unambiguously expressed act of self-determination in accord with a basic moral right.

In formulating this second condition, I have in mind epidemiologic research as it is conducted under normal circumstances. As significant as the benefits of such research are, they are not sufficient to justify invasions involving the severe moral wrong described in the preceding paragraph. It is nevertheless conceivable that in a circumstance of true extremity, involving a health problem which fundamentally threatened the social order (e.g., in the way plagues did for much of human history), the obligation of beneficence fulfilled by epidemiologists would be powerful enough that it could justifiably permit more than a minimal invasion of privacy. Since health problems of this magnitude requiring epidemiologic analysis generally do not arise in the contemporary world, this theoretical possibility has not been considered in formulating justificatory conditions.

In any case, the epidemiologist's use of identifiable information rarely—if ever—approximates the extreme invasion sketched above. The moral wrong typically in question consists only in the failure to determine what the subject's actual intention is, a failure brought on by the impossibility of incorporating effective informed consent procedures in epidemiology. Given this impossibility, the researcher is permitted only indirect clues as to the true intentions of the subjects. These may range from the implication of refusal suggested by the traditional but unspoken confidentiality of the doctor-patient relationship, to the implication of consent suggested when a blanket consent has been obtained. At the worst, then, epidemiology may involve the use of information about a person when there are ambiguous reasons for supposing that the person would not want that information to be known.

   3.   *The Research Must Additionally Present Only an Insignificant Risk of Specifiable Harms to the Interests of Subjects.* Moral wrongs are not the only negative consequences of human actions. To borrow a distinction both from the Introduction to this volume and from Alasdair MacIntyre's contribution to it, such actions can additionally cause specifiable harms to the interests of others. A hypothetical situation from biomedical experimentation will serve to illustrate this distinction. Suppose a researcher wished to test for the therapeutic effects of a new drug by administering it instead of the accepted treatment to a group of patients with the condition for which the drug was expected to be useful. If the researcher conducted the experiment without first obtaining the consent of the subjects, the moral duty to respect their rights would go unfulfilled and a moral wrong would thereby be committed. But the drug might also produce an unanticipated or previously unconfirmed physical reaction involving pain, debilitation, or disfigurement. Since people can be presumed to take an interest in their physical health and appearance, such a reaction would represent a specifiable harm to the subjects' interests over and above the moral wrong entailed by the failure to obtain consent.

The terminology thus employed to distinguish "moral wrongs" from "harms to interests" should not be taken as suggesting that the latter class of consequences does not have any *moral* relevance. It is true, however, that the particular moral relevance of harms to interests will likely differ from that of moral wrongs. In the case of epidemiology, the presence of significant harms to interests beyond any moral wrong involved in violating subject privacy would be sufficient to render epidemiologic research morally unjustifiable—though, as with the previous condition, a truly extreme health hazard threatening the continued existence of the social order would present a conceivable exception to this stipulation. One of the traditional purposes of informed consent requirements is to offer research subjects an opportunity to accept or reject for themselves the risk of specifiable harms entailed by participation in research. If that risk were appreciable in epidemiologic research that proceeds without obtaining consent, the failure to respect a person's privacy would be compounded by a failure to fulfill this additional function of consent requirements. In my opinion, any appreciable risk would therefore render the epidemiologist's inability to obtain consent morally unjustifiable.

This requirement will no doubt be indeterminate in its implications as long as expressions such as "insignificant threat" and "appreciable risk" remain undefined. I do not intend by these expressions to condemn epidemiologic research in which the data collected has the *potential* to harm subjects in specifiable ways. It is undeniable that much of the information in epidemiologists' possession is of a highly sensitive nature. In psychiatric epidemiology and in research on venereal disease, to cite but two examples, the data collected could cause any number of harms to subject interests if it were made public in an identifiable fashion. A person's interests in reputation, in social standing, and perhaps even in a marital prospect or in employment could all be damaged in consequence of such publicity. Other specifiable harms to interests that epidemiologic data could potentially cause include legal jeopardy (from, say, illegal drug use), blackmail, and various kinds of economic loss.

In this potential for harming subject interests, epidemiologic data is probably not much different from the information collected by government agencies or commercial credit companies. What is different about epidemiology is the *access* that is permitted to the sensitive information in question. As is widely known, credit companies routinely exchange computerized information whose content and accuracy remain mysterious to the individuals identified. And in the worst cases from our political history, the same agencies that collected sensitive information about presumably subversive people and organizations did so with the intention of using it to discredit or otherwise harm those people and organizations. The harms thus inflicted by sensitive data do not result from the mere fact that some person other than the subject possesses the information. Rather, they stem from the information's being available to a particular kind of audience, one with the inclination to use the information in a way that could damage the subject, or in a position inadvertently to do so. Members of this kind of audience might include employers, journalists, law enforcement officials, and even friends and acquaintances of the person to whom the collected information pertains. If the information is not available to such parties, as it is not in epidemiologic research, then it has in effect not been publicized at all (at least for purposes of identifying harms); and it can consequently be said to pose no "significant threat" or "appreciable risk" to the subject.

In the light of these considerations, it appears that epidemiologic research presents only an insignificant threat of specifiably harming subject interests. In most instances, the identifiable information collected is seen only by the epidemiologists and assistants working on the project for which the information is compiled. This group can be trusted not to harbor intentions of using the information in a way that could harm subjects, and their professional standards and precautions make even inadvertently risky or threatening uses of the information unlikely. If information is retained after the study is completed, it is kept in strict confidence, with later use being restricted to other legitimate research studies. Furthermore, the results of epidemiologic research are always presented in aggregate or anonymous form, so that the restriction of direct access means that no one other than professional research personnel sees the information which is collected.

Of course, this argument rests on broad generalizations subject to disconfirming counterexamples. It might be objected that not all epidemiologists deserve such complete trust; surely, epidemiologists sometimes conduct studies that do not incorporate adequate confidentiality protections. Even if documented cases could be cited, this objection would suggest nothing more than that some particular epidemiologic projects may not meet the conditions of justifiability outlined above—a conclusion I am willing to accept. Still, it seems highly improbable that epidemiologic projects deficient with respect to this condition are in fact conducted, given the context of procedural safeguards discussed in the next section of the paper.

A far more important problem concerns the possibility of legal subpoena. If the data in epidemiologists' files were subpoenaed for legal purposes (e.g., a grand jury investigation or civil suit), and the subpoena were not resisted, the data would become available to parties outside the professional research community. This possibility means that for all their elaborate precautions and safeguards, epidemiologists cannot guarantee that identifiable information in their possession will not be seen by parties who are in a position to harm the interests of research subjects in specifiable ways. The threat of legal subpoena thus compromises the epidemiologist's ability to satisfy the third condition. To remedy this situation, future legislative initiatives must grant immunity from subpoena to information obtained for research purposes.

Once such a legal guarantee has been provided, no doubt should remain about the insignificance of the risks posed by epidemiologic research. To say this is not to deny that the acquisition of sensitive identifiable information presents a constant potential for abuse. It is, however, to contend that the bare possibility of harmful consequences does not automatically make epidemiologic research risky or threatening. Significant levels of risk emerge only when information is accessible to a particular kind of audience, and the identifiable information collected by epidemiologists is not accessible in that way.

4. *The Results of the Research Must Be Likely to Bring Social Benefits of a Significant Nature.* This condition specifies the aspect of epidemiologic

research that most obviously makes its performance a beneficent activity. As suggested above, however, it is not merely the fact that the research yields benefits but the nature and degree of those benefits that are important. And it is in this connection that the contrast with other intuitively unjustifiable invasions of privacy in our society is most pronounced. Credit companies may appeal to the individually chosen benefit of obtaining consumer credit, but it is arguable whether that benefit is in any way great enough to justify the techniques they sometimes employ (especially since those techniques do not always seem necessary to realize the benefits described). Similarly, the benefit of "national security" invoked to justify certain government agency activities would be disputed in many instances by members of our society. Few would question the importance of the issues raised when one nation presents a direct military threat to another. It is quite a different matter, however, in cases of political dissidence that trigger government surveillance activities. Here, controversies are sure to develop over whether national security is really challenged in a way that could conceivably justify the invasion of citizen privacy in question.

The benefits of epidemiologic research, on the other hand, are both far less controversial and in many instances far more significant. Less controversial, because they clearly further an interest that is as basic and universal as any in the human experience: the interest in physical health and survival. More significant, both because of the fundamental nature of this interest, and because the benefits to that interest are justly and broadly distributed throughout the population. These features should clarify the somewhat nebulous expression "social benefits of a significant nature" found in the formulation of this fourth condition. They suggest that the condition would be satisfied neither by trivial benefits (e.g., a one-dollar tax rebate) distributed equally to all members of the population, nor by a great benefit (e.g., a dramatic lifesaving medical technology) unjustly distributed only to those who could afford its considerable expense. The benefits of epidemiologic research easily qualify as both substantial and significant in this way; indeed, even those individuals whose right to privacy is violated by epidemiologic research would be unlikely to question the fundamental importance of the benefits thereby made available. A brief but representative sample of specific epidemiologic studies and their results will bear out this contention more eloquently than whole pages of further generalization:[1]

a. Cancer. Studies that demonstrated (i) the relationship of cigarette smoking to lung cancer, bladder cancer, and other conditions; (ii) an increased cancer risk associated with occupational exposure to substances such as asbestos and vinyl chloride; (iii) the increased risk of several types of cancer that follows exposure to radiation; (iv) the risk of vaginal cancer faced by the daughters of women who received the hormone diethylstilbestrol (DES) during pregnancy; and (v) the increased risk of endometrial or uterine cancer faced by women taking estrogens for menopausal symptoms.

  b. Cardiovascular Diseases. Studies that demonstrated (i) that high
blood lipids, high blood pressure, and smoking shorten life expectancy,
particularly through coronary disease; (ii) that women taking oral contraceptives
stand at an increased risk of developing thromboembolism or stroke; and (iii) that
administration of anticoagulants to patients with myocardial infarctions is
associated with lower postinfarction mortality rates.

  c. Infectious Diseases. Studies that led to the development of vaccines for
poliomyelitis, measles, and other infectious diseases, and studies which showed
that cases of polio subsequent to polio immunization in 1955 resulted from a
vaccine lot contaminated with live virus.

  d. Child Health. Studies that demonstrated (i) that the administration of
high concentrations of oxygen to premature infants results in blindness; (ii) that
rubella (German measles) or other viral infection of the mother during pregnancy
can produce congenital malformations in the infant; (iii) that radiation exposure
of the mother during pregnancy is associated with a risk of congenital
malformations and childhood cancer in her offspring; (iv) that Rh disease
(erythroblastosis fetalis) in newborns can be prevented; and (v) that comprehensive care programs for inner-city children and youth are effective in
reducing rates of rheumatic fever.

  These examples are illustrative of results routinely produced by epidemiologic research. If the beneficial consequences of epidemiology were less
significant—e.g., by being unjustly distributed through the population—the
beneficent obligation fulfilled by the research might not be sufficient to override
the important duty to respect another's right to privacy. Conversely, social
benefits of even greater significance would make epidemiology a beneficent
activity important enough to justifiably entail greater risks and more substantial
moral wrongs. Nevertheless, given the extreme implausibility of such extraordinary benefits from epidemiology—or from any other activity, for that
matter—the four conditions, as thus far described, should suffice to govern
judgments about the moral justifiability of epidemiologic research in which
consent is not obtained.

The Context of the Research Activity: Procedural and
Institutional Safeguards

  In arguing that epidemiologic research generally satisfies these four
conditions, I may seem to have made implausibly magnanimous assumptions
about the impartiality and trustworthiness of epidemiologists. I maintained,
for instance, that because of the integrity of epidemiologists as a group, their
access to possibly sensitive identifiable information does not threaten to harm
the specifiable interests of subjects. Yet it would be unfortunate if the
satisfaction of so important a condition of justifiability were entirely contingent
on individual vagaries of character. The moral justifiability of epidemiologic
research, however, is not dependent on any such contingency, for that research

is performed in a context of procedural and institutional safeguards which largely guarantee that the conditions described above are satisfied.

The safeguards to which I here refer consist mainly in federally mandated mechanisms for ensuring that research conform to certain basic moral standards. Central among these mechanisms are the Institutional Review Boards responsible for reviewing all human subjects research at institutions that receive federal research funds. As papers throughout this volume attest, the appropriateness of IRB review in much social science research remains a hotly contested issue. In epidemiology, however, it seems to me that IRB review performs a salutary function. At its best, it ensures that epidemiologists take adequate steps to preserve the confidentiality of the data they collect, requiring that they specify who will have access to the data, how and at what point in the research personal information will be separated from other data, and whether the data will be retained at the conclusion of the study. IRB reviewers also require a thorough description of interview instruments and questionnaires, and they make sure that the informed consent of subjects will be obtained before interviews are conducted.

Perhaps most basically of all, IRBs require researchers to justify particular projects according to their anticipated risks and benefits. I have argued throughout this essay that epidemiologic research is justified because it constitutes an especially important beneficent activity, and I have maintained that its importance can be demonstrated by a rigorous utilitarian assessment. The same considerations can be invoked, however, to show that particular epidemiologic studies which do not promise sufficient benefits, or which fail to meet one of the other criteria, are not morally justifiable. As suggested above, this is a conclusion I willingly embrace, and I therefore support the requirement that IRBs assess the anticipated harms and benefits of proposed research projects.

The practical value of these procedural and institutional safeguards can be illustrated by considering epidemiologic research from the standpoint of the clinical physician. Physicians, of course, traditionally recognize a moral and professional obligation to protect the confidentiality of information collected about their patients. They may also recognize the overriding importance of the benefits made possible by epidemiology and wish to contribute data to an epidemiologic study. Few physicians have either the time or the background to evaluate proposed epidemiologic studies for their moral justifiability; yet fewer still would be willing to betray their responsibilities to patients by divulging identifiable information about them to researchers whose studies might not incorporate adequate confidentiality safeguards or promise sufficient benefits. The role of IRB review for physicians confronted with this dilemma should be obvious.

The proven value of the existing IRB process notwithstanding, government officials and university administrators ought to pay particular attention to three important issues as regulatory standards and mechanisms are revised and refined in the coming years. The first of these is the threat of legal subpoena discussed in the previous section of the essay. The second issue concerns the retention of records after a study is complete. IRBs are responsible for checking that an investigator either destroy those records that include identifiers at the end of a study or justify the retention of such records. In the latter case, the researcher must specify the length of time for which records are to be kept and the steps taken to protect the confidentiality of the data during that period. Often the reason for retaining records is an investigator's intention to conduct a follow-up study of the population to which the records pertain. When the researcher has such specific plans in mind, the justifications for data retention recognized by IRBs are clear and straightforward.

Retention of data can, however, also be justifiable when the researcher has not developed plans for conducting a follow-up study by the conclusion of the original project. Much of the expense and effort associated with epidemiologic research goes into identifying and tracing a group of diseased people and a control group without the disease. Even if no follow-up study can be envisaged at the time when the original research is performed, it is conceivable that later research uses of the data may become apparent as new health-related problems arise. To destroy those data might therefore entail a considerable inefficiency in the performance of later epidemiologic studies, an inefficiency whose costs would most likely be borne by the public. For this reason, IRBs should be free to adopt a flexible policy on the question of data retention, approving that procedure even in the absence of specific plans for further research use. Of course, it is incumbent on researchers to maintain the confidentiality of data that have been retained, and it is in this connection that statistical procedures such as those described by Robert Boruch will be of most service. IRBs often insist, for example, that data held beyond the completion of a study be identified only by individual numbers assigned to patients at the hospital, with all names and address identifiers being expunged. While this step does not protect absolutely against breaches of informational confidentiality, it does discourage outsiders who inappropriately seek to identify particular research subjects. At the same time, it permits efficient reidentification of those subjects for later research purposes.

A third and related issue involves the redisclosure of data for research and health statistical purposes. Though researchers should generally retain identifiable information in confidence, much of the point of data retention would be lost if its release to other researchers were not permitted. IRBs would be employing a misguided ideal of privacy if they prohibited such release of identifiable information out of hand. The moral problems raised by this procedure are essentially the same as the problems posed by the original use of the information for research purposes. In neither case is it possible to obtain the informed consent of the subjects who are identified, and the central question is whether this invasion of privacy is justified. Given this basic similarity of the issues involved in original and secondary release of identifiable information, it would seem only appropriate that identical standards of justifiability be applied in both instances. Thus, while IRBs should not prohibit rerelease of data for research purposes, they should review the studies in which the data will be used to ensure that those studies meet fundamental conditions of moral justifiability.

These minor refinements in the system of existing safeguards would facilitate the conduct of epidemiology while strengthening the guarantees that morally unjustifiable research will not be conducted. Even without these refinements, however, the mechanisms of institutional ethical review perform a critically important function. In conjunction with the four necessary and sufficient substantive conditions, the context of existing safeguards serves to distinguish epidemiologic research from the notorious activities in our society which unjustifiably involve a violation of privacy rights. Those safeguards mean that not only will there be clear lines foreclosing the dangerous consequences of the slippery slope, but the lines will consistently be observed in the practice of epidemiologic research. My preference for beneficent obligations in these circumstances, however, is open to criticisms of a more fundamental nature. In closing, I shall briefly consider two such criticisms and sketch a tentative response to them.

Conclusion: Alternative Approaches

Valid moral arguments are traditionally held to be universalizable. That is, the same moral considerations that justify a particular action in one set of circumstances justify a relevantly similar action in all relevantly similar circumstances. This stipulation suggests that if the arguments I have adduced are valid, they must justify not only epidemiologic research but any human subjects research that similarly satisfies the four stated conditions.

It is in thus contemplating the broader implications of my position that many social scientists are likely to adopt a dissenting view. For it will probably seem that I have drawn the justifying conditions of research more strictly than is necessary. By insisting, for example, that research must promise benefits as significant and uncontroversial as improvements to health, I may seem to have made it impossible to justify certain important social scientific studies whose benefits are of a less fundamental nature. While this is indeed a potential implication of my position, it by no means renders that position invalid or implausible. After all, it is not inconceivable that an activity of some indisputable importance—such as similar kinds of social science research—might nevertheless appear unjustifiable when subjected to rigorous ethical analysis, and counterarguments based solely on this possibility are less than wholly compelling.

Moreover, it seems doubtful that my position is so intuitively implausible as it may at first appear to social scientists. My conclusion is not that *all* research must promise substantial and significant social benefits, or that justifiable research can *never* involve more than a minimal risk. Rather, I maintain only that research which does not obtain the informed consent of subjects must meet these strict conditions. The reader who remains unconvinced by this position would do well to compare it with the conclusion reached by the psychologist Alan C. Elms earlier in this volume. Elms contends that deceptive practices in social science research are justifiable only when they meet a set of conditions substantially similar to those endorsed in this essay. Disputes will no doubt persist, however, concerning the commensurability of the social benefits of biomedical research with those of research in the social sciences.

If my position might thus appear unnecessarily strict to some proponents of human subjects research, many others will undoubtedly find it dangerously permissive. People strongly committed to the principle of autonomy in particular are likely to contend that my arguments turn on a fundamental misinterpretation of the nature of beneficent obligations. Focusing on the conflict between duties to respect privacy and duties to provide social benefits at the core of the moral dilemma in epidemiology, such opponents would argue that the latter duties are never sufficient to override the former. Beneficent considerations, they would maintain, always describe supererogatory obligations; while the positive production of benefits for others is morally praiseworthy in itself, it is not *obligatory* on moral grounds. But if this characterization is accurate, the conflict between duties that lies at the heart of epidemiologic research can uncontroversially be decided. No one would deny that supererogatory duties ought to give way when they inhibit the performance of obligatory duties.

The position espoused by Hans Jonas on the use of human subjects in biomedical experimentation can be taken as representative of this strong alternative to my conclusions.[2] Jonas does not disagree that the results of biomedical experimentation—including the benefits to health produced by epidemiology—are desirable, or even that we have come to take those desirable results for granted. He contends, however, that the production of such results is properly regarded as an optional service rather than as an obligatory duty. The activity is progressive and meliorative, involving an improvement in the social condition and not the minimal preservation of it. Yet on Jonas's account, only activities of the latter sort—i.e., those that are strictly necessary for the continued existence of society—can justifiably extract a sacrifice in aspects of human autonomy such as the right to privacy. This conclusion can be formulated in terms of the social contract underlying political and social relations. In Jonas's view, that contract simply does not entail a commitment to the continual improvement of the human lot over and above the basic preservation of social order. Participation in projects aimed at essentially meliorative goals is therefore not something that should be expected of citizens as a matter of course; rather it ought to be a fully voluntary matter left entirely to each individual to decide. It is not hard to glean the implications of Jonas's general view for the use of identifiable data in epidemiology without the informed consent of subjects.

This position seems to express an intuitively satisfying moral presumption against violations of human autonomy. Indeed, it is persuasive enough to render implausible an increasingly popular line of argument on behalf of human subjects research such as epidemiology: the defense grounded in the scientist's moral right to conduct research. While I do not dispute the accuracy and explanatory utility of positing such a moral right, I would consider that right to be far less than absolute. Like other rights, the right to conduct research should not be protected when its exercise interferes with the basic moral rights of others. Since much research that fails to secure the informed consent of its subjects uncontroversially involves a violation of subjects' moral rights, it is difficult to imagine how the positing of a right to conduct research could possibly settle the outstanding disagreements about certain practices in human subjects research.

Instead, I have chosen an explicitly utilitarian approach grounded in a commitment to the beneficent duties in the circumstances. By doing so, I have meant to shift the focus of debate to the results of epidemiologic research. Those results bring undeniably significant social benefits, and to recognize this fact should give pause to even the most devoted among Jonas's allies as to whether the presumption against violations of autonomy might not have its limits, after all.

At bottom, a recognition of such limitations will depart from Jonas's position in seeing certain meliorative social benefits as more than merely optional. An implication of my position, then, is that some beneficent activities, including epidemiologic research, *are* morally obligatory—and not merely supererogatory—social services. Since beneficent activities are sometimes not understood to be morally obligatory, this outcome may well challenge the intuitions of many readers. But I hope that in contemplating my utilitarian approach in the light of the alternatives I have described, such readers will find this outcome progressively more compelling.

Notes

1.   For detailed documentation of these studies, see Leon Gordis and Ellen Gold, "Privacy, Confidentiality, and the Use of Medical Records in Research," *Science* 207 (January 11, 1980): 153-56. With the permission of Professors Gordis and Gold, the specific examples and much of the language in the following four paragraphs borrow directly from this article.

2.   Hans Jonas, "Philosophical Reflections on Experimenting with Human Subjects," as reprinted in Tom L. Beauchamp and LeRoy Walters, eds., *Contemporary Issues in Bioethics* (Belmont, Calif.: Wadsworth Publishing Co., 1978), pp. 411-20.

14

Methods for Resolving Privacy Problems in Social Research

ROBERT F. BORUCH

Mark Twain defined an ethical man as a Christian holding four aces. This paper is dedicated to providing decent cards, if not aces, to the researcher who would be ethical. It summarizes recent attempts to clarify privacy problems in social research and, more importantly, to develop solutions to them. It also updates an earlier, relentlessly detailed monograph on multiple approaches to resolving privacy problems in social research.[1] The first section outlines objectives and working definitions. The material that follows covers procedural, statistical, and statutory approaches to resolving privacy problems in research, and considers special problems in audit and secondary analysis. The last section focuses on discriminating between settings in which individual privacy is a fundamental problem, and these solutions are then relevant, and settings in which other problems are more critical despite advertising that privacy is *the* issue.

Principles, Definitions, and Premises

I subscribe to the principle that diminution of individual privacy can be minimized without needlessly abridging our ability to do good research.[2] The proviso on abridgment is crucial and protects us from naive attempts to "maximize privacy." Others have espoused a similar principle with equal piety, and to advance beyond it I propose the use of multiple approaches for actualizing the principle. The presumption is that no single solution to privacy problems is adequate, simply because the character of problems varies so much. The emphasis here is on concrete solutions rather than on trust in the researcher. This is not meant to disparage trust, merely to reduce the need for it.

It is a pleasure to acknowledge the National Science Foundation's support of research on this topic, the volume editors' assistance in reducing the number of my lexical sins, and Art Caplan for his criticism.

Privacy is defined here as a property of the individual, confidentiality as a property of information, and security as a property of information-handling procedures. This definition, vague and useful only in context, is similar to one made by the statistical community. An older and more important distinction is between information collected for *administrative* purposes, i.e., to make decisions or judgments about a particular identifiable individual, and information collected for *research* purposes, in which the individual's identity is incidental and the function of the information is not tied to decisions about the individual.[3]

The latter distinction, between types of information, is important partly because it influences the constraints on researchers' access to information. Its recognition by the U.S. Privacy Protection Study Commission puts the commission's thinking well beyond the United Kingdom's Younger Commission, the Swedish Parliament's Privacy Act of 1973, and some Canadian and German efforts. The distinction has some meaning for the public, judging from people's willingness to undergo personality tests in the interest of research but not in the interest of meeting job screening requirements.[4] The distinction can also be corrupted, judging from the results of R. Baxter's investigation of sales campaigns thinly disguised as market research in the United States and from Madgwich and Smythe's research on private detectives masquerading as pollsters in the United Kingdom.[5] The distinction is not always made carefully. For instance, P. Hewitt's otherwise interesting volume for Britain's National Council for Civil Liberties lumps the United Kingdom's census bureau with administrative agencies, indiscriminately ignoring differences in functions and rules governing information from each source.[6]

Procedural Solutions

Procedural solutions are nontechnical approaches to handling information that avoid diminishing individual privacy or sustain confidentiality of records on identifiable respondents. Asking for anonymous responses to a questionnaire is an example. The procedures can be deceptively simple, as this one is, or unnervingly complex. They are more vulnerable to corruption than one might expect. Most such procedures are cumbersome and must be tailored to the research design. The following description covers alternative procedures and the research designs to which they have been adopted.

Cross-Sectional Studies

Consider a research design in which a different sample of hospital patients is surveyed each year to estimate the incidence of drug abuse. The strategies invented for such cross-sectional studies include: (*a*) eliciting anonymous responses directly from the respondent; (*b*) eliciting identified response in the interest of assuring sampling validity, then destroying identifiers; (c) using the custodian of a list of patients as intermediary where even identification (of, say, mental patients) is sensitive, and obtaining anonymous responses directly from the respondent; and (d) using the list custodian as intermediary in both eliciting information and as an interim recipient of responses where identification itself is sensitive and there is some risk of deductive disclosure. The methods are sturdy despite their simplicity. And they have been tested often; see, for instance, the applications in the National Survey on Drug Abuse of 1977[7] and countless others. They have the merit of not diminishing an individual's privacy even with respect to the honest researcher.

They also have notable disadvantages. For instance, three of the methods make assuring validity of the sample difficult. To accommodate the problem in mail surveys about record-keeping practices, we have asked respondents to send us postcards to verify that they did indeed respond on separate questionnaires. Anonymous response, of course, precludes tracking individuals and makes long term studies of a particular group very difficult.

The methods can be subverted. Despite a statement that the response is anonymous, one might covertly identify questionnaires, as a marketing research firm did in its survey of *National Observer* readers. One need not even construct invisible identifiers: collateral information on an individual or institution known to have responded can sometimes be used to deduce identification from a nominally anonymous questionnaire. For instance, in the National Academy of Sciences study of institutional record-keeping practices, we could have established the link for at least a third of banks responding anonymously to the questionnaire by postmark alone.[8] That some respondents will recognize the possibility of deductive disclosure is clear. What is not clear is what proportion do so, under what circumstances the problem appears, and how severe the problem is.

Longitudinal Studies

Longitudinal studies require that one be able to link individual records obtained periodically over some time span. So, for instance, one may repeatedly survey a sample of former mental patients in the interest of understanding when, how, and why rehospitalization occurs. In legitimate research of this sort, the individual's identification serves only as a vehicle for linkage. To accomplish the linkage, yet avoid diminution of privacy or threats to confidentiality, a variety of methods have been field tested. The simplest is asking that respondents use an alias. Nominal aliases have been tried out with some success in short-term studies. Peter Rossi and others have tried to use numerical aliases constructed by algorithm in studies of drug abuse. Their algorithm depended, incidentally, on the respondent's knowing his or parents' birthdates, a flawed assumption it appears. The alias approach can, of course, be employed in conjunction with one which elicits fully identified information.

It may be used when an intermediary agency is necessary to transmit the inquiry, and indeed a variation has been used in field evaluation of the Emergency School Assistance Act.

Alternatives have been developed for situations in which aliases are not satisfactory. The link file system developed at the American Council on Education is an example. The process involved using a code dictionary of researcher created aliases, kept outside the United States, as a vehicle for linking information collected periodically from a sample of college students. The use of the dictionary reduces the need to hold identified records, and because the dictionary is kept outside the country, it lowers the likelihood that nonresearchers will appropriate data for purposes other than scholarly research. Variations on the strategy include direct provision of numerical aliases to respondents, eliminating clear identifiers in response entirely, the use of intermediaries in transmitting inquiry and response or analyses, and the use of several principles to construct parts of a given numerical alias.

Such methods have clear disadvantages. Those that rely on the respondents to generate aliases prevent quality control of sampling and investigation of response validity unless special measures are taken. The devices may be objectionable on other grounds, e.g., Oklahoma police involved in the police assaults study objected to their being asked to use aliases partly because they reckoned that "only criminals use aliases." The possibility of deductive disclosure or covert identification is no different from that in the strategies described earlier. And the procedures impede linkage with other dependent sources of information, making validation studies difficult or impossible.

Linking Records from Independent Sources

Records from independent archives must occasionally be linked in the interest of assessing the relative accuracy of records, reducing respondent burden, or for other reasons. So, for instance, in a study of a delinquency prevention program, one might link police records, court records, and survey data on the same individuals to understand effects of the program. The rules governing disclosure of identifiable records from each source may, however, prevent direct merger. Consequently, a variety of methods have been developed to link records without violating disclosure rules.

Consider, for example, a variant on the "mutually insulated data bank" approach, used by Schwartz and Orleans in their experiments on reporting income to the Internal Revenue Service. The rudimentary procedure involves two record systems, each operated under different auspices, each with a rule that identified records cannot be disclosed outside the system. To achieve linkage, the custodians of the first archive, containing information collected by a social scientist from a group of individuals, cryptographically encode all the information in the record except for individual identifiers, producing a new file without meaning to an outsider. Each encoded record and the individual identifier is transmitted to the second archive. Custodians of the latter, which might for example be a hospital, church, or taxation system, then match the encoded file with their own records, based on clear identifiers appearing in both files. When the match is completed, individual identifiers are deleted, and the linked, anonymous records are returned to the social scientist. The encoded sections of each linked record are decoded by the scientist to render the file ready for statistical analysis. Records are combined *without* violating promises or regulations against disclosure of identifiable records. New variations on this method have been used most recently with social security records.[9] T. Reve has used an elaborate version to survey commercial organizations in Norway, linking survey data with data held by the organizations' representatives and clients.[10] For other illustrations, see Boruch and Cecil.

Deductive Disclosure

E. Freidson's assertion that the only way of "absolutely assuring confidentiality of sources is to destroy all record of their identities" is of course wrong.[11] Deductive disclosure is possible despite destruction of identifiers and, in any case, there is no absolute guarantee in quantitative or qualitative social research. Witness W. Kruskal's suggestion that, in Carroll's case study of government attempts to appropriate research data, the "Chicago studies of live juries in the '50's [are] . . . not identified as such but are clearly recognizable."[12] Deductive disclosure of identities of cities or other organizations is a critical problem in institutional research when there is some justification for assuring anonymity of the organizations. For example, Gibbons neatly penetrates the "Prairie City" research on criminal justice to show it is Decatur merely by ambling through census reports on cities.[13] At the individual level, examples are easy to construct, but much less easy to find. So, for example, if in a school survey of thirty-five years ago I found anonymous data informing me that one student was a dark-haired Polish orphan who looked like a gypsy, traveled some, and demolished trains after school, I would guess that it was Jerzy Kosinski.

The strategies developed to protect privacy in record linkage are vulnerable in varying degrees to deductive disclosure. For instance, it would be easy to create records for linkage that had unique contents, assuring that deductive disclosure is possible. It would not be difficult to deduce identification after the fact in some cases. To remedy the problem, the archive supplying records to the inquiring agency may use any of the techniques normally used to impede deductive disclosure with public use data tapes. They are described later, in the section on Secondary Analysis and Audit. All such prophylactic measures are cumbersome and, if one has reason to trust the inquirer, the strategies are an unnecessary burden to the agency linking the records. Furthermore, they complicate later statistical analyses considerably. In research on relatively rare phenomena, such as rape or murder, for example, they can make the data nearly useless for any sophisticated appraisal.

Statistical Solutions: Direct Inquiry

Personal interviews with identified respondents, rather than, say, mail surveys, are sometimes essential. If the inquiry concerns sensitive topics, the respondent may be discomfited by the request to respond whether the exchange is voluntary or not. Where the inquiry bears on illegal or socially deviant behavior, the risk can be serious. The researcher's records on identified respondents may be subpoenaed or used in legal proceedings against the respondent, an event which breaches the promise of confidentiality and may disrupt the research.

To resolve these problems, a variety of statistical procedures have been developed. They permit one to elicit data even in interviews without gaining information about a *particular* respondent's state. At the same time, they permit the statistician to develop elementary statistical summaries for the sample and the question at hand. Like any solution discussed here, they engender still other problems.

Randomized Response

The best known class of approaches is the randomized response tactic developed by S. L. Warner and extended creatively by Greenberg, Abernathy, Horvitz, and others in the United States, by Dalenius, Lanke, Swensson, and Erichsson in Sweden, by Warner in Canada, Moore in Holland, and by others.[14] In a simple variation on the approach, the social scientist simultaneously presents a sensitive inquiry to an individual, e.g., "Did you cheat on your income taxes this year?" and an innocuous one, the answers to which must be unrelated to those generated by the sensitive question, e.g., "Do you prefer potatoes over noodles?" The individual is then instructed to roll a die and to respond to the first question if a one or a two shows and to the second question if a three, four, five, or six appears. He is also told to refrain from giving the interviewer any indication of which question was answered. When the process is carried out on two large samples of individuals, the odds on asking each question being changed from one sample to the next, and when the instructions are followed by the respondent, it is possible to estimate the proportion of individuals in the sample who have cheated on their income tax and the proportion who prefer noodles. In particular, knowing some fundamental laws of probability, the odds on answering one or the other question in each sample, and the observed proportion of "yes" responses, the estimation is a matter of solving two independent equations in two unknowns.

The technique permits researchers to establish the statistical character of sensitive properties of groups of individuals. Moreover, it does so *without* disclosing to the interviewer or social scientist any information about a particular individual. There is no observed, deterministic link between the state of the individual and his response. At best, the approach will also reduce embarrassment or distress associated with questions. The extent to which it does so is measurable in principle, though the question has not been considered in field research. The main limitation of the method is that it requires a large sample. Current variations are useless with small samples and narrative material.

This and related methods are novel, and some experts are skeptical about their effectiveness. L. R. Bergman, R. Hanve, and J. Rapp, for instance, argue that "It appears doubtful if a randomized response technique ... has any advantages in this situation" (namely, their study of cooperation rates in Swedish surveys of living conditions).[15] They offer no evidence for their contention, however. Judging from the results of field tests listed in table 14.1, I conclude that variations on the method work about half the time. The

TABLE 14.1
FIELD RESULTS OF RANDOMIZED RESPONSE METHODS

	Sample Size for RR	Percentage Response to RR	Percentage Response to Standard	Crude Reduction in Response Bias
Abernathy, Greenberg, Horvitz	3113	97	NR	yes
I-cheng, Chow, Rider	1021	89	89	yes
Liu, Chen, Chow	353	85	NR	yes
Krotki and Fox	352	97	73	inc
Shimizu and Bonham	9797	99	NR	yes
Goodstadt and Gruson	431	95	87	yes
Brown and Harding	1100	NR	NR	inc
Brown (mail)	2114	18-50	32-65	inc
Reaser, Hartsock, Hoehn (mail)	2400	23	26	yes
Barth and Sandler	64	100	NR	yes
Berman, McCombs, Boruch	156	100	100	inc
Dawes	270	100	NR	NR
Zdep and Rhodes	995	98	75-85	yes
Locander, Sudman, Bradburn	233	60-78	48-90	inc
Folsom	423	100		
Erickson	76	97	NR	inc
Fidler and Kleinknecht	132	100	100*	yes
Illinois Institute of Technology	1200	100	NR	inc
Kim and Flueck (1)	54	NR	NR	NR
Kim and Flueck (2)	50	NR	NR	NR
Fox and Tracy	530	NR	NR	yes
Aitken and Bonneville	1825	NR	NR	yes
Lipton, Weissman, Steer	115	60		

Note: This summarizes some results of field studies undertaken with randomized response (RR) methods. The gross number of respondents involved in a survey using the methods is reported in the first column. Cooperation, registered by crude response rate, is indexed in the second column for the randomized response sample. When an estimate of response rates for direct questions or some other standard is available and reported, that is listed in column three. NR implies that the information was not included in the report. The fourth column contains a judgment, based on the published report, as to whether the use of randomized response led to reduced bias in reporting by respondents. INC indicates that results are inconclusive; YES indicates a clear reduction in bias, relative to a standard. A blank indicates that the study was not designed to provide the information. See the text for citations and topics covered in each study. References are given in Boruch and Cecil (see note 1) except for the last three studies (see notes 16 and 17).

conditions under which they perform well *cannot* always be anticipated, however, and they must be tested in pilot studies before being adopted in main surveys. Statisticians such as Jong-Ik Kim and John Flueck, have recently developed variations on the method that are more attractive to respondents and more efficient relative to statistical standards.[16]

A recent study of drug use among Canadian high school students by M. S. Goodstadt, G. Cook, and V. Gruson illustrates field tests of the methods. They executed a randomized field test in which students were randomly assigned among various ways of eliciting information about drug abuse. One of the ways consisted of the randomized response method as described earlier, changing the odds from one subsample to the next. The sensitive question concerned six drugs. The inoffensive one concerned entertainment, aside from drugs, that is. All groups were of equal size and *all* respondents were anonymous, whether they were in the randomized condition or not. The field test resulted in the findings that despite uniform anonymity, the randomized response method elicited notably more cooperation: there was a remarkable increase in the rate at which students answered questions, and mean reported drug use was significantly higher with this method than with direct questions.[17]

Microaggregation of Response

A related class of approaches is based on aggregation of responses. The individual is asked not to respond to each item in a set of questions but to give an aggregate response to the set. In one variation on the theme, the respondent adds up numerical values corresponding to each answer of each question in a set. If "Yes" is assigned a value of 1 and "No" a value of -1, for example, the response to a set of three questions each answerable with a Yes or No is a single number whose permissible range is -3 to +3. In a second independent sample of the same population, respondents are asked to subtract item 1 from the sum of items 2 and 3, rather than add the numerical value of all responses. And in a third subsample, another linear combination is used, e.g., subtracting item 2 from the sum corresponding to items 1 and 3. Given the Yes responses in each sample, one needs a little algebra—notably methods for solving a system of three simultaneous equations—to estimate the proportions of individuals in the total sample who have each of the three properties. The statistical properties of the estimate can also be derived.[18]

Again, the technique permits one to elicit even sensitive information in direct interview situations without any direct link between an identified response to the researcher's question and the actual status of the individual. Deductive disclosure of an individual response is possible for some combinations of traits, but the possibility of that can be eliminated in variations on the method. The approach has not been field-tested frequently. Its principal operating disadvantage, apart from asking the respondent to participate in a task he may not understand at all, is the requirement that the respondent be able to handle arithmetic.

Microaggregation of Sampling Units

The third major class of statistical techniques is aggregation of units in the sample. Here, one obtains data not on each identified individual, but on small and carefully constructed clusters of individuals. If the cluster's composition remains the same over time, each cluster can, under certain conditions, be regarded as a synthetic person, a composite of the properties of the small set of individuals it comprises. Informative data analyses can be conducted on the aggregated individuals and, insofar as aggregation helps to assure anonymity of individual response, there is no reduction of individual privacy.

Sample microaggregation has, so far, been limited to economic research on commercial organizations and to dissemination rather than to collection of information. Banks, for example, are reluctant to release information about their operations to an independent economist. They are willing, however, to have the social scientist analyze aggregates of banks, reconciling the need for bank privacy with the need for the research. In fact, a system for data maintenance and dissemination has been developed on this theme at the University of Wisconsin.[19]

Secondary Analysis and Audit

Reanalyzing research data in the interest of verifying original conclusions or testing new hypotheses, generates some confidentiality problems. So does the execution of an audit on a large-scale policy research. In either case, disclosure of identifiable records can, for example, violate a promise of confidentiality or a law governing the disclosure of the records.[20] Deductive disclosure is a small but notable risk. The remedies that have been developed capitalize on both procedural and statistical methods.

To eliminate unwarranted or accidental disclosure of records on identifiable individuals, the members of the National Academy of Sciences Committee on Federal Program Evaluation recommended routine deletion of identifiers from released records.[21] To impede the possibility of deductive disclosure, the recommendations were to:

> withhold lists of identifiers of all individuals whose records are on file;
> disclose anonymous records on samples rather than on the entire target population;
> minimize the number of items within records disclosed;
> adjust exactness of responses contained within each record to prevent exact deductive disclosure;
> adjust the reliability of response; and
> microaggregate records.

These actions should not be taken simultaneously. Indeed, deletion of identifiers and withholding a listing of research participants are sufficient protection in many cases. Where these are not feasible or appropriate, as in research on rare, unstable, or imperfectly measured traits, then secondary analysis by prescription is a natural option. That is, the archive performs the computations for the outside secondary analyst, providing summary statistics rather than anonymous microrecords. While this option has obvious advantages, it impedes normally interactive analysis and so is not especially useful except where data are simple. A different two-tier system in operation at the Social Security Administration (SSA) helps to resolve this last problem. Public use tapes, containing microrecords, are released for no risk data. Restricted use tapes are created when agreements can be reached that risks of disclosure are negligible. Risk assessment for SSA hinges on file content, sampling fraction, and availability of collateral information.

The new strategies for reducing the possibility of deductive disclosure in release of microrecords are worth noting. Denning's proposed strategy, random sample queries, is to generate a random subsample as a basis for answering several queries, under the constraint that a large proportion of relevant records is included in the query set. The construction of each subsample is determined so that probability of selection is controlled, and a mathematical screening function is used to reduce the likelihood of deducting disclosure. A second approach, by Tore Dalenius and S. P. Reiss, focuses on release of records and the use of *data swapping* to control deductive disclosure. So, for example, one may switch a record of Vonnegut's daily beer ration for De Vries's, when the complete record on each contains additional information, without changing the average ration computed from a sample of authors' records. To establish when substitutions of various kinds yield the same statistic, such as an average, the investigators developed an arithmetic theory of order equivalence. Both random sample queries and data swapping are experimental; mathematical and empirical work continues on each.[22]

The problem of deductive disclosure based on microrecords is in principle no different from disclosure based on statistical tables. The technology for tables has a longer history and was developed along unique lines, however, on account of census bureaus' interest in disclosure avoidance. The general idea is to eliminate the possibility of deducing new identifiable information from published tables or combinations of them, without diminishing the utility of the tables. Of the new approaches, the U.S. Census Bureau's is among the best documented. Briefly, a mathematical model is used to represent the table; impermissible values of entries to the table, susceptible to deductive disclosure, are represented as mathematical constraints.[23] The statistician tries to maximize the information available in tables and simultaneously minimize the number of tables containing entries which are susceptible to deductive disclosure. The computations are sufficiently formidable to have been developed only for two-way tables. Variations on this approach and on the statistical approaches described next are used by bureaus in North America and Western Europe. No analogous mathematical work has been done on published case study material.

As for audit, such agencies as the U.S. General Accounting Office (GAO) are empowered to review applied social research when it is sponsored by the federal government. One aspect of review is assaying quality of the research data, and this may involve disclosing records on identifiable respondents to an audit agency or reinterviewing respondents. If so, a promise of confidentiality made to respondents may be breached in the process. If breached, the research itself may be impeded or degraded in quality. The problem occurred in 1977-78, with the GAO pitted against the researchers involved in the Experimental Housing Allowance Program, and again in 1980 when the target of investigation was research on food stamp work fare projects run by the U.S. Departments of Labor and Agriculture.

To reconcile GAO interests with those of the researchers, Boruch and Cecil proposed guidelines that were adopted by the Social Science Committee on Program Evaluation. SSRC later proposed them to the GAO, and GAO revised and adopted them.[24] The guidelines include distinguishing research which incorporates access for auditors as part of normal operations from prototypes which cannot provide access for scientific reasons. They also recognize that reinterviews of survey respondents may not yield what is expected in that conditions of interview implied by an auditor can produce results which differ from those obtained by an independent research group. Moreover, such reinterviews may disrupt research because of inept auditor-interviewers or the respondent's mistrust of audit.

The options for avoiding direct reinterview of research respondents by an audit agency include:

drawing an independent sample from the target population of the research, to compare auditor results against research results on statistical grounds;

using surrogate auditors, i.e., a group that is independent of both audit agency and research agencies and has the skills required to undertake reinterview;

drawing a subsample of the original sample for the auditors' use, with consent of respondent, so as to minimize risk of disrupting the research; and

employing the linkage strategies described earlier to couple independent sources of information in the interest of verification without reinterview or breach of assurances.

In its investigation of the Experimental Housing Allowance Program, GAO elected first to elicit permission for reinterview from a sample of respondents in the Program. Permission was elicited through the original research unit and the GAO then conducted verification interviews. In the GAO's investigation of the food stamp work fare program, the GAO guidelines appear to have been ignored entirely.

Contemporary Law as a Solution

A small set of laws provide some protection against government appropriation of research information on identifiable respondents. They facilitate researchers' adherence to a promise of confidentiality, making the legal, if not ethical, responsibility explicit. To the extent that research participants find legal protection compelling, these statutes can enhance cooperation rates.

TABLE 14.2
STATUTES PROVIDING GRANTS OF QUALIFIED IMMUNITY
FOR RESEARCH INFORMATION AND THEIR PROVISIONS

Statute	1	2	3	4	5	6	7
Public Health Services Act Sections 303(a) and 308(d). Pub. L. 91-513, 42 U.S.C.A. & 242a(a)	Y	N	N	Y	Y	Y	Y
Crime Control Act of 1973. Pub. L. 93-83, 42 U.S.C.A. & 3771	Y	Y	Y	Y	Y	N	Y
Juvenile Justice and Delinquency Prevention Act of 1977. Pub. L. 95-115	Y	Y	Y	Y	Y	N	Y
Controlled Substances Act, Section 502(c). Pub. L. 91-513, 21 U.S.C.A. & 872c	Y	N	N	Y	Y	Y	N
Drug Abuse Office & Treatment Act. Pub. L. 92-255, Amended, Section 408 Pub. L. 93-282, 21 U.S.C. & 1175a	Y	Y	Y	YC	N	YC	Y
Alcohol Abuse Act. Pub. L. 93-282, 45 U.S.C.A. & 4582a	Y	Y	Y	YC	N	YC	Y
Privacy of Research Records Act	Y	Y	Y	Y	Y	Y	Y
Confidentiality of Federal Statistical Records Act	Y	Y	N	Y	Y	Y	Y

1. Protects identification if research data
2. Protects identifiable information
3. Automatic, rather than authorized
4. Immunity from administrative inquiry
5. Immunity from judicial inquiry
6. Immunity from legislative inquiry
7. Provisions for secondary analysis, in
   regulations or law

Y = Yes, covered explicitly
N = No, not covered explicitly
YC = Court order required for disclosure

Each statute focuses on a different arena of federally supported research—mental health, criminal research, and so on. Each contains slightly different provisions affecting quality and level of protection. They are described briefly here, and summarized with legal citations in table 14.2. More detailed analysis is given in the book by Boruch and Cecil referred to in note 1.

Federal agencies with responsibility for collection or dissemination of statistical information, and an assortment of nonfederal organizations periodically issue reports describing new rules.[25] The standard we have used to assess quality of the law includes: whether immunity is automatic rather than authorized separately for each research project; whether immunity refers to administrative, judicial, and legislative agencies seeking to appropriate records; whether all information or just the identification of respondents is covered; and whether provisions for secondary analysis are created.

Public Health Services Act

The secretary of health and human services is permitted to:

authorize persons engaged in research on mental health, including research on the use and effect of alcohol and psychoactive drugs, to protect the privacy of individuals who are subjects of such research by withholding from all persons not connected with the conduct of such research the names or other identifying characteristics of such individuals. Persons so authorized to protect the privacy of such individuals may not be compelled in any federal, state, or local civil, criminal, administrative, legislative, or other proceeding to identify such individuals.

The act can be of considerable importance to mental health researchers in the sense that the identity of respondents can be protected legally. Moreover, the reference to "other identifying characteristics" assures that the researcher can prevent deductive disclosure. However, if a government agency already knows the identity of a respondent, the researcher can be compelled to disclose the research record on that respondent.

The privilege must be conferred formally by the secretary. Consequently, researchers who investigate politically controversial topics, such as the effect of marijuana on sexual behavior, are at risk of not obtaining the grant of immunity or of having it rescinded. There are no provisions for disclosure of records for secondary analysis in the law.

Omnibus Crime Control and Safe Streets Act

Enacted in 1973, the statute specifies that information contained in research records, or copies of them, must not be disclosed by the researcher or other record keeper to anyone for any purpose other than the one for which it was collected. Unlike the Public Health Services Act, this act provides automatic immunity to all research information on individuals, not just identifiers. Because statistical information is also referred to explicitly in the act, deductive disclosure can be prevented. The act provides immunity from legal process in judicial and administrative proceedings, but it does not prevent a legislative committee's appropriation of identified records as evidence in its hearings. A "Privacy Certificate," required of all researchers, describes the research project and the limitations and agreements on disclosure of the information. Implementing regulations define conditions under which identifiable records can be released to other researchers for secondary analysis without the respondent's consent. The statutory provisions are duplicated in the Juvenile Justice Act of 1977.

Controlled Substances Act

The act authorizes the attorney general to permit persons engaged in research on controlled substances to withhold identification of research participants from legislative, administrative, criminal or other proceedings.

It is an important statute for statisticians, industrial researchers, physiologists, and others who are engaged in drug abuse research. Like that of the Public Health Services Act, the grant of immunity depends on the discretion of a federal executive. Consequently, it is subject to the same problem: pressure to refuse or rescind a grant on political rather than scientific grounds. Like the

Public Health Services Act, the Controlled Substances Act does not protect research data on identifiable individuals if identification has already been made. Nor are there any provisions for disclosure of identifiable records for research purposes.

Drug Abuse Office and Treatment Act

The act protects "records of patients maintained in connection with drug abuse prevention programs assisted by the federal government." The implementing regulations maintain that coverage includes records maintained for research purposes.

Unlike the Controlled Substances Act, this law covers material *other* than identification of the subject, and it is automatic rather than dependent on executive authorization. But the immunity is limited severely; a court may in fact subpoena the identification and identified records. In *People* v. *Newman,* the court affirmed the drug researcher's right to refuse to disclose respondent identification under the immunity grant of the Controlled Substances Act, despite the exemption of the Drug Abuse Office and Treatment Act. The law provides for release of identifiable records without respondent consent for research purposes.

Other Statutes

The provisions of the Alcohol Abuse Act are essentially the same as those for the Drug Abuse Office and Treatment Act, but apply to treatment of alcoholics and alcoholism research. The Health Services Research, Health Statistics, and Medical Libraries Act of 1974, provides immunity from subpoena to NCHS researchers collecting data in health surveys and evaluations. Disclosure of identification of participants in venereal disease studies is prohibited under special legislation. Amendments to social security legislation provide protection to government researchers involved in social security studies.

Advantages and Disadvantages

The extant legislation then is fragmented: Each statute focuses on a different area, each differs in nature of protection. The Public Health Services Act is the most general. It deals with mental health, a topic which can be defined very broadly. The most complete in its protection is the Crime Control Act, which makes immunity automatic, covers both identification of a research participant and the identified information, provides immunity against use of the information in administrative and judicial proceedings. This act provides no protection against legislative investigations, however. While the Public Health Services Act and the Controlled Substances Act provide immunity against legislative, as well as administrative and judicial, inquiry, they must be

authorized on a case-by-case basis. Not all acts clearly provide for secondary
analysis or audit of the data. Those which do include the Crime Control Act,
the Drug Abuse Office and Treatment Act, and the Alcohol Abuse Act.

The statutes have some advantages over the statistical and procedural
devices described earlier. The major ones are that the statutes protect
qualitative and case study information as well as quantitative data, and they
are applicable to small as well as large samples. They also afford official
protection, and it is reasonable to speculate that this will reduce some
respondents' reluctance to cooperate in research because they demand legal
assurance or because they are confused by or distrust other methods for
assuring confidentiality. However, there is no hard evidence supporting this
hypothesis. Finally, the statutes are specific enough to discourage legal
harassment. The statistical and some procedural strategies, on the other hand,
are unlikely to be understood by the average attorney, and their complexity
may actually invite a litigation strategy based on confusion.

State Law

State governments have not been active in promoting confidentiality of
research records. But there have been a few special executive actions and some
new legislation (see note 25). Gubernatorial protection has been extended, for
instance, to respondents in roadside surveys of drivers, to assure their
cooperation in research on drinking and driving. Among the recent state laws is
a New York statute which authorizes special investigation units to study motor
vehicle accidents. It provides that a unit's staff "shall not be required to
produce their records on identifiable respondents or evidence contained in
them in any legal action or other proceeding." The main justification for the
statute is the reluctance that accident victims have in talking about an accident,
together with the fact that "specialized accident-investigation units have, in the
past, made invaluable discoveries concerning causation by alcohol and
mechanical defects of vehicles" (State of New York, S. 7626. A. 8606).

Executive Privilege

I know of no scholarly investigation on the extent to which executive
privilege has been employed by government officials to assure the confidentiality of *research* records. But examples do exist.

Albert Biderman of the Bureau of Social Science Research, for instance,
reports that in post-Korean War research on prisoners of war, the chief of staff
agreed to provide a guarantee of confidentiality to the researchers. The
assurance was that data would not be used for nonresearch purposes, including
"legal process or . . . individual personnel actions." Biderman and his colleagues invoked the assurance prior to Senate hearings on POW issues when
Senate staff demanded some research information on POWs. In subsequent
negotiation among military legal counsel and committee staff, agreement was
reached to drop the demand, partly, it appears, on the basis of the assurance.[26]

*The Future: Privacy of Research Records Act and
the Confidentiality of Statistical Records Act*

On April 2, 1979, President Carter submitted a bill, the "Privacy of Research Records Act," to Congress. Part of a broader privacy program, it is the most important proposal yet made to assure confidentiality of research data and privacy of research respondents. Briefly, the bill states that research records on identifiable respondents, collected under federal auspices, will be confidential and cannot be used in administrative, legislative, or judicial hearings, as evidence against the respondent. To accommodate the need for secondary analysis of data, the bill permits disclosure of identifiable records to the legitimate independent researcher when disclosure is essential, poses no unwarranted risk to the individual, and does not violate assurances given in the original data collection. Regulations binding the original analyst also bind the secondary analyst. Further, follow-up of respondents by an independent researcher is explicitly permitted provided that recontact is essential and the risks to the respondent are minimized and outweighed by the value of the research.

The bill contains four major exemptions to the general prohibition against disclosure of identified records. The first permits the respondent to give consent to have his or her record revealed, in a court hearing, for example. The researcher need not disclose it, however. A second exemption is that disclosure is permitted under bona fide medical emergency or to prevent a future crime of violence. The third permits access for program evaluation or audit. The final exemption is that access is permitted in a court case against the researcher, but the respondent is permitted to contest the judicial demand for the record. Violation of any of these provisions is defined as a misdemeanor and carries a fine. In addition, the respondent's right to sue for damages is explicit.

A second proposal, the Confidentiality of Federal Statistical Records Bill, deals only with statistical information, rather than with research data more generally. Briefly, "Protected Statistical Centers" are created as a device to assure the confidentiality of statistical files they maintain; such centers would include the Census Bureau and the National Center for Health Statistics. The confidentiality assurance is automatic for any files they hold, so long as they continue in their protected status. Discontinuance of power is vested in the new office of the chief statistician and may be exercised if the center fails to adhere to the standard. Individually identifiable information in a center's files must be kept confidential, is immune from legal process, and cannot be used as evidence in judicial, administrative, or legislative proceedings at any level of government. Secondary analysis is accommodated by a provision that permits the chief statistician to disclose identifiable records when disclosure is essential for research. Redisclosure is prohibited and procedures for confidentiality binding the center also bind the secondary analyst.

The Federal Statistical Records Bill contains a variety of exemptions. Unlike the Research Records Act, there is no provision for disclosure with respondent consent; nor is there an exemption for medical emergency or to prevent a future crime. There is a provision for disclosure for audit and evaluation, but the identified record must be maintained as confidential in other respects. Records may also be disclosed in court action against violators of the act, so long as the record is not made public and not used for any action against respondents.

Red Herrings, Errors, and Misconceptions:
Claims about Privacy and Social Research

Some controversies are labeled as privacy problems when in fact individual privacy is not the fundamental issue. It is relatively easy, for example, to find hypocritical espousal of privacy rights made in the interest of protecting an institution from examination by the Office of Civil Rights or by the National Institute of Occupational Safety and Health. It is similarly easy to find privacy entrained in a complex political argument, inflating the argument's importance, giving it misleading dignity, and distracting attention from more important matters. In suspected problems of privacy, the business of deciding what the problem is, rather than what it's alleged to be, is often extremely difficult. Some stereotypical mislabeling is discussed below, on the premise that if the problem is indeed mislabeled, solutions described here are bound to be immaterial. More generally, they constitute interesting targets for research and development.

Computer as Scapegoat

Fear of machinery and of numbers, and the hostility that each engenders, are not unusual and they achieve a peculiar confluence in assaults on computers. Recent Louis Harris polls for 1979, for instance, suggest that a majority (54 percent) of the public thinks computers are a threat to privacy. Rule's survey suggests that people believe these machines affect them negatively in regard to privacy.[27] Louis Harris issues solemn warnings based on the 1979 Sentry Survey on Privacy: "The results are a literal warning shot across our national bow" (p. 1).[28] Sweden's Privacy Act controls computerized records and ignores manual systems, and recent British proposals are similar. Part of the absurdity here lies in the fact that manual access record systems are considerably more common than computerized ones. Moreover, manual systems are often less accurate than computerized systems, and it is doubtful that they can provide any more confidentiality protection than computerized systems.[29] Hewitt's claim that magnetic tape "is far more susceptible to theft . . . than manual systems" is not supported by systematic evidence or theory.[30] The absence of any evidence that there has been misuse has not prevented restrictive law or general political statement. The United Kingdom's White Paper on Computers and Privacy, for instance, recognizes explicitly that there is no evidence of misuse, but does make sweeping recommendations to prevent problems.

Incompetence Mislabeled

The mundane problem of incompetence is often labeled as a "privacy issue," giving the matter more dignity and popular appeal than it would otherwise have. So, for example, when, as Hewitt suggests, credit bureaus "fail to provide supporting evidence or signatures . . . rely on bits of paper containing illegible scrawls,"[31] the problem ought to be labeled for what it is: incompetent record keeping. Researcher incompetence also has its place, judging from the *National Observer* episode: a market researcher used invisible ink on purportedly anonymous questionnaires ostensibly to permit tracking nonrespondents, when other less deceptive methods exist to achieve the same end—assuring validity of sampling. Violation of privacy is an effect of the incompetence and ignoring the latter problem by focusing on the former is misleading. It is also wasteful, judging from the large number of privacy bills submitted to legislatures over the last few years.

Ignorance as Obstacle

A minority of the public (40 percent) believe themselves to be up to date on what the federal government is doing, according to 1973 Harris polls, and a much smaller fraction (11 percent) have any direct contact with the federal government in the sense of getting help.[32] It is little wonder then that 40 percent of the public say that they are not confident that the Census Bureau doesn't share identified data with other federal agencies; 10 percent are not sure of what protection they get. That a large fraction of the public doesn't realize assurances exist, even when told directly, is clear from other surveys.

The most recent gem in this mine comes from the 1979 Harris poll for the Sentry Insurance Company which reports that about 9 percent of Americans feel their phone has been tapped.[33] Putting aside the interesting bioelectronic question of how one "feels" this, we may infer, if the public is right, that the annual tap rate is about 900,000 per year, demands 4.5 million man-hours each year, and occupies a staff as large as the FBI, CIA, and ten big city police departments. This is absurd, of course, and it implies that the public opinion on this issue is absurd, if one regards it as proxy for what actually happens in the field. It is clear that pollsters are not particularly thoughtful about the matter.

Errors in Reporting

Errors in reporting on privacy matters are so common that it does not seem fair to criticize them. They have been made by influential agencies, however. We examine two recent examples to illustrate. Consider first Hewitt's complaint, under the auspices of the British Council on Civil Liberties (BCCL), that the United Kingdom's Office of Population Census and Surveys (OPCS) released identifiers for follow-up in nursing studies. It is not clear that the office did so, since follow-up does not require release of identifiers. Hewitt's accusation is unsupported by verifiable evidence and, in any event, release would result in a court case because it is illegal. The BCCL report also claims that published small-area statistics permit deductive disclosure. But it provides neither analytical nor empirical proof and does not recognize the avoidance techniques normally used by OPCS. The claim parallels an earlier, equally erroneous one by lawyer Arthur Miller on deductive disclosure in the United States.[34]

The second example concerns chapter 10 of the Privacy Protection Study Commission's report, on educational research.[35] The tone of the text is harsh, involving claims that schools find it difficult to resist demands for records used for research purposes and to control access to records in such research, and that they are bothered by a "serious problem . . . of surveys" that are intrusive and about which people complain. The only study cited in support of the commission's views is a product of the National Committee for Citizens in Education (NCCE).[36] Because the NCCE report seems to be so important and because its treatment of educational research is peculiarly imbalanced relative to, say, the commission's remarks on statistical research, the use of NCCE research warrants examination.

On page 412 of the Privacy Commission's report, I find the first reference to NCCE research on abuses of records, page 309 of Rioux and Sandow. I find the second on page 421 of the commission's report, recognition of parental complaints about intrusive surveys and a citation of Rioux and Sandow's work in support. The first reference, to page 309 of Rioux and Sandow, is incorrect: the page's contents bear no relation to the commission's text. Suspecting that the abuses to which the commission alludes are lodged elsewhere in Rioux and Sandow, I poked carefully through their text to find the major source of substantive examples in appendix 2: thirty-two excerpts of letters from parents, all from two to five sentences in length. *Not a single excerpt deals even indirectly with researcher collection of data from students or with research use of student records.* Most deal with parents' difficulty in assessing data on their children, a few deal with amateur (teacher) diagnosis of children's emotional problems. In fact, the only mention of educational research or surveys in Rioux and Sandow's book concerns a state statute which permits disclosure of anonymous records for statistical research purposes. They cite it as an exemplar, with minor qualifications.

The point is that the Privacy Commission's statements about educational research, surveys, or researcher access to school records cannot be supported by using the NCCE supported research. The NCCE work is valuable in other respects. It is worthless in this one.

Mislabeling Research Projects as Administrative Ones

Systems have been created to routinely predict individual behavior and to take action on the basis of the prediction. For example, the likelihood of parolee recidivism might be judged by a parole board or a psychologist. Teachers may judge school children's likelihood of future problems and children may be referred to social services based on the judgments. Despite their being labeled as administrative systems, to be followed routinely, they are often *not* based on verifiably accurate predictions. To the extent that the evidence is absent, the system ought to be regarded as a research enterprise rather than as an administrative one. The distinction is crude, but has some notable implications for privacy problems engendered by the prediction and subsequent action.

In the United States for example, *Mirreken* v. *Cressman* involved termination of a delinquency prevention program because it was intrusive. Specific children were identified on the basis of tests as being at risk of social or psychological problems. They were referred to a wide variety of social service agencies as a result, and their identities were made known to a variety of professionals in the system. Had it been created as a research system rather than as an administrative one, the intrusiveness issue might have been resolved by using an alias or other approaches, the data needed to support or reject the utility of the system could certainly have been collected, and the matter of intrusiveness in administrative systems might have been resolved later. In the United Kingdom, Hewitt announced, on the basis of intuition rather than good evidence, that Britain's Registry of Children at Risk is a good idea, although it does pose privacy problems. It poses considerably more problems than this, judging by our limited ability to predict human behavior. If one adopts the idea that such projects ought to be regarded first as research enterprise, to verify the system's use in prediction without taking action on prediction, to permit the invention of prophylactics against scapegoating, and so on, then other problems including privacy, are more tractable.

Concluding Remarks

In a paper of this sort, conclusions are bound to be temporary. Statutory approaches to resolving privacy problems are good but limited in scope and not always persuasive and unambiguous. This will change as law changes. The statistical assurances are clever and workable, but they may be supplanted by generically different mathematical approaches as the art develops. The procedural techniques are simpler and sturdy in many respects, but their vulnerability cannot be ignored and their robustness is likely to be improved as new variations are invented. The approaches are indeed durable in character and they are fundamental to a larger armamentarium.

The themes that underly this disquisition are at least as important, and probably more durable, than specific solutions. The first of the themes is that in the social sciences one must invent an array of solutions to ethical problems simply because each problem will not have a unitary character. This is by no means novel, but it is often industriously ignored. Second, the whole matter requires disciplinary catholicity for both understanding and invention. This theme is reflected in the classes of techniques discussed here and more generally in other papers of the volume. It is an admirable feature of some work in the less well developed sciences, and a small prophylactic for the premature specialization that academic research often engenders. Third, there are mistakes and red herrings in this arena as others—creation of problems where none need exist. Identifying these is important. Finally, the stress here on concrete solutions rather than on clarification of problems is distinctive and generalizable. The distinction lies less in discontent with essays that clarify than in an interest in the inchoate union of engineering and ethics, both defined broadly. The emphasis on solutions is generalizable to other areas of conflict between ethics or law and social research. Indeed, similar work has been undertaken to create classes of solutions to issues raised by randomized experiments, statistical prediction of violent behavior, and burdens on the research participant. These efforts are crucial to the progress of research and can, I believe, expand what we understand about law and ethics as well.

Notes

1.   This paper extends earlier work reported in a monograph by Robert F. Boruch and Joe S. Cecil, *Assuring the Confidentiality of Social Research Data* (Philadelphia: University of Pennsylvania Press, 1979).
2.   The focus here is on privacy of individuals, not of institutions or groups of individuals. Privacy problems involving the latter two are fascinating but I cannot treat them here. See E. J. Bloustein, *Individual and Group Privacy* (New Brunswick, N.J.: Transaction Books, 1978) for relevant legal theory; D. Donnison and others, *Survey Research and Privacy* (London: Centre for Survey Samples, Social and Community Planning Research, 1978) for some policy implications; and the text of this paper for a few illustrations. The definition of "research" here stresses enterprise of the quantitative sort. For an analysis of how some of this fits into a broader framework of ethical standards in research, see P. D. Reynolds, *Ethical Dilemma and Social Science Research* (San Francisco: Jossey-Bass, 1979).
3.   See Tore Dalenius, "Computers and Individual Privacy" (Paper presented at the 41st Session of the International Statistical Institute in New Delhi, December 5-15, 1977) on the definition of privacy, confidentiality, and security. The distinction between administrative and research functions of data was introduced in R. F. Boruch, "Maintaining Confidentiality in Educational Research: A Systemic Analysis," *American Psychologist* 22 (1967): 308–11.
4.   D. W. Fiske, "The Subject Reacts to Tests," *American Psychologist* 22 (1967): 287-96.
5.   See R. Baxter, "An Inquiry into the Misuse of the Survey Technique by Sales Solicitors," *Public Opinion Quarterly* 28 (1964): 124-34, and J. A. Barnes, *Who Should Know What?* (Cambridge: Cambridge University Press, 1979).
6.   See P. Hewitt, *The Information Gatherers* (London: National Council for Civil Liberties, 1977). The United Kingdom's more recent Data Protection Committee recognizes the distinction but leaves it up to a bureaucracy to interpret it, according to J. Durbin, "Statistics and the Report of the Data Protection Committee," *Journal of the Royal Statistical Society* 142 (1978): 299-306. For more ecumenical views and interesting historical notes on the United Kingdom's problems, see M. Bulmer, ed., *Censuses, Surveys, and Privacy* (London: MacMillan, 1979).
7.   J. D. Miller, I. H. Cisin, and A. V. Harrell, *Highlights from the National Survey on Drug Abuse; 1977,* Reproduced Report (Washington, D.C.: George Washington University, 1978).

8. See chapter 4 of Boruch and Cecil, *Assuring Confidentiality of Social Research Data.*

9. L. A. Alexander and T. B. Jabine, "Access to Social Security Microdata Files for Research and Statistical Purposes," *Social Security Bulletin* 41 (1978): 3-17.

10. T. Reve, "Interorganizational Relations in Distribution Channels" (Ph.D. dissertation, Graduate School of Management, Northwestern University, 1979).

11. E. Freidson, "Comment," *American Sociologist* 3 (1978): 159.

12. W. H. Kruskal, "Letter to Margaret Martin," Department of Statistics, University of Chicago, Chicago, Ill. (June 13, 1975).

13. D. C. Gibbons, "Unidentified Research Sites and Fictitious Names," *American Sociologist* 10 (1975): 32-36.

14. See S. L. Warner, "Randomized Response," *Journal of the American Statistical Association* 60 (1965): 63-69, for the original idea. References to the work in the United States, Canada, Sweden, Holland, and Germany are given in Tore Dalenius, *Information Privacy and Statistics* (Washington, D.C.: U.S. Department of Commerce, Bureau of the Census, July 1978) and in D. H. Flaherty, E. H. Harris, and S. P. Mitchell, *Privacy and Access to Government Data for Research* (London: Mansell, 1979). Review of the work up to 1979 is given in the Boruch-Cecil volume cited in note 1.

15. L. R. Bergman, R. Hanve, and J. Rapp, "Why Do Some People Refuse to Participate in Interview Surveys?," *Sartryck vr Statistisk Tidskrift* 5 (1978): 342–56.

16. See Jong-Ik Kim and John Flueck, "Modifications of Randomized Response Technique for Sampling without Replacement," *Proceedings of the American Statistical Association: Survey Research Methods, 1978* (Washington, D.C.: American Statistical Association, 1978), pp. 346-50; and Jong-Ik Kim and John Flueck, "Additive Randomized Response Model," *Proceedings of the American Statistical Association: Survey Research Methods, 1978* (Washington, D.C.: American Statistical Association, 1978), pp. 351-55. The gaps in what we know about respondents' reactions to randomized response methods are discussed in A. D. Biderman, "Sources of Data on Victimology" (Paper presented at the Victimology Research Meetings, Mitre Corporation, McLean, Va., March 10-11, 1980), in S. S. Aitken and L. Bonneville, "A General Taxpayer Opinion Survey" (Washington, D.C.: Office of Planning and Research, Internal Revenue Service, 1980), and in D. S. Lipton, A. N. Weissman, and R. A. Steer, *Types of Refusals with the Randomized Response Technique: A Research Note.* (Radnor, Pa.: Chilton Research Services, 1981).

17. See M. S. Goodstadt, G. Cook, and V. Gruson, "The Validity of Reported Drug Use: The Randomized Response Technique," *International Journal of Addictions* 13 (1978): 359-67. The only flaw in the paper is a reference to indecently small samples used by Berman and Boruch in their research on the topic; samples were much larger than the Goodstadt group advertises. Other researchers have attempted to validate the technique by comparing estimates of, say, arrest rates based on randomized response to rates based on police records. See, for instance, P. E. Tracy and J. A. Fox, "A Field Validation of the Quantitative Randomized Response Approach," *Proceedings of the American Statistical Association: Survey Research Methods, 1980* (Washington, D.C.: American Statistical Association, 1980), and R. R. Rosenblatt and E. L. Kelly, "A Comparison of the Sensitivity of the Unrelated Question Randomized Response Model with Other Data Accumulation Techniques Using Examination Cheating as a Model," *Proceedings of the American Statistical Association: Survey Research Methods* (Washington, D.C.: American Statistical Association, 1978), pp. 356-61.

18. See Boruch and Cecil, *Assuring Confidentiality of Social Research Data,* pp. 136-40.

19. G. H. Orcutt, H. W. Watts, and J. B. Edwards, "Data Aggregation and Information Loss," *American Economic Review* 58 (1968): 773-87.

20. Laws and regulations governing researcher access to government data in North America and Europe are outlined in D. H. Flaherty, *Privacy and Government Data Banks: An International Perspective* (London: Mansell, 1980), and in E. Mochman and P. J. Muller, eds., *Data Protection and Social Science Research* (New York and Frankfurt: Campus Verlag, 1979). The purposes and products of analyzing data from archives are discussed in R. F. Boruch, P. M. Wortman, and D. S. Cordray, *eds., Reanalyzing Program Evaluations* (San Francisco: Jossey-Bass, 1981).

21. D. T. Campbell, et al., "Confidentiality Preserving Modes of Access to Files and to Interfile Exchange for Useful Statistical Analysis," *Evaluation Studies Review Annual* 2 (1977): 239-69.

22. See, respectively, D. E. Denning, "Secure Statistical Data Bases with Random Sample Queries," Reproduced Report (Lafayette, Ind.: Purdue University, 1979) and Tore Dalenius and S. P. Reiss, "Data Swapping: A Technique for Disclosure Control," Confidentiality in Surveys Report no. 31 (Stockholm, Sweden: Department of Statistics, Stockholm University, May 30, 1978).

23. See L. H. Cox, "Automated Statistical Disclosure Control," *Proceedings of the American Statistical Association: Survey Research Methods, 1978* (Washington, D.C.: American Statistical Association, 1978), pp. 172-82, and Boruch and Cecil, *Assuring Confidentiality of Social Research Data.*

24. See U.S., General Accounting Office, *Exposure Draft: A Framework for Balancing Privacy and Accountability Needs in Evaluation Research* (Washington, D.C.: GAO, 1979) and the critique of the guidelines by E. Chelimsky, Letter to Keith Marvin, GAO (McLean, Va.: Mitre Corporation, December 11, 1978).

25. The Privacy and Security Staff of the U.S. Department of Justice, directed by Carol Kaplan, is very productive. Over ten monographs dealing with privacy in criminal justice research have been issued, e.g. Privacy and Security Staff, National Criminal Justice Information and Statistics Service, *Confidentiality of Research and Statistical Data* (Washington, D.C.: Government Printing Office, 1978). The National Commission on Confidentiality of Health Records focuses its attention on confidentiality records generally. See, for instance, M. Perron, *Decisions* (Washington, D.C.: NCCHR, 1979), for court action, and T. M. Levin, *Health Records Confidentiality Law in the States* (Washington, D.C.: NCCHR, 1979), for a list of state statutes, some of which deal with research. In education, see R. Werksman and L. Schwartz, *Privacy, Protection of Human Subjects, Freedom of Information, and Forms Clearance: Update of Laws, DHEW Regulations and Publications: Report* (Washington, D.C.: National Institute of Education, 1979).

26. A. D. Biderman, "Letter to Robert F. Boruch," Bureau of Social Science Research, Washington, D.C., April 23, 1980. For a general legal review and analysis of executive privilege, see D. B. Frohnmayer, *An Essay on Executive Privilege* (Chicago: American Bar Foundation, 1974).

27. *Mosaic* (July-August, 1978), p. 8.

28. See Louis Harris and Associates, *The Dimensions of Privacy* (Stevens Point, Wis.: Sentry Insurance, 1979), and L. Harris "Remarks at the Sentry Press Conference on 'Dimensions of Privacy,'" New York, May 3-5, 1970.

29. A. F. Westin et al., *Data Banks in a Free Society* (New York: Quadrangle, 1972).

30. See note 6 above.

31. Ibid.

32. A. C. Michalos, "A Brief to the Commission on Freedom of Information and Individual Privacy," Report (Guelph, Ont.: University of Guelph, September 1977).

33. See note 8 above.

34. See U.S., Department of Commerce, "Report on Statistical Disclosure and Disclosure Avoidance Techniques," Statistical Working Paper no. 2, (Washington, D.C.: U.S. Department of Commerce, 1978), and T. B. Jabine, "Discussion," *Proceedings of the American Statistical Association: Survey Research Methods* (Washington, D.C.: American Statistical Association, 1978).

35. Privacy Protection Study Commission, *Personal Privacy in an Information Society* (Washington, D.C.: Government Printing Office, 1977).

36. J. W. Rioux and S. A. Sandow, eds., *Children, Parents, and School Records* (Columbia, Md.: National Committee for Citizens in Education, 1974).

15

On Privacy and Confidentiality in Social Science Research

ARTHUR L. CAPLAN

Why Worry about Privacy?

Worries about privacy play a key role in arguments for the regulation of inquiry in the social sciences. Many social scientists have argued that the amount of physical or mental suffering caused by social science research is so small as to make the need for regulation, both internal and external, nonexistent.[1] Physical harm, when it occurs in social scientific inquiry, is almost always a matter of malpractice, misconduct, or error. Psychological harm is difficult to assess and often transient in duration. Violations of privacy, confidentiality, or dignity, by contrast, are often felt to be at the heart of moral concern about the activities of social scientists.

Social scientists often *do* seem to infringe upon persons' privacy. Covert observation, random surveys, and the analysis of information pertaining to identifiable individuals or groups are all examples of common activities in social science where privacy can be jeopardized. This is particularly apparent when behaviors such as drug use, sexual activity, or criminal activity are the topics of social scientific inquiry. Social scientists are interested in studying a wide variety of human activities which many consider private and personal. It is a concern over the intrusive and invasive nature of the activities and methods of social science research that fuels much of the interest in, and discussion of, ethical issues about such research.

If this is so, then it becomes important in discussions of ethical issues in social science research to know exactly what is meant by the concept of privacy, and to discuss the status of this concept relative to other moral goods and evils present in everyday life. If worries about privacy and its violations are the source of most moral musings about research in the social sciences, the analysis of the meaning and weight of this concept becomes pivotal.

At first glance, this claim might appear to be only an instance of the typical philosopher's refrain—"Before we can decide what to do about *x*, in this case the regulation and promotion of social scientific inquiry, we must come to a clear understanding of concepts such as *y*, in this case privacy. Such concepts are loosely bandied about in all the extant ethical and legal discussions of this topic." This refrain is solemnly intoned by philosophers at the outset of nearly every discussion of an ethical matter, the solemnity displayed for nonphilosophers being balanced by a certain amount of internal glee. The philosopher's glee issues from the anticipation of yet another exciting ethical safari during which numerous thorny cases will be slashed clear, many dangerous conceptual pitfalls avoided, and terrifying counterexamples wrestled into logically consistent submission. The nonphilosopher, or at least the nonphilosopher with some prior travel experience in the company of philosophers, is likely to pale at the prospect of another gloomy and endless journey through the conceptual moral bush. These trips consume time and often result in undersized or worthless conceptual trophies.

I mention this safari metaphor because I fear that many persons may have come away from Professor Terry Pinkard's contribution to this volume in particular with a keen sense of disappointment. For the meager quarry flushed out of his conceptual analysis seems to be that privacy has no clear meaning. It is a concept, Professor Pinkard suggests, that is "essentially contested." Its meaning is to be understood in terms of what is deemed appropriate behavior in various social roles, and the contestable nature of the concept "appropriate" breeds a relativistic morass from which no clear-cut definition of privacy can ever be culled.

It must be noted that Professor Pinkard is not alone in his view of the slapdash nature of the concept of privacy. As he himself points out, the concept of privacy in the law is a jerry-built affair that includes activities having to do with disclosure, misrepresentation, intrusion, and restrictions of personal liberty. Frederick Davis provides a useful summary of this view of privacy when he states: "Invasion of privacy is, in reality, a complex of more fundamental wrongs. . . . The individual's interest in privacy itself, however real, is derivative and a state better vouchsafed by protecting more immediate rights."[2]

Philosophers have also found themselves puzzled by the notion of a *right* to privacy. Judith Thomson, in a recent article on privacy, notes that

> Nobody seems to have any very clear idea what the right to privacy is. . . . The right to privacy is "derivative" in this sense: it is possible to explain in the case of each right in the cluster how we have it without ever once mentioning the right to privacy. Indeed, the wrongness of every violation of the right to privacy can be explained without ever once mentioning it.[3]

For Thomson, privacy is a concept which is only useful as a placeholder to capture a complex set of concepts concerning ownership, liberty, freedom, and harm.

In a recent review of the literature on privacy, H. J. McCloskey comes to a similar conclusion about the derivative nature of privacy. He writes:

> Any right to privacy will be a derivative one from other rights and other goods. This means that it will be a conditional right, and not always a right. Whether or not it will

be a derivative right . . . will depend on practical considerations as to whether respect for privacy is necessary for the enjoyment of these [other] rights.[4]

McCloskey realizes that if privacy is a placeholder concept or a derivative right useful only as a means for achieving justice, freedom, or autonomy, then privacy becomes a topic of derivative or secondary moral concern. He notes:

> Each restriction of privacy for the sake of liberty must be weighed against the loss of liberty involved in the legal protection of privacy and in the light of the liberty that is protected. A blanket protection of privacy is not justified by this argument from liberty. Much liberty, more importantly, the liberty to inquire and to gain knowledge, more particularly about man and men, the liberty to engage in psychological, historical, biographical inquiries, and to publish and share with other scientists, historians, thinkers, the world, what one has discovered is a basic liberty, one that is the very core of the structure of our liberal society. So to protect privacy that this liberty, and similar kinds of liberties, are curtailed or lost, is to threaten the very life of our society as a liberal society.[5]

McCloskey, Thomson, Davis, and others[6] who think of privacy as a derivative or instrumental right raise a central problem for those concerned to defend the right of privacy as a legitimate area of central concern in assessing social inquiry. If privacy is a derivative moral concept, either reducible to more basic moral notions or a convenient placeholder for a diverse range of relatively minor worries and concerns, much of the starch goes out of the view that respect for privacy ought to be a dominant concern in conducting social inquiry. On these suppositions, concerns about liberty, autonomy, justice, and benefits will (a) be most appropriate to discussions of the ethics of social research and (b) will always trump worries about privacy. As R. Jay Wallace, Jr., argues in his essay, privacy will often wind up taking a back seat to social benefits when inquirer and subject meet.

Since Pinkard believes not only that the concept of privacy is derivative, but that it is also essentially contestable, his arguments deserve careful scrutiny. If he is right and privacy is ultimately in the eye of the beholder, there will be little point in going to the lengths described by Wallace, Robert F. Boruch, and Pinkard himself to protect it.

Is Privacy an Essentially Contested Concept?

Elsewhere in this volume Pinkard argues for two significant attributes of the concept of privacy—that it is "essentially contestable," and that it is derivative from the principle of respect for persons. He appeals to these features to adduce a definition of an invasion to privacy, and uses this definition in turn to formulate a right to privacy which there can be no "utilitarian or knowledge-based justification for overriding."[7] I think his arguments are flawed at a number of points. Since, however, Pinkard and I both agree that privacy is worth taking seriously as a matter of moral concern in doing and evaluating social research, these flaws must be exposed and repaired.

Pinkard notes that a number of senses of privacy float around in the legal, philosophical, and scientific literature. These senses, plus the facts that privacy is appraisive in character, internally complex, admits of different worths, and is relative to changing circumstances, lead him straight to the essential contestability of the concept. One obvious problem with these points is the ease with which they can be applied to any and every concept in ethics, aesthetics, and large chunks of the sciences. Consider the notion of "width." It is appraisive, complex, admits of different descriptions, and varies with changing circumstances. Does this make "width" an essentially contestable concept? If so, then every normative term will be essentially contestable. This may be so, but it will not help much in the analysis of privacy and its importance to know that the essentially contestable concept of privacy must be balanced against the essentially contestable concepts of justice, rights, dignity, autonomy, freedom, liberty, etc. We already know that much.

Pinkard has been deceived by the multiplicity of meanings available for privacy and by its diverse cultural and social manifestations into thinking that privacy is essentially a relativistic morass. This is a conclusion unwarranted by either definition or cultural pluralism. It is surely erroneous to conclude that since different people have different standards of privacy, the concept has no core meaning. This is simply ethical relativism in miniature.

Pinkard is undaunted by his own assessment, for he takes the messy notion of privacy developed in the first part of his essay and refines it substantially in order to demonstrate that a right to privacy exists. He writes:

> It is surely a truism that control over one's life entails control (to some degree) over what is known by others about oneself and control over some set of crucial (private) areas of one's life. From the general moral principle of respect for persons an abstract right to privacy thus follows.[8]

There are some puzzling features in this passage. First, all the alleged vagaries of meaning about privacy have evaporated. Control over what is known about one's life becomes Pinkard's "unattainable" definition. This mysterious attainment of the impossible—a definition of privacy—can best be explained in two ways. Pinkard tacitly realizes that there is another option besides essential contestability when faced with a multiplicity of definitions and assessments of a concept: trim the excess. Some things lumped together in legal definitions of privacy—say, freedom of choice regarding abortions—merit culling, and Pinkard's definition reflects this need.

Moreover, the fact that people disagree over what counts as privacy or how much privacy is enough does not show that they do not agree about what privacy is. It may be that they disagree about the scope or applicability of the definition. Contestability, after all, can be a product both of definitions *and* of the criteria for satisfying them.

Somewhat more puzzling than the appearance of a definition for a notion that is essentially contestable is the argument in this same passage that privacy is derivable from the principle of respect for persons. On Pinkard's view, privacy is a subset of personal autonomy; the principle of respect for persons demands that we respect autonomy and, thus, privacy. The problems with this argument for a right to privacy are numerous. Pinkard gives no defense of the principle of respect for persons. Without such a defense, it is unclear whether this principle is one that any rational agent must follow, and what type of rights would be contingent on such a principle. Nor is it clear that respect for a person's autonomy demands a respect for personal privacy. One might watch or study various forms of behavior without affecting autonomy. Simply knowing or learning something about persons does not necessarily impair their capability for "forming conceptions of their own good and how they should lead their lives" or their ability to "act according to those conceptions."[9] Knowing things about others does not in itself affect their ability to act freely or autonomously. A social scientist who knows something about my personal habits in my bedroom or bathroom can only threaten my autonomy by acting on such knowledge in some way. Knowing is not sufficient.

Pinkard has not given us sufficient reasons for his view that there are no utilitarian or knowledge-based justifications for overriding privacy. It is not clear that privacy is a part of autonomy, for it is not clear that free and informed action licenses control over the access of information concerning such action. Nor is it clear that a right to autonomy could not be overridden by a right to liberty or certain goods, such as knowledge or health. Moreover, it is not at all clear that we cannot know precisely what we are talking about when we invoke the concept of privacy.

What Is Privacy and How Important Is It?

In writing about the characteristics of total institutions, Erving Goffman remarks upon the phenomenon he calls "mortification of self." In many prisons, hospitals, religious orders, and schools, there is an interest in changing or remaking the person who enters. One of the central ways in which this is done is to invade or destroy the privacy of the person. Goffman writes:

> Beginning with admission, a kind of contaminative exposure occurs. On the outside, the individual can hold objects of self-feeling—such as his body, his immediate actions, his thoughts, and some of his possessions—clear of contact with alien and contaminating things. But in total institutions these territories of the self are violated; the boundary that the individual places between his being and the environment is invaded and the embodiments of self profaned.[10]

Goffman's perceptive remarks indicate that privacy plays a key role in self-identity and personhood.[11] The ability to control access to thoughts or actions is closely tied to our notions of personhood, personal identity and selfhood.

Those who run political prisons or concentration camps realize that the key to destroying personal identity and selfhood is to remove any sense or possibility of privacy. Political prisoners often report that during imprisonment they found it necessary to create a sense of mental isolation or seclusion in such environments in order to maintain their sanity and identity as persons.

Anthropologists have noted that all cultures, even the most open and highly exposed, make some provision for the privacy of their members. The Mehinacu Indians of Brazil, who live in an almost totally nonprivate society—lacking doors, barriers, and many natural obstructions such as hills—still have some provisions for seclusion. Even in this community where individual behavior quickly can become a matter of public knowledge (and comment), individuals "have a number of ways of establishing a measure of privacy for themselves even though they are often hard-pressed to do so."[12] These include various taboos, social conventions, ceremonies, affinal avoidances, and the practice of civil inattention whereby certain public events are consciously and studiously ignored.

The universality of at least some cultural practices for attaining privacy[13] is paralleled in other areas of social life in both man and animals. Territoriality and conventions as to social distance and social spacing are well known among various animal species and human cultures. The deleterious effects of crowding, of constant violations of cultural norms as to territory and spacing, and the negative effects of prolonged residential density on health and behavior are amply documented in the literature of biology and psychology.[14]

The importance of space seclusion and territory in animal and human behavior, and the deleterious effects of many practices within total institutions on personal identity, reveal what is at the core of the concept of privacy. Privacy refers to the human need for voluntary access to an exclusive space or environment. Human beings, if they are to be well-functioning persons, require noninvaded personal control over some part of their environment if that environment is publicly accessible to others.

Privacy is a basic human need. Without privacy, it is not possible to develop or maintain a sense of self or personhood. In deriving privacy from autonomy, Pinkard has the cart before the proverbial horse. Autonomy and self-determination are concepts that can only be predicated of persons. But to be a person and to remain a person, human beings require a modicum of privacy. Although questions as to exactly how much space, or what degree of spatial exclusivity, remain unsettled, the findings of social scientists and biologists clearly show that some measure of privacy is requisite for personhood. Without privacy, self-governance or autonomy becomes impossible, because there are no selves or persons to govern or be governed.

The claim that privacy is a basic human need on a par with needs for food, shelter, liberty, etc., is borne out by the deleterious consequences which result from the denial of privacy. If privacy is a basic human need, then negative consequences should accompany its absence. This is precisely what the literature in psychology and medicine reveals. In the absence of privacy, cognitive functioning is impaired, physical and mental disorders occur, the individual's sense of well-being is harmed, and the sense of personhood and of self is injured.[15]

Ironically, science provides the best available answer to the question of how important privacy is relative to other human goods. If the core notion of privacy concerns the control of personal space, then privacy is as basic and as fundamental a need as any other basic human need. Indeed, respecting the rights persons have to privacy is as basic a requirement as there can be in ethics; in the absence of privacy, there are no persons to serve as either the subjects or agents of moral action and moral description.

The Buying Power of Privacy in the Moral Marketplace

Privacy is not a derivative or secondary right. It stands as a basic human need and as such is on a par with rights rooted in other basic human needs. If this analysis is correct, it means that we must take the right to privacy seriously when it collides with the rights of other humans or with social practices. While Professor Pinkard and I disagree about why it is so, we both agree that there must be good reasons given for overriding so fundamental a right as the right to privacy.

Wallace agrees that the right to privacy is a serious and basic right. But he maintains that utilitarian considerations of the social or common good may sometimes justify violations of an individual's right to privacy. The main problem with this view is a pragmatic one—the calculation of utility may not often produce the kind of disciplinary privacy waiver Wallace seeks. Wallace is particularly concerned to provide a justification for the violation of privacy rights by epidemiologists. He notes that the driving forces behind social inquiry in epidemiological research are the prevention and control of disease— both widely accepted social goods. If these goals are to be obtained, Wallace maintains, certain conditions have to be met in epidemiological research. These conditions can be reconstructed from his discussion as follows:

1. Individually identifiable medical and vital information must be available to researchers.

2. The rerelease of identifiable health information should be permitted.

3. Most medical records should be retained.

4. Researchers should be granted immunity from the subpoena power of the state.

What is the likely response to the suggestion that people must give up some freedom and privacy for the general good of the public? Note that this request issues from the public health community and not the police or duly elected legislators. It is easy to imagine one sort of response coming from certain libertarian circles—peals of laughter, followed by "not one iota of freedom, not one infringement or invasion of privacy." On this view, no one can or should be compelled to help, aid, or abet the good of another, much less the *general public*—whoever that unwashed mass might be—at a cost of individual rights.

This claim obviously arises in response to Wallace's overtly utilitarian argument that more benefits will accrue to the public if a policy of leniency is adopted toward privacy concerns vis-à-vis the health benefits of vigorous epidemiological research. A large group of persons is unlikely to be moved by this logic. Their freedom and privacy are not barterable. No one, for any reason, can infringe on basic rights and feel morally justified about the infringement. For this crowd, a utilitarian argument for infringing on privacy is entirely wrongheaded. The concern with privacy, as I have tried to suggest, is rooted in basic human needs. Defenders of individual rights are not likely to be assuaged by appeals to greater public goods. In fact, it is just this impassioned defense of privacy that is behind some of the current pleas of social scientists against any form of regulation.[16] Why not argue that scientists qua scientists have basic rights to freedom and privacy, too, and let the libertarians hash out how the various and inevitable rights conflicts will be resolved? One does not have to resort to utilitarianism to justify one person's invasion of another's privacy.

Another objection to public-spirited arguments for allowing some transgression of privacy in the name of public health is based on the claim that epidemiology can provide the promised public goods even if all of Wallace's conditions for research are not fulfilled. One might argue, following Robert Boruch, that Wallace overstates the case for the need for identifiable health information. Clever statistical maneuvering may suffice to protect privacy while allowing the promotion of public health. Similarly, one might say that making medical records available to researchers is necessary, but that a ten-year shield law before release might permit roughly the same degree of prophylaxis and cure at a lower cost to privacy.

Wallace's plan for utilitarian exemptions for epidemiology can even be challenged on his own utilitarian grounds by questioning the accuracy of his moral calculations. He argues that disease prevention and health are worth the cost of some confidentiality and privacy. But his calculations are not complete. A few well-placed subpoenas may provide social utility far in excess of the cost of the privacy of a few individuals, the autonomy of a few epidemiologists, or a few days in jail for the overprotective public health officer. Or perhaps there are other, more efficient paths to health than the long route of epidemiological detective work. Imposing strict pollution controls and modifying personal behavior in light of present knowledge may go further toward prevention and cure at less cost to privacy than further epidemiological research. Once one's foot is firmly planted on the utilitarian path, it may be hard to avoid all the directions in which this road leads.

Finally, one could critique the ordering of goods found in the utilitarian calculus. Health may be nice, but a maximization of liberty, or sexual pleasure, or the thrills of risk and danger may be just as desirable, if not more so. This line of criticism is compelling when one realizes that determinations of public goods will, in Wallace's view, be made by small groups of health professionals in IRBs. Wallace's utilitarianism and concern for the public weal thus may not take him where he wants to go. Even on utilitarian grounds, it is far from clear that the cost-benefit calculation will come out the way he thinks it will. The IRBs upon which Wallace depends, may require drastically different research practices from those anticipated by the author. I am willing to walk down the utilitarian primrose path quite a way in thinking about reasons for overriding privacy. But danger lurks down this road—there are libertarian muggers all about, and the road may lead elsewhere if epidemiology cannot really deliver on its promise of concrete improvements in public health.

Protecting Privacy Can Be Good for Scientific Health

I have few criticisms to offer about Boruch's contribution to this volume. While I make no claims to competency in assessing the adequacy of the various statistical stratagems and techniques Boruch describes, I applaud his attempts to protect privacy in the course of social research. His goal of max-imization of research opportunity and minimization of privacy risks is laudable. Sometimes humanists rebel at the suggestion that technical solutions might be available for solving ethical worries. However, this intolerance is silly. If Boruch and his colleagues can devise clever modes of protecting privacy and confidentiality while retaining an acceptable basis for scientific inquiry, then hurrah for them!

One of the delicious ironies of Boruch's presentation is that it illustrates how moral concerns have fueled imaginative advances in statistical research methodology. If moral worries were at least responsible for the evolution of some of the techniques Boruch reports, this would give the lie to the old chestnut that moralists are only concerned with restraining or prohibiting free scientific inquiry. Boruch provides an example of the way moral worries about science can lead to better, or at least richer, science. Perhaps by putting ethics courses into the graduate curriculum of schools of social science, we might further advance scientific methodology and technique! Unlike many of his colleagues in the social sciences, Boruch has responded to moral concern with cleverness and respect rather than whining and special pleading.

This being so, let us consider some criticisms, quibbles, and whinings of my own. One might reasonably ask, "How widely applicable are the techniques and methods Boruch discusses?" I pose this question with a number of senses of applicablity in mind. First, what is the realistic scope of techniques involving the aggregation of data or the avoidance of identifiers through linkage for all areas of social inquiry? What are participant observers to do about their privacy and confidentiality problems? Second, how widely known are these techniques? Has the profession devoted sufficient time in training and continuing education to make the utilization of these methods a reality? Third, how feasible are these methods? Professor Boruch is at a large university where he is the director of a program explicitly devoted to methodology and evaluation research. The facilities and staff available at his institution may simply not be available to other persons at other places. What is the poor survey researcher at Green Acres State to do, given his or her limited resources?

Next, consider the possible moral problems posed by the availability of nonidentifiable statistical information that can be used or linked with other bits of data. Social research on identifiable social groups sometimes poses examples of what Herbert C. Kelman calls risks of social harms.[17] When people sign on for an experiment or agree to be in a survey, they have consented to these procedures and to nothing else. But when eager researchers begin to search for anonymous data with which to do other studies, different sorts of problems may appear. Minority groups, for example, may see their social or economic status as contingent upon various scientific findings in the social sciences. People who agree to participate in one sort of study (say reading ability) may be shocked to see anonymous data about them used in other studies (say busing) whose results may pose serious harms to them. Personal privacy is no guarantee of group privacy. The protection of an individual's privacy may not be sufficient for preventing harm to the individual if the individual is a member of an easily identifiable social group.

This sort of moral problem can elicit some odd complaints from scientists. Some charge that worries about the social implications of publicly available social knowledge are reflective of ideological biases or blind political commitments. But the issue involved is one of control over information. It seems morally suspicious not to inform potential research subjects that data they provide may be pooled, aggregated, linked, or reused (in anonymous form) by others. If this seems to be an excessive restriction on social science— medical researchers and natural scientists rarely worry about the social impact of their work—the excess nonetheless seems justified. This is an area where social science is different in a morally relevant way from other modes of scientific inquiry. Policies are made, money distributed, and interests met on the basis of social science findings. The keen interest of government in social science research is legitimate, but also legitimates special protections for those who might become subject to government programs based upon the work of social science researchers.

This point brings me to my last comment. Boruch sometimes writes as if the empirical demonstration of a lack of concern about privacy or disclosure on the part of subjects is evidence of, or constitutes a rationale for, a diminished concern in social science about confidentiality and privacy. Politically speaking, he is probably right. Ethically speaking, he is probably wrong. Surveys in certain U.S. communities in the 1920s would have revealed a significant number of persons (perhaps a majority) who thought that blacks should sit at the rear of public buses. But the common man's opinion is far from binding on moral inquiry. It is of interest, but hardly definitive, whether research shows that most people do not consciously care about privacy. This, in itself, would not constitute proof that we ought to loosen regulatory policies governing privacy. Majority opinion does not, as a matter of course, override minority concerns in all moral matters. Protecting the rights of the uninformed, the uninterested, or the incompetent may be paternalistic, but it is still morally important. As I have tried to argue, social science itself reveals a fact which we ignore at our peril: privacy is a basic human need and, thus, a basic human right.

Notes

1. See E. L. Pattullo's contribution to this volume; also Ithiel de Sola Pool, "The New Censorship of Social Research," *Public Interest* 57 (1980): 57-66.
2. Frederick Davis, "What Do We Mean by 'Right' to Privacy?" *South Dakota Law Review* (1959): 20.
3. Judith J. Thomson, "The Right to Privacy," *Philosophy and Public Affairs* 4 (1975): 331-32.
4. H. J. McCloskey, "Privacy and the Right to Privacy," *Philosophy* 55 (1980): 37.
5. Ibid., p. 35.
6. S. I. Benn, "Privacy, Freedom and Respect for Persons," *Nomos* 13 (1971): 1–26.
7. Terry Pinkard, "Invasions of Privacy in Social Science Research," this volume, p. 272.
8. Ibid., p. 264.
9. Ibid.
10. Erving Goffman, "The Mortification of Self," in R. Flacks, ed., *Conformity, Resistance and Self-Determination* (Boston: Little, Brown & Co., 1973), p. 178.
11. See also J. H. Reiman, "Privacy, Intimacy and Personhood," *Philosophy and Public Affairs* 6 (1976): 26-44.
12. J.M. Roberts and T. Gregor, "Privacy: A Cultural View," *Nomos 13* (1971): 209.
13. Margaret Mead, "Neighborhoods and Human Needs," *Ekistics* 123 (1966): 124-26; K. Greenawalt, "Privacy," *Encyclopedia of Bioethics*, ed. W. Reich (New York: Free Press, 1978), vol. 3, pp. 1356-64.
14. J. Rodin, "Density, Perceived Choice, and Responses to Controllable and Uncontrollable Outcomes," *Journal of Experimental Social Psychology* 12 (1976): 564-78; D. Stokols, "Environmental Psychology," *Annual Review of Psychology* 29 (1978): 253–95; D.P. Barash, *Sociobiology and Behavior* (New York: Elsevier, 1977).
15. J. B. Calhoun, "Population Density and Social Pathology," *Scientific American* 206 (1962): 139-48; P. B. Paulus et al., "Density Does Affect Task Performance," *Journal of Personality and Social Psychology*, 34 (1976): 248-53; S. D. Webb, "Privacy and Psychosomatic Stress: An Empirical Analysis," *Social Behavior and Personality* 8 (1978): 227-33; L. M. Dean et al., "Spatial and Perceptual Components of Crowding: Effects on Health and Satisfaction," *Environment and Behavior* 7 (1975): 225-36; J. W. Chapman, "Personality and Privacy," *Nomos* 13 (1971): 236-55; and P. M. Insel and H. C. Lindgren, *Too Close for Comfort* (Englewood Cliffs, N.J.: Prentice-Hall, 1978).
16. Lauren H. Seiler and J. M. Murtha, "Federal Regulations of Social Research Using 'Human Subjects': A Critical Assessment," *American Sociologist* 15 (1980): 146-57.
17. Herbert C. Kelman, *A Time to Speak: On Human Values and Social Research* (San Francisco: Jossey-Bass, 1968). Kelman's later and more elaborate reflections on these problems are found earlier in the present volume, chapter 2.

PART FIVE

Government Regulation

16

The Regulatory Context of Social and Behavioral Research

BRADFORD H. GRAY

The literature on the ethics of behavioral and social research[1] with human subjects is increasingly focusing on regulatory issues.[2] Of concern are the legitimacy and necessity of regulating certain types of research, the extent to which the existing regulatory approach accomplishes stated goals of protecting the rights and welfare of human subjects, the relationship between the regulatory framework and investigators' own responsibilities, and the possible effects of the regulatory structure on researchers' ability to conduct important and valid research. Much of the discussion of these issues was prompted by the work of the National Commission for the Protection of Human Subjects and by revised regulations proposed by the Department of Health, Education, and Welfare (HEW) in August 1979. The debate about research regulation in the behavioral sciences has moved from professional journals and newsletters to the pages of major newspapers and periodicals. Many assertions and predictions about the consequences of the regulations have been made in hopes of influencing the policy process during a period of flux. Deeply held values about the rights and responsibilities of scientists are clearly at stake in the regulation of research.

The basic elements of the current framework for protection of human subjects are a set of regulations having the force of law and a set of local decision-making committees known generically as institutional review boards (IRBs). The location of the review function at institutions that conduct research, rather than in governmental offices, places the reviw process relatively close to the conduct of the research—too close in the view of some critics—and keeps the government a step removed from the actual review process.

IRBs now exist at more than 550 medical schools, colleges and universities, hospitals, research institutions, institutions for the mentally ill and retarded, and other institutions where research is conducted. IRBs have become a relatively permanent feature of institutional landscapes; most boards meet regularly and have a slow turnover of membership. A significant proportion of researchers who submit proposals to IRBs have done so previously, and many applicants have also served as IRB members. The basic system is sufficiently well established and is so widely accepted that the National Commission for the Protection of Human Subjects had no extended discussions regarding the possibility of abandoning the institutional review system. However, the need for a number of changes in the system has become apparent.

In this chapter, I will review the evolution of the current regulatory framework for research involving human subjects and present some data on the impact of institutional review boards on behavioral research. I will then summarize and comment on the major issues that arise in the regulation for protection of human subjects in behavioral research, paying particular attention to how these issues have been addressed by the National Commission for the Protection of Human Subjects and by the Department of Health and Human Services (HHS).

The Development of the Present Regulatory Structure

The original review requirements were developed in a biomedical context and became known first to researchers who sought funds under the Public Health Services Act. By the mid-1970s as much as 40 percent of the research reviewed by IRBs was social and behavioral research using interviews and questionnaires, psychological or educational tests, observation, or behavioral interventions.[3]

However, the application of a single set of regulatory requirements to many different types of research conducted in various types of institutions has been a persistent source of difficulty. For example, social scientists frequently complain that the regulations appear to have been drafted to fit the so-called biomedical model. Such criticisms, however, frequently overlook the extent to which similar issues arise out of concern with ethical problems in biomedical research. Furthermore, the requirements have explicitly applied to social and behavioral research almost from the beginning. The early requirements even acknowledged some characteristics of such research that required flexibility in the interpretation of the Public Health Service (PHS) institutional review policy.

Public Health Service Policy

The current regulatory framework has evolved from policies adopted by PHS in 1966. Review committees had been used since the early 1950s for research conducted intramurally by the National Institutes of Health. By the time the 1966 PHS policy was announced, many biomedical research institutions had already voluntarily established review procedures; nonetheless, cries that echo today were then heard about freedom of inquiry and the inhibition of scientific progress.[4] On February 8, 1966, the surgeon general issued the PHS policy document that initiated the review requirement for grantee institutions.[5] The institutional review requirement was seen as operating in tandem with the review of research proposals in study sections at the National Institutes of Health (and the National Institute of Mental Health); ethical review was seen as the responsibility of the institution seeking funds, while scientific review was seen as the funding agency's responsibility.[6]

In response to questions raised by PHS policy, the surgeon general issued a "clarification" of the policy on December 12, 1966, making explicit that the requirement of institutional review "applies to all investigations that involve human subjects, including investigations in the behavioral and social sciences."[7] With regard to the latter type of research, he noted that

> there is a large range of social and behavioral research in which no personal risk to the subject is involved. In these circumstances, regardless of whether the investigation is classified as behavioral, social, medical or other, the issues of concern are the fully voluntary nature of the participation of the subject, the maintenance of confidentiality of information obtained from the subject, and the protection of the subject from misuse of the findings.

The surgeon general's statement went on to note that the social and behavioral sciences use procedures which "may in some instances not require the fully informed consent of the subject or even his knowledgeable participation." Thus, early PHS policy gave explicit attention to issues that arise with particular force in social and behavioral research. However, the original PHS policy contained no systematic analysis of the ethical issues at stake in research involving human subjects, nor was an explanation offered for the surgeon general's position that the requirement for informed consent in social and behavioral research had less force than in biomedical research.

HEW Policy

At least two revised statements of PHS policy were issued between 1966 and 1971, both of which made reference to social and behavioral research and the types of risks that may be involved therein.[8] However, the next important development came in 1971 with the publication of the well-known pamphlet "The Institutional Guide to DHEW Policy on Protection of Human Subjects."[9] The "yellow book," as it became known, contains the most detailed discussion of IRB review responsibilities that has been issued to date by HHS. The basic IRB functions specified in the yellow book were quite similar to those that appeared three years later in the regulations. However, the yellow book is particularly notable not only for its influence as HEW policy, but also for its explicit attention to social and behavioral research, to which there were frequent references.

The yellow book defined subjects to include "informants and normal volunteers," and stated that they were to be considered "at risk" if they were "exposed to the possibility of harm—physical, psychological, sociological [sic], or other—as a consequence of any activity which goes beyond the application of those established and accepted methods necessary to meet [their] needs." In attempting to make the risk formulation applicable in social and behavioral research, this somewhat confused statement refers to an issue that is of concern primarily in fields in which it is important to distinguish between activities undertaken for research purposes and activities taken to provide a service to the subject. While that distinction has been the object of much discussion in biomedical research ethics, it has little relevance to most social research.

The yellow book gave explicit attention to ethical concerns in research in which the risk of physical harm is not a concern. It did not distinguish social and behavioral research from medical research when it noted that

> there is a wide range of medical, social, and behavioral projects and activities in which no immediate physical risk to the subject is involved; e.g., those utilizing personality inventories, interviews, questionnaires, or the use of observation, photographs, taped records, or stored data. However, some of these procedures may involve varying degrees of discomfort, harassment, invasion of privacy, or may constitute a threat to the subject's dignity through the imposition of demeaning or dehumanizing conditions.

Thus, 1971 HEW policy made clear that there were issues of concern to IRBs even in research (including social and behavioral research) that posed no immediate physical risk to subjects.

There were also several paragraphs in the yellow book about privacy and confidentiality. IRBs should be sure that information that could be traced to or identified with subjects would be "safeguarded," and methods ranging from the design of questionnaires to the physical protection of data were mentioned. IRBs were to make sure that the secondary use of data was "within the scope of the original consent."

Regarding consent, the yellow book provided a list of topics for disclosure to subjects, but gave IRBs considerable latitude by stating that consent could be (*a*) oral or written, (*b*) obtained "after the fact following debriefing," or (*c*) "implicit in voluntary participation in an adequately advertised activity." However, not present in the yellow book was the language that had appeared in the earlier PHS policy statements about the acceptability of departures from "full informed consent" in the social and behavioral sciences. In contrast, there were two paragraphs about the physician's so-called "therapeutic privilege" to withhold information, even in a research context.

HEW Regulations

The next significant development was HEW's issuance on May 30, 1974, of its regulations for the protection of human subjects.[10] Between 1974 and 1981 the regulations were amended only to incorporate some specific provisions for research involving the human fetus and pregnant women and for requiring disclosures to subjects about the availability of compensation for physical harm. From the standpoint of social and behavioral research, these changes were not of much significance.

The 1974 regulations state that protection of human subjects is "primarily" the responsibility of institutions seeking funds from HEW for research involving human subjects. They further specify that HEW will not support any activity involving human subjects unless an IRB has reviewed and approved the activity. The IRB is to determine whether subjects will be placed at risk (defined as the possibility of "physical, psychological or social injury"), and, if so, whether the risks to the subjects are outweighed by the sum of the benefits to subjects and the importance of the knowledge sought; whether the rights and welfare of the subjects are adequately protected; and whether "legally effective informed consent" will be obtained by "adequate and appropriate methods."

Although this statement of the IRB's functions seems reasonably clear, the IRB composition requirements suggest that IRBs may have other functions. The regulations require that an IRB be composed of at least five persons of varying backgrounds, including individuals who are able "to ascertain the acceptability of proposals in terms of institutional commitments and regulations, applicable law, standards of professional conduct and practice, and community attitudes." I have elsewhere argued that this formulation gives IRBs license to object to research for reasons that have more to do with politics than with protecting the legitimate interests of subjects.[11] While there have been few reports of IRBs behaving in this fashion, the possibility of the political suppression of research in the name of subjects' interests is a continuing concern, particularly in the social sciences.

The regulations indicate that informed consent should ordinarily be documented in writing, although there are both implicit and explicit conditions under which this requirement might be waived. Implicitly, the requirement for documentation may not apply in research in which no subjects are at risk, since the IRB is directed to give attention to informed consent only if it determines that the research would place subjects at risk. However, "at risk" is defined so that the presence of any risk, no matter how minor or improbable, means that subjects are "at risk." Thus, an IRB that is inclined to do so can always find that subjects are at risk. The explicit provisions for waiving written consent are unclear and difficult to understand, but they appear to establish very difficult conditions for the waiver of the requirement to document consent.[12] Even a reasonable IRB acting in good faith could interpret the regulations' conditions for waiving written consent as constituting null sets, and indeed some IRBs have established a general policy of requiring written consent in all research. Given the realities of observational research and of research involving records, telephone interviews, and the like, it is not surprising that the regulations concerning informed consent, and concerning the documentation thereof, have been a particularly controversial aspect of HEW policy.

National Commission for the Protection of Human Subjects

The current period of flux in the HEW regulations has its roots in the creation (in the National Research Act of 1974) of the National Commission for the Protection of Human Subjects of Biomedical and Behavioral Research. The commission was directed to advise HEW and Congress about a number of complex topics, including issues that arise in research involving such populations as human fetuses and pregnant women, children, prisoners, and the institutionalized mentally ill and mentally retarded. As noted earlier, the commission was also directed to examine the institutional review board system. Two general points about the commission's mandate are worthy of special note.

First, rather than being directed to study means of preventing harm to research subjects, the commission was given an affirmative task: to identify the basic ethical principles that should underlie the conduct of research involving human subjects and to recommend ways to assure that research is conducted in accordance with those principles.[13] This is consistent with many current analyses of the ethics of research, which see the investigator's obligations to subjects in terms of respect for their personal integrity or autonomy, not only (or even primarily) in terms of avoidance of harm to subjects.[14] As a practical matter, this part of its mandate meant that research with relatively low levels of risk to subjects was nevertheless a matter of serious concern to the commission.

The second noteworthy point about the legislation creating the commission concerns its role regarding social research. The words "social research" do not appear in the commission's mandate ("behavioral research" is left undefined) and there is little evidence that separate concern about social research had any role in the creation of the commission.[15] Nevertheless, for at least two reasons, fulfillment of the commission's mandate inevitably had consequences for social research. First, the commission was directed to study and make recommendations regarding IRBs, and, as was noted earlier, IRBs have been responsible for reviewing social research for many years. Second, the commission was directed "to identify the basic ethical principles that should underlie the conduct of research involving human subjects." It would be difficult for social scientists to convince policy makers that "research involving human subjects" does not include much empirical work in the social sciences, although the term "subject" is not always used in such research. It would also be difficult to argue that social and biomedical research should be conducted according to different sets of basic ethical principles.[16] Thus, social research could not be ignored by the commission.

The Commission and Social and Behavioral Research

In creating the commission, Congress specified that no more than five of the eleven members of the commission could be persons who had conducted research involving human subjects. Three physicians and two psychologists filled those slots. Thus, the commission's expertise in the social sciences was very limited, although there was social science representation on the commission staff. The commission sought widespread public input through hearings and informal contact at commission meetings and tried to be responsive to concerns in fields with which its members were relatively unfamiliar—for example, survey research and anthropology. Nevertheless, the fact that no one on the commission fully understood certain fields of research and the issues that arise therein undoubtedly had consequences.

The commission did seek the perspective of social scientists when it undertook the parts of its mandate to which their view seemed relevant. While such consultation was helpful, it was complicated by the fact that researchers do not speak with one voice about these complex matters. For example, in a paper prepared at the request of the commission, the sociologist Bernard Barber, on the basis of his experiences as chairman of an IRB that reviews primarily social research, argued that IRBs could operate responsibly and effectively under existing regulations, provided that reasonable interpretations were made. On the other hand, the sociologist Albert Reiss, in another paper prepared for the commission, stressed problems of informed consent and confidentiality that were not adequately handled by existing regulations.[17] Social and behavioral scientists were quite active in making their views known to the commission, both in correspondence and hearings. A variety of real or potential problems, including many discussed in the second half of this essay, were identified through these means. Some of these problems resulted from inadequacies of the regulations, while others resulted from idiosyncratic actions by IRBs. Most of the complaints pertained to harm done to research interests while providing no benefit to the interests of subjects.[18] Virtually all of the complaints were addressed, at least to some extent, by the commission in its reports. However, the commission's response was not always the one sought by complainants.

Survey of Institutional Review Boards

In addition to conducting hearings and commissioning papers, the commission sought more systematic information on the activities of IRBs through a contract with the Survey Research Center at the University of Michigan. This study involved a sample of 61 institutions (medical schools, universities, hospitals, etc.) and interviews with more than 2,000 researchers, 800 members of IRBs, and 1,000 research subjects. The focus was on projects reviewed by IRBs between mid-1974 and mid-1975. The major findings from the study have been reported elsewhere;[19] they can be summarized briefly as follows.

First, based on comparisons with a survey conducted by Barber and his associates in 1969, it was apparent that IRBs had become more active by the mid-1970s in requiring modifications in proposed research.[20] More than 40 percent of the researchers whose proposals were approved by IRBs reported that their proposals had been modified as a result of formal or informal IRB actions. By far the most frequent substantive change pertained to informed consent, with changes reported in one-fourth of all proposals reviewed by IRBs. Modifications regarding scientific design, selection of subjects, risks and discomforts, and confidentiality were reported in a small number of projects (around 3 percent in each case).

Second, examination of the distribution of risks and benefits in research approved by IRBs revealed two important trends. First, risks and benefits tend to vary together, so that research that is relatively risky is most likely to be intended to benefit its subjects. Second, poor and minority subjects were not differentially selected into research that is particularly risky or into research that is not expected to provide benefits to subjects. Whether these results can be directly attributed to the actions of IRBs is questionable, since IRBs reject very few projects and require only infrequent changes regarding reduction of risk or selection of subjects. Yet it is important that in research approved by IRBs, risks and benefits are not distributed in the aggregate in a way that raises serious ethical concern.

Third, researchers (as well as IRB members) proved to be generally supportive of the existing system of review (table 16.1). Almost all said that the human subject review process has protected the rights and welfare of human subjects, at least to some extent; two-thirds said that the review process had improved the quality of research conducted at the institution; and almost all said that the procedure runs with reasonable efficiency. Substantial minorities, however, felt that the review process is an unwarranted intrusion on the investigator's autonomy, that the IRB gets into areas that are not appropriate to its function, that it makes judgments it is not qualified to make, and that it has impeded the progress of research. On balance, however, only about 8 percent of the researchers felt that the difficulties of the review process outweigh its benefits in protecting human subjects (data not shown).

The preceding is the basic survey evidence that the commission found to support the continuation of the IRB system, although many specific suggestions for changes were made by persons who were interviewed in the study. The study, however, raised two general areas of concern. The first pertains to IRB performance regarding informed consent; the second pertains to IRBs and behavioral research.

Although informed consent was clearly the focus of much IRB activity, virtually all modifications made by IRBs pertained to consent *forms,* rather than to the way that consent would be obtained. Previous research had shown that the manner in which consent is sought is at least as important as the consent form itself.[21] Thus, IRB concern with informed consent appears to be excessively narrow and, perhaps, legalistic. In addition, however, the study also raised questions about IRB performance regarding consent forms themselves. Consent forms approved by IRBs tended to be incomplete and difficult to read; they were generally couched in scientific and academic language, with few medical and technical terms explained. And, when the readability and completeness of original, rejected consent forms were com-

Table 16.1

ACTIONS FORMALLY REQUIRED OF THE INVESTIGATOR BY THE REVIEW BOARD,
AS PERCENTAGES OF PROJECTS BY TYPE OF INSTITUTION

			Type of Institution			
Action Required	Universities (N=514)	Medical School (N=1425)	Hospitals (N=254)	Institutions for Mentally Infirm (N=101)	Other (N=95)	All (N=2389)
More information	33%	30%	39%	28%	21%	32%
Modification in consent forms and procedures	19	25	31	14	13	24
Modification in scientific design	—[a]	2	6	8	1	3
Modification in subject selection	–	3	5	7	1	3
Modification regarding risks, discomfort	3	4	4	7	9	4
Modification regarding confidentiality	6	2	3	6	6	3
Other modifications	5	3	7	7	9	5
Informal suggestion for modifications[b]	13	15	13	19	15	15

Note: Percentages need not add to 100 percent since respondents might indicate fewer or more than one action required. Ns vary slightly within columns due to missing data. The percentages exclude missing data.
[a]Less than 0.5 percent but greater than zero.
[b]Row includes all projects modified as a result of informal discussions with IRB members, whether or not the review board formally requested modifications.

pared with those aspects of the modified, approved consent forms, no measurable change could be found. Further analysis showed poorly prepared consent forms were not more likely than good forms to have been modified by IRBs. Thus, with regard to informed consent, IRBs have not been performing up to expectations.

The second problem pertained to behavioral and social research. Inspection of table 16.2 reveals that researchers from these fields tended to be less supportive of the review system than were biomedical researchers. In addition, doubts about the IRBs' fairness were more common among behavioral researchers: asked whether their IRB treats all departments fairly, 61 percent of biomedical researchers, but only 43 percent of behavioral researchers, said so (data not shown). Twelve percent of the behavioral researchers found the difficulties of the review process to outweigh its benefits; seven percent of the biomedical researchers felt this way (data not shown).

What accounts for the less favorable attitudes among behavorial researchers? The reason was not that more behavioral researchers have proposals modified by IRBs; the percentage of their proposals approved without any modification was the same in universities and in medical schools and was only slightly lower in hospitals.[22] Few proposals are actually turned down by IRBs, and this had happened to more biomedical than behavioral researchers in the sample.[23] The most frequent modifications made by IRBs pertained to informed consent, a frequent topic of contention among researchers who have complained about past HEW regulations. Yet, biomedical projects (27 percent) were slightly more likely than behavioral projects (20 percent) to have undergone consent modifications at the hands of an IRB.

My own speculations concerning the relative dissatisfaction of behavioral researchers center on two factors. One concerns the possibility that changes made in the name of ethics are more likely to have methodological consequences in the behavioral sciences than in the biomedical sciences. There is, for example, greater concern that disclosures to subjects will result in biased research results, either through selection, suggestion, or some other process. Secondly, behavioral and biomedical researchers may differ in their general orientation toward authority structures and in their perceptions regarding the politics of research. Behavioral researchers may be more fearful than biomedical researchers that their research will be restricted because of content or subject matter. Furthermore, researchers in a medical school setting may be more accustomed to operating within a structure in which review procedures are an accepted part of the environment. Behavioral researchers seem more likely to view the review process as inconsistent with the very concept of freedom of inquiry, and they may therefore be more concerned than biomedical researchers about the possibility that ideological factors will impinge on the review of proposed research.

Table 16.2

ATTITUDES OF DIFFERENT TYPES OF INVESTIGATORS AND REVIEW COMMITTEE MEMBERS
TOWARD THE REVIEW PROCEDURE AND COMMITTEES

| | Percent Agreeing with Each Statement | | | | | |
| | Review Board Members | | | Research Investigators | | |
Attitude	Biomedical Sciences (N=370)[a]	Behavioral & Social Sciences (N=135)[a]	Other (N=220)[a]	Biomedical Sciences (N=940)[a]	Behavioral & Social Sciences (N=395)	Other (N=180)
The human subjects review procedure has protected the rights and welfare of human subjects—at least to some extent.	99%	99%	99%	99%	96%	98%
The review procedure has improved the quality of scientific research done at this institution—at least to some extent.	78	62	70	69	55	83
The review procedure runs with reasonable efficiency—at least to some extent.	99	96	99	96	94	94
The review procedure is an unwarranted intrusion on an investigator's autonomy—at least to some extent.	13	11	6	25	38	23
The review committee gets into areas which are not appropriate to its function—at least to some extent.	39	24	27	50	49	39
The review committee makes judgments that it is not qualified to make—at least to some extent.	70	71	70	43	49	25
The review procedure has impeded the progress of research done at this institution—at least to some extent.	26	30	22	43	54	36

[a]Ns are approximate, since nonresponse varied from item to item.

The IRB study data were not originally analyzed in a way that would show differences among the different disciplines categorized as "behavioral and social." While I was preparing this essay, Robert A. Cooke and I undertook the beginnings of such an analysis, looking at the responses of approximately 525 "behavioral and social" scientists from the overall sample. Respondents were classified on the basis of their self-reported fields of training. Only three subgroups contained sufficient numbers for reliable reporting: psychologists, who constituted almost 60 percent of the group; persons trained in education, who made up 12 percent of the group; and sociologists, who made up 8 percent of the group.

The most striking pattern in the responses of these researchers is the relative dissatisfaction of the sociologists with the regulations and review process. On the attitudinal items shown in table 16.1, the sociologists tended to be less favorable on the positive items and more negative on the items critical of the IRB, although the differences were not huge. For example, while 97 percent of the psychologists and 100 percent of those in education agreed that the human subjects review process protects human subjects, at least to some extent, only 84 percent of the sociologists agreed. Sociologists differed little from psychologists on most items that negatively evaluated IRBs, but differed markedly on their overall evaluation of the review process. Twenty-two percent of the sociologists indicated that the difficulties caused by the review process outweighed the benefits to subjects, compared to 12 percent of the psychologists, 10 percent of those in education, and 7 percent of the biomedical researchers. Interestingly, the sociologists were not more likely than the psychologists to have ever had an IRB return a proposal for more information (48 percent of the psychologists and 46 percent of the sociologists had had that experience), and psychologists were more likely than sociologists to have ever had to modify a proposal (50 percent vs. 31 percent) or to have had a proposal rejected (3 percent vs. none).

The information received by the commission through letters, hearings, and the complaints and suggestions reported in the Michigan survey identified a variety of problems regarding the language of the regulations and the behavior of IRBs. Yet it is not clear that there is a close correspondence between negative experiences with IRBs and negative attitudes toward the review process. While some negative attitudes may be rooted in problems in the functioning of the IRB system, other negative attitudes are based in ideological factors that are inconsistent with *any* review process (such as the belief that the review of research prior to its conduct violates the concept of academic freedom or even the First Amendment to the Constitution of the United States). There are obvious dangers in using expressions of negative attitudes as indicators of genuine problems; the goal of the review process cannot be the elimination of complaints from researchers. Nevertheless, some complaints seem well founded, and various elements in the commission's IRB recommendations and in the subsequent actions of the Department of Health and

Human Services (and its predecessor, HEW) respond to some genuine problems that have been identified in the application of past HEW regulations to survey research, fieldwork, and research based on existing records.

Outline of Revised Regulations for the Protection of Human Subjects

In the final days of the Carter administration, HHS Secretary Patricia Harris signed new regulations that replaced the original HEW regulations that has been promulgated in 1974. These 1981 regulations—which were based on the proposed revised regulations published in August 1979—represent a strong move away from federal requirements for the review of social research by (a) confining the applicability of the regulations to federally funded research and (b) exempting certain types of federally funded research from the regulations. These 1981 regulations were in part responsive to the recommendations of the National Commission for the Protection of Human Subjects, and also reflected a growing concern among social scientists about negative aspects of a set of regulations that were seen as based on biomedical research models intended to protect subjects from types of harms that were more typical of biomedical than of social research.[24] The remainder of this paper presents a brief summary of the new regulatory structure, as it affects social and behavioral research, and comments on some continuing issues in federal policy in this area.

What Should Be Reviewed by IRBs?

The question of what IRBs should review encompasses three more specific issues, namely, (1) the definition of research involving human subjects, (2) the source of funding for research, and (3) the type of research by level of risk or research methodology.

Definition of Research Involving Human Subjects. The original regulations (1974-81) for research involving human subjects defined neither "research" nor "human subjects." The reason was mainly historical: the policy was originally developed as a part of the review process for research to be funded by HEW. If the activity in question was to be submitted for funding as research, then presumably it *was* research. This assumption caused some demonstration programs that basically involved only service delivery to be considered as research, but apparently these problems were not severe enough to stimulate a definition of research.

However, the national commission felt it necessary to define research, and a similar definition was adopted in the new HHS regulations: "Research means a systematic investigation designed to develop or contribute to generalizable knowledge." This definition is, no doubt, imperfect. Questions may arise, for example, about teaching activities or about studies involving description rather than generalization. Research that emerges gradually from other activities will also create definitional problems. But the definition does rule out some clearly nonresearch activities, such as installation of new plumbing in a hospital research unit, an activity that was purportedly reviewed by one IRB because it might put subjects at risk.

The need for a definition of "human subject" became clear as questions were raised about observational research, research involving records or data that had been collected for other purposes, and research involving pathology samples.

The new regulations, closely following the national commission, define a human subject as "a living individual about whom an investigator (whether professional or student) conducting research obtains (*a*) data through intervention or interaction with the individual, or (*b*) identifiable private information." Under this definition, observational studies would not be included, unless identifiable private information were being collected, nor would studies of data from which identifiers have been removed or studies of information in the public record. Questions may still arise about what counts as "private information,"* and the application of the definition in research on aggregates (e.g., organizations).

Should the Source of Research Support Affect the Need for IRB Review? Whether the government should require IRB review of research not supported by federal grants and contracts has been a matter of confusion and controversy. The National Research Act of 1974 (which says that institutions receiving Public Health Service funds for research involving human subjects must establish IRBs to review research "conducted at or sponsored by" the institution) was seen by some as requiring review without regard to funding source and, thus, as inconsistent with the original HEW regulations, which, on their face, applied only to research sponsored by HEW. HEW, however, used the formal process under which institutions gave assurances of compliance with the regulations to require institutions to adopt a policy of reviewing all research, regardless of funding source.

In its consideration of the issue, the national commission concluded that the source of research support is largely irrelevant to the need for review. Thus, it recommended to HEW that it issue regulations applicable to all research over which HEW has regulatory authority, and it recommended to Congress that new legislation be developed to cover human subjects in all research over which the federal government might have regulatory authority. This recommendation was rooted in the ideas that IRB review is an essential element in

---

*Under the regulations, "private information" includes "information about behavior that occurs in a context in which an individual can reasonably expect that no observation or recording is taking place, and information which has been provided for specific purposes by an individual and which the individual can reasonably expect will not be made public (for example, a medical record)."

the ethical conduct of research and that consistency within institutions was desirable.

However, the commission's recommendation that IRB requirements be extended to the limits of federal authority was offered during a period of growing opposition to federal regulation, in general. Although the regulations proposed by HEW in August 1979 included requirements for IRB review of nonfederally funded research, this stipulation provoked an outcry from researchers, particularly social researchers, who saw this as a form of censorship, at least in its potential. Objections were also heard from persons with more general concerns about the policy of attaching conditions to federal dollars as a lever for change in areas not immediately touched by those dollars. In response to these concerns, the President's Commission for the Study of Ethical Problems in Medicine and in Biomedical and Behavioral Research, which began its work in early 1980, wrote to the Secretary of HEW indicating that it did not believe that the language of the National Research Act was sufficiently clear to justify the extension of the HEW regulations to non-HEW research. This view was apparently accepted, because the 1981 HHS regulations apply only to research funded by HHS, although language is also included that indicates that HHS continues to be concerned that the interests of all subjects be protected at institutions where HHS is supporting research with human subjects.

Need All Types of Research Be Reviewed?   Perhaps the most common criticism of the current regulatory structure is that IRBs spend most of their time reviewing research that presents trivial levels of risk to subjects. Not only is this a source of aggravation to researchers who may encounter delays, but it may also prevent IRBs from devoting sufficient time to research that does present serious risks to subjects. The national commission recommended revision of the regulations to allow for expedited review procedures, through which low-risk research would need to be reviewed by as few as one IRB representative.

The 1981 HHS regulations accepted and extended this idea in ways that have great importance for social and behavioral research. Not only do the regulations contain provisions for expedited review, but they would also exempt from the regulations certain categories of low-risk research and certain types of research ill suited to the consent model embodied in the regulations. Specifically, the 1981 regulations exempt from coverage (1) research in educational settings on new or established instructional strategies and techniques, curricula, or classroom management methods; (2) research involving the use of educational tests, if identifiers cannot be linked to the subjects; (3) survey and interview research and observational research in public places, unless identifiers are being collected and the data pertain to sensitive subject behavior (such as illegal conduct, drug use, sexual behavior, or use of alcohol) the disclosure of which could put the subject at risk of criminal or civil liability or could damage the subject's financial standing or employability; (4) studies using existing data, documents, records and the like, if these materials are publicly available or if the data will not be recorded in a manner that would allow linkage with individuals.

Although it appears that most social research is now exempt from the regulations either because it is specifically exempted or because it is not federally supported, the extent to which IRBs will actually continue to review such research remains to be seen. Whether IRBs stop reviewing research that is exempt from the regulations is a matter of policy at the institutions that create them. For example, many institutions may continue to require IRB review for all research involving persons for whom the institution has responsibility (such as patients). Such IRBs may follow many provisions of the regulations as they review such research. Thus, the regulations' flexibility regarding such matters as informed consent may be important even for research that the regulations may appear to exempt.

Issues of Informed Consent

At least four major informed consent issues arise in IRB review of research: (1) the necessity for informed consent; (2) determination of what must be disclosed to subjects; (3) the permissibility of deception; and (4) the necessity of documentation through consent forms. (The circumstances under which consent is sought, and consent procedures for vulnerable subjects, such as children or the mentally ill, are also important but are not discussed here.)

When Is Informed Consent Not Necessary?   The 1974 HEW regulations mentioned no categories of research for which informed consent requirements were not applicable. Thus, it is not surprising that complaints were heard from researchers whose IRBs were attaching informed consent requirements to observational research and studies based on existing records, data, or materials such as pathology samples that would otherwise be discarded. Since it was not clear what a "human subject" was, and since the regulations made no provision for waiving informed consent in any studies in which "human subjects" were involved, social researchers, epidemiologists, and other researchers occasionally were presented with consent requirements that appeared to make no sense.

The 1981 regulations' definition of human subjects, following the national commission's definition, excludes some research activities that some IRBs had been reviewing, including both observational research in public places and records studies that do not involve private behavior. Furthermore, the exempted categories of research are not covered by the regulatory requirements.

A possible problem with the exemption approach is that it may be read as an official statement that informed consent is not ethically necessary in the categories covered. Most persons who have analyzed the ethics of research would sharply disagree in many cases. This raises the issue of the relationship of ethics to regulations. In my view, it is neither necessary nor desirable that all ethical questions be covered in governmental regulations. The exemptions from the regulations are properly read not as a statement that no matters of ethical concern exist in the exempted categories but as a statement about costs and benefits of the review process itself. For example, the kinds of survey research exempted in the 1981 regulations involve very little risk and minor ethical issues, and IRBs can more productively devote their energies elsewhere. It can further be argued that a potential for mischief always exists in a review process, a potential that is difficult to outweigh in research that involves very little risk and only trivial ethical issues. None of this is to say that a person should not be given a fair explanation before being asked to complete a questionnaire.

Even though several types of research are exempt from the 1981 regulations, they continue to cover some types of research for which the full consent requirements (such as were required under the 1974 regulations) may not be appropriate. These might include, for example, some studies of records or of public behavior in which identifiers are being recorded. It is desirable that IRBs be given some flexibility in applying informed consent requirements to such research. The 1981 regulations provide that an IRB may approve studies that do not include some or all of the elements of informed consent if the IRB finds that the research involves no more than minimal risk, that the rights and welfare of the subjects will not be adversely affected, that the research could not practicably be carried out if the regular consent requirements were applied, and, where appropriate, that subjects will be given additional pertinent information about participation. These provisions may allow some forms of deception in research, although the topic is not addressed explicitly. (The national commission acknowledged that deception may be acceptable under some conditions.)

The regulations also provide for waiver of consent in research that is conducted for the purpose of demonstrating or evaluating "federal, state or local benefit or service programs" or for demonstrating or evaluating procedures for obtaining benefits under, or changes in, or alternatives to, these programs, provided that the research could not practicably be carried out without the alteration in the consent procedure.

Thus, the consent provisions in the 1981 regulations give IRBs increased flexibility in considering proposals that depart significantly from the basic research model for which the regulations were designed.

What Must Be Disclosed to Subjects?   The 1981 regulations, like the recommendations of the national commission, expand the categories of information that are to be disclosed to subjects in order to obtain informed consent. Section 46.116 of the 1981 rules requires that subjects are to be provided with:

(1) A statement that the study involves research, an explanation of the purposes of the research and the duration of the subject's participation, a description of the

procedures to be followed, and identification of any procedures which are experimental;

(2) A description of any reasonably foreseeable risks or discomforts to the subject;

(3) A description of any benefits to the subject or to others which may reasonably be expected from the research;

(4) A disclosure of appropriate alternative procedures or courses of treatment, if any, that might be advantageous to the subject;

(5) A statement describing the extent, if any, to which confidentiality of records identifying the subject will be maintained;

(6) For research involving more than minimal risk, an explanation as to whether any compensation and medical treatments are available if injury occurs and, if so, what they consist of, or where further information may be obtained;

(7) An explanation of whom to contact for answers to pertinent questions about the research and research subjects' rights, and whom to contact in the event of a research-related injury to the subject; and

(8) A statement that participation is voluntary, refusal to participate will involve no penalty or loss of benefits to which the subject is otherwise entitled, and the subject may discontinue participation at any time without penalty or loss of benefits to which the subject is otherwise entitled.

The regulations also list several other items that may need to be disclosed in some studies where the particular circumstances warrant it (e.g., if participation might result in additional costs to subjects or if withdrawal from the study might involve risks to subjects, as it does in some drug studies). As noted above, the regulations also give IRBs authority to waive elements of consent under certain circumstances.

When Are Consent Forms Not Needed?   Although the 1974 regulations stated that consent forms need not always be used, the conditions set forth for dispensing with consent forms were ambiguous at best and impossible to meet at worst. Some IRBs' inflexible insistence on written consent became one of the most common complaints about the regulations, particularly in the realm of social research (e.g., in fieldwork or telephone surveys).

This problem was addressed by the national commission and in the 1981 regulations, which allow IRBs to waive the requirement for a signed consent form if it finds that either (*a*) the consent form itself would be the only document linking the subject to the research and the principal risk in the research stems from the possibility of a breach of confidentiality (in which circumstances the regulations give *subjects* the option of disposing of the consent documentation requirement), or (*b*) when the research presents no more than minimal risk of harm to subjects and involves no procedures for which written consent is normally required outside the research context. In these circumstances, the IRB may still require investigators to provide subjects with a written statement about the research. The first of these exceptions arises from concern that in some studies of illegal or stigmatizing behavior, the signed consent form (and its vulnerability to subpoena) may itself create risk for subjects. The second exception applies to methods such as asking questions (e.g., via an interview). One does not usually ask another person for written consent in order to ask him or her a question; since this is the case, the regulation says, it is not necessary to obtain written consent just because the question happens to be asked for research purposes.

Risk-Benefit Issues

A central responsibility of IRBs continues to be an assessment of whether the risks of the research are reasonable in relation to the anticipated benefits to subjects and the importance of the knowledge that may reasonably be expected to result. The 1981 regulations also direct the IRB to eliminate unnecessary risks to subjects. The intent behind the risk-benefit language of the 1981 regulations appears to be the same as that in the 1974 regulations. IRBs' responsibility to assess the risks and benefits of proposed research has raised several controversial issues in the past, five of which are discussed briefly below.

Is the Risk-Benefit Approach Appropriate to Social and Behavioral Research? The requirement that an IRB must judge whether risks to subjects are reasonable in relation to anticipated benefits to subjects and the importance of the knowledge to be gained applies, of course, to any social and behavioral research that is not exempted from the regulations. While the level of risk in social and behavioral research is ordinarily low, it is often quite difficult to show that basic research in these fields produces "benefit," unless one considers any increment of knowledge to be a benefit. There is no conveniently available and widely accepted value such as "health" that can plausibly be seen as the ultimate research goal. Most people are willing to accept the possibility that basic biomedical research will eventually prove beneficial, and they can perceive the researcher's motivations in such terms. However, the value of much basic social and behavioral research is not as intuitively obvious. Further, many problems for study are undoubtedly selected because of the personal values of the researcher or because the problem seems "interesting," not out of a belief that the research will lead to some utilitarian benefit. Thus, many social and behavioral scientists are uncomfortable with having the acceptability of their research judged in risk-benefit terms.

Furthermore, researchers from these fields are likely to perceive the risk-benefit judgment as subjective, likely to be influenced by a wide variety of social and psychological factors, and somewhat capricious. Some comfort can be taken from the fact that IRBs have rejected very little social and psychological research on risk-benefit grounds. Nonetheless, a disturbing potential exists that research with low levels of risk may be rejected rather arbitrarily on these grounds. Concern about this will undoubtedly grow if this potential is realized.

Should Possible "Harmful" Results Be Considered in Risk-Benefit Judgments by IRBs? The 1974 regulations directed IRB concerns toward risks to subjects while participating in research, such as the risks of ingesting a drug, receiving an electric shock, or disclosing sensitive information. It has also been argued, however, that subjects may be harmed by the results of research, as when the research results are unfavorable to a category of which the subjects are members. The harm might be a stigma or might result from policy decision based on the research. Concerns about research on race and IQ, and on violence and the XYY karyotype, are prominent examples, but the concern could arise in many, perhaps most, social research contexts.

Whether IRBs should consider possible research results *as risks* when making risk-benefit judgments has been intensively debated at some institutions (most notably at the University of California at Berkeley) and by the national commission. The argument on the one side is that future risks are as real as the hypothetical future benefits that IRBs are asked to weigh against the risks to subjects, and that symmetry demands that both be considered. This symmetry, incidentally, would not confine the risks of concern to those that affect subjects; in reaching its judgments the IRB might be concerned with any future risk.

The national commission rejected these arguments, and both its recommendations and the 1981 HHS regulations state explicitly that IRBs should not consider such risks. This decision was, I believe, based upon the recognition that such risk-benefit determination would be highly problematic for a series of reasons. First, the predictions are speculative. Second, the judgments are essentially political. Consider, for example, studies of such topics as welfare cheating or investment of foreign capital in the United States. The results of either study could influence social policies and affect the interest of certain groups of which the subjects might be members. But surely the proper forum for the policy debate is not a local IRB, and the debate about the policy implications of the research is not best conducted before the research takes place. (Incidentally, arguments in favor of IRB review of such risks often makes naive assumptions of some automatic link between research and policy.) Third, the issues involved are in no way peculiar to research involving human subjects. The same issues would arise when a George Will, or a James Reston, or a Joan Didion undertakes policy analysis or social commentary. The issue, however, remains very troublesome, and will, I suspect, continue to be seriously debated in the future. There may continue to be pressure to have IRBs reject research because of its "social risk."

Should IRBs Be Concerned about Whether "Sensitive Questions" Will Be Asked in the Research?   The 1974 regulations made no reference to the sensitivity of the questions asked in research, nor did the national commission's recommendations. Some IRBs, however, apparently have made the sensitivity of the questions asked in social or psychological research a factor in their risk-benefit judgments. The 1981 regulations may encourage this practice by making the collection of "sensitive aspects of an individual's behavior such as illegal conduct, drug use, sexual behavior, or use of alcohol" a factor in determining whether certain social and behavioral research will exempt from the regulations. Although this language has an understandable purpose of focusing review on studies in which there is risk to subjects, presumably so that adequate precautions can be taken to assure confidentiality, it may also encourage IRBs to attempt to screen out questions (on grounds of protecting subjects) because of subject matter.

The possibility is troublesome for First Amendment reasons and because those within and outside the relevant fields of research may well have different ideas about (a) what may be "sensitive" and (b) what subjects or respondents will do when asked a question about matters that *they* consider to be sensitive. Outsiders sometimes seem to assume that respondents have no defense against such questions, while social and behavioral researchers are keenly aware that respondents have many defenses, that great care must be taken in approaching certain topic areas, and that certain areas are very difficult to approach through particular research methods (such as survey research). The researcher, therefore, may well believe that subjects—at least competent, adult subjects— do not need a review board to protect them from having to respond to certain questions. Clearly, there is some potential for future conflict between researchers and IRBs with regard to this issue.

Should IRBs Consider Scientific Quality of Research? Although the 1974 regulations did not direct IRBs to review research design or scientific quality, IRB consideration of this aspect of proposed studies has been one of the most controversial areas of IRB activities. Some commentators argue that no risks to subjects can be justified if research is so poorly designed as to produce no valid information.[25] This logic perhaps explains why some IRBs have become concerned with the quality of research designs; responsibility to do so can be seen as resting on their responsibility to make risk-benefit decisions. (Interestingly, there is a widespread perception among researchers that IRBs have positively contributed to the quality of research.)[26]

The national commission recommended (and HEW subsequently proposed) to give IRBs explicit responsibility to make these judgments. In its early reports (e.g., its report on research involving children), the commission said that IRBs should make sure that proposed research involving vulnerable populations is "scientifically sound." In response to arguments about how conceptions of "scientific soundness" may vary to some extent across disciplines—it could be argued, for example, that all research that does not involve random assignment to treatments is not "scientifically sound"—the commission in its IRB report changed its language slightly, stating that the IRB should determine that the methods are appropriate in light of the objectives of the research and the field of study. Thus, presumably, a descriptive, observational sociological study should not be judged by criteria that might be applied to clinical drug trials. The proposed HEW regulations of 1979 adopted the language from the commission's IRB report.

Objections to having IRBs review and approve the scientific quality of proposed research are at least twofold. First, scientific review is the function of study sections (at NIH or ADAMHA) and these study sections, unlike IRBs, are designed to represent the scientific expertise necessary to make this judgment. The assumption that adequate expertise could be assembled in hundreds of local IRBs (and that such IRBs would have time to make a careful review of scientific quality) is questionable, raising the concern that IRBs were being given a responsibility that they would frequently be unable to fulfill. This concern would threaten their legitimacy and distract them from other responsibilities. Second, concepts of appropriate methodology are constantly changing and are a matter of legitimate and serious dispute within, and between, many scientific fields. Thus, it was feared that IRBs might attempt to enforce methodological orthodoxy or particular conceptions of scientific quality. (This same criticism, of course, is often directed at study sections and must be taken seriously there as well.)

For such reasons, the 1981 regulations do not require IRBs to review the appropriateness of the scientific methods. The extent to which such issues will continue to arise in the context of IRB risk-benefit judgments remains to be seen. Since the regulations apply only to federally funded research, which in most cases will go through a peer review process for assessment of scientific merit, problems may arise only infrequently.

Should IRBs Address Questions Regarding Confidentiality? The protection of confidentiality of data ranks high on most social scientists' lists of ethical responsibilities of researchers. The 1974 regulations did not address this issue at all, and this ommission was often cited to demonstrate the irrelevance of the regulations to social research. Some IRBs were concerned with such issues, but not because of explicit regulatory requirements.

Following the national commission's recommendations, the 1981 regulations indicate that the review of research by IRBs should include a determination that adequate provisions have been made to protect the privacy of subjects and to maintain the confidentiality of data. IRB responsibility to reduce unnecessary risk may also apply to confidentiality problems. Since much of the social research that is not exempted from the regulations involves the collection of sensitive personal information, IRB concern with confidentiality issues seems all the more appropriate. The provisions of the 1981 regulations will increase the relevancy of the regulations and IRBs' activities to social and behavioral research. How IRBs discharge these responsibilities merits careful attention as the 1981 regulations are translated into practice.

Other Issues

Composition of IRBs. The 1974 regulations required a mixture of competencies—members who could judge research in terms of such matters as "law, institutional commitments, and community attitudes." The national commission recommended that IRBs must be composed so as to be acceptable both to investigators and to the community served by the institutions in which they are located. The 1981 regulations state that, among other qualifications, the IRB membership should have sufficient "sensitivity to community attitudes" to promote respect for IRB decisions; the IRB should also be able to judge proposed research in terms of "institutional commitments and regulations, applicable law, and standards of professional conduct and practice." Thus, it appears that a potential area of future controversy will be in situations where IRBs may judge the acceptability of proposed research in terms of perceptions of community attitudes or the image of the institution. The conflict with the concept of freedom of inquiry is obvious.

Another issue pertains to the numbers of scientific and nonscientific members on the board. The 1974 regulations stated the need for diversity, but contained no particular formula. The national commission suggested that between one-third and two-thirds of IRB members should be scientists. This would presumably have resulted in an increase in the nonscientific representation, because the minimum acceptable level would approximate the existing average level—one-third nonscientists. The 1981 regulations, however, are similar to the 1974 regulations, stating only that an IRB must include at least one member "whose primary concerns are in nonscientific areas."

Appeals Process for IRB Decisions. Although neither the national commission's recommendations nor the 1981 regulations have provisions for an appeals process, many people have been troubled by the lack of provisions for appealing IRB decisions. Thus, although IRBs may take unjustified actions (either to approve or disapprove a proposal), there has been no institutionalized effort to seek corrective action other than through the courts. (Very few projects have been turned down by IRBs, however.)[27] A few institutions have instituted an appeals process; by and large, these are institutions in which several IRBs operate under the aegis of a larger, superordinate IRB. Thus, if the latter IRB approves the research, the regulatory requirement of IRB approval is met.[28]

This suggests the major conceptual difficulty with an appeals process. If the requirement is established that a body that is constituted in a certain way must approve research according to a set of regulatory criteria, how can the judgment of that body be overruled by an individual or group that does not meet the regulatory requirements? Unless an institution were to establish an IRB to be used for appeals purposes (which institutions are now free to do), it is difficult to integrate an appeals process with the IRB requirement.

Although the national commission did not recommend an appeals process, it did recommend that IRBs announce their policies and procedures, that investigators be notified in writing of IRB decisions and the basis for the decision, and that investigators be given an opportunity to respond in person or in writing.[29] The 1981 regulations basically accepted these recommendations. However, the possibility remains that an injustice could be done for which there is no remedy. Presumably, if the injustice is substantial, the case could end up in the courts; some of the legal questions that have been raised regarding IRBs may then be answered. To the best of my knowledge, the courts have been asked to intervene in no negative decisions by IRBs and in only one positive decision. This suggests that, however unreasonable some initial decisions by IRBs may be, ultimately most are resolved in ways that are at least minimally acceptable to the affected parties. Even so, the idea of an appeals process merits further consideration.

Conclusion

This paper has reviewed the history of the regulation of research that involves human subjects in the social and behavioral sciences. After a period in the late 1970s of vocal concern from social scientists about these regulatory issues, a new period has begun with the publication in January 1981 of revised regulations. In my view, the new regulations exempt most social research and provide for more flexibility in the review of research that is not exempted. Many institutions, however, may of their own volition continue to review research that is exempt from the regulations, and some old sources of tension may continue. Awareness of the IRB process, however, has clearly grown among social and behavioral scientists; further empirical study of this process can be expected in the future.

Notes

1. Possible distinctions between the terms *social research* and *behavioral research* are not germane to this paper, and the terms are used interchangeably. Similarly, possible distinctions between the terms *human subjects* and other terms frequently used in certain types of social and behavioral research (e.g., *respondents* in survey research and *informants* in ethnographic research) are not examined.

2. Numerous federal departments and agencies (and several states) have policies and regulations regarding protection of human subjects. (The National Commission for the Protection of Human Subjects of Biomedical and Behavioral Research summarized the policies of federal agencies in "Staff Report on the Protection of Human Subjects in Research Conducted or Supported by Federal Agencies," published in 1978.) In some cases, important regulations affecting social and behavioral research may be found under rubrics other than "protection of human subjects." The Law Enforcement Assistance Administration's regulations to maintain the confidentiality of research data are an example. However, with the exception of such special purpose regulations, most governmental regulations are modeled after the regulations issued by the Department of Health, Education, and Welfare in 1974 *(Code of Federal Regulations,* Title 45, Part 46). This HEW (now HHS) regulatory structure is the focus of this paper. (Although some other regulations, such as those focusing particularly on privacy, have substantial importance for some behavioral research, they are not addressed in this chapter.)

3. Robert A. Cooke, Arnold S. Tannenbaum, and Bradford H. Gray, "A Survey of Institutional Review Boards and Research Involving Human Subjects," *Report and Recommendations on Institutional Review Boards of the National Commission for the Protection of Human Subjects* (Washinton, D.C.: Government Printing Office, 1977), appendix, p. 105.

4. For example, the prestigious journal *Science* published a letter in its April 22, 1966, issue predicting that 1966 would be looked back on as the year that medical progress stopped.

5. U.S. Public Health Service, PPO #129, February 8, 1966. For an examination of the origins of the PHS policy, see William J. Curran, "Governmental Regulation of the Use of Human Subjects in Medical Research: The Approach of Two Federal Agencies," *Daedalus* 98 (1969): 542–94; and Mark S. Frankel, "The Public Health Service Guidelines Governing Research Involving Human Subjects: An Analysis of the Policy-Making Process" (Washington, D.C.: George Washington University Program in Policy Studies in Science and Technology, 1972).

6. Until recent years, the functions of ethical review and scientific review were generally seen as distinct and separable from each other. This view is challenged by the National Commission for the Protection of Human Subjects and others who argue that justification is required if subjects are asked to undergo even minor risk or inconvenience, that this justification rests substantially on the scientific benefits of the research, and that no scientific benefits can result from unsound research designs. By this logic the quality of the research design becomes an issue in the risk-benefit assessment by which research is justified.

7. Memorandum from the Surgeon General to Heads of Institutions Receiving Public Health Service Grants, December 12, 1966.

8. In March 1968, a small green pamphlet was issued by HEW under the title "Public Health Service Policy for the Protection of the Individual as a Subject of Investigation." This contained language similar to the surgeon general's December 1966 statement. It noted the types of risk in social and behavioral research and the ethical issues of concern in such research (voluntary participation, maintenance of confidentiality, and protection of the subject from "misuse of findings"), and it acknowledged that "fully informed consent" and "knowledgeable participation" may not be always necessary. On May 1, 1969, a new PHS policy statement was published. This was a blue pamphlet entitled "Protection of the Individual as a Research Subject: Grants, Awards, Contracts." This statement was brief in its treatment of social and behavioral research, did not discuss it separately from biomedical research, and eliminated earlier statements regarding flexibility in consent. The entire discussion was as follows:

There is a wide range of medical, social, and behavioral research in which no immediate physical risk to the subject is involved. However, some of these may impose varying degrees of discomfort, irritation, and harassment. In addition there may be substantial potential injury to the subject's rights if attention is not given to maintenance of the confidentiality of information obtained from the subject and the protection of the subject from misuse of findings.

9. "The Institutional Guide to DHEW Policy on Protection of Human Subjects" (Washington, D.C.: DHEW, 1971).

10. *Code of Federal Regulations,* Title 45, Part 46.

11. Bradford H. Gray, "The Functions of Human Subjects Review Committees," *American Journal of Psychiatry* 134 (1977): 907-10.

12. An IRB can waive written consent requirements providing that it determines that the risk to subjects in the research was minimal [undefined in the regulations], that written consent would "surely invalidate objectives of considerable immediate importance," *and* "that any reasonable alternative means for attaining these objectives would be less advantageous to the subjects" (*Code of Federal Regulations,* Title 45, Part 46.106).

13. National Commission for the Protection of Human Subjects of Biomedical and Behavioral Research, *The Belmont Report: Ethical Principles and Guidelines for the Protection of Human Subjects of Research,* DHEW Publication no. (OS) 78-0014 (Washington, D.C.: Government Printing Office, 1978).

14. H. Tristram Engelhardt, "Basic Ethical Principles in the Conduct of Biomedical and Behavioral Research Involving Human Subjects," in National Commission for the Protection of Human Subjects of Biomedical and Behavioral Research, *Belmont Report,* appendix; Paul Ramsey, *The Patient as Person* (New Haven: Yale University Press, 1970); Robert M. Veatch, "Three Theories of Informed Consent: Philosophical Foundations and Policy Implications," in National Commission for the Protection of Human Subjects of Biomedical and Behavioral Research, *Belmont Report,* appendix.

15. U.S. Senate, Hearings on the Quality of Health Care: Human Experimentation. (Washington, D.C.: Government Printing Office, 1973).

16. There may, nevertheless, be some relevant differences among research methodologies regarding, for example, the extent to which the procedures used in the research (*a*) have some

protection under the U.S. Constitution and (*b*) would require informed consent even if their use did not involve research. On both counts research that involves only written or oral interaction between researcher and subject would differ from research that involves surgical intervention.

17. Both the Barber and Reiss papers are published in the appendix to the commission's *Belmont Report.* This volume also includes a paper by Donald Campbell and Joe S. Cecil on issues in program evaluation and social experimentation, a pair of contrasting papers by Diana Baumrind and Leonard Berkowitz on deception in research, and a paper by Gregory Kimble on risk-benefit analysis in psychological research. Several other papers by nonbehavioral scientists also examined various aspects of the ethics of research in the social and behavioral sciences.

18. A partial listing of the problems raised in commission hearings is:

a. IRBs' insistence on *written* consent when it was not needed and would damage the research;

b. Infringements of academic freedom resulting from IRBs' application of risk-benefit criteria;

c. The general lack of fit between the regulations and the ethical issues that arise in some types of research (e.g., ethnography);

d. The failure of the regulations to address explicitly certain issues (e.g., deception, privacy, confidentiality of data, and the use of research for teaching purposes) and certain types of research (e.g., fieldwork or evaluation research);

e. The conflict that can develop between written consent requirements and researchers' responsibility to assure confidentiality of the identity of subjects;

f. The lack of clear definition of the applicability of the regulations (e.g., just what *is* a human subject?);

g. The harm to research that can result from application of consent requirements to certain research, such as observation studies in public places and studies based on existing records;

h. The use of IRBs to protect vested interests (e.g., the alleged tendency of IRBs in some medical schools and hospitals to discourage social research within their walls);

i. Some IRBs' lack of reasonable flexibility in interpreting regulatory language;

j. Some IRBs' lack of qualifications to review certain types of studies;

k. The application of review requirements to research not funded by the federal government; and

l. The lack of appeal procedures.

19. Cooke et al., "Survey of Institutional Review Boards"; Bradford H. Gray, Robert A. Cooke, and Arnold S. Tannenbaum, "Research Involving Human Subjects," *Science* 201 (September 22, 1978): 1094–1101; Bradford H. Gray and Robert A. Cooke, "The Impact of Institutional Review Boards on Research," *Hastings Center Report* 10, no. 1 (February 1980): 36–41.

20. Bernard Barber et al., *Research on Human Subjects* (New York: Russell Sage Foundation, 1973).

21. For example, see Bradford H. Gray, *Human Subjects in Medical Experimentation* (New York: Wiley-Interscience, 1975).

22. Gray, Cooke, and Tannenbaum, "Research Involving Human Subjects," p. 1096.

23. When asked if they had ever had a proposal turned down by an IRB, 6 percent of biomedical researchers and 1 percent of behavioral researchers answered affirmatively. This difference is probably partially due to the fact that, on average, biomedical researchers have had more proposals reviewed by IRBs.

24. Carol Levine, "Social Scientists Form Committee to Protest Regulations," *IRB: A Review of Human Subjects Research* 1, no. 8 (December 8, 1979).

25. David Rutstein, "The Ethical Design of Human Experiments," *Daedalus* 98 (Spring 1969): 523–41.

26. Gray, Cooke, and Tannenbaum, "Research Involving Human Subjects."

27. Bradford H. Gray and Robert A. Cooke, "The Impact of Human Subjects Regulations on Research," *Hastings Center Report* 10, no. 1 (February 1980): 36–41.

28. The preamble to the *Federal Register* publication of the January 1981 regulations stated that "The National Commission did not recommend a mechanism for appeal from IRB determinations, since it felt that the IRB is the final authority at the institution regarding the ethical acceptability of proposed research involving human subjects. HHS does not rule out the possibility of an institution establishing an appeals process in order to provide a second review of research activities that were disapproved by an IRB. However, under such circumstances, the

appellate body established must meet all of the requirements of the regulation, including those specifying membership requirements." See Officè of the Secretary, Department of Health and Human Services, "Final Regulations Amending Basic HHS Policy for the Protection of Human Research Subjects," *Federal Register* 46, no. 16 (January 26, 1981): 8374.

29.   For other suggestions to improve the functioning of IRBs, see John A. Robertson, "Ten Ways to Improve IRBs," *Hastings Center Report* 9, no. 1 (February 1979): 29–33.

17

The Social Scientist's Right to Research and the IRB System

JOHN A. ROBERTSON

The federal government, by requiring institutional review board (IRB) review of human subject research at institutions receiving federal research funds, now indirectly regulates most of the social science research occuring in American universities. While some social scientists view this regulatory system as unnecessary, overbroad, rigid, and destructive of good research, others question the very legitimacy of any government regulation of social research.[1] In their view scientists have a right to plan and conduct research as they see fit, subject only to judgments of their peers based on canons of scientific validity. This right, they assert, is inherent in the role of scientist and in doctrines of academic freedom and is protected by the free speech clause of the First Amendment. If it is not honored, the scientific enterprise may wither, and the fruits of scientific knowledge may be lost.

In this chapter I attempt to show that governmental regulation of social research through the IRB system violates no moral or legal rights of scientists and is constitutionally legitimate. I argue that disputes over the structure and scope of the IRB system are disputes of policy rather than rights, and that the establishment of this system is well within the legitimate authority of government and university administrators. I then show that the IRB system embodies two different kinds of policy: substantive norms and procedural mechanisms for implementing those norms. These distinctions can help clarify the policy issues that arise in the IRB system and point the way to improvement.

The Moral Legitimacy of Regulation

One may be sympathetic to the pleas of social scientists to be free of government restrictions and still believe that public regulation is morally legitimate. When scientists claim a right of free inquiry—the right to conduct research unrestricted by any governmental regulation—they may be seen as making a claim based on two important moral principles: the principle of autonomy and the principle of beneficence. Since regulation of research prevents a scientist from fulfilling or carrying out the role of scientist as he or she sees fit, it violates the scientist's autonomy. Similarly, to the extent that regulation reduces the amount of knowledge and resulting benefits produced for others, regulation limits the good that scientists do and thus violates the principle of beneficence.

If the claim to freedom of inquiry is grounded on basic moral principles, thus creating a moral presumption in favor of free inquiry, then any regulatory system that limits scientific inquiry would be morally permissible only if it were also based on important ethical principles. For example, the autonomy of scientists could justifiably be limited if its exercise harms others or prevents their exercise of autonomy. Similarly, actions motivated by beneficence may clash with the moral principle of nonmaleficence—the duty not to harm others. It is these competing moral considerations that undermine the argument that any regulation of research is morally impermissible. For the scientist's exercise of autonomy in his or her role as researcher, even if motivated by pursuit of the good of others, can violate the autonomy or cause harm to other persons in morally significant ways. A public policy choice to prevent those moral violations, even at some cost to scientists, would not be morally impermissible.

The moral legitimacy of research regulation becomes clearer if we recall the ways in which research may burden others, and hence implicate competing moral principles. Scientific research may create morally relevant burdens in at least three ways, raising ethical and social policy issues that could each justify some form of public intervention. First, there is the opportunity cost of research. The decision to use public or private resources to do research removes those resources from use in other socially useful activities, including some which may produce a higher utility. Resources spent on basic research in physics cannot be used to deliver health care to poor children. Similarly, the resources used in research to reduce mortality in heart transplants may produce a higher health return if devoted to research in prevention of parasitic diseases.[2] The opportunity costs of research funding decisions suggest a legitimate role for government in setting budgetary priorities, at least when public funds are in question, for the scientist's choice of priorities may not coincide with the choice of the community for how best to serve the good of others.

A second set of costs supporting regulation arises in the conduct of research. In carrying out research, particularly research with human subjects, the researcher may violate moral duties to respect and refrain from harming subjects, laboratory personnel, or the surrounding community. While such burdens are more likely in biomedical research, they may also occur in social research, as Herbert C. Kelman, Donald P. Warwick, and others have documented.[3] Situational pressures on the researcher to perform research may lead him or her to underestimate the importance of these costs. Since the burdens generated by the research process may outweigh the benefits, regulation to reduce the burdens or assure an optimal mix would, on both deontological and utilitarian grounds, seem legitimate.

Finally, scientific research can burden others in ethically and socially significant ways as a result of the uses to which the resulting knowledge leads. The products of research permit people to manipulate their environment and fellow men in ways that can have serious consequences for the health, well-being, and social position of others. Thus the moral duty not to do harm may conflict with a scientist's perceived duty to create or advance knowledge.[4] Surely scientists alone should not resolve these conflicts, for they may overestimate the gains and minimize the harms, ignore the interests of those most affected, or decide them according to a set of values not shared by the community at large. Thus some role for public regulation, though perhaps a more limited one, would seem legitimate here as well.

A regulatory system that aims to reduce some or all of the costs generated by research would seem to be morally legitimate, in terms of the same moral premises on which the scientist's claim of a moral right to research rests. The moral legitimacy of research regulation is perhaps most evident in the case of regulation that aims to reduce harms and violations of autonomy generated by the research process. Thus a regulatory system that aimed to minimize harm and protect the autonomy of research subjects by requiring researchers to obtain their informed consent and to assure that the benefits of the research outweighed the risks would be consistent with moral principle of nonmaleficence and autonomy. A regulatory system set up to honor these principles by requiring researchers to submit to prior ethical review would, in light of the risk of researcher bias, seem reasonable. As long as regulation by prior review did not impose costs greater than the benefits provided, it would be morally legitimate and not undermine the moral presumption in favor of free scientific inquiry.

The Constitutional Legitimacy of Governmental Regulation of Research

While some public regulation of the funding, conduct, and product of research to maximize net utility may seem morally appropriate, the legitimacy of governmental regulation of research in the United States through the IRB system has been challenged on constitutional grounds as well. Scientific research, it is claimed, produces knowledge and information relevant to basic individual and social choices, and thus is protected by the free speech clause of the First Amendment. If research is a kind or part of protected speech, then is not federal regulation an unconstitutional and illegitimate restriction of free speech?

Persons arguing that the IRB system violates free speech are in my view correct that research is a form of protected speech.[5] Although the First Amendment most clearly protects against state restrictions on publication of already acquired information, the Supreme Court has recently extended protection to the receipt or acquisition of information.[6] Indeed, if publication is to be fully protected, predissemination activities essential for publication, such as the acquisition or gathering of information through research, should also be protected. Otherwise the government could cut off the flow of protected information by focusing restrictions clearly unacceptable at the publication stage on activities essential if publication is to occur. Although the Supreme Court has not yet had to decide a case raising this question, evolving First Amendment precedents strongly suggest that the Court would recognize a constitutional right to acquire scientific information from willing sources through research and experimentation. The scientist's right to research, at least with voluntary subjects and materials under his or her lawful control, is thus constitutionally protected.

It is incorrect, however, to conclude that all restrictions on research are therefore unconstitutional. The protection accorded research depends upon the nature and scope of a constitutional right to research. An important point that is often overlooked in discussing constitutional rights is the distinction between positive and negative rights.

Positive rights give the holder a claim (and thus impose a duty) on another to provide services or resources, while negative rights merely impose a duty not to interfere with the holder's freedom of action.[7] Most constitutional rights, including rights of free speech and research, are negative rights. They protect the holder against (or negate) governmental interference with an individual's decision to exercise the right. But they create no entitlement in the holder to have the state provide the services or resources necessary for its exercise. For example, the state may not stop a citizen from going to Washington to protest governmental policies, but it is not obligated to give him or her a plane ticket to do so.[8] Similarly, a constitutional right to research, being a negative right, creates a duty in the government not to interfere without sufficient justification with a scientist's choice of research topics or methods. It imposes no duty on the state to provide the resources essential to conduct the research, or to provide research funds free of restrictions on their use.[9]

This distinction between negative and positive rights is crucial for understanding the scope of a constitutional right to research and its implications for the IRB system. Since the right to research is a negative right, it protects the researcher only against governmental restrictions directed at privately funded research. The right requires the government to show a compelling justification for any restriction on privately funded research. However, since the right creates no obligation on the government to fund research, it sets few limits on the state's power to restrict the research that it directly funds.

Restrictions on Publicly Funded Research

In contrast to restrictions on privately funded research, the constitutional right to research, being a negative right, gives almost no protection against government decisions to fund research. Governmental funding decisions have a powerful influence on the research agendas of scientists. But since the government is not constitutionally obligated to fund any research, its funding decisions are prudential questions of social policy that generally do not violate constitutional rights. Thus the state may choose to fund only that research which it thinks will promote the general welfare and may withhold funds from research topics that in its view do not.

An important implication of the state's power to fund is the corollary power to set content and method restrictions on the use of its funds that would be beyond its power to impose directly on privately funded research. Thus a government funding agency may give grants only to those who conduct certain kinds of research, and then only when they agree to use methods that protect the health and safety of subjects and the surrounding community. Just as the funding agency is free to allocate research funds according to its view of what best serves the general welfare, it may choose to fund only those methods of producing the desired knowledge that protect third-party interests threatened by the research. Because the researcher has no right to receive funds for particular research ends, *a fortiori* he or she has no right to receive such funds free of restrictions on the manner of conducting the research.

Broad authority over funding decisions also exists at the state and institutional level. State institutions may allocate research funds and positions according to the research agendas and method criteria that they choose. A public university may legally staff research positions with those persons who agree to research certain topics, to conduct research in a certain manner, or to abide by university rules for the conduct of research.[10] Thus it may condition the hiring of faculty on their agreeing to submit research to human subject review committees, even though these involve prior restraints that would raise serious constitutional problems if the state imposed them directly on privately funded research.

An important issue raised by the conditional spending power—the power to condition receipt of public funds on the recipient's taking certain other actions—is the extent to which the funding vehicle can be used to regulate activities that are not directly funded. For example, the National Research Act,[11] which is the statutory authority for the institutional review board system, requires that institutions receiving federal research funds review, in addition to federally funded research, all nonfederally funded research that they conduct or sponsor. Since this provision requires institutions to extend the IRB system to a wide variety of nonpublicly funded research in the social sciences, it has disturbed many social scientists and led to claims of unconstitutional regulation of research. Many scientists accept the federal government's legal authority to regulate federally funded research, but find illegitimate the imposition of federal restrictions on nonfederally funded research.

The use of the conditional funding power as a vehicle to regulate an institution's nonfunded research activities does raise important questions about the limits of the federal funding power, but it is unlikely that the question will be decided against Congress. Neither scientists nor institutions have challenged in court the power of Congress to impose such conditions, perhaps because the Supreme Court, if ever faced with the question, is likely to construe Congress's conditional spending power broadly and to approve such conditions. At most, the Court might require that the attached condition rationally further the purpose of the spending.[12] On this standard the National Research Act requirement would appear to be constitutional, for institutional review of all research is rationally related to enhancing the ethics of publicly funded research. In any event, even if such conditions were found to be outside Congress's power, it would mean only that the federal government could not require that institutions, as a condition of funding, review nonfederally funded research. However, it would remain within an institution's legal authority over its employees and activities to require on its own that all institutionally sponsored or conducted research be first reviewed by the institution's ethical review board.

One limitation on the federal funding power deserves mention. The legal doctrine of unconstitutional conditions would prohibit distribution of research funds on the basis of the researcher's exercise of a constitutional right in some area unrelated to the research.[13] Under this doctrine neither the federal government in making grants, nor a state institution in hiring, could give research resources only to non-Marxists, Democrats, antiabortionists, or those researchers who on their own time conduct certain kinds of research.[14]

Restrictions on Privately Funded Research

Where government is not funding the research or the institution conducting it, it has much less authority to regulate research. The scope of the protection afforded privately funded research depends upon the source of the harm engendering governmental restrictions and the precise form that regulation takes. Restrictions on unfunded research directed to the effects or uses to be made of the research product would seldom be justified. Under the First Amendment the government may not keep information from the public by stopping publication or by stopping the acquisition of information from voluntary subjects on which publication depends. Restrictions on research topics would have to meet the exacting standard for bans on publication of the resulting knowledge. This would require the government to show that the ban on research is necessary to prevent imminent lawless action or a high probability of substantial harm from occurring.[15] Thus a law which made it a crime to investigate the genetic basis of intelligence would, like a law that banned publication of a book arguing the proposition, in almost all cases be unconstitutional.

The government would have greater leeway in restricting privately funded research if the regulation, rather than banning the acquisition of knowledge, merely restricted research methods that threatened harm to subjects. The right of free speech does not prevent the government from restricting the time, place, and manner of speech in a public forum to protect privacy or other interests that are affected by the act of speech itself rather than its content. Similarly, the government may require researchers to alter their research methods to protect the rights and welfare of research subjects, the surrounding community, or other interests that might be harmed by unrestricted choice of research methods.[16] Thus laws that require researchers in privately funded research to obtain subject consent, respect their privacy, and the like are constitutionally valid, for they aim to prevent harms that arise in the research process independent of the topic under investigation and do not prevent study of an area altogether.[17]

In keeping with the status of research as a negative right, we find almost no governmental restrictions on privately funded research occurring outside institutions receiving federal research funds.[18] There are no laws that penalize researchers for seeking certain categories or types of knowledge, no matter how offensive or potentially dangerous the resulting information. No law, for example, prohibits researchers from acquiring knowledge about behavior control, racial inferiority, genetic engineering, and the like, even if the resulting knowledge might lead to social unrest, drastic changes in our living habits, loss of personal freedom, injustice for minorities, or other harmful or undesirable effects.

Some state regulation of privately funded research does occur through laws of general applicability that indirectly prohibit use of certain research methods. A social researcher, for example, could be penalized under burglary or trespass laws for breaking into a house to spy on the occupants, or under assault laws for delivering an electric shock without consent. Privacy laws may also penalize disclosures of confidential information or invasions of private space when consent has not been obtained.[19] Sometimes these method regulations may impede or prevent research, but they do not prohibit research altogether. If an acceptable method can be found (as is usually the case) the research may go on. For example, the federal law passed after hearings on surreptitious recording of jury deliberations in the Wichita Jury Study makes it difficult to obtain data on how jurors actually deliberate.[20] The law, however, does not prohibit jury researchers from investigating the jury process as long as they use techniques such as simulation or postverdict interviews with jurors which do not record actual jury deliberations.

The Constitutional Legitimacy of the IRB System

From this analysis it should be clear that the IRB system does not violate First Amendment rights of researchers and is constitutionally legitimate. The federal government does not require IRB review of all research, just research in institutions that receive *federal research funds*. Since institutions and researchers have no constitutional rights to have federal research funds provided, they have no right to have federal funds provided free of restrictions aimed at protecting the interests of research subjects. If they choose to accept federal funds, they cannot legitimately complain that the funds come with strings attached.

Nor is the researcher who is conducting nonfederally funded research at an institution that receives federal research funds and thus is required to obtain IRB review in a better position to complain. Whether responding to a federal carrot or genuinely concerned about subjects, institutions may as a condition of employment require that researchers comply with institutional rules for human subject research. A social scientist may disagree with, or question the motives for, an institution's concern with research ethics, but its preference for research efficiency is not an issue of constitutional legitimacy.

Social scientists thus are treated no differently from journalists. Both are subject to employer constraints on the topics they investigate and methods they use. Newspapers, like universities, could require their journalists to submit projects to in-house ethics review, and fire journalists who refused.[21] Both have constitutional protection against government interference with privately funded activities, but both are subject to restrictions attached to grants of public funds. If the government gave grants to newspapers to foster investigative reporting, it could, as it does with human subject research funds, condition them on reporters having a publisher's ethics committee approve their investigative techniques.

The IRB System and Public Policy

The preceding sections of this chapter have shown that government regulation of research is neither morally nor constitutionally impermissible. This conclusion, however, does not resolve the entirely separate question of whether any particular regulation, such as the IRB system, is a wise or desirable public policy. Here the inquiry shifts from the moral problem of reconciling competing moral principles of autonomy, beneficence, and nonmaleficence, and the constitutional problem of discerning the limits of the First Amendment, to the pragmatic question of whether a regulatory system effectively implements public goals for how the research transaction should occur. A policy evaluation of a regulatory system cannot be divorced from the ethical goals that inform the policy. The relevant question, then, is whether a particular regulatory system most effectively achieves the policy goals that have been chosen.

The IRB system, thus, must be judged in terms of the moral goals it seeks to achieve. These goals appear to be a compromise between subject and researcher interests that stresses the primacy of the subject's right to self-determination and to be protected against harm, yet which does not totally ignore the preeminent value of scientific knowledge and the autonomy of scientists. Once this moral commitment is acknowledged, the policy question becomes whether the IRB system most effectively achieves this goal: that is, does it increase subject autonomy and reduce harm at an acceptable cost to researchers and institutions? Such a cost-benefit analysis is appropriate, not as a moral requirement, but as a matter of practical policy, given a prior commitment to protect subject interests without undue cost to science. If the cost of protecting subjects is too great relative to the benefits, then changes in, or regulatory devices other than, the IRB system may have to be considered, or, indeed, the basic commitment to subject interests over those of scientists may have to be rethought. Rather than attempt a detailed assessment of the costs and benefits of government regulation or of the IRB system, I want to clarify the inquiry by drawing a distinction between substantive and procedural government regulatory policies. Objections to government regulation often do not distinguish between these two kinds of regulatory policies, but since the costs and benefits of each differ, the distinction is crucial if research regulatory policy is to be evaluated properly.

Substantive Policies

One way in which government might regulate research is to prescribe norms or standards, in the form either of rules or principles, for research with human subjects. The standards could be hortatory or mandatory, with penalties for violation, and they could be implemented through a variety of prior or after-the-fact enforcement mechanisms. Indeed, the federally mandated IRB system consists in part of a set of designated substantive standards for the conduct of research, which institutions receiving federal research funds apply through IRB review to research that they sponsor or conduct. The substantive standards for research contained in the federal regulations state that research with human subjects should respect the rights and welfare of subjects by obtaining legally effective informed consent and by not imposing risks incommensurate with the benefits of the research to the subject and others.[22]

Persons who object to governmental regulation of research as a matter of policy may object to these substantive policies on two grounds: (1) the state should not set substantive standards for research, even research that it funds; and (2) the standards set do not properly balance the interests of subjects and the scientific and social interest in new knowledge.

Objections based on the first ground, the fact that government is setting substantive standards, do not seem persuasive, for the benefits of government action in designating standards appear to outweigh the costs. As noted earlier, research interactions may affect the interests, autonomy, and rights of subjects and others in morally significant ways, which researchers, with their interest in producing knowledge, may ignore or undervalue. Since researchers alone or through professional self-regulation[23] cannot assure adequate regard for these interests, it is appropriate, if subject interests are to be protected, that the state promulgate rules and standards for researcher-subject interactions. It is particularly appropriate that government designate substantive norms for publicly funded research, but there is a role for government articulation of substantive research norms even in privately funded research. Governmentally prescribed standards should more accurately reflect community values about priorities between researcher and subject interests than standards devised by researchers alone. Given the societal interest in how researcher-subject trade-offs are resolved, and doubts about the ability of researchers to reflect accurately the community consensus, the claim that researchers rather than government should set the norms for conducting science is simply not persuasive.

But while the government may legitimately and appropriately set norms for researcher-subject interactions, the second objection challenges the substantive validity of the norms selected. Here the claim is that the norms overprotect (or underprotect) research subjects, and thus give inadequate (or more than adequate) weight to the valid interests of scientists and the beneficiaries of scientific knowledge.[24] But while state-set substantive norms could be unreasonably skewed in favor of (or against) subjects, it is difficult to see that this is the case with the risk-benefit and consent rules of the federal regulations. They incorporate norms of respect for persons and nonmaleficence found in research codes, legal policies, and generally accepted morals of the community concerning harm, consent, and privacy.[25] True, compliance with the norms could prevent use of research techniques that may be more efficient and preferred by researchers and might indirectly prevent some kinds of research altogether. But that is precisely the point of the norm—to express a communal preference for subject welfare over the benefits of unrestricted research. Objections to the substantive norms must therefore be directed to the normative conclusion that the rights and welfare of subjects are more important than unrestricted research. One might, for example, argue that the consent norm undervalues the benefits of the research thereby prevented, and that using subjects against their will is justified by the importance of the knowledge gained. However, unless the gain is very great relative to the loss of autonomy, it is unlikely that the community will accept norms that give higher priority to science than to respect for subjects.[26]

Another kind of objection to the substantive norms could be that the norms are inapplicable because the research impinges only trivially or not at all on the interests and values they seek to protect. Thus many social scientists argue that written prior consent should not be required for telephone interviews, household surveys, observation studies, secondary data analysis, and many kinds of fieldwork because subject autonomy is not implicated by the research maneuvers in ways that prior written consent could avoid. If their claims are true and there are ways to make the substantive standard more precise without impeding its effectiveness for the research that is problematic, the solution is to exempt these activities from the reach of the substantive standard.

In sum, whether government-prescribed substantive standards for research are good policy depends on an ethical evaluation of trade-offs between researcher and subject interests that they incorporate. Objections based on the fact of government involvement will be less persuasive than objections that the norms are unnecessarily broad or insensitive to the burdens they impose on science. The recently revised HHS regulations, which exempt certain categories of research from mandatory review and allow expedited review of other research, seem better attuned than the previous federal regulations to the varying impact of subject interests in different research settings.[27] In general, researchers have acquiesced in the value trade-offs of the federal norms, for they too share in the community's normative consensus that subject autonomy and welfare is a value greater than research efficiency.

Procedural Policies

Another way in which government might regulate research is to require that researchers or research institutions follow certain procedures to assure implementation of the substantive norms. Procedural policies assume the existence of a body of research norms, but are logically independent of who sets the substantive norms or the values that the norms reflect. The government could require implementing procedures even if professional groups, institutions, or researchers themselves decided on the norms. Since the purpose of government-imposed procedural policies is to assure that substantive norms are in fact followed in practice, the main policy question is whether the costs of the implementing procedure are greater than the gains in increased compliance from use of this procedure.

The IRB system required of institutions receiving federal research funds is, as should be clear, a procedural system for implementing substantive research norms. Institutions, in return for federal research funds, appoint a review board and delegate to it power to review research and to modify or stop studies that do not meet the institutionally adopted federal norms of consent and risk.[28] The investigator is required by the institution (and by the federal government if requesting federal research funds) to obtain IRB certification that his or her research methods meet these norms. IRB review is thus a mechanism for assuring compliance with ethical norms for the conduct of research. The investigator who fails to submit to the IRB process or who ignores its restrictions risks institutional sanctions and, in federally funded research, the loss of research funds.

As a procedure for implementing substantive norms, the institutionally based prior review of the IRB system has distinct advantages over either noninstitutional prior review, or after-the-fact review. Compared to noninstitutional prior review, such as review by a government or community review board, an institutional review system is probably cheaper and easier to run, less likely to induce hostility from investigators, and more likely to be attuned to the problems of conducting research in particular institutions. After-the-fact review, on the other hand, whether or not institutionally run, is less likely to prevent ethical violations in advance. Moreover, it faces the dilemma either of reviewing all research that has occurred, which could be costly (though it may serve monitoring functions), or reviewing research on a selective basis, and thus overlooking some individual norm violations. Selective after-the-fact review is particularly likely to miss norm violations where review is triggered by complaints of alleged violations, for people other than the investigator are rarely in a position to identify violations, and even then may lack incentives to complain. An institutional prior review system thus can be preventive and educative in ways that after-the-fact review cannot. Moreover, it applies across the board and does not depend for its triggering upon an aggrieved subject. Conducted by colleagues close to the situation, it is less rigid and distant than noninstitutional review, and may be a useful policy device to assure that the substantive research standards are followed in practice.[29]

Overinclusivity.   Despite these advantages over after-the-fact and non-institutional prior review, a procedural policy of prior institutional review has costs that must be carefully examined in assessing its merits. One significant cost arises when the procedural policy requires, as the IRB system now does, prior review of all research with human subjects occurring at an institution. While such a blanket policy assures that all research is reviewed, and thus minimizes the chance that research detrimental to subjects will escape review, it exacts a high cost in the time of researchers and board members. Researchers must prepare and submit proposals, suffer delays, make revisions, and the like for every research project, whatever the risks to subjects or chance that the researcher will ignore the applicable norms. Similarly, board members, who serve without pay at the cost of time taken from other activities, must review every project, and because of the workload may end up spending less time on those projects that warrant closer scrutiny. Some kinds of research, however, involve such minor or negligible risks that the costs to subjects of norm violation may be of no great concern. In these cases the added protection review provides to subjects may not justify the costs.

There is growing consensus[30] that the IRB system has been overinclusive in requiring review of all research with human subjects, regardless of the risk and the relationship between subject and investigators, and that sharper lines that exclude low-risk research from review altogether and require expedited review of other research should be drawn. Refining the category requiring prior review should reduce some of the burden of overinclusivity on researchers and reviewers and enhance the credibility of the system. Since a catalogue of research risks by severity is possible, the exemption of certain kinds of low-risk research from mandatory review in the current federal regulations is generally justified. While institutions should continue to regulate some of the exempted research, they need not require complete IRB review in every case.

Procedural Due Process for Investigators. Once IRB prior review is modified to reflect the low-risk nature of some social science research, the main problem with a prior institutional review procedure for implementing substantive norms is the possibility of arbitrary actions. IRBs have authority, derived from the institution's legal authority over research that its staff conducts, to restrict, modify, delay, or even stop a research project. Since the substantive standards leave much room for the play of discretion, and IRBs are not easily held accountable for their decisions, arbitrary or improper IRB action is possible.

The frequency of IRB arbitrariness, however, has probably been exaggerated, and is not a sufficient reason to eliminate the entire system. IRBs could, for example, arbitrarily weigh risks and benefits and prohibit research from occurring at all. Or they might apply their own personal substantive standards of research ethics, rather than the HEW or institutionally designated standards, as if they decided on the desirability of the resulting knowledge rather than the risks of the research process. IRB members could act like a board of research censors and approve only research that promotes their political and social goals. They could also disapprove projects because they dislike the politics or personality of the researcher.

Such decisions would be corruptions or abuses of the IRB system and are not endemic in a prior review system, particularly one structured like the IRB system to favor researchers. Indeed, there are several features of the IRB system that suggest that arbitrary or corrupt use of IRB power is likely to be rare. IRBs are dominated by peers of the researcher, with only token noninstitutional membership. Both the institutions creating them and board members themselves have strong vested interests in promoting research. Although literal, overcautious, or even corrupt decisions are possible, IRBs have few incentives to be overrestrictive toward research and many incentives to interpret the norms in favor of researchers. The available data on IRB performance supports this impression. The National Commission for Protection of Human Subjects' survey of IRBs found that they rarely stop research outright, and modify proposals only in a quarter of the cases, with nearly all modifications aimed at the wording of the consent form.[31] A more important problem with the discretionary aspects of the IRB sytem may be a structural bias in favor of research, rather than overzealous or arbitrary protection of subjects.

Although the risk of arbitrary IRB action is probably small, and certainly not great enough to warrant scrapping the system altogether, recognizing the rights of researchers to procedural due process in all IRB proceedings would reduce the possibility of abuse. Since IRB decisions can adversely affect careers and access to funds, researchers should be treated fairly in IRB proceedings. Fairness requires at a minimum that researchers be informed of the rules and standards applied by the IRBs and given a chance to respond in person to IRB claims that their research falls short.[32] For example, the mandate, authority and norms to be applied by the IRB should be clearly stated in a charter available to all researchers. Deferral or changes in research proposals should always be based on these written norms, with reasons for finding a violation stated in writing. Investigators should be permitted to appear before the IRB to present their case for using methods found objectionable. A review mechanism outside the institution should be available to appeal claims of arbitrary denial. Providing investigators the procedural due process that they deserve should deter arbitrary IRB decisions and quiet fears about political abuse.[33]

Conclusion

The important issues about the IRB system and social science research thus involve questions of policy and prudence, and not legitimacy and rights. Agencies funding research, and the institutions hiring researchers, may, without violating academic freedom or free speech, require that researchers follow procedures to minimize the costs to subjects of the research that they conduct. Since they are not obligated to fund any research at all, they are not obligated to permit the research that they do fund to occur without restrictions on research methods. The reasonableness or appropriateness of research restrictions thus involves the prudential question of what policies will adequately protect subjects while minimizing the costs (including the costs to researchers) of doing so. This question requires, in turn, decisions about substantive ethical norms for regulating the researcher-subject transaction, and about procedures for applying these norms in practice.

The IRB system represents one policy choice among many available procedures for implementing ethical norms in the practice of research. Its premise is that issues of consent and harm arise frequently enough to justify a prior institutional peer review system to assure compliance with ethical norms. But the risks to subjects in many kinds of social science research are so slight or trivial that the costs of prior IRB review of all research is not justified. If researchers do not significantly implicate subject rights and welfare, there is little reason to require them to go through a procedure designed for situations where subjects can be harmed. The problem is to identify those categories of research which, because of the minimal risk they pose, may be exempted from review altogether or subjected to an informal, expedited review procedure without substantial loss in subject protection.

The views of social scientists are relevant here, but ultimately the question requires a community judgment about the morality of research interactions in varying situations of relative power between subject and researcher. The line-drawing necessary here will not please everyone. Reasonable people will differ over how important individual autonomy and privacy are relative to research. In addition, the categories drawn will to some extent inevitably be overinclusive (requiring review of research that need not be reviewed) and underinclusive (exempting research that needs review). But with the accumulating experience of IRBs with social science research, there is good reason to think that the federal government and institutions will draw finer lines for mandatory review than they have in the past.

A better-tuned IRB system is in the interests of both subjects and researchers. In the final analysis, ethical research practice depends on the administrative structures devised to implement the ethical norms that we want researchers to follow.

Notes

1. Ithiel de Sola Pool, "Prior Restraint," *New York Times*, December 16, 1979, p. E-19; idem, "The New Censorship of Social Research," *Public Interest* 59 (Spring 1980): 56–68; E. L. Pattullo, "Who Risks What in Social Research," *IRB: A Journal of Human Subject Research* 2 (March 1980): 1–3, 12; Lauren H. Seiler and James M. Murtha, "Federal Regulation of Social Research," *Society*, November/December 1980, pp. 23–31.

2. While the examples in the text involve biomedical research, the same point applies to social science research. The federal funds that have supported countless repetitions of the Milgram obedience studies might well produce greater social utility if spent in other social or biomedical research.

3. Herbert C. Kelman, *A Time to Speak: On Human Values and Social Research* (San Francisco: Jossey-Bass, 1968); Donald P. Warwick, "Types of Harm in Social Research," pp. 101–24 in this volume.

4. For a useful discussion of the problem, see David H. Smith, "Scientific Knowledge and Forbidden Truths," *Hastings Center Report* 8, no. 6 (December 1978): 30–35.

5. John A. Robertson, "The Scientist's Right to Research: A Constitutional Analysis," *Southern California Law Review* 51 (1979): 1203–81.

6. *Virginia State Board of Pharmacy v. Virginia Citizens Consumers Council, Inc.*, 425 U.S. 748 (1976); *Procunier v. Martinez*, 416 U.S. 396 (1974); *Martin v. Struthers*, 319 U.S. 141 (1973); *Stanley v. Georgia*, 394 U.S. 477 (1969); *Lamont v. Postmaster General*, 381 U.S. 301 (1965).

7. For a philosophical discussion of the distinction between negative and positive rights, see Gerald Macallum, "Negative and Positive Freedom," *Philosophical Review* 76 (July 1967): 312–14.

8. This is true even if the citizen is indigent and is unable to travel to Washington at all without government help.

9. The government's failure to fund, or its decision to deny access to persons under its control, may mean that the research will not occur. But since the right to research is only a negative right, denial of funds or access is not a denial of the researcher's rights, as it would be if the right were a positive one.

10. This statement is true as long as the institution has imposed the restrictions in accordance with faculty or staff governance procedures incorporated into the researcher's employment contract with the institution. See John A. Robertson, "The Law of Institutional Review Boards," *UCLA Law Review* 26 (1979): 511–16.

11. 42 U.S.C. §2891 (a) (1976). The current federal regulations have retreated from requiring IRB review of all research conducted or sponsored by an institution regardless of funding source. Now the institution must in its assurances to HHS only provide "a statement of principles governing the institution in the discharge of its responsibilities for protecting

the rights and welfare of human subjects of research conducted at or sponsored by the institution regardless of source of funding" (45 C.F.R. 46.103 [b] [10]).

12. Further argument for this assertion may be found in Robertson, "The Law of Institutional Review Boards," pp. 506–10.

13. Ibid., p. 500; William Van Alstyne, "The Demise of the Right-Privilege Distinction in Constitutional Law," *Harvard Law Review* 81 (1979): 1439, 1445–57.

14. The distinction is between researchers who on their own time outside their institutional duties conduct research and those who conduct research on time or in facilities funded by their employing institution. The institution may generally exercise no control over the former, though it may over the latter.

15. For further discussion of the legal standard for state restrictions on publication, and hence on research necessary for publication to occur, see Robertson, "The Scientist's Right to Research," pp. 1248–52.

16. To be valid, a governmental restriction on research methods in privately funded research must "further an important or substantial government interest . . . unrelated to the suppression of free expression," with any content restriction incidental to achieving the governmental interest involved. *United States* v. *O'Brien,* 391 U.S. 367, 376 (1968); *Procunier* v. *Martinez,* 416 U.S. 396 (1974).

17. Concerns such as confidentiality may be considered concerns about research methods, since the harm occurs from violation of a condition—an explicit or implicit pledge of confidentiality—under which the research occurred, rather than from the applications which the resulting knowledge made possible.

18. One exception may be laws which a few states have enacted to protect research subjects in all research, regardless of whether the state has funded it. See New York Public Health Law, §2440–2446 (McKinney); Wisconsin Statutes, § 57.61 (1978).

19. A case illustrating the point with journalists rather than social researchers is *Le Mistral, Inc.* v. *CBS,* 61 App. Div. 2d 491, 402 N.Y.S. 2d 815 (1978) (damages awarded to restaurant against television station for entering restaurant without consent, with cameras rolling to record health code violations).

20. Jay Katz, ed., with the assistance of Alexander Morgan Capron, and Eleanor Swift Glass, *Experimentation with Human Beings* (New York: Russell Sage Foundation, 1972), pp. 67–109. The law enacted after the study prohibits recording of jury proceedings even with the consent of all other jurors. However, it does not prevent jurors from talking to researchers after the verdict, or jurors from making written notes of their experience as they go along.

21. An illustration of this power may be drawn from the film of Heinrich Boll's, *The Lost Honor of Katharina Blum,* which shows an aggressive journalist pretending to be a doctor to get a story from a dying woman. A newspaper publisher would clearly be within his legal authority in prohibiting its reporters from using unethical reporting techniques.

22. 45 C.F.R. § 46.102(b) (1977).

23. For the defects of professional self-regulation of research activities, see William Blackstone, "The American Psychological Association Code of Ethics for Research Involving Human Participants: An Appraisal," *Southern Journal of Philosophy* 13 (Winter 1975): 407–18; J. Galliher, "The Protection of Human Subjects: A Re-examination of the Professional Code of Ethics," *American Sociologist* 8 (August 1973): 96.

24. Although this article is considering the substantive norm from the perspective of the researcher, the text states the point in the alternative to remind the reader that the substantive norms could be written in favor of researcher interests. Indeed the procedures for implementing these norms seem heavily weighted toward researcher interests. See note 30 below.

25. The federal research regulations, for example, follow very closely such influential ethical codes as the Nuremburg Code, reprinted in Katz et al., *Experimentation with Human Beings,* pp. 305–6. For legal sources, see George Annas, Leonard Glantz, and Barbara Katz, *Informed Consent to Human Experimentation: The Subject's Dilemma* (Cambridge, Mass.: Ballinger Publishing Co., 1977).

26. However, some limited exceptions to the substantive norms would probably be accepted when the benefit of honoring the norm is greatly outweighed by the benefits to others of violating it. For an illustrative instance, see Norman P. Fost and John A. Robertson, "Case Study: Deferring Consent with Incompetent Patients in an Intensive Care Unit," *IRB: A Journal of Human Subjects Research* 2 (August—September 1980): 5–6.

27. 45 C.F.R. 46 (January 26, 1981). While the exemptions from mandatory review seem generally justified, in some respects they are broader than warranted, as in not requiring review of surveys or interviews concerning sensitive matters where the answers will not be recorded in identifiable form (45 C.F.R. 46.101[b]). Institutions retain authority to regulate such research, and would be justified in requiring IRB review of some research now exempted from mandatory review.

28. Since it is often forgotten, it is worth repeating that the IRB is a creature of the institution creating it and not an agent of the federal government. Though institutions usually set up IRBs in response to federal funding requirements, the IRBs come into existence and have powers only if the institution decides to create them. Though the federal government sets minimum standards for their structure and operation, institutions retain great discretion over composition, procedures, powers, and other aspects of IRB operation.

29. The danger, of course, is that a review structure so heavily oriented toward researchers may underprotect subjects. For a fuller discussion of this problem, see Robertson, "The Law of Institutional Review Boards," pp. 544–49.

30. National Commission for the Protection of Human Subjects of Biomedical and Behavioral Research, *Report and Recommendations: Institutional Review Boards*, DHEW Publication no. (OS) 78-0008 (1978), pp. 30–35. The consensus is also reflected in the regulations proposed on August 14, 1979, 44 Fed. Reg. 47698, § 46.101(c). See also Judith P. Swazey, "A Commentary on Exempted Research and Responses to DHEW's Proposed Regulations," *IRB: A Journal of Human Subjects Research* 2 (March 1980): 4–6.

31. National Commission for the Protection of Human Subjects of Biomedical and Behavioral Research, *Report and Recommendations: Institutional Review Boards*, pp. 60–61.

32. *Mathews* v. *Eldridge*, 424 U.S. 319 (1976). For a discussion of the extent to which investigators currently have a legal right to procedural due process before IRBs, see Robertson, "The Law of Institutional Review Boards," pp. 516–24.

33. Indeed, the fears expressed by de Sola Pool, Seiler and Murtha, and others (note 1 above) that IRBs will stop research on political grounds has been greatly exaggerated. IRBs have a very different mandate, structure, and process than the Loyalty Security Boards that were part of the McCarthy witch-hunt era. See David Caute, *The Great Fear: The Anti-Communist Purge under Truman and Eisenhower* (New York: Simon & Schuster, 1978), pp. 271–73.

18

Modesty Is the Best Policy:
The Federal Role in Social Research

E. L. PATTULLO

Fifteen years ago the federal government issued regulations intended to protect human subjects involved in biomedical and behavioral research. It was high time, and few questioned the necessity. In August 1979, the Department of Health, Education, and Welfare (now the Department of Health and Human Services—HHS) proposed to extend its controls to studies, in any field, that seek "generalizable" knowledge by methods that include the collection of information by which individuals, living or dead, may be identified. The principal instrument of control is prior review and approval of research by an Institutional Review Board (IRB).[1]

Not until January 1981, did the departing Carter administration finally withdraw this proposal, replacing it with final regulations of much more limited scope. For eighteen months, hundreds of individuals, some principally concerned with maintaining a healthy research enterprise and some alarmed at basic incursions upon accustomed freedoms, devoted thousands of hours to persuading those who write the regulations that single-minded concentration on precluding every possibility of harm to subjects had produced a proposal that threatened much greater social harm than any it might possibly prevent.

Had HEW proceeded as it intended in 1979, a political scientist perusing the *New York Times* for information about individual politicians, and seeking to form a general conclusion, first would have had to get permission from the university's IRB. A sociologist studying leisure activities would have been required to obtain prior approval before making systematic notes on Carl Yastrzemski's behavior at Fenway Park. A student of contemporary history would have violated the proposed regulations had he or she interviewed members of Congress, intending to identify them, without the board's approval.

In this mistaken effort to protect "subjects" from minuscule possibilities of harm that those same subjects—like all of us—risk and suffer daily in other areas of life, the government was on the brink of a most dangerous encroachment upon freedom of speech. Nor was it only the *proposed* regulations that went too far; the rules in force for the past six years interfere with relationships between consenting adults in a way that none would tolerate were the activities not characterized as research.[2]

In this paper I will argue that the protection of research subjects is the shared responsibility of subjects, scientists, and government, and that the role of the latter should be confined to circumstances that present risks of harm that are unfamiliar or tangible in their consequences. Legal restraints to prevent moral harm should be avoided by a nation that values individual freedom.

Historical Background

For those unfamiliar with the problem, let me sketch the background and give one view of where we are and how we got there. (A fuller and less polemical account may be found in Bradford H. Gray's essay; see also Richard A. Tropp's contribution for a view from within the regulatory agencies.) In 1963 public attention focused on a research project directed by a nationally famed cancer researcher at the Jewish Chronic Disease Hospital in New York.[3] "Live cancer cells," said the headlines, had been injected into elderly, noncancerous patients, many of whom were not competent to give free and informed consent. A member of the hospital's board, outraged at the apparently cavalier procedures and frustrated by the adminstration's response to his objections, appealed to the courts for help. At about the same time, Timothy Leary and Richard Alpert, soon to become gurus of the drugs-for-fun movement, created a storm of controversy with their free-wheeling dispensation of psilocybin and LSD to willing (all too willing) Harvard and Radcliffe undergraduates.[4] Initially, in that innocent era, they identified their endeavor as "research" and cast the students in the role of "subjects." Then, in the early seventies, it was revealed that U.S. Public Health Service officials, for the preceding forty years, had allowed a group of recognized syphilitics, all black and all poor, to go untreated as part of a long-term study of the effects of that disease.[5]

Though the most shocking events and the most lurid fantasies about future possibilities had to do with research in the biomedical sciences, there were instances also of objectionable procedures being used in psychology and the social sciences. In 1953, a University of Chicago study (conducted by a future U.S. attorney general), which involved recording federal jury deliberations without the knowledge of the jurors, brought congressional hearings and legislation intended to preclude a repetition.[6] At Yale, Stanley Milgram's "obedience to authority" experiments outraged many. In these studies some subjects, given the illusion that they were inflicting painful electric shock on others, were reduced to tears and visible paroxysms of remorse.[7] Parents and teachers in schools across the country encountered projects (often involving sex questionnaires) to which they took vehement exception, perceiving that innocent pupils were being misused by pseudoscientific investigators with a personal, social, or political axe to grind.[8] Nor were the parents and teachers always mistaken, though sometimes their own motivations were suspect.

These and other dramatic and well-publicized episodes occured against a backdrop of vivid memories of the Nazis' use of Jews and other ethnic minorities as human sacrifices to a science gone insane. The incidents demonstrated that well-meaning physicians and scholars were sometimes capable of shocking insensitivity toward the dignity and welfare of patients and subjects, especially prisoners, the poor, and the incompetent. At about the same time, and for unrelated reasons, the hitherto sacrosanct status of science was being called into question. We were moving into an era of uncommonly active concern for the rights and welfare of segments of the population that had traditionally been neglected or exploited. The pressure for governmental regulation of the research process rose rapidly, the demand seeming the more legitimate because a large proportion of the work in question was directly supported by federal funds.

As a result, the surgeon general of the United States issued regulations in 1966 governing the use of subjects by scientists whose work was funded by the National Institutes of Health. A vast majority of those grants went to the bio-medical sciences, and most of the projects that involved human subjects were of a kind that included physical interventions, usually carried out in a laboratory, clinic, or hospital. But NIH also supported a modest amount of work in the social sciences, one discipline of which—psychology—bridges the social and natural sciences; research in that field may include physical interventions or may consist simply of questions and answers—conversation of a kind. What to do? The easiest course for the agency was to make its regulations applicable across the board, ignoring basic differences in the ways in which subjects were involved in various kinds of research. That is the course the surgeon general chose. It was made yet easier, in that era when the federal gravy train was really rolling, because social scientists, eager to catch a ride, positively yearned to be identified with natural scientists. Even the anthropologists, their work supported by the National Institute of Mental Health, thought Institutional Review Board perusal of their research a small price to pay for the status (and fiscal rewards) of being lumped together with more macho trades. Members of that particular profession, at just about that time, had quarreled bitterly over Project Camelot, a Department of Defense sponsored study of a number of South American countries. Some anthropologists concluded from this experience that their work could be misused and that, in certain circumstances, the happy villagers who innocently cooperated with them might suffer for their pains.[9]

Thus, a combination of bureaucratic sloth, social science vanity, and honest concern for the laymen involved in social research led to easy acceptance of subject-protection regulation in areas of study far removed from the bio-medical one in which abuse was most feared. In addition, the scope of the regulatory activity spread slowly, moving like Down East fog, from a scarcely perceptible mist to an impenetrable shroud.

Title 45, Part 46, of the *Code of Federal Regulations* (revised as of November 6, 1975) says that "no activity involving human subjects to be supported by [HEW] grants and contracts shall be undertaken unless an Institutional Review Board has reviewed and approved such activity." Until a few years ago, paying close attention to those words, most universities operated a two-track system that obscured many problems inherent in the rules because the absolute requirement for prior review was applied only to projects funded by HEW. But then came the National Research Act of 1974 that combined with the HEW regulations in such a way as to extend the requirement for IRB approval to *all* biomedical and behavioral research involving human subjects done at an institution that *ever* receives HHS support for such work. (The new regulations issued on January 26, 1981, again specifically limit the applicability of the rules to research supported by HHS and exempt entirely most work in the social sciences and much that is physically noninvasive in other areas.)

Throughout, the rulemakers have proceeded on the basis of a syllogism that appears to be this: (1) Research can harm subjects; (2) Only impartial outsiders can judge the risk of harm; (3) Therefore, all research must be approved by an impartial outside group. Let us consider where that syllogism has led. A strange case came to my own IRB some time ago (fortunately, we did not have to resolve it because the student who proposed the study, incredulous at our existence, sloped off in some other direction). The investigator was an undergraduate editor of the *Harvard Crimson* who sought permission to proceed with a "participant observer" study of the process by which the paper's editorial group reached decisions. That is, he would keep his eyes and ears open and make systematic observations of how he and his friends went about their business. The work was to be his senior thesis in psychology, and thus, *research*. His fellow editors therefore became his *subjects*, and review and approval by the board was legally prerequisite to his doing the study. Had he proposed to undertake precisely the same inquiry in his role of reporter, rather than in that of scholar, it would not have occurred to anyone to require that he obtain the university's permission.

In addition to looking at the poor *Crimson* editor's aborted thesis, our board has had to make arrangements to provide timely review for scores of miniprojects undertaken by undergraduates as part of their regular course work, most of which involve using each other as subjects. These studies range from administering Thematic Apperception Tests, to asking each other about political attitudes, to conducting open-ended interviews about family relationships or sexual preferences. (There seems to be rather a lot of the latter!) At the very least, this is a terrible logistical headache. Most students do not pretend to be professional; their plans are seldom worked out very far in advance, and more likely than not the protocol will change completely between breakfast and lunch. In addition to these, we solemnly review such things as a psychophysicist's scheme to recruit sophomores to distinguish beeps of differing tones, a linguist's study of a child's developing speech capacity, a Radcliffe College inquiry into the reasons many women avoid the natural sciences, a graduate student's plan to ask members of the Clamshell Alliance why they joined, and an anthropologist's proposal to live with Eskimos in order to observe their way of life. None of these projects seems to our IRB to present possibilities of the kind of harm that justifies our intrusion into the transaction.

One somewhat unusual episode set me wondering about how differently we perceive identical activities depending on whether or not they are categorized as research. About two years ago I received a call from Richard Tropp, then a member of Secretary Califano's immediate staff at the Department of Health, Education, and Welfare (now HHS). He was advising Mr. Califano about how he should respond to the regulations that other staff members were proposing the department issue in August of 1979. He asked a long series of questions about my experience with our IRB, and the conversation concluded with his request that I send him a letter answering further questions too complex to be dealt with orally. As I sat down, quill poised, it suddenly struck me: "This guy is doing research, and I'm his subject!" My letter to him began as follows:

> Had you been a member of this University and had Mr. Califano asked you to mount the inquiry which led to our recent telephone conversation there would have been a necessary hiatus while you figured out precisely who you wished to interview, how you would approach them, how you would obtain their informed consent, how that would be documented, what questions you would ask, whether you could assure confidentiality and anonymity, and how you proposed to guarantee that assurance. Having worked it out in your own mind you would have had to write it out, persuasively, in the form of an application to our IRB for approval of your research plan. I would then have circulated your application to our scattered members (after chastising you for not planning sufficiently far in advance to be able to wait for a regular meeting). After an uncertain interval, depending on the alacrity of members' responses (and assuming that none perceived risks that had escaped you, e.g., might the respondent's institution be identified somehow and subjected to penalties in consequence of a careless response?), it is to be presumed that a quorum would have approved and that you could proceed. If, in the process of the inquiry, you were persuaded that significant changes in the form of the interviews were desirable (a not infrequent occurrence in research), you would have had to stop and repeat the process in order to obtain IRB review and approval of the change.
>
> A memo for the Secretary by Labor Day? Never!
>
> The above is not an overly exaggerated description of what an [HHS] grantee, as opposed to an [HHS] staff member, would encounter in doing precisely what you are doing. Is it what the government intends? Is it necessary to protect me, your subject?

The Risks of Research and of Everyday Life

In its proposed regulations of August 1979 (now withdrawn), HEW leapt from the frying pan straight into the fire by proposing to extend its rules beyond biomedical and behavioral research and to require prior review of any study in any field when the subjects were identifiable. The error of this proposal lay in its failure to distinguish between the kind of harm risked in some biomedical (and behavioral) research and the kind of harm that can occur in some social research. They are very different, and it is the latter that must be weighed against the harm society risks by imposing prior restraint on the exchange of information.

I am indebted to Dr. Donald Seldin, a former member of the National Commission for the Protection of Human Subjects of Biomedical and Behavioral Research, for the following general schema. It exaggerates by emphasizing polarities, yet is useful in suggesting the several dimensions on which social and biomedical studies may differ:

	Biomedical	Social Science
Subject matter	individual human beings	aggregate human behavior
Intervention	intervention with drugs and physical manipulations	impersonal interview and data collection
Benefits	personal benefit; benefit to others with the same disease; impersonal new knowledge	impersonal new knowledge of an aggregate type
Costs	personal harm	erosion of free speech
Setting	hospital or clinic	university or society at large

Clearly the compartments are not mutually exclusive and instances can easily be found where the two kinds of research converge. Yet, the schema reflects the differences, both prototypical and common, that are significant in considering the ways in which, and the means by which, research subjects should be protected. In personal life each of us does for our own purposes what, in professional life, the social scientist does for a general purpose. Our subject matter is the behavior of those who concern us; our intervention is to ask questions and otherwise seek information; the benefit is our increased understanding; the cost is the pain (for us or others) often resultant from free inquiry; and the setting is our daily lives. As we all speak prose (to the astonishment of some, according to Molière), so we are all social scientists. Those who call themselves such refine the common methods, proceed more systematically, and seek wider goals, but the differences are of degree, not kind. The curing of disease, mending of bodies, and study of man's physical corpus, on the other hand, involve activities that are mostly, to most of us, wholly unfamiliar—just as the hospitals and laboratories in which such activities take place are strange, intimidating settings.

There is a long tradition, reflected both in common law and statutes, that recognizes injury done by one person to another through physical intervention or deprivation. Such injury is palpable and objectively verifiable. Though the damage is often less obvious, legal protections against some kinds of social harm are similarly well established, as evidenced by laws pertaining to libel, slander, blackmail, and contract. To a large extent, redress is available only when the injured party can demonstrate a tangible loss of some kind. Few, if any, have ever been harmed in that way by virtue of participation in social research.[10] To consider the case thus, as Donald P. Warwick makes clear in his contribution to this volume, is to use a narrow definition of harm.[11] Yet such a definition may be useful when we inquire into the role that it is appropriate for the *government* to play in encouraging ethical behavior in the research enterprise. To single out one sphere of social activity and subject it to legal constraints based on a concept of harm that the law does not recognize elsewhere is, at least, unusual. The need should be clear and compelling. Unless the circumstances are plainly unique to research we ought to wonder at the fairness of the action, and it is only prudent to worry about setting a precedent that can be used to justify similar controls over other activities posing similar risks.

In arguing in favor of restricting the government's role, I do not mean to deny the possibility that subjects may suffer real harm by participating in some studies that I would exempt from control. I believe that there should be no required, prior, third-party review of research that uses competent subjects, is not deceitful, and poses no risk of physical harm. This would leave scholars free to do with their subjects the same things the rest of us are free to do with each other in every other area of life. Clearly, that means that a risk of harm remains and that both scholars and subjects will continue to confront the range of ethical issues that all of us face, or refuse to face, daily. They are as relevant—no more and no less—to scientist and subject as they are to teacher and student, merchant and customer, parent and child, husband and wife, to friends, or to strangers. The ethical problems of every social interaction are real, constant, and difficult. In an open society, consensus as to their proper resolution is, probably, never attainable.

While resolutely denying the wisdom of trying (as the government is now trying) to define solutions and impose them on individuals, I do not disagree with those honest ethicists who seek to raise our consciousness and widen our conception of what constitutes an ethical problem. There is a large and growing literature about the moral dangers that inhere in the relationships essential to biographical studies, sociological and anthropological field work, social policy experimentation, political science—every field whose object of study is mankind.[12] Few of the problems detected are entirely new, but they are being seen in a wider perspective that is prompting many to reconsider established habits of inquiry that were long thought unproblematic. If this increased sensitivity on the part of those who make professional ethics their profession can be translated into a general consensus that guides scientists as effectively as did widely shared values in the past, all will gain. If, instead, the impulse is translated into an attempt to impose the values of some on all, much will be lost—morally, scientifically, and socially.

Let us consider, briefly, the intangible kinds of harm that Donald Warwick addresses in his article. (I must note that the cases he mentions are familiar, being the same few repeatedly cited by those who advocate prior restraints on social research. This suggests to me that examples of abuse are rare.) I agree with Warwick that the problem at issue is not one that can be fully resolved by reference to hard data; the nature of the phenomenon is such as to defy objective measurement. That is, of course, amongst the reasons that incline me to argue that government effort to guard against the kind of injury alleged, by imposing third-party control, is ill advised. Not only is the possibility of injury speculative in prospect, but after the fact, the question of whether injury occurred is usually equally speculative. Often it depends entirely on how the putative victim feels; an experience that one individual regards as welcome and salutary may be seen by another as aversive and injurious.

Needless to say, examples of social research can be found that raise questions, at least, in the minds of all but a few. By now the classic case in psychology has become the "obedience to authority" studies conducted by Stanley Milgram. That many of his subjects endured the harm of an emotionally stressful experience is undeniable and is attested to, in graphic terms, by Milgram's own account of the work. Prompted in part by the ethical controversy aroused by the studies, Professor Milgram persuaded a surprising ninety-two percent of his subjects to report, some time later, their assessment of the experience, and found that only 1.3 percent regretted their participation while four-fifths believed that further, similar work should be conducted. Warwick dismisses this attempt to disprove psychological injury as lacking in rigor.[13] He is right in the sense that deeper probing of the subjects' psyches might reveal that they were only fooling themselves (and Milgram) in an effort to defend against the discomfort that contemplation of their own experience brings. It is also possible that many learned something about themselves that they have since put to good use, and thus genuinely benefited from participation in the research. Still, as Diana Baumrind has forcefully reminded us, the fact that an imposition finally results in conferring a benefit ("inflicted insight") does not remove the moral taint from the original act.[14]

I have no illusion that in a few sentences I can dissuade any who have already decided that Milgram's study was unethical and unjustified. The question has been argued endlessly; equally honest and ethical people continue to make differing judgments. That, however, confirms my point. The prolonged discussion of the work within psychology (Milgram's experiments were conducted in the early sixties) attests to the fact that ethical concern is not lacking in the profession. The fact that many subjects, many psychologists, and many laymen continue to believe that the knowledge gained is worth the harm done cannot settle the moral argument, but it strongly suggests the danger of settling it by empowering those who judge the case negatively to forbid similar work in the future.

In addition to the possibility of psychological abuse or injury (e.g., Milgram), Warwick discusses six other kinds of harm that might befall individual subjects of social research: death, physical abuse, damaged personal relations, legal jeopardy, economic damage, and lost privacy.

Though the likelihood of the different harms being incurred varies from almost infinitesimal to considerable, none will wholly dismiss any of the possibilities he limns. His discussion is useful, and the responsibility of scholars to do all that they can to protect subjects from such consequences is obvious. In the case of competent subjects invited to participate in research where the objectives and procedures are apparent, however, the very respect for individual autonomy that Warwick invokes argues that scientist and subject should be free to make their own bargain, rather than being denied that opportunity by the paternalistic interventions of others. (I should add that there is nothing in Warwick's paper to suggest that he would necessarily disagree. His purpose is to provide a taxonomy of harms, rather than to describe the means by which they may best be avoided.) Finally, my concern is principally with the role of government in regulating research practices; government has thus far confined itself to measures designed to protect individual subjects, explicitly abjuring any intention to control the consequences that may flow from increased knowledge, so I will not comment on Warwick's discussion of the harm that science and society, as distinct from individual subjects, may suffer from social research.

Most people agree that there is a world of difference between the things that hurt us physically and those that hurt or offend us psychically and socially. That a considerable number of social studies have resulted in subjects experiencing boredom, self-doubt, humiliation, and outrage is unquestionable. Further, it would be surprising if there were none in which breaches of confidentiality, especially, have led to more dire consequences. Still, a lost job can be distinguished from a lost leg. Though neither is desirable, the difference between the two is significant if our concern for protecting subjects is to be matched by a concern for preserving freedom of speech.

We have not yet considered the harm done to subjects that *is* measurable by reasonably objective standards. I cannot have been alone in having taken for granted, during the years we awaited the report of the National Commission for the Protection of Human Subjects and observed the consolidation of federal controls, that undergirding these events was a mountain of solid research establishing the fact of significant injury inflicted upon subjects. The *Belmont Report*[15] was philosophic and confined itself to analysis of the principles applying to research ethics, but the commission's IRB report included fat appendices that were filled with empirical data.[16] For some months after its publication (not wanting, perhaps, to confront the evidence of my colleagues' offenses) I did not even trouble to burrow into the appendices to examine the information I presumed they contained about who had been harmed (and how). I was soundly rebuked for my neglect by an anonymous reviewer for *Science* who, savaging an article in which I had petulantly asserted that I knew of no instances of serious harm being done by research that did not involve physical interventions, sardonically questioned whether I was aware of the "large amount of careful work which has been done on the topic over the past decade." He or she specifically recommended the "hard data, empirical studies" done by the national commission.

Sheepishly, and laggardly, I opened the relevant volume and this is what I found: on the basis of reports from investigators (admittedly a biased group), "harmful effects occurred" in 79 research projects out of a total of 2,384 surveyed, or 3 percent. Of the total, 1,655 were in the biomedical area, and 75 of them (4.5 percent) reported the occurrence of harmful effects, a majority having to do with drug administration. The behavioral sciences accounted for 729 of the total, and "harmful effects occurred" in 4 of these or 0.5 percent. In all of the projects surveyed, 158 subjects were reported to have been harmed. (Unfortunately no data are given on the total number of subjects involved.) The authors say only this about the nature of the harm: "These effects generally were considered trivial or only temporarily disabling. Three investigators reported fatal effects; in each of two projects one subject died and in one project three subjects died. Each of these projects involved cancer research and in two of the projects at least, subjects were in a terminal stage at the time of their participation in the research."[17] So far as I can tell, no information was collected about projects in fields outside the biomedical and behavioral sciences, e.g., history, government, or economics.

I repeat, these data were collected from investigators and it would not be surprising if the data reflected their interest in underreporting the occurrence of injury. Nevertheless, do not such figures in the largest—indeed, so far as I know the only—systematic inquiry into the dangers of research give reason to wonder? Thousands of hours and millions of dollars are being diverted from the pursuit of knowledge to the tasks involved in ensuring prior review of proposed studies. (The 1974–75 costs at the University of California, Berkeley, were estimated to be $100,000.)[18] HEW's aborted proposal of August 1979, would have decreased this somewhat by exempting certain kinds of work, but would have also expanded it manyfold by extending the requirement for review beyond biomedical and behavioral science to all scholarly disciplines. Is it naive to think it absurd (and frightening, given the source of the proposal) that so complex a system should have been proposed in the absence of any more substantial demonstration of need than I have just reviewed? I resonate to the despairing wail of sociologist Howard Higman of the University of Colorado, "So, in 30 years of no problems, suddenly we have an enormous solution!"

An alarming development can been seen in several of the essays that appear in this collection. Both Bradford Gray and John A. Robertson, for instance, appear to be moving toward a position (or has it always been so?) that obviates the need for those who advocate external control to justify it by demonstrating that subjects may suffer injury. The appeal instead is to an ideal standard of ethical conduct that, it is urged, should be made mandatory. The harm to be avoided is simply the violation of that standard. For example, I as subject must be adequately informed of your purpose and give my consent before you ask me a question; otherwise my autonomy has been compromised—which Gray and Robertson find offensive whether or not, in the circumstance, it offends either you or me. If this example caricatures their position it does not misrepresent it. Such a stand drastically changes the nature of the debate, and an appeal to the research record revealing scant evidence of harm is of no avail. The stark proposition now is that society should determine and impose ethical standards to which private citizens must conform. Mr. Robertson is at pains to trace the ways in which this can be done without offense to constitutional guarantees,[19] and I have no legal grounds on which to dispute him. However, the problem then becomes, as he suggests, one of prudence: is it wise for a society that values freedom of conscience to legislate ethical standards in the absence of clear and present dangers?

Our Mutual Interest in Discovery

I agree with Robertson that a distinction should be made between the government's responsibility for research that it sponsors and research supported by private agencies. Like him, I find it hard to question the right of a sponsor to set almost any conditions it chooses for work it commissions. Between 1966 and 1974, when HEW regulations were applicable only to research supported by HEW, it was appropriate to debate the wisdom of the rules but not their legitimacy. An excellent case can be made that the best way to promote fruitful basic research is to minimize external control of both objectives and methods; however, that is for the sponsor to decide.

But the fact that, for six years, the government has required university scholars to submit almost all of their research for prior review, however financed, has meant that a single sponsor's control extends to most of the basic (and much of the applied) research done in the United States. Giving the government control over all such research is very different from acknowledging its right to set conditions for the research it funds. It is my impression that few yet understand the full implications of the difference. To date the argument about it has been confined to that segment of the population that actively observes or participates in the research process. If the legitimacy of government control over so broad an area is accepted, however—and when, further, it is recognized that the interactions and problems in social research are often indistinguishable from those in other social activities—then a strong precedent will exist for imposing standards of ethical conduct in other areas that traditionally have been the preserve of individual conscience.

Particularly obvious is the case of the press and the business of gathering and reporting news. I have already mentioned the *Harvard Crimson* reporter who was brought up short when he thought to do as a research project what he might otherwise have done, with no external restraint, as a journalist. To an extent, the two professions (social science and journalism) are simply working different sides of the same street, the difference often being little other than one of perspective. Think about the teams of investigative reporters who, since Watergate, have been so widely admired. Many of these are famous, or infamous, for their penetrating inquiries into socially significant topics, a process frequently involving the use of such investigative methods as hidden cameras, deception of informants, and purloining of confidential documents. In addition to the public service sometimes done, the results of these investigations include blasted careers, emotional trauma, ruined reputations, lost income, prison sentences, and shattered egos—even an occasional suicide has been attributed to them. The psychological and social harm suffered by the subjects, some of whom are innocent of wrongdoing, is apparent, but this is taken for granted as the necessary price to be paid for a free press. While few social scientists would wish to emulate the methods of journalists, many legislators and administrators (and some of the public) appear to believe that far less serious risks are yet too high a price to pay for knowledge about ourselves and society, when it is collected by scholars doing "research."

In considering how best to protect research subjects, it is important to consider also Jay Katz's proposition that at least three parties have equally legitimate interests in the research process: the investigator, the subjects, and society.[20] No question about the enterprise can be answered adequately until the interest of each has been examined.

The investigator's stake in the activity is readily apparent. Its particulars vary greatly, however, ranging from the tepid motivation of a reluctant undergraduate assigned a research paper, through the not dissimilar interest that moves some assistant professors hungry for tenure, to the feverish dedication of an unknown M. or Mme. Curie. It is the immediacy of the investigator's interest that gives us reason to think that he or she cannot always be trusted to weigh fairly the possible consequences of the research for its subjects or for society.

The subject's interest is equally apparent in research that is undertaken principally for the subject's own benefit. A cancer victim may be desperately eager to submit to great risk in a trial that offers the only hope of a cure. In most research, however, the case is seldom so clear and only a small proportion of subjects are sustained by the thought that their own situation will improve should the research succeed. Many, especially in the biomedical area, are motivated by the likelihood that their service as subjects will benefit others. The possibility that the tests or procedures to which one submits may help others in a reasonably proximate future is, for most people, a sufficient reason to justify participation.

This same admirable motive becomes attenuated, without completely disappearing, as one moves across the spectrum into behavioral and social research. The possibility that any given study, or even series of studies, is going to produce a significant social benefit dwindles, and individuals become increasingly dependent on their general respect for knowledge and the possible welfare of others in deciding what interest, if any, they have in serving as subjects. Some would not wish to sacrifice even ten minutes' time for so nebulous and uncertain a good, but many (particularly in light of the limited possibilities for harm and the fact that participation is often intrinsically interesting) are happy to help and pleased to be able to contribute whatever they can.

The interests of society (which, of course, includes the professions) both subsume and transcend those of investigators and subjects. It must determine, through its multiple organs—of which government is but one—what place research shall have in our order of values and how the issue is to be resolved when differing values conflict. Society is avid for knowledge that will benefit particular living individuals, as it is for that which will help generations unborn. Extremely important in our culture is the fact that knowledge is highly valued for its own sake, quite apart from other benefits it may bring.

At this juncture it is apropos to reemphasize one aspect of the history of federal intervention: It did not arise as a result of careful analysis of the several interests involved, but rather as a political response to a handful of notorious cases in which subjects were reportedly mistreated. From the beginning, therefore, government policy contained an understandable bias toward subject protection as opposed to being an evenhanded effort to balance competing, legitimate interests. I would not overstate this suggestion; there was never a time, so far as I know, when either elected officials or administrators were blind to the fact that society and scientists shared the subjects' interest in the research process. Further, individuals whose concern is primarily subject protection can make a good case that in the early regulatory years IRBs were overly solicitous of the scientists' interests. However, unmistakable evidence of the underlying bias is to be seen in HEW's 1979 proposal to extend regulation to the humanities and social sciences, in the absence of popular demand or palpable injury, and on the basis of uncertain legislative authority.

The only reason that society and science and subjects have not suffered more damage than they yet have from federal intervention is that the rules have tended to be honored more in the breach than in the observance. The unsung heroes of the past decade are countless review board members who have had the wit and courage to act on the premise that the rules cannot possibly mean what they say! Yet HEW, basing its original proposal for new regulations on the recommendations of the prestigious National Commission for the Protection of Human Subjects (though distorting these in important respects), would have taken a major step toward eliminating the very ambiguities that have permitted us to act sensibly. To eliminate ambiguities is, of course, the job of the bureaucracy. Thus I find myself in the odd position of arguing that it is the increasing effectiveness of the system that makes it impossible to ignore the dangers implicit in some of our policies. The gradual extension—indeed, the perfectly logical refinement—of regulation has brought us to the threshold of an era in which government control will be an ever-present threat to the integrity of social research.

This conclusion pains me because if we cannot function optimally with federal regulation, neither can we function optimally without a federal presence. Given the collective interest in scientific inquiry (including increasingly urgent questions about the use of some of its findings, as discussed by both Warwick and Robertson), and given the predictable failure of scientists, left to themselves, to understand or protect all of the interests involved, the public has good reason to insist on some government role. It has equal reason—because its interests include, but go far beyond, the protection of subjects—to demand that legislators and officials devise a system of regulation that confines itself to the need and does not unnecessarily impede the research process. I firmly believe this is possible if only those charged with the task will trouble to understand the complexity of the problem. After all, it is simply not the case that the single instrument of control available is prior review. That regulatory mechanism is precisely appropriate to some circumstances. In others, however, it is a foolish impediment, while in still others it is patently inadequate. For instance, problems resulting from breaches of confidentiality seldom, if ever, arise from flaws in the research design; the real dangers lurk in failures of the safeguards that every trained investigator includes in his or her protocols. Prior review helps not one whit to guard against the loose tongue of a careless staff member, nor against the subpoena obtained by a zealous district attorney.

Responsibility for Research Ethics

Unfortunately, some who are concerned with research ethics appear willing to sacrifice all other interests to that of protecting subjects, without sufficient regard to what else may be lost or, even, to the subjects' need or desire for protection. Judith P. Swazey, professor of socio-medical sciences at Boston University and executive director of Medicine in the Public Interest, Inc., is a case in point. Writing in the March 1980 *IRB* and concerned that social scientists' objections to some of HEW's proposed rules might prove persuasive, she could imagine no better alternative than to throw the baby out with the bath! Responding, specifically, to arguments—such as the one I offered above—that there is something amiss when scholars must obtain prior review for activities newspaper reporters undertake daily, she writes, "I would rather see journalists subject to the same types of social controls as are researchers, regarding the protection of human subjects, rather than researchers being given the same 'privileges' as the press.[21] The only such "privilege" claimed thus far by social scientists, so far as I know, is the American citizen's right to free speech. I note with sinking heart that in this volume John Robertson, too, discusses with fine equanimity the conditions under which it would be legitimate to apply to journalists the restrictions now being fashioned for scholars.[22]

Let us return to the syllogism that, I suggested, has underlain federal regulatory policy to date: Research can harm subjects. Only impartial outsiders can judge the risk of harm. Therefore, all research must be reviewed by an impartial outside group in advance. It is apparent that the harm research can do to its subjects falls on a continuum extending from mild affront to sudden death. Therefore, without altering the major premise (research can cause harm) we see it in a different light. Most of the harm encountered in social research is of a kind that we decided long ago must be risked if we are to live as free men and women. I continue to doubt that the Congress ever meant to protect subjects from risks that are inherent in American society, although after reading Bradford Gray's essay in this volume I concede that may be the intention of HHS. A wiser purpose of government would be simply to try to ensure that research does not expose us to unaccustomed risks of harm. The problem then is to find a workable distinction between research that poses unique dangers and that whose risks and harms are familiar.

It is not difficult: federal regulation for the purpose of protecting the rights and welfare of competent subjects should be limited to research that involves the possibility of physical harm, deprives subjects of accustomed resources, or significantly deceives them. While the January 1981 HHS final regulations take a giant step in this direction, they stop well short of accepting it completely.

Note that this proposal leaves under the "prior review" shield all research that poses any risk of physical danger, all research that involves serious deception, and all research that utilizes subjects incapable of making their own decisions. It exposes competent subjects to familiar risks of psychic or social harm on the assumption that they are autonomous individuals and can learn, if they do not already know, that not all scientists are saints. It emphatically does *not* mean that research excluded from prior review will proceed without regard to ethical norms any more than it has in the past.

Often it seems to be forgotten that legal sanctions are but one, and seldom the most effective, means of social control. None of the scholarly professions has ever been wholly bereft of standards of ethical conduct. Few professions (probably fortunately, on balance) have easily available means for drumming out those who offend, and all tend to be overprotective of their members. Yet, it is also true that any who would rise in a profession must be jealous of their reputations and have to be concerned that they not violate the prevailing consensus on ethical conduct. One of the benefits of federal intervention (they do exist, as Bradford Gray has pointed out in an excellent summary in the February 1980 *Hastings Center Report*)[23] has been rapidly rising self-consciousness on the part of scholars about their modes of procedure. This has stimulated a more active interest throughout the scientific community than previously existed, and has caused many to reexamine practices that were long taken for granted. This volume is witness to the fact.

Yet even prior to the present activity, the great majority of scholars shared agreement about ethical standards that did not differ greatly from the agreement prevailing amongst laymen. Ordinarily, within the fields of the social sciences it is taken for granted that one obtains the subjects' consent; indeed, it is usually difficult to proceed without it. Though deception is common in social psychology, that field has also long been riven by debate about its need and ethicality. Few social scientists have ever been unconcerned about protecting the confidentiality of data and ensuring the anonymity of subjects. On the other hand, there are many research circumstances in which neither confidentiality nor anonymity nor formal consent are matters of grave concern (at least to the participants). In such cases investigators tend to ₊worry no more than do their subjects. Of course, individual scholars may become careless. Further, there are always a few who consciously hold to an ethical standard that differs from the prevailing one. Finally, alas, there are some sadly lacking in character.

There is no doubt that adoption of my suggestion for exempting broad categories of research from prior review will mean that a few subjects will encounter harm that might otherwise have been avoided. To accept that risk is to accept the same risk that is the necessary condition of a free society, namely, that men and women will sometimes act foolishly and suffer in consequence. Those who value free speech must advocate such a choice, even knowing that a substantial body of law favors a definition of speech so broad as to leave open the possibility of abuse. As subjects we could be entrapped, exposed, and embarrassed with only the laws of slander, libel, privacy, and contract to protect us. But we are thus exposed already to friends, enemies, journalists, acquaintances, and strangers. Neither history nor any present danger justifies the imposition of prior restraint in the research setting more than in other areas of life.

Conclusion

I have proposed what I believe to be the proper limit of the government's responsibility for securing a high standard of ethical conduct. I have insisted that, traditionally, individual scholars and the professions have been concerned with ethical matters and have generally adhered to a high-standard in practice. I have suggested that research subjects should be prepared, as free women and men, to assume reasonable responsibility for their own protection. What else might be done, by any or all of these, as an alternative to the overexpansion of the governmental role proposed by HEW and favored by some students of research ethics? Amongst the possibilities are the following:

1. Encourage scholarly journals to require that contributors discuss the ethical considerations relevant to their use of subjects, just as a methods section is now customarily required. It is hard to imagine an innovation more effective than this in making such problems salient to all within every profession.

2. In cooperation with investigators, HHS should establish a regular procedure for sampling the experience of subjects in federally supported

research, both of the kind receiving prior review and of the kind that should be exempt from that requirement. If results demonstrate recurring, significant problems in a particular area, the department will have reason to consider remedies appropriate to the need.

3. Charge IRBs with responsibility for disseminating word amongst subject populations that the boards are available to hear complaints about unethical procedures. In addition to any action the sponsoring institutions might take in a particular case, the boards could be required to report annually to HHS on the number and nature of complaints, thus providing another channel to complement the agency surveys suggested above. This procedure would have the additional advantage of giving individual subjects an opportunity to air grievances that are not so serious as to merit resort to the courts.

4. Require IRBs to ensure that all members of their institutions are aware that the board is available to consult on ethical problems whether or not the study requires prior review. Couple this with giving the boards explicit authority to intervene in federally funded research, at their discretion, when they have reason to believe that subjects are at risk.

5. Federal granting agencies should develop a series of discussion papers detailing the ways in which subjects might be affected adversely by participation in the kinds of research they support, and the measures that can be taken to mitigate or avoid such consequences. These materials should be required reading for all grant applicants.

Others, no doubt, can imaging more and better ways of persuading those involved with the use of human subjects in research to consider carefully the moral problems the activity presents. In a nation devoted to freedom of speech and freedom of conscience, that is the appropriate way to address such problems. It is incumbent on those whose special concern is our values to resist the use of government power to impose standards of ethical conduct, except in circumstances where grave danger allows no alternative. Federal control over research ethics should be limited to studies directly sponsored by the government and to practices, peculiar to research, that pose a risk of tangible harm. Few will object if, in addition, the government uses it considerable powers of leadership to promote and encourage the search for an ever higher ethical standard—so long as it resists the temptation to claim ultimate success by enshrining that standard in law.

Notes

1. *Federal Register* 44, pp. 47693, 47695 (August 14, 1979).
2. 45 *Code of Federal Regulations* 46.102(a).

3. Jay Katz, *Experimentation with Human Beings* (New York: Russell Sage Foundation, 1972), chap. 1.

4. J.K. Benson and J.O. Smith, "The Harvard Drug Controversy," in Gideon Sjoberg, ed., *Ethics, Politics, and Social Research* (Cambridge, Mass.: Schenkman Publishing Co., 1967), chap. 5.

5. *New York Times,* July 26, 1972, p. 1.

6. Katz, *Experimentation with Human Beings,* chap. 2.

7. Stanley Milgram, *Obedience to Authority* (New York: Harper & Row, 1974).

8. Charlotte Isler, untitled, *Saturday Review* 5 (February 1966): 64–65.

9. Irving Louis Horowitz, ed., *The Rise and Fall of Project Camelot* (Cambridge, Mass.: MIT Press, 1967).

10. Edward Diener and Rick Crandall, *Ethics in Social and Behavioral Research* (Chicago: University of Chicago Press, 1978).

11. Donald P. Warwick, "Types of Harm in Social Research," this volume, pp. 103–5.

12. E.g., *Bibliography of Society, Ethics and the Life Sciences 1970–80* (Hastings-on-Hudson, N.Y.: Hastings Center, 1980).

13. Warwick, "Types of Harm," p. 106.

14. Diana Baumrind, "Nature and Definition of Informed Consent in Research Involving Deception," in National Commission for the Protection of Human Subject of Biomedical and Behavioral Research, *The Belmont Report, Ethical Principles and Guidelines for the Protection of Human Subjects of Research,* DHEW Publication no. (OS) 78–0014 (Washington, D.C.: Government Printing Office, 1978), appendix, vol. 2.

15. National Commission for the Protection of Human Subjects of Biomedical and Behavioral Research, *Belmont Report.*

16. Idem, *Report and Recommendations: Institutional Review Boards,* appendix.

17. Ibid., pp. 1–73 and 1–74.

18. Eugene J. Millstein, "The DHEW Requirements for the Protection of Human Subjects: Analysis and Impact at the University of California, Berkeley" (Unpublished paper, July 1974).

19. John A. Robertson, "The Social Scientist's Right to Research and the IRB System," this volume, pp. 358ff.

20. Katz, *Experimentation with Human Beings,* pp. 1–5.

21. Judith P. Swazey, "A Commentary on Exempted Research and Responses to DHEW's Proposed Regulations," *IRB: A Review of Human Subjects Research* 2 (March 1980): 6.

22. Robertson, "The Social Scientist's Right to Research," p. 363.

23. Bradford H. Gray and Robert A. Cooke, "The Impact of Institutional Review Boards on Research," *Hastings Center Report* 10, no. 1 (February 1980): 39–40.

19

A Regulatory Perspective on Social Science Research

RICHARD A. TROPP

> *Institutional review committees are essentially autonomous and unregulated bodies who have been given the power to determine morality for all investigators in their institution, with no guarantee of consistency through time or between institutions. . . . The privacy and lack of standardization creates an opportunity for arbitrary and capricious actions by some committees which have the potential for a serious abridgement of intellectual and academic freedom.*

> *For the state to devise a system whereby research faculty are denied the right to freely engage in face-to-face conversations with normal adults is not a matter of ethics, it is a matter of abridging civil liberties. The issue . . . affects the entire academic community. . . . The result has been to categorize college faculty with convicts, prisoners of war, and inmates of internment camps—for who else in the United States must submit their would-be conversations or correspondence to state supported boards of review?*

Under the gun of imminent congressional passage of the National Research Act, and in order to preempt a possible Senate move to include in it mandatory ethical standards governing federally sponsored research, the secretary of

I am grateful to the following for their ideas, support, and tough critique of an earlier version of this paper: Brad Gray, LeRoy Walters, Peter Shuck, Sid Moore, Dave Goslin, Jim McCullogh, Bernard Barber, Bob Boruch, Dave Florio, Mark Frankel, Paul Reynolds, Joan Sieber, Linda Wilson, Bob Bower, Bob Veatch, Hal Edgar, Beth Tanke, Joel Zimmerman, Joel Kavet, and Mick Timpane. I am also indebted to the American Enterprise Institute for Public Policy Research (AEI) for providing an office and encouragement while I was working on this project. The views expressed here are mine alone and not necessarily those either of AEI or of the colleagues who generously provided me with counsel.

The first epigraph is from David J. Kallen and Judith J. Stephenson, "Problems of Obtaining Clearance for Sex Research from University Committees on Human Subjects Investigations" (Revision of paper presented at session on "Problems of Sex Research," Society for the Study of Social Problems, September 1978; preliminary and unpublished, Department of Human Development, Michigan State University), p. 6.

The second epigraph is from Lauren H. Seiler and James M. Murtha, "Academic Freedom versus the IRB System of Prior Review: Examples from Survey Research," Unpublished (June 1979), Queens College, City University of New York, pp. 16–17.

HEW on May 22, 1974, signed a regulation on "Protection of Human Subjects" which essentially transformed the predecessor NIH guidelines into department policy. The regulation was largely a product of the "H" part of HEW, drafted without participation by those HEW agencies which customarily commission social science research products and maintain daily contact with the social science research world.

Under the Senate legislative deadline pressure, the secretary published the regulation even though interagency differences within HEW remained tense and unresolved. It was understood within the department—and alluded to in the regulation's preamble—that further negotiation would follow, to produce a consensus regulation crafted so as to be appropriate for all types of research. The urgency of the issue to the secretary's office waned, however, and that has never happened.

Almost as an afterthought, then—without systematically focusing on the problems raised by federal regulation of social science research—HEW stumbled into the legal codification of 45 C.F.R. 46, "Protection of Human Subjects." Enforcement of that regulation by Institutional Review Boards (IRBs) has now begun to arouse an incipient firestorm in the social science research community (viz., the quotations at the head of this essay).

We will here explore whether there is some fire behind that emotional smoke, and whether the problems created by the regulation are so serious as to warrant its major overhaul. After first briefly establishing the legal context within which policy issues must be framed, we will try to flush out major problems posed by key sections of the regulation, in the order in which those problems would appear to the reader thoughtfully going through the regulation. Crosscutting all of the issues, we will be focusing on three underlying themes:

1.   What are some key differences between social science research and biomedical/laboratory behavioral research which make the current regulation inappropriate to social science research?

2.   What are some of the unintended and perverse effects of treating the two types of research in the same way for regulatory purposes?

3.   What should we do to fix those problems, while vigorously protecting subjects in truly risky research?

The reader may periodically wonder, as he or she goes through this analysis, "How could those people in HEW conceivably have done *this*?" It is helpful, in considering the issues which follow, to remember the accidental nature of the "policy-making process" which produced them.

The Legal Parameters

As we consider the issues raised by the regulation, it is also important to remember the legal constraints within which we operate and which restrict our choices.

First among these constraints is *Crane* v. *Mathews*.[1] In the early 1970s the governor of Georgia decided to require Medicaid recipients to pay a percentage of their medical expenses, in order to discourage them from frivolous utilization of medical resources. The state Medicaid staff discovered that although requiring "copayment" was impermissible as an element of service delivery, it was possible if they called the copayment an experiment and secured from HEW an experimental waiver under section 1115 of the Social Security Act. The theory was that by conducting a "demonstration" or experiment, they would learn the precise level of copayment sufficient to deter frivolous service utilization, but not necessary medical care.

The National Welfare Rights Organization (NWRO) sued on several causes of action, including the allegation that if indeed this was an experiment, and not major change in service delivery cloaked in the guise of research, then it obviously presented risk to the subjects and therefore required prior review by an IRB. A federal district court ruled that the copayment experiment was research, did involve human subjects, and therefore required IRB review. In making that ruling, the court affirmed that the regulation did reach beyond biomedical/laboratory research, and the court's opinion laid out how the regulation was to operate.*

Electing not to appeal the *Crane* decision, HEW—a codefendant in the NWRO suit—thereby elevated it to the status of accepted federal law. The department's acceptance of the district court decision confirmed what had previously been implicit in the regulation: (1) the protections for human subjects were to apply to social science research generally, and to social experimentation in particular, and not, only to biomedical and clinical behavioral research; (2) the threshold question for determining whether a grantee or contractor must establish an IRB is not whether risk to subjects may exist, but simply whether human subjects are involved in the research at all; and, if so, (3) the first question before an IRB is whether or not a particular project does involve risk. It is not within the discretion of a research investigator to decide that a project involving human subjects does not involve risk and, therefore, need not be submitted for IRB review.

Having found that a project does involve risk, an IRB must next consider whether the experimental design can be so modified as to reduce that risk below the "minimal" threshold of ethical acceptability. If the risk can be so

---

*In lieu of appointing his own IRB of persons familiar with social experimentation, the governor turned to an existing Georgia university IRB for review of the co-payment experiment. That IRB, composed of biomedical research specialists and under careful scrutiny by the NWRO, held that the experiment raised an unacceptable level of risk, that no modifications in research design would diminish the risk to the point of acceptability, and that the experiment ought not to proceed. It stopped.

reduced, the IRB need only certify that to HEW, and need not either consider risk-benefit trade-offs or monitor the researcher's process of securing informed consent forms from subjects. If not, the IRB must examine and approve consent and, in theory, monitor the actual securing of consents by an investigator.

Public interest groups such as the ACLU Prisoners' Rights Project, the Mental Health Law Project, and the Children's Defense Fund have quite appropriately seen the broadened human subjects regulation—as explicated by the *Crane* court—as a vehicle for protecting the interests of their constituencies. Like the NWRO in *Crane*, they have used it—mostly by judicious threats to IRBs and to federal funding agencies—to compel changes in welfare reform and health services delivery demonstration projects, on behalf of their clients.

Public assistance client groups, for example, held up the Work Equity Project (WEP) in Minnesota for nearly a year, and pressured the state of Minnesota and the Department of Labor (DOL) into accepting an expensive dozen-page list of conditions* as a prerequisite to their assent to WEP. DOL has considered scrapping major parts† of the demonstration to avoid the acrimonious IRB process, and the local university IRB has vowed that it will never again handle a politically charged issue for the state government. Public assistance directors and governors in other states are refusing to participate in the DOL welfare demonstrations, for fear that they too will be embroiled in a political catfight similar to Minnesota's.

Another legal constraint is the HEW-Labor appropriations bill, which every year has required the secretary to ensure that no HEW (now HHS) funds be spent on "any program, project, or course which is of an experimental nature, or any other activity involving human participants" (i.e., demonstrations and service delivery, as well as research) unless the secretary ensures that informed consent is secured, and sets up the procedures (i.e., IRBs) necessary to enforce that requirement.[2] This rider has annually been inserted in the appropriations legislation governing HHS, Labor, and related agencies, and it is clearly not restricted to biomedical research—or, in fact, to research at all.

The last legal constraint which we need to keep in mind is the application of the civil rights analogy to the protection of human subjects. Some have argued that HHS has no business, and no legal authority for, regulating privately funded or unfunded research in institutions which receive federal funds for other purposes. The same argument was made by those who opposed extension of the civil rights statutes to all parts of a university campus, beyond the departments or projects which actually received federal dollars. They lost in court, several times in several different types of cases, on "equal protection" (Fourteenth Amendment) grounds.

*E.g., an on-site advocate for every welfare client involved in the demonstration.
†E.g., recapture of welfare savings and their rechanneling into social services for the same clients.

That civil rights legal precedent applies exactly to the issues of protection of subjects in nonfederally funded research. The precedent requires that IRBs assert their authority over all research on a campus (or in a private survey research organization) which receives any federal dollars at all. Given the effective scrutiny of the public interest groups, it would be an unwise university which failed to protect privately funded or unfunded research subjects, and it would be an unwise—and inconsistent—department which failed to insist that universities and other research organizations do so.

Having established the legal context, we turn now to the policy issues.

The Scope of Regulatory Jurisdiction

The "Applicability" section of the regulation is all-inclusive, based upon the assumption that—as in the biomedical research model—all categories of social science research may pose risk, and therefore all should be reviewed by an IRB and regulated. Because the assumption is incorrect, we spend IRB time on *pro forma* review of reams of proposals which pose no risk to subjects, while diverting the attention of IRBs from those truly risky categories of proposals in which subjects may need intensive IRB attention to protect their interests.

The Conceptual Problem

We can identify classes of nonrisky social science research that need not be regulated. There are several categories of social science research which are nearly always nonrisky, assuming the use of normal adult populations not in particularly vulnerable situations (not prisoners, clinic or ward patients in the institution conducting the research or being compensated to permit the research, students of the research investigator, military personnel subject to the command authority of the research investigator, alcohol or drug abusers, public assistance or Medicaid recipients when the research focuses on their client status, *inter alia*). These nonrisky classes of research include:

Secondary analyses of data in medical, criminal, education, public assistance, and other records, including secondary analysis for program evaluation, provided that individual identifiers are either not available to the investigator, not collected, or immediately expunged after initial use for research purposes;

Sociological and anthropological observation studies (including ethnography, field research, and folklore) of public behavior, assuming that (*a*) the researcher does not keep identifiers (such as photographs) of persons who engage in stigmatized or illegal behavior, and (*b*) the researcher merely observes his environment (whether unobtrusively or as a participant) and does not alter its natural state in order to study what then happens;

Standardized and criterion-referenced education achievement and aptitude tests, including "competency-based testing";

Most changes in instructional techniques and curriculum design within a single classroom, school, or school district;

Surveys—whether by mail, telephone, or visiting interviewer—provided that they restrict their collection and use of identifiers (as in secondary analysis), and *except* those surveys which ask questions in particularly sensitive areas which may cause unacceptable stress to the respondent (e.g., alcohol or drug abuse, sexuality, family violence, consideration of suicide);

Linguistics, oral history, English, journalism, and other interview studies, with the same two caveats as in surveys;

Standardized psychological laboratory exercises which do not involve deception; and

Demonstration programs on systems of service delivery, where what is being tested is different variations of the *delivery* system and not the actual *service* provided to subjects (e.g., patients).

It must be stressed again, at the risk of redundancy, that these categories of research can be considered nonrisky only when (*a*) they are conducted on normal adults not in any of the classes vulnerable to either explicitly or implicitly coerced consent, and (*b*) identifiers are either not collected or immediately expunged. The exception to the first rule is harmless educational testing and research, which of necessity involves children.

Some biomedical research, such as study of unidentified blood or hair specimens, can also be categorized as nonrisky. Most biomedical research cannot be so classified, however, while in social science research *most* of the categories—within the constraints stipulated above—can reasonably be treated as nonrisky.

The Effects of the Problem

The current "Applicability" section applies itself to social science research as if this difference did not exist, with several effects:

Human Subjects Regulations Often Ignored.   IRB members are not stupid, and are perfectly aware that much social science research is nonrisky. In many institutions, therefore, they simply ignore the regulation on "Protection of Human Subjects," and fail to review most social science research. (In doing so, given the present scope of the regulation, they violate the law.)

With the striking exceptions of NIH, ADAMHA, FDA, and the National Institute of Education (NIE), HHS staff also ignore the regulation with respect to behavioral and social science research. Most agency staffs are unaware that the regulation exists and that it is supposed to be applied to R & D that they support. Even where agency staffs do enforce 45 C.F.R. 46 with respect to grants, they do not generally apply it to contracts. And where they are aware that the regulation is to be enforced as to grants and contracts, they generally do not apply it to their own intramural research —and indeed are generally unaware that they are supposed to. With the exception of FDA (systematically) and NIH (randomly), no agency monitors grantees or contractors to ensure—whatever the proposals at the front end promise to do—*actual* compliance with the regulation.

Researcher Fury at IRB Intrusiveness.   Where IRBs have intensively reviewed social science research proposals, their enforcement of the regulation has aroused unusually strong emotions among research investigators. Investigators offer countless tales of what they experience as harassment and abuse of discretion by IRBs, and stories are legion of research projects which have been abandoned entirely. In some cases, the IRB regulatory process proved unreasonably costly in time and energy, while in other cases IRBs imposed requirements (e.g., written informed consent from aborigines in anthropological field work) which have effectively killed the research.

Focus on Threshold Review of Paper, Rather than Actual Monitoring of Research.   Where IRBs have tried to take the scope of the current regulation seriously and to review all social science research submitted to them, they have been drowned in threshold determinations of whether risk exists and in minor modifications of no-risk or minimal-risk research designs. The cost of this exercise has been that (*a*) they have been unable to focus adequately on the small proportion of research proposals which do seem to present significant risk, and (*b*) they have generally been unable to focus at all on "continuing review" of the actual course of research.

When they do focus on risky research, IRB energies are almost entirely expended on review of research proposals at the front end—before funding. The regulatory requirement of "continuing review" during the course of the research is a myth, and IRBs generally have no idea whether research investigators are doing what they have promised at the proposal stage. The cost of our spending IRB resources on the paper process of review of *all* proposals involving human subjects, however trivial or improbable the possible risk, is that IRBs have no time remaining to check investigators for actual compliance with requirements in those projects which do present significant risk.

IRB members are highly conscious of this problem, and chafe at the requirement that they review all research involving human subjects. They repeatedly request that IRB jurisdiction be narrowed, so that they can spend their resources on protecting the subjects involved in truly risky research.

What Is to Be Done?*

Given the differences between social science research and the kinds of research originally covered by the NIH guidelines, and given our exposition of

*The Secretary of HHS has done most of this, as well as several of the steps recommended in the following sections on "Risk" and "Informed Consent," in a "midnight" final regulation promulgated just before the end of the Carter Administration and published in the *Federal Register* (vol. 46, #16) of Monday, January 26, 1981—after the new president's inauguration—at Part X, pp. 8366–

the unintended and sometimes perverse effects of applying the current regulatory structure to social science research, what we need to do to fix the problems raised by overbroad scope of "Applicability" follows pretty straightforwardly.

We need to deregulate those classes of social science and biomedical research which we can identify as nonrisky, and *focus* IRB energies on (*a*) those classes of research which actually are risky, and (*b*) real-world "continuing review" of risky research, rather than immersion in the process of approval of a flood of paper before funding.

The Timing of IRB Review

The process of some kinds of social science research may be so different from the biomedical model as to *require IRB jurisdiction at very different procedural checkpoints.* The "Applicability" section does not confront this problem.

In anthropological research on sensitive topics (stigmatized behavior, for example), front-end consent is meaningless because neither the researcher nor the subject knows what will happen. Moreover, even if consent is formally secured, the relationship may evolve so that the subject feels unable—to his detriment—to withhold data from the researcher. If there is a need for constraint on the field researcher, the only effective point is during—not before—the research. (But, in the real world, how?)

Survey and depth interview research proposals are frequently funded before a detailed questionnaire is available—the proposal, in fact, is frequently for phase 1 funding of questionnaire design. IRBs cannot effectively review such research designs before the questionnaire is constructed. If they are truly to regulate the exceptional categories of risky survey research, they will have to examine a proposal for a second time after questionnaire construction and before the researcher goes into the field.

In anthropological field research and in survey research before a questionnaire has been constructed, the timing of IRB review at the proposal stage makes that review essentially meaningless. Without a second review when the data necessary to assess risks is available, IRBs cannot regulate those classes of research in which the risks are not evident at the proposal stage.

This could readily be solved by amendment of the "Applicability" section to authorize a second invocation of IRB jurisdiction, for these kinds of research, at that postfunding stage at which the data is sufficient to make real review possible.

---

92. While the new regulation does not resolve most of the issues raised here, it does (1) address the most critical informed consent issues, and (2) make sweeping reductions in the applicability of the regulation to riskless social science research.

The Assessment of Research Risks

The Conceptual Problem

The risks posed by social science research proposals are different from the biomedical model, and require different treatment. Because the regulation fails to define "risk" appropriately, IRBs do some things which they ought not to do, and fail to review some critical risks upon which they ought to be focusing.

In biomedical research, the investigator can generally identify and present to an IRB a limited number of specifiable risks. In much social science research, on the other hand, the possible harms are both infinite and much less specifiable, and without a definition of "risk" it is unclear to both IRB members and research investigators what the standards are against which research risk is to be judged—what we expect of them.

The current uncertainty within the research community about precisely what "risk" means has produced inconsistent interventions by IRBs at different institutions in the research designs of similar projects. An IRB at one institution may require major research design changes by an investigator, while another institution's IRB may approve the same project after only cursory review. One HHS agency may require careful IRB review of projects involving a particular kind of risk, while another agency may treat the risk as minimal and accept cursory IRB review.

Moreover, the same project may be treated by an IRB as if risks to subjects remain even after the research design has been modified in accordance with IRB suggestions, while another institution's IRB may consider all risk to have been eliminated by the same design modifications in the same project. In the first institution, the investigator will have to go through the informed consent disclosure process with his subjects and document that he has done so, while in the second institution the IRB will not check on whether he does or does not solicit informed consent.

One "risk" which presents itself most strikingly—although not exclusively—in social science research is that of breach of confidentiality. Research investigators and IRB members in a recent HEW survey overwhelmingly raised this risk as the most dangerous and the most frequent in social science research. All social scientists and virtually all IRB members contacted* were vehement about the need for uniform confidentiality protections to be incorporated into the regulation on "Protection of Human

---

*This finding, and others recited here but not supported by footnote, are based upon the HEW survey's several hundred conversations with IRB chairmen and members, social scientists, public interest group client representatives, "human subjects," academic experts, HEW funding agency staff, and others. While the sample was by no means rigorously drawn, it was not small.

Subjects," to give precise guidance to researchers on what they are supposed to do about the problem.

Except for the Alcohol, Drug Abuse, and Mental Health Administration (ADAMHA), HEW agencies generally do not require IRBs to include confidentiality protections as part of their review, effectively leaving those protections to the discretion of the research investigator. Although not required to do so, many IRBs have in practice spent much of their time modifying research designs to address this risk. HEW has treated confidentiality on an entirely separate bureaucratic track from protection of subjects, while both the community of social science research investigators and IRB members have experienced confidentiality as a part of the broader human subjects complex of issues. It appears that, by taking the initiative to address the issue on their own, IRBs have gotten out in front of the regulators.

Confidentiality has particularly been on the minds of IRB members reviewing research on illegal and stigmatizing behavior. Some IRBs have barred social science interview research (e.g., prisoner surveys on unreported criminal histories) because the institution cannot offer subjects protection against subpoena. Other IRBs have severely restricted research involving urinalysis and blood specimen study, because pathology reports could yield unanticipated information about illegal drug abuse which the institution then could not protect from prosecutors.

A second risk problem which also presents itself most commonly— although again not exclusively—in social science research is that of risk to the whole community. Members of the community within which research is done may be exposed to risk even though the research is not intended to generate data about their behavior, or to intervene in their lives. For example:

> A housing allowance experiment may drive up apartment rents generally in neighborhoods which house experimental allowance recipients. The effects of the price rise will be felt by nonparticipant neighbors of the subjects, and by those who consider moving into the neighborhood.

> An income maintenance experiment or a welfare reform demonstration project may drive labor supply prices significantly up (if subjects who receive experimental benefits opt out of the labor market) or down (if they keep working, but become willing to take much lower-paying jobs since they have the experimental income supplement). In the first case, nonparticipant employers who are part of the local labor market may be financially harmed (or, at the extreme of the marginal small business, driven out of that labor market); in the second case, nonparticipant employees competing in that labor market will be forced to accept lower wages.

> A police stress demonstration program may affect the whole community's safety, or a police deployment or patrol pattern experiment may transfer some kinds of crime from one neighborhood to another.

A health insurance experiment may increase the price of medical care to nonparticipants in the experimental community, and may both increase the price and decrease the supply of scarce medical resources in neighboring nonexperimental communities. At the extreme, a nonparticipant individual may die as a consequence of being priced out of the market for a scarce life-saving resource, which goes instead to an experimental subject whose purchase of the resource is subsidized by the research.

IRB review at the research institution level is insufficient and inappropriate for research posing risks to whole communities, to a class of persons within a state (e.g., AFDC recipients), or to a class of persons in several states. An IRB cannot do its job if it is restricted by a conceptual framework which sees risk—and the requirement for consent—only in terms of subjects who can be identified at the front end by an investigator.

A third risk issue sometimes arising in social science research on controversial topics is that of the possible harm to a group arising from *publication* or *policy application* of research *results,* as opposed to the traditional IRB focus on risks arising to individuals from the *conduct*—the process—of the research.

Social science research proposals have sometimes been challenged before an IRB on the ground that publication of a research conclusion (e.g., Arthur Jensen's comparative IQ research, or surveys of schoolchildren shortly after the introduction of forced busing within a community) would in itself be harmful to a class of persons (e.g., all blacks nationally, or all black children within a community) or to the whole community. Others have argued the same point with respect to policy changes that the government might make based upon anticipated research results (e.g., AFDC changes based upon an income maintenance or welfare cash-out demonstration project). Where this kind of issue has arisen, it has been highly politicized within the community, and has resulted in intense pressures on individual IRB members.

A related fourth problem is that of the meaning of "social injury" and "psychological injury," and of how an IRB is to apply those concepts to a particular proposal. Absent definition of these key terms in the regulation, IRBs have construed them to cover a broad range of possible harms, including (1) transient embarrassment to subjects, (2) longer-term loss of reputation and of status within the community, and (3) injury to subjects incurred solely in their capacity as members of an ethnic, racial, religious, economic, or community group. Some IRBs have also construed "psychological injury" and "social injury" to include risks to the relative or the friend of an injured subject. When risk arising from speculative injury to a group to which the subject belongs has been claimed before an IRB, the "ethical" review process has inevitably become politically supercharged.

In social experimentation, and in social science research generally, subjects may experience economic risk as more compelling than risk of physical or psychological injury. Drafted within a biomedical framework, the current regulation contains no reference to the possibility of *financial injury* raised by income maintenance experiments, health insurance research, and Medicaid and Social Security demonstrations which may involve loss of statutory benefits under a § 1115 or § 1110 waiver.

This fifth "risk" problem arising specially in social science research occurs particularly strikingly when social experimentation or Health Care Financing Administration (HCFA) demonstration coverage of medical services raises the possibility of harm *arising from loss of temporary experimental benefit:*

A recipient of temporary experimental health insurance benefits may become ill during the experiment, and may consequently be unable to resume his private health insurance coverage—or may be able to repurchase it only at a prohibitive price—once the experimental benefits have ended.

A therapy client may benefit from HCFA demonstration coverage of psychological services unsupervised by an M.D. psychiatrist, only to find in the middle of his therapy—and perhaps in the middle of an emotional crisis— that the demonstration is over, and he cannot afford to pay for the rest of the therapy himself.

One could also argue that *randomization* of the distribution of experimental benefits, when control group members do not receive those benefits, ought to be construed as "financial injury" and considered by an IRB. That argument becomes particularly compelling where control group members were statutorily entitled to the same benefits prior to HHS or DOL grant of an experimental waiver making witholding of those benefits permissible.

This fifth "risk" problem of "financial injury" is generally immaterial in biomedical research, and the concept of financial injury is not now a part of the regulation.

The Effects of the Problem

Arbitrary and Inconsistent Treatment of Proposals. Many research investigators experience themselves as having been treated arbitrarily and capriciously by IRBs, given the broad discretion which IRBs necessarily exercise in the absence of a regulatory definition of "risk." Proposals are treated inconsistently in different institutions, and over time in the same institution, and to many investigators the fate of their proposal appears primarily a function of chance, whim, and the effectiveness of their gamesmanship in dealing with an IRB.

IRB members share these feelings, and feel discomfort exercising significant discretion over investigators' careers unguided and untrammeled by federal prescription.

Confidentiality Inadequately Protected. Since no confidentiality standards are incorporated in the regulation, there are none either uniformly implemented or explained to subjects. Subject protection against breach of confidentiality is dependent upon the conscientiousness of the researcher and of the IRB in individual cases, and therefore varies tremendously within classes of research.

Promises of confidentiality are sometimes made to subjects which, given the possibility of subpoena, cannot be kept. Where researchers fail to explain risks of breach of confidentiality, and subjects are then harmed because of such breach, researchers may be exposed to legal claims of fraudulent inducement of those subjects.

Where IRBs are either conscientious or worried about suit against the research institution, surveys involving sensitive questions and/or vulnerable populations (e.g., unreported criminal histories of felony prisoners) may be disapproved after funding or terminated in midstream for fear that sensitive data will be subpoenaed or leaked, exposing subjects to irreversible harm and institutions to damages. This is particularly likely if an institution's legal counsel sits on its IRB, and advises that promises of confidentiality cannot be kept.

Political Decision Making by IRBs. Where issues involving publication and policy application of research results have been presented to IRBs, and where IRBs have chosen to take cognizance of those issues in their consideration of "risk," IRB proceedings have lost legitimacy in the eyes of the research investigators affected and their professional peers. IRB decisions have been made for what seem to be "political" reasons. In these cases, risk to individual subjects has not been the determining criterion for IRB approval, and the IRBs involved have lost respect on their campuses—and have lost, as a consequence, some of their ability to act as ethical raisers of consciousness among research faculty.

When IRBs have addressed arguments involving publication or policy application of research results, community and national public interest organizations have become part of the IRB process. On such occasions, the IRB has become a politically charged forum for issues very different from those envisioned by the regulation.

The same basic change in an IRB's nature has occurred when it chooses to interpret "psychological injury" or "social injury" as involving harm not only to individuals, but also to ethnic, racial, religious, economic, and community groups, and has then focused its attention on those issues.

Failure to Protect Subjects from Financial Injury. Absent any incorporation of the notion of "financial injury" into the definition of risk, IRBs have lacked guidance on how to deal with social experimentation and demonstration. Subjects in those modes of research have, therefore, been haphazardly and inconsistently protected.

What Is to Be Done?

To fix these problems, we need to make some additions to the current regulation.

First, and most important, we need to put some content into the expression "risk," in order to present IRBs and investigators with unambiguous guidance on what standards proposals are to be held to.

Second, the definition of risk ought to specify that the expressions "social injury" and "psychological injury" do not give IRBs license to modify research designs or to reject proposals based upon political considerations of risk to groups or communities, but rather that IRBs are to confine themselves to questions of risk to individual subjects.

The definition ought also to specify that allegations of risk arising from the possible publication or policy application of research *results*—and not from the research *process*—are not to be construed by IRBs as a legitimate basis for modifying or rejecting proposals. The granting agency, and the political process at the state and federal levels, are the appropriate forums before which those issues can be considered.

Third, the definition of risk ought to raise the issues of breach of confidentiality and of "financial injury," and to specify that IRBs must focus upon these issues. Uniform standards of confidentiality ought to be laid out in detail in the regulation, so that IRBs and investigators understand what they must do to protect against the risk of breach.

In particular, those standards ought to mention the secretary of HHS's authority to grant shields protecting some classes of research data from subpoena[3] and should require IRBs to ensure that investigators solicit that shield whenever a research proposal addresses sensitive questions and breach of confidentiality could therefore be particularly harmful to subjects.

The Definition of a "Human Subject"

The concept of "human subject" now embodied in the regulation may be appropriate to biomedical research, but it *is inadequate to protect all who may be harmed by social science research.*

Innocent bystanders may be at risk arising from social science research even though they have no contact with a research investigator, the research does not generate or examine data about them, and there is no intent to intervene in their lives (e.g., the housing allowance and income maintenance experiments, and the unlucky bystander whose photograph is taken in sensitive anthropological research).

Regulation 45 C.F.R. 46 currently protects only those who are themselves subjects of research, not those who may equally be harmed although they are nonparticipants. Risks to nonparticipants, when sufficiently visible, are dealt with through the political process at the community level, on Capitol Hill, and by the HHS secretary as they become politically charged issues. Despite the regulation's silence on this issue, some IRBs have taken the initiative to protect nonsubjects at risk, sometimes in social experimentation but particularly when relatives and friends seem at risk from subject participation in clinical psychological research or in biomedical research involving ultrahazardous materials.

Given the restricted definition of "human subject," absent any concept in that definition of "nonparticipant at risk," IRBs at best haphazardly protect innocent bystanders. We need to expand the definition, in order to communicate to IRBs that they are charged with systematically flushing out risks to innocent bystanders, as well as risks to formal participants in research.

The Requirement of Informed Consent

The Conceptual Problem

The elements of the regulation's "informed consent" disclosure model impose *unreasonably burdensome requirements on investigators in some classes of social science research,* without compensating benefit to subjects. In some kinds of research, for some categories of subjects, *the disclosure requirements may themselves create otherwise nonexistent risks for the subjects* they are supposed to protect.

Explanation of Research Purposes and Procedures.   The current definition of informed consent requires explanation to subjects of (*a*) all research procedures, regardless of whether particular procedures may cause risk to subjects, and (*b*) all purposes of the study, regardless of whether disclosure of purpose is material to the subjects' evaluation of risk.

Explanation of research purposes and of some procedures, however, may skew social science research results because the subject's otherwise natural behavior will be affected by his new knowledge. For instance:

If a subject is informed that a major purpose of an income maintenance experiment is to see whether he quits work (or elects to enter the labor market in the first place) while receiving the experimental cash benefit, his propensity to work is likely to be affected by the awareness that that is precisely what the researcher is watching.

If a subject is informed that a major purpose of a health insurance experiment is to measure his utilization of free versus subsidized experimental medical services, and to learn at what point a copayment eliminates frivolous visits to the doctor, his propensity to use the insurance to make those visits will be affected by the resulting self-consciousness.

If a child who is the subject of unobtrusive research on educational performance is told that he will be watched through a one-way mirror, his behavior will hardly be spontaneous.

If a subject in clinical psychological research involving deception must be informed at the front end (as opposed to a debriefing afterward) of the issues on which he will be deceived, his behavior obviously loses validity for research purposes.

HEW's guidelines until 1974 did not specify that purpose be disclosed, and the American Medical Association's principles still do not (although the Nuremberg Code, the Declaration of Helsinki, and the World Medical Association Code do). Several participants in the recent Brookings conference on social experimentation went out of their way to suggest that "there should be no ethical responsibility to inform subjects in analytical detail about the intent of the research."[4]

> To disclose the purpose of the research may jeopardize the scientific validity of the results. This is certainly true in social science research since it is concerned with the behavior of subjects. . . . This behavior may be influenced not only by the pure treatment, but by . . . the subject's perception of the experimenter's expectations.

The Brookings conferees generally argued that research procedures and purposes should be disclosed only insofar as the information is material to the subject's understanding of whether and how he is at risk, and therefore to his decision process on whether to participate in an experiment.

   Disclosure of Hypothetical Benefits and Alternatives.   The current definition of informed consent requires disclosure to subjects of "any benefits reasonably to be expected" from the research and of "any appropriate alternative procedures that might be advantageous for the subject."

   Explanation of benefits, like explanation of research purposes and procedures, may skew research results by affecting the subject's behavior, particularly if he is in a control group and understands the difference between the benefits he is receiving (but to which he was not entitled before the experiment began) and those which go to members of the experimental group.

   Disclosure of alternative procedures assumes that, as in much biomedical research, there actually are standard and accepted treatment options available to the subject. This model does not usually apply in social science research, and there is often an infinity of benefit permutations (how much cash and which social services could be provided in an income maintenance experiment, for instance). The social scientist who has to spend time dreaming up all possible benefit packages, and then explaining them to the subject, is burdened to no gain by the subject, since most of those packages are not available to him in the real world. Some subjects may be sufficiently confused by this recitation to opt out of the research (not, one hastens to add, a hypothetical scenario).

   Disclosure of Risks of Breach of Confidentiality.   Survey research, depth interviews, and observation research (cf. William H. Whyte's participant observation studies of juvenile gangs) raise most acutely the issue of whether the researcher should have to disclose to subjects all the possible causes of breach of confidentiality of the data which he collects from them, and all the possible consequences to them of such breach.

   This issue remains even if the researcher has taken every possible technical precaution, and even if he is fully in compliance with HHS confidentiality regulations, because the data may be subpoenaed. David Kershaw has recounted in the Brookings conference proceedings that a grand jury, at least two welfare departments, the General Accounting Office, and the Senate Finance Committee attempted to secure confidential data from the New Jersey income maintenance experiments, sometimes by subpoena, in order to track down fraudulent welfare recipients. James Carroll and Charles Knerr's survey of social scientists indicates that although actual subpoenas are rare, threats by police and prosecuters are more frequent, and that the possibility of either an actual subpoena or a threat of one can chill research into illegal or stigmatized behavior.

There is, moreover, the danger that notwithstanding all technical precautions for data security, simple gossip by survey research employees (e.g., on stigmatized sexual behavior or family violence) may harm a respondent.

Many IRBs have required opinion survey researchers to obtain written informed consent from respondents on this issue before conducting telephone or mail polls. Some IRBs have required researchers conducting house-to-house interviews to describe in detail the possible confidentiality problems, and to obtain the "anonymous" respondent's written consent at the door before beginning to ask questions.

Inevitably, some respondents have slammed the door in their faces, hung up the telephone, or signed a consent form and then given dishonest or incomplete answers.

Requiring Documentation of Informed Consent When the Documentation Itself Is Clearly Inappropriate. One candidate in sociology secured permission from the members of a local organized crime community to conduct a sociometric analysis of it, only to be told by her IRB that she would have to secure written informed consent from each of her respondents! Even after her explanation that the consent document would itself become a source of risk to her respondents far greater than anything she might do in the course of the research, the IRB would not relent. In order to go forward with her dissertation, she had to move to another university.

William C. Sturtevant, testifying on behalf of the American Anthropological Association before the national commission, emphasized that

> Signed permissions seem silly in a non-literate community, and detailed explanations in most such communities are incomprehensible, as well as in many literate communities. The legalistic procedures have been compared . . . with those of early Spanish conquistadores, who as they stepped ashore read out to the Indians a statement in Spanish or Latin putting them on notice that they were subjects of the King of Spain so that any resistance would morally and legally be treated as sedition and put down by force.[5]

One anthropology department chairman who has conducted research among preliterate Latin American Communities wrote, in an amusing letter to an HEW official:

> Signed consent forms are meaningful only to Americans (and in fact, not all of them). Elsewhere, people who are illiterate, people who are only required to sign forms when the government is getting ready to exploit them, and people who have no

concept of Western law and judicially protected rights find consent forms totally meaningless. As Sturtevant's testimony mentioned, signed consent forms in non-literate or semi-literate societies are analogous to the proclamations ready by Columbus to New World natives, converting them to subjects of Spain, subject to its laws. No one listening knew who Spain was, what a king was, or what the laws were that were involved.[6]

This anthropologist's IRB persisted in its demand that he secure written documentation of consent from each of the natives to whose community he had been admitted, with the result that he temporarily moved to another university outside the country for a base from which to conduct his research. Similarly, there are dozens of reports of IRBs which have required the submission of consent forms from respondents in research on illegal or stigmatized behavior, even though the existence of the forms themselves posed more risk than any aspect of the research.

A third case of an inappropriate requirement of documentation of consent occurs in telephone and mail surveys. Even if the consent requirement itself is considered reasonable when applied to those surveys, the question remains whether the IRB should require that each respondent sign a written consent form, and that the investigator submit all forms to the IRB, before the survey can proceed. Survey researchers experience this as an unreasonable burden often imposed by IRBs, one which makes some surveys impossible to conduct.

Deception Research.   Like biomedical research involving a placebo, some social psychological research can only proceed with incomplete front end disclosure to subjects, or even active deception. Some psychologists estimate that well over 75 percent of all psychological laboratory research necessarily involves deception. Should an IRB be able to waive the informed consent requirement in these cases, contingent upon provision of a debriefing afterward?

The Effects of the Problem

Scaring Off Survey and Interview Respondents by Too Much Disclosure. IRBs have sometimes been aware that requiring disclosure of all research procedures and purposes will inevitably skew survey and interview data. They have then simply ignored this requirement or effectively waived it through an inappropriate use of the regulation's modification clause (§ 46.110 [c]). In those cases, the seemingly stringent requirement for complete disclosure of procedures and purposes has had the real-world effect of protecting subjects less than a moderated, enforceable requirement would.

Alternatively, many IRBs have stuck to the letter of the regulation and imposed the requirement on all social science research presented to them, including telephone and mail surveys. The predictable results, recounted by dozens of social scientists, include drops in aggregate response rates, drops in the timeliness of response, and skewing of data when respondents do consent to be interviewed. Survey researchers argue that their cost per completed interview has risen significantly, and that the representativeness of their sample and the reliability of their data have diminished.[7]

Where this requirement—and that of disclosure of hypothetical benefits and alternatives—has been enforced by IRBs, survey and interview researchers have been vehement in their protests of response bias.

Unreasonable Burden of Disclosure of Confidentiality Risks. When IRBs have required that respondents be told all possible causes of breach of confidentiality, and all possible risks to them of that breach, that response bias has been particularly pronounced. Especially in surveys that present questions on illegal or stigmatized behavior, subjects have withheld information or flatly refused to answer questions.

Given the requirement that all conceivable confidentiality risks be disclosed, this problem has occurred whether or not the researcher has in fact taken all possible precautions to protect the data. IRBs have apparently failed, when they have enforced a stringent disclosure requirement, to distinguish between the researcher who has taken all possible precautions and the researcher who has taken none.

Perverse Requirements for Documentation of Informed Consent. When IRBs have been inflexible in enforcing the requirement for *documentation* of informed consent, often in order to protect themselves and their institutions from litigation, the requirement has made some research impossible and driven several researchers to other institutions or out of the country. Where researchers have tried to meet an IRB's demand, they have sometimes lost a carefully nurtured rapport with a whole respondent community, and the research has been destroyed.

This has occurred particularly when researchers have attempted to collect written informed consent from respondents in studies of illegal and stigmatized behavior. In such studies, the very existence of the signed consent document is more dangerous to the subject than anything that he can conceive the researcher doing. It has also occurred when researchers have tried to secure signatures or Xs on consent documents from primitive foreign populations, whose experience has been that when their government asks them to sign something, the government is about to take away their land or resources.

"Gestalt" of Suspicion Created by Overthorough Disclosure. Some anthropologists have argued that the very process of a detailed informed consent disclosure—the "Gestalt" which is generated by a researcher's giving a respondent a complicated and generally incomprehensible series of warnings which the respondent never thought of and finds it difficult to relate to his real world—creates an atmosphere, a feeling of suspicion and of adversary relationship. That new tone for the relationship between researcher and subject will inevitably affect response rate and quality, in a way often unwarranted by any actual risk to subjects.

Waiver of Documentation as Subterfuge for Waiver of Informed Consent Requirement. Especially in telephone and mail surveys, one result of IRB perceptions that they must apply all of the elements in the regulatory definition of "informed consent" to all social science research has been an illegitimate use of the "modification clause." That clause (§ 46.110 [c], "Documentation of Informed Consent"), intended to permit modification of the procedure used by the investigator to *document* his solicitation of informed consent, has been used—in surveys, deception research, and ethnographic and observation research—as a subterfuge to waive investigator compliance with the *substance* of informed consent requirements.

What Is to Be Done?

The "informed consent" model laid out in the regulation needs overhaul to make it appropriate to social science, as well as biomedical, research:

1. Amend the definition of the elements of "informed consent"— particularly the requirements for disclosure of all purposes, all procedures, all benefits hypothetically available, and all conceivable alternatives—so as to remove disabling and unnecessary burdens from some classes of research, while preserving the requirement that respondents be given all information material to their perception of risk and their decision on participation in the research.

2. Specify that if the researcher has met the IRB's standards of protection of confidential data, he need not recite to respondents all possible risks of breach of confidentiality. Permit the IRB to require, instead, a short-form "Miranda warning" to subjects, in a couple of sentences. In the case of research on illegal or stigmatized behavior, however, require that that warning be very clear on the possibility and the legal consequences of subpoena of the data.

3. Require, when data is collected on illegal or stigmatized behavior, by field research among primitive populations, or by telephone or mail survey, that the IRB *must* waive the requirement for *documentation* of informed consent. The burden should remain on the investigator, however, to show the IRB that he will secure oral consent, and in particular to show that as part of that oral consent process he will present to respondents a warranty of the confidentiality protections being implemented and a warning of the consequences if those protections fail.

4. Specify that psychological laboratory research involving deception is permitted without complete informed consent before the fact, assuming that (*a*) the deception does not withhold from the subject any facts material to his assessment of risk, and (*b*) a debriefing after the research will provide him with all of the information which he would otherwise have been given in a complete informed consent process beforehand.

The Abuse of IRB Discretion

The Problem

IRBs have apparently abused their discretion in order to impose their notions of good scientific methodology on investigators, to avoid embarrassment and legal threat to their institution, and to achieve political ends. Junior faculty and those in nonquantitative disciplines are particularly vulnerable to this.

HEW originally conceived of IRBs as groups which would have a fiduciary obligation to protect research subjects, and which would meet that obligation by making "ethical" judgments centered on the acceptability of *risk* to individual subjects. The drafters of the regulation deliberately left undefined the key notion of "risk," and explicitly stated that IRBs were to select the ethical code which they would then apply.

The result of this grant of broad discretion has, in all too many cases, been very different from its intent. Without local constituencies representing the interests of subjects before them, IRBs have frequently become fiduciaries not of subjects, but of their institutions, and of their own notions of conventional research methodology. Instead of focusing upon risk, they have, in dozens of cases reported to the HEW survey:

disapproved research for fear of embarrassment to their university from publication of research results (e.g., research on the effects of compulsory busing and other school desegregation devices), and for fear of general political controversy in the local community;

disapproved research upon a political judgment that research results would, if published, harm a group, organization, or community (e.g., research on comparative IQs and academic achievement of ethnic groups), and for fear of the general political consequences which might follow that harm;

disapproved research as promising no significant benefit from the research results, based upon their judgment of the competence of a research investigator rather than of the particulars of a submitted research design;

disapproved research as having insufficient merit, based upon either (a) a judgment that the research methodology embodied in a proposal is generally of no value, or (b) failure to understand a research methodology foreign to their training and their work, in both cases failing again to address the particulars of the individual submitted research design; and

required major research design modifications as a condition of approval, based upon general disrespect for a whole research methodology or academic discipline or upon a misunderstanding of the details and implications of a methodology.

Anthropologists, sociologists, other qualitative social scientists, and even clinical investigators and epidemiologists (when faced with IRBs composed of

M.D.s) commonly complain that IRBs are composed of persons who do not understand or respect their disciplines' research methodologies, and who consequently treat them and their proposals with contempt. Political scientists and sociologists have begun to complain bitterly that IRBs, by constraining their research for purposes other than protection of individual subjects, are engaging in censorship and abrogating academic freedom. There is a small but growing social science literature on this point, and it promises to become a source of intense political controversy within the academic community in the near future.

IRB members, for their part, freely admit that they are conservative in evaluating research proposals, particularly when university general counsels are IRB members, in order to prevent any conceivable litigation against (or embarrassment to) the research institution. They are also motivated by their own personal exposure to litigation, since they are not generally individually covered against suits by the liability insurance of research institutions. They have in all too many cases, then, become fiduciaries of interests quite different from those which they were originally intended to protect.

The Effects of the Problem

The regulation's broad grant of discretion to IRBs, together with its failure to define "risk" or to lay out other substantive standards to guide IRB decisions, has resulted in unnecessary IRB review of social science research which presents trivial risk. The result has been an unnecessary paperwork burden upon the researcher who must make a presentation to his IRB even though his study presents trivial risk, and the squandering of IRB resources on threshold jurisdictional issues instead of supervision of the few classes of really risky research.

The broad grant of discretion, the failure to define substantive standards, and an "Applicability" section which requires review of all research involving human subjects have all combined to make it possible for the IRB process to become politicized at some institutions, to the point that entire studies or particular survey questions have been disapproved for political—as opposed to "ethical"—reasons.

The broad scope of the "Applicability" section has, moreover, resulted in the inappropriate IRB imposition of the "informed consent" disclosure requirements even where that burden upon the researcher is not justified by a prior finding of risk.

Most frequently, however, the consequence of infinite jurisdictional scope combined with the absence of standards to inform IRB decisions has been a wholesale abdication of IRB legal responsibilities under the regulation—a wholesale throwing up of their hands in the air at the impossibility of it all. This "ritualization" of the IRB process places the researcher and the institution at risk of litigation if a subject should be harmed, and spends IRB member energies on creating a paper trail of ostensible compliance with the regulation while leaving the subject without any real protection.

What Is to Be Done?

To remedy these problems, the regulation needs amendment to provide clear guidance to IRBs on (*a*) what they are charged with doing, and (*b*) the constraints upon their authority. We ought to specify that:

1.   IRBs must put some flesh into the regulatory requirement of "continuing review," to ensure that researchers implement the protections promised to them (and to subjects) in research proposals. IRBs must, especially, monitor the real implementation and not merely the documentation of informed consent, scrutinizing with particular care the consent process when vulnerable subject classes (children, institutionalized mentally disabled, et al.) are involved.

2.   IRBs must clearly articulate to a researcher why his proposal is rejected, and must present clear guidance on what modification of the research design would make it acceptable. They must establish a formal record of their decisions over time, formally present to their institution's research community the legal and ethical standards on which they intend to base decisions, and generally treat investigators with due process and equity.

3.   They may not reject or radically redesign research proposals unless there is undue risk to individuals or an inadequate informed consent process. In particular, they may not disapprove proposals on grounds of embarrassment or legal peril to their institution, fear of anticipated political attack following publication of research findings, disrespect for a particular investigator, or disrespect for a whole research methodology or academic discipline.

Postscript: Issues on the Horizon

The steps that need to be taken to make the regulatory structure appropriate to social science research are not particularly complicated. They do, however, require recognition by HHS that the regulation is being applied by IRBs in a way which imposes needless and heavy burdens on some social science research, while protecting at best haphazardly subjects involved in the few classes of truly risky social science research.

Perhaps the major issue which emerges from this discussion is whether IRBs will continue to concentrate on reviewing paper at the front end of all human subjects research, or whether we will deregulate enough harmless research to free them to reallocate their energies into monitoring the actual conduct of risky research. If this reallocation is to take place, we need to parse out how IRBs can monitor research without so interfering in it that it becomes too expensive to perform or that its results are invalidated.

There are some other issues on the horizon, on which creative thinking needs to be done:

1. Can we generate data that demonstrate, for survey, interview, and field research, whether or not the mere asking of some kinds of questions is itself harmful because it generates an unacceptable level of emotional stress?[8]

2. If so, can we identify which topics should be considered especially sensitive and which—although they are within generally deregulated classes of research—should nonetheless trigger IRB review?

3. Can we identify precisely the technical protections of confidentiality of sensitive data which should be written into the regulation on "Protection of Human Subjects," and should therefore be required of every investigator and checked up on by IRBs?

4. How can we routinize the use of the researcher shield against compulsory subpoena by research investigators whose proposals must be approved by an IRB? How should the exceptions to that shield be drafted— the classes of information *not* to be protected, within the broader categories of information which are immunized—so as to produce a final regulation which protects most confidential social science research data, fairly balances society's interests with those of subjects, and maximizes the probability that the regulation will be upheld judicially against the inevitable challenge to its protections?

5. Under what circumstances ought a research institution to assume the responsibility of compensating an injured research subject?[9] If there is to be compensation, how is a "compensable event" to be defined and how are damages to be measured in the case of a "psychological harm"? What should be the substantive and the administrative parameters of a compensation scheme? Ought we to be discussing the issue at all, or does it open up an unmanageable Pandora's Box of litigation?

These are questions which have begun to be the focus of discussion among some policymakers involved in the regulation of federally sponsored research, demonstrations, and experimental service delivery. There is a need for the social science community to begin its own analysis of them, and to take the initiative to collect relevant empirical data, if that community wants to share in the policy process which will shape the parameters of a major chunk of its research.

Notes

1. 417 F. Supp. 532–547 (1976).

2. This legal authority has been included in every HEW-Labor appropriations bill since fiscal year 1975, when it was enacted as § 412 of P.L. 93-517. See, e.g., § 409 of P.L. 94-439 (F.Y. 1977).

3.   HEW: Public Health Service, "Protection of Identity: Research Subjects," *Federal Register* 44 (April 4, 1979): 20382–87 (regulation 42 C.F.R. Part 2 a, referencing § 303 [a] of the Public Health Service Act, as amended, codified at 42 U.S.C. 242 [a]).

4.   Alice M. Rivlin and P. Michael Timpane, eds., *Ethical and Legal Issues of Social Experimentation* (Washington, D.C.: Brookings Institution, 1975), p. 78. This and the quotation following, at p. 73, are from Robert M. Veatch, "Ethical Principles in Medical Experimentation," pp. 21-78. Edward M. Gramlich and Larry L. Orr, "The Ethics of Social Experimentation," pp. 105-14, make the same point at pp. 107 and 114.

5.   William C. Sturtevant, Testimony before the National Commission for the Protection of Human Subjects of Biomedical and Behavioral Research (Oral testimony, representing the American Anthropological Association, May 3, 1977), pp. 1–2.

6.   Letter to author, August 1, 1978.

7.   See, for example, Lloyd B. Lueptow, "Bias and Non-Response Resulting from Informed Consent Procedures in Survey Research on High School Seniors," Unpublished (HEW, Office of the Assistant Secretary for Planning and Evaluation, January 1976), pp. 43, 46.

8.   See, for example, Joseph M. Petrosko et al., "Behavioral Effects and Privacy Implications of Administering Questionnaires: A Review of Research" (Center for the Study of Evaluation, UCLA Graduate School of Education, commissioned by U.S. Office of Education, June 1974).

9.   See Rivlin and Timpane, *Ethical and Legal Issues,* pp. 11, 18, 54, 57, 63, 70, 76-77, 103-4; Richard A. Tropp, "What Problems Are Raised When the Current DHEW Regulation on Protection of Human Subjects Is Applied to Social Science Research?," in National Commission for the Protection of Human Subjects of Biomedical and Behavioral Research, *The Belmont Report: Ethical Principles and Guidelines for the Protection of Human Subjects of Research,* DHEW Publication no. (OS) 78-0014 (Washington, D.C.: Government Printing Office, 1978), appendix, vol. 2, pp. (18-1) – (18-17), p. (18-15); HEW Secretary's *Task Force on the Compensation of Injured Research Subjects* (Washington, D.C.: Office of the Secretary, HEW, 1977).

Selected Bibliography

I. General Treatments of the Ethical Issues in Social Research

Boruch, Robert F.; Ross, Jerry; and Cecil, Joe S., eds. *Conference on Ethical and Legal Problems in Applied Social Research.* Evanston, Ill.: Northwestern University, 1979. Conference proceedings and background papers.

Bower, Robert T., and de Gasparis, Priscilla R. *Ethics in Social Science Research: Protecting the Interests of Human Subjects.* New York: Praeger, 1978.

Diener, Edward, and Crandall, Rick. *Ethics in Social and Behavioral Research.* Chicago: University of Chicago Press, 1978.

Kelman, Herbert C. "Research, behavioral." In *Encyclopedia of Bioethics,* edited by Warren T. Reich, vol. 4, pp. 1470-81. New York: Free Press, 1978.

————. *A Time to Speak: On Human Values and Social Research.* Jossey-Bass Behavioral Science Series, edited by William E. Henry and Nevitt Sanford. San Francisco: Jossey-Bass, 1968.

Reynolds, Paul Davidson. *Ethical Dilemmas and Social Science Research: An Analysis of Moral Issues Confronting Investigators in Research Using Human Participants.* San Francisco: Jossey-Bass, 1979.

Warwick, Donald P. *The Teaching of Ethics in the Social Sciences.* The Teaching of Ethics, no. 6. Hastings-on-Hudson, N.Y.: Hastings Center, 1980.

II. Sources Addressing Ethical Issues That Arise in Specific Disciplines in the Social Sciences

Appell, George N. *Ethical Dilemmas in Anthropological Inquiry: A Case Book.* Waltham, Mass.: Crossroads Press, 1978.

Bermant, Gordon; Kelman, Herbert C.; and Warwick, Donald P., eds. *The Ethics of Social Intervention.* Washington, D.C.: Hemisphere Publishing Corp.; New York: Halsted Press, John Wiley & Sons, 1978.

Cassell, Joan, and Wax, Murray L., eds. "Ethical Problems of Fieldwork." *Social Problems* 27, no. 3 (February 1980). Special issue.

International Journal of Psychology 14, no. 2 (1979). Issue containing articles presenting international perspectives on ethical issues in psychological research, pp. 121–30, 137–41.

Klockars, Carl B., and O'Connor, Finbarr W., eds. *Deviance and Decency: The Ethics of Research with Human Subjects.* Sage annual reviews of studies in deviance, vol. 3. Beverly Hills, Calif.: Sage Publications, 1979.

Masters, William H.; Johnson, Virginia E.; and Kolodny, Robert, eds. *Ethical Issues in Sex Therapy and Research.* Reproductive Biology Research Foundation Conference. Boston: Little, Brown & Co., 1977.

Nejelski, Paul, ed. *Social Research in Conflict with Law and Ethics.* Cambridge, Mass.: Ballinger Publishing Co., 1976.

Riecken, Henry W., and Boruch, Robert F., eds. *Social Experimentation: A Method for Planning and Evaluating Social Intervention.* Quantitative Studies in Social Relations, edited by Peter H. Rossi. New York: Academic Press, 1974.

Rivlin, Alice M., and Timpane, P. Michael, eds. *Ethical and Legal Issues of Social Experimentation.* Washington, D.C.: Brookings Institution, 1975.

Rynkiewich, Michael A., and Spradley, James P., eds. *Ethics and Anthropology: Dilemmas in Fieldwork.* New York: John Wiley & Sons, 1976.

Schoolar, Joseph C., and Gaitz, Charles M., eds. *Research and the Psychiatric Patient.* New York: Brunner/Mazel Press, 1975.

Sherrer, Charles W., and Sherrer, M. Sylvia. *Ethical and Professional Standards for Academic Psychologists and Counsellors.* Springfield, Ill.: Charles C. Thomas Publisher, 1980.

Sjoberg, Gideon, ed. *Ethics, Politics, and Social Research.* Cambridge, Mass.: Schenkman Publishing Co., 1967.

Stolz, Stephanie B., and associates. *Ethical Issues in Behavior Modification.* Report of the American Psychological Association Commission. Jossey-Bass Social and Behavioral Science series. San Francisco: Jossey-Bass, 1978.

III. Classic Case Studies: Particular Projects in the Social Sciences That Have Generated Moral Controversy

Festinger, Leon; Riecken, Henry W.; and Schachter, Stanley. *When Prophecy Fails: A Social and Psychological Study of a Modern Group That Predicted the Destruction of the World.* Minneapolis: University of Minnesota Press, 1956.

Horowitz, Irving Louis, ed. *The Rise and Fall of Project Camelot.* Cambridge, Mass.: MIT Press, 1967.

Humphreys, Laud. *Tearoom Trade: Impersonal Sex in Public Places.* Enlarged edition. Chicago: Aldine Publishing Co., 1975.

Milgram, Stanley. *Obedience to Authority: An Experimental View.* New York: Harper & Row, 1974.

Rosenhan, David L. "On Being Sane in Insane Places." *Science* 179 (1973): 250–58.

Vidich, Arthur J., and Bensman, Joseph. *Small Town in Mass Society.* Garden City, N.Y.: Doubleday, 1960.

Zimbardo, P.G.; Haney, C.; Banks, W. C.; and Jaffe, D. "The Mind as a Formidable Jailer: A Pirandellian Prison." *New York Times Magazine,* 9 April 1973, p. 38.

IV. Studies Pertaining to the Issues Raised in the "Harm and Benefit" Section

American Academy of Arts and Sciences. "Limits of Scientific Inquiry." *Daedalus* 107, no. 2 (1978). Special issue.

Atkinson, Richard C. "Federal Support in the Social Sciences." *Science* 207 (1980): 829. Editorial.

Baram, Michael S. "Cost-Benefit Analysis: An Inadequate Basis for Health, Safety, and Environmental Regulatory Decision-making." *Ecology Law Review* 8 (1980): 473–531.

Cassell, Joan. "Risk and Benefit to Subjects of Fieldwork." *American Sociologist* 13 (1978): 134–43.

Koocher, Gerald P. "Bathroom Behavior and Human Dignity." *Journal of Personality and Social Psychology* 35 (1977): 120–21.

Lindblom, Charles E., and Cohen, Davis K. *Usable Knowledge: Social Science and Social Problem Solving.* New Haven: Yale University Press, 1979.

Milgram, Stanley. "Subject Reaction: The Neglected Factor in the Ethics of Experimentation." *Hastings Center Report* 7, no. 5 (1977): 19–23.

Miller, George A. "Psychology as a Means of Promoting Human Welfare." *American Psychologist* 24 (1969): 1063-75.

Smith, David H. "Scientific Knowledge and Forbidden Truths: Are There Things We Should Not Know?," *Hastings Center Report* 8, no. 6 (December 1978): 30-35.

Starr, Chauncey, and Whipple, Chris. "Risks of Risk Decisions." *Science* 208 (1980): 1114–19.

Veatch, Robert M. "Longitudinal Studies, Sequential Design, and Grant Renewals: What to Do with Preliminary Data." *IRB: A Review of Human Subjects Research* 1, no. 4 (June/July 1979): 1–3.

V. Studies Pertaining to the Issues Raised in the "Informed Consent" Section

Baumrind, Diana. "Nature and Definition of Informed Consent in Research Involving Deception." In *The Belmont Report: Ethical Principles and Guidelines for the Protection of Human Subjects of Research,* edited by National Commission for the Protection of Human Subjects of Biomedical and Behavioral Research, appendix, vol. 2, pp. (23-1) – (23-71). DHEW Publication no. (OS)78-0013. Washington, D.C.: Government Printing Office, 1978.

Bok, Sissela. *Lying: Moral Choice in Public and Private Life.* New York: Pantheon Books, 1978.

Brown, Peter G. "Informed Consent in Social Experimentation: Some Cautionary Notes." In *Ethical and Legal Aspects of Social Experimentation,* edited by Alice M. Rivlin and P. Michael Timpane, pp. 79–104. Brookings Studies in Social Experimentation. Washington, D.C.: Brookings Institution, 1975.

Dresser, Rebecca S. "Deception Research and the HHS Final Regulations." *IRB* 3 (April 1981): 3–4.

Homan, Robert, and Bulmer, Martin. "The Ethics of Covert Methods." *British Journal of Sociology* 31, no. 1 (March 1980): 46-65.

Kelman, Herbert C. "The Rights of the Subject in Social Research: An Analysis in Terms of Relative Power and Legitimacy." *American Psychologist* 27 (1972): 989–1015.

Mead, Margaret. "Research with Human Beings: A Model Derived from Anthropological Field Practice." *Daedalus* 98 (1969): 361–86.

Murray, Thomas H. "Commentary: Was This Deception Necessary?" *IRB: A Review of Human Subjects Research* 2, no. 10 (December 1980): 7–8. With response by

Robert A. Baron, "The 'Cost of Deception' Revisited: An Openly Optimistic Rejoinder." *IRB: A Review of Human Subjects Research* 3, no. 7 (January 1981): 8–10.

―――. "Learning to Deceive." *Hastings Center Report* 10, no. 2 (April 1980): 11–14.

Reiss, Albert J. "Conditions and Consequences of Consent in Human Subject Research." In *Regulation of Scientific Inquiry: Societal Concerns with Research,* edited by Keith M. Wulff, pp. 161–84. Boulder, Colo.: Westview Press, 1979.

―――. "Selected Issues in Informed Consent and Confidentiality with Special Reference to Behavioral/Social Science Research/Inquiry." In *The Belmont Report: Ethical Principles and Guidelines for the Protection of Human Subjects of Research,* edited by National Commission for the Protection of Human Subjects of Biomedical and Behavioral Research, appendix, vol. 2, pp. (25-1) – (25-165). DHEW Publication no. (OS)78-0013. Washington, D.C.: Government Printing Office, 1978.

Shipley, Thorne. "Misinformed Consent: An Enigma in Modern Social Science Research." *Ethics in Science and Medicine* 4 (1977): 93–106.

Singer, Eleanor. "Informed Consent: Consequences for Response Rate and Response Quality in Social Surveys." *American Sociological Review* 43 (1978): 144–62.

Warwick, Donald P. "Deceptive Research: Social Scientists Ought to Stop Lying." *Psychology Today,* February 1975, pp. 38–40, 105–6.

Weiss, Robert J. "The Use and Abuse of Deception." *American Journal of Public Health* 70, no. 10 (October 1980): 1097–98. With response by Marc Renaud, "The Ethics of Consumer Protection Research." *American Journal of Public Health* 70, no. 10 (October 1980): pp. 1098-99.

VI. Studies Pertaining to the Issues Raised in the "Privacy and Confidentiality" Section

Barnes, John Arundel. *Who Should Know What? Social Science, Privacy, and Ethics.* Cambridge: Cambridge University Press, 1980.

Bond, Kathleen, et al. "Confidentiality and the Protection of Human Subjects in Social Science Research: A Report on Recent Developments." *American Sociologist* 13, no. 3 (August 1979): 144–77.

Boruch, Robert F., and Cecil, Joe S., eds. *Assuring the Confidentiality of Social Research Data.* Philadelphia: University of Pennsylvania Press, 1979.

Dalenius, Tore, and Klevmarken, Anders, eds. *Proceedings of a Symposium on Personal Integrity and the Need for Data in the Social Sciences, Held at Häseby Slott, Stockholm March 15–17, 1976, and Sponsored by the Swedish Council for Social Science Research.* Stockholm: Statens råd för samhällsforskning: Humanistisk-samhällsvetenskapliga forskningrådet, 1976.

Dionisopoulos, P. Allan, and Ducat, Craig R. *The Right to Privacy: Essays and Cases.* St. Paul, Minn.: West Publishing Co., 1976.

Greenawalt, Kent. "Privacy." In *Encyclopedia of Bioethics,* edited by Warren T. Reich, vol. 3, pp. 1356–64. New York: Macmillan, Free Press, 1978.

Kelman, Herbert C. "Privacy and Research with Human Beings." *Journal of Social Issues* 33 (1977): 169–95.

Kelsey, Jennifer L. "Privacy and Confidentiality in Epidemiological Research Involving Patients." *IRB* 3 (February 1981): 1–4.

McCloskey, H.J. "Privacy and the Right to Privacy." *Philosophy* 55 (1980): 17–38.

Mochmann, Ekkehard, and Müller, Paul J. *Data Protection and Social Science Research.* Frankfurt: Campus Verlag, 1979.

Privacy Protection Study Commission. *Personal Privacy in an Information Society.* Washington, D.C.: Government Printing Office, 1977.

Ruebhausen, Oscar M., and Brim, Orville G., Jr. "Privacy and Behavioral Research." *Columbia Law Review* 65 (1965): 1184–1211 and *American Psychologist* 21 (1966): 423–44.

Survey Research and Privacy: Report of a Working Party. London: Social and Community Planning Research, 1973.

Thomson, Judith Jarvis. "The Right to Privacy." *Philosophy and Public Affairs* 4 (1975): 295-314.

Young, John B. *Privacy.* New York: John Wiley & Sons, 1978.

VII. Studies Pertaining to the Issues Raised in the "Government Regulation" Section

De Sola Pool, Ithiel. "The New Censorship of Social Research." *Public Interest,* no. 59 (1980), pp. 57–65.

DuVal, Benjamin S. "The Human Subjects Protection Committee: An Experiment in Decentralized Federal Regulation." *American Bar Foundation Research Journal* 1979, no. 3 (1979): 571–688.

Gray, Bradford H. "Changing Federal Regulation of IRBs, Part III: Social Research and the Proposed DHEW Regulations." *IRB: A Review of Human Subjects Research* 2, no. 1 (January 1980): 1–5, 12.

Gray, Bradford H., and Cooke, Robert A. "The Impact of Institutional Review Boards on Research." *Hastings Center Report* 10, no. 1 (February 1980): 36–41.

Hogue, L. Lynn. "Institutional Review Boards and Consumer Surveys." *American Journal of Public Health* 69, no. 7 (July 1979): 649–50.

Pattullo, E. L. "Who Risks What in Social Research." *IRB: A Review of Human Subjects Research* 2, no. 3 (March 1980): 1–3, 12, and *Hastings Center Report* 10, no. 2 (April 1980): 15–18.

_____. "Transforming a Personal Inquiry into a Research Project." *IRB* (April 1981): 5–6.

_____. "How General an Assurance?" *IRB* (May 1981): 8.

Robertson, John A. "The Law of Institutional Review Boards." *UCLA Law Review* 26, no. 3 (February 1980): 484–549.

Seiler, Lauren H., and Murtha, James M. "Government Regulation of Research." *Society,* November/December 1980, pp. 23-31.

Seiler, Lauren H., and Murtha, James M. "Federal Regulations of Social Research Using 'Human Subjects': A Critical Assessment." *American Sociologist* 15 (1980): 146-57.

Tropp, Richard A. "What Problems Are Raised When the Current DHEW Regulation on the Protection of Human Subjects Is Applied to Social Science Research?" In *The Belmont Report: Ethical Principles and Guidelines for the Protection of Human Subjects of Research,* edited by National Commission for the Protection of Human Subjects of Biomedical and Behavioral Research, appendix, vol. 2, pp. (18-1) – (18-17). DHEW Publication no. (OS)78-0013. Washington, D.C.: Government Printing Office, 1978.

Veatch, Robert M., and Wigodsky, Herman S. "Two Views of the New Research Regulations." *Hastings Center Report* 11, no. 3 (June 1981): 9–14.

Wax, Murray L. "On Fieldworkers and Those Exposed to Fieldwork: Federal Regulations and Moral Issues." *Human Organization* 36 (1977): 321-28.

Wax, Murray L., and Cassell, Joan, eds. *Federal Regulations: Ethical Issues and Social Research.* AAAS Selected Symposium, no. 36. Boulder, Colo.: Westview Press, 1979.

Contributors

TOM L. BEAUCHAMP is professor of philosophy and senior research scholar at the Kennedy Institute of Ethics, Georgetown University. He is the author of *Philosophical Ethics* and coauthor of *Hume and the Problem of Causation* and *Principles of Biomedical Ethics.* He previously served as consulting philosopher in ethics for the National Commission for the Protection of Human Subjects of Biomedical and Behavioral Research.

GORDAN BERMANT is deputy director of research at the Federal Judicial Center, in Washington, D.C. Trained as a psychologist, he was formerly coordinator of the Battelle Memorial Institute Program in the Behavioral and Social Sciences, in Seattle. He is coeditor of *Markets and Morals* and *The Ethics of Social Intervention.*

ROBERT F. BORUCH is director of policy and evaluation research in the Department of Psychology at Northwestern University. He is coeditor of *Experimental Testing of Public Policy* and *Social Experimentation,* and coauthor with Joe S. Cecil of *Assuring the Confidentiality of Social Research Data.*

ARTHUR L. CAPLAN is associate for the humanities at the Hastings Center, Institute of Society, Ethics, and the Life Sciences. He is the editor of *The Sociobiology Debate* and coeditor of the volume *Concepts of Health and Disease: Interdisciplinary Perspectives* and also of a series of volumes dealing with moral controversies and their closure in the natural and social sciences.

ALEXANDER MORGAN CAPRON is professor at the University of Pennsylvania Law School. He was executive director of the President's Commission for the Study of Ethical Problems in Medicine and Biomedical and Behavioral Research. He is the author, with Jay Katz, of *Catastrophic Diseases: Who Decides What?* He also collaborated with Katz and Eleanor Swift Glass to produce *Experimentation with Human Beings.*

JOAN CASSELL is research associate at the Center for Policy Research, in New York City. She received her Ph.D. in anthropology from Columbia University and is coeditor of *Federal Regulations: Ethical Issues and Social Research* and of a special issue of *Social Problems* devoted to "Ethical Problems of Fieldwork."

GERALD DWORKIN is professor in the Department of Philosophy, College of Liberal Arts and Sciences, at the University of Illinois at Chicago Circle. He has been Luce Fellow at the Hastings Center. He is coeditor of the books *Ethics, The IQ Controversy,* and *Markets and Morals.* He is also the author of the influential article "Autonomy and Behavior Control" (*Hastings Center Report*) and associate editor of the journal *Ethics.*

ALAN C. ELMS is professor in the Department of Psychology at the University of California, Davis. He received his Ph.D. in social psychology from Yale University, where he worked as Stanley Milgram's research assistant on the latter's famous experiments on obedience to authority. He is the author of *Social Psychology and Social Relevance.*

RUTH R. FADEN is associate professor of health services administration, behavioral sciences, and population dynamics in the School of Hygiene and Public Health, and associate professor of psychology, at The Johns Hopkins University. She is also senior research scholar at the Kennedy Institute of Ethics, Georgetown University. In addition to publishing numerous articles on research and biomedical ethics, she has served on the institutional review board of the School of Hygiene and Public Health for several years.

BRADFORD H. GRAY is senior professional associate in the Division of Legal, Ethical, and Educational Aspects of Health at the Institute of Medicine, National Academy of Sciences. He received his doctorate in sociology from Yale University, and served on the staff of the National Commission for the Protection of Human Subjects of Biomedical and Behavioral Research. He is the author of *Human Subjects in Medical Experimentation.*

HERBERT C. KELMAN is Richard Clarke Cabot Professor of Social Ethics at Harvard University, where he teaches in the Department of Psychology and Social Relations. He has been a Fellow at the Center for Advanced Study in the Behavioral Sciences and at the Woodrow Wilson International Center for Scholars. He is widely regarded as the first scholar to have addressed systematically the ethical aspects of social science research. Many of his influential early articles in the area are collected in *A Time to Speak.*

ALASDAIR MACINTYRE is professor in the Department of Philosophy at Boston University. He was previously a Fellow of University College, Oxford, and professor of sociology at the University of Essex. His many influential books include *The Unconscious, Against the Self-Images of the Age, A Short History of Ethics,* and *After Virtue.*

RUTH MACKLIN is associate professor in the Department of Community Health at Albert Einstein College of Medicine. She was formerly a research associate at the Hastings Center, Institute of Society, Ethics, and the Life Sciences. She is the author of *Man, Mind, and Morality: The Ethics of Behavior Control* and coeditor of *Moral Problems in Medicine.*

DOROTHY NELKIN is professor in the Program on Science, Technology, and Society at Cornell University. She has written widely on the political and social issues surrounding scientific research. Her recent books include *Science Textbook Controversies and the Politics of Equal Time* and *Controversy: Politics of Technical Decisions.*

E. L. PATTULLO is director of the Center for the Behavioral Sciences at Harvard University and editor-in-chief of the center's *Newsletter.* He is also senior lecturer in Psychology at Harvard.

TERRY PINKARD is associate professor in the Department of Philosophy and senior research scholar at the Kennedy Institute of Ethics, Georgetown University. He is coeditor of *Ethics and Public Policy,* and the author of "Models of the

Person" *(Canadian Journal of Philosophy)* and "Categorical Theory and Political Philosophy" *(Journal of Value Inquiry).*

JOHN A. ROBERTSON is professor in the Law School at the University of Wisconsin. His studies of the governmental, legal, and constitutional issues raised by scientific research include "The Scientist's Right to Research: A Constitutional Analysis" *(Southern California Law Review)* and "The Law of Institutional Review Boards" *(UCLA Law Review).*

RICHARD A. TROPP is in the Office of Policy at the Environmental Protection Agency. He has long been involved in the development of government policy on the regulation of research involving human participants. He contributed the paper "What Problems Are Raised When the Current DHEW Regulation on Protection of Human Subjects Is Applied to Social Science Research" to the appendix of *The Belmont Report.*

R. JAY WALLACE, JR., has been a research associate at the Kennedy Institute of Ethics, Georgetown University. He graduated from Williams College and read for the B. Phil. degree in Philosophy at Oxford University.

LEROY WALTERS is director of the Center for Bioethics, Kennedy Institute of Ethics, and associate professor of philosophy, Georgetown University. He is the editor of the annual *Bibliography of Bioethics* and coeditor of an anthology entitled *Contemporary Issues in Bioethics.* He has served as a consultant to the National Commission for the Protection of Human Subjects; the Ethics Advisory Board of the U.S. Department of Health, Education, and Welfare; and the President's Commission for the Study of Ethical Problems in Medicine and Biomedical and Behavioral Research.

DONALD P. WARWICK is Institute Fellow in the Harvard Institute for International Development. He also teaches in the Department of Sociology and in the Graduate School of Education at Harvard University. His several articles on ethical issues in social research include a well-known study of Laud Humphreys's research, "Tearoom Trade: Means and Ends in Social Research" *(Hastings Center Studies).* He is coeditor of *The Ethics of Social Intervention* and the author of *The Teaching of Ethics in the Social Sciences.*

427

Index

THE JOHNS HOPKINS UNIVERSITY PRESS

Ethical Issues in Social Science Research

This book was composed in Times Roman text
and display type by Brushwood Graphics, from
a design by Lisa Mirski. It was printed on
S. D. Warren's 50-lb. Sebago Eggshell paper
and bound in Holliston Roxite A cloth by
the Maple Press Company.